Praise for Michael Hartl's Books and Videos on Ruby on Rails

"My former company (CD Baby) was one of the first to loudly switch to Ruby on Rails, and then even more loudly switch back to PHP. (Google me to read about the drama.) This book by Michael Hartl came so highly recommended that I had to try it, and the *Ruby on Rails*™ *Tutorial* is what I used to switch back to Rails again."
    —From the Foreword by Derek Sivers (sivers.org)
        Formerly: founder of CD Baby
        Currently: founder of Thoughts Ltd.

"Michael Hartl's Rails Tutorial book is the #1 (and only, in my opinion) place to start when it comes to books about learning Rails. . . . It's an amazing piece of work and, unusually, walks you through building a Rails app from start to finish with testing. If you want to read just one book and feel like a Rails master by the end of it, pick the *Ruby on Rails*™ *Tutorial*."
    —Peter Cooper, editor, Ruby Inside

"Michael Hartl's *Ruby on Rails*™ *Tutorial* seamlessly taught me about not only Ruby on Rails, but also the underlying Ruby language, HTML, CSS, a bit of JavaScript, and even some SQL—but most importantly it showed me how to build a web application (Twitter) in a short amount of time."
    —Mattan Griffel, co-founder & CEO of One Month

"Although I'm a Python/Django developer by trade, I can't stress enough how much this book has helped me. As an undergraduate, completely detached from industry, this book showed me how to use version control, how to write tests, and, most importantly—despite the steep learning curve for setting up and getting stuff running—how the end result of perseverance is extremely gratifying. It made me fall in love with technology all over again. This is the book I direct all my friends to who want to start learning programming/building stuff. Thank you Michael!"
    —Prakhar Srivastav, software engineer, Xcite.com, Kuwait

"It has to be the best-written book of its type I've ever seen, and I can't recommend it enough."
—Daniel Hollands, administrator of Birmingham.IO

"For those wanting to learn Ruby on Rails, Hartl's *Ruby on Rails*™ *Tutorial* is (in my opinion) the best way to do it."
—David Young, software developer and author at deepinthecode.com

"This is a great tutorial for a lot of reasons, because aside from just teaching Rails, Hartl is also teaching good development practices."
—Michael Denomy, full-stack web developer

"Without a doubt, the best way I learned Ruby on Rails was by building an actual working app. I used Michael Hartl's *Ruby on Rails*™ *Tutorial*, which showed me how to get a very basic Twitter-like app up and running from scratch. I cannot recommend this tutorial enough; getting something up and going fast was key; it beats memorization by a mile."
—James Fend, serial entrepreneur, JamesFend.com

"The book gives you the theory and practice, while the videos focus on showing you in person how it's done. Highly recommended combo."
—Antonio Cangiano, software engineer, IBM

"The author is clearly an expert at the Ruby language and the Rails framework, but more than that, he is a working software engineer who introduces best practices throughout the text."
—Gregory Charles, principal software developer at Fairway Technologies

RUBY ON RAILS™ TUTORIAL

Sixth Edition

RUBY ON RAILS™ TUTORIAL

Learn Web Development with Rails

Sixth Edition

Michael Hartl

✦✦Addison-Wesley

Boston • Columbus • New York • San Francisco • Amsterdam • Cape Town
Dubai • London • Madrid • Milan • Munich • Paris • Montreal • Toronto • Delhi • Mexico City
São Paulo • Sydney • Hong Kong • Seoul • Singapore • Taipei • Tokyo

Library of Congress Control Number: 2020932223

ISBN-13: 978-0-13-670265-8
ISBN-10: 0-13-670265-1

1 2020

Vice President and Publisher
Mark L. Taub

Executive Editor
Debra Williams Cauley

Associate Editor
Manjula Anaskar

Managing Producer
Sandra Schroeder

Sr. Content Producer
Julie B. Nahil

Project Editor
diacriTech

Copy Editor
Jill Hobbs

Indexer
diacriTech

Proofreader
diacriTech

Cover Designer
Chuti Prasertsith

Compositor
diacriTech

Contents

Foreword

My former company (CD Baby) was one of the first to loudly switch to Ruby on Rails, and then even more loudly switch back to PHP (Google me to read about the drama). This book by Michael Hartl came so highly recommended that I had to try it, and the *Ruby on Rails Tutorial* is what I used to switch back to Rails again.

Though I've worked my way through many Rails books, this is the one that finally made me "get" it. Everything is done very much "the Rails way"—a way that felt very unnatural to me initially, but now after doing this book finally feels natural. This is also the only Rails book that does test-driven development the entire time, an approach that is highly recommended by the experts but that has never been so clearly demonstrated before. Finally, by including Git, GitHub, and Heroku in the demo examples, the author really gives you a feel for what it's like to do a real-world project. The tutorial's code examples are not in isolation.

The linear narrative is such a great format. Personally, I powered through the Rails Tutorial in three long days doing all the examples and challenges at the end of each chapter. [This is not typical! Most readers take much longer to finish the tutorial. —Michael] Do it from start to finish, without jumping around, and you'll get the ultimate benefit.

Enjoy!

—Derek Sivers (sivers.org)
Founder, CD Baby

Acknowledgments

The *Ruby on Rails Tutorial* owes a lot to my previous Rails book, *RailsSpace*, and hence to my coauthor Aurelius Prochazka. I'd like to thank Aure both for the work he did on that book and for his support of this one. I'd also like to thank Debra Williams Cauley, my editor on both *RailsSpace* and the *Ruby on Rails Tutorial*; as long as she keeps taking me to baseball games, I'll keep writing books for her.

I'd like to acknowledge a long list of Rubyists who have taught and inspired me over the years: David Heinemeier Hansson, Yehuda Katz, Carl Lerche, Jeremy Kemper, Xavier Noria, Ryan Bates, Geoffrey Grosenbach, Peter Cooper, Matt Aimonetti, Mark Bates, Gregg Pollack, Wayne E. Seguin, Amy Hoy, Dave Chelimsky, Pat Maddox, Tom Preston-Werner, Chris Wanstrath, Chad Fowler, Josh Susser, Obie Fernandez, Ian McFarland, Steph Bristol, Pratik Naik, Sarah Mei, Sarah Allen, Wolfram Arnold, Alex Chaffee, Giles Bowkett, Evan Dorn, Long Nguyen, James Lindenbaum, Adam Wiggins, Tikhon Bernstam, Ron Evans, Wyatt Greene, Miles Forrest, Sandi Metz, Ryan Davis, Aaron Patterson, Aja Hammerly, Richard "Schneems" Schneeman, the good people at Pivotal Labs, the Heroku gang, the thoughtbot folks, and the GitHub crew.

I'd like to thank technical reviewer Andrew Thai for his careful reading of the original manuscript and for his helpful suggestions. I'd also like to thank my cofounders at Learn Enough, Nick Merwin and Lee Donahoe, for all their help in preparing this tutorial.

Finally, many, many readers—far too many to list—have contributed a huge number of bug reports and suggestions during the writing of this book, and I gratefully acknowledge their help in making it as good as it can be.

About the Author

Michael Hartl is the creator of the *Ruby on Rails*™ *Tutorial*, one of the leading introductions to web development, and is cofounder and principal author at LearnEnough.com. Previously, he was a physics instructor at the California Institute of Technology (Caltech), where he received a Lifetime Achievement Award for Excellence in Teaching. He is a graduate of Harvard College, has a PhD in Physics from Caltech, and is an alumnus of the Y Combinator entrepreneur program.

CHAPTER 1

From Zero to Deploy

Welcome to the *Ruby on Rails Tutorial*! The purpose of this tutorial is to teach you how to develop custom web applications. The resulting skillset will put you in a great position to get a job as a web developer, start a career as a freelancer, or found a company of your own. If you already know how to develop web applications, this tutorial will quickly get you up to speed with Ruby on Rails.

The focus throughout the *Ruby on Rails Tutorial* is on general skills that are useful no matter which specific technology you end up using. Once you understand how web apps work, learning another framework can be done with *much* less effort. That being said, the framework of choice in this tutorial—namely, Ruby on Rails—has never been a better choice for learning web development (Box 1.1).

Box 1.1: The many advantages of Rails

Ruby on Rails (or just "Rails" for short) is a free and open-source web development framework written in the Ruby programming language. Upon its debut, Ruby on Rails rapidly became one of the most popular tools for building dynamic web applications. Rails is used by companies as varied as Airbnb, SoundCloud, Disney, Hulu, GitHub, and Shopify, as well as by innumerable freelancers, independent development shops, and startups.

Although there are many choices in web development, Rails stands apart for its elegance, power, and integrated approach to web applications. Using Rails, even novice developers can build a full-stack web application without ever leaving the framework—a huge boon for people learning web development for the first time. Rails also gives you flexibility going forward—for example, serving as a great back end if you want to build a single-page application or mobile app sometime down the line.

One big advantage is that Rails is not prone to the "new hotness" problem that plagues some development communities (notably JavaScript/Node.js), in which a dizzyingly complex set of technologies seems to change every six months. As Rails creator David Heinemeier Hansson once noted:

> Back then the complexity merchant of choice was J2EE, but the complaints are uncannily similar to those leveled against JavaScript today... The core premise of Rails remains in many ways as controversial today as it was when it premiered. That by formalizing conventions, eliminating valueless choices, and offering a full-stack framework that provides great defaults for anyone who wants to create a complete application, we can make dramatic strides of productivity.

Due in part to this philosophy, Rails has remained so stable at its core much of this tutorial has been the same since the third edition, launched in 2014. The things you learn here won't go out of date soon.

And yet, Rails continues to innovate. For example, the Rails 6 release includes major new features for email routing, text formatting, parallel testing, and multiple-database support. A big part of Rails 6 is being "scalable by default," which means that *Rails scales* no matter how big your app gets. All this while maintaining rock-solid dependability—indeed, the wildly popular developer platform GitHub, the hugely successful online store-builder Shopify, and the collaboration tool (and very first Rails app) Basecamp all run their sites on the pre-release versions of Rails. This means that *new versions of Rails are immediately tested by some of the largest, most successful web apps in existence.*

Not bad for a little side project cooked up by a freelance Danish web developer way back in 2004. What was an edgy choice then is an easy choice now: With its proven track-record, productive feature-set, and helpful community, Rails is a fantastic framework for building modern web applications.

There are no formal prerequisites for this book, which contains integrated tutorials for the Ruby programming language, the Unix command line, HTML, CSS, a small amount of JavaScript, and even a little SQL. That's a lot of material to absorb, though, and if you're new to software development I recommend starting with the tutorials at Learn Enough https://www.learnenough.com/, especially *Learn Enough Command Line to Be Dangerous* (www.learnenough.com/command-line) and *Learn*

Enough Ruby to Be Dangerous (www.learnenough.com/ruby).[1] On the other hand, a surprising number of complete beginners have gotten through this tutorial, so don't let me stop you if you're excited to build web apps.

The principal teaching method of this tutorial is building real working software through a series of example applications of increasing sophistication, starting with a minimal *hello* app (Figure 1.1, Section 1.2), a slightly more capable *toy* app (Figure 1.2, Chapter 2), and a real *sample* app (Figure 1.3,[2] Chapter 3 through Chapter 14). As

Figure 1.1: The beginning hello app.

---

1. Adding the rest of the Learn Enough sequence would certainly provide excellent preparation for this tutorial, but if you're in a hurry you can probably get by with just Command Line and Ruby. *Learn Enough Ruby to Be Dangerous* (www.learnenough.com/ruby) in particular has a chapter on building a simple web application using Sinatra, a Ruby-based micro-framework that serves as excellent preparation for Rails. If you get stuck in the present tutorial, I suggest giving *Learn Enough Ruby to Be Dangerous* (www.learnenough.com/ruby) and its prerequisites a try, then loop back here to see how it goes the second time.

2. Baby photo retrieved from https://www.flickr.com/photos/glasgows/338937124/ on 2014-08-25. Copyright © 2008 by M&R Glasgow and used unaltered under the terms of the CC by License.

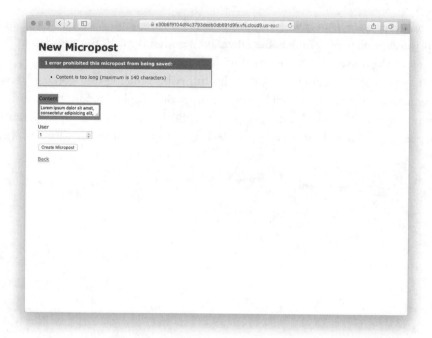

Figure 1.2: An intermediate toy app.

implied by their generic names, these applications focus on general principles, which are applicable to practically any kind of web application. In particular, the full sample application includes all the major features needed by professional-grade web apps, including user signup, login, and account management. The final version of the sample app, developed in Chapter 14, also bears more than a passing resemblance to Twitter— a website that, coincidentally, was also originally written in Rails.

Let's get started!

1.1 Up and Running

One advantage of using this tutorial is that you can get up and running fast. In particular, the Rails Tutorial has a long-running partnership with AWS Cloud9, a development environment that runs in your browser. The result is a complete system for developing all the software in this tutorial.

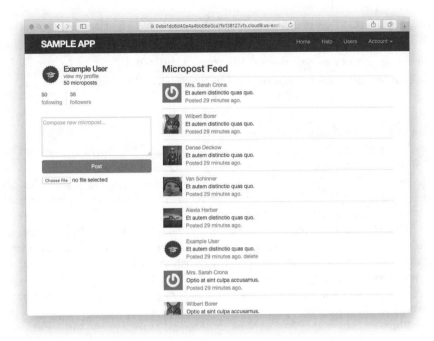

Figure 1.3: The final sample app.

This is important because, even for experienced developers, installing Ruby, Rails, and all the associated supporting software can be quite challenging. Compounding the problem is the multiplicity of environments: different operating systems, version numbers, preferences in text editors, and so on.

This is why the recommended solution, especially for newer users, is to sidestep most installation and configuration issues by using a *cloud integrated development environment*, or cloud IDE (Section 1.1.1). The cloud IDE used in this tutorial runs inside an ordinary web browser, and hence works the same across different platforms. It also maintains the current state of your work, so you can take a break from the tutorial and come back to the system just as you left it.

A second possibility is to set up your native system (Windows, macOS, or Linux) for Rails development. It is definitely recommended that you do this eventually, but it can represent significant overhead, and is likely to require a healthy amount of *technical sophistication* (Box 1.2). Instructions for setting up your native system can be found in the "Native OS setup" section of *Learn Enough Dev Environment to Be Danger-ous* (www.learnenough.com/dev-environment). (Note in particular that you'll need Ruby 2.6 or greater to run Rails 6.) If you go this route, be sure to complete the configuration and Rails installation steps in Section 1.1.2 as well.

Box 1.2: Technical Sophistication

The *Ruby on Rails Tutorial* is part of the Learn Enough family of tutorials, which develop the theme of *technical sophistication*: the combination of hard and soft skills that make it seem like you can magically solve any technical problem (as illustrated in "Tech Support Cheat Sheet" from xkcd.com).

Knowing how to code is an important component of technical sophistication, but there's more to it than that—you also have to know how to click around menu items to learn the capabilities of a particular application, how to clarify a confusing error message by Googling it, or when to give up and just reboot the darn thing.

Because web applications have so many moving parts, they offer ample oppor-tunities to develop your technical sophistication. In the context of Rails web development, some specific examples of technical sophistication include making sure you're using the right Ruby gem versions, running `bundle install` or `bundle update`, and restarting the local webserver if something doesn't work. (Don't worry if all this sounds like gibberish; we'll cover everything mentioned here in the course of completing this tutorial.)

As you proceed through this tutorial, in all likelihood you will occasionally be tripped up by things not immediately working as expected. Although some particu-larly tricky steps are explicitly highlighted in the text, it is impossible to anticipate all the things that can go wrong. I recommend you embrace these inevitable stumbling blocks as opportunities to work on improving your technical sophistication. Or, as we say in geek speak: *It's not a bug, it's a feature!*

1.1.1 Development Environment

Considering various idiosyncratic customizations, there are probably as many devel-opment environments as there are Rails programmers. To avoid this complexity, the *Ruby on Rails Tutorial* standardizes on the excellent cloud development environment Cloud9, part of Amazon Web Services (AWS). The resulting workspace environ-ment comes preconfigured with most of the software needed for Ruby on Rails web development, including Ruby, RubyGems, and Git. (Indeed, the only big piece of software we'll install separately is Rails itself, and this is intentional (Section 1.1.2).)

The cloud IDE includes the three essential components needed to develop web applications: a command-line terminal, a filesystem navigator, and a text editor (Figure 1.4). Among other features, the cloud IDE's text editor supports the "Find in Files" global search that I consider essential to navigating any large Ruby or Rails project. Finally, even if you decide not to use the cloud IDE exclusively in real life (and I certainly recommend learning other tools as well), it provides an excellent introduction to the general capabilities of command-line terminals, text editor, and other development tools.

Here are the steps for getting started with the cloud development environment:[3]

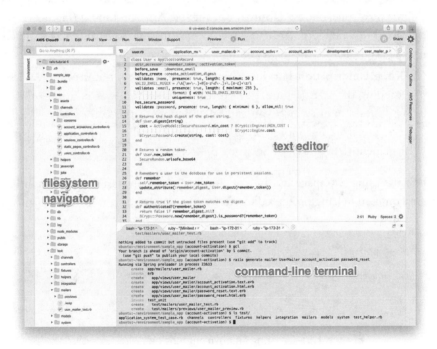

Figure 1.4: The anatomy of the cloud IDE.

---

3. Due to the constantly evolving nature of sites like AWS, details may vary; use your technical sophistication (Box 1.2) to resolve any discrepancies.

1. Because Cloud9 is part of Amazon Web Services (AWS), if you already have an AWS account you can just sign in.[4] To create a new Cloud9 workspace environment, go to the AWS console and type "Cloud9" in the search box.

2. If you don't already have an AWS account, you should sign up for a free account at AWS Cloud9.[5] To prevent abuse, AWS requires a valid credit card for signup, but the workspace is 100% free (for a year, as of this writing), and your card will not be charged. You might have to wait up to 24 hours for the account to be activated, but in my case it was ready in about 10 minutes.

3. Once you've successfully gotten to the Cloud9 administrative page (Figure 1.5), click "Create environment" and fill in the information as shown in Figure 1.6, including the name "rails-tutorial".[6] Fill in the description as shown in Figure 1.6. On the next page, choose **Ubuntu Server** (*not* Amazon Linux) (Figure 1.7), and then click "Next step." You will see a confirmation page and a best practices message right before the provisioning begins (Figure 1.8).

   Click the confirmation buttons to accept the default settings until AWS starts provisioning the IDE (Figure 1.9). You may run into a warning message about being a "root" user, which you can safely ignore at this early stage. (We'll discuss the preferred but more complicated practice, called an Identity and Access Management (IAM) user, in Section 13.4.4.)

Because using two spaces for indentation is a near-universal convention in Ruby, I also recommend changing the editor to use two spaces instead of the default four.

Figure 1.5: Creating an environment on AWS Cloud9.

---

4. https://aws.amazon.com/

5. https://www.railstutorial.org/cloud9-signup

6. If you've previously done this tutorial, you may want to use a fresh environment, with a name like "rails-tutorial-6".

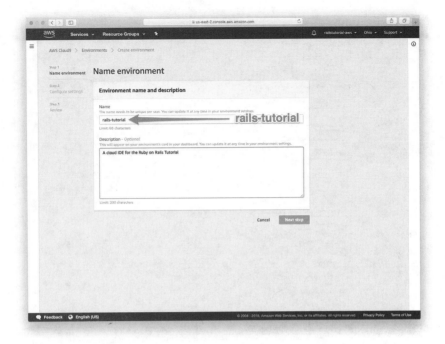

Figure 1.6: Naming a new work environment at AWS Cloud9.

As shown in Figure 1.10, you can do this by clicking the gear icon in the upper right and then clicking the minus sign in the "Soft Tabs" setting until it reaches 2. (Note that this takes effect immediately; you don't need to click a "Save" button.)

1.1.2 Installing Rails

The development environment from Section 1.1.1 includes all the software we need to get started except for Rails itself. This is by design, as installing the exact version of Rails used in this tutorial is important for getting predictable results.

First, we'll do a little preparation by adding configuration settings to prevent the time-consuming installation of local Ruby documentation, as shown in Listing 1.1.[7]

---

7. This uses the **echo** and **>>** (append) commands covered in Section 1.3 and Section 2.1 of *Learn Enough Command Line to Be Dangerous* (www.learnenough.com/command-line). Note that if the file being appended to doesn't exist, **>>** is smart enough to create it.

Figure 1.7: Selecting **Ubuntu Server**.

Note that this step needs to be done only once per system. (For more information on the command line and other conventions in this book, see Section 1.6.)

Listing 1.1: Configuring the `.gemrc` file to skip the installation of Ruby documentation.

```
$ echo "gem: --no-document" >> ~/.gemrc
```

To install Rails, we'll use the **gem** command provided by the *RubyGems* package manager, which involves typing the command shown in Listing 1.2 into your command-line terminal. (If developing on your local system, this means using a regular terminal window; if using the cloud IDE, this means using the command-line area shown in Figure 1.4.)

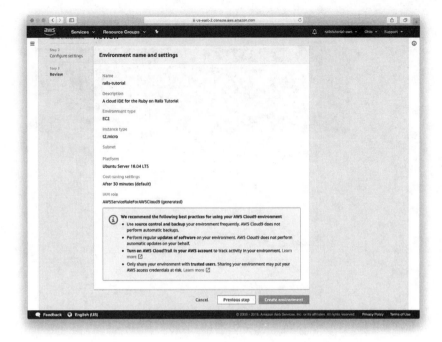

Figure 1.8: The final step before provisioning the IDE.

Listing 1.2: Installing Rails with a specific version number.

```
$ gem install rails -v 6.0.2.1
```

Here the **-v** flag ensures that the specified version of Rails gets installed. You can confirm that the installation succeeded by passing the **-v** flag to the **rails** command itself:

```
$ rails -v
Rails 6.0.2.1
```

The version number output by this command should match the version installed in Listing 1.2.

There's one more configuration step, which is to install Yarn, a program to manage software dependencies. If you're using your native OS, you should follow the Yarn

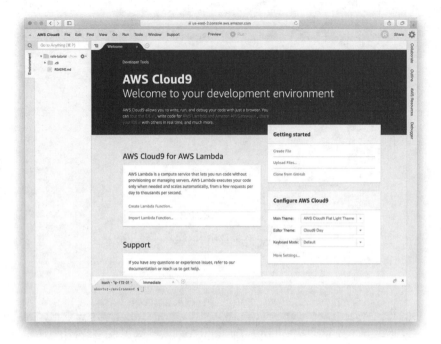

Figure 1.9: The default cloud IDE.

installation instructions for your platform. If you're on the cloud IDE, you can run this command, which downloads and executes the necessary commands from the Learn Enough CDN:

```
$ source <(curl -sL https://cdn.learnenough.com/yarn_install)
```

From time to time, you'll probably get a warning message that looks like this:

```
=======================================
  Your Yarn packages are out of date!
  Please run `yarn install --check-files` to update.
=======================================
```

All you need to do if this happens is execute the suggested **yarn** command:

```
$ yarn install --check-files
```

Figure 1.10: Setting Cloud9 to use two spaces for indentation.

That's it! You've now got a system fully configured for Ruby on Rails web development.

1.2   The First Application

Following a long tradition in computer programming, our goal for the first application is to write a "hello, world" program. In particular, we will create a simple application that displays the string "hello, world!" on a web page, both on our development environment (Section 1.2.4) and on the live web (Section 1.4).

Virtually all Rails applications start the same way, by running the **rails new** command. This handy command creates a skeleton Rails application in a directory of your choice. To get started, users *not* using the Cloud9 IDE recommended in

Section 1.1.1 should make a **environment** directory for their Rails projects if it doesn't already exist (Listing 1.3) and then change into the directory.[8]

Listing 1.3: Making an **environment** directory for Rails projects.

```
# These steps are not needed on the cloud IDE.
$ cd           ·            # Change to the home directory.
$ mkdir environment         # Make an environment directory.
$ cd environment/           # Change into the environment directory.
```

Listing 1.3 uses the Unix commands **cd** and **mkdir**; see Box 1.3 if you are not already familiar with these commands.

Box 1.3: A crash course on the Unix command line

For readers coming from Windows or macOS, the Unix command line may be unfamiliar. Luckily, if you are using the recommended cloud environment, you automatically have access to a Unix (Linux) command line running a standard shell (command-line interface) known as Bash.

The basic idea of the command line is simple: By issuing short commands, users can perform a large number of operations, such as creating directories (mkdir), moving and copying files (mv and cp), and navigating the filesystem by changing directories (cd). Although the command line may seem primitive to users mainly familiar with graphical user interfaces (GUIs), appearances are deceiving: The command line is one of the most powerful tools in the developer's toolbox. Indeed, you will rarely see the desktop of an experienced developer without several open terminal windows running command-line shells.

The general subject is deep, but for the purposes of this tutorial we will need only a few of the most common Unix command-line commands, as summarized in Table 1.1. For a more thorough introduction to the basics of the command line, see the first Learn Enough tutorial, *Learn Enough Command Line to Be Dangerous* (www.learnenough.com/command-line).

---

8. This step is designed to unify the treatment of native systems and the cloud IDE by using identical directory structures. If you are confident in your technical sophistication, feel free to omit this step, and use a directory of your choice.

Table 1.1: Some common Unix commands.

Description	Command	Example
list contents	ls	$ **ls -l**
make directory	mkdir <dirname>	$ **mkdir environment**
change directory	cd <dirname>	$ **cd environment/**
cd one directory up		$ **cd ..**
cd to home directory		$ **cd ~** or just $ **cd**
cd to path including home dir		$ **cd ~/environment/**
move file (rename)	mv <source> <target>	$ **mv foo bar**
copy file	cp <source> <target>	$ **cp foo bar**
remove file	rm <file>	$ **rm foo**
remove empty directory	rmdir <directory>	$ **rmdir environment/**
remove nonempty directory	rm -rf <directory>	$ **rm -rf tmp/**
concatenate and display file contents	cat <file>	$ **cat ~/.ssh/id_rsa.pub**

The next step on both local systems and the cloud IDE is to create the first application using the command in Listing 1.4. Note that Listing 1.4 explicitly includes the Rails version number as part of the command. This ensures that the same version of Rails we installed in Listing 1.2 is used to create the first application's file structure.

Listing 1.4: Running **rails new** (with a specific version number).

```
$ cd ~/environment
$ rails _6.0.2.1_ new hello_app
      create
      create  README.md
      create  Rakefile
      create  .ruby-version
      create  config.ru
      create  .gitignore
      create  Gemfile
         run  git init from "."
Initialized empty Git repository in /home/ubuntu/environment/hello_app/.git/
      create  package.json
```

```
create  app
create  app/assets/config/manifest.js
create  app/assets/stylesheets/application.css
create  app/channels/application_cable/channel.rb
create  app/channels/application_cable/connection.rb
create  app/controllers/application_controller.rb
create  app/helpers/application_helper.rb
  .
  .
  .
```

Notice how many files and directories the **rails** command creates. This standard directory and file structure (Figure 1.11) is one of the many advantages of Rails: It immediately gets you from zero to a functional (if minimal) application. Moreover, since the structure is common to all Rails apps, you can immediately get your bearings when looking at someone else's code.

A summary of the default Rails files appears in Table 1.2. We'll learn about most of these files and directories throughout the rest of this book. In particular, starting

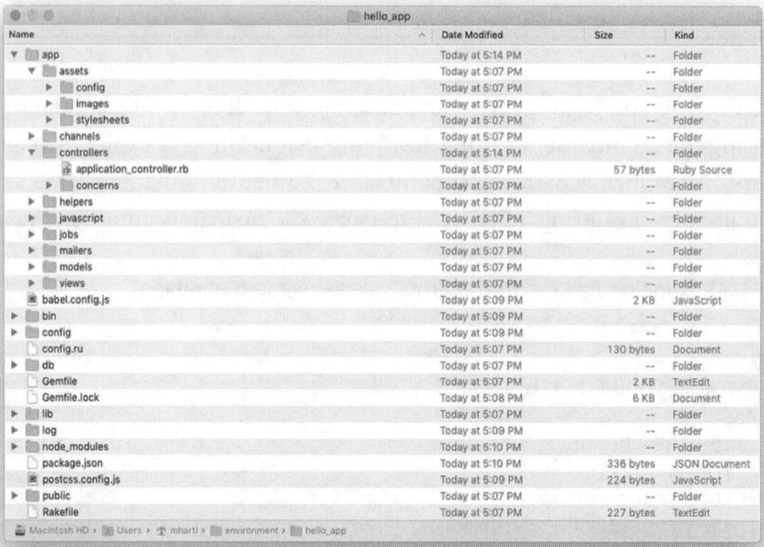

Figure 1.11: The directory structure for a newly created Rails app.

Table 1.2: A summary of the default Rails directory structure.

File/Directory	Purpose
app/	Core application (app) code, including models, views, controllers, and helpers
app/assets	Application assets such as Cascading Style Sheets (CSS) and images
bin/	Binary executable files
config/	Application configuration
db/	Database files
doc/	Documentation for the application
lib/	Library modules
log/	Application log files
public/	Data accessible to the public (e.g., via web browsers), such as error pages
bin/rails	A program for generating code, opening console sessions, or starting a local server
test/	Application tests
tmp/	Temporary files
README.md	A brief description of the application
Gemfile	Gem requirements for this app
Gemfile.lock	A list of gems used to ensure that all copies of the app use the same gem versions
config.ru	A configuration file for Rack middleware
.gitignore	Patterns for files that should be ignored by Git

in Section 5.2.1 we'll discuss the **app/assets** directory, part of the *asset pipeline* that makes it easy to organize and deploy assets such as Cascading Style Sheets and image files.

1.2.1   Bundler

After creating a new Rails application, the next step is to use *Bundler* to install and include the gems needed by the app. Bundler is run automatically (via **bundle install**) by the **rails** command in Listing 1.4, but in this section we'll make some changes to the default application gems and run Bundler again. This involves opening the **Gemfile** with a text editor. (With the cloud IDE, this involves clicking the arrow in the file navigator to open the sample app directory and double-clicking the **Gemfile** icon.) Although the exact version numbers and details may differ slightly,

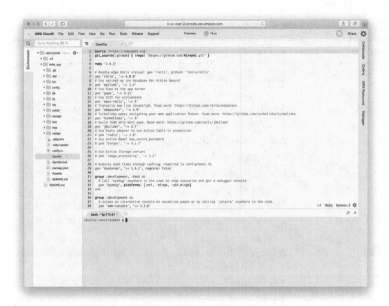

Figure 1.12: The default **Gemfile** open in a text editor.

the results should look something like Figure 1.12 and Listing 1.5. (The code in this file is Ruby, but don't worry at this point about the syntax; Chapter 4 will cover Ruby in more depth.)

If the files and directories don't appear as shown in Figure 1.12, click the file navigator's gear icon and select "Refresh File Tree." (As a general rule, you should refresh the file tree any time files or directories don't appear as expected.)[9]

Listing 1.5: The default **Gemfile** in the **hello_app** directory.

```
source 'https://rubygems.org'
git_source(:github) { |repo| "https://github.com/#{repo}.git" }

ruby '2.6.3'

# Bundle edge Rails instead: gem 'rails', github: 'rails/rails'
gem 'rails', '~> 6.0.2.1'
# Use sqlite3 as the database for Active Record
gem 'sqlite3', '~> 1.4'
# Use Puma as the app server
gem 'puma', '~> 3.11'
```

---

9. This is a typical example of technical sophistication (Box 1.2).

```
# Use SCSS for stylesheets
gem 'sass-rails', '~> 5'
# Transpile app-like JavaScript. Read more: https://github.com/rails/webpacker
gem 'webpacker', '~> 4.0'
# Turbolinks makes navigating your web application faster.
# Read more: https://github.com/turbolinks/turbolinks
gem 'turbolinks', '~> 5'
# Build JSON APIs with ease. Read more: https://github.com/rails/jbuilder
gem 'jbuilder', '~> 2.7'
# Use Redis adapter to run Action Cable in production
# gem 'redis', '~> 4.0'
# Use Active Model has_secure_password
# gem 'bcrypt', '~> 3.1.7'

# Use Active Storage variant
# gem 'image_processing', '~> 1.2'

# Reduces boot times through caching; required in config/boot.rb
gem 'bootsnap', '>= 1.4.2', require: false

group :development, :test do
  # Call 'byebug' anywhere in the code to stop execution and get a
  # debugger console
  gem 'byebug', platforms: [:mri, :mingw, :x64_mingw]
end

group :development do
  # Access an interactive console on exception pages or by calling 'console'
  # anywhere in the code.
  gem 'web-console', '>= 3.3.0'
  gem 'listen', '>= 3.0.5', '< 3.2'
  # Spring speeds up development by keeping your application running in the
  # background. Read more: https://github.com/rails/spring
  gem 'spring'
  gem 'spring-watcher-listen', '~> 2.0.0'
end

group :test do
  # Adds support for Capybara system testing and selenium driver
  gem 'capybara', '>= 2.15'
  gem 'selenium-webdriver'
  # Easy installation and use of web drivers to run system tests with browsers
  gem 'webdrivers'
end

# Windows does not include zoneinfo files, so bundle the tzinfo-data gem
gem 'tzinfo-data', platforms: [:mingw, :mswin, :x64_mingw, :jruby]
```

Many of these lines are commented out with the hash symbol **#** (Section 4.2); they are there to show you some commonly needed gems and to give examples of the Bundler syntax. For now, we won't need any gems other than the defaults.

Unless you specify a version number to the **gem** command, Bundler will automatically install the latest requested version of the gem. This is the case, for example, in the code

```
gem 'sqlite3'
```

There are also two common ways to specify a gem version range, which allows us to exert some control over the version used by Rails. The first looks like this:

```
gem 'capybara', '>= 2.15'
```

This installs the latest version of the `capybara` gem (which is used in testing) as long as it's greater than or equal to version **2.15**—even if it's, say, version **7.2**.

The second method looks like this:

```
gem 'rails', '~> 6.0.2.1'
```

This installs the gem, **rails**, as long as it's version **6.0.1** or newer but *not* **6.1** or newer. In other words, the **>=** notation always installs the latest gem, whereas the **~> 6.0.1** notation will install **6.0.2** (if available) but not **6.1.0**.[10]

Unfortunately, experience shows that even minor point releases can break Rails applications, so for the *Ruby on Rails Tutorial* we'll err on the side of caution by including exact version numbers for all gems. You are welcome to use the most up-to-date version of any gem, including using the **~>** construction in the **Gemfile** (which I generally recommend for more advanced users), but be warned that this may cause the tutorial to act unpredictably.

---

10. Similarly, **~> 6.0** would install version **6.9** of a gem but not **7.0**. This is especially useful if the project in question uses *semantic versioning* (also called "semver"), which is a convention for numbering releases designed to minimize the chances of breaking software dependencies.

Converting the **Gemfile** in Listing 1.5 to use exact gem versions results in the code shown in Listing 1.6.[11] Note that we've also taken this opportunity to arrange for the `sqlite3` gem to be included only in a development or test environment (Section 7.1.1), which prevents potential conflicts with the database used by Heroku (Section 1.4). Finally, we've removed the line from Listing 1.5 specifying the exact Ruby version number; as noted in Section 7.5.4, it's recommended to keep this line in a mission-critical app, but keeping it in a tutorial of this nature introduces potential errors and complexity. (That said, if your app fails to work without that line, you should definitely restore it.)

Important note: For all the Gemfiles in this book, you should use the version numbers listed at gemfiles-6th-ed.railstutorial.org instead of the ones listed below (although they should be identical if you are reading this online).

Listing 1.6: A **Gemfile** with an explicit version for each Ruby gem.

```
source 'https://rubygems.org'
git_source(:github) { |repo| "https://github.com/#{repo}.git" }

gem 'rails',       '6.0.2.1'
gem 'puma',        '3.12.2'
gem 'sass-rails',  '5.1.0'
gem 'webpacker',   '4.0.7'
gem 'turbolinks',  '5.2.0'
gem 'jbuilder',    '2.9.1'
gem 'bootsnap',    '1.4.5', require: false

group :development, :test do
  gem 'sqlite3', '1.4.1'
  gem 'byebug',  '11.0.1', platforms: [:mri, :mingw, :x64_mingw]
end

group :development do
  gem 'web-console',           '4.0.1'
  gem 'listen',                '3.1.5'
  gem 'spring',                '2.1.0'
  gem 'spring-watcher-listen', '2.0.1'
end
```

---

11. You can determine the exact version number for each gem by running **gem list <gem name>** at the command line, but Listing 1.6 saves you the trouble.

```
group :test do
  gem 'capybara',            '3.28.0'
  gem 'selenium-webdriver',  '3.142.4'
  gem 'webdrivers',          '4.1.2'
end

# Windows does not include zoneinfo files, so bundle the tzinfo-data gem
gem 'tzinfo-data', platforms: [:mingw, :mswin, :x64_mingw, :jruby]
```

Once you've placed the contents of Listing 1.6 into the application's **Gemfile**, install the gems using **bundle install**:[12]

```
$ cd hello_app/
$ bundle install
Fetching source index for https://rubygems.org/
 .
 .
 .
```

The **bundle install** command might take a few moments, but when it's done our application will be ready to run.

By the way, when you run **bundle install** it's possible that you'll get a message saying you need to run **bundle update** first. In this case you should ... run **bundle update** first! (Learning not to panic when things don't go exactly as planned is a key part of technical sophistication, and you'll be amazed at how often the "error" message contains the exact instructions you need to fix the problem at hand.)

1.2.2 rails server

Thanks to running **rails new** in Section 1.2 and **bundle install** in Section 1.2.1, we already have an application we can run—but how? Happily, Rails comes with a command-line program, or *script*, that runs a *local* webserver to assist us in developing our application: **rails server**.

---

12. As noted in Table 3.1, you can even leave off **install**, as the **bundle** command by itself is an alias for **bundle install**.

Before running **rails server**, it's necessary on some systems (including the cloud IDE) to allow connections to the local webserver. To enable this, you should navigate to the file **config/environments/development.rb** and paste in the two extra lines shown in Listing 1.7 and Figure 1.13.

Listing 1.7: Allowing connections to the local webserver.
config/environments/development.rb

```
Rails.application.configure do
  .
  .
  .
  # Allow connections to local server.
  config.hosts.clear

end
```

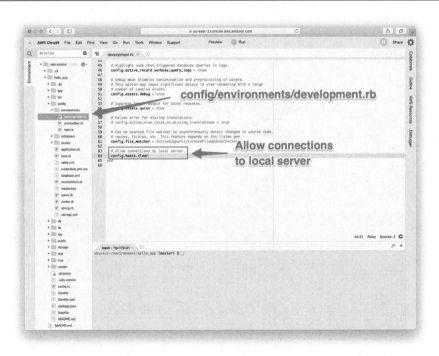

Figure 1.13: Allowing Cloud9 to connect to the Rails server.

The **rails server** command appears in Listing 1.8, which I recommend you run in a second terminal tab so that you can still issue commands in the first tab, as shown in Figure 1.14 and Figure 1.15. Note from Listing 1.8 that you can shut the server down using Ctrl-C.[13]

Listing 1.8: Running the Rails server.

```
$ cd ~/environment/hello_app/
$ rails server
=> Booting Puma
=> Ctrl-C to shutdown server
```

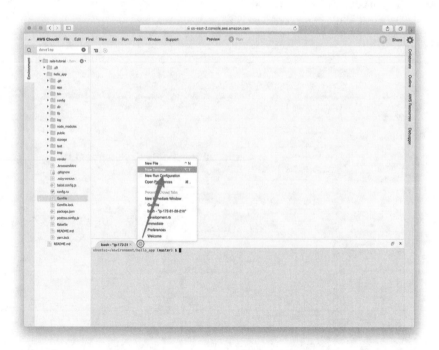

Figure 1.14: Opening a new terminal tab.

---

13. Here "C" refers to the character on the keyboard, not the capital letter, so there's no need to hold down the Shift key to get a capital "C".

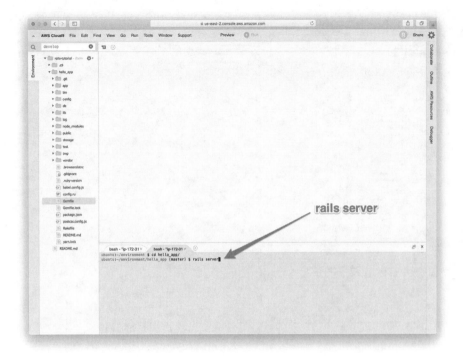

Figure 1.15: Running the Rails server in a separate tab.

To view the result of **rails server** on a native OS, paste the URL http://localhost:3000 into the address bar of your browser. On the cloud IDE, go to Preview and click "Preview Running Application" (Figure 1.16), and then open it in a full browser window or tab (Figure 1.17). In either case, the result should look something like Figure 1.18.

Exercises

The *Ruby on Rails Tutorial* contains a large number of exercises. Solving them as you proceed through the tutorial is strongly recommended.

To keep the main discussion independent of the exercises, the solutions are not generally incorporated into subsequent code listings. (In the rare circumstance that an exercise solution is used subsequently, it is explicitly solved in the main text.) This

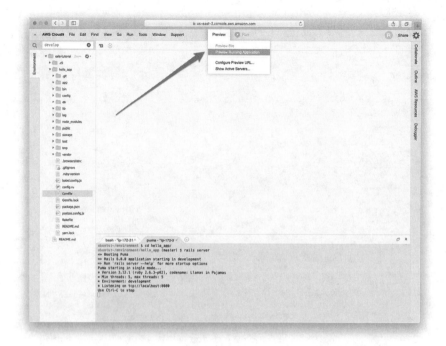

Figure 1.16: Sharing the local server running on the cloud workspace.

means that over time your code may diverge from the code shown in the tutorial due
to differences introduced in the exercises. Learning how to resolve such discrepancies
is a valuable exercise in technical sophistication (Box 1.2).

Solutions to the exercises are available to all Rails Tutorial purchasers at
https://www.railstutorial.org/aw-solutions.

To see other people's answers and to record your own, subscribe to the Rails
Tutorial course or to the Learn Enough All Access Bundle.

Many of the exercises are challenging, but we'll start out with some easy ones just
to get warmed up:

1. According to the default Rails page, what is the version of Ruby on your system?
   Confirm by running **ruby -v** at the command line.

2. What is the version of Rails? Confirm that it matches the version installed in
   Listing 1.2.

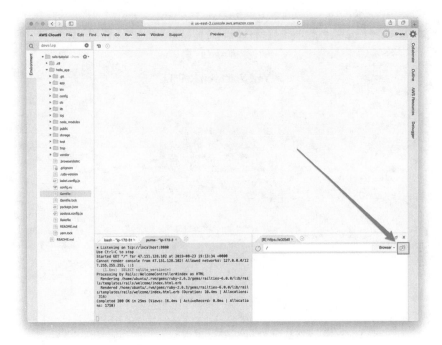

Figure 1.17: Opening the running app in a full browser window or tab.

1.2.3 Model-View-Controller (MVC)

Even at this early stage, it's helpful to get a high-level overview of how Rails applications work, as illustrated in Figure 1.19. You might have noticed that the standard Rails application structure (Figure 1.11) has an application directory called **app/**, which includes subdirectories called **models**, **views**, and **controllers** (among others). This is a hint that Rails follows the model-view-controller (MVC) architectural pattern, which enforces a separation between the data in the application (such as user information) and the code used to display it, which is a common way of structuring a GUI.

When interacting with a Rails application, a browser sends a *request*, which is received by a webserver and passed on to a Rails *controller*, which is in charge of what to do next. In some cases, the controller will immediately render a *view*, which is a template that gets converted to HTML and sent back to the browser. More commonly for dynamic sites, the controller interacts with a *model*, which is a Ruby object that

Figure 1.18: The default Rails page served by `rails server`.

represents an element of the site (such as a user) and is in charge of communicating with the database. After invoking the model, the controller then renders the view and returns the complete web page to the browser as HTML.

If this discussion seems a bit abstract right now, don't worry; we'll cover these ideas in more detail later in this book. In particular, Section 1.2.4 shows a first tentative application of MVC, while Section 2.2.2 includes a more detailed discussion of MVC in the context of the toy app. Finally, the full sample app will use all aspects of MVC: We'll cover controllers and views starting in Section 3.2 and models starting in Section 6.1, and we'll see all three working together in Section 7.1.2.

1.2.4 Hello, World!

As a first application of the MVC framework, we'll make a wafer-thin change to the first app by adding a *controller action* to render the string "hello, world!" to replace

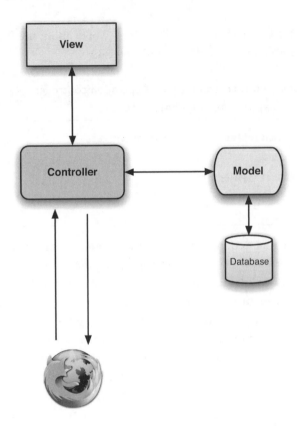

Figure 1.19: A schematic representation of the model-view-controller (MVC) architecture.

the default Rails page from Figure 1.18. (We'll learn more about controller actions starting in Section 2.2.2.)

As implied by their name, controller actions are defined inside controllers. We'll call our action **hello** and place it in the Application controller. Indeed, at this point the Application controller is the only controller we have, which you can verify by running

```
$ ls app/controllers/*_controller.rb
```

to view the current controllers. (We'll start creating our own controllers in Chapter 2.) Listing 1.9 shows the resulting definition of **hello**, which uses the **render** function to return the HTML text "hello, world!". (Don't worry about the Ruby syntax right now; it will be covered in more depth in Chapter 4.)

Listing 1.9: Adding a **hello** action to the Application controller.
`app/controllers/application_controller.rb`

```
class ApplicationController < ActionController::Base

  def hello
    render html: "hello, world!"
  end
end
```

Having defined an action that returns the desired string, we need to tell Rails to use that action instead of the default page in Figure 1.18. To do this, we'll edit the Rails *router*, which sits in front of the controller in Figure 1.19 and determines where to send requests that come in from the browser. (I've omitted the router from Figure 1.19 for simplicity, but we'll discuss it in more detail starting in Section 2.2.2.) In particular, we want to change the default page, the *root route*, which determines the page that is served on the *root URL*. Because it's the URL for an address like http://www.example.com/ (where nothing comes after the final forward slash), the root URL is often referred to as / ("slash") for short.

As seen in Listing 1.10, the Rails routes file (**config/routes.rb**) includes a comment directing us to the Rails Guide on Routing (guides.rubyonrails.org/routing.html), which includes instructions on how to define the root route. The syntax looks like this:

```
root 'controller_name#action_name'
```

In the present case, the controller name is **application** and the action name is **hello**, which results in the code shown in Listing 1.11.

Listing 1.10: The default routing file (formatted to fit).
`config/routes.rb`

```
Rails.application.routes.draw do
  # For details on the DSL available within this file,
  # see https://guides.rubyonrails.org/routing.html
end
```

Listing 1.11: Setting the root route.
`config/routes.rb`

```
Rails.application.routes.draw do
  root 'application#hello'
end
```

With the code from Listing 1.9 and Listing 1.11, the root route returns "hello, world!" as required (Figure 1.20).[14] Hello, world!

Figure 1.20: Viewing "hello, world!" in the browser.

---

14. The base URL for the Rails Tutorial Cloud9 shared URLs has changed from rails-tutorial-c9-mhartl.c9.io to one on Amazon Web Services, but in many cases the screenshots are identical, so the browser address bar will show old-style URLs in some figures (such as Figure 1.20). This is the sort of minor discrepancy you can resolve by using your technical sophistication (Box 1.2).

Exercises

Solutions to the exercises are available to all Rails Tutorial purchasers at https://www.railstutorial.org/aw-solutions.

To see other people's answers and to record your own, subscribe to the Rails Tutorial course or to the Learn Enough All Access Bundle.

1. Change the content of the **hello** action in Listing 1.9 to read "hola, mundo!" instead of "hello, world!".

2. Show that Rails supports non-ASCII characters by including an inverted exclamation point, as in "¡Hola, mundo!" (Figure 1.21).[15] To get a ¡ character on a Mac,

Figure 1.21: Changing the root route to return "¡Hola, mundo!".

---

15. Your editor may display a message like "invalid multibyte character," but this is not a cause for concern. You can Google the error message if you want to learn how to make it go away.

Figure 1.22: Changing the root route to return "goodbye, world!".

you can use Option-1; otherwise, you can always copy-and-paste the character
into your editor.

3. By following the example of the **hello** action in Listing 1.9, add a second action
   called **goodbye** that renders the text "goodbye, world!". Edit the routes file
   from Listing 1.11 so that the root route goes to **goodbye** instead of to **hello**
   (Figure 1.22).

1.3 Version Control with Git

Now that we have a working "hello, world" application, we'll take a moment for
a step that, while technically optional, would be viewed by many experienced software developers as practically essential: placing our application source code under
version control. Version control systems allow us to track changes to our project's code,

collaborate more easily, and roll back any inadvertent errors (such as accidentally deleting files). Knowing how to use a version control system is a required skill for every professional-grade software developer.

There are many options for version control, but the software development community has largely standardized on Git, a distributed version control system originally developed by Linus Torvalds to host the Linux kernel. Git is a large subject, and we'll only be scratching the surface in this book; for a more thorough introduction to the basics, see *Learn Enough Git to Be Dangerous* (www.learnenough.com/git).

Putting your source code under version control with Git is *strongly* recommended, not only because it's nearly a universal practice in the Rails world, but also because it will allow you to back up and share your code more easily (Section 1.3.3) and deploy your application right here in the first chapter (Section 1.4).

1.3.1 Installation and Setup

The cloud IDE recommended in Section 1.1.1 includes Git by default, so no installation is necessary in this case. Otherwise, *Learn Enough Git to Be Dangerous* (www.learnenough.com/git) includes instructions for installing Git on your system.

First-Time System Setup

Before using Git, you should perform a few one-time setup steps. These are *system* setups, meaning you have to do them only once per computer.

The first (and required) step is to configure your name and email address, as shown in Listing 1.12.

Listing 1.12: Configuring the name and email fields for Git.

```
$ git config --global user.name "Your Name"
$ git config --global user.email your.email@example.com
```

Note that the name and email address you use in your Git configuration will be available in any repositories you make public.

If you're using the cloud IDE, the next step is to configure a default editor for the times when Git needs one (such as editing, or "amending" changes to projects). We'll use the **nano** editor, which is relatively friendly to beginners and is the default on the cloud IDE. As of this writing, the default editor gets reset on logout, and the path is also incorrect, so we need to execute Listing 1.13, which creates a *symbolic link* (or "symlink") to the correct location of the **nano** executable.[16] (The command in Listing 1.13 is a little advanced, so don't worry about understanding it if it looks confusing.)

Listing 1.13: Configuring the default editor on the cloud IDE.

```
$ sudo ln -sf `which nano` /usr/bin
```

Next, we'll take an optional but convenient step and set up an *alias*, or synonym, for the commonly used **checkout** command, as shown in Listing 1.14.

Listing 1.14: Setting up **git co** as a checkout alias.

```
$ git config --global alias.co checkout
```

In this tutorial, I'll always use the full **git checkout** command for maximum compatibility, but in practice I almost always use **git co** for short.

The final step is to prevent Git from asking for your password every time you want to use commands like **push** or **pull** (Section 1.3.4). The options for doing this are system-dependent; see the article "Caching Your GitHub Password in Git" (help.github.com/en/github/using-git/caching-your-github-password-in-git) if you're using anything other than Linux (including the cloud IDE). If you are using Linux (including, of course, the cloud IDE), you can simply set a *cache timeout* as shown in Listing 1.15.

Listing 1.15: Configuring Git to remember passwords for a set length of time.

```
$ git config --global credential.helper "cache --timeout=86400"
```

---

16. Vim is actually my Git preferred editor in this context, and is recommended for people who have Minimum Viable Vim or better (as described in *Learn Enough Text Editor to Be Dangerous*, www.learnenough.com/text-editor). To use **vim** in Listing 1.13, just replace `which nano` with `which vim`

Listing 1.15 configures Git to remember any passwords you use for 86,400 seconds (one day).[17] If you're highly security-conscious, you can use a shorter timeout, such as the default 900 seconds, or 15 minutes.

First-Time Repository Setup

Now we come to some steps that are necessary each time you create a new *repository* (sometimes called a *repo* for short). The first step is to navigate to the root directory of the hello app and initialize a new repository:

```
$ cd ~/environment/hello_app    # Just in case you weren't already there
$ git init
Reinitialized existing Git repository in
/home/ubuntu/environment/hello_app/.git/
```

Note that Git outputs a message that the repository has been *re*initialized. This is because, as of Rails 6, running **rails new** (Listing 1.4) automatically initializes a Git repository (a strong indication of how ubiquitous Git's use is in tech). Thus, the **git init** step isn't technically necessary in our case, but this won't hold for general Git repositories, so always running **git init** is a good habit to cultivate.

The next step is to add all the project files to the repository using **git add -A**:[18]

```
$ git add -A
```

This command adds all the files in the current directory apart from those that match the patterns in a special file called **.gitignore**. The **rails new** command automatically generates a **.gitignore** file appropriate to a Rails project, but you can add additional patterns as well.[19]

---

17. In theory, you could use a longer timeout, but on the cloud IDE the timer seems to gets reset every day or so, so entering a timeout of more than 86,400 seconds appears to have little effect in this case.

18. Many developers use the nearly equivalent **git add .**, where **.** ("dot") represents the current directory. In the rare cases where the two differ, what you usually want is **git add -A**, and this is what's used in the official Git documentation, so that's what we go with here.

19. Although we'll never need to edit it in the main tutorial, an example of adding a rule to the **.gitignore** file appears in Section 3.6.2, which is part of the optional advanced testing setup in Section 3.6.

The added files are initially placed in a *staging area*, which contains pending changes to our project. We can see which files are in the staging area by using the **status** command:

```
$ git status
On branch master

No commits yet

Changes to be committed:
  (use "git rm --cached <file>..." to unstage)

        new file:   .browserslistrc
        new file:   .gitignore
        new file:   .ruby-version
        new file:   Gemfile
        new file:   Gemfile.lock
        .
        .
        .
```

To tell Git we want to keep the changes, we use the **commit** command:

```
$ git commit -m "Initialize repository"
[master (root-commit) df0a62f] Initialize repository
.
.
.
```

The **-m** flag lets us add a *message* for the commit; if we omit **-m**, Git will open the system's default editor and have us enter the message there. (All the examples in this tutorial will use the **-m** flag.)

It is important to note that Git commits are *local*, recorded only on the machine on which the commits occur. We'll see how to push the changes up to a remote repository (using **git push**) in Section 1.3.4.

By the way, we can see a list of the commit messages using the **log** command:

```
$ git log
commit b981e5714e4d4a4f518aeca90270843c178b714e (HEAD -> master)
Author: Michael Hartl <michael@michaelhartl.com>
Date:   Sun Aug 18 17:57:06 2019 +0000

    Initialize repository
```

Depending on the length of the repository's log history, you may have to type **q** to quit. (As explained in *Learn Enough Git to Be Dangerous* (www.learnenough.com/git), **git log** uses the **less** interface covered in *Learn Enough Command Line to Be Dangerous* (www.learnenough.com/command-line).)

1.3.2 What Good Does Git Do for You?

If you've never used version control before, it may not be entirely clear at this point what benefits it provides, so let's look at just one example. Suppose you've made some accidental changes, such as (D'oh!) deleting the critical **app/controllers/** directory.

```
$ ls app/controllers/
application_controller.rb  concerns/
$ rm -rf app/controllers/
$ ls app/controllers/
ls: app/controllers/: No such file or directory
```

Here we're using the Unix **ls** command to list the contents of the **app/controllers/** directory and the **rm** command to remove it (Table 1.1). As noted in *Learn Enough Command Line to Be Dangerous* (www.learnenough.com/command-line), the **-rf** flag means "recursive force," which recursively removes all files, directories, subdirectories, and so on, without asking for explicit confirmation of each deletion.

Let's check the status to see what changed:

```
$ git status
On branch master
Changes not staged for commit:
  (use "git add/rm <file>..." to update what will be committed)
  (use "git checkout -- <file>..." to discard changes in working directory)

        deleted:    app/controllers/application_controller.rb
        deleted:    app/controllers/concerns/.keep

no changes added to commit (use "git add" and/or "git commit -a")
```

We see here that a file has been deleted, but the changes are only on the "working tree"; they haven't been committed yet. This means we can still undo the changes by using the **checkout** command with the **-f** flag to force overwriting of the current changes:

```
$ git checkout -f
$ git status
On branch master
nothing to commit, working tree clean
$ ls app/controllers/
application_controller.rb  concerns/
```

The missing files and directories are back. That's a relief!

1.3.3 GitHub

Now that we've put our project under version control with Git, it's time to push our code up to GitHub, a site optimized for hosting and sharing Git repositories.[20] Putting a copy of your Git repository at GitHub serves two purposes: It provides a full backup of your code (including the full history of commits), and it makes any future collaboration much easier.

Getting started with GitHub is straightforward: Just sign up for a GitHub account if you don't already have one (Figure 1.23).

Once you've signed up or signed in, click on the + sign dropdown menu and select "New repository" (Figure 1.24).

On the new repository page, fill the fields with the repository name (**hello_app**) and optional description, and take special care to select the "Private" option, as shown in Figure 1.25. Although Rails apps are, in principle, safe to expose as public repositories, so many things can go wrong (such as accidentally exposing passwords or private keys) that making all such repositories private is a prudent default.[21]

After clicking the "Create repository" button, you should see something like Figure 1.26, with commands for adding an existing repository to GitHub. Click on the HTTPS option,[22] and then copy the commands in the section for an existing repository. I suggest clicking the small icon on the right side of the screen, which

---

20. Bitbucket and GitLab are also excellent choices. Like GitHub, GitLab is written in Rails.

21. GitHub allows unlimited public and private repositories.

22. The SSH option shown in Figure 1.26 is excellent for more advanced users, so feel free to use it if you're comfortable with generating and configuring SSH keys. Among other things, this option allows your system to cache your password automatically, rendering the setup step in Listing 1.15 unnecessary.

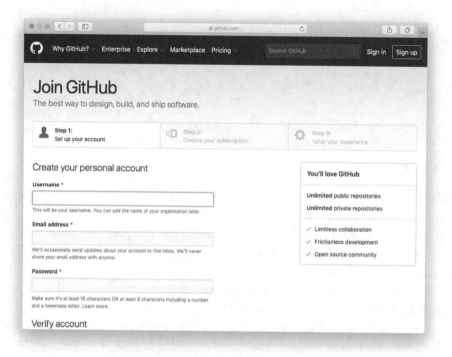

Figure 1.23: Signing up for GitHub.

automatically copies the commands shown in Listing 1.16 to your pasteboard buffer, allowing you to paste them into the command-line terminal.

Finally, run the commands in Listing 1.16. You will have to type your GitHub password, but you won't need to do so the next time (as long as it's within the cache timeout period) due to the configuration in Listing 1.15.

Listing 1.16: Adding GitHub as a remote origin and pushing up the repository.

```
$ git remote add origin https://github.com/<username>/hello_app.git
$ git push -u origin master
```

The commands in Listing 1.16 first tell Git that you want to add GitHub as the *origin* for your repository, and then push your repository up to the remote origin. (Don't

Figure 1.24: Selecting the "New repository" option.

worry about what the **-u** flag does; if you're curious, do a web search for "git set upstream".) Of course, you should replace **<username>** in Listing 1.16 with your actual username. For example, the command I ran looked like this:

```
$ git remote add origin https://github.com/mhartl/hello_app.git
```

The result is a page at GitHub for the hello_app repository, with file browsing, full commit history, and lots of other features (Figure 1.27).

1.3.4 Branch, Edit, Commit, Merge

If you've followed the steps in Section 1.3.3, you might have noticed that GitHub automatically rendered the repository's README file, as shown in Figure 1.28. This

Figure 1.25: Creating a private repository at GitHub.

file, called **README.md**, was generated automatically by the command in Listing 1.4. As indicated by the filename extension **.md**, it is written in *Markdown*,[23] a human-readable markup language designed to be easy to convert to HTML—which is exactly what GitHub has done.

This automatic rendering of the README is convenient, but of course it would be better if we tailored the contents of the file to the project at hand. In this section, we'll customize the README by adding some Rails Tutorial–specific content. In the process, we'll see a first example of the branch, edit, commit, merge workflow that I recommend using with Git.[24]

---

23. See *Learn Enough Text Editor to Be Dangerous*, www.learnenough.com/text-editor and *Learn Enough Git to Be Dangerous* (www.learnenough.com/git) for more information about Markdown.

24. For a convenient way to visualize Git repositories, take a look at Atlassian's SourceTree app.

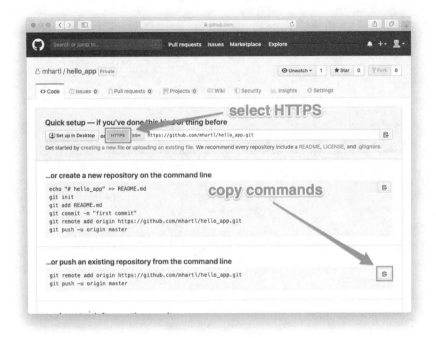

Figure 1.26: Code for adding an existing repository.

Branch

Git is incredibly good at making *branches*, which are effectively copies of a repository where we can make (possibly experimental) changes without modifying the parent files. In most cases, the parent repository is the *master* branch, and we can create a new topic branch by using **checkout** with the **-b** flag:

```
$ git checkout -b modify-README
Switched to a new branch 'modify-README'
$ git branch
  master
* modify-README
```

Here the second command, **git branch**, just lists all the local branches, and the asterisk * identifies which branch we're currently on. Note that **git checkout -b modify-README** both creates a new branch and switches to it, as indicated by the asterisk in front of the **modify-README** branch.

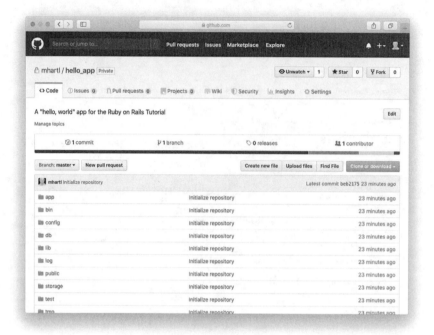

Figure 1.27: A GitHub repository page.

The full value of branching becomes clear only when you're working on a project with multiple developers,[25] but branches are helpful even for a single-developer tutorial such as this one. In particular, because the master branch is insulated from any changes we make to the topic branch, even if we *really* mess things up we can always abandon the changes by checking out the master branch and deleting the topic branch. We'll see how to do this at the end of the section.

By the way, for a change as small as this one, I wouldn't normally bother with a new branch (opting instead to work directly on the master branch), but in the present context it's a prime opportunity to start practicing good habits.

Edit

After creating the topic branch, we'll edit the README to add custom content, as shown in Listing 1.17 and Figure 1.29.

---

25. See, for example, the section on Collaborating in *Learn Enough Git to Be Dangerous* (www.learnenough.com/git).

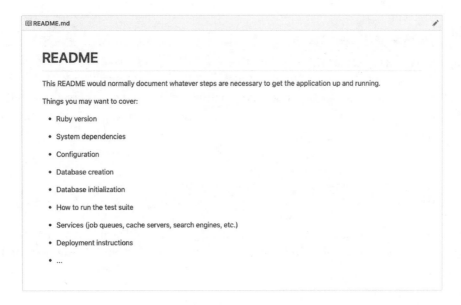

Figure 1.28: GitHub's rendering of the default Rails README.

Listing 1.17: The new **README** file.
README.md

```
# Ruby on Rails Tutorial

## "hello, world!"

This is the first application for the
[*Ruby on Rails Tutorial*](https://www.railstutorial.org/)
by [Michael Hartl](https://www.michaelhartl.com/). Hello, world!
```

Commit

With the changes made, we can take a look at the status of our branch:

```
$ git status
On branch modify-README
Changes not staged for commit:
  (use "git add <file>..." to update what will be committed)
  (use "git checkout -- <file>..." to discard changes in working directory)
```

```
        modified:   README.md

no changes added to commit (use "git add" and/or "git commit -a")
```

At this point, we could use **git add -A** as in Section 1.3.1, but **git commit** provides
the **-a** flag as a shortcut for the (very common) case of committing all modifications
to existing files:

```
$ git commit -a -m "Improve the README file"
[modify-README 34bb6a5] Improve the README file
 1 file changed, 5 insertions(+), 22 deletions(-)
```

Be careful about using the **-a** flag improperly; if you have added any new files to the
project since the last commit, you still have to tell Git about them by using **git add
-A** first.

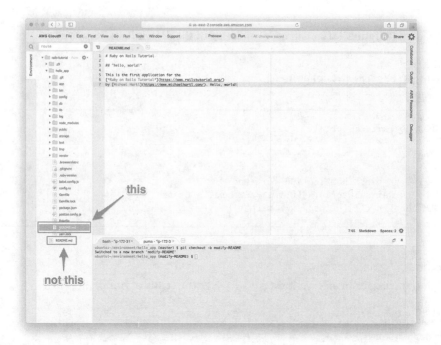

Figure 1.29: Editing the README file.

Note that we write the commit message in the *present* tense (and, technically speaking, the imperative mood). Git models commits as a series of patches, and in this context it makes sense to describe what each commit *does*, rather than what it did. Moreover, this usage matches up with the commit messages generated by the Git commands themselves. See Committing to Git from *Learn Enough Git to Be Dangerous* (www.learnenough.com/git) for more information.

Merge

Now that we've finished making our changes, we're ready to *merge* the results back into our master branch:

```
$ git checkout master
Switched to branch 'master'
$ git merge modify-README
Updating b981e57..015008c
Fast-forward
 README.md | 27 +++++----------------------
 1 file changed, 5 insertions(+), 22 deletions(-)
```

Note that the Git output frequently includes things like **34f06b7**, which are related to Git's internal representation of repositories. Your exact results will differ in these details, but otherwise should essentially match the output just shown.

After you've merged in the changes, you can tidy up your branches by deleting the topic branch using **git branch -d** if you're done with it:

```
$ git branch -d modify-README
Deleted branch modify-README (was 015008c).
```

This step is optional, and in fact it's quite common to leave the topic branch intact. This way you can switch back and forth between the topic and master branches, merging in changes every time you reach a natural stopping point.

As mentioned earlier, it's also possible to abandon your topic branch changes, in this case with **git branch -D**:

```
# For illustration only; don't do this unless you mess up a branch
$ git checkout -b topic-branch
$ <really mess up the branch>
```

```
$ git add -A
$ git commit -a -m "Make major mistake"
$ git checkout master
$ git branch -D topic-branch
```

Unlike the **-d** flag, the **-D** flag will delete the branch even though we haven't merged in the changes.

Push

Now that we've updated the **README**, we can push the changes up to GitHub to see the result. Since we have already done one push (Section 1.3.3), on most systems we can omit **origin master**, and simply run **git push**:

```
$ git push
```

As with the default **README**, GitHub nicely converts the Markdown in our updated **README** to HTML (Figure 1.30).

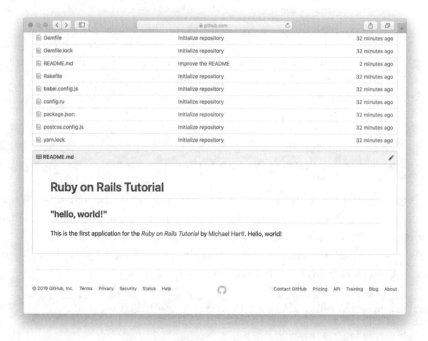

Figure 1.30: The improved **README** file at GitHub.

1.4 Deploying

Even though this is only the first chapter, we're already going to deploy our Rails application to production! As with the version control setup in Section 1.3, this step is technically optional, but deploying early and often allows us to catch any deployment problems early in our development cycle. The alternative—deploying only after laborious effort sealed away in a development environment—often leads to terrible integration headaches when launch time comes.[26]

Deploying Rails applications used to be a pain, but the Rails deployment ecosystem has matured rapidly in the past few years, and now there are several great options. These include shared hosts or virtual private servers running Phusion Passenger (a module for the Apache and Nginx[27] webservers), full-service deployment companies such as Engine Yard and Rails Machine, and cloud deployment services such as Engine Yard Cloud and Heroku.

My favorite Rails deployment option is Heroku, which is a hosted platform built specifically for deploying Rails and other web applications. (As you might guess, Heroku itself is written in Rails.) Heroku makes deploying Rails applications ridiculously easy, as long as your source code is under version control with Git—which is yet another reason to follow the Git setup steps in Section 1.3 if you haven't already done so. In addition, for many purposes, including for this tutorial, Heroku's free tier is more than sufficient.

The rest of this section is dedicated to deploying our first application to Heroku. Some of the ideas are fairly advanced, so don't worry about understanding all the details; what's important is that by the end of the process we'll have deployed our application to the live web.

1.4.1 Heroku Setup and Deployment

Heroku uses the PostgreSQL database (pronounced "post-gres-cue-ell," and often called "Postgres" for short), which means that we need to add the pg gem in the production environment to allow Rails to talk to Postgres:

---

26. Though it shouldn't matter for the example applications in the Rails Tutorial, if you're worried about accidentally making your app public too soon there are several options; see Section 1.4.2 for one.

27. Pronounced "Engine X."

```
group :production do
  gem 'pg', '1.1.4'
end
```

Also be sure to incorporate the changes made in Listing 1.6 that prevent the `sqlite3` gem from being included in a production environment, since the SQLite database isn't supported at Heroku:[28]

```
group :development, :test do
  gem 'sqlite3', '1.4.1'
  gem 'byebug',  '11.0.1', platforms: [:mri, :mingw, :x64_mingw]
end
```

The resulting **Gemfile** appears as in Listing 1.18.

Important note: For all the Gemfiles in this book, you should use the version numbers listed at gemfiles-6th-ed.railstutorial.org instead of the ones listed below (although they should be identical if you are reading this online).

Listing 1.18: A **Gemfile** with added and rearranged gems.

```
source 'https://rubygems.org'
git_source(:github) { |repo| "https://github.com/#{repo}.git" }

gem 'rails',      '6.0.2.1'
gem 'puma',       '3.12.2'
gem 'sass-rails', '5.1.0'
gem 'webpacker',  '4.0.7'
gem 'turbolinks', '5.2.0'
gem 'jbuilder',   '2.9.1'
gem 'bootsnap',   '1.4.5', require: false

group :development, :test do
  gem 'sqlite3', '1.4.1'
  gem 'byebug',  '11.0.1', platforms: [:mri, :mingw, :x64_mingw]
end

group :development do
  gem 'web-console',          '4.0.1'
  gem 'listen',               '3.1.5'
```

---

28. SQLite is widely used as an embedded database—for instance, it's ubiquitous in mobile phones—and Rails uses it locally by default because it's so easy to set up, but it isn't designed for database-backed web applications. See Section 3.1 for more information.

```
  gem 'spring',                '2.1.0'
  gem 'spring-watcher-listen', '2.0.1'
end

group :test do
  gem 'capybara',            '3.28.0'
  gem 'selenium-webdriver',  '3.142.4'
  gem 'webdrivers',          '4.1.2'
end

group :production do
  gem 'pg', '1.1.4'
end

# Windows does not include zoneinfo files, so bundle the tzinfo-data gem
gem 'tzinfo-data', platforms: [:mingw, :mswin, :x64_mingw, :jruby]
```

To prepare the system for deployment to production, we run **bundle install** with a special flag to prevent the local installation of any production gems (which in this case consists of the pg gem), as shown in Listing 1.19.

Listing 1.19: Bundling without production gems.

```
$ bundle install --without production
```

Because the only gem added in Listing 1.18 is restricted to a production environment, right now the command in Listing 1.19 doesn't actually install any additional local gems, but it's needed to update **Gemfile.lock** with the pg gem. We can commit the resulting change as follows:

```
$ git commit -a -m "Update Gemfile for Heroku"
```

Next we have to create and configure a new Heroku account. The first step is to sign up for Heroku. Then check to see if your system already has the Heroku command-line client installed:

```
$ heroku --version
```

This will display the current version number if the **heroku** command-line interface (CLI) is available, but on most systems it will be necessary to install the Heroku CLI by hand.[29] In particular, if you're working on the cloud IDE, you can install Heroku using the command shown in Listing 1.20.

Listing 1.20: The command to install Heroku on the cloud IDE.

```
$ source <(curl -sL https://cdn.learnenough.com/heroku_install)
```

After running the command in Listing 1.20, you should now be able to verify the installation by displaying the current version number (details may vary):

```
$ heroku --version
heroku/7.27.1 linux-x64 node-v11.14.0
```

Once you've verified that the Heroku command-line interface is installed, use the **heroku** command to log in with the mail address and password you used when signing up (the **--interactive** option prevents **heroku** from trying to spawn a browser):

```
$ heroku login --interactive
```

Finally, use the **heroku create** command to create a place on the Heroku servers for the sample app to live (Listing 1.21).

Listing 1.21: Creating a new application at Heroku.

```
$ heroku create
Creating app... done, □ blooming-bayou-75897
https://blooming-bayou-75897.herokuapp.com/ |
https://git.heroku.com/blooming-bayou-75897.git
```

The **heroku** command creates a new subdomain just for our application, available for immediate viewing. There's nothing there yet, though, so let's get busy deploying.

Heroku Deployment, Step 1
The first step is to use Git to push the master branch up to Heroku:

---

29. toolbelt.heroku.com

```
$ git push heroku master
```

(You may see some warning messages, which you should ignore for now. We'll discuss them further in Section 7.5.)

Heroku Deployment, Step 2

There is no step two! We're already done. To see your newly deployed application, visit the address that you saw when you ran **heroku create** (i.e., Listing 1.21).[30] The result appears in Figure 1.31. The page is identical to Figure 1.20, but now it's running in a production environment on the live web.[31]

Figure 1.31: The first Rails Tutorial application running on Heroku.

---

30. If you're working on your local machine instead of the cloud IDE, you can use **heroku open** to open the site automatically in a web browser.

31. Your results may differ if you completed the exercises in Section 1.2.4.

Exercises

Solutions to the exercises are available to all Rails Tutorial purchasers at https://www.railstutorial.org/aw-solutions.

To see other people's answers and to record your own, subscribe to the Rails Tutorial course or to the Learn Enough All Access Bundle.

1. By making the same change as in Section 1.2.4, arrange for your production app to display "hola, mundo!".

2. As in Section 1.2.4, arrange for the root route to display the result of the **goodbye** action. When deploying, confirm that you can omit **master** in the Git push, as in **git push heroku**.

1.4.2 Heroku Commands

There are many Heroku commands, and we'll barely scratch the surface of the many possibilities in this book. Let's take a minute to show just one of them by renaming the application as follows:

```
$ heroku rename rails-tutorial-hello
```

Don't use this name yourself; it's already taken by me! In fact, you probably shouldn't bother with this step right now; using the default address supplied by Heroku is fine. But if you do want to rename your application, you can arrange for it to be reasonably secure by using a random or obscure subdomain, such as the following:

```
hwpcbmze.herokuapp.com
seyjhflo.herokuapp.com
jhyicevg.herokuapp.com
```

With a random subdomain like this, someone could visit your site only if you gave them the address.[32] (By the way, as a preview of Ruby's compact awesomeness, here's the code I used to generate the random subdomains:

---

32. This solution, known as "security through obscurity," is fine for hobby projects, but for sites that require greater initial security I recommend using Rails HTTP basic authentication. This is a much more advanced technique, though, and requires significantly more technical sophistication (Box 1.2) to implement. (Thanks to Alfie Pates for raising this issue.)

```
('a'..'z').to_a.shuffle[0..7].join
```

We'll return to this bit of code in Chapter 4.)[33]

In addition to supporting subdomains, Heroku supports custom domains. (In fact, the Ruby on Rails Tutorial site lives at Heroku; if you're reading this book online, you're looking at a Heroku-hosted site right now!) See the Heroku documentation for more information about custom domains and other Heroku topics.

Exercises

Solutions to the exercises are available to all Rails Tutorial purchasers at https://www.railstutorial.org/aw-solutions.

To see other people's answers and to record your own, subscribe to the Rails Tutorial course or to the Learn Enough All Access Bundle.

1. Run **heroku help** to see a list of Heroku commands. What is the command to display logs for an app?

2. Use the command identified in the previous exercise to inspect the activity on your application. What was the most recent event? (This command is often useful when debugging production apps.)

1.5 Conclusion

We've come a long way in this chapter: development environment setup, installation, version control, and deployment. In the next chapter, we'll build on the foundation from Chapter 1 to make a database-backed *toy app*, which will give us our first real taste of what Rails can do.

If you'd like to share your progress at this point, feel free to send a tweet or Facebook status update with something like this:

I'm learning Ruby on Rails with the @railstutorial! https://www.railstutorial.org/

---

33. As is often the case, this code can be made even *more* compact using a built-in part of Ruby, in this case something called **sample**: **('a'..'z').to_a.sample(8).join**. Thanks to alert reader Stefan Pochmann for pointing this out—I didn't even know about **sample** until he told me!

I also recommend signing up for the Rails Tutorial email list,[34] which will ensure that you receive priority updates (and exclusive coupon codes) regarding the *Ruby on Rails Tutorial*.

1.5.1 What We Learned in this Chapter

- Ruby on Rails is a web development framework written in the Ruby programming language.

- Installing Rails, generating an application, and editing the resulting files is easy using a preconfigured cloud environment.

- Rails comes with a command-line command called **rails** that can generate new applications (**rails new**) and run local servers (**rails server**).

- We added a controller action and modified the root route to create a "hello, world" application.

- We protected against data loss while enabling collaboration by placing our application source code under version control with Git and pushing the resulting code to a private repository at GitHub.

- We deployed our application to a production environment using Heroku.

1.6 Conventions Used in this Book

The conventions used in this book are mostly self-explanatory. In this section, we'll go over some that may not be.

This tutorial makes frequent use of command-line commands. For simplicity, all command-line examples use a Unix-style command-line prompt (a dollar sign), as follows:

```
$ echo "hello, world"
hello, world
```

---

34. railstutorial.org/email

Rails comes with many commands that can be run at the command line. For example, in Section 1.2.2 we'll run a local development webserver with the **rails server** command:

```
$ rails server
```

As with the command-line prompt, the Rails Tutorial uses the Unix convention for directory separators (i.e., a forward slash **/**). For example, the sample application **production.rb** configuration file appears as follows:

```
config/environments/production.rb
```

This *file path* should be understood as being relative to the application's root directory, which will vary by system. For example, on the cloud IDE (Section 1.1.1) it looks like this:

```
/home/ubuntu/environment/sample_app/
```

Thus, the full path to **production.rb** is

```
/home/ubuntu/environment/sample_app/config/environments/production.rb
```

I will typically omit the application path and write just **config/environments/-production.rb** for short.

The Rails Tutorial often shows output from various programs. Because of the innumerable small differences between different computer systems, the output you see may not always agree exactly with what is shown in the text, but this is not cause for concern. In addition, some commands may produce errors depending on your system; rather than attempt the Sisyphean task of documenting all such errors in this tutorial, I will delegate to the "Google the error message" algorithm, which among other things is good practice for real-life software development (Box 1.2). If you run into any problems while following the tutorial, I suggest consulting the resources listed at the Rails Tutorial Help page.[35]

---

35. https://www.railstutorial.org/help

Because the Rails Tutorial covers testing of Rails applications, it is often helpful to know if a particular piece of code causes the test suite to fail (indicated by the color red) or pass (indicated by the color green). For convenience, code resulting in a failing test is thus indicated with RED, while code resulting in a passing test is indicated with GREEN.

Finally, for convenience the *Ruby on Rails Tutorial* adopts two conventions designed to make the many code samples easier to understand. First, some code listings include one or more highlighted lines, as seen here:

```
class User < ApplicationRecord
  validates :name,  presence: true
  validates :email, presence: true
end
```

Such highlighted lines typically indicate the most important new code in the given sample, and often (though not always) represent the difference between the present code listing and previous listings. Second, for brevity and simplicity many of the book's code listings include vertical dots, as follows:

```
class User < ApplicationRecord
  .
  .
  .
  has_secure_password
end
```

These dots represent omitted code and should not be copied literally.

CHAPTER 2

A Toy App

In this chapter, we develop a toy demo application to show off some of the power of Rails. The purpose is to get a high-level overview of Ruby on Rails programming (and web development in general) by rapidly generating an application using *scaffold generators*, which create a large amount of functionality automatically. As discussed in Box 2.1, the rest of the book will take the opposite approach, developing a full sample application incrementally and explaining each new concept as it arises, but for a quick overview (and some instant gratification) there is no substitute for scaffolding. The resulting toy app will enable us to interact with it through its URLs, giving us insight into the structure of a Rails application, including a first example of the *REST architecture* favored by Rails.

As with the forthcoming sample application, the toy app will consist of *users* and their associated *microposts* (thus constituting a minimalist Twitter-style app). The functionality will be utterly under-developed, and many of the steps will seem like magic, but worry not: We will develop a similar application from the ground up starting in Chapter 3, and I will provide plentiful forward-references to later material. In the meantime, have patience and a little faith—the whole point of this tutorial is to take you *beyond* this superficial, scaffold-driven approach to achieve a deeper understanding of Rails.

Box 2.1: Scaffolding: Quicker, Easier, More Seductive

From the beginning, Rails has benefited from a palpable sense of excitement, starting with the famous 15-minute weblog video (youtu.be/Gzj723LkRJY) by Rails creator David Heinemeier Hansson. That video and its successors are a great way to get a taste of Rails' power, and I recommend watching them. But be warned: They accomplish their amazing 15-minute feat using a feature called *scaffolding*, which relies heavily on *generated code*, magically created by the Rails `generate scaffold` command.

When writing a Ruby on Rails tutorial, it is tempting to rely on the scaffolding approach—it's quicker, easier, more seductive. But the complexity and sheer amount of code in the scaffolding can be utterly overwhelming to a beginning Rails developer; you may be able to use it, but you probably won't understand it. Following the scaffolding approach risks turning you into a virtuoso script generator with little (and brittle) actual knowledge of Rails.

In the *Ruby on Rails Tutorial*, we'll take the (nearly) polar opposite approach: Although this chapter will develop a small toy app using scaffolding, the core of the Rails Tutorial is the sample app, which we'll start writing in Chapter 3. At each stage of developing the sample application, we will write *small, bite-sized* pieces of code—simple enough to understand, yet novel enough to be challenging. The cumulative effect will be a deeper, more flexible knowledge of Rails, giving you a good background for writing nearly any type of web application.

2.1 Planning the Application

In this section, we'll outline our plans for the toy application. As in Section 1.2, we'll start by generating the application skeleton using the **rails new** command with a specific Rails version number:

```
$ cd ~/environment
$ rails _6.0.2.1_ new toy_app
$ cd toy_app/
```

If you're using the cloud IDE as recommended in Section 1.1.1, note that this second app can be created in the same environment as the first. It is not necessary to create a new environment. To get the files to appear, you may need to click the gear icon in the file navigator area and select "Refresh File Tree."

Next, we'll use a text editor to update the **Gemfile** needed by Bundler with the contents of Listing 2.1.

Important note: For all the Gemfiles in this book, you should use the version numbers listed at gemfiles-6th-ed.railstutorial.org instead of the ones listed below (although they should be identical if you are reading this online).

Listing 2.1: A **Gemfile** for the toy app.

```
source 'https://rubygems.org'
git_source(:github) { |repo| "https://github.com/#{repo}.git" }

gem 'rails',      '6.0.2.1'
gem 'puma',       '3.12.2'
gem 'sass-rails', '5.1.0'
gem 'webpacker',  '4.0.7'
gem 'turbolinks', '5.2.0'
gem 'jbuilder',   '2.9.1'
gem 'bootsnap',   '1.4.5', require: false

group :development, :test do
  gem 'sqlite3', '1.4.1'
  gem 'byebug',  '11.0.1', platforms: [:mri, :mingw, :x64_mingw]
end

group :development do
  gem 'web-console',          '4.0.1'
  gem 'listen',               '3.1.5'
  gem 'spring',               '2.1.0'
  gem 'spring-watcher-listen', '2.0.1'
end

group :test do
  gem 'capybara',           '3.28.0'
  gem 'selenium-webdriver', '3.142.4'
  gem 'webdrivers',         '4.1.2'
end

group :production do
  gem 'pg', '1.1.4'
end

# Windows does not include zoneinfo files, so bundle the tzinfo-data gem
gem 'tzinfo-data', platforms: [:mingw, :mswin, :x64_mingw, :jruby]
```

Note that Listing 2.1 is identical to Listing 1.18.

As in Section 1.4.1, we'll install the local gems while preventing the installation of production gems using the **--without production** option:

```
$ bundle install --without production
```

As noted in Section 1.2.1, you may need to run **bundle update** as well (Box 1.2).

Finally, we'll put the toy app under version control with Git:

```
$ git init
$ git add -A
$ git commit -m "Initialize repository"
```

You should also create a new repository at GitHub by following the same steps as in Section 1.3.3 (taking care to make it private as in Figure 2.1), and then push up to the remote repository:

Figure 2.1: Creating the toy app repository at GitHub.

```
$ git remote add origin https://github.com/<username>/toy_app.git
$ git push -u origin master
```

Finally, it's never too early to deploy, which I suggest doing by following the same "hello, world!" steps from Section 1.2.4, as shown in Listing 2.2 and Listing 2.3.

Listing 2.2: Adding a **hello** action to the Application controller.
app/controllers/application_controller.rb

```
class ApplicationController < ActionController::Base

  def hello
    render html: "hello, world!"
  end
end
```

Listing 2.3: Setting the root route.
config/routes.rb

```
Rails.application.routes.draw do
  root 'application#hello'
end
```

Then commit the changes and push up to Heroku, and, at the same time, GitHub—it's a good idea to keep the two copies in sync:

```
$ git commit -am "Add hello"
$ heroku create
$ git push && git push heroku master
```

Here we've used the double ampersand operator **&&** (read "and") to combine the pushes to GitHub and Heroku; the second command will execute only if the first one succeeds.[1]

---

1. The **&&** operator is described in Chapter 4 of *Learn Enough Command Line to Be Dangerous* (www.learnenough.com/command-line).

As in Section 1.4, you may see some warning messages, which you should ignore for now. We'll deal with them in Section 7.5. Apart from the URL of the Heroku app, the result should be the same as in Figure 1.31.

2.1.1 A Toy Model for Users

Now we're ready to start making the app itself. The typical first step when making a web application is to create a *data model*, which is a representation of the structures needed by our application, including the relationships between them. In our case, the toy app will be a Twitter-style microblog, with only users and short (micro)posts. Thus, we'll begin with a model for *users* of the app in this section, and then we'll add a model for *microposts* (Section 2.1.2).

There are as many choices for a user data model as there are different registration forms on the web; for simplicity, we'll go with a distinctly minimalist approach. Users of our toy app will have a unique identifier called **id** (of type **integer**), a publicly viewable **name** (of type **string**), and an **email** address (also of type **string**) that will double as a unique username. (Note that there is no **password** attribute at this point, which is part of what makes this app a "toy." We'll cover passwords starting in Chapter 6.) A summary of the data model for users appears in Figure 2.2.

As we'll see starting in Section 6.1.1, the label **users** in Figure 2.2 corresponds to a *table* in a database, and the **id**, **name**, and **email** attributes are *columns* in that table.

2.1.2 A Toy Model for Microposts

Recall from the introduction that a *micropost* is simply a short post, essentially a generic term for the brand-specific "tweet" (with the prefix "micro" motivated by Twitter's original description as a "micro-blog"). The core of the micropost data model is even

users	
id	integer
name	string
email	string

Figure 2.2: The data model for users.

simpler than the one for users: A micropost has only an **id** and a **content** field for the micropost's text (of type **text**).[2] There's an additional complication, though: We want to *associate* each micropost with a particular user. We'll accomplish this by recording the **user_id** of the owner of the post. The results are shown in Figure 2.3.

We'll see in Section 2.3.3 (and more fully in Chapter 13) how this **user_id** attribute allows us to succinctly express the notion that a user potentially has many associated microposts.

2.2 The Users Resource

In this section, we'll implement the users data model in Section 2.1.1, along with a web interface to that model. The combination will constitute a *Users resource*, which will allow us to think of users as objects that can be created, read, updated, and deleted through the web via the HTTP protocol. As promised in the introduction, our Users resource will be created by a scaffold generator program, which comes standard with each Rails project. I urge you not to look too closely at the generated code; at this stage, it will only serve to confuse you.

Rails scaffolding is generated by passing the **scaffold** command to the **rails generate** script. The argument of the **scaffold** command is the singular version of

microposts	
id	integer
content	text
user_id	integer

Figure 2.3: The data model for microposts.

---

2. Because microposts are short by design, the **string** type might actually be big enough to contain them, but using **text** better expresses our intent, while also giving us greater flexibility should we ever wish to relax the length constraint. Indeed, Twitter's change from allowing 140 to 280 characters in English-language tweets is a perfect example of why such flexibility is important: A **string** typically allows 255 ($2^8 - 1$) characters, which is big enough for 140-character tweets but not for 280-character ones. Using **text** allows a unified treatment of both cases.

the resource name (in this case, **User**), together with optional parameters for the data model's attributes:[3]

```
$ rails generate scaffold User name:string email:string
      invoke  active_record
      create    db/migrate/<timestamp>_create_users.rb
      create    app/models/user.rb
      invoke    test_unit
      create      test/models/user_test.rb
      create      test/fixtures/users.yml
      invoke  resource_route
       route    resources :users
      invoke  scaffold_controller
      create    app/controllers/users_controller.rb
      invoke    erb
      create      app/views/users
      create      app/views/users/index.html.erb
      create      app/views/users/edit.html.erb
      create      app/views/users/show.html.erb
      create      app/views/users/new.html.erb
      create      app/views/users/_form.html.erb
      invoke    test_unit
      create      test/controllers/users_controller_test.rb
      create      test/system/users_test.rb
      invoke    helper
      create      app/helpers/users_helper.rb
      invoke      test_unit
      invoke    jbuilder
      create      app/views/users/index.json.jbuilder
      create      app/views/users/show.json.jbuilder
      create      app/views/users/_user.json.jbuilder
      invoke  assets
      invoke    scss
      create      app/assets/stylesheets/users.scss
      invoke  scss
      create    app/assets/stylesheets/scaffolds.scss
```

By including **name:string** and **email:string**, we have arranged for the User model to have the form shown in Figure 2.2. (Note that there is no need to include a parameter for **id**; Rails creates it automatically for use as the *primary key* in the database.)

---

3. The name of the scaffold follows the convention of *models*, which are singular, rather than resources and controllers, which are plural. Thus, we have **User** instead of **Users**.

To proceed with the toy application, we first need to *migrate* the database using **rails db:migrate**, as shown in Listing 2.4.

Listing 2.4: Migrating the database.

```
$ rails db:migrate
== CreateUsers: migrating ======================================
-- create_table(:users)
   -> 0.0027s
== CreateUsers: migrated (0.0036s) =============================
```

The effect of Listing 2.4 is to update the database with our new **users** data model. (We'll learn more about database migrations starting in Section 6.1.1.)

Having run the migration in Listing 2.4, we can run the local webserver in a separate tab (Figure 1.15). Users of the cloud IDE should first add the same configuration as in Section 1.2.2 to allow the toy app to be served (Listing 2.5).

Listing 2.5: Allowing connections to the local web server.
config/environments/development.rb

```
Rails.application.configure do
  .
  .
  .
  # Allow Cloud9 connections.
  config.hosts.clear
end
```

Then run the Rails server as in Section 1.2.2:

```
$ rails server
```

Now the toy application should be available on the local server as described in Section 1.2.2. In particular, if we visit the root URL at / (read "slash", as noted in Section 1.2.4), we get the same "hello, world!" page shown in Figure 1.20.

2.2.1 A User Tour

In generating the Users resource scaffolding in Section 2.2, Rails created a large number of pages for manipulating users. For example, the page for listing all users is at /users, and the page for making a new user is at /users/new. The rest of this section is dedicated to taking a whirlwind tour through these user pages. As we proceed, it may help to refer to Table 2.1, which shows the correspondence between pages and URLs.

We start with the page that shows all the users in our application, called **index** and located at /users. As you might expect, initially there are no users at all (Figure 2.4).

Table 2.1: The correspondence between pages and URLs for the Users resource.

URL	Action	Purpose
/users	**index**	page to list all users
/users/1	**show**	page to show user with id **1**
/users/new	**new**	page to make a new user
/users/1/edit	**edit**	page to edit user with id **1**

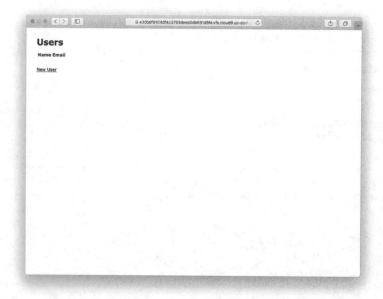

Figure 2.4: The initial index page for the Users resource (/users).

To make a new user, we can click on the New User link in Figure 2.4 to visit the **new** page at /users/new, as shown in Figure 2.5. In Chapter 7, this will become the user signup page.

We can create a user by entering name and email values in the text fields and then clicking the Create User button. The result is the user **show** page at /users/1, as seen in Figure 2.6. (The green welcome message is accomplished using the *flash*, which we'll learn about in Section 7.4.2.) Note that the URL is /users/1; as you might suspect, the number **1** is simply the user's **id** attribute from Figure 2.2. In Section 7.1, this page will become the user's profile page.

To change a user's information, we click the Edit link to visit the **edit** page at /users/1/edit (Figure 2.7). By modifying the user information and clicking the Update User button, we arrange to change the information for the user in the toy application (Figure 2.8). (As we'll see in detail starting in Chapter 6, this user data is stored in a database back end.) We'll add user edit/update functionality to the sample application in Section 10.1.

Now we'll create a second user by revisiting the **new** page at /users/new and submitting a second set of user information. The resulting user **index** is shown in

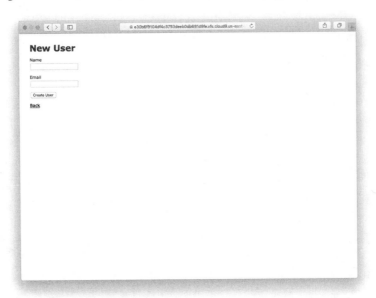

Figure 2.5: The new user page (/users/new).

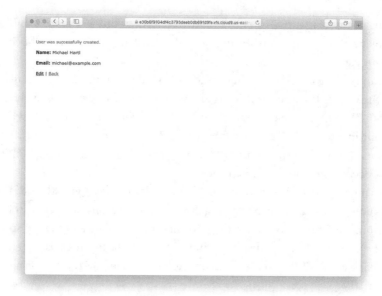

Figure 2.6: The page to show a user (/users/1).

Figure 2.7: The user edit page (/users/1/edit).

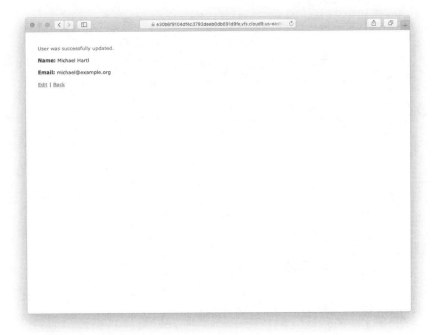

Figure 2.8: A user with updated information.

Figure 2.9. In Section 7.1, we will develop the user index into a more polished page for showing all users.

Having shown how to create, show, and edit users, we come finally to destroying them (Figure 2.10). You should verify that clicking on the link in Figure 2.10 destroys the second user, yielding an index page with only one user. (If it doesn't work, be sure that JavaScript is enabled in your browser; Rails uses JavaScript to issue the request needed to destroy a user.) Section 10.4 adds user deletion to the sample app, taking care to restrict its use to a special class of administrative users.

Exercises

Solutions to the exercises are available to all Rails Tutorial purchasers at https://www.railstutorial.org/aw-solutions.

To see other people's answers and to record your own, subscribe to the Rails Tutorial course or to the Learn Enough All Access Bundle.

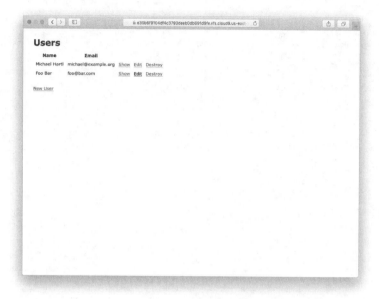

Figure 2.9: The user index page (/users) with a second user.

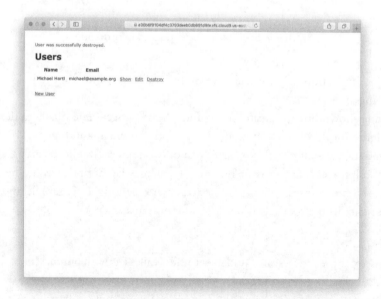

Figure 2.10: Destroying a user.

1. (For readers who know CSS) Create a new user, then use your browser's HTML inspector to determine the CSS id for the text "User was successfully created." What happens when you refresh your browser?

2. What happens if you try to create a user with a name but no email address?

3. What happens if you try create a user with an invalid email address, like "@example.com"?

4. Destroy each of the users created in the previous exercises. Does Rails display a message by default when a user is destroyed?

2.2.2 MVC in Action

Now that we've completed a quick overview of the Users resource, let's examine one particular part of it in the context of the model-view-controller (MVC) pattern introduced in Section 1.2.3. Our strategy will be to describe the results of a typical browser hit—a visit to the user index page at /users—in terms of MVC (Figure 2.11).

Here is a summary of the steps shown in Figure 2.11:

1. The browser issues a request for the /users URL.

2. Rails routes /users to the **index** action in the Users controller.

3. The **index** action asks the User model to retrieve all users (**User.all**).

4. The User model pulls all the users from the database.

5. The User model returns the list of users to the controller.

6. The controller captures the users in the **@users** variable, which is passed to the **index** view.

7. The view uses embedded Ruby to render the page as HTML.

8. The controller passes the HTML back to the browser.[4]

Now let's take a look at the these steps in more detail. We start with a request issued from the browser—that is, the result of typing a URL in the address bar or clicking on a link (Step 1 in Figure 2.11). This request hits the *Rails router* (Step 2), which

---

4. Some references indicate that the view returns the HTML directly to the browser (via a webserver such as Apache or Nginx). Regardless of the implementation details, I find it helpful to think of the controller as a central hub through which all the application's information flows.

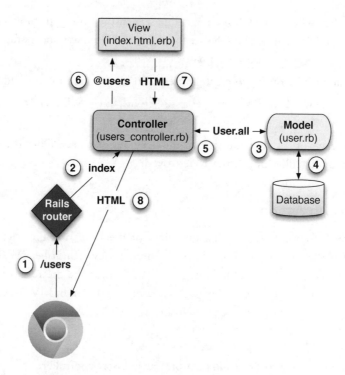

Figure 2.11: A detailed diagram of MVC in Rails.

dispatches the request to the proper *controller action* based on the URL (and, as we'll see in Box 3.2, the type of request). The code to create the mapping of user URLs to controller actions for the Users resource appears in Listing 2.6. This code effectively sets up the table of URL/action pairs seen in Table 2.1. (The strange notation `:users` is a *symbol*, which we'll learn about in Section 4.3.3.)

Listing 2.6: The Rails routes, with a rule for the Users resource.
`config/routes.rb`

```
Rails.application.routes.draw do
  resources :users
  root 'application#hello'
end
```

While we're looking at the routes file, let's take a moment to associate the root route with the users index, so that "slash" goes to /users. Recall from Listing 2.3 that we added the root route

```
root 'application#hello'
```

so that the root route went to the **hello** action in the Application controller. In the present case, we want to use the **index** action in the Users controller, which we can arrange using the code shown in Listing 2.7.

Listing 2.7: Adding a root route for users.
`config/routes.rb`

```
Rails.application.routes.draw do
  resources :users
  root 'users#index'
end
```

A *controller* contains a collection of related *actions*, and the pages from the tour in Section 2.2.1 correspond to actions in the Users controller. The controller generated by the scaffolding is shown schematically in Listing 2.8. Note the code **class UsersController < ApplicationController**, which is an example of a Ruby *class* with *inheritance*. (We'll discuss inheritance briefly in Section 2.3.4 and cover both subjects in more detail in Section 4.4.)

Listing 2.8: The Users controller in schematic form.
`app/controllers/users_controller.rb`

```
class UsersController < ApplicationController
  .
  .
  .
  def index
    .
    .
    .
  end
```

```
    def show
      .
      .
      .
    end

    def new
      .
      .
      .
    end

    def edit
      .
      .
      .
    end

    def create
      .
      .
      .
    end

    def update
      .
      .
      .
    end

    def destroy
      .
      .
      .
    end
  end
```

You might notice that there are more actions than there are pages. The **index**, **show**, **new**, and **edit** actions all correspond to pages from Section 2.2.1, but there are additional **create**, **update**, and **destroy** actions as well. These actions don't typically render pages (although they can); instead, their main purpose is to modify information about users in the database.

This full suite of controller actions, summarized in Table 2.2, represents the implementation of the REST architecture in Rails (Box 2.2), which is based on the idea of *representational state transfer*, a concept identified and named by computer scientist

Table 2.2: RESTful routes provided by the Users resource in Listing 2.6.

HTTP request	URL	Action	Purpose
GET	/users	**index**	page to list all users
GET	/users/1	**show**	page to show user with id **1**
GET	/users/new	**new**	page to make a new user
POST	/users	**create**	create a new user
GET	/users/1/edit	**edit**	page to edit user with id **1**
PATCH	/users/1	**update**	update user with id **1**
DELETE	/users/1	**destroy**	delete user with id **1**

Roy Fielding.[5] Note from Table 2.2 that there is some overlap in the URLs; for example, both the user **show** action and the **update** action correspond to the URL /users/1. The difference between them is the HTTP request method they respond to. We'll learn more about HTTP request methods starting in Section 3.3.

Box 2.2: REpresentational State Transfer (REST)

If you read much about Ruby on Rails web development, you'll see a lot of references to "REST," which is an acronym for REpresentational State Transfer. REST is an architectural style for developing distributed, networked systems and software applications such as the World Wide Web and web applications. Although REST theory is rather abstract, in the context of Rails applications REST means that most application components (such as users and microposts) are modeled as *resources* that can be created, read, updated, and deleted—operations that correspond both to the CRUD operations of relational databases and to the four fundamental HTTP request methods: POST, GET, PATCH, and DELETE. (We'll learn more about HTTP requests in Section 3.3 and especially Box 3.2.)

As a Rails application developer, the RESTful style of development helps you make choices about which controllers and actions to write: You simply structure the application using resources that get created, read, updated, and deleted. In the case of users and microposts, this process is straightforward, since they are naturally resources in their own right. In Chapter 14, we'll see an example where

---

5. Fielding, Roy Thomas. *Architectural Styles and the Design of Network-Based Software Architectures*. Doctoral dissertation, University of California, Irvine, 2000.

> REST principles allow us to model a subtler problem, "following users," in a natural and convenient way.

To examine the relationship between the Users controller and the User model, let's focus on the **index** action, shown in Listing 2.9. (Learning how to read code even when you don't fully understand it is an important aspect of technical sophistication (Box 1.2).)

Listing 2.9: The simplified user **index** action for the toy application.
`app/controllers/users_controller.rb`

```ruby
class UsersController < ApplicationController
  .
  .
  .
  def index
    @users = User.all
  end
  .
  .
  .
end
```

This **index** action includes the line **@users = User.all** (Step 3 in Figure 2.11), which asks the User model to retrieve a list of all the users from the database (Step 4), and then places them in the variable **@users** (pronounced "at-users") (Step 5).

The User model itself appears in Listing 2.10. Although it is rather plain, it comes equipped with a large amount of functionality because of inheritance (Section 2.3.4 and Section 4.4). In particular, by using the Rails library called *Active Record*, the code in Listing 2.10 arranges for **User.all** to return all the users in the database.

Listing 2.10: The User model for the toy application.
`app/models/user.rb`

```ruby
class User < ApplicationRecord
end
```

Once the **@users** variable is defined, the controller calls the *view* (Step 6), shown in Listing 2.11. Variables that start with the **@** sign, called *instance variables*, are automatically available in the views; in this case, the **index.html.erb** view in Listing 2.11 iterates through the **@users** list and outputs a line of HTML for each one. (Remember, you aren't supposed to understand this code right now. It is shown only for purposes of illustration.)

Listing 2.11: The view for the users index.
app/views/users/index.html.erb

```erb
<p id="notice"><%= notice %></p>

<h1>Users</h1>

<table>
  <thead>
    <tr>
      <th>Name</th>
      <th>Email</th>
      <th colspan="3"></th>
    </tr>
  </thead>

  <tbody>
    <% @users.each do |user| %>
      <tr>
        <td><%= user.name %></td>
        <td><%= user.email %></td>
        <td><%= link_to 'Show', user %></td>
        <td><%= link_to 'Edit', edit_user_path(user) %></td>
        <td><%= link_to 'Destroy', user, method: :delete,
                        data: { confirm: 'Are you sure?' } %></td>
      </tr>
    <% end %>
  </tbody>
</table>

<br>

<%= link_to 'New User', new_user_path %>
```

The view converts its contents to HTML (Step 7), which is then returned by the controller to the browser for display (Step 8).

Exercises

Solutions to the exercises are available to all Rails Tutorial purchasers at https://www.railstutorial.org/aw-solutions.

To see other people's answers and to record your own, subscribe to the Rails Tutorial course or to the Learn Enough All Access Bundle.

1. By referring to Figure 2.11, write out the analogous steps for visiting the URL /users/1/edit.

2. Find the line in the scaffolding code that retrieves the user from the database in the previous exercise. *Hint*: It's in a special location called **set_user**.

3. What is the name of the view file for the user edit page?

2.2.3 Weaknesses of this Users Resource

Though good for getting a general overview of Rails, the scaffold Users resource suffers from a number of severe weaknesses.

- **No data validations.** Our User model accepts data such as blank names and invalid email addresses without complaint.

- **No authentication.** We have no notion of logging in or out, and no way to prevent any user from performing any operation.

- **No tests.** This isn't technically true—the scaffolding includes rudimentary tests— but the generated tests don't test for data validation, authentication, or any other custom requirements.

- **No style or layout.** There is no consistent site styling or navigation.

- **No real understanding.** If you understand the scaffold code, you probably shouldn't be reading this book.

2.3 The Microposts Resource

Having generated and explored the Users resource, we turn now to the associated Microposts resource. Throughout this section, I recommend comparing the elements of the Microposts resource with the analogous user elements from Section 2.2; you should see that the two resources parallel each other in many ways. The RESTful structure of Rails applications is best absorbed by this sort of repetition of form. Indeed, seeing the parallel structure of Users and Microposts even at this early stage is one of the prime motivations for this chapter.

2.3.1   A Micropost Microtour

As with the Users resource, we'll generate scaffold code for the Microposts resource using **rails generate scaffold**, in this case implementing the data model from Figure 2.3:[6]

```
$ rails generate scaffold Micropost content:text user_id:integer
    invoke  active_record
    create    db/migrate/<timestamp>_create_microposts.rb
    create    app/models/micropost.rb
    invoke    test_unit
    create      test/models/micropost_test.rb
    create      test/fixtures/microposts.yml
    invoke  resource_route
     route    resources :microposts
    invoke  scaffold_controller
    create    app/controllers/microposts_controller.rb
    invoke    erb
    create      app/views/microposts
    create      app/views/microposts/index.html.erb
    create      app/views/microposts/edit.html.erb
    create      app/views/microposts/show.html.erb
    create      app/views/microposts/new.html.erb
    create      app/views/microposts/_form.html.erb
    invoke    test_unit
    create      test/controllers/microposts_controller_test.rb
    create      test/system/microposts_test.rb
    invoke    helper
    create      app/helpers/microposts_helper.rb
    invoke      test_unit
    invoke    jbuilder
    create      app/views/microposts/index.json.jbuilder
    create      app/views/microposts/show.json.jbuilder
    create      app/views/microposts/_micropost.json.jbuilder
    invoke  assets
    invoke    scss
    create      app/assets/stylesheets/microposts.scss
    invoke  scss
 identical    app/assets/stylesheets/scaffolds.scss
```

To update our database with the new data model, we need to run a migration as in Section 2.2:

---

6. As with the User scaffold, the scaffold generator for microposts follows the singular convention of Rails models; thus, we have **generate Micropost**.

```
$ rails db:migrate
== CreateMicroposts: migrating =================================================
-- create_table(:microposts)
   -> 0.0023s
== CreateMicroposts: migrated (0.0026s) ========================================
```

Now we are in a position to create microposts in the same way we created users in Section 2.2.1. As you might guess, the scaffold generator has updated the Rails routes file with a rule for Microposts resource, as seen in Listing 2.12.[7] As with users, the **resources :microposts** routing rule maps micropost URLs to actions in the Microposts controller, as seen in Table 2.3.

Listing 2.12: The Rails routes, with a new rule for Microposts resources.
`config/routes.rb`

```
Rails.application.routes.draw do
  resources :microposts
  resources :users
  root 'users#index'
end
```

Table 2.3: RESTful routes provided by the Microposts resource in Listing 2.12.

HTTP request	URL	Action	Purpose
GET	/microposts	**index**	page to list all microposts
GET	/microposts/1	**show**	page to show micropost with id **1**
GET	/microposts/new	**new**	page to make a new micropost
POST	/microposts	**create**	create a new micropost
GET	/microposts/1/edit	**edit**	page to edit micropost with id **1**
PATCH	/microposts/1	**update**	update micropost with id **1**
DELETE	/microposts/1	**destroy**	delete micropost with id **1**

---

7. The scaffold code may have extra blank lines compared to Listing 2.12. This is not a cause for concern, as Ruby ignores such extra space.

The Microposts controller itself appears in schematic form in Listing 2.13. Note that, apart from having **MicropostsController** in place of **UsersController**, Listing 2.13 is *identical* to the code in Listing 2.8. This is a reflection of the REST architecture that is common to both resources.

Listing 2.13: The Microposts controller in schematic form.
app/controllers/microposts_controller.rb

```ruby
class MicropostsController < ApplicationController
  .
  .
  .
  def index
    .
    .
    .
  end

  def show
    .
    .
    .
  end

  def new
    .
    .
    .
  end

  def edit
    .
    .
    .
  end

  def create
    .
    .
    .
  end

  def update
    .
    .
    .
  end
```

```
def destroy
  .
  .
  .
end
end
```

To make some actual microposts, we click on New Micropost on the micropost index page (Figure 2.12). We then enter information at the new microposts page, /microposts/new, as seen in Figure 2.13.

At this point, go ahead and create a micropost or two, taking care to make sure that at least one has a **user_id** of **1** to match the id of the first user created in Section 2.2.1. The result should look something like Figure 2.14.

Figure 2.12: The micropost index page (/microposts).

Figure 2.13: The new micropost page (/microposts/new).

Exercises

Solutions to the exercises are available to all Rails Tutorial purchasers at https://www.railstutorial.org/aw-solutions.

To see other people's answers and to record your own, subscribe to the Rails Tutorial course or to the Learn Enough All Access Bundle.

1. (For readers who know CSS) Create a new micropost, then use your browser's HTML inspector to determine the CSS id for the text "Micropost was successfully created." What happens when you refresh your browser?

2. Try to create a micropost with empty content and no user id.

3. Try to create a micropost with more than 140 characters of content (say, the first paragraph from the Wikipedia article on Ruby).

4. Destroy the microposts from the previous exercises.

Figure 2.14: The micropost index page with a couple of posts.

2.3.2 Putting the *Micro* in Microposts

Any *micro*post worthy of the name should have some means of enforcing the rules governing the length of the post. Implementing this constraint in Rails is easy with *validations*; to accept microposts with at most 140 characters (à la the original design of Twitter), we use a *length* validation. At this point, you should open the file **app/models/micropost.rb** in your text editor or IDE and fill it with the contents of Listing 2.14.

Listing 2.14: Constraining microposts to be at most 140 characters.
app/models/micropost.rb

```
class Micropost < ApplicationRecord
  validates :content, length: { maximum: 140 }
end
```

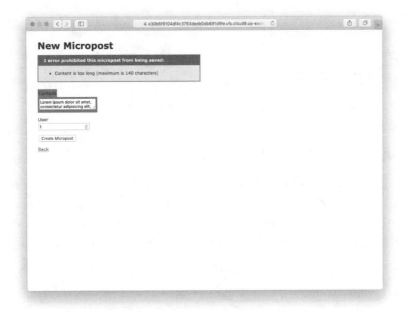

Figure 2.15: Error messages for a failed micropost creation.

The code in Listing 2.14 may look rather mysterious—we'll cover validations more thoroughly starting in Section 6.2—but its effects are readily apparent if we go to the new micropost page and enter more than 140 characters for the content of the post. As seen in Figure 2.15, Rails renders *error messages* indicating that the micropost's content is too long. (We'll learn more about error messages in Section 7.3.3.)

Exercises

Solutions to the exercises are available to all Rails Tutorial purchasers at https://www.railstutorial.org/aw-solutions.

To see other people's answers and to record your own, subscribe to the Rails Tutorial course or to the Learn Enough All Access Bundle.

1. Try to create a micropost with the same long content used in a previous exercise (Section 2.3.1). How has the behavior changed?

2. (For readers who know CSS) Use your browser's HTML inspector to determine the CSS id of the error message produced by the previous exercise.

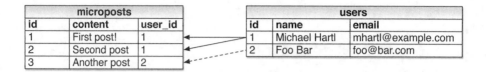

Figure 2.16: The association between microposts and users.

2.3.3 A User `has_many` **Microposts**

One of the most powerful features of Rails is the ability to form *associations* between different data models. In the case of our User model, each user potentially has many microposts. We can express this relationship in code by updating the User and Micropost models as in Listing 2.15 and Listing 2.16, respectively.

Listing 2.15: A user has many microposts.
app/models/user.rb

```
class User < ApplicationRecord
  has_many :microposts
end
```

Listing 2.16: A micropost belongs to a user.
app/models/micropost.rb

```
class Micropost < ApplicationRecord
  belongs_to :user
  validates :content, length: { maximum: 140 }
end
```

We can visualize the result of this association in Figure 2.16. Because of the **user_id** column in the **microposts** table, Rails (using Active Record) can infer the microposts associated with each user.

In Chapter 13 and Chapter 14, we will use the association of users and microposts both to display all of a user's microposts and to construct a Twitter-like micropost feed. For now, we can examine the implications of the user–micropost association by using the *console*, which is a useful tool for interacting with Rails applications. We first invoke the console with **rails console** at the command line, and then retrieve the first user from the database using **User.first** (putting the results in the variable **first_user**), as shown in Listing 2.17.[8] (I include **exit** in the last line just to demonstrate how to exit the console. On most systems, you can also use Ctrl-D for the same purpose.)[9]

Listing 2.17: Investigating the state of the application using the Rails console.

```
$ rails console
>> first_user = User.first
   (0.5ms)  SELECT sqlite_version(*)
  User Load (0.2ms)  SELECT "users".* FROM "users" ORDER BY "users"."id" ASC
  LIMIT ?  [["LIMIT", 1]]
=> #<User id: 1, name: "Michael Hartl", email: "michael@example.org",
  created_at: "2019-08-20 00:39:14", updated_at: "2019-08-20 00:41:24">
>> first_user.microposts
  Micropost Load (3.2ms)  SELECT "microposts".* FROM "microposts" WHERE
  "microposts"."user_id" = ? LIMIT ?  [["user_id", 1], ["LIMIT", 11]]
=> #<ActiveRecord::Associations::CollectionProxy [#<Micropost id: 1, content:
  "First micropost!", user_id: 1, created_at: "2019-08-20 02:04:13", updated_at:
  "2019-08-20 02:04:13">, #<Micropost id: 2, content: "Second micropost",
  user_id: 1, created_at: "2019-08-20 02:04:30", updated_at: "2019-08-20
  02:04:30">]>
>> micropost = first_user.microposts.first
  Micropost Load (0.2ms)  SELECT "microposts".* FROM "microposts" WHERE
  "microposts"."user_id" = ? ORDER BY "microposts"."id" ASC LIMIT ?
  [["user_id", 1], ["LIMIT", 1]]
=> #<Micropost id: 1, content: "First micropost!", user_id: 1, created_at:
  "2019-08-20 02:04:13", updated_at: "2019-08-20 02:04:13">
>> micropost.user
=> #<User id: 1, name: "Michael Hartl", email: "michael@example.org",
  created_at: "2019-08-20 00:39:14", updated_at: "2019-08-20 00:41:24"
>> exit
```

There's a lot going on in Listing 2.17, and teasing out the relevant parts is a good exercise in technical sophistication (Box 1.2). The output includes the actual return

---

8. Your console prompt might be something like **2.6.3 :001 >**, but the examples use **>>** since Ruby versions will vary.

9. As in the case of Ctrl-C, the capital "D" refers to the key on the keyboard, not the capital letter, so you don't have to hold down the Shift key along with the Ctrl key.

values, which are raw Ruby objects, as well as the structured query language (SQL) code that produced them.

In addition to retrieving the first user with **User.first**, Listing 2.17 shows two other things: (1) how to access the first user's microposts using the code **first_user.microposts**, which automatically returns all the microposts with **user_id** equal to the id of **first_user** (in this case, **1**); and (2) how to return the user corresponding to a particular post using **micropost.user**. We'll learn much more about the Ruby involved in Listing 2.17 in Chapter 4, and more about the association facilities in Active Record in Chapter 13 and Chapter 14.

Exercises

Solutions to the exercises are available to all Rails Tutorial purchasers at https://www.railstutorial.org/aw-solutions.

To see other people's answers and to record your own, subscribe to the Rails Tutorial course or to the Learn Enough All Access Bundle.

1. Edit the user show page to display the content of the user's first micropost. (Use your technical sophistication (Box 1.2) to guess the syntax based on the other content in the file.) Visit /users/1 to confirm that it worked.

2. The code in Listing 2.18 shows how to add a validation for the presence of micropost content to ensure that microposts can't be blank. Verify that you get the behavior shown in Figure 2.17.

3. Update Listing 2.19 by replacing **FILL_IN** with the appropriate code to validate the presence of name and email attributes in the User model (Figure 2.18).

Listing 2.18: Code to validate the presence of micropost content.
`app/models/micropost.rb`

```
class Micropost < ApplicationRecord
  belongs_to :user
  validates :content, length: { maximum: 140 },
                      presence: true
end
```

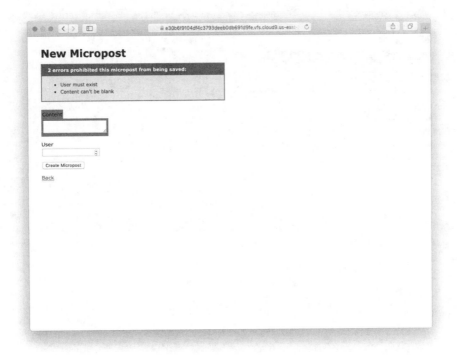

Figure 2.17: The effect of a micropost presence validation.

Listing 2.19: Adding presence validations to the User model.
app/models/user.rb

```
class User < ApplicationRecord
  has_many :microposts
    validates FILL_IN, presence: true    # Replace FILL_IN with the right code.
    validates FILL_IN, presence: true    # Replace FILL_IN with the right code.
end
```

2.3.4   Inheritance Hierarchies

We end our discussion of the toy application with a brief description of the controller and model class hierarchies in Rails. This discussion will make more sense if you

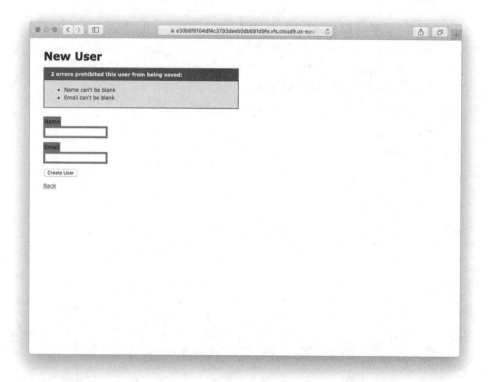

Figure 2.18: The effect of presence validations on the User model.

have some experience with object-oriented programming (OOP), particularly *classes*. Don't worry if it's confusing for now; we'll discuss these ideas more thoroughly in Section 4.4.

We start with the inheritance structure for models. Comparing Listing 2.20 and Listing 2.21, we see that both the User model and the Micropost model inherit (via the left angle bracket **<**) from **ApplicationRecord**, which in turn inherits from **ActiveRecord::Base**, which is the base class for models provided by Active Record; a diagram summarizing this relationship appears in Figure 2.19. By inheriting from **ActiveRecord::Base**, our model objects gain the ability to communicate with the database, treat the database columns as Ruby attributes, and so on.

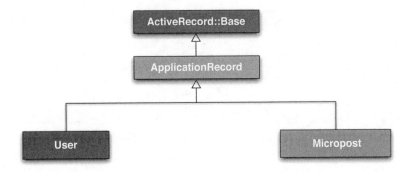

Figure 2.19: The inheritance hierarchy for the User and Micropost models.

Listing 2.20: The **User** class, highlighting inheritance.
app/models/user.rb

```
class User < ApplicationRecord
  .
  .
  .
end
```

Listing 2.21: The **Micropost** class, highlighting inheritance.
app/models/micropost.rb

```
class Micropost < ApplicationRecord
  .
  .
  .
end
```

The inheritance structure for controllers is essentially the same as that for models. Comparing Listing 2.22 and Listing 2.23, we see that both the Users controller and the Microposts controller inherit from the Application controller. Examining Listing 2.24, we see that **ApplicationController** itself inherits from **ActionController::Base**, which is the base class for controllers provided by the Rails library Action Pack. The relationships between these classes are illustrated in Figure 2.20.

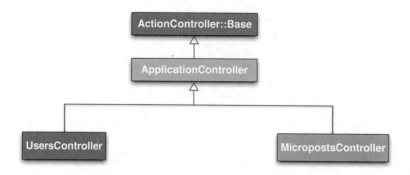

Figure 2.20: The inheritance hierarchy for the Users and Microposts controllers.

Listing 2.22: The **UsersController** class, highlighting inheritance.
app/controllers/users_controller.rb

```
class UsersController < ApplicationController
  .
  .
  .
end
```

Listing 2.23: The **MicropostsController** class, highlighting inheritance.
app/controllers/microposts_controller.rb

```
class MicropostsController < ApplicationController
  .
  .
  .
end
```

Listing 2.24: The **ApplicationController** class, highlighting inheritance.
app/controllers/application_controller.rb

```
class ApplicationController < ActionController::Base
  .
  .
  .
end
```

As with model inheritance, both the Users and Microposts controllers gain a large amount of functionality by inheriting from a base class (in this case, **ActionController::Base**), including the capability to manipulate model objects, filter inbound HTTP requests, and render views as HTML. Since all Rails controllers inherit from **ApplicationController**, all rules defined in the Application controller automatically apply to every action in the application. For example, in Section 9.1 we'll see how to include helpers for logging in and logging out of all of the sample application's controllers.

Exercises

Solutions to the exercises are available to all Rails Tutorial purchasers at https://www.railstutorial.org/aw-solutions.

To see other people's answers and to record your own, subscribe to the Rails Tutorial course or to the Learn Enough All Access Bundle.

1. By examining the contents of the Application controller file, find the line that causes **ApplicationController** to inherit from **ActionController::Base**.

2. Is there an analogous file containing a line where **ApplicationRecord** inherits from **ActiveRecord::Base**? *Hint*: It would probably be a file called something like **application_record.rb** in the **app/models** directory.

2.3.5 Deploying the Toy App

With the completion of the Microposts resource, now is a good time to push the repository up to GitHub:

```
$ git status     # It's a good habit to check the status before adding
$ git add -A
$ git commit -m "Finish toy app"
$ git push
```

Ordinarily, you should make smaller, more frequent commits, but for the purposes of this chapter a single big commit at the end is fine.

At this point, you can also deploy the toy app to Heroku as is described in Section 1.4:

```
$ git push heroku
```

(This assumes you created the Heroku app in Section 2.1. Otherwise, you should run **heroku create** and then **git push heroku master**.)

At this point, visiting the page at Heroku yields an error message, as shown in Figure 2.21. We can track down the problem by inspecting the Heroku logs:

```
$ heroku logs
```

Scrolling up in the logs, you should see a line that includes something like this:

```
ActionView::Template::Error (PG::UndefinedTable: ERROR:  relation "users" does
not exist
```

This line is a big hint that there is a missing **users** table. Luckily, we learned how to handle that problem way back in Listing 2.4: All we need to do is run the database migrations (which will create the **microposts** table as well).

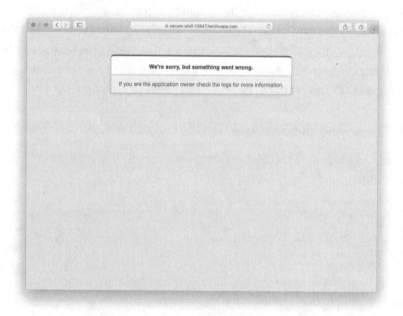

Figure 2.21: An error page at Heroku.

The way to execute this sort of command at Heroku is to prefix the usual Rails command with **heroku run**, like this:

```
$ heroku run rails db:migrate
```

This updates the database at Heroku with the user and micropost data models as required. After running the migration, you should be able to use the toy app in production, with a real PostgreSQL database back end (Figure 2.22).[10]

Finally, if you completed the exercises in Section 2.3.3, you will have to remove the code to display the first user's micropost to get the app to load properly. In this case, simply delete the offending code, make another commit, and push again to Heroku.

Figure 2.22: Running the toy app in production.

---

10. The production database should work without any additional configuration, but in fact some configuration is recommended by the official Heroku documentation. We'll take care of this detail in Section 7.5.3.

Exercises

Solutions to the exercises are available to all Rails Tutorial purchasers at https://www.railstutorial.org/aw-solutions.

To see other people's answers and to record your own, subscribe to the Rails Tutorial course or to the Learn Enough All Access Bundle.

1. Create a few users on the production app.

2. Create a few production microposts for the first user.

3. By trying to create a micropost with content exceeding 140 characters, confirm that the validation from Listing 2.14 works on the production app.

2.4 Conclusion

We've come now to the end of the high-level overview of a Rails application. The toy app developed in this chapter has several strengths and a host of weaknesses.

Strengths

- High-level overview of Rails

- Introduction to MVC

- First taste of the REST architecture

- Beginning data modeling

- A live, database-backed web application in production

Weaknesses

- No custom layout or styling

- No static pages (such as "Home" or "About")

- No user passwords

- No user images

- No logging in

- No security

- No automatic user/micropost association

- No notion of "following" or "followed"
- No micropost feed
- No meaningful tests
- **No real understanding**

The rest of this tutorial is dedicated to building on the strengths and eliminating the weaknesses.

2.4.1 What We Learned in this Chapter

- Scaffolding automatically creates code to model data and interact with it through the web.
- Scaffolding is good for getting started quickly but is bad for understanding.
- Rails uses the model-view-controller (MVC) pattern for structuring web applications.
- As interpreted by Rails, the REST architecture includes a standard set of URLs and controller actions for interacting with data models.
- Rails supports data validations to place constraints on the values of data model attributes.
- Rails comes with built-in functions for defining associations between different data models.
- We can interact with Rails applications at the command line using the Rails console.

CHAPTER **3**

Mostly Static Pages

In this chapter, we will begin developing the professional-grade sample application that will serve as our example throughout the rest of this tutorial. Although the sample app will eventually have users, microposts, and a full login and authentication framework, we will begin with a seemingly limited topic: the creation of static pages. Despite its apparent simplicity, making static pages is a highly instructive exercise, rich in implications—a perfect start for our nascent application.

Although Rails is designed for making database-backed dynamic websites, it also excels at making the kind of static pages we might create using raw HTML files. In fact, even using Rails for static pages yields a distinct advantage: We can easily add just a *small* amount of dynamic content. In this chapter we'll learn how. Along the way, we'll get our first taste of *automated testing*, which will help us be more confident that our code is correct. Moreover, having a good test suite will allow us to *refactor* our code with confidence, changing its form without changing its function.

3.1 Sample App Setup

As in Chapter 2, before getting started we need to create a new Rails project, this time called **sample_app**, as shown in Listing 3.1.[1]

---

1. If you're using the cloud IDE, it's often useful to use the "Go to Anything" command (under the "Go" menu), which makes it easy to navigate the filesystem by typing in partial filenames. In this context, having the hello, toy, and sample apps present in the same project can be inconvenient due to the many common filenames. For example, when searching for a file called "Gemfile", six possibilities will show up, because each project has matching files called **Gemfile** and **Gemfile.lock**. Thus, you may want to consider removing the first two apps before proceeding, which you can do by navigating to the **environment** directory and

Listing 3.1: Generating a new sample app.

```
$ cd ~/environment
$ rails _6.0.2.1_ new sample_app
$ cd sample_app/
```

(As in Section 2.1, note that users of the cloud IDE can create this project in the same environment as the applications from the previous two chapters. It is not necessary to create a new environment.)

Note: For convenience, a reference implementation of the sample app is available at GitHub,[2] with a separate branch for each chapter in the tutorial.

As in Section 2.1, our next step is to use a text editor to update the **Gemfile** with the gems needed by our application. Listing 3.2 is identical to Listing 1.6 and Listing 2.1 apart from the gems in the **test** group, which are needed for the optional advanced testing setup (Section 3.6) and integration testing starting in Section 5.3.4. *Note*: If you would like to install *all* the gems needed for the sample application, you should use the code in Listing 13.72 at this time.

Important note: For all the Gemfiles in this book, you should use the version numbers listed at gemfiles-6th-ed.railstutorial.org instead of the ones listed below (although they should be identical if you are reading this online).

Listing 3.2: A **Gemfile** for the sample app.

```
source 'https://rubygems.org'
git_source(:github) { |repo| "https://github.com/#{repo}.git" }

gem 'rails',      '6.0.2.1'
gem 'puma',       '3.12.2'
gem 'sass-rails', '5.1.0'
gem 'webpacker',  '4.0.7'
gem 'turbolinks', '5.2.0'
gem 'jbuilder',   '2.9.1'
gem 'bootsnap',   '1.4.5', require: false

group :development, :test do
```

---

running **rm -rf hello_app/ toy_app/** (Table 1.1). (As long as you pushed the corresponding repositories up to GitHub, you can always recover them later.)

2. https://github.com/mhartl/sample_app_6th_ed

```
  gem 'sqlite3', '1.4.1'
  gem 'byebug',  '11.0.1', platforms: [:mri, :mingw, :x64_mingw]
end

group :development do
  gem 'web-console',          '4.0.1'
  gem 'listen',               '3.1.5'
  gem 'spring',               '2.1.0'
  gem 'spring-watcher-listen', '2.0.1'
end

group :test do
  gem 'capybara',                   '3.28.0'
  gem 'selenium-webdriver',         '3.142.4'
  gem 'webdrivers',                 '4.1.2'
  gem 'rails-controller-testing',   '1.0.4'
  gem 'minitest',                   '5.11.3'
  gem 'minitest-reporters',         '1.3.8'
  gem 'guard',                      '2.15.0'
  gem 'guard-minitest',             '2.4.6'
end

group :production do
  gem 'pg', '1.1.4'
end

# Windows does not include zoneinfo files, so bundle the tzinfo-data gem
gem 'tzinfo-data', platforms: [:mingw, :mswin, :x64_mingw, :jruby]
```

As in the previous two chapters, we run **bundle install** to install and include the gems specified in the **Gemfile**, while skipping the installation of production gems using the option **--without production**:[3]

```
$ bundle install --without production
```

This arranges to skip the pg gem for PostgreSQL in development and use SQLite for development and testing. Heroku recommends against using different databases in development and production, but for the sample application it won't make any

---

3. It's worth noting that **--without production** is a "remembered option," which means it will be included automatically the next time we run **bundle install**.

difference, and SQLite is *much* easier than PostgreSQL to install and configure locally.[4] In case you've previously installed a version of a gem (such as Rails itself) other than the one specified by the **Gemfile**, it's a good idea to *update* the gems with **bundle update** to make sure the versions match:

```
$ bundle update
```

With that, all we have left is to initialize the Git repository:

```
$ git init
$ git add -A
$ git commit -m "Initialize repository"
```

As with the first application, I suggest updating the README file to be more helpful and descriptive by replacing the default contents of **README.md** with the Markdown shown in Listing 3.3. The README includes instructions for getting started with the application.[5] (We won't actually need to run **rails db:migrate** until Chapter 6, but it does no harm to include it now.)

Note: For convenience, the full reference app README contains additional advanced information not present in Listing 3.3.

Listing 3.3: An improved README file for the sample app.
README.md

```
# Ruby on Rails Tutorial sample application

This is the sample application for
[*Ruby on Rails Tutorial:
Learn Web Development with Rails*](https://www.railstutorial.org/)
(6th Edition)
by [Michael Hartl](https://www.michaelhartl.com/).
```

---

4. Generally speaking, it's a good idea for the development and production environments to match as closely as possible, which includes using the same database, so I recommend eventually learning how to install and configure PostgreSQL in development—but now is not that time. When the time comes, Google "install configure postgresql <your system>" and "rails postgresql setup", and prepare for a challenge. (On the cloud IDE, <your system> is Linux.)

5. The README also makes reference to a LICENSE file, which I've added by hand to the official reference implementation, but it isn't present by default. You can download a copy from the reference implementation repository if you want it for completeness, but it's not necessary for completing the tutorial.

```
## License

All source code in the [Ruby on Rails Tutorial](https://www.railstutorial.org/)
is available jointly under the MIT License and the Beerware License. See
[LICENSE.md](LICENSE.md) for details.

## Getting started

To get started with the app, clone the repo and then install the needed gems:

```
$ bundle install --without production
```

Next, migrate the database:

```
$ rails db:migrate
```

Finally, run the test suite to verify that everything is working correctly:

```
$ rails test
```

If the test suite passes, you'll be ready to run the app in a local server:

```
$ rails server
```

For more information, see the
[*Ruby on Rails Tutorial* book](https://www.railstutorial.org/book).
```

Then commit the changes as follows:

```
$ git commit -am "Improve the README"
```

You may recall from Section 1.3.4 that we used the Git command **git commit -a
-m "Message"**, with flags for "all changes" (**-a**) and a message (**-m**). As shown in the
second command above, Git also lets us roll the two flags into one using **git commit
-am "Message"**.

Figure 3.1: Creating the main sample app repository at GitHub.

You should also create a new repository at GitHub by following the same steps as in Section 1.3.3 (taking care to make it private, as in Figure 3.1), and then push up to the remote repository:

```
$ git remote add origin https://github.com/<username>/sample_app.git
$ git push -u origin master
```

If you're using the cloud IDE, you'll need to prepare the application to be served locally by editing the **development.rb** file as in the previous two chapters (Listing 3.4).

Listing 3.4: Allowing connections to the local webserver.
config/environments/development.rb

```
Rails.application.configure do
  .
  .
  .
```

```
  # Allow connections to local server.
  % config.hosts.clear
end
```

To avoid integration headaches later on, it's also a good idea to deploy the app to
Heroku even at this early stage. As in Chapter 1 and Chapter 2, I suggest following the
"hello, world!" steps in Listing 3.5 and Listing 3.6. (The main reason for this is that
the default Rails page typically breaks at Heroku, which makes it hard to tell whether
the deployment was successful.)

Listing 3.5: Adding a **hello** action to the Application controller.
app/controllers/application_controller.rb

```
class ApplicationController < ActionController::Base

  def hello
    render text: "hello, world!"
  end
end
```

Listing 3.6: Setting the root route.
config/routes.rb

```
Rails.application.routes.draw do
  root 'application#hello'
end
```

Then commit the changes and push up to GitHub and Heroku:

```
$ git commit -am "Add hello"
$ git push
$ heroku create
$ git push heroku master
```

As in Section 1.4, you may see some warning messages, which you should ignore for
now. We'll deal with them in Section 7.5. Apart from the address of the Heroku app,
the result should be the same as in Figure 1.31.

As you proceed through the rest of the book, I recommend pushing and deploying the application regularly, which automatically makes remote backups and lets you catch any production errors as soon as possible. If you run into problems at Heroku, make sure to take a look at the production logs to try to diagnose the problem:

```
$ heroku logs        # to see the most recent events
$ heroku logs --tail # to see events as they happen, Ctrl-C to quit
```

Note: If you do end up using Heroku for a real-life application, be sure to follow the production webserver configuration in Section 7.5.

Exercises

Solutions to the exercises are available to all Rails Tutorial purchasers at https://www.railstutorial.org/aw-solutions.

To see other people's answers and to record your own, subscribe to the Rails Tutorial course or to the Learn Enough All Access Bundle.

1. Confirm that GitHub renders the Markdown for the README in Listing 3.3 as HTML (Figure 3.2).

2. By visiting the root route on the production server, verify that the deployment to Heroku succeeded.

3.2 Static Pages

With all the preparation from Section 3.1 finished, we're ready to get started developing the sample application. In this section, we'll take a first step toward making dynamic pages by creating a set of Rails *actions* and *views* containing only static HTML.[6] Rails actions come bundled together inside *controllers* (the C in MVC from Section 1.2.3), which contain sets of actions related by a common purpose. We got a glimpse of controllers in Chapter 2, and will come to a deeper understanding once we explore the REST architecture more fully (starting in Chapter 6). To

---

6. Our method for making static pages is probably the simplest, but it's not the only way. The optimal method really depends on your needs; if you expect a *large* number of static pages, using a Static Pages controller can get quite cumbersome, but in our sample app we'll need only need a few. If you do need a lot of static pages, take a look at the `high_voltage` gem from thoughtbot.

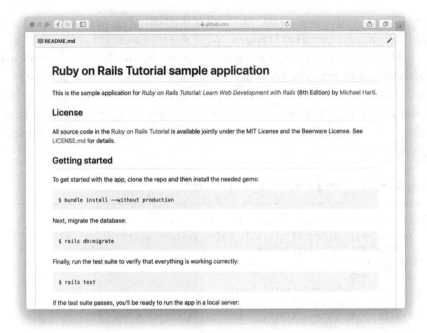

Figure 3.2: The sample app README at GitHub.

get our bearings, it's helpful to recall the Rails directory structure from Section 1.2 (Figure 1.11). In this section, we'll be working mainly in the **app/controllers** and **app/views** directories.

Recall from Section 1.3.4 that, when using Git, it's a good practice to do our work on a separate topic branch rather than the master branch. If you're using Git for version control, you should run the following command to check out a topic branch for static pages:

```
$ git checkout -b static-pages
```

3.2.1 Generated Static Pages

To get started with static pages, we'll first generate a controller using the same Rails **generate** script we used in Chapter 2 to generate scaffolding. Since we'll be making a controller to handle static pages, we'll call it the Static Pages controller, designated by the CamelCase name **StaticPages**. We'll also plan to make actions for a Home page, a Help page, and an About page, designated by the lowercase action names **home**, **help**, and **about**. The **generate** script takes an optional list of actions, so we'll include actions for the Home and Help pages directly on the command line, while intentionally leaving off the action for the About page so that we can see how to add it (Section 3.3). The resulting command to generate the Static Pages controller appears in Listing 3.7.

Listing 3.7: Generating a Static Pages controller.

```
$ rails generate controller StaticPages home help
      create  app/controllers/static_pages_controller.rb
       route  get 'static_pages/home'
get 'static_pages/help'
      invoke  erb
      create    app/views/static_pages
      create    app/views/static_pages/home.html.erb
      create    app/views/static_pages/help.html.erb
      invoke  test_unit
      create    test/controllers/static_pages_controller_test.rb
      invoke  helper
      create    app/helpers/static_pages_helper.rb
      invoke    test_unit
      invoke  assets
      invoke    scss
      create      app/assets/stylesheets/static_pages.scss
```

Incidentally, it's worth noting that **rails g** is a shortcut for **rails generate**, which is only one of several shortcuts supported by Rails (Table 3.1). For clarity, this tutorial always uses the full command, but in real life most Rails developers use one or more of the shortcuts shown in Table 3.1.[7]

Before moving on, if you're using Git it's a good idea to add the files for the Static Pages controller to the remote repository:

---

[7]. In fact, many Rails developers add an *alias* (as described in *Learn Enough Text Editor to Be Dangerous*, www.learnenough.com/text-editor) for the **rails** command, typically shortening it to just **r**. This allows us to run, for example, a Rails server using the compact command **r s**.

Table 3.1: Some Rails shortcuts.

Full command	Shortcut
`$ rails server`	`$ rails s`
`$ rails console`	`$ rails c`
`$ rails generate`	`$ rails g`
`$ rails test`	`$ rails t`
`$ bundle install`	`$ bundle`

```
$ git add -A
$ git commit -m "Add a Static Pages controller"
$ git push -u origin static-pages
```

The final command here arranges to push the **static-pages** topic branch up to GitHub. Subsequent pushes can omit the other arguments and write simply

```
$ git push
```

This commit and push sequence represents the kind of pattern I would ordinarily follow in real-life development, but for simplicity I'll typically omit such intermediate commits from now on. (When following this tutorial, a good rule of thumb is to make a Git commit at the end of each section.)

In Listing 3.7, note that we have passed the controller name as CamelCase (so called because it resembles the humps of a Bactrian camel), which leads to the creation of a controller file written in snake case, so that a controller called StaticPages yields a file called **static_pages_controller.rb**. This is merely a convention, and in fact using snake case at the command line also works: the command

```
$ rails generate controller static_pages ...
```

also generates a controller called **static_pages_controller.rb**. Because Ruby uses CamelCase for class names (Section 4.4), my preference is to refer to controllers using their CamelCase names, but this is a matter of taste. (Since Ruby filenames typically use snake case, the Rails generator converts CamelCase to snake case using the underscore method.)

By the way, if you ever make a mistake when generating code, it's useful to know how to reverse the process. See Box 3.1 for some techniques on how to undo things in Rails.

Box 3.1: Undoing Things

Even when you're very careful, things can sometimes go wrong when developing Rails applications. Happily, Rails has some facilities to help you recover.

One common scenario is wanting to undo code generation—for example, when you change your mind about the name of a controller and want to eliminate the generated files. Because Rails creates a substantial number of auxiliary files along with the controller (as seen in Listing 3.7), this isn't as easy as removing the controller file itself; undoing the generation means removing not only the principal generated file, but all the ancillary files as well. (In fact, as we saw in Section 2.2 and Section 2.3, rails generate can make automatic edits to the routes.rb file, which we also want to undo automatically.) In Rails, this can be accomplished with rails destroy followed by the name of the generated element. In particular, these two commands cancel each other out:

```
$ rails generate controller StaticPages home help
$ rails destroy  controller StaticPages home help
```

Similarly, in Chapter 6 we'll generate a *model* as follows:

```
$ rails generate model User name:string email:string
```

This can be undone using

```
$ rails destroy model User
```

(In this case, it turns out we can omit the other command-line arguments. When you get to Chapter 6, see if you can figure out why.)

Another technique related to models involves undoing *migrations*, which we saw briefly in Chapter 2 and will see much more frequently starting in Chapter 6. Migrations change the state of the database using the command

```
$ rails db:migrate
```

We can undo a single migration step using

```
$ rails db:rollback
```

To go all the way back to the beginning, we can use

```
$ rails db:migrate VERSION=0
```

As you might guess, substituting any other number for 0 migrates to that version number, where the version numbers come from listing the migrations sequentially. With these techniques in hand, we are well equipped to recover from the inevitable development snafus.

The Static Pages controller generation in Listing 3.7 automatically updates the routes file (**config/routes.rb**), which we first saw in Section 1.2.4 when we edited the root route for the hello app (Listing 1.11), and which we most recently saw in Listing 3.6. The routes file is responsible for implementing the router (seen in Figure 2.11) that defines the correspondence between URLs and web pages. The routes file is located in the **config** directory, where Rails collects files needed for the application configuration (Figure 3.3).

Since we included the **home** and **help** actions in Listing 3.7, the routes file already has a rule for each one, as seen in Listing 3.8.

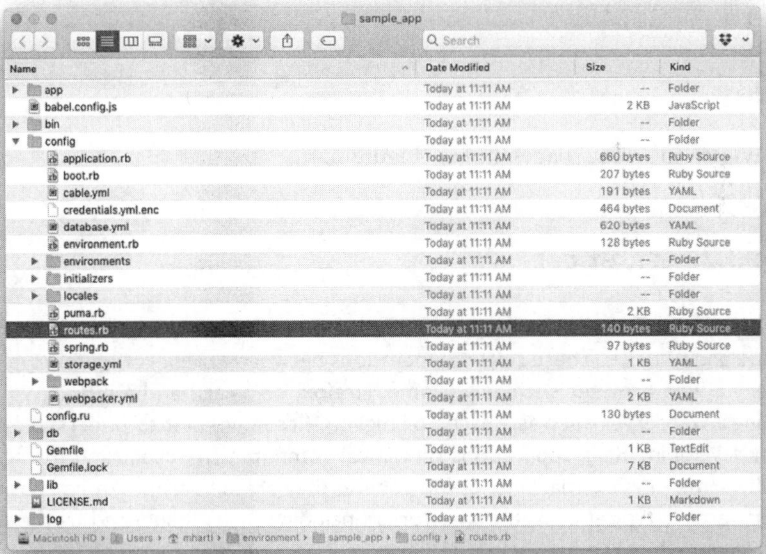

Figure 3.3: Contents of the sample app's **config** directory.

Listing 3.8: The routes for the **home** and **help** actions in the Static Pages controller.
config/routes.rb

```
Rails.application.routes.draw do
  get  'static_pages/home'
  get  'static_pages/help'
  root 'application#hello'
end
```

Here the rule

```
get 'static_pages/home'
```

maps requests for the URL /static_pages/home to the **home** action in the Static Pages controller. Moreover, by using **get** we arrange for the route to respond to a GET request, which is one of the fundamental *HTTP verbs* supported by the Hypertext Transfer Protocol (Box 3.2). In our case, this means that when we generate a **home** action inside the Static Pages controller, we automatically get a page at the address /static_pages/home. To see the result, start a Rails development server as described in Section 1.2.2:

```
$ rails server
```

Then navigate to /static_pages/home (Figure 3.4).

Box 3.2: GET, et cet.

The Hypertext Transfer Protocol (HTTP) defines the basic operations GET, POST, PATCH, and DELETE. These refer to operations between a *client* computer (typically running a web browser such as Chrome, Firefox, or Safari) and a *server* (typically running a webserver such as Apache or Nginx). (It's important to understand that, when developing Rails applications on a local computer, the client and the server are the same physical machine, but in general they are different.) An emphasis on HTTP verbs is typical of web frameworks (including Rails) influenced by the *REST architecture*, which we saw briefly in Chapter 2 and will start learning more about in Chapter 7.

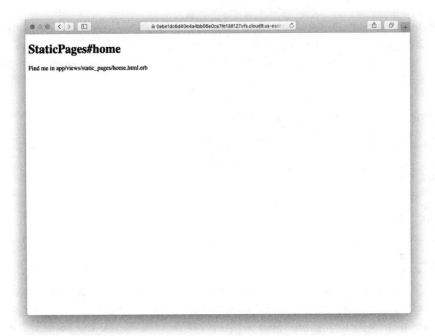

Figure 3.4: The raw home view (/static_pages/home).

GET is the most common HTTP operation, used for *reading* data on the web; it just means "get a page." Every time you visit a site like https://www.google. com/ or https://www.wikipedia.org/ your browser is submitting a GET request. POST is the next most common operation; it is the request sent by your browser when you submit a form. In Rails applications, POST requests are typically used for *creating* things (although HTTP also allows POST to perform updates). For example, the POST request sent when you submit a registration form creates a new user on the remote site. The other two verbs, PATCH and DELETE, are designed for *updating* and *destroying* things on the remote server. These requests are less common than GET and POST since browsers are incapable of sending them natively, but some web frameworks (including Ruby on Rails) have clever ways of making it *seem* like browsers are issuing such requests. As a result, Rails supports all four of the request types GET, POST, PATCH, and DELETE.

To understand where this page comes from, let's start by examining the Static Pages controller in a text editor, which should look something like Listing 3.9. You may note that, unlike the demo Users and Microposts controllers from Chapter 2, the Static Pages controller does not use the standard REST actions. This is normal for a collection of static pages: The REST architecture isn't the best solution to every problem.

Listing 3.9: The Static Pages controller made by Listing 3.7.
`app/controllers/static_pages_controller.rb`

```
class StaticPagesController < ApplicationController
  def home
  end

  def help
  end
end
```

We see from the **class** keyword in Listing 3.9 that **static_pages_controller.rb** defines a *class*, in this case called **StaticPagesController**. Classes are simply a convenient way to organize *functions* (also called *methods*) like the **home** and **help** actions, which are defined using the **def** keyword. As discussed in Section 2.3.4, the angle bracket **<** indicates that **StaticPagesController** *inherits* from the Rails class **ApplicationController**; as we'll see in a moment, this means that our pages come equipped with a large amount of Rails-specific functionality. (We'll learn more about both classes and inheritance in Section 4.4.)

In the case of the Static Pages controller, both of its methods are initially empty:

```
def home
end

def help
end
```

In plain Ruby, these methods would simply do nothing. In Rails, the situation is different. **StaticPagesController** is a Ruby class, but because it inherits from **ApplicationController** the behavior of its methods is specific to Rails: When visiting the URL /static_pages/home, Rails looks in the Static Pages controller and executes the code in the **home** action, and then renders the *view* (the V in MVC from Section 1.2.3) corresponding to the action. In the present case, the **home** action is empty, so all visiting /static_pages/home does is render the view. So, what does a view look like, and how do we find it?

If you take another look at the output in Listing 3.7, you might be able to guess the correspondence between actions and views: An action like **home** has a corresponding view called **home.html.erb**. We'll learn in Section 3.4 what the **.erb** part means; from the **.html** part you probably won't be surprised that it basically looks like HTML (Listing 3.10).

Listing 3.10: The generated view for the Home page.
app/views/static_pages/home.html.erb

```
<h1>StaticPages#home</h1>
<p>Find me in app/views/static_pages/home.html.erb</p>
```

The view for the **help** action is analogous (Listing 3.11).

Listing 3.11: The generated view for the Help page.
app/views/static_pages/help.html.erb

```
<h1>StaticPages#help</h1>
<p>Find me in app/views/static_pages/help.html.erb</p>
```

Both of these views are just placeholders: They have a top-level heading (inside the **h1** tag) and a paragraph (**p** tag) with the full path to the corresponding file.

Exercises

Solutions to the exercises are available to all Rails Tutorial purchasers at https://www.railstutorial.org/aw-solutions.

To see other people's answers and to record your own, subscribe to the Rails Tutorial course or to the Learn Enough All Access Bundle.

1. Generate a controller called **Foo** with actions **bar** and **baz**.

2. By applying the techniques described in Box 3.1, destroy the **Foo** controller and its associated actions.

3.2.2 Custom Static Pages

We'll add some (very slightly) dynamic content starting in Section 3.4, but as they stand the files shown in Listing 3.10 and Listing 3.11 underscore an important point: Rails views can simply contain static HTML. This means we can begin customizing the Home and Help pages even with no knowledge of Rails, as shown in Listing 3.12 and Listing 3.13.

Listing 3.12: Custom HTML for the Home page.
`app/views/static_pages/home.html.erb`

```
<h1>Sample App</h1>
<p>
  This is the home page for the
  <a href="https://www.railstutorial.org/">Ruby on Rails Tutorial</a>
  sample application.
</p>
```

Listing 3.13: Custom HTML for the Help page.
`app/views/static_pages/help.html.erb`

```
<h1>Help</h1>
<p>
  Get help on the Ruby on Rails Tutorial at the
  <a href="https://www.railstutorial.org/help">Rails Tutorial Help page</a>.
  To get help on this sample app, see the
  <a href="https://www.railstutorial.org/book"><em>Ruby on Rails Tutorial</em>
  book</a>.
</p>
```

The results of Listing 3.12 and Listing 3.13 are shown in Figure 3.5 and Figure 3.6.

3.3 Getting Started with Testing

Having created and filled in the Home and Help pages for our sample app (Section 3.2.2), now we're going to add an About page as well. When making a change of this nature, it's a good practice to write an *automated test* to verify that the feature is implemented correctly. Developed over the course of building an application, the

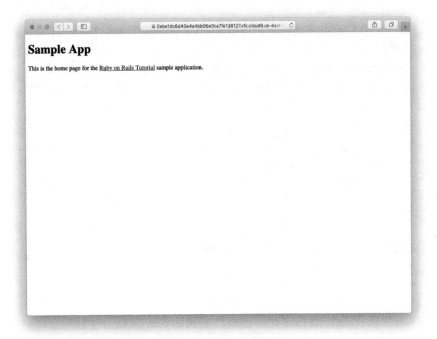

Figure 3.5: A custom Home page.

resulting *test suite* serves as a safety net and as executable documentation of the application source code. When done right, writing tests also allows us to develop *faster* despite requiring extra code, because we'll end up wasting less time trying to track down bugs. This is true only once we get good at writing tests, though, which is one reason it's important to start practicing as early as possible.

Although virtually all Rails developers agree that testing is a good idea, there is a diversity of opinion on the details. There is an especially lively debate over the use of test-driven development (TDD),[8] a testing technique in which the programmer writes failing tests first, and then writes the application code to get the tests to pass. The *Ruby on Rails Tutorial* takes a lightweight, intuitive approach to testing, employing TDD when convenient without being dogmatic about it (Box 3.3).

---

8. See, for example, "TDD is dead. Long live testing." by Rails creator David Heinemeier Hansson.

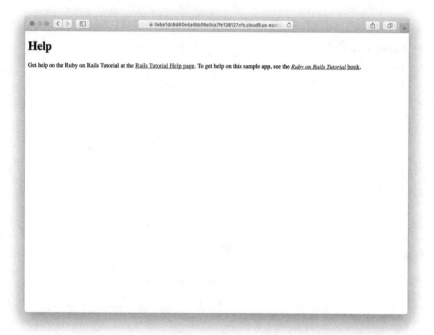

Figure 3.6: A custom Help page.

Box 3.3: When to Test

When deciding when and how to test, it's helpful to understand *why* to test. In my view, writing automated tests has three main benefits:

1. Tests protect against *regressions*, where a functioning feature stops working for some reason.

2. Tests allow code to be *refactored* (i.e., changing its form without changing its function) with greater confidence.

3. Tests act as a *client* for the application code, thereby helping determine its design and its interface with other parts of the system.

Although none of these benefits *requires* that tests be written first, there are many circumstances where test-driven development (TDD) is a valuable tool to have in your kit. Deciding when and how to test depends in part on how comfortable you are writing tests; many developers find that, as they get better at writing tests, they are more inclined to write them first. It also depends on how difficult the test is relative to the application code, how precisely the desired features are known, and how likely the feature is to break in the future.

In this context, it's helpful to have a set of guidelines on when we should test first (or test at all). Here are some suggestions based on my own experience:

- When a test is especially short or simple compared to the application code it tests, lean toward writing the test first.

- When the desired behavior isn't yet crystal clear, lean toward writing the application code first, then write a test to codify the result.

- Because security is a top priority, err on the side of writing tests of the security model first.

- Whenever a bug is found, write a test to reproduce it and protect against regressions, then write the application code to fix it.

- Lean against writing tests for code (such as detailed HTML structure) likely to change in the future.

- Write tests before refactoring code, focusing on testing error-prone code that's especially likely to break.

In practice, these guidelines mean that we'll usually write controller and model tests first and integration tests (which test functionality across models, views, and controllers) second. And when we're writing application code that isn't particularly brittle or error-prone, or is likely to change (as is often the case with views), we'll often skip testing altogether.

Our main testing tools will be *controller tests* (starting in this section), *model tests* (starting in Chapter 6), and *integration tests* (starting in Chapter 7). Integration tests are especially powerful, as they allow us to simulate the actions of a user interacting with our application using a web browser. Integration tests will eventually be our primary testing technique, but controller tests give us an easier place to start.

3.3.1 Our First Test

Now it's time to add an About page to our application. As we'll see, the test is short and simple, so we'll follow the guidelines from Box 3.3 and write the test first. We'll then use the failing test to drive the writing of the application code.

Getting started with testing can be challenging, requiring extensive knowledge of both Rails and Ruby. At this early stage, writing tests might thus seem hopelessly intimidating. Luckily, Rails has already done the hardest part for us, because **rails generate controller** (Listing 3.7) automatically generated a test file to get us started:

```
$ ls test/controllers/
static_pages_controller_test.rb
```

Let's take a look at it (Listing 3.14).

Listing 3.14: The default tests for the StaticPages controller. GREEN
test/controllers/static_pages_controller_test.rb

```ruby
require 'test_helper'

class StaticPagesControllerTest < ActionDispatch::IntegrationTest

  test "should get home" do
    get static_pages_home_url
    assert_response :success
  end

  test "should get help" do
    get static_pages_help_url
    assert_response :success
  end
end
```

It's not important at this point to understand the syntax in Listing 3.14 in detail, but we can see that there are two tests, one for each controller action we included on the command line in Listing 3.7. Each test simply gets a URL and verifies (via an *assertion*) that the result is a success. Here the use of **get** indicates that our tests expect the Home and Help pages to be ordinary web pages, accessed using a GET request (Box 3.2). The response **:success** is an abstract representation of the underlying HTTP status code (in this case, 200 OK). In other words, a test like

```ruby
test "should get home" do
  get static_pages_home_url
  assert_response :success
end
```

says, "Let's test the Home page by issuing a GET request to the Static Pages **home** URL and then making sure we receive a 'success' status code in response."

To begin our testing cycle, we need to run our test suite to verify that the tests currently pass. We can do this with the **rails** command as follows:

Listing 3.15: GREEN

```
$ rails db:migrate      # Necessary on some systems
$ rails test
2 tests, 2 assertions, 0 failures, 0 errors, 0 skips
```

As required, initially our test suite is passing (GREEN). (Some systems won't actually display the color green unless you add the minitest reporters from the optional Section 3.6.1, but the terminology is common even when literal colors aren't involved.) Note that here and throughout this tutorial, I'll generally omit some lines from the test output to highlight only the most imporant parts.

By the way, on some systems you may see generated files of the form

```
/db/test.sqlite3-0
```

show up in the **db** directory. To prevent these generated files from being added to the repository, I suggest adding a rule to the **.gitignore** file (Section 1.3.1) to ignore them, as shown in Listing 3.16.

Listing 3.16: Ignoring generated database files.
.gitignore

```
.
.
.
# Ignore db test files.
db/test.*
```

3.3.2 Red

As noted in Box 3.3, test-driven development involves writing a failing test first, writing the application code needed to get it to pass, and then refactoring the code if necessary. Because many testing tools represent failing tests with the color red and passing tests with the color green, this sequence is sometimes known as the "Red, Green, Refactor" cycle. In this section, we'll complete the first step in this cycle, getting to RED by writing a failing test. Then we'll get to GREEN in Section 3.3.3, and refactor in Section 3.4.3.[9]

Our first step is to write a failing test for the About page. By following the models from Listing 3.14, can you guess what it should be? The answer appears in Listing 3.17.

Listing 3.17: A test for the About page. RED
`test/controllers/static_pages_controller_test.rb`

```ruby
require 'test_helper'

class StaticPagesControllerTest < ActionDispatch::IntegrationTest

  test "should get home" do
    get static_pages_home_url
    assert_response :success
  end

  test "should get help" do
    get static_pages_help_url
    assert_response :success
  end

  test "should get about" do
    get static_pages_about_url
    assert_response :success
  end
end
```

We see from the highlighted lines in Listing 3.17 that the test for the About page is the same as the Home and Help tests with the word "about" in place of "home" or "help".

As required, the test initially fails:

---

9. On some systems, **rails test** shows red when the tests fail but doesn't show green when the tests pass. To arrange for a true Red–Green cycle, see Section 3.6.1.

Listing 3.18: RED

```
$ rails test
3 tests, 2 assertions, 0 failures, 1 errors, 0 skips
```

3.3.3 Green

Now that we have a failing test (RED), we'll use the failing test's error messages to guide us to a passing test (GREEN), thereby implementing a working About page.

We can get started by examining the error message output by the failing test:

Listing 3.19: RED

```
$ rails test
NameError: undefined local variable or method `static_pages_about_url'
```

The error message here says that the Rails code for the About page URL is undefined, which is a hint that we need to add a line to the routes file. We can accomplish this by following the pattern in Listing 3.8, as shown in Listing 3.20.

Listing 3.20: Adding the **about** route. RED
config/routes.rb

```
Rails.application.routes.draw do
  get  'static_pages/home'
  get  'static_pages/help'
  get 'static_pages/about'
  root 'application#hello'
end
```

The highlighted line in Listing 3.20 tells Rails to route a GET request for the URL /static_pages/about to the **about** action in the Static Pages controller. This automatically creates a helper called

```
static_pages_about_url
```

Running our test suite again, we see that it is still RED, but now the error message has changed:

Listing 3.21: RED

```
$ rails test
AbstractController::ActionNotFound:
The action 'about' could not be found for StaticPagesController
```

The error message now indicates a missing **about** action in the Static Pages controller, which we can add by following the model provided by **home** and **help** in Listing 3.9, as shown in Listing 3.22.

Listing 3.22: The Static Pages controller with added **about** action. RED
`app/controllers/static_pages_controller.rb`

```
class StaticPagesController < ApplicationController

  def home
  end

  def help
  end

  def about
  end
end
```

As before, our test suite is still RED, but the error message has changed again:

```
$ rails test
ActionController::UnknownFormat: StaticPagesController#about is missing
a template for this request format and variant.
```

This indicates a missing template, which in the context of Rails is essentially the same thing as a view. As described in Section 3.2.1, an action called **home** is associated with a view called **home.html.erb** located in the **app/views/static_pages** directory, which means that we need to create a new file called **about.html.erb** in the same directory.

The way to create a file varies by system setup, but most text editors will let you control-click inside the directory where you want to create the file to bring up a menu with a "New File" menu item. Alternatively, you can use the File menu to create a new file and then pick the proper directory when saving it. Finally, you can use my favorite trick by applying the Unix touch command as follows:

```
$ touch app/views/static_pages/about.html.erb
```

As mentioned in *Learn Enough Command Line to Be Dangerous* (www.learnenough. com/command-line), **touch** is designed to update the modification timestamp of a file or directory without otherwise affecting it, but as a side effect it creates a new (blank) file if one doesn't already exist. (If you're using the cloud IDE, you may have to refresh the file tree as described in Section 1.2.1. This is a good example of technical sophistication (Box 1.2).)

Once you've created the **about.html.erb** file in the right directory, you should fill it with the content shown in Listing 3.23.

Listing 3.23: Code for the About page. GREEN
app/views/static_pages/about.html.erb

```
<h1>About</h1>
<p>
  The <a href="https://www.railstutorial.org/"><em>Ruby on Rails
  Tutorial</em></a>, part of the
  <a href="https://www.learnenough.com/">Learn Enough</a> family of
  tutorials, is a
  <a href="https://www.railstutorial.org/book">book</a> and
  <a href="https://screencasts.railstutorial.org/">screencast series</a>
  to teach web development with
  <a href="https://rubyonrails.org/">Ruby on Rails</a>.
  This is the sample app for the tutorial.
</p>
```

At this point, running **rails test** should get us back to GREEN:

Listing 3.24: GREEN

```
$ rails test
3 tests, 3 assertions, 0 failures, 0 errors, 0 skips
```

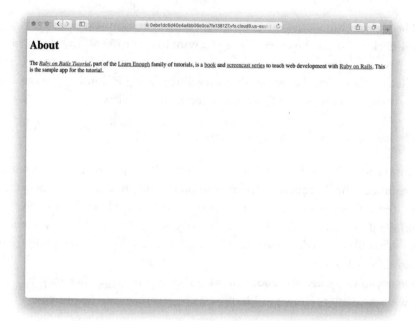

Figure 3.7: The new About page (/static_pages/about).

Of course, it's never a bad idea to take a look at the page in a browser to make sure our tests aren't leading us astray (Figure 3.7).

3.3.4 Refactor

Now that we've gotten to GREEN, we are free to refactor our code with confidence. When developing an application, often code will start to "smell," meaning that it gets ugly, bloated, or filled with repetition. The computer doesn't care what the code looks like, of course, but humans do, so it is important to keep the code base clean by refactoring frequently. Although our sample app is a little too small to refactor right now, code smell seeps in at every crack, and we'll get started refactoring in Section 3.4.3.

3.4 Slightly Dynamic Pages

Now that we've created the actions and views for some static pages, we'll make them *slightly* dynamic by adding some content that changes on a per-page basis: We'll have

Table 3.2: The (mostly) static pages for the sample app.

Page	URL	Base title	Variable title
Home	/static_pages/home	`"Ruby on Rails Tutorial Sample App"`	`"Home"`
Help	/static_pages/help	`"Ruby on Rails Tutorial Sample App"`	`"Help"`
About	/static_pages/about	`"Ruby on Rails Tutorial Sample App"`	`"About"`

the title of each page change to reflect its content. Whether a changing title represents *truly* dynamic content is debatable, but in any case it lays the necessary foundation for unambiguously dynamic content in Chapter 7.

Our plan is to edit the Home, Help, and About pages to make page titles that change on each page. This will involve using the **`<title>`** tag in our page views. Most browsers display the contents of the title tag at the top of the browser window, and it is also important for search-engine optimization. We'll be using the full "Red, Green, Refactor" cycle: first by adding simple tests for our page titles (RED), then by adding titles to each of our three pages (GREEN), and finally using a *layout* file to eliminate duplication (Refactor). By the end of this section, all three of our static pages will have titles of the form "<page name> | Ruby on Rails Tutorial Sample App," where the first part of the title will vary depending on the page (Table 3.2).

The **rails new** command (Listing 3.1) creates a layout file by default, but it's instructive to ignore it initially, which we can do by changing its name:

```
$ mv app/views/layouts/application.html.erb layout_file    # temporary change
```

You wouldn't normally do this in a real application, but it's easier to understand the purpose of the layout file if we start by disabling it.

3.4.1   Testing Titles (Red)

To add page titles, we need to learn (or review) the structure of a typical web page, which takes the form shown in Listing 3.25. (This is covered in much more depth in *Learn Enough HTML to Be Dangerous*, www.learnenough.com/html.)

Listing 3.25: The HTML structure of a typical web page.

```
<!DOCTYPE html>
<html>
  <head>
```

```
  <title>Greeting</title>
 </head>
 <body>
  <p>Hello, world!</p>
 </body>
</html>
```

The structure in Listing 3.25 includes a *document type*, or doctype, declaration at the top to tell browsers which version of HTML we're using (in this case, HTML5);[10] a **head** section, in this case with "Greeting" inside a **title** tag; and a **body** section, in this case with "Hello, world!" inside a **p** (paragraph) tag. (The indentation is optional—HTML is not sensitive to whitespace, and ignores both tabs and spaces—but it makes the document's structure easier to see.)

We'll write simple tests for each of the titles in Table 3.2 by combining the tests in Listing 3.17 with the **assert_select** method, which lets us test for the presence of a particular HTML tag (sometimes called a "selector"—hence the name):[11]

```
assert_select "title", "Home | Ruby on Rails Tutorial Sample App"
```

In particular, this code checks for the presence of a **<title>** tag containing the string "Home | Ruby on Rails Tutorial Sample App". Applying this idea to all three static pages gives the tests shown in Listing 3.26.

Listing 3.26: The Static Pages controller test with title tests. RED
`test/controllers/static_pages_controller_test.rb`

```
require 'test_helper'

class StaticPagesControllerTest < ActionDispatch::IntegrationTest

  test "should get home" do
    get static_pages_home_url
    assert_response :success
```

---

10. HTML changes with time; by explicitly making a doctype declaration we make it likelier that browsers will render our pages properly in the future. The simple doctype **<!DOCTYPE html>** is characteristic of the latest HTML standard, HTML5.

11. For a list of common minitest assertions, see the table of available assertions in the Rails Guides testing article.

```
      assert_select "title", "Home | Ruby on Rails Tutorial Sample App"
  end

  test "should get help" do
    get static_pages_help_url
    assert_response :success
    assert_select "title", "Help | Ruby on Rails Tutorial Sample App"
  end

  test "should get about" do
    get static_pages_about_url
    assert_response :success
    assert_select "title", "About | Ruby on Rails Tutorial Sample App"
  end
end
```

With the tests from Listing 3.26 in place, you should verify that the test suite is currently RED:

Listing 3.27: RED

```
$ rails test
3 tests, 6 assertions, 3 failures, 0 errors, 0 skips
```

3.4.2   Adding Page Titles (Green)

Now we'll add a title to each page, getting the tests from Section 3.4.1 to pass in the process. Applying the basic HTML structure from Listing 3.25 to the custom Home page from Listing 3.12 yields Listing 3.28.

Listing 3.28: The view for the Home page with full HTML structure. RED
`app/views/static_pages/home.html.erb`

```
<!DOCTYPE html>
<html>
  <head>
    <title>Home | Ruby on Rails Tutorial Sample App</title>
  </head>
  <body>
```

```
<h1>Sample App</h1>
<p>
  This is the home page for the
  <a href="https://www.railstutorial.org/">Ruby on Rails Tutorial</a>
  sample application.
</p>
</body>
</html>
```

The corresponding web page appears in Figure 3.8. Note that the browser used in the screenshots (Safari) displays the page title only if you include an additional tab, which explains the second tab shown in Figure 3.8.

Following this model for the Help page (Listing 3.13) and the About page (Listing 3.23) yields the code in Listing 3.29 and Listing 3.30.

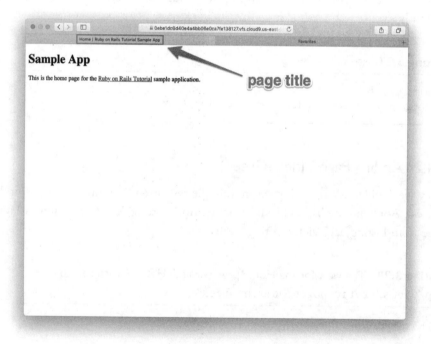

Figure 3.8: The Home page with a title.

Listing 3.29: The view for the Help page with full HTML structure. RED
`app/views/static_pages/help.html.erb`

```
<!DOCTYPE html>
<html>
  <head>
    <title>Help | Ruby on Rails Tutorial Sample App</title>
  </head>
  <body>
    <h1>Help</h1>
    <p>
      Get help on the Ruby on Rails Tutorial at the
      <a href="https://www.railstutorial.org/help">Rails Tutorial help
      page</a>.
      To get help on this sample app, see the
      <a href="https://www.railstutorial.org/book"><em>Ruby on Rails
      Tutorial</em> book</a>.
    </p>
  </body>
</html>
```

Listing 3.30: The view for the About page with full HTML structure. GREEN
`app/views/static_pages/about.html.erb`

```
<!DOCTYPE html>
<html>
  <head>
    <title>About | Ruby on Rails Tutorial Sample App</title>
  </head>
  <body>
    <h1>About</h1>
    <p>
      The <a href="https://www.railstutorial.org/"><em>Ruby on Rails
      Tutorial</em></a>, part of the
      <a href="https://www.learnenough.com/">Learn Enough</a> family of
      tutorials, is a
      <a href="https://www.railstutorial.org/book">book</a> and
      <a href="https://screencasts.railstutorial.org/">screencast series</a>
      to teach web development with
      <a href="https://rubyonrails.org/">Ruby on Rails</a>.
      This is the sample app for the tutorial.
    </p>
  </body>
</html>
```

At this point, the test suite should be back to GREEN:

Listing 3.31: GREEN

```
$ rails test
3 tests, 6 assertions, 0 failures, 0 errors, 0 skips
```

Exercise

Solutions to the exercises are available to all Rails Tutorial purchasers at https://www.railstutorial.org/aw-solutions.

To see other people's answers and to record your own, subscribe to the Rails Tutorial course or to the Learn Enough All Access Bundle.

Beginning in this section, we'll start making modifications to the applications in the exercises that won't generally be reflected in future code listings. The reason is so that the text makes sense to readers who don't complete the exercises, but as a result your code will diverge from the main text if you *do* solve them. Learning to resolve small discrepancies like this is an excellent example of technical sophistication (Box 1.2).

1. You may have noticed some repetition in the Static Pages controller test (Listing 3.26). In particular, the base title, "Ruby on Rails Tutorial Sample App," is the same for every title test. Using the special function **setup**, which is automatically run before every test, verify that the tests in Listing 3.32 are still GREEN. (Listing 3.32 uses an *instance variable*, seen briefly in Section 2.2.2 and covered further in Section 4.4.5, combined with *string interpolation*, which is covered further in Section 4.2.2.)

Listing 3.32: The Static Pages controller test with a base title. GREEN
`test/controllers/static_pages_controller_test.rb`

```
require 'test_helper'

class StaticPagesControllerTest < ActionDispatch::IntegrationTest
  def setup
    @base_title = "Ruby on Rails Tutorial Sample App"
  end

  test "should get home" do
    get static_pages_home_url
    assert_response :success
```

```
     assert_select "title", "Home | #{@base_title}"
   end

   test "should get help" do
     get static_pages_help_url
     assert_response :success
     assert_select "title", "Help | #{@base_title}"
   end

   test "should get about" do
     get static_pages_about_url
     assert_response :success
     assert_select "title", "About | #{@base_title}"
   end
end
```

3.4.3 Layouts and Embedded Ruby (Refactor)

We've achieved a lot already in this section, generating three valid pages using Rails controllers and actions, but they are purely static HTML and hence don't show off the power of Rails. Moreover, they suffer from terrible duplication:

- The page titles are almost (but not quite) exactly the same.
- "Ruby on Rails Tutorial Sample App" is common to all three titles.
- The entire HTML skeleton structure is repeated on each page.

This repeated code is a violation of the important "Don't Repeat Yourself" (DRY) principle; in this section we'll "DRY out our code" by removing the repetition. At the end, we'll re-run the tests from Section 3.4.2 to verify that the titles are still correct.

Paradoxically, we'll take the first step toward eliminating duplication by first adding some more: We'll make the titles of the pages, which are currently quite similar, match *exactly*. This will make it much simpler to remove all the repetition at a stroke.

The technique involves using *embedded Ruby* in our views. Since the Home, Help, and About page titles have a variable component, we'll use a special Rails function called **provide** to set a different title on each page. We can see how this works by replacing the literal title "Home" in the **home.html.erb** view with the code in Listing 3.33.

Listing 3.33: The view for the Home page with an embedded Ruby title. GREEN
`app/views/static_pages/home.html.erb`

```erb
<% provide(:title, "Home") %>
<!DOCTYPE html>
<html>
  <head>
    <title><%= yield(:title) %> | Ruby on Rails Tutorial Sample App</title>
  </head>
  <body>
    <h1>Sample App</h1>
    <p>
      This is the home page for the
      <a href="https://www.railstutorial.org/">Ruby on Rails Tutorial</a>
      sample application.
    </p>
  </body>
</html>
```

Listing 3.33 is our first example of embedded Ruby, also called *ERb* (or ERB). (Now you know why HTML views have the file extension `.html.erb`.) ERb is the primary template system for including dynamic content in web pages.[12] The code

```erb
<% provide(:title, "Home") %>
```

indicates using **<% ... %>** that Rails should call the **provide** function and associate the string **"Home"** with the label **:title**.[13] Then, in the title, we use the closely related notation **<%= ... %>** to insert the title into the template using Ruby's **yield** function:[14]

```erb
<title><%= yield(:title) %> | Ruby on Rails Tutorial Sample App</title>
```

(The distinction between the two types of embedded Ruby is that **<% ... %>** *executes* the code inside, while **<%= ... %>** executes it *and inserts* the result into the template.)

---

12. There is a second popular template system called Haml (note: not "HAML"), which I personally love, but it's not *quite* standard enough for use in an introductory tutorial.

13. Experienced Rails developers might have expected the use of **content_for** at this point, but it doesn't work well with the asset pipeline. The **provide** function is its replacement.

14. If you've studied Ruby before, you might suspect that Rails is *yielding* the contents to a block, and your suspicion would be correct. But you don't need to know this to develop applications with Rails.

The resulting page is exactly the same as before, only now the variable part of the title is generated dynamically by ERb.

We can verify that all this works by running the tests from Section 3.4.2 and confirming that they are still GREEN:

Listing 3.34: GREEN

```
$ rails test
3 tests, 6 assertions, 0 failures, 0 errors, 0 skips
```

Then we can make the corresponding replacements for the Help and About pages (Listing 3.35 and Listing 3.36).

Listing 3.35: The view for the Help page with an embedded Ruby title. GREEN
`app/views/static_pages/help.html.erb`

```erb
<% provide(:title, "Help") %>
<!DOCTYPE html>
<html>
  <head>
    <title><%= yield(:title) %> | Ruby on Rails Tutorial Sample App</title>
  </head>
  <body>
    <h1>Help</h1>
    <p>
      Get help on the Ruby on Rails Tutorial at the
      <a href="https://www.railstutorial.org/help">Rails Tutorial help
      section</a>.
      To get help on this sample app, see the
      <a href="https://www.railstutorial.org/book"><em>Ruby on Rails
      Tutorial</em> book</a>.
    </p>
  </body>
</html>
```

Listing 3.36: The view for the About page with an embedded Ruby title. GREEN
`app/views/static_pages/about.html.erb`

```erb
<% provide(:title, "About") %>
<!DOCTYPE html>
<html>
  <head>
```

```
    <title><%= yield(:title) %> | Ruby on Rails Tutorial Sample App</title>
  </head>
  <body>
    <h1>About</h1>
    <p>
      The <a href="https://www.railstutorial.org/"><em>Ruby on Rails
      Tutorial</em></a>, part of the
      <a href="https://www.learnenough.com/">Learn Enough</a> family of
      tutorials, is a
      <a href="https://www.railstutorial.org/book">book</a> and
      <a href="https://screencasts.railstutorial.org/">screencast series</a>
      to teach web development with
      <a href="https://rubyonrails.org/">Ruby on Rails</a>.
      This is the sample app for the tutorial.
    </p>
  </body>
</html>
```

Now that we've replaced the variable part of the page titles with ERb, each of our pages looks something like this:

```
<% provide(:title, "Page Title") %>
<!DOCTYPE html>
<html>
  <head>
    <title><%= yield(:title) %> | Ruby on Rails Tutorial Sample App</title>
  </head>
  <body>
    Contents
  </body>
</html>
```

In other words, all the pages are identical in structure, including the contents of the title tag, with the sole exception of the material inside the **body** tag.

To factor out this common structure, Rails comes with a special *layout* file called **application.html.erb**, which we renamed in the beginning of this section (Section 3.4) and which we'll now restore:

```
$ mv layout_file app/views/layouts/application.html.erb
```

To get the layout to work, we have to replace the default title with the embedded Ruby from the preceding examples:

```
<title><%= yield(:title) %> | Ruby on Rails Tutorial Sample App</title>
```

The resulting layout appears in Listing 3.37.

Listing 3.37: The sample application site layout. GREEN
`app/views/layouts/application.html.erb`

```erb
<!DOCTYPE html>
<html>
  <head>
    <title><%= yield(:title) %> | Ruby on Rails Tutorial Sample App</title>
    <meta charset="utf-8">
    <%= csrf_meta_tags %>
    <%= csp_meta_tag %>

    <%= stylesheet_link_tag 'application', media: 'all',
                                           'data-turbolinks-track': 'reload' %>
    <%= javascript_pack_tag 'application', 'data-turbolinks-track': 'reload' %>
  </head>

  <body>
    <%= yield %>
  </body>
</html>
```

Note here the special line

```erb
<%= yield %>
```

This code is responsible for inserting the contents of each page into the layout. It's not important to know exactly how this works; what matters is that using this layout ensures that, for example, visiting the page /static_pages/home converts the contents of **home.html.erb** to HTML and then inserts it in place of **<%= yield %>**.

Listing 3.37 also includes the "character set", which in this case is utf-8 for displaying Unicode.

Finally, it's worth noting that the default Rails layout includes several additional lines:

```
<%= csrf_meta_tags %>
<%= csp_meta_tag %>
<%= stylesheet_link_tag ... %>
<%= javascript_pack_tag "application", ... %>
```

This code arranges to include the application stylesheet and JavaScript, which are part of the asset pipeline (Section 5.2.1), together with the Rails method **csp_meta_tag**, which implements Content Security Policy (CSP) to mitigate cross-site scripting (XSS) attacks, and **csrf_meta_tags**, which mitigates cross-site request forgery (CSRF) attacks. (One huge advantage of using a mature framework like Rails is that it worries about such things so that we don't have to.)

Even though the tests are passing, there one detail left to deal with: The views in Listing 3.33, Listing 3.35, and Listing 3.36 are still filled with all the HTML structure included in the layout. Since it's redundant (and indeed leads to invalid HTML markup), we should remove it and leave only the interior contents. The resulting cleaned-up views appear in Listing 3.38, Listing 3.39, and Listing 3.40.

Listing 3.38: The Home page with HTML structure removed. GREEN
`app/views/static_pages/home.html.erb`

```
<% provide(:title, "Home") %>
<h1>Sample App</h1>
<p>
  This is the home page for the
  <a href="https://www.railstutorial.org/">Ruby on Rails Tutorial</a>
  sample application.
</p>
```

Listing 3.39: The Help page with HTML structure removed. GREEN
`app/views/static_pages/help.html.erb`

```
<% provide(:title, "Help") %>
<h1>Help</h1>
<p>
  Get help on the Ruby on Rails Tutorial at the
  <a href="https://www.railstutorial.org/help">Rails Tutorial Help page</a>.
  To get help on this sample app, see the
  <a href="https://www.railstutorial.org/book"><em>Ruby on Rails Tutorial</em>
  book</a>.
</p>
```

Listing 3.40: The About page with HTML structure removed. GREEN
`app/views/static_pages/about.html.erb`

```erb
<% provide(:title, "About") %>
<h1>About</h1>
<p>
  The <a href="https://www.railstutorial.org/"><em>Ruby on Rails
  Tutorial</em></a>, part of the
  <a href="https://www.learnenough.com/">Learn Enough</a> family of
  tutorials, is a
  <a href="https://www.railstutorial.org/book">book</a> and
  <a href="https://screencasts.railstutorial.org/">screencast series</a>
  to teach web development with
  <a href="https://rubyonrails.org/">Ruby on Rails</a>.
  This is the sample app for the tutorial.
</p>
```

With these views defined, the Home, Help, and About pages are the same as before, but they have much less duplication.

Experience shows that even fairly simple refactoring is error-prone and can easily go awry. This is one reason why having a good test suite is so valuable. Rather than double-checking every page for correctness—a procedure that isn't too hard early on but rapidly becomes unwieldy as an application grows—we can simply verify that the test suite is still GREEN:

Listing 3.41: GREEN

```
$ rails test
3 tests, 6 assertions, 0 failures, 0 errors, 0 skips
```

This isn't a *proof* that our code is still correct, but it greatly increases the probability, thereby providing a safety net to protect us against future bugs.

Exercise

Solutions to the exercises are available to all Rails Tutorial purchasers at https://www.railstutorial.org/aw-solutions.

To see other people's answers and to record your own, subscribe to the Rails Tutorial course or to the Learn Enough All Access Bundle.

1. Make a Contact page for the sample app.[15] Following the model in Listing 3.17, first write a test for the existence of a page at the URL /static_pages/contact by testing for the title "Contact | Ruby on Rails Tutorial Sample App." Get your test to pass by following the same steps as when making the About page in Section 3.3.3, including filling the Contact page with the content from Listing 3.42.

Listing 3.42: Code for a proposed Contact page.
`app/views/static_pages/contact.html.erb`

```erb
<% provide(:title, "Contact") %>
<h1>Contact</h1>
<p>
  Contact the Ruby on Rails Tutorial about the sample app at the
  <a href="https://www.railstutorial.org/contact">contact page</a>.
</p>
```

3.4.4 Setting the Root Route

Now that we've customized our site's pages and gotten a good start on the test suite, let's set the application's root route before moving on. As in Section 1.2.4 and Section 2.2.2, this involves editing the **routes.rb** file to connect / to a page of our choice, which in this case will be the Home page. (At this point, I also recommend removing the **hello** action from the Application controller if you added it in Section 3.1.) As shown in Listing 3.43, this means changing the **root** route from

```
root 'application#hello'
```

to

```
root 'static_pages#home'
```

This arranges for requests for / to be routed to the **home** action in the Static Pages controller. The resulting routes file is shown in Figure 3.9.

---

15. This exercise is solved in Section 5.3.1.

Figure 3.9: The Home page at the root route.

Listing 3.43: Setting the root route to the Home page.
config/routes.rb

```
Rails.application.routes.draw do
  root 'static_pages#home'
  get  'static_pages/home'
  get  'static_pages/help'
  get  'static_pages/about'
end
```

Exercises

Solutions to the exercises are available to all Rails Tutorial purchasers at https://www.railstutorial.org/aw-solutions.

To see other people's answers and to record your own, subscribe to the Rails Tutorial course or to the Learn Enough All Access Bundle.

1. Adding the root route in Listing 3.43 leads to the creation of a Rails helper called **root_url** (in analogy to helpers like **static_pages_home_url**). By filling in the code marked **FILL_IN** in Listing 3.44, write a test for the root route.

2. Due to the code in Listing 3.43, the test in the previous exercise is already GREEN. In such a case, it's harder to be confident that we're actually testing what we think we're testing, so modify the code in Listing 3.43 by commenting out the root route to get to RED (Listing 3.45). (We'll talk more about Ruby comments in Section 4.2.) Then uncomment it (thereby restoring the original Listing 3.43) and verify that you get back to GREEN.

Listing 3.44: A test for the root route. GREEN
`test/controllers/static_pages_controller_test.rb`

```ruby
require 'test_helper'

class StaticPagesControllerTest < ActionDispatch::IntegrationTest

  test "should get about" do
    get FILL_IN
    assert_response FILL_IN
  end

  test "should get home" do
    get static_pages_home_url
    assert_response :success
  end

  test "should get help" do
    get static_pages_help_url
    assert_response :success
  end

  test "should get about" do
    get static_pages_about_url
    assert_response :success
  end
end
```

Listing 3.45: Commenting out the root route to get a failing test. RED
`config/routes.rb`

```
Rails.application.routes.draw do
#   root 'static_pages#home'
  get  'static_pages/home'
  get  'static_pages/help'
  get  'static_pages/about'
end
```

3.5 Conclusion

Seen from the outside, this chapter hardly accomplished anything: We started with static pages, and ended with … *mostly* static pages. But appearances are deceiving: By developing in terms of Rails controllers, actions, and views, we are now in a position to add arbitrary amounts of dynamic content to our site. Seeing exactly how this plays out is the task for the rest of this tutorial.

Before moving on, let's take a minute to commit the changes on our topic branch and merge them into the master branch. Back in Section 3.2 we created a Git branch for the development of static pages. If you haven't been making commits as we've been moving along, first make a commit indicating that we've reached a stopping point:

```
$ git add -A
$ git commit -m "Finish static pages"
```

Then merge the changes back into the master branch using the same technique as in Section 1.3.4:[16]

```
$ git checkout master
$ git merge static-pages
```

---

16. If you get an error message saying that the Spring process id (pid) file would be overwritten by the merge, just remove the file using **rm -f *.pid** at the command line.

Once you reach a stopping point like this, it's usually a good idea to push your code up to a remote repository (which, if you followed the steps in Section 1.3.3, will be GitHub):

```
$ git push
```

I also recommend deploying the application to Heroku:

```
$ rails test
$ git push heroku
```

Here we've taken care to run the test suite before deploying, which is a good habit to develop.

3.5.1 What We Learned in this Chapter

- For a third time, we went through the full procedure of creating a new Rails application from scratch, installing the necessary gems, pushing it up to a remote repository, and deploying it to production.

- The **rails** script generates a new controller with **rails generate controller ControllerName <optional action names>**.

- New routes are defined in the file **config/routes.rb**.

- Rails views can contain static HTML or embedded Ruby (ERb).

- Automated testing allows us to write test suites that drive the development of new features, allow for confident refactoring, and catch regressions.

- Test-driven development uses a "Red, Green, Refactor" cycle.

- Rails layouts allow the use of a common template for pages in our application, thereby eliminating duplication.

3.6 Advanced Testing Setup

This optional section describes the testing setup used in the *Ruby on Rails Tutorial* screencast series. There are two main elements: an enhanced pass/fail reporter (Section 3.6.1) and an automated test runner that detects file changes and automatically runs the corresponding tests (Section 3.6.2). The code in this section is advanced and is presented for convenience only; you are not expected to understand it at this time.

The changes in this section should be made on the master branch:

```
$ git checkout master
```

3.6.1 Minitest Reporters

Although many systems, including the cloud IDE, will show the appropriate colors for RED and GREEN test suites, adding *minitest reporters* lends a degree of pleasant polish to the test outputs, so I recommend adding the code in Listing 3.46 to your test helper file,[17] thereby making use of the `minitest-reporters` gem included in Listing 3.2.

Listing 3.46: Configuring the tests to show RED and GREEN.
test/test_helper.rb

```ruby
ENV['RAILS_ENV'] ||= 'test'
require_relative '../config/environment'
require 'rails/test_help'
require "minitest/reporters"
Minitest::Reporters.use!

class ActiveSupport::TestCase
  # Run tests in parallel with specified workers
  parallelize(workers: :number_of_processors)

  # Setup all fixtures in test/fixtures/*.yml for all tests in alphabetical order.
  fixtures :all

  # Add more helper methods to be used by all tests here...
end
```

The resulting transition from RED to GREEN in the cloud IDE appears as in Figure 3.10.

---

17. The code in Listing 3.46 mixes single- and double-quoted strings. This is because **rails new** generates single-quoted strings, whereas the minitest reporters documentation uses double-quoted strings. This mixing of the two string types is common in Ruby; see Section 4.2.2 for more information.

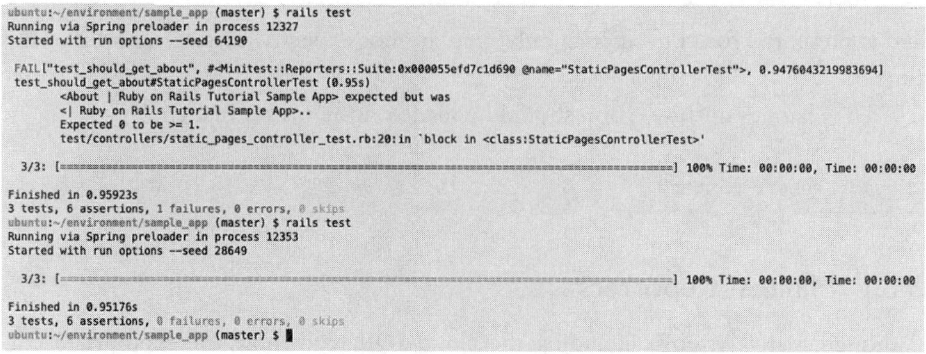

```
ubuntu:~/environment/sample_app (master) $ rails test
Running via Spring preloader in process 12327
Started with run options --seed 64190

 FAIL["test_should_get_about", #<Minitest::Reporters::Suite:0x000055efd7c1d690 @name="StaticPagesControllerTest">, 0.9476043219983694]
 test_should_get_about#StaticPagesControllerTest (0.95s)
        <About | Ruby on Rails Tutorial Sample App> expected but was
        <| Ruby on Rails Tutorial Sample App>..
        Expected 0 to be >= 1.
        test/controllers/static_pages_controller_test.rb:20:in 'block in <class:StaticPagesControllerTest>'

  3/3: [===============================================================================] 100% Time: 00:00:00, Time: 00:00:00

Finished in 0.95923s
3 tests, 6 assertions, 1 failures, 0 errors, 0 skips
ubuntu:~/environment/sample_app (master) $ rails test
Running via Spring preloader in process 12353
Started with run options --seed 28649

  3/3: [===============================================================================] 100% Time: 00:00:00, Time: 00:00:00

Finished in 0.95176s
3 tests, 6 assertions, 0 failures, 0 errors, 0 skips
ubuntu:~/environment/sample_app (master) $ █
```

Figure 3.10: Going from RED to GREEN in the cloud IDE.

3.6.2 Automated Tests with Guard

One annoyance associated with using the **rails test** command is having to switch to the command line and run the tests by hand. To avoid this inconvenience, we can use *Guard* to automate the running of the tests. Guard monitors changes in the filesystem so that, for example, when we change the **static_pages_controller_test.rb** file, only those tests get run. Even better, we can configure Guard so that when, say, the **home.html.erb** file is modified, the **static_pages_controller_test.rb** automatically runs.

The **Gemfile** in Listing 3.2 has already included the guard gem in our application, so to get started we just need to initialize it:

```
$ bundle exec guard init
Writing new Guardfile to /home/ec2-user/environment/sample_app/Guardfile
00:51:32 - INFO - minitest guard added to Guardfile, feel free to edit it
```

We then edit the resulting **Guardfile** so that Guard will run the right tests when the integration tests and views are updated, which will look something like Listing 3.47. For maximum flexibility, I recommend using the version of the **Guardfile** listed in the reference application, which if you're reading this online should be identical to Listing 3.47:

- Reference **Guardfile** at railstutorial.org/guardfile

Listing 3.47: A custom **Guardfile**.

```ruby
# Defines the matching rules for Guard.
guard :minitest, spring: "bin/rails test", all_on_start: false do
  watch(%r{^test/(.*)/?(.*)_test\.rb$})
  watch('test/test_helper.rb') { 'test' }
  watch('config/routes.rb') { interface_tests }
  watch(%r{app/views/layouts/*}) { interface_tests }
  watch(%r{^app/models/(.*?)\.rb$}) do |matches|
    "test/models/#{matches[1]}_test.rb"
  end
  watch(%r{^app/controllers/(.*?)_controller\.rb$}) do |matches|
    resource_tests(matches[1])
  end
  watch(%r{^app/views/([^/]*?)/.*\.html\.erb$}) do |matches|
    ["test/controllers/#{matches[1]}_controller_test.rb"] +
    integration_tests(matches[1])
  end
  watch(%r{^app/helpers/(.*?)_helper\.rb$}) do |matches|
    integration_tests(matches[1])
  end
  watch('app/views/layouts/application.html.erb') do
    'test/integration/site_layout_test.rb'
  end
  watch('app/helpers/sessions_helper.rb') do
    integration_tests << 'test/helpers/sessions_helper_test.rb'
  end
  watch('app/controllers/sessions_controller.rb') do
    ['test/controllers/sessions_controller_test.rb',
     'test/integration/users_login_test.rb']
  end
  watch('app/controllers/account_activations_controller.rb') do
    'test/integration/users_signup_test.rb'
  end
  watch(%r{app/views/users/*}) do
    resource_tests('users') +
    ['test/integration/microposts_interface_test.rb']
  end
end

# Returns the integration tests corresponding to the given resource.
def integration_tests(resource = :all)
  if resource == :all
    Dir["test/integration/*"]
  else
    Dir["test/integration/#{resource}_*.rb"]
  end
end
```

```ruby
# Returns all tests that hit the interface.
def interface_tests
  integration_tests << "test/controllers/"
end

# Returns the controller tests corresponding to the given resource.
def controller_test(resource)
  "test/controllers/#{resource}_controller_test.rb"
end

# Returns all tests for the given resource.
def resource_tests(resource)
  integration_tests(resource) << controller_test(resource)
end
```

On the cloud IDE, there's one additional step, which is to run the following rather obscure commands to allow Guard to monitor all the files in the project:

```
$ echo fs.inotify.max_user_watches=524288 | sudo tee -a /etc/sysctl.conf
$ sudo sysctl -p
```

Once Guard is configured, you should open a new terminal (as with the Rails server in Section 1.2.2) and run it at the command line as follows (Figure 3.11):

```
$ bundle exec guard
```

Figure 3.11: Using Guard on the cloud IDE.

The rules in Listing 3.47 are optimized for this tutorial, automatically running (for example) the integration tests when a controller is changed. To run *all* the tests, simply hit return at the **guard>** prompt.

To exit Guard, press Ctrl-D. To add additional matchers to Guard, refer to the examples in Listing 3.47, the Guard README, and the Guard wiki.

If the test suite fails without apparent cause, try exiting Guard, stopping Spring (which Rails uses to preload information to help speed up tests), and restarting:

```
$ bin/spring stop     # Try this if the tests mysteriously start failing.
$ bundle exec guard
```

Before proceeding, you should add your changes and make a commit:

```
$ git add -A
$ git commit -m "Complete advanced testing setup"
```

CHAPTER 4
Rails-Flavored Ruby

Grounded in examples from Chapter 3, this chapter explores some elements of the Ruby programming language that are important for Rails. Ruby is a big language, but fortunately the subset needed to be productive as a Rails developer is relatively small. It also differs somewhat from the usual material covered in an introduction to Ruby. This chapter is designed to give you a solid foundation in Rails-flavored Ruby, whether or not you have prior experience in the language. It covers a lot of material, and it's OK not to get it all on the first pass. We'll refer back to it frequently in future chapters.[1]

4.1 Motivation

As we saw in the last chapter, it's possible to develop the skeleton of a Rails application, and even start testing it, with essentially no knowledge of the underlying Ruby language. We did this by relying on the test code provided by the tutorial and addressing each error message until the test suite was passing. This situation can't last forever, though, and we'll open this chapter with an addition to the site that brings us face-to-face with our Ruby limitations.

As in Section 3.2, we'll use a separate topic branch to keep our changes self-contained:

```
$ git checkout -b rails-flavored-ruby
```

---

1. For a more systematic introduction to Ruby, see *Learn Enough Ruby to Be Dangerous* (www.learnenough.com/ruby).

We'll merge our changes into **master** in Section 4.5.

4.1.1 Built-in Helpers

When we last saw our new application, we had just updated our mostly static pages to use Rails layouts to eliminate duplication in our views, as shown in Listing 4.1 (which is the same as Listing 3.37).

Listing 4.1: The sample application site layout.
`app/views/layouts/application.html.erb`

```erb
<!DOCTYPE html>
<html>
  <head>
    <title><%= yield(:title) %> | Ruby on Rails Tutorial Sample App</title>
    <meta charset="utf-8">
    <%= csrf_meta_tags %>
    <%= csp_meta_tag %>

    <%= stylesheet_link_tag 'application', media: 'all',
                                           'data-turbolinks-track': 'reload' %>
    <%= javascript_pack_tag 'application', 'data-turbolinks-track': 'reload' %>
  </head>

  <body>
    <%= yield %>
  </body>
</html>
```

Let's focus on one particular line in Listing 4.1:

```erb
<%= stylesheet_link_tag 'application', media: 'all',
                                       'data-turbolinks-track': 'reload' %>
```

This uses the built-in Rails function **stylesheet_link_tag** (which you can read more about at the Rails API)[2] to include **application.css** for all media types (including computer screens and printers). To an experienced Rails developer, this

---

2. An "API" is an application programming interface, which is a set of methods and other conventions that serves as an abstraction layer for interacting with a software system. The practical effect is that we as developers don't need to understand the program internals; we need only be famliar with the public-facing API. In the

line looks simple, but there are at least four potentially confusing Ruby ideas: built-in Rails methods, method invocation with missing parentheses, symbols, and hashes. We'll cover all of these ideas in this chapter.

4.1.2 Custom Helpers

In addition to coming equipped with a large number of built-in functions for use in the views, Rails allows the creation of new ones. Such functions are called *helpers*. To see how to make a custom helper, let's start by examining the title line from Listing 4.1:

```erb
<%= yield(:title) %> | Ruby on Rails Tutorial Sample App
```

This relies on the definition of a page title (using **provide**) in each view, as in

```erb
<% provide(:title, "Home") %>
<h1>Sample App</h1>
<p>
  This is the home page for the
  <a href="https://www.railstutorial.org/">Ruby on Rails Tutorial</a>
  sample application.
</p>
```

But what if we don't provide a title? It's a good convention to have a *base title* we use on every page, with an optional page title if we want to be more specific. We've *almost* achieved that with our current layout, with one wrinkle: As you can see if you delete the **provide** call in one of the views, in the absence of a page-specific title the full title appears as follows:

```
| Ruby on Rails Tutorial Sample App
```

In other words, there's a suitable base title, but there's also a leading vertical bar character | at the beginning.

To solve the problem of a missing page title, we'll define a custom helper called **full_title**. The **full_title** helper returns a base title, "Ruby on Rails Tutorial

---

present case, this means that, rather than be concerned with how **stylesheet_link_tag** is implemented, we need only know how it behaves.

Sample App," if no page title is defined, and adds a vertical bar preceded by the page title if one is defined (Listing 4.2).[3]

Listing 4.2: Defining a **full_title** helper.
`app/helpers/application_helper.rb`

```ruby
module ApplicationHelper

  # Returns the full title on a per-page basis.
  def full_title(page_title = '')
    base_title = "Ruby on Rails Tutorial Sample App"
    if page_title.empty?
      base_title
    else
      page_title + " | " + base_title
    end
  end
end
```

Now that we have a helper, we can use it to simplify our layout by replacing

```erb
<title><%= yield(:title) %> | Ruby on Rails Tutorial Sample App</title>
```

with

```erb
<title><%= full_title(yield(:title)) %></title>
```

as seen in Listing 4.3.

Listing 4.3: The site layout with the **full_title** helper. GREEN
`app/views/layouts/application.html.erb`

```erb
<!DOCTYPE html>
<html>
  <head>
    <title><%= full_title(yield(:title)) %></title>
```

---

3. If a helper is specific to a particular controller, you should put it in the corresponding helper file; for example, helpers for the Static Pages controller generally go in **app/helpers/static_pages_helper.rb**. In our case, we expect the **full_title** helper to be used on all the site's pages, and Rails has a special helper file for this case: **app/helpers/application_helper.rb**.

```
  <meta charset="utf-8">
  <%= csrf_meta_tags %>
  <%= csp_meta_tag %>

  <%= stylesheet_link_tag 'application', media: 'all',
                               'data-turbolinks-track': 'reload' %>
  <%= javascript_pack_tag 'application', 'data-turbolinks-track': 'reload' %>
  </head>
  <body>
    <%= yield %>
  </body>
</html>
```

To put our helper to work, we can eliminate the unnecessary word "Home" from the Home page, allowing it to revert to the base title. We do this by first updating our test with the code in Listing 4.4, which updates the previous title test and adds one to test for the absence of the custom **"Home"** string in the title.

Listing 4.4: An updated test for the Home page's title. RED
`test/controllers/static_pages_controller_test.rb`

```ruby
require 'test_helper'

class StaticPagesControllerTest < ActionDispatch::IntegrationTest

  test "should get home" do
    get static_pages_home_url
    assert_response :success
    assert_select "title", "Ruby on Rails Tutorial Sample App"
  end

  test "should get help" do
    get static_pages_help_url
    assert_response :success
    assert_select "title", "Help | Ruby on Rails Tutorial Sample App"
  end

  test "should get about" do
    get static_pages_about_url
    assert_response :success
    assert_select "title", "About | Ruby on Rails Tutorial Sample App"
  end
end
```

Let's run the test suite to verify that one test fails:[4]

Listing 4.5: RED

```
$ rails test
3 tests, 6 assertions, 1 failures, 0 errors, 0 skips
```

To get the test suite to pass, we'll remove the **provide** line from the Home page's view, as seen in Listing 4.6.

Listing 4.6: The Home page with no custom page title. GREEN
`app/views/static_pages/home.html.erb`

```
<h1>Sample App</h1>
<p>
  This is the home page for the
  <a href="https://www.railstutorial.org/">Ruby on Rails Tutorial</a>
  sample application.
</p>
```

At this point the tests should pass:

Listing 4.7: GREEN

```
$ rails test
```

(Previous examples have included partial output of running **rails test**, including the number of passing and failing tests, but for brevity these will usually be omitted from now on.)

As with the line to include the application stylesheet in Section 4.1.1, the code in Listing 4.2 may look simple to the eyes of an experienced Rails developer, but it's *full* of important Ruby ideas: modules, method definition, optional method arguments, comments, local variable assignment, booleans, control flow, string concatenation, and return values. This chapter will cover all of these ideas as well.

---

4. I'll generally run the test suite explicitly for completeness, but in practice I usually just use Guard as described in Section 3.6.2.

4.2 Strings and Methods

Our principal tool for learning Ruby will be the *Rails console*, a command-line program for interacting with Rails applications first seen in Section 2.3.3. The console itself is built on top of interactive Ruby (**irb**), and thus has access to the full power of the Ruby language. (As we'll see in Section 4.4.4, the console also has access to the Rails environment.)

If you're using the cloud IDE, there are a couple of irb configuration parameters I recommend including. Using the simple **nano** text editor, open a file called **.irbrc** in the home directory:[5]

```
$ nano ~/.irbrc
```

Then fill it with the content of Listing 4.8, which arranges to simplify the **irb** prompt and suppress some annoying auto-indent behavior.

Listing 4.8: Adding some irb configuration.
`~/.irbrc`

```
IRB.conf[:PROMPT_MODE] = :SIMPLE
IRB.conf[:AUTO_INDENT_MODE] = false
```

Finally, exit **nano** with Ctrl-X and save **~/.irbrc** by typing **y** to confirm.

We can now start the console at the command line as follows:

```
$ rails console
Loading development environment
>>
```

By default, the console starts in a *development environment*, which is one of three separate environments defined by Rails (the others are *test* and *production*). This distinction won't be important in this chapter, but it will in the future, and we'll learn more about environments in Section 7.1.1.

---

5. The **nano** editor is easier for beginners, but for this sort of short edit I would almost always use Vim instead. To learn Minimum Viable Vim, see *Learn Enough Text Editor to Be Dangerous*, www.learnenough.com/text-editor.

The console is a great learning tool, and you should feel free to explore it. Don't worry—you (probably) won't break anything. When using the console, type Ctrl-C if you get stuck, or type Ctrl-D to exit the console altogether. As with a regular terminal shell, you can also use up-arrow to retrieve previous commands, which can be a significant time-saver.

Throughout the rest of this chapter, you might find it helpful to consult the Ruby API. It's packed (perhaps even *too* packed) with information. For example, to learn more about Ruby strings you can look at the Ruby API entry for the **String** class.

During this discussion, we'll sometimes use Ruby *comments*, which start with the pound sign **#** (also called the "hash mark" or, more poetically, the "octothorpe") and extend to the end of the line. Ruby ignores comments, but they are useful for human readers (including, often, the original author!). In the code

```
# Returns the full title on a per-page basis.
def full_title(page_title = '')
  .
  .
  .
end
```

the first line is a comment indicating the purpose of the subsequent function definition.

You don't ordinarily include comments in console sessions, but for instructional purposes I'll include some comments in what follows, like this:

```
$ rails console
>> 17 + 42   # Integer addition
=> 59
```

If you follow along in this section by typing or copying-and-pasting commands into your own console, you can of course omit the comments if you like; the console will ignore them in any case.

4.2.1 Strings

Strings are probably the most important data structure for web applications, since web pages ultimately consist of strings of characters sent from the server to the browser. Let's start exploring strings with the console:

```
$ rails console
>> ""          # An empty string
=> ""
>> "foo"       # A nonempty string
=> "foo"
```

These are *string literals* (also called *literal strings*), created using the double quote character **"**. The console prints the result of evaluating each line, which in the case of a string literal is just the string itself.

We can also concatenate strings with the **+** operator:

```
>> "foo" + "bar"     # String concatenation
=> "foobar"
```

Here the result of evaluating **"foo"** plus **"bar"** is the string **"foobar"**.[6]

Another way to build up strings is via *interpolation* using the special syntax **#{}**:[7]

```
>> first_name = "Michael"     # Variable assignment
=> "Michael"
>> "#{first_name} Hartl"      # String interpolation
=> "Michael Hartl"
```

Here we've *assigned* the value **"Michael"** to the variable **first_name** and then interpolated it into the string **"#{first_name} Hartl"**. We could also assign both strings a variable name:

```
>> first_name = "Michael"
=> "Michael"
>> last_name = "Hartl"
=> "Hartl"
>> first_name + " " + last_name     # Concatenation, with a space in between
=> "Michael Hartl"
>> "#{first_name} #{last_name}"     # The equivalent interpolation
=> "Michael Hartl"
```

---

6. For more on the origins of "foo" and "bar"—and, in particular, the possible *non*-relation of "foobar" to "FUBAR"—see the Jargon File entry on "foo." (www.catb.org/jargon/html/F/foo.html).

7. Programmers familiar with Perl or PHP should compare this to the automatic interpolation of dollar sign variables in expressions like **"foo $bar"**.

Note that the final two expressions are equivalent, but I prefer the interpolated version; having to add the single space **" "** seems a bit awkward.

Printing

To *print* a string to the screen, the most commonly used Ruby function is **puts** (pronounced "put ess," for "put string," though some people do pronounce it like the word "puts" instead):

```
>> puts "foo"      # put string
foo
=> nil
```

The **puts** method operates as a *side effect*: The expression **puts "foo"** prints the string to the screen and then returns literally nothing—**nil** is a special Ruby value for "nothing at all." (In what follows, I'll sometimes suppress the **=> nil** part for simplicity.)

As seen in the preceding examples, using **puts** automatically includes a new line after the string gets printed (the same as the behavior of the **echo** command covered in *Learn Enough Command Line to Be Dangerous*). The closely related **print** command prints the raw string without the extra line:

```
>> print "foo"     # print string without extra line
foo=> nil
```

You can see here that the output **foo** bumps right up against the prompt in the second line.

The technical name for an extra line of blank space is a *newline*, typically represented by "backslash n" **\n**. We can arrange for **print** to replicate the behavior of **puts** by including an explicit newline character in the string:

```
>> print "foo\n"  # Same as puts "foo"
foo
=> nil
```

Single-quoted Strings

All the examples so far have used *double-quoted strings*, but Ruby also supports *single-quoted* strings. For many uses, the two types of strings are effectively identical:

```
>> 'foo'          # A single-quoted string
=> "foo"
>> 'foo' + 'bar'
=> "foobar"
```

There's an important difference, though; Ruby won't interpolate into single-quoted strings:

```
>> '#{foo} bar'      # Single-quoted strings don't allow interpolation
=> "\#{foo} bar"
```

Note how the console returns values using double-quoted strings, which requires a backslash to *escape* special character combinations such as **#{**.

If double-quoted strings can do everything that single-quoted strings can do, and interpolate to boot, what's the point of single-quoted strings? They are often useful because they are truly literal, containing exactly the characters you type. For example, the "backslash" character is special on most systems, as in the literal newline **\n**. If you want a variable to contain a literal backslash, single quotes make it easier:

```
>> '\n'          # A literal 'backslash n' combination
=> "\\n"
```

As with the **#{** combination in our previous example, Ruby needs to escape the backslash with an additional backslash; inside double-quoted strings, a literal backslash is represented with *two* backslashes. For a small example like this, there's not much savings, but if there are lots of things to escape it can be a real help:

```
>> 'Newlines (\n) and tabs (\t) both use the backslash character \.'
=> "Newlines (\\n) and tabs (\\t) both use the backslash character \\."
```

Finally, it's worth noting that, in the common case that both single and double quotes work just fine, you'll often find that the source code switches between the two without any apparent pattern. There's really nothing to be done about this, except to say, "Welcome to Ruby! You'll get used to it soon enough."

Exercises

Solutions to the exercises are available to all Rails Tutorial purchasers at https://www.railstutorial.org/aw-solutions.

To see other people's answers and to record your own, subscribe to the Rails Tutorial course or to the Learn Enough All Access Bundle.

1. Assign variables **city** and **state** to your current city and state of residence. (If you reside outside the United States, substitute the analogous quantities.)

2. Using interpolation, print (using **puts**) a string consisting of the city and state separated by a comma and a space, as in "Los Angeles, CA".

3. Repeat the previous exercise but with the city and state separated by a tab character.

4. What is the result if you replace double quotes with single quotes in the previous exercise?

4.2.2 Objects and Message Passing

Everything in Ruby, including strings and even **nil**, is an *object*. We'll see the technical meaning of this in Section 4.4.2, but I don't think anyone ever understood objects by reading the definition in a book; you have to build up your intuition for objects by seeing lots of examples.

It's easier to describe what objects *do*, which is respond to messages. An object like a string, for example, can respond to the message **length**, which returns the number of characters in the string:

```
>> "foobar".length       # Passing the "length" message to a string
=> 6
```

Typically, the messages that get passed to objects are *methods*, which are functions defined on those objects.[8] Strings also respond to the **empty?** method:

```
>> "foobar".empty?
=> false
>> "".empty?
=> true
```

---

8. Apologies in advance for switching haphazardly between *function* and *method* throughout this chapter. In Ruby, they're the same thing: All methods are functions, and all functions are methods, because everything is an object.

Note the question mark at the end of the **empty?** method. This is a Ruby convention indicating that the return value is *boolean*: **true** or **false**. Booleans are especially useful for *control flow*:

```
>> s = "foobar"
>> if s.empty?
>>    "The string is empty"
>> else
>>    "The string is nonempty"
>> end
=> "The string is nonempty"
```

To include more than one clause, we can use **elsif** (**else** + **if**):

```
>> if s.nil?
>>    "The variable is nil"
>> elsif s.empty?
>>    "The string is empty"
>> elsif s.include?("foo")
>>    "The string includes 'foo'"
>> end
=> "The string includes 'foo'"
```

Booleans can also be combined using the **&&** ("and"), **||** ("or"), and **!** ("not") operators:

```
>> x = "foo"
=> "foo"
>> y = ""
=> ""
>> puts "Both strings are empty" if x.empty? && y.empty?
=> nil
>> puts "One of the strings is empty" if x.empty? || y.empty?
"One of the strings is empty"
=> nil
>> puts "x is not empty" if !x.empty?
"x is not empty"
=> nil
```

Since everything in Ruby is an object, it follows that **nil** is an object, so it, too, can respond to methods. One example is the **to_s** method, which can convert virtually any object to a string:

```
>> nil.to_s
=> ""
```

This certainly appears to be an empty string, as we can verify by passing multiple methods to **nil**, a technique known as *method chaining*:

```
>> nil.empty?
NoMethodError: undefined method `empty?' for nil:NilClass
>> nil.to_s.empty?        # Message chaining
=> true
```

We see here that the **nil** object doesn't itself respond to the **empty?** method, but **nil.to_s** does.

There's a special method for testing for **nil**-ness, which you might be able to guess:

```
>> "foo".nil?
=> false
>> "".nil?
=> false
>> nil.nil?
=> true
```

The code

```
puts "x is not empty" if !x.empty?
```

also shows an alternative use of the **if** keyword: Ruby allows you to write a statement that is evaluated only if the statement following **if** is true. There's a complementary **unless** keyword that works the same way:

```
>> string = "foobar"
>> puts "The string '#{string}' is nonempty." unless string.empty?
The string 'foobar' is nonempty.
=> nil
```

It's worth noting that the **nil** object is special, in that it is the *only* Ruby object that is false in a boolean context, apart from **false** itself. We can see this using **!!** (read "bang bang"), which negates an object twice, thereby coercing it to its boolean value:

```
>> !!nil
=> false
```

In particular, all other Ruby objects are *true*, even 0:

```
>> !!0
=> true
```

Exercises

Solutions to the exercises are available to all Rails Tutorial purchasers at https://www.railstutorial.org/aw-solutions.

To see other people's answers and to record your own, subscribe to the Rails Tutorial course or to the Learn Enough All Access Bundle.

1. What is the length of the string "racecar"?

2. Confirm using the **reverse** method that the string in the previous exercise is the same when its letters are reversed.

3. Assign the string "racecar" to the variable **s**. Confirm using the *comparison operator* **==** that **s** and **s.reverse** are equal.

4. What is the result of running the code shown in Listing 4.9? How does it change if you reassign the variable **s** to the string "onomatopoeia"? *Hint*: Use up-arrow to retrieve and edit previous commands

Listing 4.9: A simple palindrome test.

```
>> puts "It's a palindrome!" if s == s.reverse
```

4.2.3 Method Definitions

The console allows us to define methods the same way we did with the **home** action from Listing 3.8 or the **full_title** helper from Listing 4.2. (Defining methods in the console is a bit cumbersome, and ordinarily you would use a file, but it's convenient for demonstration purposes.) For example, let's define a function **string_message** that takes a single *argument* and returns a message based on whether the argument is empty:

```
>> def string_message(str = '')
>>   if str.empty?
>>     "It's an empty string!"
>>   else
>>     "The string is nonempty."
>>   end
```

```
>> end
=> :string_message
>> puts string_message("foobar")
The string is nonempty.
>> puts string_message("")
It's an empty string!
>> puts string_message
It's an empty string!
```

As seen in the final example, it's possible to leave out the argument entirely (in which case we can also omit the parentheses). This is because the code

```
def string_message(str = '')
```

contains a *default* argument, which in this case is the empty string. This makes the **str** argument optional, and if we leave it off it automatically takes the given default value.

Note that Ruby functions have an *implicit return*, meaning they return the last statement evaluated—in this case, one of the two message strings, depending on whether the method's argument **str** is empty. Ruby also has an explicit return option; the following function is equivalent to the one above:

```
>> def string_message(str = '')
>>   return "It's an empty string!" if str.empty?
>>   return "The string is nonempty."
>> end
```

(The alert reader might notice at this point that the second **return** here is actually unnecessary. As the last expression in the function, the string **"The string is nonempty."** will be returned regardless of the **return** keyword, but using **return** in both places has a pleasing symmetry to it.)

It's also important to understand that the name of the function argument is irrelevant as far as the caller is concerned. In other words, the first example above could replace **str** with any other valid variable name, such as **the_function_argument**, and it would work just the same:

```
>> def string_message(the_function_argument = '')
>>   if the_function_argument.empty?
>>     "It's an empty string!"
>>   else
>>     "The string is nonempty."
>>   end
>> end
=> nil
```

```
>> puts string_message("")
It's an empty string!
>> puts string_message("foobar")
The string is nonempty.
```

Exercises

Solutions to the exercises are available to all Rails Tutorial purchasers at https://www.railstutorial.org/aw-solutions.

To see other people's answers and to record your own, subscribe to the Rails Tutorial course or to the Learn Enough All Access Bundle.

1. By replacing **FILL_IN** with the appropriate comparison test shown in Listing 4.10, define a method for testing palindromes. *Hint*: Use the comparison shown in Listing 4.9.

2. By running your palindrome tester on "racecar" and "onomatopoeia," confirm that the first is a palindrome and the second isn't.

3. By calling the **nil?** method on **palindrome_tester("racecar")**, confirm that its return value is **nil** (i.e., calling **nil?** on the result of the method should return **true**). This is because the code in Listing 4.10 prints its responses instead of returning them.

Listing 4.10: A simple tester for palindromes.

```
>> def palindrome_tester(s)
>>   if FILL_IN
>>     puts "It's a palindrome!"
>>   else
>>     puts "It's not a palindrome."
>>   end
>> end
```

4.2.4   Back to the Title Helper

We are now in a position to understand the **full_title** helper from Listing 4.2,[9] which appears with commented annotations in Listing 4.11.

---

9. Well, there will still be *one* thing left that we don't understand, which is how Rails ties this all together: mapping URLs to actions, making the **full_title** helper available in views, etc. This is an interesting subject, and I encourage you to investigate it further, but knowing exactly *how* Rails works is not necessary when *using* Rails.

Listing 4.11: An annotated `title_helper`.
`app/helpers/application_helper.rb`

```
module ApplicationHelper

  # Returns the full title on a per-page basis.     # Documentation comment
  def full_title(page_title = '')                   # Method def, optional arg
    base_title = "Ruby on Rails Tutorial Sample App"  # Variable assignment
    if page_title.empty?                            # Boolean test
      base_title                                    # Implicit return
    else
      page_title + " | " + base_title               # String concatenation
    end
  end
end
```

These elements—function definition (with an optional argument), variable assignment, boolean tests, control flow, and string concatenation[10]—come together to make a compact helper method for use in our site layout. The final element is **module ApplicationHelper**: Modules give us a way to package together related methods, which can then be *mixed in* to Ruby classes using **include**. When writing ordinary Ruby, you often write modules and include them explicitly yourself, but in the case of a helper module Rails handles the inclusion for us. The result is that the **full_title** method is automagically available in all our views.

4.3 Other Data Structures

Although web apps are ultimately about strings, actually *making* those strings requires using other data structures as well. In this section, we'll learn about some Ruby data structures important for writing Rails applications.

4.3.1 Arrays and Ranges

An array is just a list of elements in a particular order. We haven't discussed arrays yet in the Rails Tutorial, but understanding them gives a good foundation for understanding

---

10. It's tempting to use string interpolation instead—indeed, this was the technique used in all previous versions of the tutorial—but in fact the call to **provide** converts the string into a so-called SafeBuffer object instead of an ordinary string. Interpolating and inserting into a view template then over-escapes any inserted HTML, so a title such as "Help's on the way" would be converted to "Help&#39;s on the way". (Thanks to reader Jeremy Fleischman for pointing out this subtle issue.)

hashes (Section 4.3.3) and for aspects of Rails data modeling (such as the **has_many** association seen in Section 2.3.3 and covered more in depth in Section 13.1.3).

So far we've spent a lot of time understanding strings, and there's a natural way to get from strings to arrays using the **split** method:

```
>> "foo bar    baz".split    # Split a string into a three-element array.
=> ["foo", "bar", "baz"]
```

The result of this operation is an array of three strings. By default, **split** divides a string into an array by splitting on whitespace, but you can split on nearly anything else as well:

```
>> "fooxbarxbaz".split('x')
=> ["foo", "bar", "baz"]
```

As is conventional in most computer languages, Ruby arrays are *zero-offset*, which means that the first element in the array has index 0, the second has index 1, and so on:

```
>> a = [42, 8, 17]
=> [42, 8, 17]
>> a[0]              # Ruby uses square brackets for array access.
=> 42
>> a[1]
=> 8
>> a[2]
=> 17
>> a[-1]             # Indices can even be negative!
=> 17
```

We see here that Ruby uses square brackets to access array elements. In addition to this bracket notation, Ruby offers synonyms for some commonly accessed elements:[11]

```
>> a                # Just a reminder of what 'a' is
=> [42, 8, 17]
>> a.first
=> 42
```

---

11. The **second** method used here isn't currently part of Ruby itself, but rather is added by Rails. It works in this case because the Rails console automatically includes the Rails extensions to Ruby.

```
>> a.second
=> 8
>> a.last
=> 17
>> a.last == a[-1]     # Comparison using ==
=> true
```

This last line introduces the equality comparison operator **==**, which Ruby shares with many other languages, along with the associated **!=** ("not equal") and other operators:

```
>> x = a.length        # Like strings, arrays respond to the 'length' method.
=> 3
>> x == 3
=> true
>> x == 1
=> false
>> x != 1
=> true
>> x >= 1
=> true
>> x < 1
=> false
```

In addition to **length** (seen in the first line above), arrays respond to a wealth of other methods:

```
>> a
=> [42, 8, 17]
>> a.empty?
=> false
>> a.include?(42)
=> true
>> a.sort
=> [8, 17, 42]
>> a.reverse
=> [17, 8, 42]
>> a.shuffle
=> [17, 42, 8]
>> a
=> [42, 8, 17]
```

Note that none of these methods changes **a** itself. To *mutate* the array, use the corresponding "bang" methods (so called because the exclamation point is usually pronounced "bang" in this context):

```
>> a
=> [42, 8, 17]
>> a.sort!
=> [8, 17, 42]
>> a
=> [8, 17, 42]
```

You can also add to arrays with the **push** method or its equivalent operator, **<<**, called the "shovel operator":

```
>> a.push(6)              # Pushing 6 onto an array
=> [42, 8, 17, 6]
>> a << 7                 # Pushing 7 onto an array
=> [42, 8, 17, 6, 7]
>> a << "foo" << "bar"    # Chaining array pushes
=> [42, 8, 17, 6, 7, "foo", "bar"]
```

This last example shows that you can chain pushes together, and also that, unlike arrays in many other languages, Ruby arrays can contain a mixture of different types (in this case, integers and strings).

Earlier we saw **split** convert a string to an array. We can also go the other way with the **join** method:

```
>> a
=> [42, 8, 17, 6, 7, "foo", "bar"]
>> a.join                 # Join on nothing.
=> "4281767foobar"
>> a.join(', ')           # Join on comma-space.
=> "42, 8, 17, 6, 7, foo, bar"
```

Closely related to arrays are *ranges*, which can probably most easily be understood by converting them to arrays using the **to_a** method:

```
>> 0..9
=> 0..9
>> 0..9.to_a              # Oops, call to_a on 9.
NoMethodError: undefined method `to_a' for 9:Fixnum
>> (0..9).to_a            # Use parentheses to call to_a on the range.
=> [0, 1, 2, 3, 4, 5, 6, 7, 8, 9]
```

Though **0..9** is a valid range, the second expression shows that we need to add parentheses to call a method on it.

Ranges are useful for pulling out array elements:

```
>> a = %w[foo bar baz quux]        # Use %w to make a string array.
=> ["foo", "bar", "baz", "quux"]
>> a[0..2]
=> ["foo", "bar", "baz"]
```

A particularly useful trick is to use the index -1 at the end of the range to select every element from the starting point to the end of the array without explicitly having to use the array's length:

```
>> a = (0..9).to_a
=> [0, 1, 2, 3, 4, 5, 6, 7, 8, 9]
>> a[2..(a.length-1)]              # Explicitly use the array's length.
=> [2, 3, 4, 5, 6, 7, 8, 9]
>> a[2..-1]                        # Use the index -1 trick.
=> [2, 3, 4, 5, 6, 7, 8, 9]
```

Ranges also work with characters:

```
>> ('a'..'e').to_a
=> ["a", "b", "c", "d", "e"]
```

Exercises

Solutions to the exercises are available to all Rails Tutorial purchasers at https://www.railstutorial.org/aw-solutions.

To see other people's answers and to record your own, subscribe to the Rails Tutorial course or to the Learn Enough All Access Bundle.

1. Assign **a** to be to the result of splitting the string "A man, a plan, a canal, Panama" on comma-space.

2. Assign **s** to the string resulting from joining **a** on nothing.

3. Split **s** on whitespace and rejoin on nothing. Use the palindrome test from Listing 4.10 to confirm that the resulting string **s** is *not* a palindrome by the current definition. Using the **downcase** method, show that **s.downcase** *is* a palindrome.

4. What is the result of selecting element 7 from the range of letters **a** through **z**? What about the same range reversed? *Hint*: In both cases you will have to convert the range to an array.

4.3.2 Blocks

Both arrays and ranges respond to a host of methods that accept *blocks*, which are simultaneously one of Ruby's most powerful and most confusing features:

```
>> (1..5).each { |i| puts 2 * i }
2
4
6
8
10
=> 1..5
```

This code calls the **each** method on the range **(1..5)** and passes it the block **{ |i| puts 2 * i }**. The vertical bars around the variable name in **|i|** are Ruby syntax for a block variable, and it's up to the method to know what to do with the block. In this case, the range's **each** method can handle a block with a single local variable, which we've called **i**, and it just executes the block for each value in the range.

Curly braces are one way to indicate a block, but there is a second way as well:

```
>> (1..5).each do |i|
?>    puts 2 * i
>> end
2
4
6
8
10
=> 1..5
```

Blocks can be more than one line, and often are. In the Rails Tutorial we'll follow the common convention of using curly braces only for short one-line blocks and the **do..end** syntax for longer one-liners and for multi-line blocks:

```
>> (1..5).each do |number|
?>    puts 2 * number
>>    puts '--'
>> end
2
--
4
```

```
--
6
--
8
--
10
--
=> 1..5
```

Here I've used **number** in place of **i** just to emphasize that any variable name will do.

Unless you already have a substantial programming background, there is no shortcut to understanding blocks; you just have to see them a lot, and eventually you'll get used to them.[12] Luckily, humans are quite good at making generalizations from concrete examples; here are a few more, including a couple using the **map** method:

```
>> 3.times { puts "Betelgeuse!" }    # 3.times takes a block with no variables.
"Betelgeuse!"
"Betelgeuse!"
"Betelgeuse!"
=> 3
>> (1..5).map { |i| i**2 }           # The ** notation is for 'power'.
=> [1, 4, 9, 16, 25]
>> %w[a b c]                         # Recall that %w makes string arrays.
=> ["a", "b", "c"]
>> %w[a b c].map { |char| char.upcase }
=> ["A", "B", "C"]
>> %w[A B C].map { |char| char.downcase }
=> ["a", "b", "c"]
```

As you can see, the **map** method returns the result of applying the given block to each element in the array or range. In the final two examples, the block inside **map** calls a particular method on the block variable, and in this case there's a commonly used shorthand called "symbol-to-proc":

```
>> %w[A B C].map { |char| char.downcase }
=> ["a", "b", "c"]
>> %w[A B C].map(&:downcase)
=> ["a", "b", "c"]
```

---

12. Programming experts, on the other hand, might benefit from knowing that blocks are *closures*, which are one-shot anonymous functions with data attached.

(This strange-looking but compact code uses a *symbol*, which we'll discuss in Section 4.3.3.) One interesting thing about this construction is that it was originally added to Ruby on Rails, and people liked it so much that it has now been incorporated into core Ruby.

As one final example of blocks, we can take a look at an individual test from the file in Listing 4.4:

```
test "should get home" do
  get static_pages_home_url
  assert_response :success
  assert_select "title", "Ruby on Rails Tutorial Sample App"
end
```

It's not important to understand the details (and in fact *I* don't know the details offhand), but we can infer from the presence of the **do** keyword that the body of the test is a block. The **test** method takes in a string argument (the description) and a block, and then executes the body of the block as part of running the test suite.

By the way, we're now in a position to understand the line of Ruby I threw into Section 1.4.2 to generate random subdomains:[13]

```
('a'..'z').to_a.shuffle[0..7].join
```

Let's build it up step-by-step:

```
>> ('a'..'z').to_a                    # An alphabet array
=> ["a", "b", "c", "d", "e", "f", "g", "h", "i", "j", "k", "l", "m", "n", "o",
"p", "q", "r", "s", "t", "u", "v", "w", "x", "y", "z"]
>> ('a'..'z').to_a.shuffle            # Shuffle it.
=> ["c", "g", "l", "k", "h", "z", "s", "i", "n", "d", "y", "u", "t", "j", "q",
"b", "r", "o", "f", "e", "w", "v", "m", "a", "x", "p"]
>> ('a'..'z').to_a.shuffle[0..7]       # Pull out the first eight elements.
=> ["f", "w", "i", "a", "h", "p", "c", "x"]
>> ('a'..'z').to_a.shuffle[0..7].join  # Join them together to make one string.
=> "mznpybuj"
```

---

13. As noted in Chapter 1, in this case the code **('a'..'z').to_a.sample(8).join** is an even more compact way of getting the same result.

Exercises

Solutions to the exercises are available to all Rails Tutorial purchasers at https://www.railstutorial.org/aw-solutions.

To see other people's answers and to record your own, subscribe to the Rails Tutorial course or to the Learn Enough All Access Bundle.

1. Using the range **0..16**, print out the first 17 powers of 2.

2. Define a method called **yeller** that takes in an array of characters and returns a string with an ALLCAPS version of the input. Verify that **yeller(['o', 'l', 'd'])** returns **"OLD"**. *Hint*: Combine **map**, **upcase**, and **join**.

3. Define a method called **random_subdomain** that returns a randomly generated string of eight letters.

4. By replacing the question marks in Listing 4.12 with the appropriate methods, combine **split**, **shuffle**, and **join** to write a function that shuffles the letters in a given string.

Listing 4.12: Skeleton for a string shuffle function.

```
>> def string_shuffle(s)
>>    s.?('').?.?
>> end
>> string_shuffle("foobar")
=> "oobfra"
```

4.3.3 Hashes and Symbols

Hashes are essentially arrays that aren't limited to integer indices. (In fact, some languages, especially Perl, sometimes call hashes *associative arrays* for this reason.) Instead, hash indices, or *keys*, can be almost any object. For example, we can use strings as keys:

```
>> user = {}                        # {} is an empty hash.
=> {}
>> user["first_name"] = "Michael"   # Key "first_name", value "Michael"
=> "Michael"
>> user["last_name"] = "Hartl"      # Key "last_name", value "Hartl"
=> "Hartl"
>> user["first_name"]               # Element access is like arrays.
```

```
=> "Michael"
>> user                              # A literal representation of the hash
=> {"last_name"=>"Hartl", "first_name"=>"Michael"}
```

Hashes are indicated with curly braces containing key-value pairs; a pair of braces with no key-value pairs—that is, **{}**—is an empty hash. It's important to note that the curly braces for hashes have nothing to do with the curly braces for blocks. (Yes, this can be confusing.) Although hashes resemble arrays, one important difference is that hashes don't generally guarantee that they will keep their elements in a particular order.[14] If order matters, use an array.

Instead of defining hashes one item at a time using square brackets, it's easy to use a literal representation with keys and values separated by **=>**, called a "hashrocket":

```
>> user = { "first_name" => "Michael", "last_name" => "Hartl" }
=> {"last_name"=>"Hartl", "first_name"=>"Michael"}
```

Here I've used the usual Ruby convention of putting an extra space at the two ends of the hash—a convention ignored by the console output. (Don't ask me why the spaces are conventional; probably some early influential Ruby programmer liked the look of the extra spaces, and the convention stuck.)

So far we've used strings as hash keys, but in Rails it is much more common to use *symbols* instead. Symbols look kind of like strings, but are prefixed with a colon instead of surrounded by quotes. For example, **:name** is a symbol. You can think of symbols as basically strings without all the extra baggage.[15]

```
>> "name".split('')
=> ["n", "a", "m", "e"]
>> :name.split('')
NoMethodError: undefined method `split' for :name:Symbol
>> "foobar".reverse
=> "raboof"
>> :foobar.reverse
NoMethodError: undefined method `reverse' for :foobar:Symbol
```

---

14. Ruby versions 1.9 and later actually guarantee that hashes keep their elements in the same order entered, but it would be unwise ever to count on a particular ordering.

15. As a result of having less baggage, symbols are easier to compare to each other; strings need to be compared character by character, while symbols can be compared all in one go. This makes them ideal for use as hash keys.

Symbols are a special Ruby data type shared with very few other languages, so they may seem weird at first, but Rails uses them a lot, so you'll get used to them fast. Unlike strings, not all characters are valid:

```
>> :foo-bar
NameError: undefined local variable or method `bar' for main:Object
>> :2foo
SyntaxError
```

As long as you start your symbols with a letter and stick to normal word characters, you should be fine.

In terms of symbols as hash keys, we can define a **user** hash as follows:

```
>> user = { :name => "Michael Hartl", :email => "michael@example.com" }
=> {:name=>"Michael Hartl", :email=>"michael@example.com"}
>> user[:name]                # Access the value corresponding to :name.
=> "Michael Hartl"
>> user[:password]            # Access the value of an undefined key.
=> nil
```

We see here from the last example that the hash value for an undefined key is simply **nil**.

Because it's so common for hashes to use symbols as keys, version 1.9 Ruby supports a new syntax just for this special case:

```
>> h1 = { :name => "Michael Hartl", :email => "michael@example.com" }
=> {:name=>"Michael Hartl", :email=>"michael@example.com"}
>> h2 = { name: "Michael Hartl", email: "michael@example.com" }
=> {:name=>"Michael Hartl", :email=>"michael@example.com"}
>> h1 == h2
=> true
```

The second syntax replaces the symbol/hashrocket combination with the name of the key followed by a colon and a value:

```
{ name: "Michael Hartl", email: "michael@example.com" }
```

This construction more closely follows the hash notation in other languages (such as JavaScript) and enjoys growing popularity in the Rails community. Because both hash syntaxes are still in common use, it's essential to be able to recognize both of them. Unfortunately, this can be confusing, especially since **:name** is valid on its own (as a stand-alone symbol) but **name:** has no meaning by itself. The bottom line is that **:name =>** and **name:** are effectively the same *only inside literal hashes*, so that

```
{ :name => "Michael Hartl" }
```

and

```
{ name: "Michael Hartl" }
```

are equivalent, but otherwise you need to use **:name** (with the colon coming first) to denote a symbol.

Hash values can be virtually anything, even other hashes, as seen in Listing 4.13.

Listing 4.13: Nested hashes.

```
>> params = {}          # Define a hash called 'params' (short for 'parameters').
=> {}
>> params[:user] = { name: "Michael Hartl", email: "mhartl@example.com" }
=> {:name=>"Michael Hartl", :email=>"mhartl@example.com"}
>> params
=> {:user=>{:name=>"Michael Hartl", :email=>"mhartl@example.com"}}
>>  params[:user][:email]
=> "mhartl@example.com"
```

These sorts of hashes-of-hashes, or *nested hashes*, are heavily used by Rails, as we'll see starting in Section 7.3.

Like arrays and ranges, hashes respond to the **each** method. For example, consider a hash named **flash** with keys for two conditions, **:success** and **:danger**:

```
>> flash = { success: "It worked!", danger: "It failed." }
=> {:success=>"It worked!", :danger=>"It failed."}
>> flash.each do |key, value|
?>   puts "Key #{key.inspect} has value #{value.inspect}"
>> end
Key :success has value "It worked!"
Key :danger has value "It failed."
```

Note that, while the **each** method for arrays takes a block with only one variable, **each** for hashes takes two, a *key* and a *value*. Thus, the **each** method for a hash iterates through the hash one key-value *pair* at a time.

The last example uses the useful **inspect** method, which returns a string with a literal representation of the object it's called on:

```
>> puts (1..5).to_a          # Put an array as a string.
1
2
3
4
5
>> puts (1..5).to_a.inspect    # Put a literal array.
[1, 2, 3, 4, 5]
>> puts :name, :name.inspect
name
:name
>> puts "It worked!", "It worked!".inspect
It worked!
"It worked!"
```

By the way, using **inspect** to print an object is common enough that there's a shortcut for it, the **p** function:[16]

```
>> p :name               # Same output as 'puts :name.inspect'
:name
```

Exercises

Solutions to the exercises are available to all Rails Tutorial purchasers at https://www.railstutorial.org/aw-solutions.

To see other people's answers and to record your own, subscribe to the Rails Tutorial course or to the Learn Enough All Access Bundle.

1. Define a hash with the keys **'one'**, **'two'**, and **'three'**, and the values **'uno'**, **'dos'**, and **'tres'**. Iterate over the hash, and for each key-value pair print out **"'#{key}' in Spanish is '#{value}'"**.

---

16. There's actually a subtle difference, which is that **p** returns the object being printed while **puts** always returns **nil**. (Thanks to reader Katarzyna Siwek for pointing this out.)

2. Create three hashes called **person1**, **person2**, and **person3**, with first and last names under the keys **:first** and **:last**. Then create a **params** hash so that **params[:father]** is **person1**, **params[:mother]** is **person2**, and **params[:child]** is **person3**. Verify that, for example, **params[:father][:first]** has the right value.

3. Define a hash with symbol keys corresponding to name, email, and a "password digest," and values equal to your name, your email address, and a random string of 16 lowercase letters.

4. Find an online version of the Ruby API and read about the Hash method **merge**. What is the value of the following expression?

```
{ "a" => 100, "b" => 200 }.merge({ "b" => 300 })
```

4.3.4 CSS Revisited

It's time now to revisit the line from Listing 4.1 used in the layout to include the Cascading Style Sheets:

```
<%= stylesheet_link_tag 'application', media: 'all',
                                       'data-turbolinks-track': 'reload' %>
```

We are now nearly in a position to understand this. As mentioned briefly in Section 4.1, Rails defines a special function to include stylesheets, and

```
stylesheet_link_tag 'application', media: 'all',
                                   'data-turbolinks-track': 'reload'
```

is a call to this function. But there are several mysteries. First, where are the parentheses? In Ruby, they are optional, so these two are equivalent:

```
# Parentheses on function calls are optional.
# This:
stylesheet_link_tag('application', media: 'all',
                                   'data-turbolinks-track': 'reload')
# is the same as this:
stylesheet_link_tag 'application', media: 'all',
                                   'data-turbolinks-track': 'reload'
```

Second, the **media** argument sure looks like a hash, but where are the curly braces? When hashes are the *last* argument in a function call, the curly braces are optional, so these two are equivalent:

```
# Curly braces on final hash arguments are optional.
# This:
stylesheet_link_tag 'application', { media: 'all',
                                     'data-turbolinks-track': 'reload' }
# is the same as this:
stylesheet_link_tag 'application', media: 'all',
                                   'data-turbolinks-track': 'reload'
```

Finally, why does Ruby correctly interpret the lines

```
stylesheet_link_tag 'application', media: 'all',
                                   'data-turbolinks-track': 'reload'
```

even with a line break between the final elements? The answer is that Ruby doesn't distinguish between newlines and other whitespace in this context.[17] The *reason* I chose to break the code into pieces is that I prefer to keep lines of source code to fewer than 80 characters for legibility.[18]

So, we see now that the line

```
stylesheet_link_tag 'application', media: 'all',
                                   'data-turbolinks-track': 'reload'
```

calls the **stylesheet_link_tag** function with two arguments: a string, indicating the path to the stylesheet, and a hash with two elements, indicating the media type and telling Rails to use the turbolinks feature added in Rails 4.0. Because of the **<%= ... %>** brackets, the results are inserted into the template by ERb, and if you view the source of the page in your browser you should see the HTML needed to include a stylesheet (Listing 4.14). (The extra stuff in Listing 4.14, like **?body=1** and the long

---

17. A newline is what comes at the end of a line, thereby starting a new line. As noted in Section 4.2.1, it is typically represented by the character **\n**.

18. Constantly having to check the column number is rather inconvenient, so many text editors have a visual aid to help you. For example, if you take a look back at Figure 1.12, you may be able to make out the small vertical line on the right side of the screen, which is designed to help keep code under 80 characters. (It's very subtle, so you may not be able to see it in the screenshot.) The cloud IDE (Section 1.1.1) includes such a line by default. In Sublime Text, you can use View > Ruler > 78 or View > Ruler > 80.

string of hexadecimal digits are, inserted by Rails to ensure that browsers reload the CSS when it changes on the server. Because the hex string is by design unique, your exact version of Listing 4.14 will differ.)

Listing 4.14: The HTML source produced by the CSS includes.

```
<link rel="stylesheet" media="all" href="/assets/application.self-
f0d704deea029cf000697e2c0181ec173a1b474645466ed843eb5ee7bb215794.css?body=1"
data-turbolinks-track="reload" />
```

4.4   Ruby Classes

We've said before that everything in Ruby is an object, and in this section we'll finally get to define some of our own. Ruby, like many object-oriented languages, uses *classes* to organize methods; these classes are then *instantiated* to create objects. If you're new to object-oriented programming, this may sound like gibberish, so let's look at some concrete examples.

4.4.1   Constructors

We've seen lots of examples of using classes to instantiate objects, but we have yet to do so explicitly. For example, we instantiated a string using the double quote characters, which is a *literal constructor* for strings:

```
>> s = "foobar"        # A literal constructor for strings using double quotes
=> "foobar"
>> s.class
=> String
```

We see here that strings respond to the method **class**, and simply return the class they belong to.

Instead of using a literal constructor, we can use the equivalent *named constructor*, which involves calling the **new** method on the class name:[19]

---

19. These results will vary based on the version of Ruby you are using. This example assumes you are using Ruby 1.9.3 or later.

```
>> s = String.new("foobar")    # A named constructor for a string
=> "foobar"
>> s.class
=> String
>> s == "foobar"
=> true
```

This is equivalent to the literal constructor, but it's more explicit about what we're doing.

Arrays work the same way as strings:

```
>> a = Array.new([1, 3, 2])
=> [1, 3, 2]
```

Hashes, in contrast, are different. While the array constructor **Array.new** takes an initial value for the array, **Hash.new** takes a *default* value for the hash, which is the value of the hash for a nonexistent key:

```
>> h = Hash.new
=> {}
>> h[:foo]             # Try to access the value for the nonexistent key :foo.
=> nil
>> h = Hash.new(0)   # Arrange for nonexistent keys to return 0 instead of nil.
=> {}
>> h[:foo]
=> 0
```

When a method gets called on the class itself, as in the case of **new**, it's called a *class method*. The result of calling **new** on a class is an object of that class, also called an *instance* of the class. A method called on an instance, such as **length**, is called an *instance method*.

Exercises

Solutions to the exercises are available to all Rails Tutorial purchasers at https://www.railstutorial.org/aw-solutions.

To see other people's answers and to record your own, subscribe to the Rails Tutorial course or to the Learn Enough All Access Bundle.

1. What is the literal constructor for the range of integers from 1 to 10?

2. What is the constructor using the **Range** class and the **new** method? *Hint*: **new** takes two arguments in this context.

3. Confirm using the **==** operator that the literal and named constructors from the previous two exercises are identical.

4.4.2 Class Inheritance

When learning about classes, it's useful to find out the *class hierarchy* using the **superclass** method:

```
>> s = String.new("foobar")
=> "foobar"
>> s.class                       # Find the class of s.
=> String
>> s.class.superclass            # Find the superclass of String.
=> Object
>> s.class.superclass.superclass # Ruby has a BasicObject base class as of 1.9
=> BasicObject
>> s.class.superclass.superclass.superclass
=> nil
```

A diagram of this inheritance hierarchy appears in Figure 4.1. We see here that the superclass of **String** is **Object** and the superclass of **Object** is **BasicObject**, but

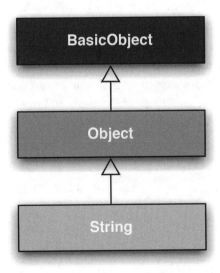

Figure 4.1: The inheritance hierarchy for the **String** class.

BasicObject has no superclass. This pattern is true of every Ruby object: Trace back the class hierarchy far enough and every class in Ruby ultimately inherits from **BasicObject**, which has no superclass itself. This is the technical meaning of "everything in Ruby is an object."

To understand classes a little more deeply, there's no substitute for making one of our own. Let's make a **Word** class with a **palindrome?** method that returns **true** if the word is the same spelled forward and backward:

```
>> class Word
>>   def palindrome?(string)
>>     string == string.reverse
>>   end
>> end
=> :palindrome?
```

We can use it as follows:

```
>> w = Word.new              # Make a new Word object.
=> #<Word:0x22d0b20>
>> w.palindrome?("foobar")
=> false
>> w.palindrome?("level")
=> true
```

If this example strikes you as a bit contrived, good—this is by design. It's odd to create a new class just to create a method that takes a string as an argument. Since a word *is a* string, it's more natural to have our **Word** class *inherit* from **String**, as seen in Listing 4.15. (You should exit the console and re-enter it to clear out the old definition of **Word**.)

Listing 4.15: Defining a **Word** class in the console.

```
>> class Word < String         # Word inherits from String.
>>   # Returns true if the string is its own reverse.
>>   def palindrome?
>>     self == self.reverse     # self is the string itself.
>>   end
>> end
=> nil
```

Here **Word < String** is the Ruby syntax for inheritance (discussed briefly in Section 3.2), which ensures that, in addition to the new **palindrome?** method, words have all the same methods as strings:

```
>> s = Word.new("level")    # Make a new Word, initialized with "level".
=> "level"
>> s.palindrome?            # Words have the palindrome? method.
=> true
>> s.length                 # Words also inherit all the normal string methods.
=> 5
```

Since the **Word** class inherits from **String**, we can use the console to see the class hierarchy explicitly:

```
>> s.class
=> Word
>> s.class.superclass
=> String
>> s.class.superclass.superclass
=> Object
```

This hierarchy is illustrated in Figure 4.2.

In Listing 4.15, note that checking that the word is its own reverse involves accessing the word inside the **Word** class. Ruby allows us to do this using the **self** keyword: Inside the **Word** class, **self** is the object itself, which means we can use

```
self == self.reverse
```

to check if the word is a palindrome. In fact, inside the String class the use of **self.** is optional on a method or attribute (unless we're making an assignment), so

```
self == reverse
```

would work as well.

Exercises

Solutions to the exercises are available to all Rails Tutorial purchasers at https://www.railstutorial.org/aw-solutions.

To see other people's answers and to record your own, subscribe to the Rails Tutorial course or to the Learn Enough All Access Bundle.

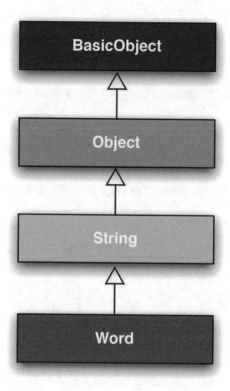

Figure 4.2: The inheritance hierarchy for the (non-built-in) **Word** class from Listing 4.15.

1. What is the class hierarchy for a range? For a hash? For a symbol?
2. Confirm that the method shown in Listing 4.15 works even if we replace **self.reverse** with just **reverse**.

4.4.3 Modifying Built-in Classes

While inheritance is a powerful idea, in the case of palindromes it might be even more natural to add the **palindrome?** method to the **String** class itself, so that (among other things) we can call **palindrome?** on a string literal, which we currently can't do:

```
>> "level".palindrome?
NoMethodError: undefined method `palindrome?' for "level":String
```

Amazingly, Ruby lets you do just this. Ruby classes can be *opened* and modified, allowing ordinary mortals such as ourselves to add methods to them:

```
>> class String
>>   # Returns true if the string is its own reverse.
>>   def palindrome?
>>     self == self.reverse
>>   end
>> end
=> nil
>> "deified".palindrome?
=> true
```

(I don't know which is cooler: that Ruby lets you add methods to built-in classes, or that **"deified"** is a palindrome.)

Modifying built-in classes is a powerful technique, but with great power comes great responsibility, and it's considered bad form to add methods to built-in classes without having a *really* good reason for doing so. Rails does have some good reasons. For example, in web applications we often want to prevent variables from being *blank*—for instance, a user's name should be something other than spaces and other whitespace—so Rails adds a **blank?** method to Ruby. Since the Rails console automatically includes the Rails extensions, we can see an example here (this won't work in plain **irb**):

```
>> "".blank?
=> true
>> "      ".empty?
=> false
>> "      ".blank?
=> true
>> nil.blank?
=> true
```

We see that a string of spaces is not *empty*, but it is *blank*. Note also that **nil** is blank; since **nil** isn't a string, this is a hint that Rails actually adds **blank?** to **String**'s base class, which (as we saw at the beginning of this section) is **Object** itself. We'll see some other examples of Rails additions to Ruby classes in Section 9.1.

Exercises

Solutions to the exercises are available to all Rails Tutorial purchasers at https://www.railstutorial.org/aw-solutions.

To see other people's answers and to record your own, subscribe to the Rails Tutorial course or to the Learn Enough All Access Bundle.

1. Verify that "racecar" is a palindrome and "onomatopoeia" is not. What about the name of the South Indian language "Malayalam"? *Hint*: Downcase it first.

2. Using Listing 4.16 as a guide, add a **shuffle** method to the **String** class. *Hint*: Refer to Listing 4.12.

3. Verify that Listing 4.16 works even if you remove **self.**.

Listing 4.16: Skeleton for a **shuffle** method attached to the **String** class.

```
>> class String
>>   def shuffle
>>     self.?('').?.?
>>   end
>> end
>> "foobar".shuffle
=> "borafo"
```

4.4.4 A Controller Class

All this talk about classes and inheritance may have triggered a flash of recognition, because we have seen both before, in the Static Pages controller (Listing 3.20):

```
class StaticPagesController < ApplicationController

  def home
  end

  def help
  end

  def about
  end
end
```

You're now in a position to appreciate, at least vaguely, what this code means: **StaticPagesController** is a class that inherits from **ApplicationController**, and comes equipped with **home**, **help**, and **about** methods. Since each Rails console session loads the local Rails environment, we can even create a controller explicitly and examine its class hierarchy:[20]

```
>> controller = StaticPagesController.new
=> #<StaticPagesController:0x22855d0>
>> controller.class
=> StaticPagesController
>> controller.class.superclass
=> ApplicationController
>> controller.class.superclass.superclass
=> ActionController::Base
>> controller.class.superclass.superclass.superclass
=> ActionController::Metal
>> controller.class.superclass.superclass.superclass.superclass
=> AbstractController::Base
>> controller.class.superclass.superclass.superclass.superclass.superclass
=> Object
```

A diagram of this hierarchy appears in Figure 4.3.

We can even call the controller actions inside the console, which are just methods:

```
>> controller.home
=> nil
```

Here the return value is **nil** because the **home** action is blank.

But wait—actions don't have return values, at least not ones that matter. The point of the **home** action, as we saw in Chapter 3, is to render a web page, not to return a value. And I sure don't remember ever calling **StaticPagesController.new** anywhere. What's going on?

What's going on is that Rails is *written in* Ruby, but Rails isn't Ruby. Some Rails classes are used like ordinary Ruby objects, but some are just grist for Rails' magic mill. Rails is *sui generis*, and should be studied and understood separately from Ruby.

---

20. You don't have to know what each class in this hierarchy does. *I* don't know what they all do, and I've been programming in Ruby on Rails since 2005. This means either that (a) I'm grossly incompetent or (b) you can be a skilled Rails developer without knowing all its innards. I hope for both our sakes that it's the latter.

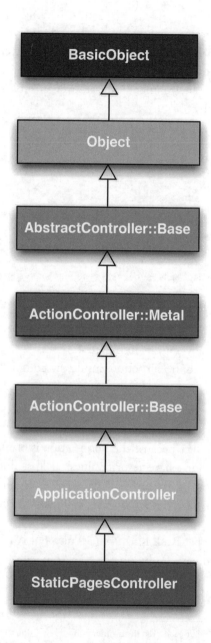

Figure 4.3: The inheritance hierarchy for the Static Pages.

Exercises

Solutions to the exercises are available to all Rails Tutorial purchasers at https://www.railstutorial.org/aw-solutions.

To see other people's answers and to record your own, subscribe to the Rails Tutorial course or to the Learn Enough All Access Bundle.

1. By running the Rails console in the toy app's directory from Chapter 2, confirm that you can create a **user** object using **User.new**.

2. Determine the class hierarchy of the **user** object.

4.4.5   A User Class

We end our tour of Ruby with a complete class of our own, a **User** class that anticipates the User model coming up in Chapter 6.

So far we've entered class definitions at the console, but this quickly becomes tiresome; instead, create the file **example_user.rb** in your application root directory and fill it with the contents of Listing 4.17.

Listing 4.17: Code for an example user.
example_user.rb

```ruby
class User
  attr_accessor :name, :email

  def initialize(attributes = {})
    @name  = attributes[:name]
    @email = attributes[:email]
  end

  def formatted_email
    "#{@name} <#{@email}>"
  end
end
```

There's quite a bit going on here, so let's take it step by step. The first line,

```ruby
attr_accessor :name, :email
```

creates *attribute accessors* corresponding to a user's name and email address. This creates "getter" and "setter" methods that allow us to retrieve (get) and assign (set) **@name** and **@email** *instance variables*, which were mentioned briefly in Section 2.2.2 and Section 3.4.2. In Rails, the principal importance of instance variables is that they are automatically available in the views, but in general they are used for variables that need to be available throughout a Ruby class. (We'll have more to say about this in a moment.) Instance variables always begin with an **@** sign, and are **nil** when undefined.

The first method, **initialize**, is special in Ruby: It's the method called when we execute **User.new**. This particular **initialize** takes one argument, **attributes**:

```
def initialize(attributes = {})
  @name  = attributes[:name]
  @email = attributes[:email]
end
```

Here the **attributes** variable has a *default value* equal to the empty hash, so that we can define a user with no name or email address. (Recall from Section 4.3.3 that hashes return **nil** for nonexistent keys, so **attributes[:name]** will be **nil** if there is no **:name** key, and similarly for **attributes[:email]**.)

Finally, our class defines a method called **formatted_email** that uses the values of the assigned **@name** and **@email** variables to build up a nicely formatted version of the user's email address using string interpolation (Section 4.2.1):

```
def formatted_email
  "#{@name} <#{@email}>"
end
```

Because **@name** and **@email** are both instance variables (as indicated with the **@** sign), they are automatically available in the **formatted_email** method.

Let's fire up the console, **require** the example user code, and take our User class out for a spin:

```
>> require './example_user'      # This is how you load the example_user code.
=> true
>> example = User.new
=> #<User:0x224ceec @email=nil, @name=nil>
>> example.name                  # nil since attributes[:name] is nil
=> nil
>> example.name = "Example User"          # Assign a non-nil name
```

```
=> "Example User"
>> example.email = "user@example.com"          # and a non-nil email address
=> "user@example.com"
>> example.formatted_email
=> "Example User <user@example.com>"
```

Here the `'.'` is Unix for "current directory," and `'./example_user'` tells Ruby to look for an example user file relative to that location. The subsequent code creates an empty example user and then fills in the name and email address by assigning directly to the corresponding attributes (assignments made possible by the **attr_accessor** line in Listing 4.17). When we write

```
example.name = "Example User"
```

Ruby is setting the **@name** variable to **"Example User"** (and similarly for the **email** attribute), which we then use in the **formatted_email** method.

Recalling from Section 4.3.4 that we can omit the curly braces for final hash arguments, we can create another user by passing a hash to the **initialize** method to create a user with predefined attributes:

```
>> user = User.new(name: "Michael Hartl", email: "mhartl@example.com")
=> #<User:0x225167c @email="mhartl@example.com", @name="Michael Hartl">
>> user.formatted_email
=> "Michael Hartl <mhartl@example.com>"
```

We will see starting in Chapter 7 that initializing objects using a hash argument, a technique known as *mass assignment*, is common in Rails applications.

Exercises

Solutions to the exercises are available to all Rails Tutorial purchasers at https://www.railstutorial.org/aw-solutions.

To see other people's answers and to record your own, subscribe to the Rails Tutorial course or to the Learn Enough All Access Bundle.

1. In the example User class, change from **name** to separate first and last name attributes, and then add a method called **full_name** that returns the first and last names separated by a space. Use it to replace the use of **name** in the formatted email method.

2. Add a method called **alphabetical_name** that returns the last name and first name separated by comma-space.

3. Verify that **full_name.split** is the same as **alphabetical_name.split(', ').reverse**.

4.5 Conclusion

This concludes our overview of the Ruby language. In Chapter 5, we'll start putting it to good use in developing the sample application.

We won't be using the **example_user.rb** file from Section 4.4.5, so I suggest removing it:

```
$ rm example_user.rb
```

Then commit the other changes to the main source code repository and merge into the **master** branch, push up to GitHub, and deploy to Heroku:

```
$ git commit -am "Add a full_title helper"
$ git checkout master
$ git merge rails-flavored-ruby
```

As a reality check, it's a good practice to run the test suite before pushing or deploying:

```
$ rails test
```

Then push up to GitHub:

```
$ git push
```

Finally, deploy to Heroku:

```
$ git push heroku
```

4.5.1 What We Learned in this Chapter

• Ruby has a large number of methods for manipulating strings of characters.

• Everything in Ruby is an object.

- Ruby supports method definition via the **def** keyword.
- Ruby supports class definition via the **class** keyword.
- Rails views can contain static HTML or embedded Ruby (ERb).
- Built-in Ruby data structures include arrays, ranges, and hashes.
- Ruby blocks are a flexible construct that (among other things) allow natural iteration over enumerable data structures.
- Symbols are labels, like strings without any additional structure.
- Ruby supports object inheritance.
- It is possible to open up and modify built-in Ruby classes.
- The word "deified" is a palindrome.

CHAPTER 5
Filling in the Layout

In the process of taking a brief tour of Ruby in Chapter 4, we learned about including the application stylesheet into the sample application (Section 4.1), but (as noted in Section 4.3.4) the stylesheet doesn't yet contain any CSS. In this chapter, we'll start filling in the custom stylesheet by incorporating a CSS framework into our application, and then we'll add some custom styles of our own.[1] We'll also start filling in the layout with links to the pages (such as Home and About) that we've created so far (Section 5.1). Along the way, we'll learn about partials, Rails routes, and the asset pipeline, including an introduction to Sass (Section 5.2). We'll end by taking a first important step toward letting users sign up to our site (Section 5.4).

Most of the changes in this chapter involve adding and editing markup in the sample application's site layout, which (based on the guidelines in Box 3.3) is exactly the kind of work that we wouldn't ordinarily test-drive, or even test at all. As a result, we'll spend most of our time in our text editor and browser, using TDD only to add a Contact page (Section 5.3.1). We will add an important new test, though, writing our first *integration test* to check that the links on the final layout are correct (Section 5.3.4).

5.1 Adding Some Structure

The *Ruby on Rails Tutorial* is a book on web development, not web design, but it would be depressing to work on an application that looks like *complete* garbage, so in

---

1. Thanks to reader Colm Tuite for his excellent work in helping to convert the sample application over to the Bootstrap CSS framework.

this section we'll add some structure to the layout and give it some minimal styling with CSS. In addition to using some custom CSS rules, we'll make use of *Bootstrap*, an open-source web design framework from Twitter.[2] (This design will initially be optimized for desktop/laptop computers, but we'll include some additional some rules for mobile devices in Section 8.2.3.) We'll also give our *code* some styling, so to speak, using *partials* to tidy up the layout once it gets a little cluttered.

When building web applications, it is often useful to get a high-level overview of the user interface as early as possible. Throughout the rest of this book, we will thus often consider *mockups* (in a web context often called *wireframes*), which are rough sketches of what the eventual application will look like.[3] In this chapter, we will principally be developing the static pages introduced in Section 3.2, including a site logo, a navigation header, and a site footer. A mockup for the most important of these pages, the Home page, appears in Figure 5.1. You can see the final result in Figure 5.9. You'll note that it differs in some details—for example, we'll end up adding a Rails logo on the page—but that's fine, since a mockup need not be exact.

As usual, if you're using Git for version control, now would be a good time to make a new branch:

```
$ git checkout -b filling-in-layout
```

5.1.1 Site Navigation

As a first step toward adding links and styles to the sample application, we'll update the site layout file **application.html.erb** (last seen in Listing 4.3) with additional HTML structure. This includes some additional divisions, some CSS classes, and the start of our site navigation. The full file is in Listing 5.1; explanations for the various pieces follow immediately thereafter. If you'd rather not delay gratification, you can see the results in Figure 5.2. (*Note*: It's not (yet) very gratifying.)

---

2. Although more recent versions of Bootstrap are now available, this tutorial standardizes on Bootstrap 3 in order to retain compatibility with the design and HTML structure from previous editions. The latest version of Bootstrap is similar, so the skills you learn here are highly transferable.

3. The mockups in the *Ruby on Rails Tutorial* are made with an excellent online mockup application called Mockingbird.

Figure 5.1: A mockup of the sample application's Home page.

Listing 5.1: The site layout with added structure.
app/views/layouts/application.html.erb

```
<!DOCTYPE html>
<html>
  <head>
    <title><%= full_title(yield(:title)) %></title>
    <meta charset="utf-8">
    <%= csrf_meta_tags %>
    <%= csp_meta_tag %>

    <%= stylesheet_link_tag 'application', media: 'all',
                                           'data-turbolinks-track': 'reload' %>
    <%= javascript_pack_tag 'application', 'data-turbolinks-track': 'reload' %>
    <!--[if lt IE 9]>
      <script src="//cdnjs.cloudflare.com/ajax/libs/html5shiv/r29/html5.min.js">
```

```
      </script>
    <![endif]-->
  </head>
  <body>
    <header class="navbar navbar-fixed-top navbar-inverse">
      <div class="container">
        <%= link_to "sample app", '#', id: "logo" %>
        <nav>
          <ul class="nav navbar-nav navbar-right">
            <li><%= link_to "Home",   '#' %></li>
            <li><%= link_to "Help",   '#' %></li>
            <li><%= link_to "Log in", '#' %></li>
          </ul>
        </nav>
      </div>
    </header>
    <div class="container">
      <%= yield %>
    </div>
  </body>
</html>
```

Let's look at the new elements in Listing 5.1 from top to bottom. As alluded to
briefly in Section 3.4.1, Rails uses HTML5 by default (as indicated by the doctype
<!DOCTYPE html>) which at this point most browsers support, but we can make our
site more accessible to older browsers by adding some JavaScript code, known as an
"HTML5 shim (or shiv)":[4]

```
<!--[if lt IE 9]>
  <script src="//cdnjs.cloudflare.com/ajax/libs/html5shiv/r29/html5.min.js">
  </script>
<![endif]-->
```

The somewhat odd syntax

```
<!--[if lt IE 9]>
```

---

4. The words *shim* and *shiv* are used interchangably in this context. The former is the proper term, based on
the English word whose meaning is "a washer or thin strip of material used to align parts, make them fit,
or reduce wear," while the latter (meaning "a knife or razor used as a weapon") is apparently a play on the
name of the shim's original author, Sjoerd Visscher.

includes the enclosed line only if the version of Microsoft Internet Explorer (IE) is less than 9 (**if lt IE 9**). The weird **[if lt IE 9]** syntax is *not* part of Rails; it's actually a conditional comment supported by Internet Explorer browsers for just this sort of situation. It's a good thing, too, because it means we can include the HTML5 shim *only* for IE browsers less than version 9, leaving other browsers such as Firefox, Chrome, and Safari unaffected.

The next section includes a **header** for the site's (plain-text) logo, a couple of divisions (using the **div** tag), and a list of elements with navigation links:

```
<header class="navbar navbar-fixed-top navbar-inverse">
  <div class="container">
    <%= link_to "sample app", '#', id: "logo" %>
    <nav>
      <ul class="nav navbar-nav navbar-right">
        <li><%= link_to "Home",   '#' %></li>
        <li><%= link_to "Help",   '#' %></li>
        <li><%= link_to "Log in", '#' %></li>
      </ul>
    </nav>
  </div>
</header>
```

Here the **header** tag indicates elements that should go at the top of the page. We've given the **header** tag three *CSS classes*,[5] called **navbar**, **navbar-fixed-top**, and **navbar-inverse**, separated by spaces:

```
<header class="navbar navbar-fixed-top navbar-inverse">
```

All HTML elements can be assigned both classes and *ids*;[6] these are merely labels, and are useful for styling with CSS (Section 5.1.2). The main difference between classes and ids is that classes can be used multiple times on a page, but ids can be used only once. In the present case, all the navbar classes have special meaning to the Bootstrap framework, which we'll install and use in Section 5.1.2.

---

5. These are completely unrelated to Ruby classes.

6. Short for "identification" and pronounced as the separate letters "I D". The usual convention in English is to use all-caps ("ID,") reserving "id" for a term in Freudian psychoanalysis. Because HTML is usually typed in all lowercase letters, though, it's more common in this context to write "id" instead.

Inside the **header** tag, we see a **div** tag:

```
<div class="container">
```

The **div** tag is a generic division; it doesn't do anything apart from divide the document into distinct parts. In older-style HTML, **div** tags are used for nearly all site divisions, but HTML5 adds the **header**, **nav**, and **section** elements for divisions common to many applications. In this case, the **div** has a CSS class as well (**container**). As with the **header** tag's classes, this class has special meaning to Bootstrap.

After the div, we encounter some embedded Ruby:

```
<%= link_to "sample app", '#', id: "logo" %>
<nav>
  <ul class="nav navbar-nav navbar-right">
    <li><%= link_to "Home",   '#' %></li>
    <li><%= link_to "Help",   '#' %></li>
    <li><%= link_to "Log in", '#' %></li>
  </ul>
</nav>
```

This uses the Rails helper **link_to** to create links (which we created directly with the anchor tag **a** in Section 3.2.2); the first argument to **link_to** is the link text, while the second is the URL. We'll fill in the URLs with *named routes* in Section 5.3.3, but for now we use the stub URL **'#'** commonly used in web design (i.e., **'#'** is just a "stub," or placeholder, for the real URL). The third argument is an options hash, in this case adding the CSS id **logo** to the sample app link. (The other three links have no options hash, which is fine since it's optional.) Rails helpers often take options hashes in this way, giving us the flexibility to add arbitrary HTML options without ever leaving Rails.

The second element inside the divs is a list of navigation links, made using the *unordered list* tag **ul**, together with the *list item* tag **li**:

```
<nav>
  <ul class="nav navbar-nav navbar-right">
    <li><%= link_to "Home",   '#' %></li>
    <li><%= link_to "Help",   '#' %></li>
    <li><%= link_to "Log in", '#' %></li>
  </ul>
</nav>
```

The **<nav>** tag, though formally unnecessary here, is used to more clearly communicate the purpose of the navigation links. Meanwhile, the **nav**, **navbar-nav**, and **navbar-right** classes on the **ul** tag have special meaning to Bootstrap and will be styled automatically when we include the Bootstrap CSS in Section 5.1.2. As you can verify by inspecting the navigation in your browser,[7] once Rails has processed the layout and evaluated the embedded Ruby the list looks like this:[8]

```
<nav>
  <ul class="nav navbar-nav navbar-right">
    <li><a href="#">Home</a></li>
    <li><a href="#">Help</a></li>
    <li><a href="#">Log in</a></li>
  </ul>
</nav>
```

This is the text that will be returned to the browser.

The final part of the layout is a **div** for the main content:

```
<div class="container">
  <%= yield %>
</div>
```

As before, the **container** class has special meaning to Bootstrap. As we learned in Section 3.4.3, the **yield** method inserts the contents of each page into the site layout.

Apart from the site footer, which we'll add in Section 5.1.3, our layout is now complete, and we can look at the results by visiting the Home page. To take advantage of the upcoming style elements, we'll add some extra elements to the **home.html.erb** view (Listing 5.2).

Listing 5.2: The Home page with a link to the signup page.
app/views/static_pages/home.html.erb

```
<div class="center jumbotron">
  <h1>Welcome to the Sample App</h1>
```

---

7. All modern browsers have the capability to inspect the HTML source of a page. If you've never used a web inspector before, do a web search for something like "web inspector <name of browser>" to learn more.

8. The spacing might look slightly different, which is fine because (as noted in Section 3.4.1) HTML is insensitive to whitespace.

```
<h2>
  This is the home page for the
  <a href="https://www.railstutorial.org/">Ruby on Rails Tutorial</a>
  sample application.
</h2>

<%= link_to "Sign up now!", '#', class: "btn btn-lg btn-primary" %>
</div>

<%= link_to image_tag("rails.svg", alt: "Rails logo", width: "200"),
                    "https://rubyonrails.org/" %>
```

In preparation for adding users to our site in Chapter 7, the first **link_to** creates a
stub link of the form

```
<a href="#" class="btn btn-lg btn-primary">Sign up now!</a>
```

In the **div** tag, the **jumbotron** CSS class has a special meaning to Bootstrap, as do the
btn, **btn-lg**, and **btn-primary** classes in the signup button.

The second **link_to** shows off the **image_tag** helper, which takes as arguments
the path to an image and an optional options hash, in this case setting the **alt** and
width attributes of the image tag using symbols. For this to work, there needs to be an
image called **rails.svg**, which you should download from the Learn Enough website at https://cdn.learnenough.com/rails.svg and place in the **app/assets/images/**
directory.

If you're using the cloud IDE or another Unix-like system, you can accomplish
this with the **curl** utility, as shown in Listing 5.3.[9]

Listing 5.3: Downloading an image.

```
$ curl -o app/assets/images/rails.svg -OL https://cdn.learnenough.com/rails.svg
```

Because we used the **image_tag** helper in Listing 5.2, Rails will automatically find any
images in the **app/assets/images/** directory using the asset pipeline (Section 5.2).

---

9. See *Learn Enough Command Line to Be Dangerous* (www.learnenough.com/command-line) for more
information about **curl**.

Figure 5.2: The Home page with no custom CSS.

Now we're finally ready to see the fruits of our labors. You may have to restart the Rails server to see the changes (Box 1.2), and the results should appear as shown in Figure 5.2.

To make the effects of **image_tag** clearer, let's look at the HTML it produces by inspecting the image in our browser:[10]

```
<img alt="Rails logo" width="200px" src="/assets/rails-<long string>.svg">
```

Here the **<long string>** is a random value added by Rails to ensure that the filename is unique, which causes browsers to load images properly when they have been updated

---

10. You might notice that the **img** tag, rather than looking like <img>...</img>, instead looks like <img ... />. Tags that follow this form are known as *self-closing* tags.

(instead of retrieving them from the browser cache). Note that the **src** attribute *doesn't* include **images**, instead using an **assets** directory common to all assets (e.g., images, JavaScript, CSS). On the server, Rails associates images in the **assets** directory with the proper **app/assets/images** directory, but as far as the browser is concerned all the assets look like they are in the same directory, which allows them to be served faster. Meanwhile, the **alt** attribute will be displayed if the page is accessed by a program that can't display images (such as screen readers for people with visual impairments).

As for the result shown in Figure 5.2, it might look a little underwhelming. Happily, though, we've done a good job of giving our HTML elements sensible classes, which puts us in a great position to add style to the site with CSS.

Exercises

Solutions to the exercises are available to all Rails Tutorial purchasers at https://www.railstutorial.org/aw-solutions.

To see other people's answers and to record your own, subscribe to the Rails Tutorial course or to the Learn Enough All Access Bundle.

1. It's well known that no web page is complete without a cat image. Using the command in Listing 5.4, arrange to download the kitten pic shown in Figure 5.3.[11]

2. Using the **mv** command, move **kitten.jpg** to the correct asset directory for images (Section 5.2.1).

3. Using **image_tag**, add **kitten.jpg** to the Home page, as shown in Figure 5.4.

Listing 5.4: Downloading a cat picture from the Internet.

```
$ curl -OL https://cdn.learnenough.com/kitten.jpg
```

5.1.2 Bootstrap and Custom CSS

In Section 5.1.1, we associated many of the HTML elements with CSS classes, which gives us considerable flexibility in constructing a layout based on CSS. As noted in

---

11. Image retrieved from https://www.flickr.com/photos/deborah_s_perspective/14144861329 on 2016-01-09. Copyright © 2009 by Deborah and used unaltered under the terms of the Creative Commons Attribution 2.0 Generic license.

Figure 5.3: An obligatory kitten pic.

Section 5.1.1, many of these classes are specific to Bootstrap, a CSS framework that makes it easy to add nice web design and user interface elements to an HTML5 application. In this section, we'll combine Bootstrap with some custom CSS rules to start adding some style to the sample application. It's worth noting that using Bootstrap automatically makes our application's design *responsive*, ensuring that it looks sensible across a wide range of devices.

Our first step is to add Bootstrap, which in Rails applications can be accomplished with the `bootstrap-sass` gem, as shown in Listing 5.5.[12] The Bootstrap framework natively uses the Less CSS language for making dynamic stylesheets, but the Rails asset pipeline supports the (very similar) Sass language by default (Section 5.2), so `bootstrap-sass` converts Less to Sass and makes all the necessary Bootstrap files available to the current application.

---

12. As always, you should use the version numbers listed at gemfiles-6th-ed.railstutorial.org instead of the ones listed here.

Figure 5.4: The result of adding a kitten image to the Home page.

Listing 5.5: Adding the bootstrap-sass gem to the **Gemfile**.

```
source 'https://rubygems.org'

gem 'rails',          '6.0.2.1'
gem 'bootstrap-sass', '3.4.1'
gem 'puma',           '3.12.2'
.
.
.
```

To install Bootstrap, we run **bundle install** as usual:

```
$ bundle install
```

Although **rails generate** automatically creates a separate CSS file for each controller, it's surprisingly hard to include them all properly and in the right order, so for simplicity we'll put all of the CSS needed for this tutorial in a single file. The first step toward getting custom CSS to work is to create such a custom CSS file:

```
$ touch app/assets/stylesheets/custom.scss
```

(This uses the **touch** trick from Section 3.3.3 en route, but you can create the file however you like.) Here both the directory name and the filename extension are important. The directory

```
app/assets/stylesheets/
```

is part of the asset pipeline (Section 5.2), and any stylesheets in this directory will automatically be included as part of the **application.css** file included in the site layout. Furthermore, the filename **custom.scss** includes the **.scss** extension, which indicates a "Sassy CSS" file and arranges for the asset pipeline to process the file using Sass. (We won't use Sass until Section 5.2.2, but it's needed now for the bootstrap-sass gem to work its magic.)

Inside the file for the custom CSS, we can use the **@import** function to include Bootstrap (together with the associated Sprockets utility), as shown in Listing 5.6.[13]

Listing 5.6: Adding Bootstrap CSS.

app/assets/stylesheets/custom.scss

```
@import "bootstrap-sprockets";
@import "bootstrap";
```

The two lines in Listing 5.6 include the entire Bootstrap CSS framework. After restarting the webserver to incorporate the changes into the development application (by pressing Ctrl-C and then running **rails server** as in Section 1.2.2), the results appear as in Figure 5.5. The placement of the text isn't good and the logo doesn't have any style, but the colors and signup button look promising.

---

13. If these steps seem mysterious, take heart: I'm just following the instructions from the bootstrap-sass README file.

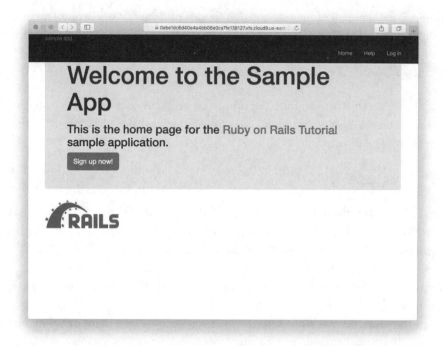

Figure 5.5: The sample application with Bootstrap CSS.

Next we'll add some CSS that will be used site-wide for styling the layout and each individual page, as shown in Listing 5.7. The result is shown in Figure 5.6. (There are quite a few rules in Listing 5.7; to get a sense of what a CSS rule does, it's often helpful to comment it out using CSS comments—that is, by putting it inside **/*** ... **/***—and seeing what changes.)

Listing 5.7: Adding CSS for some universal styling applying to all pages.
`app/assets/stylesheets/custom.scss`

```scss
@import "bootstrap-sprockets";
@import "bootstrap";

/* universal */

body {
```

```
    padding-top: 60px;
}

section {
  overflow: auto;
}

textarea {
  resize: vertical;
}

.center {
  text-align: center;
}

.center h1 {
  margin-bottom: 10px;
}
```

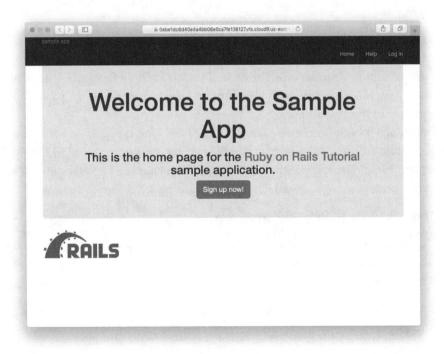

Figure 5.6: Adding some spacing and other universal styling.

Note that the CSS in Listing 5.7 has a consistent form. In general, CSS rules refer either to a class, an id, an HTML tag, or some combination thereof, followed by a list of styling commands. For example,

```
body {
  padding-top: 60px;
}
```

puts 60 pixels of padding at the top of the page. Because of the **navbar-fixed-top** class in the **header** tag, Bootstrap fixes the navigation bar to the top of the page, so the padding serves to separate the main text from the navigation. (Because the default navbar color changed after Bootstrap 2.0, we need the **navbar-inverse** class to make it dark instead of light.) Meanwhile, the CSS in the rule

```
.center {
  text-align: center;
}
```

associates the **center** class with the **text-align: center** property. In other words, the dot **.** in **.center** indicates that the rule styles a class. (As we'll see in Listing 5.9, the pound sign **#** identifies a rule to style a CSS *id*.) This rule means that elements inside any tag (such as a **div**) with class **center** will be centered on the page. (We saw an example of this class in Listing 5.2.)

Although Bootstrap comes with CSS rules for nice typography, we'll also add some custom rules for the appearance of the text on our site, as shown in Listing 5.8. (Not all of these rules apply to the Home page, but each rule here will be used at some point in the sample application.) The result of Listing 5.8 is shown in Figure 5.7.

Listing 5.8: Adding CSS for nice typography.
app/assets/stylesheets/custom.scss

```
@import "bootstrap-sprockets";
@import "bootstrap";
.
.
.
/* typography */

h1, h2, h3, h4, h5, h6 {
  line-height: 1;
}
```

```
h1 {
  font-size: 3em;
  letter-spacing: -2px;
  margin-bottom: 30px;
  text-align: center;
}

h2 {
  font-size: 1.2em;
  letter-spacing: -1px;
  margin-bottom: 30px;
  text-align: center;
  font-weight: normal;
  color: #777;
}

p {
  font-size: 1.1em;
  line-height: 1.7em;
}
```

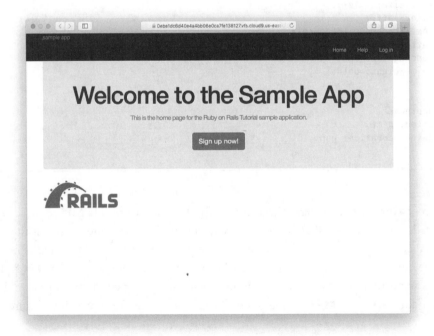

Figure 5.7: Adding some typographic styling.

Finally, we'll add some rules to style the site's logo, which simply consists of the text "sample app." The CSS in Listing 5.9 converts the text to uppercase and modifies its size, color, and placement. (We've used a CSS id because we expect the site logo to appear on the page only once, but you could use a class instead.)

Listing 5.9: Adding CSS for the site logo.
`app/assets/stylesheets/custom.scss`

```scss
@import "bootstrap-sprockets";
@import "bootstrap";
.
.
.
/* header */

#logo {
  float: left;
  margin-right: 10px;
  font-size: 1.7em;
  color: #fff;
  text-transform: uppercase;
  letter-spacing: -1px;
  padding-top: 9px;
  font-weight: bold;
}

#logo:hover {
  color: #fff;
  text-decoration: none;
}
```

Here **color: #fff** changes the color of the logo to white. HTML colors can be coded with three pairs of base-16 (hexadecimal) numbers, one each for the primary colors red, green, and blue (in that order). The code **#ffffff** maxes out all three colors, yielding pure white, and **#fff** is a shorthand for the full **#ffffff**. The CSS standard also defines a large number of synonyms for common HTML colors, including **white** for **#fff**. The result of the CSS in Listing 5.9 is shown in Figure 5.8.

Figure 5.8: The sample app with nicely styled logo.

Exercises

Solutions to the exercises are available to all Rails Tutorial purchasers at https://www.railstutorial.org/aw-solutions.

To see other people's answers and to record your own, subscribe to the Rails Tutorial course or to the Learn Enough All Access Bundle.

1. Using code like that shown in Listing 5.10, comment out the cat image from Section 5.1.1. Verify using a web inspector that the HTML for the image no longer appears in the page source.

2. By adding the CSS in Listing 5.11 to **custom.scss**, hide all images in the application (currently just the Rails logo on the Home page). Verify with a web inspector that, although the image doesn't appear, the HTML source is still present.

Listing 5.10: Code to comment out embedded Ruby.

```
<%#= image_tag("kitten.jpg", alt: "Kitten") %>
```

Listing 5.11: CSS to hide all images.

```
img {
  display: none;
}
```

5.1.3 Partials

Although the layout in Listing 5.1 serves its purpose, it's getting a little cluttered. The HTML shim takes up three lines and uses weird IE-specific syntax, so it would be nice to tuck it away somewhere on its own. In addition, the header HTML forms a logical unit, so it should all be packaged up in one place. The way to achieve this in Rails is to use a facility called *partials*. Let's first take a look at what the layout looks like after the partials are defined (Listing 5.12).

Listing 5.12: The site layout with partials for the stylesheets and header.
`app/views/layouts/application.html.erb`

```
<!DOCTYPE html>
<html>
  <head>
    <title><%= full_title(yield(:title)) %></title>
    <meta charset="utf-8">
    <%= csrf_meta_tags %>
    <%= csp_meta_tag %>

    <%= stylesheet_link_tag 'application', media: 'all',
                                      'data-turbolinks-track': 'reload' %>
    <%= javascript_pack_tag 'application', 'data-turbolinks-track': 'reload' %>
    <%= render 'layouts/shim' %>
  </head>
  <body>
    <%= render 'layouts/header' %>
    <div class="container">
      <%= yield %>
    </div>
  </body>
</html>
```

In Listing 5.12, we've replaced the HTML shim stylesheet lines with a single call to a Rails helper called **render**:

```
<%= render 'layouts/shim' %>
```

The effect of this line is to look for a file called **app/views/layouts/_shim. html.erb**, evaluate its contents, and insert the results into the view.[14] (Recall that **<%= ... %>** is the embedded Ruby syntax needed to evaluate a Ruby expression and then insert the results into the template.) Note the leading underscore on the filename **_shim.html.erb**; this underscore is the universal convention for naming partials, and among other things makes it possible to identify all the partials in a directory at a glance.

To get the partial to work, we have to create the corresponding file and fill it with some content. In the case of the shim partial, this is just the three lines of shim code from Listing 5.1. The result appears in Listing 5.13.

Listing 5.13: A partial for the HTML shim.
app/views/layouts/_shim.html.erb

```
<!--[if lt IE 9]>
  <script src="//cdnjs.cloudflare.com/ajax/libs/html5shiv/r29/html5.min.js">
  </script>
<![endif]-->
```

Similarly, we can move the header material into the partial shown in Listing 5.14 and insert it into the layout with another call to **render**. (As usual with partials, you will have to create the file by hand using your text editor.)

Listing 5.14: A partial for the site header.
app/views/layouts/_header.html.erb

```
<header class="navbar navbar-fixed-top navbar-inverse">
  <div class="container">
    <%= link_to "sample app", '#', id: "logo" %>
    <nav>
```

---

14. Many Rails developers use a **shared** directory for partials shared across different views. I prefer to use the **shared** folder for utility partials that are useful on multiple views, while putting partials that are literally on every page (as part of the site layout) in the **layouts** directory. (We'll create the **shared** directory starting in Chapter 7.) That seems to me a logical division, but putting them all in the **shared** folder certainly works fine, too.

```
    <ul class="nav navbar-nav navbar-right">
      <li><%= link_to "Home",   '#' %></li>
      <li><%= link_to "Help",   '#' %></li>
      <li><%= link_to "Log in", '#' %></li>
    </ul>
  </nav>
  </div>
</header>
```

Now that we know how to make partials, let's add a site footer to go along with the header. By now you can probably guess that we'll call it **_footer.html.erb** and put it in the layouts directory (Listing 5.15).[15]

Listing 5.15: A partial for the site footer.
app/views/layouts/_footer.html.erb

```
<footer class="footer">
  <small>
    The <a href="https://www.railstutorial.org/">Ruby on Rails Tutorial</a>
    by <a href="https://www.michaelhartl.com/">Michael Hartl</a>
  </small>
  <nav>
    <ul>
      <li><%= link_to "About",   '#' %></li>
      <li><%= link_to "Contact", '#' %></li>
      <li><a href="https://news.railstutorial.org/">News</a></li>
    </ul>
  </nav>
</footer>
```

As with the header, in the footer we've used **link_to** for the internal links to the About and Contact pages and stubbed out the URLs with **'#'** for now. (As with **header**, the **footer** tag is new in HTML5.)

We can render the footer partial in the layout by following the same pattern as the stylesheets and header partials (Listing 5.16).

---

15. You may wonder why we use both the **footer** tag and **.footer** class. The answer is that the tag has a clear meaning to human readers, and the class is used by Bootstrap. Using a **div** tag in place of **footer** would work as well.

Listing 5.16: The site layout with a footer partial.
`app/views/layouts/application.html.erb`

```erb
<!DOCTYPE html>
<html>
  <head>
    <title><%= full_title(yield(:title)) %></title>
    <meta charset="utf-8">
    <%= csrf_meta_tags %>
    <%= csp_meta_tag %>

    <%= stylesheet_link_tag 'application', media: 'all',
                                           'data-turbolinks-track': 'reload' %>
    <%= javascript_pack_tag 'application', 'data-turbolinks-track': 'reload' %>
    <%= render 'layouts/shim' %>
  </head>
  <body>
    <%= render 'layouts/header' %>
    <div class="container">
      <%= yield %>
      <%= render 'layouts/footer' %>
    </div>
  </body>
</html>
```

Next, we'll add some styling for the footer, as shown in Listing 5.17. The results appear in Figure 5.9.

Listing 5.17: Adding the CSS for the site footer.
`app/assets/stylesheets/custom.scss`

```scss
.
.
.
/* footer */

footer {
  margin-top: 45px;
  padding-top: 5px;
  border-top: 1px solid #eaeaea;
  color: #777;
}

footer a {
  color: #555;
```

```
}

footer a:hover {
  color: #222;
}

footer small {
  float: left;
}

footer ul {
  float: right;
  list-style: none;
}

footer ul li {
  float: left;
  margin-left: 15px;
}
```

Figure 5.9: The Home page with an added footer.

Exercises

Solutions to the exercises are available to all Rails Tutorial purchasers at https://www.railstutorial.org/aw-solutions.

To see other people's answers and to record your own, subscribe to the Rails Tutorial course or to the Learn Enough All Access Bundle.

1. Replace the default Rails head with the call to **render** shown in Listing 5.18. *Hint*: For convenience, cut the default header rather than just deleting it.

2. Because we haven't yet created the partial needed by Listing 5.18, the tests should be RED. Confirm that this is the case.

3. Create the necessary partial in the **layouts** directory, paste in the contents, and verify that the tests are now GREEN again.

Listing 5.18: Replacing the default Rails head with a call to **render**.
`app/views/layouts/application.html.erb`

```
<!DOCTYPE html>
<html>
  <head>
    <title><%= full_title(yield(:title)) %></title>
    <meta charset="utf-8">
    <%= render 'layouts/rails_default' %>
    <%= render 'layouts/shim' %>
  </head>
  <body>
    <%= render 'layouts/header' %>
    <div class="container">
      <%= yield %>
      <%= render 'layouts/footer' %>
    </div>
  </body>
</html>
```

5.2 Sass and the Asset Pipeline

One of the most useful features of Rails is the *asset pipeline*, which significantly simplifies the production and management of static assets such as CSS and images. The asset pipeline also works well in parallel with Webpack (a JavaScript asset bundler) and Yarn (a dependency manager mentioned in Section 1.1.2), both of which are supported by default in Rails. This section first gives a high-level overview of the asset pipeline, and then shows how to use *Sass*, a powerful tool for writing Cascading Style Sheets (CSS).

5.2.1   The Asset Pipeline

From the perspective of a typical Rails developer, there are three main features to understand about the asset pipeline: asset directories, manifest files, and preprocessor engines.[16] Let's consider each in turn.

Asset Directories

The Rails asset pipeline uses three standard directories for static assets, each with its own purpose:

- **app/assets**: assets specific to the present application
- **lib/assets**: assets for libraries written by your dev team
- **vendor/assets**: assets from third-party vendors (not present by default)

Each of these directories has a subdirectory for each of two asset classes—images and CSS:

```
$ ls app/assets/
config  images  stylesheets
```

At this point, we're in a position to understand the motivation behind the location of the custom CSS file in Section 5.1.2: **custom.scss** is specific to the sample application, so it goes in **app/assets/stylesheets**.

Manifest Files

Once you've placed your assets in their logical locations, you can use *manifest files* to tell Rails (via the Sprockets gem) how to combine them to form single files. (This applies to CSS and JavaScript but not to images.) As an example, let's take a look at the default manifest file for app stylesheets (Listing 5.19).

---

16. The original structure of this section was based on the excellent blog post "The Rails 3 Asset Pipeline in (About) 5 Minutes" by Michael Erasmus.

Listing 5.19: The manifest file for app-specific CSS.
app/assets/stylesheets/application.css

```
/*
 * This is a manifest file that'll be compiled into application.css, which will
 * include all the files listed below.
 *
 * Any CSS and SCSS file within this directory, lib/assets/stylesheets, or any
 * plugin's vendor/assets/stylesheets directory can be referenced here using a
 * relative path.
 *
 * You're free to add application-wide styles to this file and they'll appear at
 * the bottom of the compiled file so the styles you add here take precedence
 * over styles defined in any other CSS/SCSS files in this directory. Styles in
 * this file should be added after the last require_* statement.
 * It is generally better to create a new file per style scope.
 *
 *= require_tree .
 *= require_self
 */
```

The key lines here are actually CSS comments, but they are used by Sprockets to include the proper files:

```
/*
 .
 .
 .
 *= require_tree .
 *= require_self
 */
```

Here

```
*= require_tree .
```

ensures that all CSS files in the **app/assets/stylesheets** directory (including the tree subdirectories) are included into the application CSS. The line

```
*= require_self
```

specifies where in the loading sequence the CSS in **application.css** itself gets included.

Rails comes with sensible default manifest files, and in the Rails Tutorial we won't need to make any changes, but the Rails Guides entry on the asset pipeline (http://guides.rubyonrails.org/asset_pipeline.html) has more detail if you need it.

Preprocessor Engines

After you've assembled your assets, Rails prepares them for the site template by running them through several preprocessing engines and using the manifest files to combine them for delivery to the browser. We tell Rails which processor to use using filename extensions; the two most common cases are `.scss` for Sass and `.erb` for embedded Ruby (ERb). We first covered ERb in Section 3.4.3 and cover Sass in Section 5.2.2.

Efficiency in Production

One of the best things about the asset pipeline is that it automatically results in assets that are optimized to be efficient in a production application. Traditional methods for organizing CSS involve splitting functionality into separate files and using nice formatting (with lots of indentation). While convenient for the programmer, this is inefficient in production. In particular, including multiple full-sized files can significantly slow page-load times, which is one of the most important factors affecting the quality of the user experience.

With the asset pipeline, we don't have to choose between speed and convenience: We can work with multiple nicely formatted files in development, and then use the asset pipeline to make efficient files in production. In particular, the asset pipeline combines all the application stylesheets into one CSS file (`application.css`) and then *minifies* it to remove the unnecessary spacing and indentation that bloats file size. The result is the best of both worlds: convenience in development and efficiency in production.

5.2.2 Syntactically Awesome Stylesheets

Sass is a language for writing stylesheets that improves on CSS in many ways. In this section, we cover two of the most important improvements, *nesting* and *variables*. (A third technique, *mixins*, is introduced in Section 7.1.1.)

As noted briefly in Section 5.1.2, Sass supports a format called SCSS (indicated with a `.scss` filename extension), which is a strict superset of CSS itself. That is, SCSS only *adds* features to CSS, rather than defining an entirely new syntax.[17] This means that every valid CSS file is also a valid SCSS file, which is convenient for projects with existing style rules. In our case, we used SCSS from the start to take advantage of Bootstrap. Since the Rails asset pipeline automatically uses Sass to process files with the **.scss** extension, the **custom.scss** file will be run through the Sass preprocessor before being packaged up for delivery to the browser.

Nesting

A common pattern in stylesheets is having rules that apply to nested elements. For example, in Listing 5.7 we have rules both for **.center** and for **.center h1**:

```
.center {
  text-align: center;
}

.center h1 {
  margin-bottom: 10px;
}
```

We can replace this in Sass with

```
.center {
  text-align: center;

  h1 {
    margin-bottom: 10px;
  }
}
```

Here the nested **h1** rule automatically inherits the **.center** context.

There's a second candidate for nesting that requires a slightly different syntax. In Listing 5.9, we have the code

```
#logo {
  float: left;
  margin-right: 10px;
```

17. Sass also supports an alternative syntax that does define a new language that is less verbose (and has fewer curly braces) but is less convenient for existing projects and is harder to learn for those already familiar with CSS.

```
    font-size: 1.7em;
    color: #fff;
    text-transform: uppercase;
    letter-spacing: -1px;
    padding-top: 9px;
    font-weight: bold;
}

#logo:hover {
    color: #fff;
    text-decoration: none;
}
```

Here the logo id **#logo** appears twice, once by itself and once with the **hover** attribute (which controls its appearance when the mouse pointer hovers over the element in question). To nest the second rule, we need to reference the parent element **#logo**; in SCSS, this is accomplished with the ampersand character **&** as follows:

```
#logo {
    float: left;
    margin-right: 10px;
    font-size: 1.7em;
    color: #fff;
    text-transform: uppercase;
    letter-spacing: -1px;
    padding-top: 9px;
    font-weight: bold;
    &:hover {
      color: #fff;
      text-decoration: none;
    }
}
```

Sass changes **&:hover** into **#logo:hover** as part of converting from SCSS to CSS.

Both of these nesting techniques apply to the footer CSS in Listing 5.17, which can be transformed into the following:

```
footer {
  margin-top: 45px;
  padding-top: 5px;
  border-top: 1px solid #eaeaea;
  color: #777;
  a {
```

```
    color: #555;
    &:hover {
      color: #222;
    }
  }
  small {
    float: left;
  }
  ul {
    float: right;
    list-style: none;
    li {
      float: left;
      margin-left: 15px;
    }
  }
}
```

Converting Listing 5.17 by hand is a good exercise (Section 5.2.2), and you should verify that the CSS still works properly after the conversion.

Variables

Sass allows us to define *variables* to eliminate duplication and write more expressive code. For example, looking at Listing 5.8 and Listing 5.17, we see that there are repeated references to the same color:

```
h2 {
  .
  .
  .
  color: #777;
}
.
.
.
footer {
  .
  .
  .
  color: #777;
}
```

In this case, **#777** is a light gray, and we can give it a name by defining a variable as follows:

```
$light-gray: #777;
```

This allows us to rewrite our SCSS like this:

```
$light-gray: #777;
.
.
.
h2 {
  .
  .
  .
  color: $light-gray;
}
.
.
.
footer {
  .
  .
  .
  color: $light-gray;
}
```

Because variable names such as **$light-gray** are more descriptive than **#777**, it's often useful to define variables even for values that aren't repeated. Indeed, the Bootstrap framework defines a large number of variables for colors, available online on the Bootstrap page of Less variables. That page defines variables using Less, not Sass, but the `bootstrap-sass` gem provides the Sass equivalents. It is not difficult to guess the correspondence: Where Less uses an "at" sign **@**, Sass uses a dollar sign **$**. For example, looking at the Bootstrap variable page, we see that there is a variable for light gray:

```
@gray-light: #777;
```

This means that, via the `bootstrap-sass` gem, there should be a corresponding SCSS variable **$gray-light**. We can use this to replace our custom variable, **$light-gray**, which gives

```
h2 {
  .
  .
  .
```

```
    color: $gray-light;
}
  .
  .
  .
footer {
  .
  .
  .
  color: $gray-light;
}
```

Applying the Sass nesting and variable definition features to the full SCSS file gives the file in Listing 5.20. This uses both Sass variables (as inferred from the Bootstrap Less variable page) and built-in named colors (i.e., **white** for **#fff**). Note in particular the dramatic improvement in the rules for the **footer** tag.

Listing 5.20: The initial SCSS file converted to use nesting and variables.
app/assets/stylesheets/custom.scss

```scss
@import "bootstrap-sprockets";
@import "bootstrap";

/* mixins, variables, etc. */

$gray-medium-light: #eaeaea;

/* universal */

body {
  padding-top: 60px;
}

section {
  overflow: auto;
}

textarea {
  resize: vertical;
}

.center {
  text-align: center;
  h1 {
```

```
    margin-bottom: 10px;
  }
}

/* typography */

h1, h2, h3, h4, h5, h6 {
  line-height: 1;
}

h1 {
  font-size: 3em;
  letter-spacing: -2px;
  margin-bottom: 30px;
  text-align: center;
}

h2 {
  font-size: 1.2em;
  letter-spacing: -1px;
  margin-bottom: 30px;
  text-align: center;
  font-weight: normal;
  color: $gray-light;
}

p {
  font-size: 1.1em;
  line-height: 1.7em;
}


/* header */

#logo {
  float: left;
  margin-right: 10px;
  font-size: 1.7em;
  color: white;
  text-transform: uppercase;
  letter-spacing: -1px;
  padding-top: 9px;
  font-weight: bold;
  &:hover {
    color: white;
    text-decoration: none;
  }
}
```

```
/* footer */

footer {
  margin-top: 45px;
  padding-top: 5px;
  border-top: 1px solid $gray-medium-light;
  color: $gray-light;
  a {
    color: $gray;
    &:hover {
      color: $gray-darker;
    }
  }
  small {
    float: left;
  }
  ul {
    float: right;
    list-style: none;
    li {
      float: left;
      margin-left: 15px;
    }
  }
}
```

Sass gives us even more ways to simplify our stylesheets, but the code in Listing 5.20 uses the most important features and gives us a great start. See the Sass website for more details.

Exercise

Solutions to the exercises are available to all Rails Tutorial purchasers at https://www.railstutorial.org/aw-solutions.

To see other people's answers and to record your own, subscribe to the Rails Tutorial course or to the Learn Enough All Access Bundle.

1. As suggested in Section 5.2.2, go through the steps to convert the footer CSS from Listing 5.17 to Listing 5.20 to SCSS by hand.

5.3 Layout Links

Now that we've finished a site layout with decent styling, it's time to start filling in the links we've stubbed out with **'#'**. Because plain HTML is valid in Rails ERb templates, we could hard-code links like

Table 5.1: Route and URL mapping for site links.

Page	URL	Named route
Home	/	**root_path**
About	/about	**about_path**
Help	/help	**help_path**
Contact	/contact	**contact_path**
Sign up	/signup	**signup_path**
Log in	/login	**login_path**

```
<a href="/static_pages/about">About</a>
```

but that isn't the Rails Way™. For one, it would be nice if the URL for the about page were /about rather than /static_pages/about. Moreover, Rails conventionally uses *named routes*, which involves code like

```
<%= link_to "About", about_path %>
```

This way the code has a more transparent meaning, and it's also more flexible since we can change the definition of **about_path** and have the URL change everywhere **about_path** is used.

The full list of our planned links appears in Table 5.1, along with their mapping to URLs and routes. We took care of the first route in Section 3.4.4, and we'll have implemented all but the last one by the end of this chapter. (We'll make the last one in Chapter 8.)

5.3.1 Contact Page

For completeness, we'll add the Contact page, which was left as an exercise in Chapter 3. The test appears as in Listing 5.21, which simply follows the model last seen in Listing 3.26.

Listing 5.21: A test for the Contact page. RED
test/controllers/static_pages_controller_test.rb

```
require 'test_helper'

class StaticPagesControllerTest < ActionDispatch::IntegrationTest
```

```
test "should get home" do
  get static_pages_home_url
  assert_response :success
  assert_select "title", "Ruby on Rails Tutorial Sample App"
end

test "should get help" do
  get static_pages_help_url
  assert_response :success
  assert_select "title", "Help | Ruby on Rails Tutorial Sample App"
end

test "should get about" do
  get static_pages_about_url
  assert_response :success
  assert_select "title", "About | Ruby on Rails Tutorial Sample App"
end

test "should get contact" do
  get static_pages_contact_url
  assert_response :success
  assert_select "title", "Contact | Ruby on Rails Tutorial Sample App"
end
end
```

At this point, the tests in Listing 5.21 should be RED:

Listing 5.22: RED

```
$ rails test
```

The application code parallels the addition of the About page in Section 3.3: First we update the routes (Listing 5.23), then we add a **contact** action to the Static Pages controller (Listing 5.24), and finally we create a Contact view (Listing 5.25).

Listing 5.23: Adding a route for the Contact page. RED
config/routes.rb

```
Rails.application.routes.draw do
  root 'static_pages#home'
  get  'static_pages/home'
```

```
get   'static_pages/help'
get   'static_pages/about'
get   'static_pages/contact'
end
```

Listing 5.24: Adding an action for the Contact page. RED
`app/controllers/static_pages_controller.rb`

```
class StaticPagesController < ApplicationController
  .
  .
  .
  def contact
  end
end
```

Listing 5.25: The view for the Contact page. GREEN
`app/views/static_pages/contact.html.erb`

```
<% provide(:title, 'Contact') %>
<h1>Contact</h1>
<p>
  Contact the Ruby on Rails Tutorial about the sample app at the
  <a href="https://www.railstutorial.org/contact">contact page</a>.
</p>
```

Now make sure that the tests are GREEN:

Listing 5.26: GREEN

```
$ rails test
```

5.3.2 Rails Routes

To add the named routes for the sample app's static pages, we'll edit the routes file, **config/routes.rb**, that Rails uses to define URL mappings. We'll begin by reviewing the route for the Home page (defined in Section 3.4.4), which is a special case, and then define a set of routes for the remaining static pages.

So far, we've seen three examples of how to define a root route, starting with the code

```
root 'application#hello'
```

in the hello app (Listing 1.11), the code

```
root 'users#index'
```

in the toy app (Listing 2.7), and the code

```
root 'static_pages#home'
```

in the sample app (Listing 3.41). In each case, the **root** method arranges for the root path / to be routed to a controller and action of our choice. Defining the root route in this way has a second important effect: It creates named routes that enable us to refer to routes by a name rather than by the raw URL. In this case, these routes are **root_path** and **root_url**, with the only difference being that the latter includes the full URL:

```
root_path -> '/'
root_url  -> 'http://www.example.com/'
```

In the Rails Tutorial, we'll follow the common convention of using the **_path** form except when doing redirects, where we'll use the **_url** form. (This is because the HTTP standard technically requires a full URL after redirects, though in most browsers it will work either way.)

Because the default routes used in, for example, Listing 5.21 are rather verbose, we'll also take this opportunity to define shorter named routes for the Help, About, and Contact pages. To do this, we need to make changes to the **get** rules from Listing 5.23, transforming lines like

```
get 'static_pages/help'
```

to

```
get '/help', to: 'static_pages#help'
```

This new pattern routes a GET request for the URL /help to the **help** action in the Static Pages controller. As with the rule for the root route, this creates two named routes, **help_path** and **help_url**:

```
help_path -> '/help'
help_url  -> 'http://www.example.com/help'
```

Applying this rule change to the remaining static page routes from Listing 5.23 gives Listing 5.27.

Listing 5.27: Routes for static pages. RED
config/routes.rb

```
Rails.application.routes.draw do
  root 'static_pages#home'
  get  '/help',    to: 'static_pages#help'
  get  '/about',   to: 'static_pages#about'
  get  '/contact', to: 'static_pages#contact'
end
```

Note that Listing 5.27 also removes the route for **'static_pages/home'**, as we'll always use **root_path** or **root_url** instead.

Because the tests in Listing 5.21 used the old routes, they are now RED. To get them GREEN again, we need to update the routes as shown in Listing 5.28. Note that we've taken this opportunity to update to the (optional) convention of using the ***_path** form of each named route.

Listing 5.28: The static pages tests with the new named routes. GREEN
test/controllers/static_pages_controller_test.rb

```
require 'test_helper'

class StaticPagesControllerTest < ActionDispatch::IntegrationTest

  test "should get home" do
    get root_path
    assert_response :success
    assert_select "title", "Ruby on Rails Tutorial Sample App"
  end
```

```
test "should get help" do
  get help_path
    assert_response :success
    assert_select "title", "Help | Ruby on Rails Tutorial Sample App"
  end

  test "should get about" do
  get about_path
   assert_response :success
    assert_select "title", "About | Ruby on Rails Tutorial Sample App"
  end

  test "should get contact" do
  get contact_path
    assert_response :success
    assert_select "title", "Contact | Ruby on Rails Tutorial Sample App"
  end
end
```

Exercises

Solutions to the exercises are available to all Rails Tutorial purchasers at https://www.railstutorial.org/aw-solutions.

To see other people's answers and to record your own, subscribe to the Rails Tutorial course or to the Learn Enough All Access Bundle.

1. It's possible to use a named route other than the default by using the **as:** option. Drawing inspiration from a famous *Far Side* comic strip, change the route for the Help page to use **helf** (Listing 5.29).

2. Confirm that the tests are now RED. Get them to GREEN by updating the route in Listing 5.28.

3. Revert the changes from these exercises using Undo.

Listing 5.29: Changing 'help' to 'helf'.

```
Rails.application.routes.draw do
  root 'static_pages#home'
  get  '/help',    to: 'static_pages#help', as: 'helf'
  get  '/about',   to: 'static_pages#about'
  get  '/contact', to: 'static_pages#contact'
end
```

5.3.3 Using Named Routes

With the routes defined in Listing 5.27, we're now in a position to use the resulting named routes in the site layout. This simply involves filling in the second arguments of the **link_to** functions with the proper named routes. For example, we'll convert

```erb
<%= link_to "About", '#' %>
```

to

```erb
<%= link_to "About", about_path %>
```

and so on.

We'll start in the header partial, **_header.html.erb** (Listing 5.30), which has links to the Home and Help pages. While we're at it, we'll follow a common web convention and link the logo to the Home page as well.

Listing 5.30: Header partial with links.
app/views/layouts/_header.html.erb

```erb
<header class="navbar navbar-fixed-top navbar-inverse">
  <div class="container">
    <%= link_to "sample app", root_path, id: "logo" %>
    <nav>
      <ul class="nav navbar-nav navbar-right">
        <li><%= link_to "Home",    root_path %></li>
        <li><%= link_to "Help",    help_path %></li>
        <li><%= link_to "Log in", '#' %></li>
      </ul>
    </nav>
  </div>
</header>
```

We won't have a named route for the "Log in" link until Chapter 8, so we've left it as **'#'** for now.

The other place with links is the footer partial, **_footer.html.erb**, which has links to the About and Contact pages (Listing 5.31).

Listing 5.31: Footer partial with links.
`app/views/layouts/_footer.html.erb`

```erb
<footer class="footer">
  <small>
    The <a href="https://www.railstutorial.org/">Ruby on Rails Tutorial</a>
    by <a href="https://www.michaelhartl.com/">Michael Hartl</a>
  </small>
  <nav>
    <ul>
      <li><%= link_to "About",   about_path %></li>
      <li><%= link_to "Contact", contact_path %></li>
      <li><a href="https://news.railstutorial.org/">News</a></li>
    </ul>
  </nav>
</footer>
```

With that, our layout has links to all the static pages created in Chapter 3, so that, for example, /about goes to the About page (Figure 5.10).

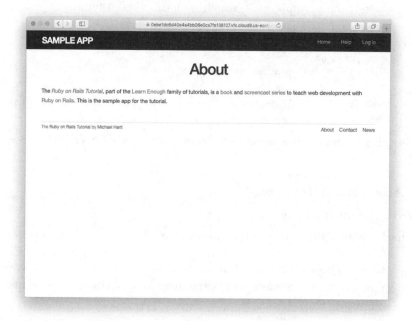

Figure 5.10: The About page at /about.

Exercises

Solutions to the exercises are available to all Rails Tutorial purchasers at https://www.railstutorial.org/aw-solutions.

To see other people's answers and to record your own, subscribe to the Rails Tutorial course or to the Learn Enough All Access Bundle.

1. Update the layout links to use the **helf** route from Listing 5.29.
2. Revert the changes using Undo.

5.3.4 Layout Link Tests

Now that we've filled in several of the layout links, it's a good idea to test them to make sure they're working correctly. We could do this by hand with a browser, first visiting the root path and then checking the links by hand, but this quickly becomes cumbersome. Instead, we'll simulate the same series of steps using an *integration test*, which allows us to write an end-to-end test of our application's behavior. We can get started by generating a template test, which we'll call **site_layout**:

```
$ rails generate integration_test site_layout
      invoke  test_unit
      create    test/integration/site_layout_test.rb
```

Note that the Rails generator automatically appends **_test** to the name of the test file.

Our plan for testing the layout links involves checking the HTML structure of our site:

1. Get the root path (Home page).
2. Verify that the right page template is rendered.
3. Check for the correct links to the Home, Help, About, and Contact pages.

Listing 5.32 shows how we can use Rails integration tests to translate these steps into code, beginning with the **assert_template** method to verify that the Home page is rendered using the correct view.[18]

---

18. Some developers insist that a single test shouldn't contain multiple assertions. I find this practice to be unnecessarily complicated, while also incurring extra overhead if common setup tasks are needed before

Listing 5.32: A test for the links on the layout. GREEN
test/integration/site_layout_test.rb

```ruby
require 'test_helper'

class SiteLayoutTest < ActionDispatch::IntegrationTest

  test "layout links" do
    get root_path
    assert_template 'static_pages/home'
    assert_select "a[href=?]", root_path, count: 2
    assert_select "a[href=?]", help_path
    assert_select "a[href=?]", about_path
    assert_select "a[href=?]", contact_path
  end
end
```

Listing 5.32 uses some of the more advanced options of the **assert_select** method, seen before in Listing 3.26 and Listing 5.21. In this case, we use a syntax that allows us to test for the presence of a particular link–URL combination by specifying the tag name **a** and attribute **href**, as in

```ruby
assert_select "a[href=?]", about_path
```

Here Rails automatically inserts the value of **about_path** in place of the question mark (escaping any special characters if necessary), thereby checking for an HTML tag of the form

```html
<a href="/about">...</a>
```

Note that the assertion for the root path verifies that there are *two* such links (one each for the logo and navigation menu element):

```ruby
assert_select "a[href=?]", root_path, count: 2
```

This ensures that both links to the Home page defined in Listing 5.30 are present.

---

each test. In addition, a well-written test tells a coherent story, and breaking it up into individual pieces disrupts the narrative. I thus have a strong preference for including multiple assertions in a test, relying on Ruby (via minitest) to tell me the exact lines of any failed assertions.

Table 5.2: Some uses of **assert_select**.

Code	Matching HTML
assert_select "div"	<div>foobar</div>
assert_select "div", "foobar"	<div>foobar</div>
assert_select "div.nav"	<div class="nav">foobar</div>
assert_select "div#profile"	<div id="profile">foobar</div>
assert_select "div[name=yo]"	<div name="yo">hey</div>
assert_select "a[href=?]", '/', count: 1	<a href="/">foo</a>
assert_select "a[href=?]", '/', text: "foo"	<a href="/">foo</a>

Some other uses of **assert_select** appear in Table 5.2. While **assert_select** is flexible and powerful (having many more options than the ones shown here), experience shows that it's wise to take a lightweight approach by testing only HTML elements (such as site layout links) that are unlikely to change much over time.

To check that the new test in Listing 5.32 passes, we can run just the integration tests using the following Rake task:

Listing 5.33: GREEN

```
$ rails test:integration
```

If all went well, you should run the full test suite to verify that all the tests are GREEN:

Listing 5.34: GREEN

```
$ rails test
```

With the added integration test for layout links, we are now in a good position to catch regressions quickly using our test suite.

Exercises

Solutions to the exercises are available to all Rails Tutorial purchasers at https://www.railstutorial.org/aw-solutions.

To see other people's answers and to record your own, subscribe to the Rails Tutorial course or to the Learn Enough All Access Bundle.

1. In the footer partial, change **about_path** to **contact_path** and verify that the tests catch the error.

2. It's convenient to use the **full_title** helper in the tests by including the Application helper into the test helper, as shown in Listing 5.35. We can then test for the right title using code like Listing 5.36. This is brittle, though, because now any typo in the base title (such as "Ruby on Rails Tutoial") won't be caught by the test suite. Fix this problem by writing a direct test of the **full_title** helper, which involves creating a file to test the application helper and then filling in the code indicated with **FILL_IN** in Listing 5.37. (Listing 5.37 uses **assert_equal <expected>, <actual>**, which verifies that the expected result matches the actual value when compared with the **==** operator.)

Listing 5.35: Including the Application helper in tests.
`test/test_helper.rb`

```ruby
ENV['RAILS_ENV'] ||= 'test'
.
.
.
class ActiveSupport::TestCase
  fixtures :all
  include ApplicationHelper
  .
  .
  .
end
```

Listing 5.36: Using the **full_title** helper in a test. GREEN
`test/integration/site_layout_test.rb`

```ruby
require 'test_helper'

class SiteLayoutTest < ActionDispatch::IntegrationTest

  test "layout links" do
    get root_path
    assert_template 'static_pages/home'
```

```
    assert_select "a[href=?]", root_path, count: 2
    assert_select "a[href=?]", help_path
    assert_select "a[href=?]", about_path
    assert_select "a[href=?]", contact_path
    get contact_path
    assert_select "title", full_title("Contact")
  end
end
```

Listing 5.37: A direct test of the **full_title** helper.
test/helpers/application_helper_test.rb

```
require 'test_helper'

class ApplicationHelperTest < ActionView::TestCase
  test "full title helper" do
    assert_equal full_title,          FILL_IN
    assert_equal full_title("Help"), FILL_IN
  end
end
```

5.4 User Signup: A First Step

As a capstone to our work on the layout and routing, in this section we'll make a route for the signup page, which will mean creating a second controller along the way. This is an important first step toward allowing users to register for our site; we'll take the next step, modeling users, in Chapter 6, and we'll finish the job in Chapter 7.

5.4.1 Users Controller

We created our first controller, the Static Pages controller, in Section 3.2. It's time to create a second one, the Users controller. As before, we'll use **generate** to make the simplest controller that meets our present needs—namely, one with a stub signup page for new users. Following the conventional REST architecture favored by Rails, we'll call the action for new users **new**, which we can arrange to create automatically by passing **new** as an argument to **generate**. The result is shown in Listing 5.38.

Listing 5.38: Generating a Users controller (with a **new** action).

```
$ rails generate controller Users new
      create  app/controllers/users_controller.rb
       route  get 'users/new'
      invoke  erb
      create    app/views/users
      create    app/views/users/new.html.erb
      invoke  test_unit
      create    test/controllers/users_controller_test.rb
      invoke  helper
      create    app/helpers/users_helper.rb
      invoke    test_unit
      invoke  assets
      invoke    scss
      create      app/assets/stylesheets/users.scss
```

As required, Listing 5.38 creates a Users controller with a **new** action (Listing 5.39) and a stub user view (Listing 5.40). It also creates a minimal test for the new user page (Listing 5.41).

Listing 5.39: The initial Users controller, with a **new** action.
app/controllers/users_controller.rb

```
class UsersController < ApplicationController

  def new
  end
end
```

Listing 5.40: The initial **new** view for Users.
app/views/users/new.html.erb

```
<h1>Users#new</h1>
<p>Find me in app/views/users/new.html.erb</p>
```

Listing 5.41: The generated test for the new user page. GREEN
test/controllers/users_controller_test.rb

```
require 'test_helper'

class UsersControllerTest < ActionDispatch::IntegrationTest
```

```
  test "should get new" do
    get users_new_url
    assert_response :success
  end
end
```

At this point, the tests should be GREEN:

Listing 5.42: GREEN

```
$ rails test
```

Exercises

Solutions to the exercises are available to all Rails Tutorial purchasers at https://www.railstutorial.org/aw-solutions.

To see other people's answers and to record your own, subscribe to the Rails Tutorial course or to the Learn Enough All Access Bundle.

1. Per Table 5.1, change the route in Listing 5.41 to use **signup_path** instead of **users_new_url**.

2. The route in the previous exercise doesn't yet exist, so confirm that the tests are now RED. (This is intended to help us get comfortable with the RED/GREEN flow of test-driven development (TDD, Box 3.3); we'll get the tests back to GREEN in Section 5.4.2.)

5.4.2 Signup URL

With the code from Section 5.4.1, we already have a working page for new users at /users/new, but recall from Table 5.1 that we want the URL to be /signup instead. We'll follow the examples from Listing 5.27 and add a **get '/signup'** rule for the signup URL, as shown in Listing 5.43.

Listing 5.43: A route for the signup page. RED
config/routes.rb

```
Rails.application.routes.draw do
  root 'static_pages#home'
```

```
get  '/help',    to: 'static_pages#help'
get  '/about',   to: 'static_pages#about'
get  '/contact', to: 'static_pages#contact'
get  '/signup',  to: 'users#new'
end
```

With the routes in Listing 5.43, we also need to update the test generated in Listing 5.38 with the new signup route, as shown in Listing 5.44.

Listing 5.44: Updating the Users controller test to use the signup route. GREEN
test/controllers/users_controller_test.rb

```
require 'test_helper'

class UsersControllerTest < ActionDispatch::IntegrationTest

  test "should get new" do
    get signup_path
    assert_response :success
  end
end
```

Next, we'll use the newly defined named route to add the proper link to the button on the Home page. As with the other routes, **get 'signup'** automatically gives us the named route **signup_path**, which we put to use in Listing 5.45. Adding a test for the signup page is left as an exercise (Section 5.3.2.)

Listing 5.45: Linking the button to the signup page.
app/views/static_pages/home.html.erb

```
<div class="center jumbotron">
  <h1>Welcome to the Sample App</h1>

  <h2>
    This is the home page for the
    <a href="https://www.railstutorial.org/">Ruby on Rails Tutorial</a>
    sample application.
  </h2>

  <%= link_to "Sign up now!", signup_path, class: "btn btn-lg btn-primary" %>
```

```
</div>

<%= link_to image_tag("rails.svg", alt: "Rails logo", width: "200"),
                      "https://rubyonrails.org/" %>
```

Finally, we'll add a custom stub view for the signup page (Listing 5.46).

Listing 5.46: The initial (stub) signup page.
`app/views/users/new.html.erb`

```
<% provide(:title, 'Sign up') %>
<h1>Sign up</h1>
<p>This will be a signup page for new users.</p>
```

With that, we're done with the links and named routes—at least until we add a route for logging in (Chapter 8). The resulting new user page (at the URL /signup) appears in Figure 5.11.

Figure 5.11: The new signup page at /signup.

Exercises

Solutions to the exercises are available to all Rails Tutorial purchasers at https://www.railstutorial.org/aw-solutions.

To see other people's answers and to record your own, subscribe to the Rails Tutorial course or to the Learn Enough All Access Bundle.

1. If you didn't solve the exercise in Section 5.4.1, change the test in Listing 5.41 to use the named route **signup_path**. Because of the route defined in Listing 5.43, this test should initially be GREEN.

2. To verify the correctness of the test in the previous exercise, comment out the **signup** route to get to RED, then uncomment it to get to GREEN.

3. In the integration test from Listing 5.32, add code to visit the signup page using the **get** method and verify that the resulting page title is correct. *Hint*: Use the **full_title** helper as in Listing 5.36.

5.5 Conclusion

In this chapter, we've hammered our application layout into shape and polished up the routes. The rest of the book is dedicated to fleshing out the sample application: first, by adding users who can sign up, log in, and log out; next, by adding user microposts; and, finally, by adding the ability to follow other users.

At this point, if you are using Git, you should merge your changes back into the master branch:

```
$ git add -A
$ git commit -m "Finish layout and routes"
$ git checkout master
$ git merge filling-in-layout
```

Then push up to GitHub (running the test suite first for safety):

```
$ rails test
$ git push
```

Finally, deploy to Heroku:

```
$ git push heroku
```

Figure 5.12: The sample application in production.

The result of the deployment should be a working sample application on the production server (Figure 5.12).

5.5.1   What We Learned in this Chapter

- Using HTML5, we can define a site layout with logo, header, footer, and main body content.

- Rails partials are used to place markup in a separate file for convenience.

- CSS allows us to style the site layout based on CSS classes and ids.

- The Bootstrap framework makes it easy to create a nicely designed site quickly.

- Sass and the asset pipeline allow us to eliminate duplication in our CSS while packaging up the results efficiently for production.

- Rails allows us to define custom routing rules, thereby providing named routes.

- Integration tests effectively simulate a browser clicking from page to page.

CHAPTER 6

Modeling Users

In Chapter 5, we ended with a stub page for creating new users (Section 5.4). Over the course of the next six chapters, we'll fulfill the promise implicit in this incipient signup page. In this chapter, we'll take the first critical step by creating a *data model* for users of our site, together with a way to store that data. In Chapter 7, we'll give users the ability to sign up for our site and create a user profile page. Once users can sign up, we'll let them log in and log out as well (Chapter 8 and Chapter 9), and in Chapter 10 (Section 10.2.1) we'll learn how to protect pages from improper access. Finally, in Chapter 11 and Chapter 12 we'll add account activations (thereby confirming a valid email address) and password resets. Taken together, the material in Chapter 6 through Chapter 12 develops a full Rails login and authentication system. As you may know, various pre-built authentication solutions are available for Rails; Box 6.1 explains why, at least at first, it's probably a better idea to roll your own.

Box 6.1: Rolling Your Own Authentication System

Virtually all web applications require a login and authentication system of some sort. As a result, most web frameworks end up with one or more standardized libraries for doing so, and Rails is no exception. In particular, the Devise gem has emerged as a robust solution for a wide variety of uses, and represents a strong choice for professional-grade applications.

Nevertheless, I believe it is a mistake to use a pre-built system like Devise in a tutorial like this one. Off-the-shelf systems can be "black boxes" with potentially mysterious innards, and the complicated data models used by such systems would

---

be utterly overwhelming for beginners (or even for experienced developers not familiar with data modeling). For learning purposes, it's essential to introduce the subject more gradually.

Happily, Rails makes it possible to take such a gradual approach while still developing an industrial-strength login and authentication system suitable for production applications. This way, even if you *do* end up using a third-party system later on, you'll be in a much better position to understand and modify it to meet your particular needs.

6.1   User Model

Although the ultimate goal of the next three chapters is to make a signup page for our site (as mocked up in Figure 6.1), it would do little good now to accept information

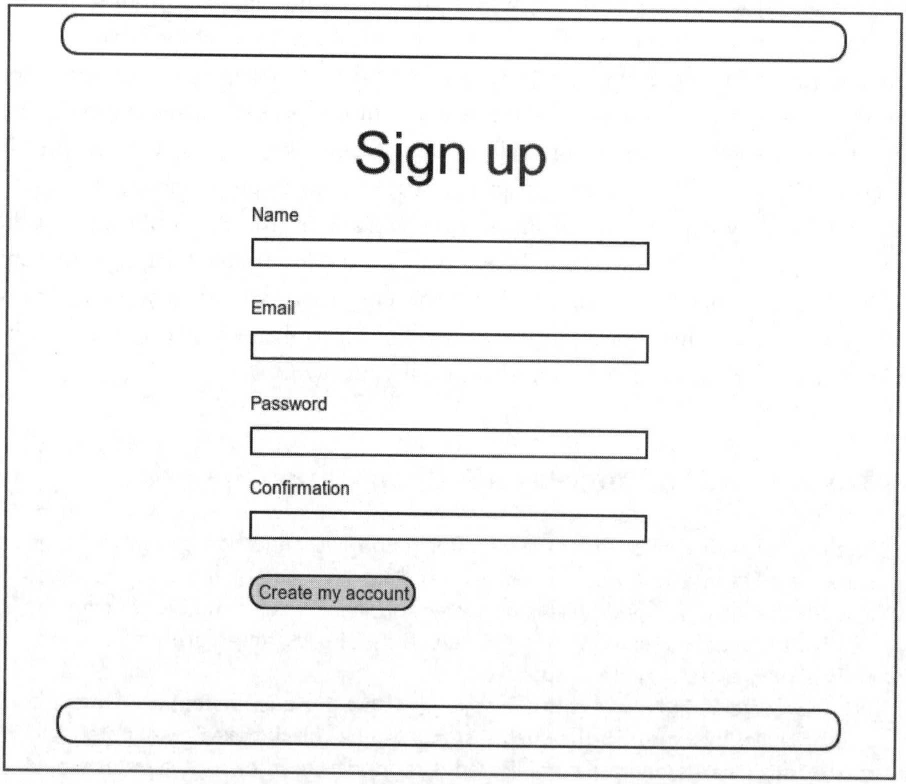

Figure 6.1: A mockup of the user signup page.

for new users: We don't currently have any place to put it. Thus, the first step in signing up users is to make a data structure to capture and store their information.

In Rails, the default data structure for a data model is called, naturally enough, a *model* (the M in MVC from Section 1.2.3). The default Rails solution to the problem of persistence is to use a *database* for long-term data storage, and the default library for interacting with the database is called *Active Record*.[1] Active Record comes with a host of methods for creating, saving, and finding data objects, all without having to use the structured query language (SQL)[2] used by relational databases. Moreover, Rails has a feature called *migrations* to allow data definitions to be written in pure Ruby, without having to learn an SQL data definition language (DDL). The effect is that Rails insulates you almost entirely from the details of the database. In this book, by using SQLite for development and PostgreSQL (via Heroku) for deployment (Section 1.4), we have developed this theme even further, to the point where we barely ever have to think about how Rails stores data, even for production applications.

As usual, if you're following along using Git for version control, now would be a good time to make a topic branch for modeling users:

```
$ git checkout -b modeling-users
```

6.1.1   Database Migrations

You may recall from Section 4.4.5 that we have already encountered, via a custom-built **User** class, user objects with **name** and **email** attributes. That class served as a useful example, but it lacked the critical property of *persistence*: When we created a User object at the Rails console, it disappeared as soon as we exited. Our goal in this section is to create a model for users that won't disappear quite so easily.

As with the User class in Section 4.4.5, we'll start by modeling a user with two attributes, a **name** and an **email** address, the latter of which we'll use as a unique

---

1. The name comes from the "active record pattern," identified and named in *Patterns of Enterprise Application Architecture* by Martin Fowler.

2. Officially pronounced "ess-cue-ell," though the alternate pronunciation "sequel" is also common. You can differentiate an individual author's preference by the choice of indefinite article: Those who write "a SQL database" prefer "sequel," whereas those who write "an SQL database" prefer "ess-cue-ell." As you'll soon see, I prefer the latter.

username.[3] (We'll add an attribute for passwords in Section 6.3.) In Listing 4.17, we did this with Ruby's **attr_accessor** method:

```
class User
  attr_accessor :name, :email
  .
  .
  .
end
```

In contrast, when using Rails to model users, we don't need to identify the attributes explicitly. As noted briefly earlier, to store data Rails uses a relational database by default, which consists of *tables* composed of data *rows*, where each row has *columns* of data attributes. For example, to store users with names and email addresses, we'll create a **users** table with **name** and **email** columns (with each row corresponding to one user). An example of such a table appears in Figure 6.2, corresponding to the data model shown in Figure 6.3. (Figure 6.3 is just a sketch; the full data model appears in Figure 6.4.) By naming the columns **name** and **email**, we can let Active Record figure out the User object attributes for us.

You may recall from Listing 5.38 that we created a Users controller (along with a **new** action) using the command

```
$ rails generate controller Users new
```

users		
id	name	email
1	Michael Hartl	mhartl@example.com
2	Sterling Archer	archer@example.gov
3	Lana Kane	lana@example.gov
4	Mallory Archer	boss@example.gov

Figure 6.2: A diagram of sample data in a **users** table.

---

3. By using an email address as the username, we open the possibility of communicating with our users at a future date (Chapter 11 and Chapter 12).

users	
id	integer
name	string
email	string

Figure 6.3: A sketch of the User data model.

The analogous command for making a model is **`generate model`**, which we can use to generate a User model with **`name`** and **`email`** attributes, as shown in Listing 6.1.

Listing 6.1: Generating a User model.

```
$ rails generate model User name:string email:string
      invoke  active_record
      create    db/migrate/<timestamp>_create_users.rb
      create    app/models/user.rb
      invoke    test_unit
      create      test/models/user_test.rb
      create      test/fixtures/users.yml
```

(Note that, in contrast to the plural convention for controller names, model names are singular: a *Users* controller, but a *User* model.) By passing the optional parameters **`name:string`** and **`email:string`**, we tell Rails about the two attributes we want, along with which types those attributes should be (in this case, **`string`**). Compare this with how we included the action names in Listing 3.6 and Listing 5.38.

One of the results of the **`generate`** command in Listing 6.1 is a new file called a *migration*. Migrations provide a way to alter the structure of the database incrementally, so that our data model can adapt to changing requirements. In the case of the User model, the migration is created automatically by the model generation script; it creates a **`users`** table with two columns, **`name`** and **`email`**, as shown in Listing 6.2. (We'll see starting in Section 6.2.5 how to make a migration from scratch.)

Listing 6.2: Migration for the User model (to create a **users** table).
`db/migrate/[timestamp]_create_users.rb`

```ruby
class CreateUsers < ActiveRecord::Migration[6.0]
  def change
    create_table :users do |t|
      t.string :name
      t.string :email

      t.timestamps
    end
  end
end
```

Note that the name of the migration file is prefixed by a *timestamp* based on when the migration was generated. In the early days of migrations, the filenames were prefixed with incrementing integers, which caused conflicts for collaborating teams if multiple programmers had migrations with the same number. Barring the improbable scenario of migrations generated the same second, using timestamps conveniently avoids such collisions.

The migration itself consists of a **change** method that determines the change to be made to the database. In the case of Listing 6.2, **change** uses a Rails method called **create_table** to create a table in the database for storing users. The **create_table** method accepts a block (Section 4.3.2) with one block variable, in this case called **t** (for "table"). Inside the block, the **create_table** method uses the **t** object to create **name** and **email** columns in the database, both of type **string**.[4] Here the table name is plural (**users**) even though the model name is singular (User), which reflects a linguistic convention followed by Rails: A model represents a single user, whereas a database table consists of many users. The final line in the block, **t.timestamps**, is a special command that creates two *magic columns* called **created_at** and **updated_at**, which are timestamps that automatically record when a given user is created and updated. (We'll see concrete examples of the magic columns starting in Section 6.1.3.) The full data model represented by the migration in Listing 6.2 is shown in Figure 6.4. (Note the addition of the magic columns, which weren't present in the sketch shown in Figure 6.3.)

---

4. Don't worry about exactly how the **t** object manages to do this; the beauty of *abstraction layers* is that we don't have to know. We can just trust the **t** object to do its job.

users	
`id`	integer
`name`	string
`email`	string
`created_at`	datetime
`updated_at`	datetime

Figure 6.4: The User data model produced by Listing 6.2.

We can run the migration, known as "migrating up," using the **db:migrate** command as follows:

```
$ rails db:migrate
```

(You may recall that we ran this command in a similar context in Section 2.2.) The first time **db:migrate** is run, it creates a file called **db/development.sqlite3**, which is an SQLite[5] database. We can see the structure of the database by opening **development.sqlite3** with DB Browser for SQLite. (If you're using the cloud IDE, you should first download the database file to the local disk, as shown in Figure 6.5.) The result appears in Figure 6.6; compare it with the diagram in Figure 6.4. You might note that Figure 6.6 includes one column not accounted for in the migration: the **id** column. As noted briefly in Section 2.2, this column is created automatically, and is used by Rails to identify each row uniquely.

Exercises

Solutions to the exercises are available to all Rails Tutorial purchasers at https://www.railstutorial.org/aw-solutions.

To see other people's answers and to record your own, subscribe to the Rails Tutorial course or to the Learn Enough All Access Bundle.

---

5. Officially pronounced "ess-cue-ell-ite," although the (mis)pronunciation "sequel-ite" is also common.

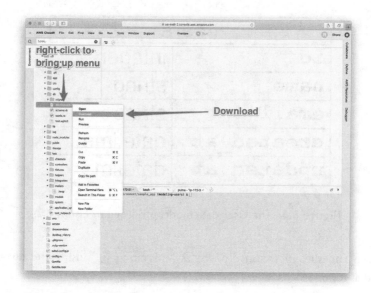

Figure 6.5: Downloading a file from the cloud IDE.

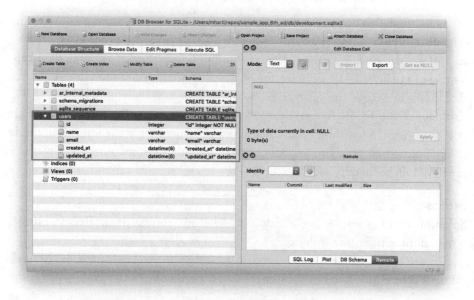

Figure 6.6: DB Browser with our new **users** table.

1. Rails uses a file called **schema.rb** in the **db/** directory to keep track of the structure of the database (called the *schema*, hence the filename). Examine your local copy of **db/schema.rb** and compare its contents to the migration code in Listing 6.2.

2. Most migrations (including all the ones in this tutorial) are *reversible*, which means we can "migrate down" and undo them with a single command, called **db:rollback**:

```
$ rails db:rollback
```

   After running this command, examine **db/schema.rb** to confirm that the rollback was successful. (See Box 3.1 for another technique useful for reversing migrations.) Under the hood, this command executes the **drop_table** command to remove the users table from the database. The reason this works is that the **change** method knows that **drop_table** is the inverse of **create_table**, which means that the rollback migration can be easily inferred. In the case of an irreversible migration, such as one to remove a database column, it is necessary to define separate **up** and **down** methods in place of the single **change** method. Read about migrations in the Rails Guides (guides.rubyonrails.org/migrations.html) for more information.

3. Rerun the migration by executing **rails db:migrate** again. Confirm that the contents of **db/schema.rb** have been restored.

6.1.2 The Model File

We've seen how the User model generation in Listing 6.1 generated a migration file (Listing 6.2), and we saw in Figure 6.6 the results of running this migration: It updated a file called **development.sqlite3** by creating a table **users** with columns **id**, **name**, **email**, **created_at**, and **updated_at**. Listing 6.1 also created the model itself. The rest of this section is dedicated to understanding it.

We begin by looking at the code for the User model, which lives in the file **user.rb** inside the **app/models/** directory. It is, to put it mildly, very compact (Listing 6.3).

Listing 6.3: The brand-new User model.
`app/models/user.rb`

```
class User < ApplicationRecord
end
```

Recall from Section 4.4.2 that the syntax **class User < ApplicationRecord** means that the **User** class *inherits* from the **ApplicationRecord** class, which in turn inherits from **ActiveRecord::Base** (Figure 2.19), so that the User model automatically has all the functionality of the **ActiveRecord::Base** class. Of course, this knowledge doesn't do us any good unless we know what **ActiveRecord::Base** contains, so let's get started with some concrete examples.

Exercises

Solutions to the exercises are available to all Rails Tutorial purchasers at https://www.railstutorial.org/aw-solutions.

To see other people's answers and to record your own, subscribe to the Rails Tutorial course or to the Learn Enough All Access Bundle.

1. In a Rails console, use the technique from Section 4.4.4 to confirm that **User.new** is of class **User** and inherits from **ApplicationRecord**.

2. Confirm that **ApplicationRecord** inherits from **ActiveRecord::Base**.

6.1.3 Creating User Objects

As in Chapter 4, our tool of choice for exploring data models is the Rails console. Since we don't (yet) want to make any changes to our database, we'll start the console in a *sandbox*:

```
$ rails console --sandbox
Loading development environment in sandbox
Any modifications you make will be rolled back on exit
>>
```

As indicated by the helpful message "Any modifications you make will be rolled back on exit," when started in a sandbox the console will "roll back" (i.e., undo) any database changes introduced during the session.

In the console session in Section 4.4.5, we created a new user object with
User.new, which we had access to only after requiring the example user file in Listing 4.17. With models, the situation is different: As you may recall from Section 4.4.4,
the Rails console automatically loads the Rails environment, which includes the
models. This means that we can make a new user object without any further
work:

```
>> User.new
=> #<User id: nil, name: nil, email: nil, created_at: nil, updated_at: nil>
```

We see here the default console representation of a user object.

When called with no arguments, **User.new** returns an object with all **nil**
attributes. In Section 4.4.5, we designed the example User class to take an *initialization hash* to set the object attributes; that design choice was motivated by Active
Record, which allows objects to be initialized in the same way:

```
>> user = User.new(name: "Michael Hartl", email: "michael@example.com")
=> #<User id: nil, name: "Michael Hartl", email: "michael@example.com",
created_at: nil, updated_at: nil>
```

Here we see that the name and email attributes have been set as expected.

The notion of *validity* is important for understanding Active Record model
objects. We'll explore this subject in more depth in Section 6.2, but for now it's worth
noting that our initial **user** object is valid, which we can verify by calling the boolean
valid? method on it:

```
>> user.valid?
true
```

So far, we haven't touched the database: **User.new** only creates an object *in memory*, while **user.valid?** merely checks to see if the object is valid. To save the User
object to the database, we need to call the **save** method on the **user** variable:

```
>> user.save
  (0.1ms)  SAVEPOINT active_record_1
  SQL (0.8ms)  INSERT INTO "users" ("name", "email", "created_at",
"updated_at") VALUES (?, ?, ?, ?) [["name", "Michael Hartl"],
["email", "michael@example.com"], ["created_at", "2019-08-22 01:51:03.453035"],
```

```
["updated_at", "2019-08-22 01:51:03.453035"]]
  (0.1ms)  RELEASE SAVEPOINT active_record_1
=> true
```

The **save** method returns **true** if it succeeds and **false** otherwise. (Currently, all saves should succeed because there are as yet no validations; we'll see cases in Section 6.2 when some will fail.) For reference, the Rails console also shows the SQL command corresponding to **user.save** (namely, **INSERT INTO "users"**...). We'll hardly ever need raw SQL in this book,[6] and I'll omit discussion of the SQL commands from now on, but you can learn a lot by reading the SQL corresponding to Active Record commands.

You may have noticed that the new user object had **nil** values for the **id** and the magic columns **created_at** and **updated_at** attributes. Let's see if our **save** changed anything:

```
>> user
=> #<User id: 1, name: "Michael Hartl", email: "michael@example.com",
created_at: "2019-08-22 01:51:03", updated_at: "2019-08-22 01:51:03">
```

We see that the **id** has been assigned a value of **1**, while the magic columns have been assigned the current time and date.[7] Currently, the created and updated timestamps are identical; we'll see them differ in Section 6.1.5.

As with the User class in Section 4.4.5, instances of the User model allow access to their attributes using a dot notation:

```
>> user.name
=> "Michael Hartl"
>> user.email
```

---

6. The only exception is in Section 14.3.3.

7. The timestamps are recorded in Coordinated Universal Time (UTC), which for most practical purposes is the same as Greenwich Mean Time. But why call it UTC? From the NIST Time and Frequency FAQ: **Q:** Why is UTC used as the acronym for Coordinated Universal Time instead of CUT? **A:** In 1970 the Coordinated Universal Time system was devised by an international advisory group of technical experts within the International Telecommunication Union (ITU). The ITU felt it was best to designate a single abbreviation for use in all languages in order to minimize confusion. Since unanimous agreement could not be achieved on using either the English word order, CUT, or the French word order, TUC, the acronym UTC was chosen as a compromise.

```
=> "michael@example.com"
>> user.updated_at
=> Thu, 22 Aug 2019 01:51:03 UTC +00:00
```

As we'll see in Chapter 7, it's often convenient to make and save a model in two steps as we have done here, but Active Record also lets you combine them into one step with **User.create**:

```
>> User.create(name: "A Nother", email: "another@example.org")
#<User id: 2, name: "A Nother", email: "another@example.org", created_at:
"2019-08-22 01:53:22", updated_at: "2019-08-22 01:53:22">
>> foo = User.create(name: "Foo", email: "foo@bar.com")
#<User id: 3, name: "Foo", email: "foo@bar.com", created_at: "2019-08-22
01:54:03", updated_at: "2019-08-22 01:54:03">
```

Note that **User.create**, rather than returning **true** or **false**, returns the User object itself, which we can optionally assign to a variable (such as **foo** in the second command above).

The inverse of **create** is **destroy**:

```
>> foo.destroy
  (0.1ms)  SAVEPOINT active_record_1
  SQL (0.2ms)  DELETE FROM "users" WHERE "users"."id" = ?  [["id", 3]]
  (0.1ms)  RELEASE SAVEPOINT active_record_1
=> #<User id: 3, name: "Foo", email: "foo@bar.com", created_at: "2019-08-22
01:54:03", updated_at: "2019-08-22 01:54:03">
```

Like **create**, **destroy** returns the object in question, though I can't recall ever having used the return value of **destroy**. In addition, the destroyed object still exists in memory:

```
>> foo
=> #<User id: 3, name: "Foo", email: "foo@bar.com", created_at: "2019-08-22
01:54:03", updated_at: "2019-08-22 01:54:03">
```

So how do we know if we really destroyed an object? And for saved and non-destroyed objects, how can we retrieve users from the database? To answer these questions, we need to learn how to use Active Record to find user objects.

Exercises

Solutions to the exercises are available to all Rails Tutorial purchasers at https://www.railstutorial.org/aw-solutions.

To see other people's answers and to record your own, subscribe to the Rails Tutorial course or to the Learn Enough All Access Bundle.

1. Confirm that **user.name** and **user.email** are of class **String**.

2. Of what class are the **created_at** and **updated_at** attributes?

6.1.4 Finding User Objects

Active Record provides several options for finding objects. Let's use them to find the first user we created while verifying that the third user (**foo**) has been destroyed. We'll start with the existing user:

```
>> User.find(1)
=> #<User id: 1, name: "Michael Hartl", email: "michael@example.com",
created_at: "2019-08-22 01:51:03", updated_at: "2019-08-22 01:51:03">
```

Here we've passed the id of the user to **User.find**; Active Record returns the user with that id.

Let's see if the user with an **id** of **3** still exists in the database:

```
>> User.find(3)
ActiveRecord::RecordNotFound: Couldn't find User with ID=3
```

Since we destroyed our third user in Section 6.1.3, Active Record can't find it in the database. Instead, **find** raises an *exception*, which is a way of indicating an exceptional event in the execution of a program—in this case, a nonexistent Active Record id, leading **find** to raise an **ActiveRecord::RecordNotFound** exception.[8]

In addition to the generic **find**, Active Record enables us to find users by specific attributes:

```
>> User.find_by(email: "michael@example.com")
=> #<User id: 1, name: "Michael Hartl", email: "michael@example.com",
created_at: "2019-08-22 01:51:03", updated_at: "2019-08-22 01:51:03">
```

---

8. Exceptions and exception handling are somewhat advanced Ruby subjects, and we won't need them much in this book. They are important, though, and I suggest learning about them using one of the Ruby books recommended in Section 14.4.1.

Since we will be using email addresses as usernames, this sort of **find** will be useful when we learn how to let users log in to our site (Chapter 7). If you're worried that **find_by** will be inefficient if there are a large number of users, you're ahead of the game; we'll cover this issue, and its solution via database indices, in Section 6.2.5.

We'll end with a couple of more general ways of finding users. First, there's **first**:

```
>> User.first
=> #<User id: 1, name: "Michael Hartl", email: "michael@example.com",
created_at: "2019-08-22 01:51:03", updated_at: "2019-08-22 01:51:03">
```

Naturally, **first** just returns the first user in the database. There's also **all**:

```
>> User.all
=> #<ActiveRecord::Relation [#<User id: 1, name: "Michael Hartl", email:
"michael@example.com", created_at: "2019-08-22 01:51:03", updated_at:
"2019-08-22 01:51:03">, #<User id: 2, name: "A Nother", email:
"another@example.org", created_at: "2019-08-22 01:53:22", updated_at:
"2019-08-22 01:53:22">]>
```

As you can see from the console output, **User.all** returns all the users in the database as an object of class **ActiveRecord::Relation**, which is effectively an array (Section 4.3.1).

Exercises

Solutions to the exercises are available to all Rails Tutorial purchasers at https://www.railstutorial.org/aw-solutions.

To see other people's answers and to record your own, subscribe to the Rails Tutorial course or to the Learn Enough All Access Bundle.

1. Find the user by **name**. Confirm that **find_by_name** works as well. (You will often encounter this older style of **find_by** in legacy Rails applications.)

2. For most practical purposes, **User.all** acts like an array, but confirm that in fact it's of class **User::ActiveRecord_Relation**.

3. Confirm that you can find the length of **User.all** by passing it the **length** method (Section 4.2.2). Ruby's ability to manipulate objects based on how they act rather than on their formal class type is called *duck typing*, based on the aphorism that "If it looks like a duck, and it quacks like a duck, it's probably a duck."

6.1.5 Updating User Objects

Once we've created objects, we often want to update them. There are two basic ways
to do this. First, we can assign attributes individually, as we did in Section 4.4.5:

```
>> user              # Just a reminder about our user's attributes
=> #<User id: 1, name: "Michael Hartl", email: "michael@example.com",
created_at: "2019-08-22 01:51:03", updated_at: "2019-08-22 01:51:03">
>> user.email = "mhartl@example.net"
=> "mhartl@example.net"
>> user.save
=> true
```

Note that the final step is necessary to write the changes to the database. We can see
what happens without a save by using **reload**, which reloads the object based on the
database information:

```
>> user.email
=> "mhartl@example.net"
>> user.email = "foo@bar.com"
=> "foo@bar.com"
>> user.reload.email
=> "mhartl@example.net"
```

Now that we've updated the user by running **user.save**, the magic columns
differ, as promised in Section 6.1.3:

```
>> user.created_at
=> Thu, 22 Aug 2019 01:51:03 UTC +00:00
>> user.updated_at
=> Thu, 22 Aug 2019 01:58:08 UTC +00:00
```

The second main way to update multiple attributes is to use **update**:[9]

```
>> user.update(name: "The Dude", email: "dude@abides.org")
=> true
>> user.name
=> "The Dude"
>> user.email
=> "dude@abides.org"
```

---

9. Formerly **update_attributes**.

The **update** method accepts a hash of attributes, and on success performs both the update and the save in one step (returning **true** to indicate that the save went through). Note that if any of the validations fail, such as when a password is required to save a record (as implemented in Section 6.3), the call to **update** will fail. If we need to update only a single attribute, using the singular **update_attribute** bypasses this restriction by skipping the validations:

```
>> user.update_attribute(:name, "El Duderino")
=> true
>> user.name
=> "El Duderino"
```

Exercises

Solutions to the exercises are available to all Rails Tutorial purchasers at https://www.railstutorial.org/aw-solutions.

To see other people's answers and to record your own, subscribe to the Rails Tutorial course or to the Learn Enough All Access Bundle.

1. Update the user's name using assignment and a call to **save**.

2. Update the user's email address using a call to **update**.

3. Confirm that you can change the magic columns directly by updating the **created_at** column using assignment and a save. Use the value **1.year.ago**, which is a Rails way to create a timestamp one year before the present time.

6.2 User Validations

The User model we created in Section 6.1 now has working **name** and **email** attributes, but they are completely generic: Any string (including an empty one) is currently valid in either case. And yet, names and email addresses are more specific than this. For example, **name** should be non-blank, and **email** should match the specific format characteristic of email addresses. Moreover, since we'll be using email addresses as unique usernames when users log in, we shouldn't allow email duplicates in the database.

In short, we shouldn't allow **name** and **email** to be just any strings; we should enforce certain constraints on their values. Active Record allows us to impose such constraints using *validations* (seen briefly in Section 2.3.2). In this section, we'll cover several of the most common cases, validating *presence*, *length*, *format*, and *uniqueness*. In Section 6.3.2 we'll add a final common validation, *confirmation*. And we'll see in Section 7.3 how validations give us convenient error messages when users make submissions that violate them.

6.2.1 A Validity Test

As noted in Box 3.3, test-driven development isn't always the right tool for the job, but model validations are exactly the kind of features for which TDD is a perfect fit. It's difficult to be confident that a given validation is doing exactly what we expect it to without writing a failing test and then getting it to pass.

Our method will be to start with a *valid* model object, set one of its attributes to something we want to be invalid, and then test that it in fact is invalid. As a safety net, we'll first write a test to make sure the initial model object is valid. This way, when the validation tests fail we'll know it's for the right reason (and not because the initial object was invalid in the first place).

In what follows, and when doing TDD generally, it's convenenient to work with your editor split into two *panes*, with the test code on the left and the application code on the right. My preferred setup with the cloud IDE is shown in Figure 6.7.

To get us started, the command in Listing 6.1 produced an initial test for testing users, though in this case it's practically blank (Listing 6.4).

Listing 6.4: The practically blank default User test.
`test/models/user_test.rb`

```ruby
require 'test_helper'

class UserTest < ActiveSupport::TestCase
  # test "the truth" do
  #   assert true
  # end
end
```

To write a test for a valid object, we'll create an initially valid User model object **@user** using the special **setup** method (discussed briefly in the Chapter 3 exercises), which automatically gets run before each test. Because **@user** is an instance variable,

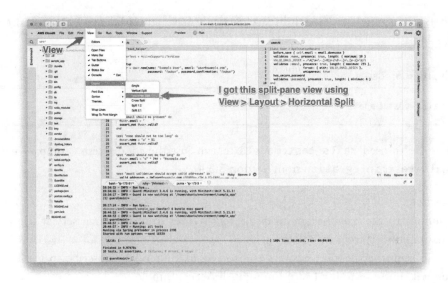

Figure 6.7: TDD with a split pane.

it's automatically available in all the tests, and we can test its validity using the **valid?** method (Section 6.1.3). The result appears in Listing 6.5.

Listing 6.5: A test for an initially valid user. GREEN
test/models/user_test.rb

```
require 'test_helper'

class UserTest < ActiveSupport::TestCase

  def setup
    @user = User.new(name: "Example User", email: "user@example.com")
  end

  test "should be valid" do
    assert @user.valid?
  end
end
```

Listing 6.5 uses the plain **assert** method, which in this case succeeds if **@user.valid?** returns **true** and fails if it returns **false**.

Because our User model doesn't currently have any validations, the initial test should pass:

Listing 6.6: GREEN

```
$ rails test:models
```

Here we've used **rails test:models** to run just the model tests (compare it to **rails test:integration** from Section 5.3.4).

Exercises

Solutions to the exercises are available to all Rails Tutorial purchasers at https://www.railstutorial.org/aw-solutions.

To see other people's answers and to record your own, subscribe to the Rails Tutorial course or to the Learn Enough All Access Bundle.

1. In the console, confirm that a new user is currently valid.

2. Confirm that the user created in Section 6.1.3 is also valid.

6.2.2 Validating Presence

Perhaps the most elementary validation is *presence*, which simply verifies that a given attribute is present. For example, in this section we'll ensure that both the name and email fields are present before a user gets saved to the database. In Section 7.3.3, we'll see how to propagate this requirement up to the signup form for creating new users.

We'll start with a test for the presence of a **name** attribute by building on the test in Listing 6.5. As seen in Listing 6.7, all we need to do is set the **@user** variable's **name** attribute to a blank string (in this case, a string of spaces) and then check (using the **assert_not** method) that the resulting User object is not valid.

Listing 6.7: A test for validation of the **name** attribute. RED
test/models/user_test.rb

```
require 'test_helper'

class UserTest < ActiveSupport::TestCase

  def setup
```

```
    @user = User.new(name: "Example User", email: "user@example.com")
  end

  test "should be valid" do
    assert @user.valid?
  end

  test "name should be present" do
    @user.name = "         "
    assert_not @user.valid?
  end
end
```

At this point, the model tests should be RED:

Listing 6.8: RED

```
$ rails test:models
```

As we saw briefly in the Chapter 2 exercises, the way to validate the presence of the name attribute is to use the **validates** method with argument **presence: true**, as shown in Listing 6.9. The **presence: true** argument is a one-element *options hash*; recall from Section 4.3.4 that curly braces are optional when passing hashes as the final argument in a method. (As noted in Section 5.1.1, the use of options hashes is a recurring theme in Rails.)

Listing 6.9: Validating the presence of a **name** attribute. GREEN
app/models/user.rb

```
class User < ApplicationRecord
  validates :name, presence: true
end
```

Listing 6.9 may look like magic, but **validates** is just a method. An equivalent formulation of Listing 6.9 using parentheses is as follows:

```
class User < ApplicationRecord
  validates(:name, presence: true)
end
```

Let's drop into the console to see the effects of adding a validation to our User model:[10]

```
$ rails console --sandbox
>> user = User.new(name: "", email: "michael@example.com")
>> user.valid?
=> false
```

Here we check the validity of the **user** variable using the **valid?** method, which returns **false** when the object fails one or more validations, and **true** when all validations pass. In this case, we have only one validation, so we know which one failed, but it can still be helpful to check using the **errors** object generated on failure:

```
>> user.errors.full_messages
=> ["Name can't be blank"]
```

(The error message is a hint that Rails validates the presence of an attribute using the **blank?** method, which we saw at the end of Section 4.4.3.)

Because the user isn't valid, an attempt to save the user to the database automatically fails:

```
>> user.save
=> false
```

As a result, the test in Listing 6.7 should now be GREEN:

Listing 6.10: GREEN

```
$ rails test:models
```

By following the model in Listing 6.7, writing a test for **email** attribute presence is easy (Listing 6.11), as is the application code to get it to pass (Listing 6.12).

---

10. I'll omit the output of console commands when they are not particularly instructive—for example, the results of **User.new**.

Listing 6.11: A test for validation of the **email** attribute. RED
`test/models/user_test.rb`

```ruby
require 'test_helper'

class UserTest < ActiveSupport::TestCase

  def setup
    @user = User.new(name: "Example User", email: "user@example.com")
  end

  test "should be valid" do
    assert @user.valid?
  end

  test "name should be present" do
    @user.name = ""
    assert_not @user.valid?
  end

  test "email should be present" do
    @user.email = "     "
    assert_not @user.valid?
  end
end
```

Listing 6.12: Validating the presence of an **email** attribute. GREEN
`app/models/user.rb`

```ruby
class User < ApplicationRecord
  validates :name,  presence: true
  validates :email, presence: true
end
```

At this point, the presence validations are complete, and the test suite should be
GREEN:

Listing 6.13: GREEN

```
$ rails test
```

Exercises

Solutions to the exercises are available to all Rails Tutorial purchasers at https://
www.railstutorial.org/aw-solutions.

To see other people's answers and to record your own, subscribe to the Rails Tutorial course or to the Learn Enough All Access Bundle.

1. Make a new user called **u** and confirm that it's initially invalid. What are the full error messages?

2. Confirm that **u.errors.messages** is a hash of errors. How would you access just the email errors?

6.2.3 Length Validation

We've constrained our User model to require a name for each user, but we should go further: The users' names will be displayed on the sample site, so we should enforce some limit on their length. With all the work we did in Section 6.2.2, this step is easy.

There's no science to picking a maximum length; we'll just pull **50** out of thin air as a reasonable upper bound, which means verifying that names of **51** characters are too long. In addition, although it's unlikely ever to be a problem, there's a chance that a user's email address could overrun the maximum length of strings, which for many databases is 255. Because the format validation in Section 6.2.4 won't enforce such a constraint, we'll add one in this section for completeness. Listing 6.14 shows the resulting tests.

Listing 6.14: Tests for **name** and **email** length validations. RED
test/models/user_test.rb
***

```
require 'test_helper'

class UserTest < ActiveSupport::TestCase

  def setup
    @user = User.new(name: "Example User", email: "user@example.com")
  end
  .
  .
  .
  test "name should not be too long" do
    @user.name = "a" * 51
    assert_not @user.valid?
  end

  test "email should not be too long" do
```

```
      @user.email = "a" * 244 + "@example.com"
      assert_not @user.valid?
  end
end
```

For convenience, we've used "string multiplication" in Listing 6.14 to make a string 51 characters long. We can see how this works using the console:

```
>> "a" * 51
=> "aaaaaaaaaaaaaaaaaaaaaaaaaaaaaaaaaaaaaaaaaaaaaaaaaaa"
>> ("a" * 51).length
=> 51
```

The email length validation arranges to make a valid email address that's one character too long:

```
>> "a" * 244 + "@example.com"
=> "aaaaaaaaaaaaaaaaaaaaaaaaaaaaaaaaaaaaaaaaaaaaaaaaaaaaaaaaaaaaaaaaaaaaaaaaa
aaaaaaaaaaaaaaaaaaaaaaaaaaaaaaaaaaaaaaaaaaaaaaaaaaaaaaaaaaaaaaaaaaaaaaaaaaaaa
aaaaaaaaaaaaaaaaaaaaaaaaaaaaaaaaaaaaaaaaaaaaaaaaaaaaaaaaaaaaaaaaaaaaaaaaaaaaa
aaaaaaaaaa@example.com"
>> ("a" * 244 + "@example.com").length
=> 256
```

At this point, the tests in Listing 6.14 should be RED:

Listing 6.15: RED

```
$ rails test
```

To get them to pass, we need to use the validation argument to constrain length, which is just **length**, along with the **maximum** parameter to enforce the upper bound (Listing 6.16).

Listing 6.16: Adding a length validation for the **name** attribute. GREEN
app/models/user.rb

```
class User < ApplicationRecord
  validates :name,  presence: true, length: { maximum: 50 }
  validates :email,  presence: true, length: { maximum: 255 }
end
```

Now the tests should be GREEN:

Listing 6.17: GREEN

```
$ rails test
```

With our test suite passing again, we can move on to a more challenging validation: email format.

Exercises

Solutions to the exercises are available to all Rails Tutorial purchasers at https://www.railstutorial.org/aw-solutions.

To see other people's answers and to record your own, subscribe to the Rails Tutorial course or to the Learn Enough All Access Bundle.

1. Make a new user with a too-long name and email and confirm that it's not valid.

2. What are the error messages generated by the length validation?

6.2.4 Format Validation

Our validations for the **name** attribute enforce only minimal constraints—any non-blank name with fewer than 51 characters will do—but of course the **email** attribute must satisfy the more stringent requirement of being a valid email address. So far we've rejected only blank email addresses; in this section, we'll require email addresses to conform to the familiar pattern **user@example.com**.

Neither the tests nor the validation will be exhaustive, just good enough to accept most valid email addresses and reject most invalid ones. We'll start with a couple of tests involving collections of valid and invalid addresses. To make these collections, it's worth knowing about the useful **%w[]** technique for making arrays of strings, as seen in this console session:

```
>> %w[foo bar baz]
=> ["foo", "bar", "baz"]
>> addresses = %w[USER@foo.COM THE_US-ER@foo.bar.org first.last@foo.jp]
=> ["USER@foo.COM", "THE_US-ER@foo.bar.org", "first.last@foo.jp"]
>> addresses.each do |address|
?>   puts address
>> end
USER@foo.COM
```

```
THE_US-ER@foo.bar.org
first.last@foo.jp
```

Here we've iterated over the elements of the **addresses** array using the **each** method (Section 4.3.2). With this technique in hand, we're ready to write some basic email format validation tests.

Because email format validation is tricky and error-prone, we'll start with some passing tests for *valid* email addresses to catch any errors in the validation. In other words, we want to make sure not just that invalid email addresses like *user@example,com* are rejected, but also that valid addresses like *user@example.com* are accepted, even after we impose the validation constraint. (Right now they'll be accepted because all non-blank email addresses are currently valid.) The result for a representative sample of valid email addresses appears in Listing 6.18.

Listing 6.18: Tests for valid email formats. GREEN
`test/models/user_test.rb`

```
require 'test_helper'

class UserTest < ActiveSupport::TestCase

  def setup
    @user = User.new(name: "Example User", email: "user@example.com")
  end
  .
  .
  .
  test "email validation should accept valid addresses" do
    valid_addresses = %w[user@example.com USER@foo.COM A_US-ER@foo.bar.org
                         first.last@foo.jp alice+bob@baz.cn]
    valid_addresses.each do |valid_address|
      @user.email = valid_address
      assert @user.valid?, "#{valid_address.inspect} should be valid"
    end
  end
end
```

Note that we've included an optional second argument to the assertion with a custom error message, which in this case identifies the address causing the test to fail:

```
assert @user.valid?, "#{valid_address.inspect} should be valid"
```

(This uses the interpolated **inspect** method mentioned in Section 4.3.3.) Including
the specific address that causes any failure is especially useful in a test with an **each**
loop like Listing 6.18; otherwise, any failure would merely identify the line number,
which is the same for all the email addresses, and which wouldn't be sufficient to
identify the source of the problem.

Next we'll add tests for the *invalidity* of a variety of invalid email addresses, such as
user@example,com (comma in place of dot) and *user_at_foo.org* (missing the '@' sign).
As in Listing 6.18, Listing 6.19 includes a custom error message to identify the exact
address causing any failure.

Listing 6.19: Tests for email format validation. RED
test/models/user_test.rb

```
require 'test_helper'

class UserTest < ActiveSupport::TestCase

  def setup
    @user = User.new(name: "Example User", email: "user@example.com")
  end
  .
  .
  .
  test "email validation should reject invalid addresses" do
    invalid_addresses = %w[user@example,com user_at_foo.org user.name@example.
                           foo@bar_baz.com foo@bar+baz.com]
    invalid_addresses.each do |invalid_address|
      @user.email = invalid_address
      assert_not @user.valid?, "#{invalid_address.inspect} should be invalid"
    end
  end
end
```

At this point, the tests should be RED:

Listing 6.20: RED

```
$ rails test
```

The application code for email format validation uses the **format** validation,
which works like this:

```
validates :email, format: { with: /<regular expression>/ }
```

This validates the attribute with the given *regular expression* (or *regex*), which is a powerful (and often cryptic) language for matching patterns in strings. It means we need to construct a regular expression to match valid email addresses while *not* matching invalid ones.

There actually exists a full regex for matching email addresses according to the official email standard, but it's enormous, obscure, and quite possibly counterproductive.[11] In this tutorial, we'll adopt a more pragmatic regex that has proven to be robust in practice. Here's what it looks like:

```
VALID_EMAIL_REGEX = /\A[\w+\-.]+@[a-z\d\-.]+\.[a-z]+\z/i
```

To help understand where this comes from, Table 6.1 breaks it into bite-sized pieces.[12]

Table 6.1: Breaking down the valid email regex.

Expression	Meaning
/\A[\w+\-.]+@[a-z\d\-.]+\.[a-z]+\z/i	full regex
/	start of regex
\A	match start of a string
[\w+\-.]+	at least one word character, plus, hyphen, or dot
@	literal "at sign"
[a-z\d\-.]+	at least one letter, digit, hyphen, or dot
\.	literal dot
[a-z]+	at least one letter
\z	match end of a string
/	end of regex
i	case-insensitive

---

11. For example, did you know that **"Michael Hartl"@example.com**, with quotation marks and a space in the middle, is a valid email address according to the standard? Incredibly, it is—but it's absurd.

12. Note that, in Table 6.1, "letter" really means "lowercase letter," but the **i** at the end of the regex enforces case-insensitive matching.

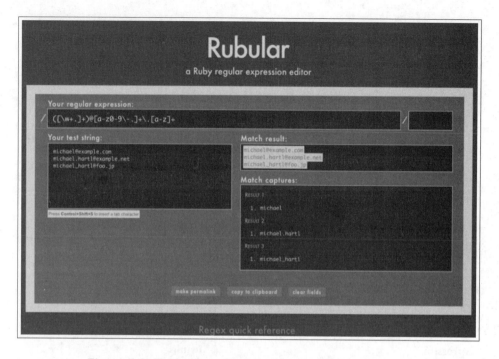

Figure 6.8: The awesome Rubular regular expression editor.

Although you can learn a lot by studying Table 6.1, to really understand regular expressions I consider using an interactive regular expression matcher like Rubular to be essential (Figure 6.8).[13] The Rubular website has a beautiful interactive interface for making regular expressions, along with a handy regex quick reference. I encourage you to study Table 6.1 with a browser window open to Rubular—no amount of reading about regular expressions can replace playing with them interactively. (*Note*: If you use the regex from Table 6.1 in Rubular, I recommend leaving off the **\A** and **\z** characters so that you can match more than one email address at a time in the given test string. Also note that the regex consists of the characters *inside* the slashes **/.../**, so you should omit those when using Rubular.)

Applying the regular expression from Table 6.1 to the **email** format validation yields the code in Listing 6.21.

---

13. If you find it as useful as I do, I encourage you to donate to Rubular to reward developer Michael Lovitt for his wonderful work.

Listing 6.21: Validating the email format with a regular expression. GREEN
`app/models/user.rb`

```
class User < ApplicationRecord
  validates :name,  presence: true, length: { maximum: 50 }
  VALID_EMAIL_REGEX = /\A[\w+\-.]+@[a-z\d\-.]+\.[a-z]+\z/i
  validates :email, presence: true, length: { maximum: 255 },
                    format: { with: VALID_EMAIL_REGEX }
end
```

Here the regex **VALID_EMAIL_REGEX** is a *constant*, indicated in Ruby by a name starting with a capital letter. The code

```
VALID_EMAIL_REGEX = /\A[\w+\-.]+@[a-z\d\-.]+\.[a-z]+\z/i
validates :email, presence: true, length: { maximum: 255 },
                  format: { with: VALID_EMAIL_REGEX }
```

ensures that only email addresses that match the pattern will be considered valid. (This expression has one minor weakness: It allows invalid addresses that contain consecutive dots, such as **foo@bar..com**. Updating the regex in Listing 6.21 to fix this blemish is left as an exercise (Section 6.2.4).)

At this point, the tests should be GREEN:

Listing 6.22: GREEN

```
$ rails test:models
```

This means that there's only one constraint left: enforcing email uniqueness.

Exercises

Solutions to the exercises are available to all Rails Tutorial purchasers at https://www.railstutorial.org/aw-solutions.

To see other people's answers and to record your own, subscribe to the Rails Tutorial course or to the Learn Enough All Access Bundle.

1. By pasting in the valid addresses from Listing 6.18 and invalid addresses from Listing 6.19 into the test string area at Rubular, confirm that the regex from Listing 6.21 matches all of the valid addresses and none of the invalid ones.

2. As noted earlier, the email regex in Listing 6.21 allows invalid email addresses with consecutive dots in the domain name—that is, addresses of the form *foo@bar..com*. Add this address to the list of invalid addresses in Listing 6.19 to get a failing test, and then use the more complicated regex shown in Listing 6.23 to get the test to pass.

3. Add *foo@bar..com* to the list of addresses at Rubular, and confirm that the regex shown in Listing 6.23 matches all the valid addresses and none of the invalid ones.

Listing 6.23: Disallowing double dots in email domain names. GREEN
`app/models/user.rb`

```ruby
class User < ApplicationRecord
  validates :name, presence: true, length: { maximum: 50 }
  VALID_EMAIL_REGEX = /\A[\w+\-.]+@[a-z\d\-]+(\.[a-z\d\-]+)*\.[a-z]+\z/i
  validates :email, presence:  true, length: { maximum: 255 },
                    format:      { with: VALID_EMAIL_REGEX }
end
```

6.2.5 Uniqueness Validation

To enforce uniqueness of email addresses (so that we can use them as usernames), we'll be using the **:uniqueness** option to the **validates** method. But be warned: There's a *major* caveat, so don't just skim this section—read it carefully.

We'll start with some short tests. In our previous model tests, we've mainly used **User.new**, which just creates a Ruby object in memory, but for uniqueness tests we actually need to put a record into the database.[14] The initial duplicate email test appears in Listing 6.24.

Listing 6.24: A test for the rejection of duplicate email addresses. RED
`test/models/user_test.rb`

```ruby
require 'test_helper'

class UserTest < ActiveSupport::TestCase
```

---

14. As noted briefly in the introduction to this section, there is a dedicated test database, **db/test.sqlite3**, for this purpose.

```
def setup
  @user = User.new(name: "Example User", email: "user@example.com")
end
  .
  .
  .
test "email addresses should be unique" do
  duplicate_user = @user.dup
  @user.save
  assert_not duplicate_user.valid?
end
end
```

The method here is to make a user with the same email address as **@user** using **@user.dup**, which creates a duplicate user with the same attributes. Since we then save **@user**, the duplicate user has an email address that already exists in the database, and hence should not be valid.

We can get the new test in Listing 6.24 to pass by adding **uniqueness: true** to the **email** validation, as shown in Listing 6.25.

Listing 6.25: Validating the uniqueness of email addresses. GREEN
app/models/user.rb

```
class User < ApplicationRecord
  validates :name,  presence: true, length: { maximum: 50 }
  VALID_EMAIL_REGEX = /\A[\w+\-.]+@[a-z\d\-.]+\.[a-z]+\z/i
  validates :email, presence: true, length: { maximum: 255 },
                    format: { with: VALID_EMAIL_REGEX },
                    uniqueness: true
end
```

We're not quite done, though. Email addresses are typically processed as if they were case-insensitive—that is, **foo@bar.com** is treated the same as **FOO@BAR.COM** or **FoO@BAr.coM**—so our validation should incorporate this as well.[15] It's thus important to test for case-insensitivity, which we do with the code in Listing 6.26.

---

15. Technically, only the domain part of the email address is case-insensitive: *foo@bar.com* is actually different from *Foo@bar.com*. In practice, though, it is a bad idea to rely on this fact; as noted at about.com, "Since the case sensitivity of email addresses can create a lot of confusion, interoperability problems and widespread headaches, it would be foolish to require email addresses to be typed with the correct case. Hardly any email

Listing 6.26: Testing case-insensitive email uniqueness. RED
`test/models/user_test.rb`

```ruby
require 'test_helper'

class UserTest < ActiveSupport::TestCase

  def setup
    @user = User.new(name: "Example User", email: "user@example.com")
  end
  .
  .
  .
  test "email addresses should be unique" do
    duplicate_user = @user.dup
    duplicate_user.email = @user.email.upcase
    @user.save
    assert_not duplicate_user.valid?
  end
end
```

Here we are using the **upcase** method on strings (seen briefly in Section 4.3.2). This test does the same thing as the initial duplicate email test, but with an uppercase email address instead. If this test feels a little abstract, go ahead and fire up the console:

```
$ rails console --sandbox
>> user = User.create(name: "Example User", email: "user@example.com")
>> user.email.upcase
=> "USER@EXAMPLE.COM"
>> duplicate_user = user.dup
>> duplicate_user.email = user.email.upcase
>> duplicate_user.valid?
=> true
```

Of course, **duplicate_user.valid?** is currently **true** because the uniqueness validation is case-sensitive, but we want it to be **false**. Fortunately, **:uniqueness** accepts an option, **:case_sensitive**, for just this purpose (Listing 6.27).

---

service or ISP does enforce case sensitive email addresses, returning messages whose recipient's email address was not typed correctly (in all upper case, for example)." Thanks to reader Riley Moses for pointing this out.

Listing 6.27: Validating the uniqueness of email addresses, ignoring case. GREEN
`app/models/user.rb`

```ruby
class User < ApplicationRecord
  validates :name,  presence: true, length: { maximum: 50 }
  VALID_EMAIL_REGEX = /\A[\w+\-.]+@[a-z\d\-.]+\.[a-z]+\z/i
  validates :email, presence: true, length: { maximum: 255 },
                    format: { with: VALID_EMAIL_REGEX },
                    uniqueness: case_sensitive: false
end
```

Note that we have simply replaced **true** in Listing 6.25 with **case_sensi
tive: false** in Listing 6.27. (Rails infers that **uniqueness** should be **true**
as well.)

At this point, our application—with an important caveat—enforces email uniqueness, and our test suite should pass:

Listing 6.28: GREEN

```
$ rails test
```

There's just one small problem, which is that *the Active Record uniqueness validation
does not guarantee uniqueness at the database level.* Here's a scenario that explains why:

1. Alice signs up for the sample app, with address alice@wonderland.com.

2. Alice accidentally clicks on "Submit" *twice*, sending two requests in quick
   succession.

3. The following sequence occurs: Request 1 creates a user in memory that passes
   validation, request 2 does the same, request 1's user gets saved, request 2's user gets
   saved.

4. Result: two user records with the exact same email address, despite the uniqueness
   validation.

If this sequence seems implausible, believe me, it isn't: It can happen on any Rails website with significant traffic (which I once learned the hard way). Luckily, the solution
is straightforward to implement: We just need to enforce uniqueness at the database

level as well as at the model level. Our method is to create a database *index* on the email column (Box 6.2), and then require that the index be unique.

Box 6.2: Database Indices

When creating a column in a database, it is important to consider whether we will need to *find* records by that column. Consider, for example, the `email` attribute created by the migration in Listing 6.2. When we allow users to log in to the sample app starting in Chapter 7, we will need to find the user record corresponding to the submitted email address. Unfortunately, based on the naïve data model, the only way to find a user by email address is to look through *each* user row in the database and compare its email attribute to the given email—which means we might have to examine *every* row (since the user could be the last one in the database). This is known in the database business as a *full-table scan*, and for a real site with thousands of users it is a Bad Thing.

Putting an index on the email column fixes the problem. To understand a database index, it's helpful to consider the analogy of a book index. In a book, to find all the occurrences of a given string, say "foobar," you would have to scan each page for "foobar"—the paper version of a full-table scan. With a book index, on the other hand, you can just look up "foobar" in the index to see all the pages containing "foobar." A database index works essentially the same way.

The email index represents an update to our data modeling requirements, which (as discussed in Section 6.1.1) is handled in Rails using migrations. We saw in Section 6.1.1 that generating the User model automatically created a new migration (Listing 6.2); in the present case, we are adding structure to an existing model, so we need to create a migration directly using the **migration** generator:

```
$ rails generate migration add_index_to_users_email
```

Unlike the migration for users, the email uniqueness migration is not pre-defined, so we need to fill in its contents with Listing 6.29.[16]

---

16. Of course, we could just edit the migration file for the **users** table in Listing 6.2, but that would require rolling back and then migrating back up. The Rails Way™ is to use migrations every time we discover that our data model needs to change.

Listing 6.29: The migration for enforcing email uniqueness.
db/migrate/[timestamp]_add_index_to_users_email.rb

```
class AddIndexToUsersEmail < ActiveRecord::Migration[6.0]
  def change
    add_index :users, :email, unique: true
  end
end
```

This uses a Rails method called **add_index** to add an index on the **email** column of the **users** table. The index by itself doesn't enforce uniqueness, but the option **unique: true** does.

The final step is to migrate the database:

```
$ rails db:migrate
```

(If the migration fails, make sure to exit any running sandbox console sessions, which can lock the database and prevent migrations.)

At this point, the test suite should be RED due to a violation of the uniqueness constraint in the *fixtures*, which contain sample data for the test database. User fixtures were generated automatically in Listing 6.1, and as shown in Listing 6.30 the email addresses are not unique. (They're not *valid* either, but fixture data doesn't get run through the validations.)

Listing 6.30: The default user fixtures. RED
test/fixtures/users.yml

```
# Read about fixtures at https://api.rubyonrails.org/classes/ActiveRecord/
# FixtureSet.html

one:
  name: MyString
  email: MyString

two:
  name: MyString
  email: MyString
```

Because we won't need fixtures until Chapter 8, for now we'll just remove them, leaving an empty fixtures file (Listing 6.31).

Listing 6.31: An empty fixtures file. GREEN
`test/fixtures/users.yml`

```
# empty
```

Having addressed the uniqueness caveat, there's one more change we need to make to be assured of email uniqueness. Some database adapters use case-sensitive indices, considering the strings "Foo@ExAMPle.CoM" and "foo@example.com" to be distinct, but our application treats those addresses as the same. To avoid this incompatibility, we'll standardize on all lower-case addresses, converting "Foo@ExAMPle.CoM" to "foo@example.com" before saving it to the database. The way to do this is with a *callback*, which is a method that gets invoked at a particular point in the life cycle of an Active Record object.

In the present case, that point is before the object is saved, so we'll use a **before_save** callback to downcase the email attribute before saving the user.[17] The result appears in Listing 6.32. (This is just a first implementation; we'll discuss this subject again in Section 11.1, where we'll use the preferred *method reference* convention for defining callbacks.)

Listing 6.32: Ensuring email uniqueness by downcasing the email attribute. RED
`app/models/user.rb`

```
class User < ApplicationRecord
  before_save { self.email = email.downcase }
  validates :name,  presence: true, length: { maximum: 50 }
  VALID_EMAIL_REGEX = /\A[\w+\-.]+@[a-z\d\-.]+\.[a-z]+\z/i
  validates :email, presence: true, length: { maximum: 255 },
                    format: { with: VALID_EMAIL_REGEX },
                    uniqueness: true
end
```

The code in Listing 6.32 passes a block to the **before_save** callback and sets the user's email address to a lowercase version of its current value using the **downcase** string method. Note also that Listing 6.32 reverts the **uniqueness** constraint back to **true**,

---

17. See the Rails API entry on callbacks for more information on which callbacks Rails supports.

since case-sensitive matching works fine if all of the email addresses are lowercase. Indeed, this practice prevents problems applying the database index from Listing 6.29, since many databases have difficulty using an index when combined with a case-insensitive match.[18]

Restoring the original constraint does break the test in Listing 6.26, but that's easy to fix by reverting the test to its previous form from Listing 6.24, as shown again in Listing 6.33.

Listing 6.33: Restoring the original email uniqueness test. GREEN
`test/models/user_test.rb`

```ruby
require 'test_helper'

class UserTest < ActiveSupport::TestCase

  def setup
    @user = User.new(name: "Example User", email: "user@example.com")
  end
  .
  .
  .
  test "email addresses should be unique" do
    duplicate_user = @user.dup
    @user.save
    assert_not duplicate_user.valid?
  end
end
```

By the way, in Listing 6.32 we could have written the assignment as

```ruby
self.email = self.email.downcase
```

(where **self** refers to the current user), but inside the User model the **self** keyword is optional on the right-hand side:

```ruby
self.email = email.downcase
```

---

18. Thanks to reader Alex Friedman for pointing this out.

We encountered this idea briefly in the context of **reverse** in the **palindrome** method (Section 4.4.2), which also noted that **self** is *not* optional in an assignment, so

```
email = email.downcase
```

wouldn't work. (We'll discuss this subject in more depth in Section 9.1.)

At this point, the Alice scenario described earlier will work fine: The database will save a user record based on the first request, and it will reject the second save because the duplicate email address violates the uniqueness constraint. (An error will appear in the Rails log, but that doesn't do any harm.) Moreover, adding this index on the email attribute accomplishes a second goal, alluded to briefly in Section 6.1.4: As noted in Box 6.2, the index on the **email** attribute fixes a potential efficiency problem by preventing a full-table scan when finding users by email address.

Exercises

Solutions to the exercises are available to all Rails Tutorial purchasers at https://www.railstutorial.org/aw-solutions.

To see other people's answers and to record your own, subscribe to the Rails Tutorial course or to the Learn Enough All Access Bundle.

1. Add a test for the email downcasing from Listing 6.32, as shown in Listing 6.34. This test uses the **reload** method for reloading a value from the database and the **assert_equal** method for testing equality. To verify that Listing 6.34 tests the right thing, comment out the **before_save** line to get to RED, then uncomment it to get to GREEN.

2. By running the test suite, verify that the **before_save** callback can be written using the "bang" method **email.downcase!** to modify the **email** attribute directly, as shown in Listing 6.35.

Listing 6.34: A test for the email downcasing from Listing 6.32.
test/models/user_test.rb

```ruby
require 'test_helper'

class UserTest < ActiveSupport::TestCase

  def setup
    @user = User.new(name: "Example User", email: "user@example.com")
```

```
  end
  .
  .
  .
  test "email addresses should be unique" do
    duplicate_user = @user.dup
    @user.save
    assert_not duplicate_user.valid?
  end

  test "email addresses should be saved as lowercase" do
    mixed_case_email = "Foo@ExAMPle.CoM"
    @user.email = mixed_case_email
    @user.save
    assert_equal mixed_case_email.downcase, @user.reload.email
  end
end
```

Listing 6.35: An alternative callback implementation. GREEN
app/models/user.rb

```
class User < ApplicationRecord
  before_save { email.downcase! }
  validates :name, presence: true, length: { maximum: 50 }
  VALID_EMAIL_REGEX = /\A[\w+\-.]+@[a-z\d\-.]+\.[a-z]+\z/i
  validates :email, presence: true, length: { maximum: 255 },
                    format: { with: VALID_EMAIL_REGEX },
                    uniqueness: true
end
```

6.3 Adding a Secure Password

Now that we've defined validations for the name and email fields, we're ready to add the last of the basic User attributes: a secure password. The method is to require each user to have a password (with a password confirmation), and then store a *hashed* version of the password in the database. (There is some potential for confusion here. In the present context, a *hash* refers not to the Ruby data structure from Section 4.3.3 but rather to the result of applying an irreversible hash function to input data.) We'll also add a way to *authenticate* a user based on a given password, a method we'll use in Chapter 8 to allow users to log in to the site.

The method for authenticating users will be to take a submitted password, hash it, and compare the result to the hashed value stored in the database. If the two match, then the submitted password is correct and the user is authenticated. By comparing hashed values instead of raw passwords, we will be able to authenticate users without storing the passwords themselves. This means that, even if our database is compromised, our users' passwords will still be secure.

6.3.1 A Hashed Password

Most of the secure password machinery will be implemented using a single Rails method called **has_secure_password**, which we'll include in the User model as follows:

```
class User < ApplicationRecord
  .
  .
  .
  has_secure_password
end
```

When included in a model as shown here, this one method adds the following functionality:

- The ability to save a securely hashed **password_digest** attribute to the database

- A pair of virtual attributes[19] (**password** and **password_confirmation**), including presence validations upon object creation and a validation requiring that they match

- An **authenticate** method that returns the user when the password is correct (and **false** otherwise)

The only requirement for **has_secure_password** to work its magic is for the corresponding model to have an attribute called **password_digest**. (The name *digest*

---

19. In this context, *virtual* means that the attributes exist on the model object but do not correspond to columns in the database.

users	
`id`	integer
`name`	string
`email`	string
`created_at`	datetime
`updated_at`	datetime
`password_digest`	string

Figure 6.9: The User data model with an added `password_digest` attribute.

comes from the terminology of cryptographic hash functions. In this context, *hashed password* and *password digest* are synonyms.)[20] In the case of the User model, this leads to the data model shown in Figure 6.9.

To implement the data model in Figure 6.9, we first generate an appropriate migration for the **password_digest** column. We can choose any migration name we want, but it's convenient to end the name with **to_users**, since in this case Rails automatically constructs a migration to add columns to the **users** table. The result, with migration name **add_password_digest_to_users**, appears as follows:

```
$ rails generate migration add_password_digest_to_users password_digest:string
```

Here we've also supplied the argument **password_digest:string** with the name and type of attribute we want to create. (Compare this to the original

---

20. Hashed password digests are often erroneously referred to as *encrypted passwords*. For example, the source code of **has_secure_password** makes this mistake, as did the first two editions of this tutorial. This terminology is wrong because by design encryption is *reversible*—the ability to encrypt implies the ability to *decrypt* as well. In contrast, the whole point of calculating a password's hash digest is to be *irreversible*, so that it is computationally intractable to infer the original password from the digest. (Thanks to reader Andy Philips for pointing out this issue and for encouraging me to fix the broken terminology.)

generation of the **users** table in Listing 6.1, which included the arguments **name:string** and **email:string**.) By including **password_digest:string**, we've given Rails enough information to construct the entire migration for us, as seen in Listing 6.36.

Listing 6.36: The migration to add a **password_digest** column.
`db/migrate/[timestamp]_add_password_digest_to_users.rb`

```
class AddPasswordDigestToUsers < ActiveRecord::Migration[6.0]
  def change
    add_column :users, :password_digest, :string
  end
end
```

Listing 6.36 uses the **add_column** method to add a **password_digest** column to the **users** table. To apply it, we just migrate the database:

```
$ rails db:migrate
```

To make the password digest, **has_secure_password** uses a state-of-the-art hash function called bcrypt. By hashing the password with bcrypt, we ensure that attackers won't be able to log in to the site even if they manage to obtain a copy of the database. To use bcrypt in the sample application, we need to add the bcrypt gem to our **Gemfile** (Listing 6.37).[21]

Listing 6.37: Adding **bcrypt** to the **Gemfile**.

```
source 'https://rubygems.org'

gem 'rails',           '6.0.2.1'
gem 'bcrypt',          '3.1.13'
gem 'bootstrap-sass', '3.4.1'
 .
 .
 .
```

---

21. As always, you should use the version numbers listed at gemfiles-6th-ed.railstutorial.org instead of the ones listed here.

Then run **bundle install** as usual:

```
$ bundle install
```

6.3.2 User Has Secure Password

Now that we've supplied the User model with the required **password_digest** attribute and installed bcrypt, we're ready to add **has_secure_password** to the User model, as shown in Listing 6.38.

Listing 6.38: Adding **has_secure_password** to the User model. RED
`app/models/user.rb`

```
class User < ApplicationRecord
  before_save { self.email = email.downcase }
  validates :name, presence: true, length: { maximum: 50 }
  VALID_EMAIL_REGEX = /\A[\w+\-.]+@[a-z\d\-.]+\.[a-z]+\z/i
  validates :email, presence: true, length: { maximum: 255 },
                    format: { with: VALID_EMAIL_REGEX },
                    uniqueness: true
  has_secure_password
end
```

As indicated by the RED indicator in Listing 6.38, the tests are now failing, as you can confirm at the command line:

Listing 6.39: RED

```
$ rails test
```

The reason is that, as noted in Section 6.3.1, **has_secure_password** enforces validations on the virtual **password** and **password_confirmation** attributes, but the tests in Listing 6.26 create an **@user** variable without these attributes:

```
def setup
  @user = User.new(name: "Example User", email: "user@example.com")
end
```

So, to get the test suite passing again, we just need to add a password and its confirmation, as shown in Listing 6.40.

Listing 6.40: Adding a password and its confirmation. GREEN
`test/models/user_test.rb`

```
require 'test_helper'

class UserTest < ActiveSupport::TestCase

  def setup
    @user = User.new(name: "Example User", email: "user@example.com",
                     password: "foobar", password_confirmation: "foobar")
  end
  .
  .
  .
end
```

Note that the first line inside the **setup** method includes an additional comma at the end, as required by Ruby's hash syntax (Section 4.3.3). Leaving this comma off will produce a syntax error, and you should use your technical sophistication (Box 1.2) to identify and resolve such errors if (or, more realistically, when) they occur.

At this point the tests should be GREEN:

Listing 6.41: GREEN

```
$ rails test
```

In just a moment we'll see the benefits of adding **has_secure_password** to the User model (Section 6.3.4), but first we'll add a minimal requirement on password security.

Exercises

Solutions to the exercises are available to all Rails Tutorial purchasers at https://www.railstutorial.org/aw-solutions.

To see other people's answers and to record your own, subscribe to the Rails Tutorial course or to the Learn Enough All Access Bundle.

1. Confirm that a user with a valid name and email still isn't valid overall.

2. What are the error messages for a user with no password?

6.3.3 Minimum Password Standards

It's good practice in general to enforce some minimum standards on passwords to make them harder to guess. There are many options for enforcing password strength in Rails, but for simplicity we'll just enforce a minimum length and the requirement that the password not be blank. Picking a length of 6 as a reasonable minimum leads to the validation test shown in Listing 6.42.

Listing 6.42: Testing for a minimum password length. RED
`test/models/user_test.rb`

```ruby
require 'test_helper'

class UserTest < ActiveSupport::TestCase

  def setup
    @user = User.new(name: "Example User", email: "user@example.com",
                     password: "foobar", password_confirmation: "foobar")
  end
  .
  .
  .
  test "password should be present (nonblank)" do
    @user.password = @user.password_confirmation = " " * 6
    assert_not @user.valid?
  end

  test "password should have a minimum length" do
    @user.password = @user.password_confirmation = "a" * 5
    assert_not @user.valid?
  end
end
```

Note the use of the compact multiple assignment

```ruby
@user.password = @user.password_confirmation = "a" * 5
```

in Listing 6.42. This arranges to assign a particular value to the password and its confirmation at the same time (in this case, a string of length 5, constructed using string multiplication as in Listing 6.14).

You may be able to guess the code for enforcing a **minimum** length constraint by referring to the corresponding **maximum** validation for the user's name (Listing 6.16):

```
validates :password, length: { minimum: 6 }
```

Combining this with a **presence** validation (Section 6.2.2) to ensure non-blank passwords, this leads to the User model shown in Listing 6.43. (It turns out the **has_secure_password** method includes a presence validation, but unfortunately it applies only to records with *empty* passwords, which allows users to create invalid passwords like '   ' (six spaces).)

Listing 6.43: The complete implementation for secure passwords. GREEN
app/models/user.rb

```
class User < ApplicationRecord
  before_save { self.email = email.downcase }
  validates :name, presence: true, length: { maximum: 50 }
  VALID_EMAIL_REGEX = /\A[\w+\-.]+@[a-z\d\-.]+\.[a-z]+\z/i
  validates :email, presence: true, length: { maximum: 255 },
                    format: { with: VALID_EMAIL_REGEX },
                    uniqueness: true
  has_secure_password
  validates :password, presence: true, length: { minimum: 6 }
end
```

At this point, the tests should be GREEN:

Listing 6.44: GREEN

```
$ rails test:models
```

Exercises

Solutions to the exercises are available to all Rails Tutorial purchasers at https://www.railstutorial.org/aw-solutions.

To see other people's answers and to record your own, subscribe to the Rails Tutorial course or to the Learn Enough All Access Bundle.

1. Confirm that a user with a valid name and email but a too-short password isn't valid.

2. What are the associated error messages?

6.3.4 Creating and Authenticating a User

Now that the basic User model is complete, we'll create a user in the database as preparation for making a page to show the user's information in Section 7.1. We'll also take a more concrete look at the effects of adding **has_secure_password** to the User model, including an examination of the important **authenticate** method.

Since users can't yet sign up for the sample application through the web—that's the goal of Chapter 7—we'll use the Rails console to create a new user by hand. For convenience, we'll use the **create** method discussed in Section 6.1.3, but in the present case we'll take care *not* to start in a sandbox so that the resulting user will be saved to the database. This means starting an ordinary **rails console** session and then creating a user with a valid name and email address together with a valid password and matching confirmation:

```
$ rails console
>> User.create(name: "Michael Hartl", email: "michael@example.com",
?>             password: "foobar", password_confirmation: "foobar")
=> #<User id: 1, name: "Michael Hartl", email: "michael@example.com",
created_at: "2019-08-22 03:15:38", updated_at: "2019-08-22 03:15:38",
password_digest: [FILTERED]>
```

To check that this worked, let's look at the resulting **users** table in the development database using DB Browser for SQLite, as shown in Figure 6.10.[22] (If you're using the cloud IDE, you should download the database file as in Figure 6.5.) Note that the columns correspond to the attributes of the data model defined in Figure 6.9.

Returning to the console, we can see the effect of **has_secure_password** from Listing 6.43 by looking at the **password_digest** attribute:

---

22. If for any reason something went wrong, you can always reset the database as follows:

1. Quit the console.

2. Run **$ rm -f development.sqlite3** at the command line to remove the database. (We'll learn a more elegant method for doing this in Chapter 7.)

3. Rerun the migrations using **$ rails db:migrate**.

4. Restart the console.

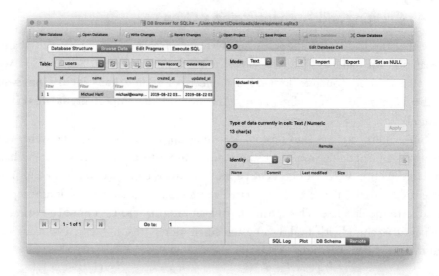

Figure 6.10: A user row in the SQLite database **db/development.sqlite3**.

```
>> user = User.find_by(email: "michael@example.com")
>> user.password_digest
=> "$2a$12$WgjER5ovLFjC2hmCItmbTe6nAXzT3bO66GiAQ83Ev03eVp32zyNYG"
```

This is the hashed version of the password (**"foobar"**) used to initialize the user object. Because it's constructed using bcrypt, it is computationally impractical to use the digest to discover the original password.[23]

As noted in Section 6.3.1, **has_secure_password** automatically adds an **authenticate** method to the corresponding model objects. This method determines if a given password is valid for a particular user by computing its digest and comparing the result to **password_digest** in the database. In the case of the user we just created, we can try a couple of invalid passwords as follows:

```
>> user.authenticate("not_the_right_password")
false
```

---

23. By design, the bcrypt algorithm produces a *salted hash*, which protects against two important classes of attacks (dictionary attacks and rainbow table attacks).

```
>> user.authenticate("foobaz")
false
```

Here **user.authenticate** returns **false** for an invalid password. If we instead authenticate with the correct password, **authenticate** returns the user itself:

```
>> user.authenticate("foobar")
=> #<User id: 1, name: "Michael Hartl", email: "michael@example.com",
created_at: "2019-08-22 03:15:38", updated_at: "2019-08-22 03:15:38",
password_digest: [FILTERED]>
```

In Chapter 8, we'll use the **authenticate** method to sign registered users into our site. In fact, it will turn out not to be important to us that **authenticate** returns the user itself; all that will matter is that it returns a value that is **true** in a boolean context. Recalling from Section 4.2.2 that **!!** converts an object to its corresponding boolean value, we can see that **user.authenticate** does the job nicely:

```
>> !!user.authenticate("foobar")
=> true
```

Exercises

Solutions to the exercises are available to all Rails Tutorial purchasers at https://www.railstutorial.org/aw-solutions.

To see other people's answers and to record your own, subscribe to the Rails Tutorial course or to the Learn Enough All Access Bundle.

1. Quit and restart the console, and then find the user created in this section.
2. Try changing the name by assigning a new name and calling **save**. Why didn't it work?
3. Update **user**'s name to use your name. *Hint*: The necessary technique is covered in Section 6.1.5.

6.4 Conclusion

Starting from scratch, in this chapter we created a working User model with name, email, and password attributes, together with validations enforcing several important constraints on their values. In addition, we have the ability to securely authenticate users using a given password. This is a remarkable amount of functionality for only 12 lines of code.

In Chapter 7, we'll make a working signup form to create new users, together with a page to display each user's information. In Chapter 8, we'll then use the authentication machinery from Section 6.3 to let users log into the site.

If you're using Git, now would be a good time to commit if you haven't done so in a while:

```
$ rails test
$ git add -A
$ git commit -m "Make a basic User model (including secure passwords)"
```

Then merge back into the master branch and push to the remote repository:

```
$ git checkout master
$ git merge modeling-users
$ git push
```

To get the User model working in production, we need to run the migrations at Heroku, which we can do with **heroku run**:

```
$ rails test
$ git push heroku
$ heroku run rails db:migrate
```

We can verify that this worked by running a console in production:

```
$ heroku run rails console --sandbox
>> User.create(name: "Michael Hartl", email: "michael@example.com",
?>            password: "foobar", password_confirmation: "foobar")
=> #<User id: 1, name: "Michael Hartl", email: "michael@example.com",
created_at: "2019-08-22 03:20:06", updated_at: "2019-08-22 03:20:06",
password_digest: [FILTERED]>
```

6.4.1 What We Learned in this Chapter

- Migrations allow us to modify our application's data model.

- Active Record comes with a large number of methods for creating and manipulating data models.

- Active Record validations allow us to place constraints on the data in our models.

- Common validations include presence, length, and format.

- Regular expressions are cryptic but powerful.

- Defining a database index improves lookup efficiency while allowing enforcement of uniqueness at the database level.

- We can add a secure password to a model using the built-in **has_secure_password** method.

CHAPTER 7
Sign Up

Now that we have a working User model, it's time to add a capability that few websites can live without: letting users sign up. We'll use an HTML *form* to submit user signup information to our application (Section 7.2), which will then be used to create a new user and save its attributes to the database (Section 7.4). At the end of the signup process, it's important to render a profile page with the newly created user's information, so we'll begin by making a page for *showing* users, which will serve as the first step toward implementing the REST architecture for users (Section 2.2.2). Along the way, we'll build on our work in Section 5.3.4 to write succinct and expressive integration tests.

In this chapter, we'll rely on the User model validations from Chapter 6 to increase the odds of new users having valid email addresses. In Chapter 11, we'll make *sure* of email validity by adding a separate *account activation* step to user signup.

Although this tutorial is designed to be as simple as possible while still being professional-grade, web development is a complicated subject, and Chapter 7 necessarily marks a significant increase in the difficulty of the exposition. I recommend taking your time with the material and reviewing it as necessary. (Some readers have reported simply doing the chapter twice is a helpful exercise.) You might also consider subscribing to the courses at Learn Enough to gain additional assistance, both with this tutorial and with its relevant prerequisites (especially *Learn Enough Ruby to Be Dangerous* (www.learnenough.com/ruby)).

7.1 Showing Users

In this section, we'll take the first steps toward the final profile by making a page to display a user's name and profile photo, as indicated by the mockup in Figure 7.1.[1] Our eventual goal for the user profile pages is to show the user's profile image, basic user data, and a list of microposts, as mocked up in Figure 7.2.[2] (Figure 7.2 includes

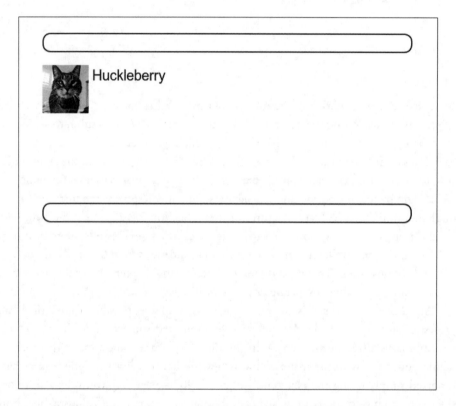

Figure 7.1: A mockup of the user profile made in this section.

---

1. Mockingbird doesn't support custom images like the profile photo in Figure 7.1; I put that in by hand using GIMP.

2. Image retrieved from https://www.flickr.com/photos/43803060@N00/24308857/ on 2014-06-16. Copyright © 2002 by Shaun Wallin and used unaltered under the terms of the Creative Commons Attribution 2.0 Generic license.

Figure 7.2: A mockup of our best guess at the final profile page.

an example of *lorem ipsum* text, which has a fascinating story that you should definitely read about some time.) We'll complete this task, and with it the sample application, in Chapter 14.

If you're following along with version control, make a topic branch as usual:

```
$ git checkout -b sign-up
```

7.1.1   Debug and Rails Environments

The profiles in this section will be the first truly dynamic pages in our application. Although the view will exist as a single page of code, each profile will be customized using information retrieved from the application's database. As preparation for adding dynamic pages to our sample application, now is a good time to add some debug information to our site layout (Listing 7.1). This displays some useful information about each page using the built-in **debug** method and **params** variable (which we'll learn more about in Section 7.1.2).

Listing 7.1: Adding some debug information to the site layout.
`app/views/layouts/application.html.erb`

```
<!DOCTYPE html>
<html>
  .
  .
  .
  <body>
    <%= render 'layouts/header' %>
    <div class="container">
      <%= yield %>
      <%= render 'layouts/footer' %>
      <%= debug(params) if Rails.env.development? %>
    </div>
  </body>
</html>
```

Since we don't want to display debug information to users of a deployed application, Listing 7.1 uses

```
if Rails.env.development?
```

to restrict the debug information to the *development environment*, which is one of three environments defined by default in Rails (Box 7.1).[3] In particular, **Rails.env.development?** is **true** only in a development environment, so the embedded Ruby

```
<%= debug(params) if Rails.env.development? %>
```

won't be inserted into production applications or tests. (Inserting the debug information into tests probably wouldn't do any harm, but it probably wouldn't do any good, either—so it's best to restrict the debug display to development only.)

---

3. You can define your own custom environments as well; see the RailsCast on adding an environment for details.

Box 7.1: Rails Environments

Rails comes equipped with three environments: test, development, and production. The default environment for the Rails console is development:

```
$ rails console
Loading development environment
>> Rails.env
=> "development"
>> Rails.env.development?
=> true
>> Rails.env.test?
=> false
```

As you can see, Rails provides a Rails object with an env attribute and associated environment boolean methods, so that, for example, Rails.env.test? returns true in a test environment and false otherwise.

If you ever need to run a console in a different environment (to debug a test, for example), you can pass the environment as a parameter to the console script:

```
$ rails console test
Loading test environment
>> Rails.env
=> "test"
>> Rails.env.test?
=> true
```

As with the console, development is the default environment for the Rails server, but you can also run it in a different environment:

```
$ rails server --environment production
```

If you view your app running in production, it won't work without a production database, which we can create by running rails db:migrate in production:

```
$ rails db:migrate RAILS_ENV=production
```

(I find it confusing that the idiomatic commands to run the console, server, and migrate commands in nondefault environments use different syntax, which is why I bothered to show all three. It's worth noting, though, that preceding any of them with RAILS_ENV=<env> will also work, as in RAILS_ENV=production rails server.)

> By the way, if you have deployed your sample app to Heroku, you can see its
> environment using `heroku run rails console`:
>
> ```
> $ heroku run rails console
> >> Rails.env
> => "production"
> >> Rails.env.production?
> => true
> ```
>
> Naturally, since Heroku is a platform for production sites, it runs each application
> in a production environment.

To make the debug output look nice, we'll add some rules to the custom stylesheet
created in Chapter 5, as shown in Listing 7.2.

Listing 7.2: Adding code for a pretty debug box, including a Sass mixin.
`app/assets/stylesheets/custom.scss`

```
@import "bootstrap-sprockets";
@import "bootstrap";

/* mixins, variables, etc. */

$gray-medium-light: #eaeaea;

@mixin box_sizing {
  -moz-box-sizing:    border-box;
  -webkit-box-sizing: border-box;
  box-sizing:         border-box;
}
.
.
.
/* miscellaneous */

.debug_dump {
  clear: both;
  float: left;
  width: 100%;
  margin-top:45px;
  @include box_sizing;
}
```

This introduces the Sass *mixin* facility, in this case called **box_sizing**. A mixin allows
a group of CSS rules to be packaged up and used for multiple elements, converting

```
.debug_dump {
    .
    .
    .
    @include box_sizing;
}
```

to

```
.debug_dump {
    .
    .
    .
    -moz-box-sizing:      border-box;
    -webkit-box-sizing:   border-box;
    box-sizing:           border-box;
}
```

We'll put this mixin to use again in Section 7.2.1. The result in the case of the debug box is shown in Figure 7.3.[4]

The debug output in Figure 7.3 gives potentially useful information about the page being rendered:

```
---
controller: static_pages
action: home
```

This is a YAML[5] representation of **params**, which is basically a hash, and in this case identifies the controller and action for the page. We'll see another example in Section 7.1.2.

Exercises

Solutions to the exercises are available to all Rails Tutorial purchasers at https:// www.railstutorial.org/aw-solutions.

To see other people's answers and to record your own, subscribe to the Rails Tutorial course or to the Learn Enough All Access Bundle.

---

4. The exact appearance of the Rails debug information is slightly version-dependent. For example, as of Rails 5 the debug information shows the **permitted** status of the information, a subject we'll cover in Section 7.3.2. Use your technical sophistication (Box 1.2) to resolve such minor discrepancies.

5. The Rails **debug** information is shown as YAML (a recursive acronym standing for "YAML Ain't Markup Language"), which is a friendly data format designed to be both machine- *and* human-readable.

Figure 7.3: The sample application Home page with debug information.

1. Visit /about in your browser and use the debug information to determine the controller and action of the **params** hash.

2. In the Rails console, pull the first user out of the database and assign it to the variable **user**. What is the output of **puts user.attributes.to_yaml**? Compare this to using the **y** method via **y user.attributes**.

7.1.2 A Users Resource

To make a user profile page, we need to have a user in the database, which introduces a chicken-and-egg problem: How can the site have a user before there is a working signup page? Happily, this problem has already been solved: In Section 6.3.4, we created a User record by hand using the Rails console, so there should be one user in the database:

```
$ rails console
>> User.count
=> 1
>> User.first
=> #<User id: 1, name: "Michael Hartl", email: "mhartl@example.com",
created_at: "2019-08-22 03:15:38", updated_at: "2019-08-22 03:15:38",
password_digest: [FILTERED]>
```

(If you don't currently have a user in your database, you should visit Section 6.3.4 now and complete it before proceeding.) We see from this console output that the user has id **1**, and our goal now is to make a page to display this user's information. We'll follow the conventions of the REST architecture favored in Rails applications (Box 2.2), which means representing data as *resources* that can be created, shown, updated, or destroyed—four actions corresponding to the four fundamental operations POST, GET, PATCH, and DELETE defined by the HTTP standard (Box 3.2).

When following REST principles, resources are typically referenced using the resource name and a unique identifier. What this means in the context of users— which we're now thinking of as a Users *resource*—is that we should view the user with id **1** by issuing a GET request to the URL /users/1. Here the **show** action is *implicit* in the type of request: When Rails' REST features are activated, GET requests are automatically handled by the **show** action.

We saw in Section 2.2.1 that the page for a user with id **1** has URL /users/1. Unfortunately, visiting that URL right now just gives an error (Figure 7.4).

We can get the routing for /users/1 to work by adding a single line to our routes file (**config/routes.rb**):

```
resources :users
```

The result appears in Listing 7.3.

Listing 7.3: Adding a Users resource to the routes file.
config/routes.rb

```
Rails.application.routes.draw do
  root 'static_pages#home'
  get  '/help',   to: 'static_pages#help'
  get  '/about',  to: 'static_pages#about'
```

```
get  '/contact', to: 'static_pages#contact'
get  '/signup',  to: 'users#new'
resources :users
end
```

Although our immediate motivation is making a page to show users, the single line **resources :users** doesn't just add a working /users/1 URL: It endows our sample application with *all* the actions needed for a RESTful Users resource,[6] along with a large number of named routes (Section 5.3.3) for generating user URLs. The resulting correspondence of URLs, actions, and named routes is shown in Table 7.1. (Compare this table to Table 2.2.) Over the course of the next three chapters, we'll

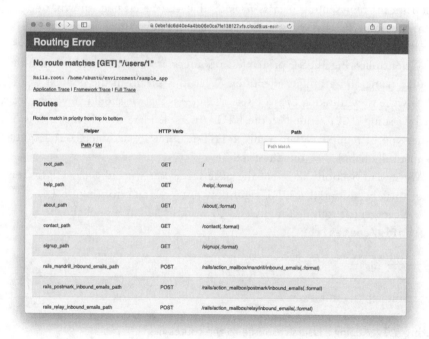

Figure 7.4: The current state of /users/1.

---

6. The *routing* works, but the corresponding pages don't necessarily work at this point. For example, /users/1/edit gets routed properly to the **edit** action of the Users controller, but since the **edit** action doesn't exist yet actually hitting that URL will return an error.

Table 7.1: RESTful routes provided by the Users resource in Listing 7.3.

HTTP request	URL	Action	Named route	Purpose
GET	/users	**index**	**users_path**	page to list all users
GET	/users/1	**show**	**user_path(user)**	page to show user
GET	/users/new	**new**	**new_user_path**	page to make a new user (signup)
POST	/users	**create**	**users_path**	create a new user
GET	/users/1/edit	**edit**	**edit_user_path(user)**	page to edit user with id **1**
PATCH	/users/1	**update**	**user_path(user)**	update user
DELETE	/users/1	**destroy**	**user_path(user)**	delete user

cover all of the other entries in Table 7.1 as we fill in all the actions necessary to make Users a fully RESTful resource.

With the code in Listing 7.3, the routing works, but there's still no page there (Figure 7.5). To fix this, we'll begin with a minimalist version of the profile page, which we'll flesh out in Section 7.1.4.

We'll use the standard Rails location for showing a user, which is **app/views/-users/show.html.erb**. Unlike the **new.html.erb** view, which we created with the generator in Listing 5.38, the **show.html.erb** file doesn't currently exist, so you'll have to create it by hand,[7] and then fill it with the content shown in Listing 7.4.

Listing 7.4: A stub view for showing user information.
app/views/users/show.html.erb

```
<%= @user.name %>, <%= @user.email %>
```

This view uses embedded Ruby to display the user's name and email address, assuming the existence of an instance variable called **@user**. Of course, eventually the real user show page will look very different (and won't display the email address publicly).

---

7. Using, for example, **touch app/views/users/show.html.erb**.

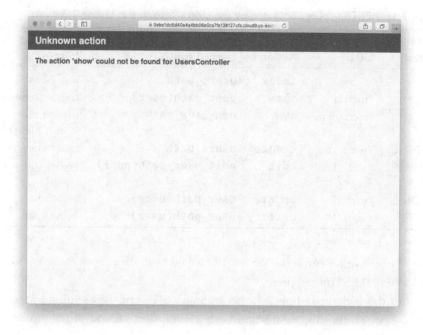

Figure 7.5: The URL /users/1 with routing but no page.

To get the user show view to work, we need to define an **@user** variable in the corresponding **show** action in the Users controller. As you might expect, we use the **find** method on the User model (Section 6.1.4) to retrieve the user from the database, as shown in Listing 7.5.

Listing 7.5: The Users controller with a **show** action.
`app/controllers/users_controller.rb`

```ruby
class UsersController < ApplicationController

  def show
    @user = User.find(params[:id])
  end

  def new
  end
end
```

Here we've used **params** to retrieve the user id. When we make the appropriate request to the Users controller, **params[:id]** will be the user id 1, so the effect is the same as that from using the **find** method **User.find(1)** we saw in Section 6.1.4. (Technically, **params[:id]** is the string **"1"**, but **find** is smart enough to convert this to an integer.)

With the user view and action defined, the URL /users/1 works perfectly, as seen in Figure 7.6. (If you haven't restarted the Rails server since adding bcrypt, you may have to do so at this time. This sort of thing is a good application of technical sophistication (Box 1.2).) Note that the debug information in Figure 7.6 confirms the value of **params[:id]**:

```
---
action: show
controller: users
id: '1'
```

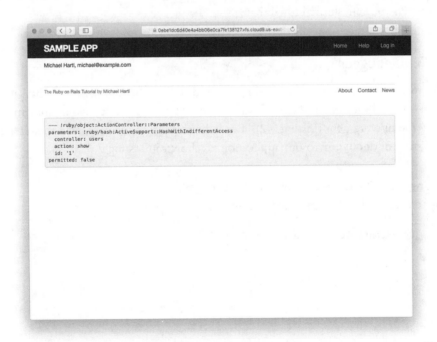

Figure 7.6: The user show page after adding a Users resource.

This is why the code

```
User.find(params[:id])
```

in Listing 7.5 finds the user with id **1**.

Exercises

Solutions to the exercises are available to all Rails Tutorial purchasers at https://www.railstutorial.org/aw-solutions.

To see other people's answers and to record your own, subscribe to the Rails Tutorial course or to the Learn Enough All Access Bundle.

1. Using embedded Ruby, add the **created_at** and **updated_at** "magic column" attributes to the user show page from Listing 7.4.

2. Using embedded Ruby, add **Time.now** to the user show page. What happens when you refresh the browser?

7.1.3 Debugger

We saw in Section 7.1.2 how the **debug** method could help us understand what's going on in our application, but there's also a more direct way to get debugging information using the byebug gem (Listing 3.2). To see how it works, we just need to add a line consisting of **debugger** to our application, as shown in Listing 7.6.

Listing 7.6: The Users controller with a debugger.
app/controllers/users_controller.rb

```ruby
class UsersController < ApplicationController

  def show
    @user = User.find(params[:id])
    debugger
  end

  def new
  end
end
```

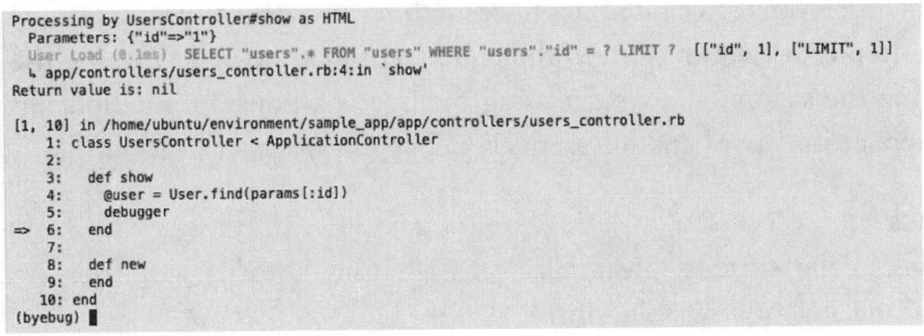

```
Processing by UsersController#show as HTML
  Parameters: {"id"=>"1"}
  User Load (0.1ms)  SELECT "users".* FROM "users" WHERE "users"."id" = ? LIMIT ?  [["id", 1], ["LIMIT", 1]]
  ↳ app/controllers/users_controller.rb:4:in `show'
Return value is: nil

[1, 10] in /home/ubuntu/environment/sample_app/app/controllers/users_controller.rb
    1: class UsersController < ApplicationController
    2:
    3:   def show
    4:     @user = User.find(params[:id])
    5:     debugger
=>  6:   end
    7:
    8:   def new
    9:   end
   10: end
(byebug)
```

Figure 7.7: The **byebug** prompt in the Rails server.

Now, when we visit /users/1, the Rails server shows a **byebug** prompt (Figure 7.7):

```
(byebug)
```

We can treat **byebug** like a Rails console, issuing commands to figure out the state of the application:

```
(byebug) @user.name
"Michael Hartl"
(byebug) @user.email
"michael@example.com"
(byebug) params[:id]
"1"
```

To release the prompt and continue execution of the application, press Ctrl-D, then remove the **debugger** line from the **show** action (Listing 7.7).

Listing 7.7: The Users controller with the debugger line removed.
app/controllers/users_controller.rb

```
class UsersController < ApplicationController

  def show
    @user = User.find(params[:id])
  end

  def new
  end
end
```

Whenever you're confused about something in a Rails application, it's a good practice to put **debugger** close to the code you think might be causing the trouble. Inspecting the state of the system using byebug is a powerful method for tracking down application errors and interactively debugging your application.

Exercises

Solutions to the exercises are available to all Rails Tutorial purchasers at https://www.railstutorial.org/aw-solutions.

To see other people's answers and to record your own, subscribe to the Rails Tutorial course or to the Learn Enough All Access Bundle.

1. With the **debugger** in the **show** action as in Listing 7.6, hit /users/1. Use **puts** to display the value of the YAML form of the **params** hash. *Hint*: Refer to the relevant exercise in Section 7.1.1. How does it compare to the debug information shown by the **debug** method in the site template?

2. Put the **debugger** in the User **new** action and hit /users/new. What is the value of **@user**?

7.1.4 A Gravatar Image and a Sidebar

Having defined a basic user page in the previous section, we'll now flesh it out a little with a profile image for each user and the first cut of the user sidebar. We'll start by adding a "globally recognized avatar," or Gravatar, to the user profile.[8] Gravatar is a free service that allows users to upload images and associate them with email addresses they control. As a result, Gravatars are a convenient way to include user profile images without going through the trouble of managing image upload, cropping, and storage; all we need to do is construct the proper Gravatar image URL using the user's email address and the corresponding Gravatar image will automatically appear. (We'll learn how to handle custom image upload in Section 13.4.)

Our plan is to define a **gravatar_for** helper function to return a Gravatar image for a given user, as shown in Listing 7.8.

---

8. In Hinduism, an avatar is the manifestation of a deity in human or animal form. By extension, the term *avatar* is commonly used to mean some kind of personal representation, especially in a virtual environment. (In the context of Twitter and other social media, the term *avi* has gained currency, which is likely a mutated form of *avatar*.)

Listing 7.8: The user show view with name and Gravatar.
`app/views/users/show.html.erb`

```
<% provide(:title, @user.name) %>
<h1>
  <%= gravatar_for @user %>
  <%= @user.name %>
</h1>
```

By default, methods defined in any helper file are automatically available in any view, but for convenience we'll put the **gravatar_for** method in the file for helpers associated with the Users controller. As noted in the Gravatar documentation, Gravatar URLs are based on an MD5 hash of the user's email address. In Ruby, the MD5 hashing algorithm is implemented using the **hexdigest** method, which is part of the **Digest** library:

```
>> email = "MHARTL@example.COM"
>> Digest::MD5::hexdigest(email.downcase)
=> "1fda4469bcbec3badf5418269ffc5968"
```

Since email addresses are case-insensitive (Section 6.2.4) but MD5 hashes are not, we've used the **downcase** method to ensure that the argument to **hexdigest** is all lowercase. (Because of the email downcasing callback in Listing 6.32, this will never make a difference in this tutorial, but it's a good practice in case the **gravatar_for** ever gets used on email addresses from other sources.) The resulting **gravatar_for** helper appears in Listing 7.9.

Listing 7.9: Defining a **gravatar_for** helper method.
`app/helpers/users_helper.rb`

```
module UsersHelper

  # Returns the Gravatar for the given user.
  def gravatar_for(user)
    gravatar_id  = Digest::MD5::hexdigest(user.email.downcase)
    gravatar_url = "https://secure.gravatar.com/avatar/#{gravatar_id}"
    image_tag(gravatar_url, alt: user.name, class: "gravatar")
  end
end
```

The code in Listing 7.9 returns an image tag for the Gravatar with a **gravatar** CSS class and alt text equal to the user's name (which is especially convenient for visually impaired users using a screen reader).

The profile page appears as in Figure 7.8, which shows the default Gravatar image, which appears because **michael@example.com** isn't a real email address. (In fact, as you can see by visiting it, the example.com domain is reserved for examples like this one.)

To get our application to display a custom Gravatar, we'll use **update_attributes** (Section 6.1.5) to change the user's email to something I control:[9]

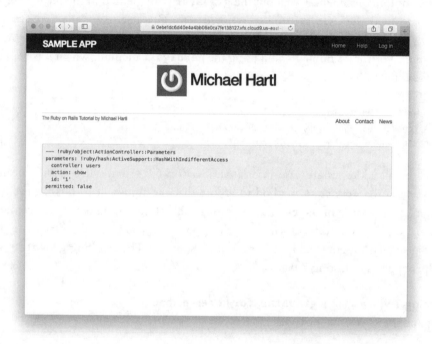

Figure 7.8: The user profile page with the default Gravatar.

---

9. The password confirmation isn't technically necessary here because **has_secure_password** (Section 6.3.1) actually allows the confirmation to be **nil**. The reason is so that apps that don't need password confirmation can simply omit the confirmation field. We do want a confirmation, though, so we'll include such a field in Listing 7.15.

```
$ rails console
>> user = User.first
>> user.update(name: "Example User",
?>            email: "example@railstutorial.org",
?>            password: "foobar",
?>            password_confirmation: "foobar")
=> true
```

Here we've assigned the user the email address **example@railstutorial.org**, which I've associated with the Rails Tutorial logo, as seen in Figure 7.9.

The last element needed to complete the mockup from Figure 7.1 is the initial version of the user sidebar. We'll implement it using the **aside** tag, which is used for content (such as sidebars) that complements the rest of the page but can also stand alone. We include **row** and **col-md-4** classes, which are both part of Bootstrap. The code for the modified user show page appears in Listing 7.10.

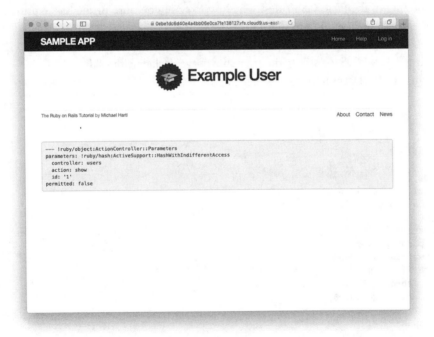

Figure 7.9: The user show page with a custom Gravatar.

Listing 7.10: Adding a sidebar to the user **show** view.
`app/views/users/show.html.erb`

```erb
<% provide(:title, @user.name) %>
<div class="row">
  <aside class="col-md-4">
    <section class="user_info">
      <h1>
        <%= gravatar_for @user %>
        <%= @user.name %>
      </h1>
    </section>
  </aside>
</div>
```

With the HTML elements and CSS classes in place, we can style the profile page
(including the sidebar and the Gravatar) with the SCSS shown in Listing 7.11.[10] (Note
the nesting of the table CSS rules, which works only because of the Sass engine used
by the asset pipeline.) The resulting page is shown in Figure 7.10.

Listing 7.11: SCSS for styling the user show page, including the sidebar.
`app/assets/stylesheets/custom.scss`

```scss
.
.
.
/* sidebar */

aside {
  section.user_info {
    margin-top: 20px;
  }
  section {
    padding: 10px 0;
    margin-top: 20px;
    &:first-child {
      border: 0;
      padding-top: 0;
    }
    span {
      display: block;
```

---

10. Listing 7.11 includes the **.gravatar_edit** class, which we'll put to work in Chapter 10.

```
      margin-bottom: 3px;
      line-height: 1;
    }
    h1 {
      font-size: 1.4em;
      text-align: left;
      letter-spacing: -1px;
      margin-bottom: 3px;
      margin-top: 0px;
    }
  }
}

.gravatar {
  float: left;
  margin-right: 10px;
}

.gravatar_edit {
  margin-top: 15px;
}
```

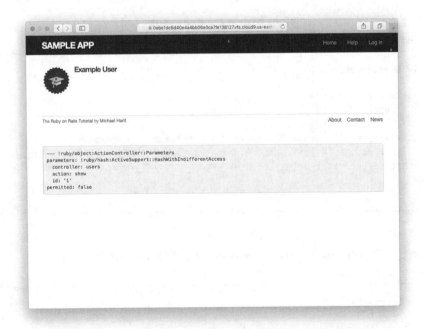

Figure 7.10: The user show page with a sidebar and CSS.

Exercises

Solutions to the exercises are available to all Rails Tutorial purchasers at https://www.railstutorial.org/aw-solutions.

To see other people's answers and to record your own, subscribe to the Rails Tutorial course or to the Learn Enough All Access Bundle.

1. Associate a Gravatar with your primary email address if you haven't already done so. What is the MD5 hash associated with the image?

2. Verify that the code in Listing 7.12 allows the **gravatar_for** helper defined in Section 7.1.4 to take an optional **size** parameter, allowing code like **gravatar_for user, size: 50** in the view. (We'll put this improved helper to use in Section 10.3.1.)

3. The options hash used in the previous exercise is still commonly used, but as of Ruby 2.0 we can use *keyword arguments* instead. Confirm that the code in Listing 7.13 can be used in place of Listing 7.12. What are the differences between the two?

Listing 7.12: Adding an options hash in the **gravatar_for** helper.
app/helpers/users_helper.rb

```ruby
module UsersHelper

  # Returns the Gravatar for the given user.
  def gravatar_for(user, options = { size: 80 })
    size         = options[:size]
    gravatar_id  = Digest::MD5::hexdigest(user.email.downcase)
    gravatar_url = "https://secure.gravatar.com/avatar/#{gravatar_id}?s=#{size}"
    image_tag(gravatar_url, alt: user.name, class: "gravatar")
  end
end
```

Listing 7.13: Using keyword arguments in the **gravatar_for** helper.
app/helpers/users_helper.rb

```ruby
module UsersHelper

  # Returns the Gravatar for the given user.
  def gravatar_for(user, size: 80)
```

```
    gravatar_id  = Digest::MD5::hexdigest(user.email.downcase)
    gravatar_url = "https://secure.gravatar.com/avatar/#{gravatar_id}?s=#{size}"
    image_tag(gravatar_url, alt: user.name, class: "gravatar")
  end
end
```

7.2 Signup Form

Now that we have a working (though not yet complete) user profile page, we're ready
to make a signup form for our site. We saw in Figure 5.11 (shown again in Figure 7.11)
that the signup page is currently blank: Right now it's useless for signing up new users.
The goal of this section is to start changing this sad state of affairs by producing the
signup form mocked up in Figure 7.12.

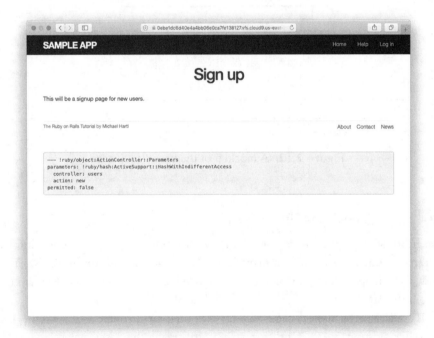

Figure 7.11: The current state of the signup page /signup.

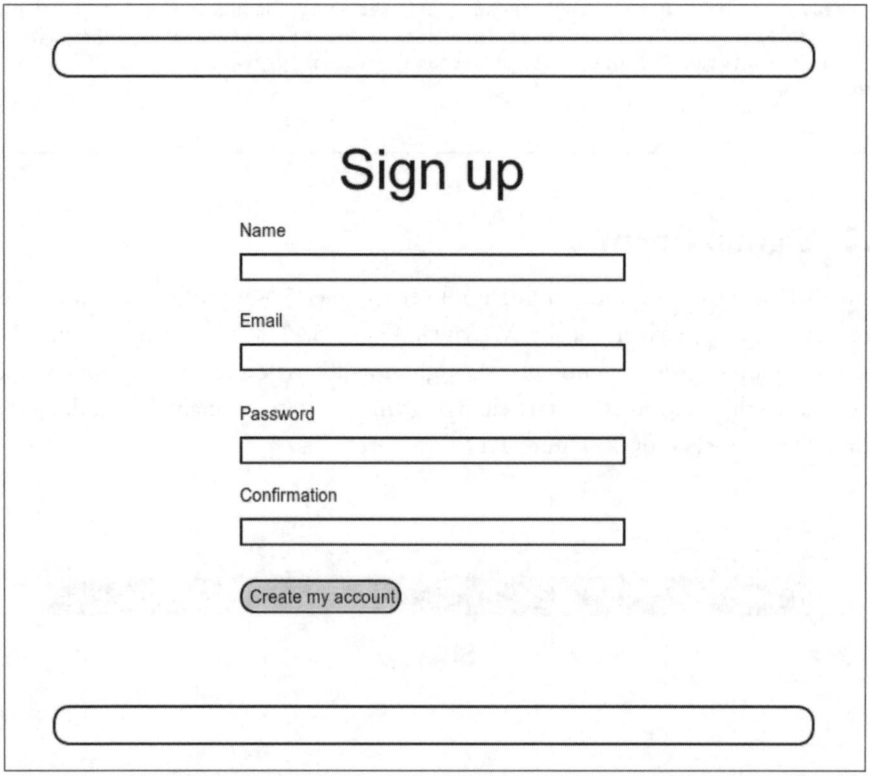

Figure 7.12: A mockup of the user signup page.

7.2.1 Using `form_with`

The heart of the signup page is a *form* for submitting the relevant signup information (name, email, password, confirmation). We can accomplish this in Rails with the `form_with` helper method, which uses an Active Record object to build a form using the object's attributes.

Recall that the signup page /signup is routed to the **new** action in the Users controller (Listing 5.43). Our first step is to create the User object required as an argument to `form_with`. The resulting `@user` variable definition appears in Listing 7.14.

Listing 7.14: Adding an **@user** variable to the **new** action.
`app/controllers/users_controller.rb`

```ruby
class UsersController < ApplicationController

  def show
    @user = User.find(params[:id])
  end

  def new
    @user = User.new
  end
end
```

The form itself appears as in Listing 7.15. We'll discuss it in detail in Section 7.2.2, but first let's style it a little with the SCSS in Listing 7.16. (Note the reuse of the **box_sizing** mixin from Listing 7.2.) Once these CSS rules have been applied, the signup page appears as in Figure 7.13.

Listing 7.15: A form to sign up new users.
`app/views/users/new.html.erb`

```erb
<% provide(:title, 'Sign up') %>
<h1>Sign up</h1>

<div class="row">
  <div class="col-md-6 col-md-offset-3">
    <%= form_with(model: @user, local: true) do |f| %>
      <%= f.label :name %>
      <%= f.text_field :name %>

      <%= f.label :email %>
      <%= f.email_field :email %>

      <%= f.label :password %>
      <%= f.password_field :password %>

      <%= f.label :password_confirmation, "Confirmation" %>
      <%= f.password_field :password_confirmation %>

      <%= f.submit "Create my account", class: "btn btn-primary" %>
    <% end %>
  </div>
</div>
```

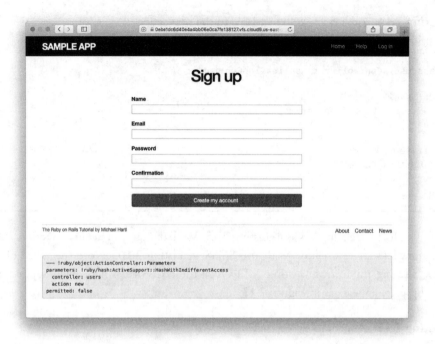

Figure 7.13: The user signup form.

Listing 7.16: CSS for the signup form.
app/assets/stylesheets/custom.scss

```
.
.
.
/* forms */

input, textarea, select, .uneditable-input {
  border: 1px solid #bbb;
  width: 100%;
  margin-bottom: 15px;
  @include box_sizing;
}

input {
  height: auto !important;
}
```

Exercise

Solutions to the exercises are available to all Rails Tutorial purchasers at https://www.railstutorial.org/aw-solutions.

To see other people's answers and to record your own, subscribe to the Rails Tutorial course or to the Learn Enough All Access Bundle.

1. Confirm by replacing all occurrences of **f** with **foobar** that the name of the block variable is irrelevant as far as the result is concerned. Why might **foobar** nevertheless be a bad choice?

7.2.2 Signup Form HTML

To understand the form defined in Listing 7.15, it's helpful to break it into smaller pieces. We'll first look at the outer structure, which consists of embedded Ruby opening with a call to **form_with** and closing with **end**:

```
<%= form_with(model: @user, local: true) do |f| %>
  .
  .
  .
<% end %>
```

The presence of the **do** keyword indicates that **form_with** takes a block with one variable, which we've called **f** (for "form"). Note the presence of the hash argument **local: true**; by default, **form_with** sends a "remote" XHR request, whereas we want a regular "local" form request, mostly so that our error messages will render properly (Section 7.3.3).

As is usually the case with Rails helpers, we don't need to know any details about the implementation, but what we *do* need to know is what the **f** object does: When called with a method corresponding to an HTML form element—such as a text field, radio button, or password field—**f** returns code for that element specifically designed to set an attribute of the **@user** object. In other words,

```
<%= f.label :name %>
<%= f.text_field :name %>
```

creates the HTML needed to make a labeled text field element appropriate for setting the **name** attribute of a User model.

If you look at the HTML for the generated form by Ctrl-clicking and using the "inspect element" function of your browser, the page's source should look something like Listing 7.17. Let's take a moment to discuss its structure.

Listing 7.17: The HTML for the form in Figure 7.13.

```
<form accept-charset="UTF-8" action="/users" class="new_user"
    id="new_user" method="post">
  <input name="authenticity_token" type="hidden"
      value="NNb6+J/j46LcrgYUC60wQ2titMuJQ5lLqyAbnbAUkdo=" />
  <label for="user_name">Name</label>
  <input id="user_name" name="user[name]" type="text" />

  <label for="user_email">Email</label>
  <input id="user_email" name="user[email]" type="email" />

  <label for="user_password">Password</label>
  <input id="user_password" name="user[password]"
      type="password" />

  <label for="user_password_confirmation">Confirmation</label>
  <input id="user_password_confirmation"
      name="user[password_confirmation]" type="password" />

  <input class="btn btn-primary" name="commit" type="submit"
      value="Create my account" />
</form>
```

We'll start with the internal structure of the document. Comparing Listing 7.15 with Listing 7.17, we see that the embedded Ruby

```
<%= f.label :name %>
<%= f.text_field :name %>
```

produces the HTML

```
<label for="user_name">Name</label>
<input id="user_name" name="user[name]" type="text" />
```

while

```
<%= f.label :email %>
<%= f.email_field :email %>
```

produces the HTML

```
<label for="user_email">Email</label>
<input id="user_email" name="user[email]" type="email" />
```

and

```
<%= f.label :password %>
<%= f.password_field :password %>
```

produces the HTML

```
<label for="user_password">Password</label>
<input id="user_password" name="user[password]" type="password" />
```

As seen in Figure 7.14, text and email fields (**type="text"** and **type="email"**) simply display their contents, whereas password fields (**type="password"**) obscure the input for security purposes, as seen in Figure 7.14. (The benefit of using an email field is that some systems treat it differently from a text field; for example, the code **type="email"** will cause some mobile devices to display a special keyboard optimized for entering email addresses.)

As we'll see in Section 7.4, the key to creating a user is the special **name** attribute in each **input**:

```
<input id="user_name" name="user[name]" - - - />
 .
 .
 .
<input id="user_password" name="user[password]" - - - />
```

These **name** values allow Rails to construct an initialization hash (via the **params** variable) for creating users using the values entered by the user, as we'll see in Section 7.3.

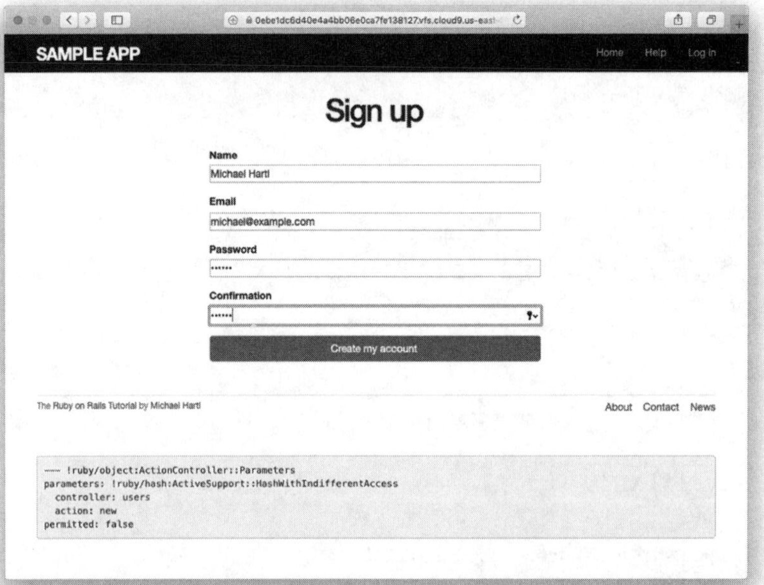

Figure 7.14: A filled-in form with **text** and **password** fields.

The second important element is the **form** tag itself. Rails creates the **form** tag using the **@user** object: Because every Ruby object knows its own class (Section 4.4.1), Rails figures out that **@user** is of class **User**. Moreover, since **@user** is a *new* user, Rails knows to construct a form with the **post** method, which is the proper verb for creating a new object (Box 3.2):

```
<form action="/users" class="new_user" id="new_user" method="post">
```

Here the **class** and **id** attributes are largely irrelevant; what's important is **action=- "/users"** and **method="post"**. Together, these constitute instructions to issue an HTTP POST request to the /users URL. In the next two sections we'll see what effects this has.

You may also have noticed the code that appears just inside the **form** tag:

```
<input name="authenticity_token" type="hidden"
       value="NNb6+J/j46LcrgYUC60wQ2titMuJQ5lLqyAbnbAUkdo=" />
```

This code, which isn't displayed in the browser, is used internally by Rails, so it's not important for us to understand what it does. Briefly, it includes an *authenticity token*, which Rails uses to thwart an attack called a *cross-site request forgery* (CSRF). Knowing when it's OK to ignore details like this is a good mark of technical sophistication (Box 1.2).[11]

Exercise

Solutions to the exercises are available to all Rails Tutorial purchasers at https://www.railstutorial.org/aw-solutions.

To see other people's answers and to record your own, subscribe to the Rails Tutorial course or to the Learn Enough All Access Bundle.

1. *Learn Enough HTML to Be Dangerous*, in which all HTML is written by hand, doesn't cover the **form** tag. Why not?

7.3 Unsuccessful Signups

Although we've briefly examined the HTML for the form in Figure 7.13 (shown in Listing 7.17), we haven't yet covered any details, and the form is best understood in the context of *signup failure*. In this section, we'll create a signup form that accepts an invalid submission and re-renders the signup page with a list of errors, as mocked up in Figure 7.15.

7.3.1 A Working Form

Recall from Section 7.1.2 that adding **resources :users** to the **routes.rb** file (Listing 7.3) automatically ensures that our Rails application responds to the RESTful URLs from Table 7.1. In particular, it ensures that a POST request to /users is handled by the **create** action. Our strategy for the **create** action is to use the form submission to make a new user object with **User.new**, try (and fail) to save that user, and then render the signup page for possible resubmission. Let's get started by reviewing the code for the signup form:

---

11. See the Stack Overflow entry on the Rails authenticity token if you're interested in the details of how this works.

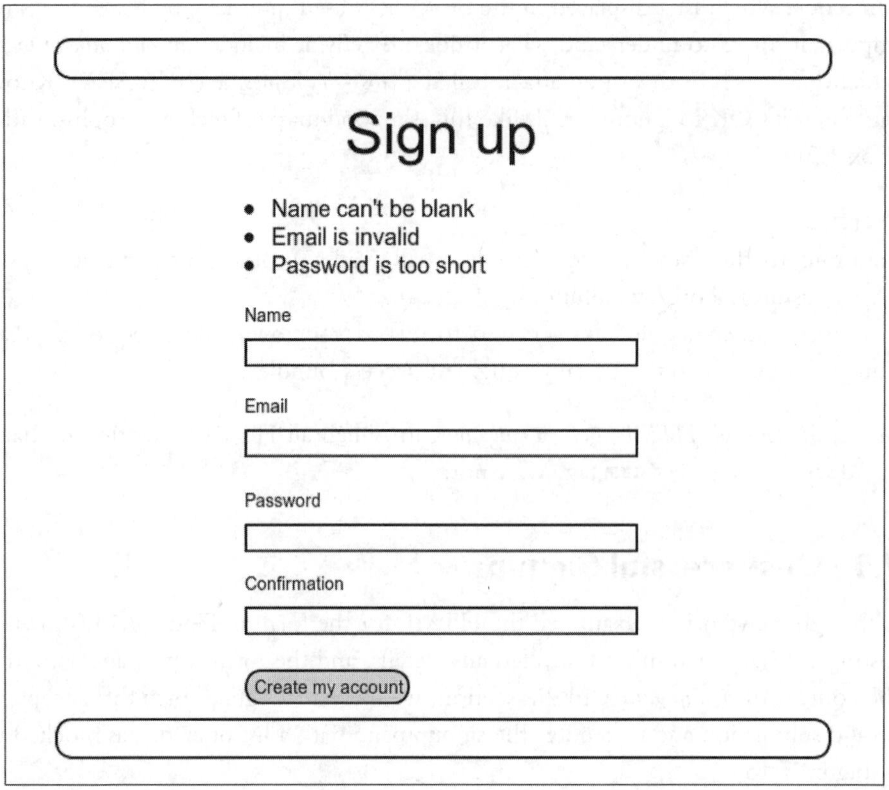

Figure 7.15: A mockup of the signup failure page.

```
<form action="/users" class="new_user" id="new_user" method="post">
```

As noted in Section 7.2.2, this HTML issues a POST request to the /users URL.

Our first step toward a working signup form is adding the code in Listing 7.18. This listing includes a second use of the **render** method, which we first saw in the context of partials (Section 5.1.3); as you can see, **render** works in controller actions as well. Note that we've taken this opportunity to introduce an **if-else** branching structure, which allows us to handle the cases of failure and success separately based on the value of **@user.save**, which (as we saw in Section 6.1.3) is either **true** or **false** depending on whether the save succeeds.

Listing 7.18: A **create** action that can handle signup failure.
app/controllers/users_controller.rb

```ruby
class UsersController < ApplicationController

  def show
    @user = User.find(params[:id])
  end

  def new
    @user = User.new
  end

  def create
    @user = User.new(params[:user])    # Not the final implementation!
    if @user.save
      # Handle a successful save.
    else
      render 'new'
    end
  end
end
```

Note the comment: This is not the final implementation. But it's enough to get us started, and we'll finish the implementation in Section 7.3.2.

The best way to understand how the code in Listing 7.18 works is to *submit* the form with some invalid signup data. The result appears in Figure 7.16, and the full debug information appears in Figure 7.17.

To get a better picture of how Rails handles the submission, let's take a closer look at the **user** part of the parameters hash from the debug information (Figure 7.17):

```ruby
"user" => { "name" => "Foo Bar",
            "email" => "foo@invalid",
            "password" => "[FILTERED]",
            "password_confirmation" => "[FILTERED]"
          }
```

This hash gets passed to the Users controller as part of **params**, and we saw starting in Section 7.1.2 that the **params** hash contains information about each request. In the case of a URL like /users/1, the value of **params[:id]** is the **id** of the corresponding

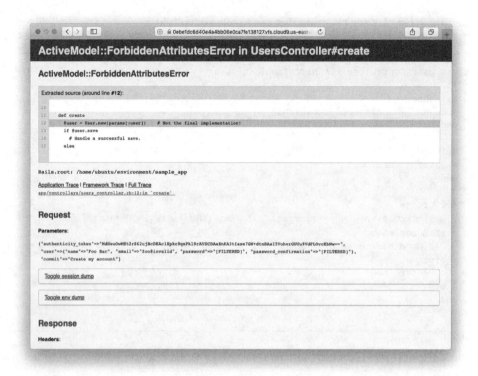

Figure 7.16: Signup failure upon submitting invalid data.

Figure 7.17: Signup failure debug information.

user (**1** in this example). In the case of posting to the signup form, **params** instead contains a hash of hashes, a construction we first saw in Section 4.3.3, which introduced the strategically named **params** variable in a console session. This debug information shows that submitting the form results in a **user** hash with attributes corresponding to the submitted values, where the keys come from the **name** attributes of the **input** tags seen in Listing 7.17. For example, the value of

```
<input id="user_email" name="user[email]" type="email" />
```

with name **"user[email]"** is precisely the **email** attribute of the **user** hash.

Although the hash keys appear as strings in the debug output, we can access them in the Users controller as symbols, so that **params[:user]** is the hash of user attributes—in fact, exactly the attributes needed as an argument to **User.new**, as seen first in Section 4.4.5 and then in Listing 7.18. This means that the line

```
@user = User.new(params[:user])
```

is mostly equivalent to

```
@user = User.new(name: "Foo Bar", email: "foo@invalid",
                 password: "foo", password_confirmation: "bar")
```

In previous versions of Rails, using

```
@user = User.new(params[:user])
```

actually worked, but it was insecure by default and required a careful and error-prone procedure to prevent malicious users from potentially modifying the application database. In Rails versions later than 4.0, this code raises an error (as seen in Figure 7.16 and Figure 7.17), which means it is secure by default.

7.3.2 Strong Parameters

We mentioned briefly in Section 4.4.5 the idea of *mass assignment*, which involves initializing a Ruby variable using a hash of values, as in

```
@user = User.new(params[:user])    # Not the final implementation!
```

The comment included in Listing 7.18 and reproduced here indicates that this is not the final implementation. The reason is that initializing the entire **params** hash is *extremely* dangerous: It arranges to pass to **User.new** *all* data submitted by a user. In particular, suppose that, in addition to the current attributes, the User model included an **admin** attribute used to identify administrative users of the site. (We will implement just such an attribute in Section 10.4.1.) The way to set such an attribute to **true** is to pass the value **admin='1'** as part of **params[:user]**, a task that is easy to accomplish using a command-line HTTP client such as **curl**. The result would be that, by passing in the entire **params** hash to **User.new**, we would allow any user of the site to gain administrative access by including **admin='1'** in the web request.

Previous versions of Rails used a method called **attr_accessible** in the *model* layer to solve this problem, and you may still see that method in legacy Rails applications. As of Rails 4.0, though, the preferred technique is to use *strong parameters* in the controller layer. This allows us to specify which parameters are *required* and which ones are *permitted*. In addition, passing in a raw **params** hash just shown will cause an error to be raised, so that Rails applications are now immune to mass assignment vulnerabilities by default.

In the present instance, we want to require the **params** hash to have a **:user** attribute, and we want to permit the name, email, password, and password confirmation attributes (but no others). We can accomplish this as follows:

```
params.require(:user).permit(:name, :email, :password, :password_confirmation)
```

This code returns a version of the **params** hash with only the permitted attributes (while raising an error if the **:user** attribute is missing).

To facilitate the use of these parameters, it's conventional to introduce an auxiliary method called **user_params** (which returns an appropriate initialization hash) and use it in place of **params[:user]**:

```
@user = User.new(user_params)
```

Since **user_params** will be used only internally by the Users controller and need not be exposed to external users via the web, we'll make it *private* using Ruby's **private** keyword, as shown in Listing 7.19. (We'll discuss **private** in more detail in Section 9.1.)

Listing 7.19: Using strong parameters in the **create** action.
`app/controllers/users_controller.rb`

```ruby
class UsersController < ApplicationController
  .
  .
  .
  def create
    @user = User.new(user_params)
    if @user.save
      # Handle a successful save.
    else
      render 'new'
    end
  end

  private

    def user_params
      params.require(:user).permit(:name, :email, :password,
                                   :password_confirmation)
    end
end
```

By the way, the extra level of indentation on the **user_params** method is designed to make it visually apparent which methods are defined after **private**. (Experience shows that this is a wise practice; in classes with a large number of methods, it is easy to define a private method accidentally, which leads to considerable confusion when it isn't available to call on the corresponding object.)

At this point, the signup form is working, at least in the sense that it no longer produces an error upon submission. Of course, as seen in Figure 7.18, it doesn't display any feedback on invalid submissions (apart from the development-only debug area), which is potentially confusing. It also doesn't actually create a new user. We'll fix the first issue in Section 7.3.3 and the second in Section 7.4.

Exercise

Solutions to the exercises are available to all Rails Tutorial purchasers at https://www.railstutorial.org/aw-solutions.

To see other people's answers and to record your own, subscribe to the Rails Tutorial course or to the Learn Enough All Access Bundle.

Figure 7.18: The signup form submitted with invalid information.

1. By hitting the URL /signup?admin=1, confirm that the **admin** attribute appears in the **params** debug information.

7.3.3 Signup Error Messages

As a final step in handling failed user creation, we'll add helpful error messages to indicate the problems that prevented successful signup. Conveniently, Rails automatically provides such messages based on the User model validations. For example, consider trying to save a user with an invalid email address and with a password that's too short:

```
$ rails console
>> user = User.new(name: "Foo Bar", email: "foo@invalid",
?>              password: "dude", password_confirmation: "dude")
>> user.save
=> false
```

```
>> user.errors.full_messages
=> ["Email is invalid", "Password is too short (minimum is 6 characters)"]
```

Here the **errors.full_messages** object (which we saw briefly before in Section 6.2.2) contains an array of error messages.

As in the console session just shown, the failed save in Listing 7.18 generates a list of error messages associated with the **@user** object. To display the messages in the browser, we'll render an error-messages partial on the user **new** page while adding the CSS class **form-control** (which has special meaning to Bootstrap) to each entry field, as shown in Listing 7.20. It's worth noting that this error-messages partial is only a first attempt; the final version appears in Section 13.3.2.

Listing 7.20: Code to display error messages on the signup form.
`app/views/users/new.html.erb`

```erb
<% provide(:title, 'Sign up') %>
<h1>Sign up</h1>

<div class="row">
  <div class="col-md-6 col-md-offset-3">
    <%= form_with(model: @user, local: true) do |f| %>
      <%= render 'shared/error_messages' %>

      <%= f.label :name %>
      <%= f.text_field :name, class: 'form-control' %>

      <%= f.label :email %>
      <%= f.email_field :email, class: 'form-control' %>

      <%= f.label :password %>
      <%= f.password_field :password, class: 'form-control' %>

      <%= f.label :password_confirmation, "Confirmation" %>
      <%= f.password_field :password_confirmation, class: 'form-control' %>

      <%= f.submit "Create my account", class: "btn btn-primary" %>
    <% end %>
  </div>
</div>
```

Notice here that we **render** a partial called **'shared/error_messages'**; this reflects the common Rails convention of using a dedicated **shared/** directory for partials expected to be used in views across multiple controllers. (We'll see this expectation fulfilled in Section 10.1.1.)

Now we have to create a new **app/views/shared** directory using **mkdir** and an error messages partial using (Table 1.1):

```
$ mkdir app/views/shared
```

We then need to create the **_error_messages.html.erb** partial file using **touch** or the text editor as usual. The contents of the partial appear in Listing 7.21.

Listing 7.21: A partial for displaying form submission error messages.
app/views/shared/_error_messages.html.erb

```erb
<% if @user.errors.any? %>
  <div id="error_explanation">
    <div class="alert alert-danger">
      The form contains <%= pluralize(@user.errors.count, "error") %>.
    </div>
    <ul>
    <% @user.errors.full_messages.each do |msg| %>
      <li><%= msg %></li>
    <% end %>
    </ul>
  </div>
<% end %>
```

This partial introduces several new Rails and Ruby constructs, including two methods for Rails error objects. The first method is **count**, which simply returns the number of errors:

```
>> user.errors.count
=> 2
```

The other new method is **any?**, which (together with **empty?**) is one of a pair of complementary methods:

```
>> user.errors.empty?
=> false
>> user.errors.any?
=> true
```

We see here that the **empty?** method, which we first encountered in Section 4.2.2 in the context of strings, also works on Rails error objects, returning **true** for an empty object and **false** otherwise. The **any?** method is just the opposite of **empty?**, returning **true** if there are any elements present and **false** otherwise. (By the way, all of these methods—**count**, **empty?**, and **any?**—work on Ruby arrays as well. We'll put this fact to good use starting in Section 13.2.)

The other new idea is the **pluralize** text helper, which is available in the console via the **helper** object:

```
>> helper.pluralize(1, "error")
=> "1 error"
>> helper.pluralize(5, "error")
=> "5 errors"
```

We see here that **pluralize** takes an integer argument and then returns the number with a properly pluralized version of its second argument. Underlying this method is a powerful *inflector* that knows how to pluralize a large number of words, including many with irregular plurals:

```
>> helper.pluralize(2, "woman")
=> "2 women"
>> helper.pluralize(3, "erratum")
=> "3 errata"
```

As a result of its use of **pluralize**, the code

```
<%= pluralize(@user.errors.count, "error") %>
```

returns **"0 errors"**, **"1 error"**, **"2 errors"**, and so on, depending on how many errors there are, thereby avoiding ungrammatical phrases such as **"1 errors"** (a distressingly common mistake in both web and desktop applications).

Note that Listing 7.21 includes the CSS id **error_explanation** for use in styling the error messages. (Recall from Section 5.1.2 that CSS uses the pound sign **#** to style ids.) In addition, after an invalid submission Rails automatically wraps the fields with errors in **div**s with the CSS class **field_with_errors**. These labels then allow us to style the error messages with the SCSS shown in Listing 7.22, which makes use of Sass's **@extend** function to include the functionality of the Bootstrap class **has-error**.

Listing 7.22: CSS for styling error messages.
`app/assets/stylesheets/custom.scss`

```scss
.
.
.
/* forms */
.
.
.
#error_explanation {
  color: red;
  ul {
    color: red;
    margin: 0 0 30px 0;
  }
}

.field_with_errors {
  @extend .has-error;
  .form-control {
    color: $state-danger-text;
  }
}
```

With the code in Listing 7.20 and Listing 7.21 and the SCSS from Listing 7.22, helpful error messages now appear when users submit invalid signup information, as seen in Figure 7.19. Because the messages are generated by the model validations, they will automatically change if you ever change your mind about, say, the format of email addresses, or the minimum length of passwords. (*Note*: Because both the presence validation and the **has_secure_password** validation catch the case of *empty* (**nil**) passwords, the signup form currently produces duplicate error messages when the user submits an empty password. We could manipulate the error messages directly to eliminate duplicates, but luckily this issue will be fixed automatically by the addition of **allow_nil: true** in Section 10.1.4.)

Exercises

Solutions to the exercises are available to all Rails Tutorial purchasers at https://www.railstutorial.org/aw-solutions.

To see other people's answers and to record your own, subscribe to the Rails Tutorial course or to the Learn Enough All Access Bundle.

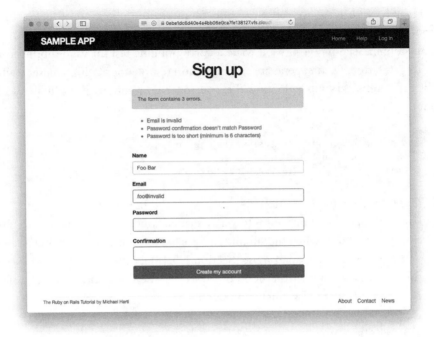

Figure 7.19: Failed signup with error messages.

1. Confirm by changing the minimum length of passwords to 5 that the error message updates automatically as well.

2. How does the URL on the unsubmitted signup form (Figure 7.13) compare to the URL for a submitted signup form (Figure 7.19)? Why don't they match?

7.3.4 A Test for Invalid Submission

In the days before powerful web frameworks with automated testing capabilities, developers had to test forms by hand. For example, to test a signup page manually, we would have to visit the page in a browser and then alternate between submitting invalid and valid data, verifying in each case that the application's behavior was correct. Moreover, we would have to remember to repeat the process anytime the application changed. This process was painful and error-prone.

Happily, with Rails we can write tests to automate the testing of forms. In this section, we'll write one such test to verify the correct behavior upon invalid form submission; in Section 7.4.4, we'll write a corresponding test for valid submission.

To get started, we first generate an integration test file for signing up users, which we'll call **users_signup** (adopting the controller convention of a plural resource name):

```
$ rails generate integration_test users_signup
      invoke  test_unit
      create    test/integration/users_signup_test.rb
```

(We'll use this same file in Section 7.4.4 to test a valid signup.)

The main purpose of our test is to verify that clicking the signup button results in *not* creating a new user when the submitted information is invalid. (Writing a test for the error messages is left as an exercise (Section 7.3.4).) The way to do this is to check the *count* of users, and under the hood our tests will use the **count** method available on every Active Record class, including **User**:

```
$ rails console
>> User.count
=> 1
```

(Here **User.count** is **1** because of the user created in Section 6.3.4, though it may differ if you've added or deleted any users in the interim.) As in Section 5.3.4, we'll use **assert_select** to test HTML elements of the relevant pages, taking care to check only elements unlikely to change in the future.

We'll start by visiting the signup path using **get**:

```
get signup_path
```

To test the form submission, we need to issue a POST request to the **users_path** (Table 7.1), which we can do with the **post** function:

```
assert_no_difference 'User.count' do
  post users_path, params: { user: { name:  "",
                                     email: "user@invalid",
                                     password:             "foo",
                                     password_confirmation: "bar" } }
end
```

Here we've included the **params[:user]** hash expected by **User.new** in the **create** action (Listing 7.27). (In versions of Rails before 5, **params** was implicit, and only the **user** hash would be passed. This practice was deprecated in Rails 5.0, and now the recommended method is to include the full **params** hash explicitly.)

By wrapping the **post** in the **assert_no_difference** method with the string argument **'User.count'**, we arrange for a comparison between **User.count** before and after the contents inside the **assert_no_difference** block. This is equivalent to recording the user count, posting the data, and verifying that the count is the same:

```
before_count = User.count
post users_path, ...
after_count  = User.count
assert_equal before_count, after_count
```

Although the two are equivalent, using **assert_no_difference** is cleaner and is more idiomatically correct Ruby.

It's worth noting that our **get** and **post** steps are technically unrelated, and it's actually not necessary to get the signup path before posting to the users path. I prefer to include both steps, though, both for conceptual clarity and to double-check that the signup form renders without error.

Putting theses ideas together leads to the test in Listing 7.23. We've also included a call to **assert_template** to check that a failed submission re-renders the **new** action. Adding lines to check for the appearance of error messages is left as an exercise (Section 7.3.4).

Listing 7.23: A test for an invalid signup. GREEN
`test/integration/users_signup_test.rb`

```
require 'test_helper'

class UsersSignupTest < ActionDispatch::IntegrationTest

  test "invalid signup information" do
    get signup_path
    assert_no_difference 'User.count' do
      post users_path, params: { user: { name:  "",
                                         email: "user@invalid",
```

```
                                           password:              "foo",
                                           password_confirmation: "bar" } }
      end
    assert_template 'users/new'
  end
end
```

Because we wrote the application code before the integration test, the test suite should be GREEN:

Listing 7.24: GREEN

```
$ rails test
```

Exercise

Solutions to the exercises are available to all Rails Tutorial purchasers at https://www.railstutorial.org/aw-solutions.

To see other people's answers and to record your own, subscribe to the Rails Tutorial course or to the Learn Enough All Access Bundle.

1. Write a test for the error messages implemented in Listing 7.20. How detailed you want to make your tests is up to you; a suggested template appears in Listing 7.25.

Listing 7.25: A template for tests of the error messages.
test/integration/users_signup_test.rb

```
require 'test_helper'

class UsersSignupTest < ActionDispatch::IntegrationTest

  test "invalid signup information" do
    get signup_path
    assert_no_difference 'User.count' do
      post users_path, params: { user: { name:  "",
                                         email: "user@invalid",
                                         password:              "foo",
                                         password_confirmation: "bar" } }
    end
    assert_template 'users/new'
```

```
      assert_select 'div#<CSS id for error explanation>'
      assert_select 'div.<CSS class for field with error>'
  end
    .
    .
    .
end
```

7.4 Successful Signups

Having handled invalid form submissions, now it's time to complete the signup form by actually saving a new user (if valid) to the database. First, we try to save the user; if the save succeeds, the user's information gets written to the database automatically, and we then *redirect* the browser to show the user's profile (together with a friendly greeting), as mocked up in Figure 7.20. If it fails, we simply fall back on the behavior developed in Section 7.3.

7.4.1 The Finished Signup Form

To complete a working signup form, we need to fill in the commented-out section in Listing 7.19 with the appropriate behavior. Currently, the form simply freezes on valid submission, as indicated by the subtle color change in the submission button (Figure 7.21), although this behavior may be system-dependent. This occurs because the default behavior for a Rails action is to render the corresponding view, and there isn't a view template corresponding to the **create** action (Figure 7.22).

Although it's possible to render a template for the **create** action, the usual practice is to *redirect* to a different page instead when the creation is successful. In particular, we'll follow the common convention of redirecting to the newly created user's profile, although the root path would also work. The application code, which introduces the **redirect_to** method, appears in Listing 7.26.

Listing 7.26: The user **create** action with a save and a redirect.
app/controllers/users_controller.rb

```
class UsersController < ApplicationController
    .
    .
    .
```

```
def create
  @user = User.new(user_params)
  if @user.save
    redirect_to @user
  else
    render 'new'
  end
end

private

  def user_params
    params.require(:user).permit(:name, :email, :password,
                                 :password_confirmation)
  end
end
```

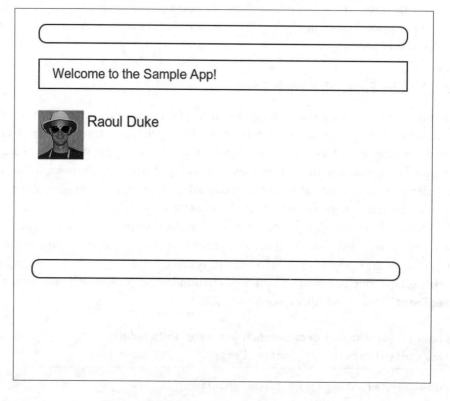

Figure 7.20: A mockup of successful signup.

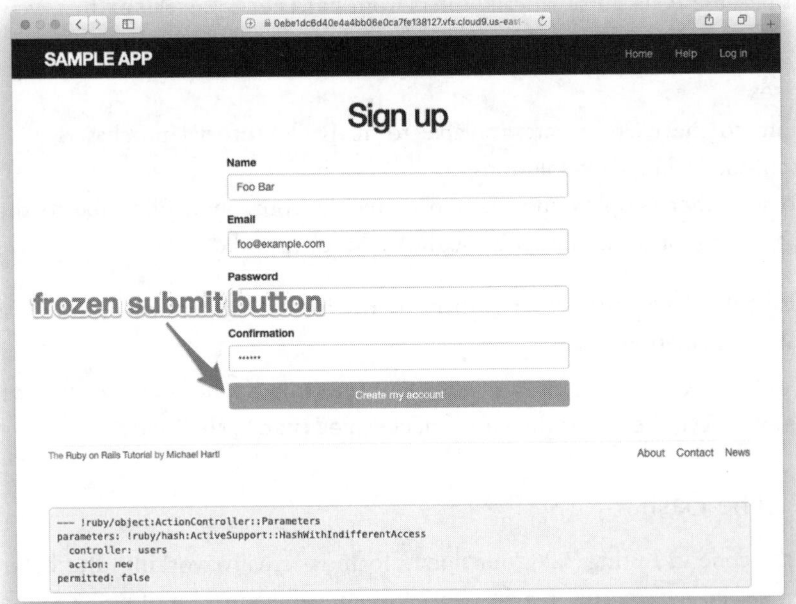

Figure 7.21: The frozen page on valid signup submission.

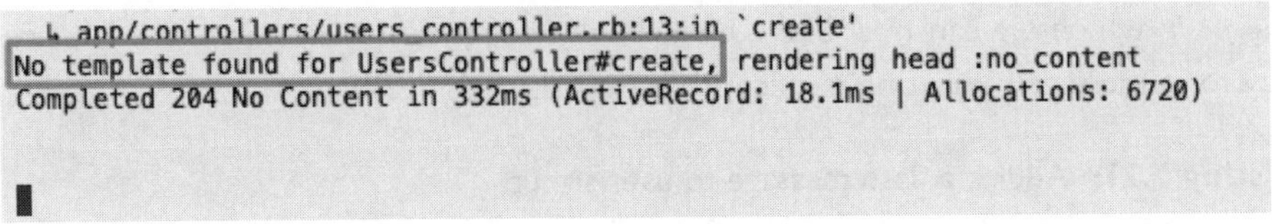

Figure 7.22: The **create** template error in the server log.

Note that we've written

```
redirect_to @user
```

where we could have used the equivalent

```
redirect_to user_url(@user)
```

This is because Rails automatically infers from **redirect_to @user** that we want to redirect to **user_url(@user)**.

Exercises

Solutions to the exercises are available to all Rails Tutorial purchasers at https://www.railstutorial.org/aw-solutions.

To see other people's answers and to record your own, subscribe to the Rails Tutorial course or to the Learn Enough All Access Bundle.

1. Using the Rails console, verify that a user is, in fact, created when the user submits valid information.

2. Confirm by updating Listing 7.26 and submitting a valid user that **redirect_to user_url(@user)** has the same effect as **redirect_to @user**.

7.4.2 The Flash

With the code in Listing 7.26, our signup form is actually working. But before submitting a valid registration in a browser, though, we'll add a bit of polish common in web applications: a message that appears on the subsequent page (in, this case, welcoming our new user to the application) and then disappears upon visiting a second page or on page reload.

The Rails way to display a temporary message is to use a special method called the *flash*, which we can treat like a hash. Rails adopts the convention of a **:success** key for a message indicating a successful result (Listing 7.27).

Listing 7.27: Adding a flash message to user signup.
`app/controllers/users_controller.rb`

```
class UsersController < ApplicationController
  .
  .
  .
  def create
    @user = User.new(user_params)
    if @user.save
      flash[:success] = "Welcome to the Sample App!"
      redirect_to @user
    else
      render 'new'
    end
```

```
  end

  private

    def user_params
      params.require(:user).permit(:name, :email, :password,
                                   :password_confirmation)
    end
end
```

By assigning a message to the **flash**, we are now in a position to display the message on the first page after the redirect. Our method is to iterate through the **flash** and insert all relevant messages into the site layout. You may recall the console example in Section 4.3.3, where we saw how to iterate through a hash using the strategically named **flash** variable (Listing 7.28).

Listing 7.28: Iterating through a **flash** hash in the console.

```
$ rails console
>> flash = { success: "It worked!", danger: "It failed." }
=> {:success=>"It worked!", danger: "It failed."}
>> flash.each do |key, value|
?>   puts "#{key}"
?>   puts "#{value}"
>> end
success
It worked!
danger
It failed.
```

By following this pattern, we can arrange to display the contents of the flash site-wide using code like this:

```
<% flash.each do |message_type, message| %>
  <div class="alert alert-<%= message_type %>"><%= message %></div>
<% end %>
```

(This code is a particularly ugly and difficult-to-read combination of HTML and ERb; making it prettier is left as an exercise (Section 7.4.4).) Here the embedded Ruby

```
alert-<%= message_type %>
```

makes a CSS class corresponding to the type of message, so that for a **:success** message the class is

```
alert-success
```

(The key **:success** is a symbol, but embedded Ruby automatically converts it to the string **"success"** before inserting it into the template.) Using a different class for each key allows us to apply different styles to different kinds of messages. For example, in Section 8.1.4 we'll use **flash[:danger]** to indicate a failed login attempt.[12] (In fact, we've already used **alert-danger** once, to style the error message **div** in Listing 7.21.) Bootstrap CSS supports styling for four such flash classes for increasingly urgent message types (**success**, **info**, **warning**, and **danger**), and we'll find occasion to use all of them in the course of developing the sample application (**info** in Section 11.2, **warning** in Section 11.3, and **danger** for the first time in Section 8.1.4).

Because the message is also inserted into the template, the full HTML result for

```
flash[:success] = "Welcome to the Sample App!"
```

appears as follows:

```
<div class="alert alert-success">Welcome to the Sample App!</div>
```

Putting the embedded Ruby just discussed into the site layout leads to the code in Listing 7.29.

Listing 7.29: Adding the contents of the **flash** variable to the site layout.
`app/views/layouts/application.html.erb`

```
<!DOCTYPE html>
<html>
  .
  .
  .
  <body>
    <%= render 'layouts/header' %>
    <div class="container">
```

---

12. Actually, we'll use the closely related **flash.now**, but we'll defer that subtlety until we need it.

```
      <% flash.each do |message_type, message| %>
        <div class="alert alert-<%= message_type %>"><%= message %></div>
      <% end %>
    <%= yield %>
    <%= render 'layouts/footer' %>
    <%= debug(params) if Rails.env.development? %>
    </div>
    .
    .
    .
  </body>
</html>
```

Exercises

Solutions to the exercises are available to all Rails Tutorial purchasers at https://www.railstutorial.org/aw-solutions.

To see other people's answers and to record your own, subscribe to the Rails Tutorial course or to the Learn Enough All Access Bundle.

1. In the console, confirm that you can use interpolation (Section 4.2.1) to interpolate a raw symbol. For example, what is the return value of **"#{:success}"**?

2. How does the previous exercise relate to the flash iteration shown in Listing 7.28?

7.4.3 The First Signup

We can see the result of all this work by signing up the first user for the sample app. Even though previous submissions didn't work properly (as shown in Figure 7.21), the **user.save** line in the Users controller still works, so users might still have been created. To clear them out, we'll reset the database as follows:

```
$ rails db:migrate:reset
```

On some systems you might have to restart the webserver (using Ctrl-C) for the changes to take effect (Box 1.2).

We'll create the first user with the name "Rails Tutorial" and email address "example@railstutorial.org", as shown in Figure 7.23. The resulting page (Figure 7.24) shows a friendly flash message upon successful signup, including nice green styling for the **success** class, which comes included with the Bootstrap CSS framework from Section 5.1.2. Then, upon reloading the user show page, the flash message disappears as promised (Figure 7.25).

Exercises

Solutions to the exercises are available to all Rails Tutorial purchasers at https://www.railstutorial.org/aw-solutions.

To see other people's answers and to record your own, subscribe to the Rails Tutorial course or to the Learn Enough All Access Bundle.

1. Using the Rails console, find by the email address to double-check that the new user was actually created. The result should look something like Listing 7.30.

Figure 7.23: Filling in the information for the first signup.

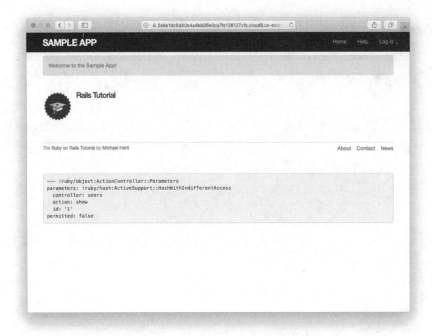

Figure 7.24: The results of a successful user signup, with flash message.

2. Create a new user with your primary email address. Verify that the Gravatar appears correctly.

Listing 7.30: Finding the newly created user in the database.

```
$ rails console
>> User.find_by(email: "example@railstutorial.org")
=> #<User id: 1, name: "Rails Tutorial", email: "example@railstutorial.
org", created_at: "2016-05-31 17:17:33", updated_at: "2016-05-31 17:17:33",
password_digest: "$2a$10$8MaeHdnOhZvMk3GmFdmpPOeG6a7u7/k2Z9TMjOanC9G...">
```

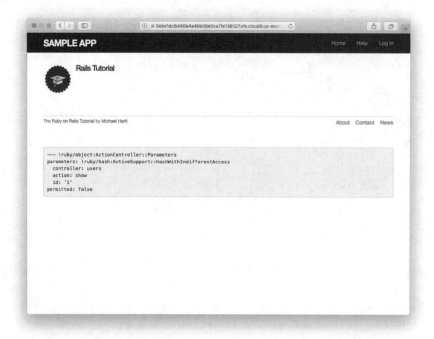

Figure 7.25: The **flash**-less profile page after a browser reload.

7.4.4 A Test for Valid Submission

Before moving on, we'll write a test for valid submission to verify our application's behavior and catch regressions. As with the test for invalid submission in Section 7.3.4, our main purpose is to verify the contents of the database. In this case, we want to submit valid information and then confirm that a user *was* created. In analogy with Listing 7.23, which used

```
assert_no_difference 'User.count' do
  post users_path, ...
end
```

here we'll use the corresponding **assert_difference** method:

```
assert_difference 'User.count', 1 do
  post users_path, ...
end
```

As with **assert_no_difference**, the first argument is the string **'User.count'**, which arranges for a comparison between **User.count** before and after the contents of the **assert_difference** block. The second (optional) argument specifies the size of the difference (in this case, 1).

Incorporating **assert_difference** into the file from Listing 7.23 yields the test shown in Listing 7.31. Note that we've used the **follow_redirect!** method after posting to the users path. This simply arranges to follow the redirect after submission, resulting in a rendering of the **'users/show'** template. (It's probably a good idea to write a test for the flash as well, which is left as an exercise (Section 7.4.4).)

Listing 7.31: A test for a valid signup. GREEN
test/integration/users_signup_test.rb

```
require 'test_helper'

class UsersSignupTest < ActionDispatch::IntegrationTest
  .
  .
  .
  test "valid signup information" do
    get signup_path
    assert_difference 'User.count', 1 do
      post users_path, params: { user: { name:  "Example User",
                                         email: "user@example.com",
                                         password:              "password",
                                         password_confirmation: "password" } }
    end
    follow_redirect!
    assert_template 'users/show'
  end
end
```

Note that Listing 7.31 also verifies that the user show template renders following successful signup. For this test to work, it's necessary for the Users routes (Listing 7.3), the Users **show** action (Listing 7.5), and the **show.html.erb** view (Listing 7.8) to work correctly. As a result, the one line

```
assert_template 'users/show'
```

is a sensitive test for almost everything related to a user's profile page. This sort
of end-to-end coverage of important application features illustrates one reason why
integration tests are so useful.

Exercises

Solutions to the exercises are available to all Rails Tutorial purchasers at https://
www.railstutorial.org/aw-solutions.

To see other people's answers and to record your own, subscribe to the Rails
Tutorial course or to the Learn Enough All Access Bundle.

1. Write a test for the flash implemented in Section 7.4.2. How detailed you want
   to make your tests is up to you; a suggested ultra-minimalist template appears in
   Listing 7.32, which you should complete by replacing **FILL_IN** with the appropriate code. (Even testing for the right key, much less the text, is likely to be
   brittle, so I prefer to test only that the flash isn't empty.)

2. As noted earlier, the flash HTML in Listing 7.29 is ugly. Verify by running the
   test suite that the cleaner code in Listing 7.33, which uses the Rails **content_tag**
   helper, also works.

3. Verify that the test fails if you comment out the redirect line in Listing 7.26.

4. Suppose we changed **@user.save** to **false** in Listing 7.26. How does this change
   verify that the **assert_difference** block is testing the right thing?

Listing 7.32: A template for a test of the flash.
test/integration/users_signup_test.rb

```
require 'test_helper'
  .
  .
  .
  test "valid signup information" do
    get signup_path
    assert_difference 'User.count', 1 do
      post users_path, params: { user: { name:  "Example User",
                                         email: "user@example.com",
                                         password:              "password",
                                         password_confirmation: "password" } }
```

```
    end
    follow_redirect!
    assert_template 'users/show'
    assert_not flash.FILL_IN
  end
end
```

Listing 7.33: The **flash** ERb in the site layout using **content_tag**.
app/views/layouts/application.html.erb

```
<!DOCTYPE html>
<html>
    .
    .
    .
    <% flash.each do |message_type, message| %>
      <%= content_tag(:div, message, class: "alert alert-#{message_type}") %>
    <% end %>
    .
    .
    .
</html>
```

7.5 Professional-Grade Deployment

Now that we have a working signup page, it's time to deploy our application and get it working in production. Although we started deploying our application in Chapter 3, this is the first time it will actually *do* something, so we'll take this opportunity to make the deployment professional-grade. In particular, we'll add an important feature to the production application to make signup secure, we'll replace the default webserver with one suitable for real-world use, and we'll add some configuration for our production database.

As preparation for the deployment, you should merge your changes into the **master** branch at this point:

```
$ git add -A
$ git commit -m "Finish user signup"
```

```
$ git checkout master
$ git merge sign-up
```

7.5.1 SSL in Production

When submitting the signup form developed in this chapter, the name, email address, and password get sent over the network, and hence are vulnerable to being intercepted by malicious users. This is a potentially serious security flaw in our application, and the way to fix it is to use Secure Sockets Layer (SSL)[13] to encrypt all relevant information before it leaves the local browser. Although we could use SSL on just the signup page, it's actually easier to implement it site-wide, which has the additional benefits of securing user login (Chapter 8) and making our application immune to the critical *session hijacking* vulnerability discussed in Section 9.1.

Although Heroku uses SSL by default, it doesn't *force* browsers to use it, thus any users of our application who rely on regular http will be interacting insecurely with the site. You can see how this works by editing the URL in the address bar to change "https" to "http"; the result appears in Figure 7.26.

Luckily, forcing browsers to use SSL is as easy as uncommenting a single line in **production.rb**, the configuration file for production applications. As shown in Listing 7.34, all we need to do is set **config.force_ssl** to **true**.

Figure 7.26: The result of using an insecure http URL in production.

---

13. Technically, SSL is now TLS, for Transport Layer Security, but everyone I know still says "SSL."

Listing 7.34: Configuring the application to use SSL in production.
`config/environments/production.rb`

```
Rails.application.configure do
  .
  .
  .
  # Force all access to the app over SSL, use Strict-Transport-Security,
  # and use secure cookies.
  config.force_ssl = true
  .
  .
  .
end
```

At this stage, we need to set up SSL on the remote server. Setting up a production site to use SSL involves purchasing and configuring an *SSL certificate* for your domain. That's a lot of work, though, and luckily we won't need it here: For an application running on a Heroku domain (such as the sample application), we can piggyback on Heroku's SSL certificate. As a result, when we deploy the application in Section 7.5.2, SSL will automatically be enabled. (If you want to run SSL on a custom domain, such as www.example.com, refer to Heroku's documentation on SSL at devcenter.heroku.com/articles/ssl.)

7.5.2 Production Webserver

Having added SSL, we now need to configure our application to use a webserver suitable for production applications. By default, Heroku uses a pure-Ruby webserver called WEBrick, which is easy to set up and run but isn't good at handling significant traffic. As a result, WEBrick isn't suitable for production use, so we'll replace WEBrick with Puma, an HTTP server that is capable of handling a large number of incoming requests.

To add the new webserver, we simply follow the Heroku Puma documentation (devcenter.heroku.com/articles/deploying-rails-applications-with-the-puma-web-server). The first step is to include the `puma` gem in our **Gemfile**, but as of Rails 5 Puma is included by default (Listing 3.2). This means we can skip right to the second step, which is to replace the default contents of the file **config/puma.rb** with the configuration shown in Listing 7.35. The code in Listing 7.35 comes straight from the Heroku documentation,[14] and there is no need to understand it (Box 1.2).

Listing 7.35: The configuration file for the production webserver.
`config/puma.rb`

```
# Puma configuration file.
max_threads_count = ENV.fetch("RAILS_MAX_THREADS") { 5 }
min_threads_count = ENV.fetch("RAILS_MIN_THREADS") { max_threads_count }
threads min_threads_count, max_threads_count
port        ENV.fetch("PORT") { 3000 }
environment ENV.fetch("RAILS_ENV") { ENV['RACK_ENV'] || "development" }
pidfile ENV.fetch("PIDFILE") { "tmp/pids/server.pid" }
workers ENV.fetch("WEB_CONCURRENCY") { 2 }
preload_app!
plugin :tmp_restart
```

We also need to make a **Procfile** to tell Heroku to run a Puma process in production, as shown in Listing 7.36. The **Procfile** should be created in your application's root directory (i.e., in the same directory as the **Gemfile**).

Listing 7.36: Defining a **Procfile** for Puma.
`./Procfile`

```
web: bundle exec puma -C config/puma.rb
```

7.5.3 Production Database Configuration

The final step in our production deployment is properly configuring the production database, which (as mentioned briefly in Section 2.3.5) is PostgreSQL. My testing indicates that PostgreSQL actually works on Heroku without any configuration, but the official Heroku documentation (devcenter.heroku.com/articles/getting-started-with-rails5) recommends explicit configuration—so we'll err on the side of caution and include it.

The actual change is easy: All we have to do is update the **production** section of the database configuration file, **config/database.yml**. The result, which I adapted from the Heroku docs, is shown in Listing 7.37.

---

14. Listing 7.35 changes the formatting slightly so that the code fits in the standard 80 columns.

Listing 7.37: Configuring the database for production.
`config/database.yml`

```
# SQLite version 3.x
#   gem install sqlite3
#
#   Ensure the SQLite 3 gem is defined in your Gemfile
#   gem 'sqlite3'
#
default: &default
  adapter: sqlite3
  pool: 5
  timeout: 5000

development:
  <<: *default
  database: db/development.sqlite3

# Warning: The database defined as "test" will be erased and
# re-generated from your development database when you run "rake".
# Do not set this db to the same as development or production.
test:
  <<: *default
  database: db/test.sqlite3

production:
  adapter: postgresql
  encoding: unicode
  # For details on connection pooling, see Rails configuration guide
  # https://guides.rubyonrails.org/configuring.html#database-pooling
  pool: <%= ENV.fetch("RAILS_MAX_THREADS") { 5 } %>
  database: sample_app_production
  username: sample_app
  password: <%= ENV['SAMPLE_APP_DATABASE_PASSWORD'] %>
```

7.5.4 Production Deployment

With the production webserver and database configuration completed, we're ready to commit and deploy:[15]

---

15. We haven't changed the data model in this chapter, so running the migration at Heroku shouldn't be necessary, but only if you followed the steps in Section 6.4. Because several readers reported having trouble, I've added **heroku run rails db:migrate** as a final step just to be safe.

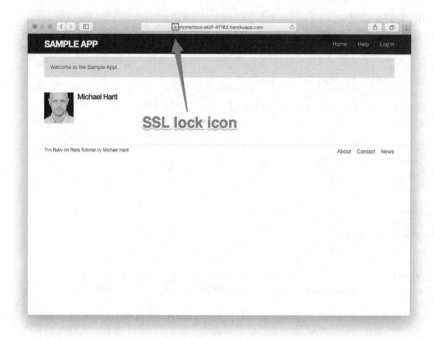

Figure 7.27: Signing up on the live web.

```
$ rails test
$ git add -A
$ git commit -m "Use SSL and the Puma webserver in production"
$ git push && git push heroku
```

The signup form is now live, and the result of a successful signup is shown in
Figure 7.27. Note the presence of a lock icon in the address bar of Figure 7.27, which
indicates that SSL is working.

Ruby Version Number

When deploying to Heroku, you may get a warning message like this one:

```
###### WARNING:
       You have not declared a Ruby version in your Gemfile.
       To set your Ruby version add this line to your Gemfile:
       ruby '2.6.3'
```

Experience shows that, at the level of this tutorial, the costs associated with including such an explicit Ruby version number outweigh the (negligible) benefits, so you should ignore this warning for now. The main issue is that keeping your sample app and system in sync with the latest Ruby version can be a huge inconvenience,[16] yet it almost never makes a difference which exact Ruby version number you use. Nevertheless, you should bear in mind that, should you ever end up running a mission-critical app on Heroku, specifying an exact Ruby version in the **Gemfile** is recommended to ensure maximum compatibility between development and production environments.

Exercises

Solutions to the exercises are available to all Rails Tutorial purchasers at https://www.railstutorial.org/aw-solutions.

To see other people's answers and to record your own, subscribe to the Rails Tutorial course or to the Learn Enough All Access Bundle.

1. Confirm on your browser that the SSL lock and **https** appear.

2. Create a user on the production site using your primary email address. Does your Gravatar appear correctly?

7.6 Conclusion

Being able to sign up users is a major milestone for our application. Although the sample app has yet to accomplish anything useful, we have laid an essential foundation for all future development. In Chapter 8 and Chapter 9, we will complete our authentication machinery by allowing users to log in and out of the application (with optional "remember me" functionality). In Chapter 10, we will allow all users to update their account information, and we will allow site administrators to delete users, thereby completing the full suite of Users resource REST actions identified in Table 7.1.

7.6.1 What We Learned in this Chapter

- Rails displays useful debug information via the **debug** method.

- Sass mixins allow a group of CSS rules to be bundled and reused in multiple places.

---

16. For example, at one point Heroku required Ruby 2.1.4, so I spent several hours trying unsuccessfully to install Ruby 2.1.4 on my local machine—only to discover that Ruby 2.1.5 had been released the previous day. (Attempts to install Ruby 2.1.5 then also failed.)

- Rails comes with three standard environments: **development**, **test**, and **production**.

- We can interact with users as a *resource* through a standard set of REST URLs.

- Gravatars provide a convenient way of displaying images to represent users.

- The **form_with** helper is used to generate forms for interacting with Active Record objects.

- Signup failure renders the new user page and displays error messages automatically determined by Active Record.

- Rails provides the **flash** as a standard way to display temporary messages.

- Signup success creates a user in the database, redirects to the user show page, and displays a welcome message.

- We can use integration tests to verify form submission behavior and catch regressions.

- We can configure our production application to use SSL for secure communications and Puma for high performance.

CHAPTER 8

Basic Login

Now that new users can sign up for our site (Chapter 7), it's time to give them the ability to log in and log out. In this chapter, we'll implement a basic but still fully functional login system: The application will maintain the logged-in state until the browser is closed by the user. The resulting authentication system will allow us to customize the site and implement an authorization model based on login status and identity of the current user. For example, we'll be able to update the site header with login/logout links and a profile link.

In Chapter 10, we'll impose a security model in which only logged-in users can visit the user index page, only the correct user can access the page for editing their information, and only administrative users can delete other users from the database. Finally, in Chapter 13, we'll use the identity of a logged-in user to create microposts associated with that user, and in Chapter 14 we'll allow the current user to follow other users of the application (thereby receiving a feed of their microposts).

The authentication system from this chapter will also serve a foundation for the more advanced login system developed in Chapter 9. Instead of "forgetting" users on browser close, Chapter 9 will start by *automatically* remembering users, and will then *optionally* remember users based on the value of a "remember me" check box. As a result, taken together Chapter 8 and Chapter 9 develop all three of the most common types of login systems on the web.

8.1 Sessions

HTTP is a *stateless protocol*, treating each request as an independent transaction that is unable to use information from any previous requests. This means there is no way within the Hypertext Transfer Protocol to remember a user's identity from page to page; instead, web applications requiring user login must use a *session*, which is a semi-permanent connection between two computers (such as a client computer running a web browser and a server running Rails).

The most common techniques for implementing sessions in Rails involve using *cookies*, which are small pieces of text placed on the user's browser. Because cookies persist from one page to the next, they can store information (such as a user id) that can be used by the application to retrieve the logged-in user from the database. In this section and in Section 8.2, we'll use the Rails method called **session** to make temporary sessions that expire automatically on browser close.[1] In Chapter 9, we'll learn how to make longer-lived sessions using the closely related **cookies** method.

It's convenient to model sessions as a RESTful resource: Visiting the login page will render a form for *new* sessions, logging in will *create* a session, and logging out will *destroy* it. Unlike the Users resource, which uses a database back end (via the User model) to persist data, the Sessions resource will use cookies, and much of the work involved in login comes from building this cookie-based authentication machinery. In this section and the next, we'll prepare for this work by constructing a Sessions controller, a login form, and the relevant controller actions. We'll then complete user login in Section 8.2 by adding the necessary session-manipulation code.

As in previous chapters, we'll do our work on a topic branch and merge in the changes at the end:

```
$ git checkout -b basic-login
```

8.1.1 Sessions Controller

The elements of logging in and out correspond to particular REST actions of the Sessions controller: The login form is handled by the **new** action (covered in this section), actually logging in is handled by sending a POST request to the **create** action

---

1. Some browsers offer an option to restore such sessions via a "continue where you left off" feature, but Rails has no control over this behavior. In such cases, the session cookie may persist even after logging out of the application.

(Section 8.2), and logging out is handled by sending a DELETE request to the **destroy** action (Section 8.3). (Recall the association of HTTP verbs with REST actions from Table 7.1.)

To get started, we'll generate a Sessions controller with a **new** action (Listing 8.1).

Listing 8.1: Generating the Sessions controller.

```
$ rails generate controller Sessions new
```

(Including **new** actually generates *views* as well, which is why we don't include actions like **create** and **destroy** that don't correspond to views.) Following the model from Section 7.2 for the signup page, our plan is to create a login form for creating new sessions, as mocked up in Figure 8.1.

Figure 8.1: A mockup of the login form.

Unlike the Users resource, which used the special **resources** method to obtain a full suite of RESTful routes automatically (Listing 7.3), the Sessions resource will use only named routes, handling GET and POST requests with the **login** route and DELETE requests with the **logout** route. The result appears in Listing 8.2 (which also deletes the unneeded routes generated by **rails generate controller**).

Listing 8.2: Adding a resource to get the standard RESTful actions for sessions. RED
`config/routes.rb`

```
Rails.application.routes.draw do
  root   'static_pages#home'
  get    '/help',    to: 'static_pages#help'
  get    '/about',   to: 'static_pages#about'
  get    '/contact', to: 'static_pages#contact'
  get    '/signup',  to: 'users#new'
  get    '/login',   to: 'sessions#new'
  get    '/login',   to: 'sessions#new'
  post   '/login',   to: 'sessions#create'
  delete '/logout',  to: 'sessions#destroy'
  resources :users
end
```

With the routes in Listing 8.2, we also need to update the test generated in Listing 8.1 with the new login route, as shown in Listing 8.3.

Listing 8.3: Updating the Sessions controller test to use the login route. GREEN
`test/controllers/sessions_controller_test.rb`

```
require 'test_helper'

class SessionsControllerTest < ActionDispatch::IntegrationTest

  test "should get new" do
    get login_path
    assert_response :success
  end
end
```

The routes defined in Listing 8.2 correspond to URLs and actions similar to those for users (Table 7.1), as shown in Table 8.1.

Table 8.1: Routes provided by the sessions rules in Listing 8.2.

HTTP request	URL	Named route	Action	Purpose
GET	/login	**login_path**	**new**	page for a new session (login)
POST	/login	**login_path**	**create**	create a new session (login)
DELETE	/logout	**logout_path**	**destroy**	delete a session (log out)

Since we've now added several custom named routes, it's useful to look at the complete list of the routes for our application, which we can generate using **rails routes**:

```
$ rails routes
   Prefix Verb   URI Pattern                Controller#Action
     root GET    /                          static_pages#home
     help GET    /help(.:format)            static_pages#help
    about GET    /about(.:format)           static_pages#about
  contact GET    /contact(.:format)         static_pages#contact
   signup GET    /signup(.:format)          users#new
    login GET    /login(.:format)           sessions#new
          POST   /login(.:format)           sessions#create
   logout DELETE /logout(.:format)          sessions#destroy
    users GET    /users(.:format)           users#index
          POST   /users(.:format)           users#create
 new_user GET    /users/new(.:format)       users#new
edit_user GET    /users/:id/edit(.:format)  users#edit
     user GET    /users/:id(.:format)       users#show
          PATCH  /users/:id(.:format)       users#update
          PUT    /users/:id(.:format)       users#update
          DELETE /users/:id(.:format)       users#destroy
```

It's not necessary to understand these results in detail, but viewing the routes in this manner gives us a high-level overview of the actions supported by our application.

Exercises

Solutions to the exercises are available to all Rails Tutorial purchasers at https://www.railstutorial.org/aw-solutions.

To see other people's answers and to record your own, subscribe to the Rails Tutorial course or to the Learn Enough All Access Bundle.

1. What is the difference between GET **login_path** and POST **login_path**?

2. By piping the results of **rails routes** to **grep**, list all the routes associated with the Users resource. Do the same for Sessions. How many routes does each resource

have? *Hint*: Refer to the section on grep in *Learn Enough Command Line to Be Dangerous* (www.learnenough.com/command-line).

8.1.2 Login Form

Having defined the relevant controller and route, now we'll fill in the view for new sessions—that is, the login form. Comparing Figure 8.1 with Figure 7.12, we see that the login form is similar in appearance to the signup form, except it has two fields (email and password) instead of four.

As seen in Figure 8.2, when the login information is invalid we want to re-render the login page and display an error message. In Section 7.3.3, we used an error-messages partial to display error messages, but we saw in that section that those

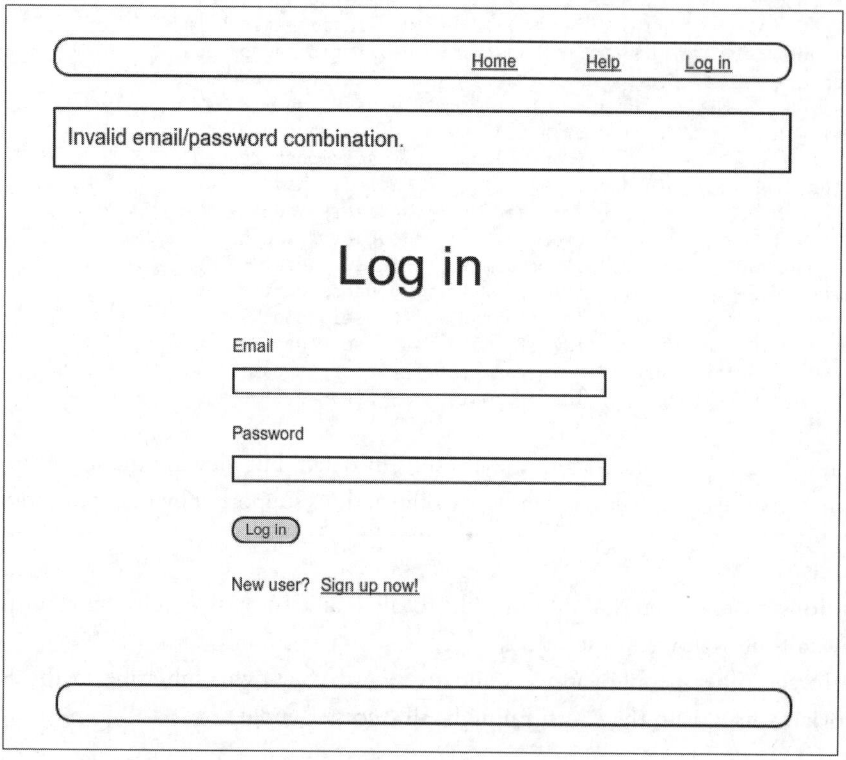

Figure 8.2: A mockup of login failure.

messages are provided automatically by Active Record. This won't work for session creation errors because the session isn't an Active Record object, so we'll render the error as a flash message instead.

Recall from Listing 7.15 that the signup form uses the **form_with** helper, taking as an argument the user instance variable **@user**:

```
<%= form_with(model: @user, local: true) do |f| %>
  .
  .
  .
<% end %>
```

The main difference between the session form and the signup form is that we have no Session model, and hence no analogue for the **@user** variable. This means that, in constructing the new session form, we have to give **form_with** slightly different information. In particular, whereas

```
form_with(model: @user, local: true)
```

enables Rails to infer that the **action** of the form should be to POST to the URL /users, in the case of sessions we need to indicate the corresponding URL, along with the *scope* (in this case, the session):

```
form_with(url: login_path, scope: :session, local: true)
```

With the proper **form_with** in hand, it's easy to make a login form to match the mockup in Figure 8.1 using the signup form (Listing 7.15) as a model, as shown in Listing 8.4.

Listing 8.4: Code for the login form.
app/views/sessions/new.html.erb

```
<% provide(:title, "Log in") %>
<h1>Log in</h1>

<div class="row">
  <div class="col-md-6 col-md-offset-3">
    <%= form_with(url: login_path, scope: :session, local: true) do |f| %>
```

```
    <%= f.label :email %>
    <%= f.email_field :email, class: 'form-control' %>

    <%= f.label :password %>
    <%= f.password_field :password, class: 'form-control' %>

    <%= f.submit "Log in", class: "btn btn-primary" %>
  <% end %>

  <p>New user? <%= link_to "Sign up now!", signup_path %></p>
  </div>
</div>
```

Note that we've added a link to the signup page for convenience. With the code in Listing 8.4, the login form appears as in Figure 8.3. (Because the "Log in" navigation link hasn't yet been filled in, you'll have to type the /login URL directly into your address bar. We'll fix this blemish in Section 8.2.3.)

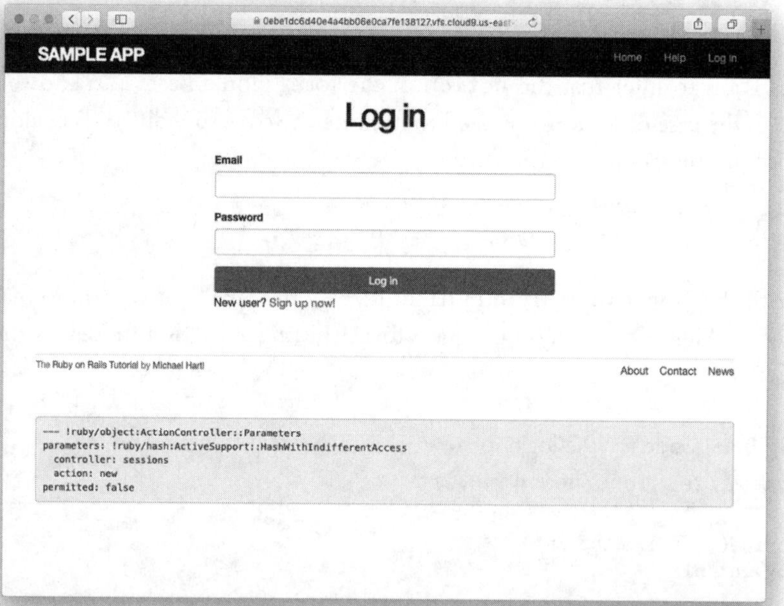

Figure 8.3: The login form.

The generated form HTML appears in Listing 8.5.

Listing 8.5: HTML for the login form produced by Listing 8.4.

```
<form accept-charset="UTF-8" action="/login" method="post">
  <input name="authenticity_token" type="hidden"
         value="NNb6+J/j46LcrgYUC60wQ2titMuJQ5lLqyAbnbAUkdo=" />
  <label for="session_email">Email</label>
  <input class="form-control" id="session_email"
         name="session[email]" type="email" />
  <label for="session_password">Password</label>
  <input id="session_password" name="session[password]"
         type="password" />
  <input class="btn btn-primary" name="commit" type="submit"
      value="Log in" />
</form>
```

Comparing Listing 8.5 with Listing 7.17, you might be able to guess that submitting this form will result in a **params** hash, where **params[:session][:email]** and **params[:session][:password]** correspond to the email and password fields, respectively.

Exercise

Solutions to the exercises are available to all Rails Tutorial purchasers at https://www.railstutorial.org/aw-solutions.

To see other people's answers and to record your own, subscribe to the Rails Tutorial course or to the Learn Enough All Access Bundle.

1. Submissions from the form defined in Listing 8.4 will be routed to the Session controller's **create** action. How does Rails know to do this? *Hint*: Refer to Table 8.1 and the first line of Listing 8.5.

8.1.3 Finding and Authenticating a User

As in the case of creating users (signup), the first step in creating sessions (login) is to handle *invalid* input. We'll start by reviewing what happens when a form gets

submitted, and then arrange for helpful error messages to appear in the case of login
failure (as mocked up in Figure 8.2). Then we'll lay the foundation for successful
login (Section 8.2) by evaluating each login submission based on the validity of its
email/password combination.

Let's start by defining a minimalist **create** action for the Sessions controller,
along with empty **new** and **destroy** actions (Listing 8.6). The **create** action in
Listing 8.6 does nothing but render the **new** view, but it's enough to get us started.
Submitting the /sessions/new form then yields the result shown in Figure 8.4 and
Figure 8.5.

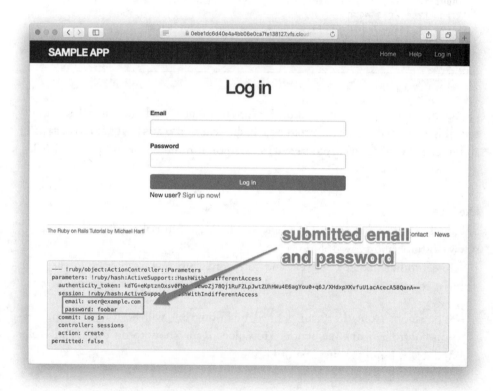

Figure 8.4: The initial failed login, with **create** as in Listing 8.6.

```
--- !ruby/object:ActionController::Parameters
parameters: !ruby/hash:ActiveSupport::HashWithIndifferentAccess
  authenticity_token: QBa8IYb8XKOlp164MhLzDzxjSnPX6aZww4LYeEFyUeFJHz16YWWJpzIA+
CgjpEtmq2GPOcr5un/nfuHa8I3YwQ==
  session: !ruby/hash:ActiveSupport::HashWithIndifferentAccess
    email: user@example.com
    password: foobar
  commit: Log in
  controller: sessions
  action: create
permitted: false
```

Figure 8.5: A closer look at the debug information from Figure 8.4.

Listing 8.6: A preliminary version of the Sessions **create** action.
app/controllers/sessions_controller.rb

```ruby
class SessionsController < ApplicationController

  def new
  end

  def create
    render 'new'
  end

  def destroy
  end
end
```

Carefully inspecting the debug information in Figure 8.5 shows that, as hinted at the end of Section 8.1.2, the submission results in a **params** hash containing the email and password under the key **session**, which (omitting some irrelevant details used internally by Rails) appears as follows:

```
---
session:
  email: 'user@example.com'
  password: 'foobar'
commit: Log in
action: create
controller: sessions
```

As with the case of user signup (Figure 7.16), these parameters form a *nested* hash like the one we saw in Listing 4.13. In particular, **params** contains a nested hash of the form

```
{ session: { password: "foobar", email: "user@example.com" } }
```

This means that

```
params[:session]
```

is itself a hash:

```
{ password: "foobar", email: "user@example.com" }
```

As a result,

```
params[:session][:email]
```

is the submitted email address and

```
params[:session][:password]
```

is the submitted password.

In other words, inside the **create** action the **params** hash has all the information needed to authenticate users by email and password. Not coincidentally, we already have exactly the methods we need: the **User.find_by** method provided by Active Record (Section 6.1.4) and the **authenticate** method provided by **has_secure_password** (Section 6.3.4). Recalling that **authenticate** returns **false** for an invalid authentication (Section 6.3.4), our strategy for user login can be summarized as shown in Listing 8.7.

Listing 8.7: Finding and authenticating a user.
`app/controllers/sessions_controller.rb`

```ruby
class SessionsController < ApplicationController

  def new
  end

  def create
    user = User.find_by(email: params[:session][:email].downcase)
    if user && user.authenticate(params[:session][:password])
      # Log the user in and redirect to the user's show page.
    else
      # Create an error message.
      render 'new'
    end
  end

  def destroy
  end
end
```

The first highlighted line in Listing 8.7 pulls the user out of the database using the submitted email address. (Recall from Section 6.2.5 that email addresses are saved as all lowercase, so here we use the **downcase** method to ensure a match when the submitted address is valid.) The next line can be a bit confusing but is fairly common in idiomatic Rails programming:

```ruby
user && user.authenticate(params[:session][:password])
```

This line uses **&&** (logical *and*) to determine if the resulting user is valid. Taking into account that any object other than **nil** and **false** itself is **true** in a boolean context (Section 4.2.2), the possibilities appear as in Table 8.2. We see from Table 8.2 that the **if** statement is **true** only if a user with the given email both exists in the database and has the given password—exactly as required.

Exercise

Solutions to the exercises are available to all Rails Tutorial purchasers at https://www.railstutorial.org/aw-solutions.

To see other people's answers and to record your own, subscribe to the Rails Tutorial course or to the Learn Enough All Access Bundle.

Table 8.2: Possible results of **user && user.authenticate(…)**.

User	Password	a && b
nonexistent	*anything*	**(nil && [anything]) == false**
valid user	wrong password	**(true && false) == false**
valid user	right password	**(true && true) == true**

1. Using the Rails console, confirm each of the values in Table 8.2. Start with **user = nil**, and then use **user = User.first**. *Hint*: To coerce the result to a boolean value, use the bang-bang trick from Section 4.2.2, as in **!!(user && user.authenticate('foobar'))**.

8.1.4 Rendering with a Flash Message

Recall from Section 7.3.3 that we displayed signup errors using the User model error messages. These errors are associated with a particular Active Record object, but this strategy won't work here because the session isn't an Active Record model. Instead, we'll put a message in the flash to be displayed upon failed login. A first, slightly incorrect, attempt appears in Listing 8.8.

Listing 8.8: An (unsuccessful) attempt at handling failed login.
app/controllers/sessions_controller.rb

```ruby
class SessionsController < ApplicationController

  def new
  end

  def create
    user = User.find_by(email: params[:session][:email].downcase)
    if user && user.authenticate(params[:session][:password])
      # Log the user in and redirect to the user's show page.
    else
      flash[:danger] = 'Invalid email/password combination' # Not quite right!
      render 'new'
    end
  end
end
```

```
 def destroy
  end
end
```

Because of the flash message display in the site layout (Listing 7.29), the **flash[:danger]** message automatically gets displayed; because of the Bootstrap CSS, it automatically gets nice styling (Figure 8.6).

Unfortunately, as noted in the text and in the comment in Listing 8.8, this code isn't quite right. The page looks fine, though, so what's the problem? The issue is that the contents of the flash persist for one *request*, but—unlike a redirect, which we used in Listing 7.27—re-rendering a template with **render** doesn't count as a request. The result is that the flash message persists one request longer than we want. For example, if we submit invalid login information and then click on the Home page, the flash gets displayed a second time (Figure 8.7). Fixing this blemish is the task of Section 8.1.5.

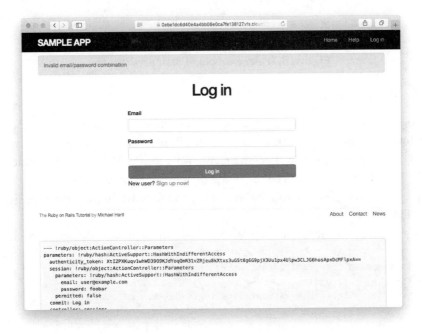

Figure 8.6: The flash message for a failed login.

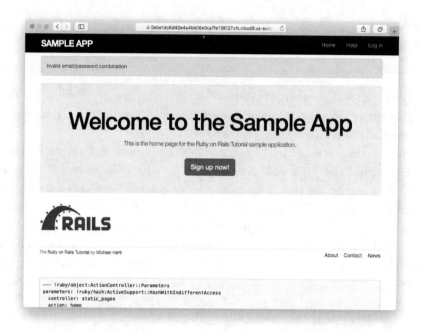

Figure 8.7: An example of flash persistence.

8.1.5 A Flash Test

The incorrect flash behavior is a minor bug in our application. According to the testing guidelines from Box 3.3, this is exactly the sort of situation where we should write a test to catch the error so that it doesn't recur. We'll thus write a short integration test for the login form submission before proceeding. In addition to documenting the bug and preventing a regression, this will give us a good foundation for further integration tests of login and logout.

We start by generating an integration test for our application's login behavior:

```
$ rails generate integration_test users_login
      invoke  test_unit
      create    test/integration/users_login_test.rb
```

Next, we need a test to capture the sequence shown in Figure 8.6 and Figure 8.7. The basic steps appear as follows:

1. Visit the login path.

2. Verify that the new sessions form renders properly.

3. Post to the sessions path with an invalid **params** hash.

4. Verify that the new sessions form gets re-rendered and that a flash message appears.

5. Visit another page (such as the Home page).

6. Verify that the flash message *doesn't* appear on the new page.

A test implementing these steps appears in Listing 8.9.

Listing 8.9: A test to catch unwanted flash persistence. RED
`test/integration/users_login_test.rb`

```ruby
require 'test_helper'

class UsersLoginTest < ActionDispatch::IntegrationTest

  test "login with invalid information" do
    get login_path
    assert_template 'sessions/new'
    post login_path, params: { session: { email: "", password: "" } }
    assert_template 'sessions/new'
    assert_not flash.empty?
    get root_path
    assert flash.empty?
  end
end
```

After adding the test in Listing 8.9, the login test should be RED:

Listing 8.10: RED

```
$ rails test test/integration/users_login_test.rb
```

This code shows how to run one (and only one) test file using **rails test** and the full path to the file.

The way to get the failing test in Listing 8.9 to pass is to replace **flash** with the special variant **flash.now**, which is specifically designed for displaying flash messages on rendered pages. Unlike the contents of **flash**, the contents of **flash.now** disappear as soon as there is an additional request, which is exactly the behavior we've tested in Listing 8.9. With this substitution, the corrected application code appears as in Listing 8.11.

Listing 8.11: Correct code for failed login. GREEN
`app/controllers/sessions_controller.rb`

```ruby
class SessionsController < ApplicationController

  def new
  end

  def create
    user = User.find_by(email: params[:session][:email].downcase)
    if user && user.authenticate(params[:session][:password])
      # Log the user in and redirect to the user's show page.
    else
      flash.now[:danger] = 'Invalid email/password combination'
      render 'new'
    end
  end

  def destroy
  end
end
```

We can then verify that both the login integration test and the full test suite are GREEN:

Listing 8.12: GREEN

```
$ rails test test/integration/users_login_test.rb
$ rails test
```

Exercise

Solutions to the exercises are available to all Rails Tutorial purchasers at https://www.railstutorial.org/aw-solutions.

To see other people's answers and to record your own, subscribe to the Rails Tutorial course or to the Learn Enough All Access Bundle.

1. Verify in your browser that the sequence from Section 8.1.4 works correctly—that is, that the flash message disappears when you click on a second page.

8.2 Logging In

Now that our login form can handle invalid submissions, the next step is to handle valid submissions correctly by actually logging a user in. In this section, we'll log the user in with a temporary session cookie that expires automatically upon browser close. In Section 9.1, we'll add sessions that persist even after closing the browser.

Implementing sessions will involve defining a large number of related functions for use across multiple controllers and views. You may recall from Section 4.2.4 that Ruby provides a *module* facility for packaging such functions in one place. Conveniently, a Sessions helper module was generated automatically when generating the Sessions controller (Section 8.1.1). Moreover, such helpers are automatically included in Rails views; by including the module into the base class of all controllers (the Application controller), we arrange to make them available in our controllers as well (Listing 8.13).[2]

Listing 8.13: Including the Sessions helper module into the Application controller.
`app/controllers/application_controller.rb`

```
class ApplicationController < ActionController::Base
  include SessionsHelper
end
```

With this configuration complete, we're now ready to write the code to log users in.

---

2. I like this technique because it connects to the pure Ruby way of including modules, but Rails 4 introduced a technique called *concerns* that can also be used for this purpose. To learn how to use concerns, run a search here for "how to use concerns in Rails."

8.2.1 The `log_in` Method

Logging a user in is simple with the help of the **session** method defined by
Rails. (This method is separate and distinct from the Sessions controller generated
in Section 8.1.1.) We can treat **session** as if it were a hash, and assign to it as
follows:

```
session[:user_id] = user.id
```

This places a temporary cookie on the user's browser containing an encrypted version of the user's id, which allows us to retrieve the id on subsequent pages using
session[:user_id]. In contrast to the persistent cookie created by the **cookies**
method (Section 9.1), the temporary cookie created by the **session** method expires
immediately when the browser is closed.

Because we'll want to use the same login technique in several places, we'll define
a method called **log_in** in the Sessions helper, as shown in Listing 8.14.

Listing 8.14: The **log_in** function.
app/helpers/sessions_helper.rb

```ruby
module SessionsHelper

  # Logs in the given user.
  def log_in(user)
    session[:user_id] = user.id
  end
end
```

Because temporary cookies created using the **session** method are automatically
encrypted, the code in Listing 8.14 is secure, and there is no way for an attacker
to use the session information to log in as the user. This applies only to temporary
sessions initiated with the **session** method, though, and is *not* the case for persistent
sessions created using the **cookies** method. Permanent cookies are vulnerable to a
session hijacking attack, so in Chapter 9 we'll have to be much more careful about the
information we place on the user's browser.

With the **log_in** method defined in Listing 8.14, we're now ready to complete the session **create** action by logging the user in and redirecting to the user's profile page. The result appears in Listing 8.15.[3]

Listing 8.15: Logging in a user.
app/controllers/sessions_controller.rb

```
 1  class SessionsController < ApplicationController
 2
 3    def new
 4    end
 5
 6    def create
 7      user = User.find_by(email: params[:session][:email].downcase)
 8      if user && user.authenticate(params[:session][:password])
 9        log_in user
10        redirect_to user
11      else
12        flash.now[:danger] = 'Invalid email/password combination'
13        render 'new'
14      end
15    end
16
17    def destroy
18    end
19  end
```

Note the compact redirect

```
redirect_to user
```

which we saw earlier in Section 7.4.1. Rails automatically converts it to the route for the user's profile page:

```
user_url(user)
```

With the **create** action defined in Listing 8.15, the login form defined in Listing 8.4 should now be working. It doesn't have any effects on the application display,

---

3. The **log_in** method is available in the Sessions controller because of the module inclusion in Listing 8.13.

though, so short of inspecting the browser session directly there's no way to tell that you're logged in. As a first step toward enabling more visible changes, in Section 8.2.2 we'll retrieve the current user from the database using the id in the session. In Section 8.2.3, we'll change the links on the application layout, including a URL to the current user's profile.

Exercises

Solutions to the exercises are available to all Rails Tutorial purchasers at https://www.railstutorial.org/aw-solutions.

To see other people's answers and to record your own, subscribe to the Rails Tutorial course or to the Learn Enough All Access Bundle.

1. Log in with a valid user and inspect your browser's cookies. What is the value of the session content? *Hint*: If you don't know how to view your browser's cookies, Google it to find out (Box 1.2).

2. What is the value of the **Expires** attribute from the previous exercise?

8.2.2 Current User

Having placed the user's id securely in the temporary session, we are now in a position to retrieve it on subsequent pages, which we'll do by defining a **current_user** method to find the user in the database corresponding to the session id. The purpose of **current_user** is to allow constructions such as

```
<%= current_user.name %>
```

and

```
redirect_to current_user
```

To find the current user, one possibility is to use the **find** method, as on the user profile page (Listing 7.5):

```
User.find(session[:user_id])
```

But recall from Section 6.1.4 that **find** raises an exception if the user id doesn't exist. This behavior is appropriate on the user profile page because it will happen only if the id is invalid, but in the present case **session[:user_id]** will often be **nil** (i.e., for non-logged-in users). To handle this possibility, we'll use the same **find_by** method we used to find by email address in the **create** method, but with **id** in place of **email**:

```
User.find_by(id: session[:user_id])
```

Rather than raising an exception, this method returns **nil** (indicating no such user) if the id is invalid.

We could now define the **current_user** method as follows:

```
def current_user
  if session[:user_id]
    User.find_by(id: session[:user_id])
  end
end
```

(If the session user id doesn't exist, the function just falls off the end and returns **nil** automatically, which is exactly what we want.) This would work fine, but it would hit the database multiple times if, for example, **current_user** appeared multiple times on a page. Instead, we'll follow a common Ruby convention by storing the result of **User.find_by** in an instance variable, which hits the database the first time but returns the instance variable immediately on subsequent invocations:[4]

```
if @current_user.nil?
  @current_user = User.find_by(id: session[:user_id])
else
  @current_user
end
```

Recalling the *or* operator || seen in Section 4.2.2, we can rewrite this as follows:

```
@current_user = @current_user || User.find_by(id: session[:user_id])
```

Because a User object is true in a boolean context, the call to **find_by** gets executed only if **@current_user** hasn't yet been assigned.

---

4. This practice of remembering variable assignments from one method invocation to the next is known as *memoization*. (This is a technical term, *not* a misspelling of "memorization"—a subtlety lost on the hapless copyeditor of a previous edition of this book.)

Although the preceding code would work, it's not idiomatically correct Ruby. Instead, the proper way to write the assignment to **@current_user** is like this:

```
@current_user ||= User.find_by(id: session[:user_id])
```

This uses the potentially confusing but frequently used **||=** ("or equals") operator (Box 8.1).

Box 8.1: What the *$@! is ||= ?

The ||= ("or equals") assignment operator is a common Ruby idiom and is thus important for aspiring Rails developers to recognize. Although at first it may seem mysterious, *or equals* is easy to understand by analogy.

We start by noting the common pattern of incrementing a variable:

```
x = x + 1
```

Many languages provide a syntactic shortcut for this operation. In Ruby (and in C, C++, Perl, Python, Java, and others), it can also appear as follows:

```
x += 1
```

Analogous constructs exist for other operators as well:

```
$ rails console
>> x = 1
=> 1
>> x += 1
=> 2
>> x *= 3
=> 6
>> x -= 8
=> -2
>> x /= 2
=> -1
```

In each case, the pattern is that x = x O y and x O= y are equivalent for any operator O.

Another common Ruby pattern is assigning to a variable if it's nil but otherwise leaving it alone. Recalling the *or* operator || seen in Section 4.2.2, we can write this as follows:

```
>> @foo
=> nil
>> @foo = @foo || "bar"
```

```
=> "bar"
>> @foo = @foo || "baz"
=> "bar"
```

Since `nil` is false in a boolean context, the first assignment to `@foo` is `nil ||` "bar", which evaluates to "bar". Similarly, the second assignment is `@foo ||` "baz", equivalent to "bar" || "baz", which also evaluates to "bar". This is because anything other than `nil` or `false` is `true` in a boolean context, and the series of `||` expressions terminates after the first true expression is evaluated. (This practice of evaluating `||` expressions from left to right and stopping on the first true value is known as *short-circuit evaluation*. The same principle applies to `&&` statements, except in this case evaluation stops on the first *false* value.)

Comparing the console sessions for the various operators, we see that `@foo = @foo ||` "bar" follows the `x = x O y` pattern with `||` in the place of `O`:

```
x    = x + 1        ->   x      += 1
x    = x * 3        ->   x      *= 3
x    = x - 8        ->   x      -= 8
x    = x / 2        ->   x      /= 2
@foo = @foo || "bar"    ->   @foo ||= "bar"
```

Thus `@foo = @foo ||` "bar" and `@foo ||=` "bar" are equivalent. In the context of the current user, this suggests the following construction:

```
@current_user ||= User.find_by(id: session[:user_id])
```

Voilà!
(Technically, Ruby evaluates the expression `@foo || @foo = "bar"`, which avoids an unnecessary assignment when `@foo` is not `nil` or `false`. But this expression doesn't explain the `||=` notation as well, so the discussion here uses the nearly equivalent `@foo = @foo ||` "bar".)

Applying the results of this discussion yields the succinct **current_user** method shown in Listing 8.16. (There's a slight amount of repetition in the use of **session[:user_id]**, which we'll eliminate in Section 9.1.2.)

Listing 8.16: Finding the current user in the session.
app/helpers/sessions_helper.rb

```
module SessionsHelper

  # Logs in the given user.
  def log_in(user)
```

```
     session[:user_id] = user.id
  end

  # Returns the current logged-in user (if any).
  def current_user
    if session[:user_id]
      @current_user ||= User.find_by(id: session[:user_id])
    end
  end
end
```

With the working **current_user** method in Listing 8.16, we're now in a position to
make changes to our application based on user login status.

Exercises

Solutions to the exercises are available to all Rails Tutorial purchasers at https://
www.railstutorial.org/aw-solutions.

   To see other people's answers and to record your own, subscribe to the Rails
Tutorial course or to the Learn Enough All Access Bundle.

1. Confirm at the console that **User.find_by(id: ...)** returns **nil** when the
   corresponding user doesn't exist.

2. In a Rails console, create a **session** hash with key **:user_id**. By fol-
   lowing the steps in Listing 8.17, confirm that the **||=** operator works as
   required.

Listing 8.17: Simulating **session** in the console.

```
>> session = {}
>> session[:user_id] = nil
>> @current_user ||= User.find_by(id: session[:user_id])
<What happens here?>
>> session[:user_id]= User.first.id
>> @current_user ||= User.find_by(id: session[:user_id])
<What happens here?>
>> @current_user ||= User.find_by(id: session[:user_id])
<What happens here?>
```

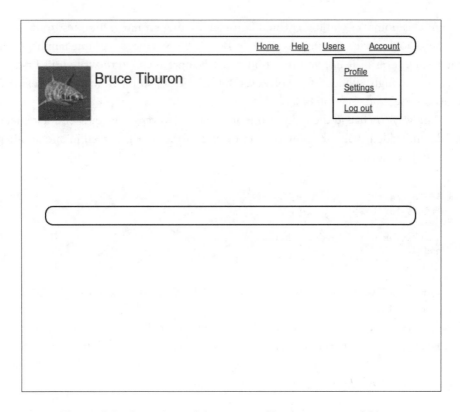

Figure 8.8: A mockup of the user profile after a successful login.

8.2.3 Changing the Layout Links

The first practical application of logging in involves changing the layout links based on login status. In particular, as seen in the Figure 8.8 mockup,[5] we'll add links for logging out, for user settings, for listing all users, and for the current user's profile page. Note in Figure 8.8 that the logout and profile links appear in a dropdown "Account" menu; we'll see in Listing 8.19 how to make such a menu with Bootstrap.

---

5. Image retrieved from https://www.flickr.com/photos/elevy/14730820387 on 2016-06-03. Copyright © 2014 by Elias Levy and used unaltered under the terms of the Creative Commons Attribution 2.0 Generic license.

At this point, in real life I would consider writing an integration test to capture the behavior described earlier. As noted in Box 3.3, as you become more familiar with the testing tools in Rails, you may find yourself more inclined to write tests first. In this case, though, such a test involves several new ideas, so for now it's best deferred to its own section (Section 8.2.4).

The way to change the links in the site layout involves using an if-else statement inside embedded Ruby to show one set of links if the user is logged in and another set of links otherwise:

```
<% if logged_in? %>
  # Links for logged-in users
<% else %>
  # Links for non-logged-in-users
<% end %>
```

This kind of code requires the existence of a **logged_in?** boolean method, which we'll now define.

A user is logged in if there is a current user in the session—that is, if **current_user** is not **nil**. Checking for this requires the use of the "not" operator (Section 4.2.2), written using an exclamation point **!** and usually read as "bang." The resulting **logged_in?** method appears in Listing 8.18.

Listing 8.18: The **logged_in?** helper method.
app/helpers/sessions_helper.rb
***

```
module SessionsHelper

  # Logs in the given user.
  def log_in(user)
    session[:user_id] = user.id
  end

  # Returns the current logged-in user (if any).
  def current_user
    if session[:user_id]
      @current_user ||= User.find_by(id: session[:user_id])
    end
  end
```

```
# Returns true if the user is logged in, false otherwise.
def logged_in?
  !current_user.nil?
end
end
```

With the addition in Listing 8.18, we're now ready to change the layout links if a user is logged in. There are four new links, two of which are stubbed out (to be completed in Chapter 10):

```
<%= link_to "Users",    '#' %>
<%= link_to "Settings", '#' %>
```

The logout link, meanwhile, uses the logout path defined in Listing 8.2:

```
<%= link_to "Log out", logout_path, method: :delete %>
```

Notice that the logout link passes a hash argument indicating that it should submit an HTTP DELETE request.[6] We'll also add a profile link as follows:

```
<%= link_to "Profile", current_user %>
```

Here we could write

```
<%= link_to "Profile", user_path(current_user) %>
```

but as usual Rails allows us to link directly to the user by automatically converting **current_user** into **user_path(current_user)** in this context. Finally, when users *aren't* logged in, we'll use the login path defined in Listing 8.2 to make a link to the login form:

```
<%= link_to "Log in", login_path %>
```

Putting everything together gives the updated header partial shown in Listing 8.19.

---

6. Web browsers can't actually issue DELETE requests; Rails fakes it with JavaScript.

Listing 8.19: Changing the layout links for logged-in users.
`app/views/layouts/_header.html.erb`

```erb
<header class="navbar navbar-fixed-top navbar-inverse">
  <div class="container">
    <%= link_to "sample app", root_path, id: "logo" %>
    <nav>
      <ul class="nav navbar-nav navbar-right">
        <li><%= link_to "Home", root_path %></li>
        <li><%= link_to "Help", help_path %></li>
        <% if logged_in? %>
          <li><%= link_to "Users", "#" %></li>
          <li class="dropdown">
            <a href="#" class="dropdown-toggle" data-toggle="dropdown">
              Account <b class="caret"></b>
            </a>
            <ul class="dropdown-menu">
              <li><%= link_to "Profile", current_user %></li>
              <li><%= link_to "Settings", "#" %></li>
              <li class="divider"></li>
              <li>
                <%= link_to "Log out", logout_path, method: "delete" %>
              </li>
            </ul>
          </li>
        <% else %>
          <li><%= link_to "Log in", login_path %></li>
        <% end %>
      </ul>
    </nav>
  </div>
</header>
```

As part of including the new links into the layout, Listing 8.19 takes advantage of Bootstrap's ability to make dropdown menus.[7] Note in particular the inclusion of the special Bootstrap CSS classes such as **dropdown**, **dropdown-menu**, and so forth. To activate the dropdown menu, we need to include Bootstrap's custom Java-Script library into our application (which is *not* included automatically as part of the `bootstrap-sass` gem in Listing 5.5), as well as the jQuery library.

---

7. See the Bootstrap components page (getbootstrap.com/docs/3.4/components) for more information.

Section 5.2 mentioned briefly that the Rails asset pipeline works in parallel with Webpack and Yarn, and we need to put both to work to include the necessary JavaScript. The first step is to install both jQuery and Bootstrap's JavaScript library in our application, which coincidentally needs the same version number for each:

```
$ yarn add jquery@3.4.1 bootstrap@3.4.1
```

To make jQuery available in our application, we need to edit Webpack's environment file and add the content shown in Listing 8.20.

Listing 8.20: Adding jQuery configuration to Webpack.
config/webpack/environment.js

```
const { environment } = require('@rails/webpacker')

const webpack = require('webpack')
environment.plugins.prepend('Provide',
  new webpack.ProvidePlugin({
    $: 'jquery/src/jquery',
    jQuery: 'jquery/src/jquery'
  })
)

module.exports = environment
```

Finally, we need to require jQuery and import Bootstrap in our **application.js** file, as shown in Listing 8.21.[8]

Listing 8.21: Requiring and importing the necessary JavaScript libraries.
app/javascript/packs/application.js

```
require("@rails/ujs").start()
require("turbolinks").start()
require("@rails/activestorage").start()
require("channels")
require("jquery")
import "bootstrap"
```

---

8. For what it's worth, I don't know offhand why one uses **require** and the other uses **import**.

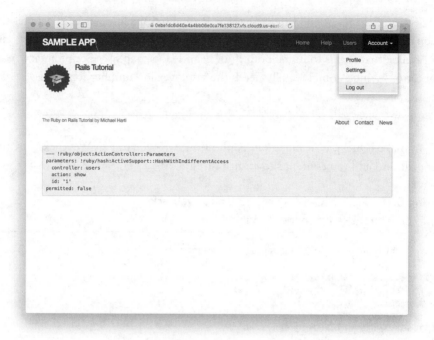

Figure 8.9: A logged-in user with new links and a dropdown menu.

At this point, you should visit the login path and log in as a valid user (username **example@railstutorial.org**, password **foobar**), which effectively tests the code in the previous three sections.[9] With the code in Listing 8.19 and Listing 8.21, you should see the dropdown menu and links for logged-in users, as shown in Figure 8.9.

If you quit your browser completely, you should also be able to verify that the application forgets your login status, requiring you to log in again to see the changes made in the previous session.[10]

Mobile styling

Now that we've got the dropdown menu working, we're going to take an opportunity to add a few design tweaks for mobile devices, thereby fulfilling a promise made in

---

9. You may have to restart the webserver to get this to work (Box 1.2).

10. If you're using the cloud IDE, I recommend using a different browser to test the login behavior so that you don't have to close down the browser running the IDE.

Section 5.1.[11] As noted in that section, this is not a tutorial on web design, so we'll be making the minimum set of changes needed to make the mobile app look nice, but you can find a much more detailed treatment of mobile styling in *Learn Enough CSS & Layout to Be Dangerous* (www.learnenough.com/css-and-layout), especially Chapter 9, "Mobile media queries".

Our first step in applying some mobile-friendly design is to view our current app as it appears in a mobile device. One possibility is simply using a smartphone to view the site, but this can be inconvenient, especially if the development app is running behind a cloud IDE login wall or on a local network (which is often inaccessible to outside devices). A more convenient alternative is to use a feature of the Safari web browser known as "Responsive Design Mode", which can be activated as shown in Figure 8.10.[12] This mode gives us the ability to view the app as it appears in any of a number of different mobile devices, as seen in Figure 8.11.[13]

Now let's take a look at the profile page from Figure 8.9 as it appears in a mobile device. As seen in Figure 8.12, the menu items currently aren't nicely aligned, and the menu itself takes over a large part of the top of the screen. Meanwhile, the footer navigation links appear in an awkward location, squished up against the other link in the footer. These are the only major issues we need to address, and we'll be able to fix both of them with a surprisingly small amount of code.

Our first step is to add a special **meta** tag called the *viewport*, which lets developers switch between desktop and mobile modes.[14] The result, which goes in the application template, appears in Listing 8.22.

Listing 8.22: Adding the viewport **meta** tag.
`app/views/layouts/application.html.erb`

```
<!DOCTYPE html>
<html>
  <head>
```

---

11. Several of these changes were based on or inspired by the excellent work of *Rails Tutorial* reader Craig Zeise.

12. See "Mobile viewport" in *Learn Enough CSS & Layout to Be Dangerous* (www.learnenough.com/css-and-layout) for yet another alternative.

13. To change the aspect ratio from portrait to landscape for any of the devices, simply double-click on the corresponding icon. Back when we were making *Learn Enough CSS & Layout to Be Dangerous* (www.learnenough.com/css-and-layout), it took me and my coauthor Lee Donahoe a surprisingly long time to figure this out.

14. See "Mobile viewport" in *Learn Enough CSS & Layout to Be Dangerous* (www.learnenough.com/css-and-layout) for more details.

```
<title><%= full_title(yield(:title)) %></title>
<meta charset="utf-8">
<meta name="viewport" content="width=device-width, initial-scale=1">
<%= csrf_meta_tags %>
<%= csp_meta_tag %>
  .
  .
  .
```

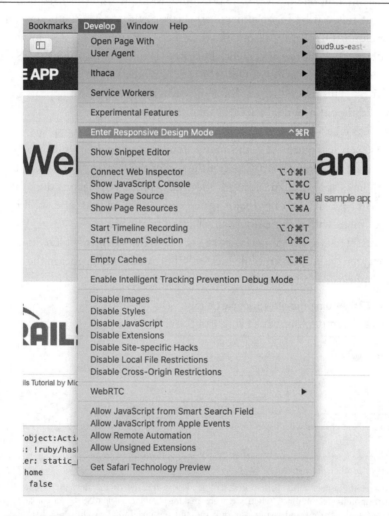

Figure 8.10: The menu item to enter Safari's Responsive Design Mode.

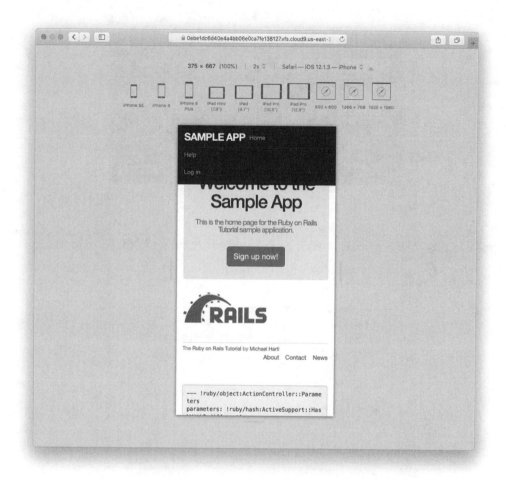

Figure 8.11: Safari's Responsive Design Mode.

To fix the menu, we'll use a so-called "hamburger menu" (named for its unintentional resemblance to a hamburger) when in mobile mode. This involves adding some markup to the header file from Listing 8.19, as shown in Listing 8.23.[15]

---

15. I might never have figured this out on my own. Thanks again to Craig Zeise for his fantastic volunteer effort.

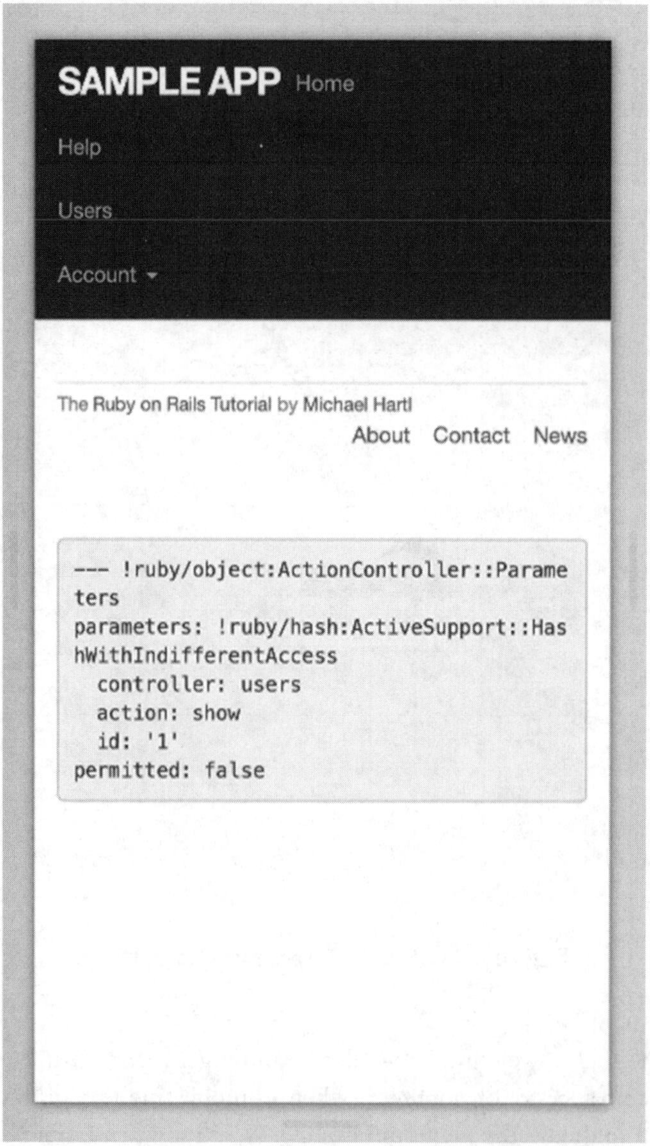

Figure 8.12: The current mobile view of a user profile.

Listing 8.23: Adding the markup for a hamburger menu.
`app/views/layouts/_header.html.erb`

```erb
<header class="navbar navbar-fixed-top navbar-inverse">
  <div class="container">
    <%= link_to "sample app", root_path, id: "logo" %>
    <nav>
      <div class="navbar-header">
        <button type="button" class="navbar-toggle collapsed"
                data-toggle="collapse"
                data-target="#bs-example-navbar-collapse-1"
                aria-expanded="false">
          <span class="sr-only">Toggle navigation</span>
          <span class="icon-bar"></span>
          <span class="icon-bar"></span>
          <span class="icon-bar"></span>
        </button>
      </div>
      <ul class="nav navbar-nav navbar-right collapse navbar-collapse"
          id="bs-example-navbar-collapse-1">
          .
          .
          .
      </ul>
    </nav>
  </div>
</header>
```

The result of Listing 8.23 appears in Figure 8.13. Pressing or clicking the hamburger icon then opens the menu, as shown in Figure 8.14. Note what a significant improvement this is compared to the default menu shown in Figure 8.12.

As a final step, we'll add a little CSS to fix the footer issue. The trick is to use a *media query* to apply different CSS for mobile devices than for desktop computers. The result, obtained after some trial-and-error in a web inspector, appears in Listing 8.24.[16] Note that the new styles will be applied when the width of the device is less than 800 pixels, which is a common threshold (known as a "breakpoint") for mobile devices.

---

16. Thanks to Learn Enough cofounder and *Learn Enough CSS & Layout to Be Dangerous* (www.learnenough.com/css-and-layout) coauthor Lee Donahoe for his assistance.

Figure 8.13: Using a hamburger menu for mobile.

Figure 8.14: The view after clicking the hamburger menu.

After refreshing the browser to apply the style in Listing 8.24, our app appears as shown in Figure 8.15.

Listing 8.24: Updating the footer CSS.
`app/assets/stylesheets/custom.scss`

```scss
.
.
.
/* footer */

footer {
  .
  .
  .
}
@media (max-width: 800px) {
  footer {
    small {
      display: block;
      float: none;
      margin-bottom: 1em;
    }
    ul {
      float: none;
      padding: 0;
      li {
        float: none;
        margin-left: 0;
      }
    }
  }
}
```

With that, our mobile styling is done, and we're ready to add some tests for the layout links added in this section.

Exercises

Solutions to the exercises are available to all Rails Tutorial purchasers at https://www.railstutorial.org/aw-solutions.

To see other people's answers and to record your own, subscribe to the Rails Tutorial course or to the Learn Enough All Access Bundle.

Figure 8.15: The footer styled for mobile.

1. Using the cookie inspector in your browser (Section 8.2.1), remove the session cookie and confirm that the layout links revert to the non-logged-in state.

2. Log in again, confirming that the layout links change correctly. Then quit your browser and start it again to confirm that the layout links revert to the non-logged-in state. (If your browser has a "remember where I left off" feature that automatically restores the session, be sure to disable it in this step (Box 1.2).)

8.2.4 Testing Layout Changes

Having verified by hand that the application is behaving properly upon successful login, before moving on we'll write an integration test to capture that behavior and catch regressions. We'll build on the test from Listing 8.9 and write a series of steps to verify the following sequence of actions:

1. Visit the login path.
2. Post valid information to the sessions path.
3. Verify that the login link disappears.
4. Verify that a logout link appears.
5. Verify that a profile link appears.

To see these changes, our test needs to log in as a previously registered user, which means that such a user must already exist in the database. The default Rails way to do this is to use *fixtures*, which are a way of organizing data for loading into the test database. We discovered in Section 6.2.5 that we needed to delete the default fixtures so that our email uniqueness tests would pass (Listing 6.31). Now we're ready to start filling in that empty file with custom fixtures of our own.

In the present case, we need only one user, whose information should consist of a valid name and email address. Because we'll need to log the user in, we also have to include a valid password to compare with the password submitted to the Sessions controller's **create** action. Referring to the data model in Figure 6.9, we see that this means creating a **password_digest** attribute for the user fixture, which we'll accomplish by defining a **digest** method of our own.

As discussed in Section 6.3.1, the password digest is created using bcrypt (via **has_secure_password**), so we'll need to create the fixture password using the same method. By inspecting the secure password source code, we find that this method is

```
BCrypt::Password.create(string, cost: cost)
```

where **string** is the string to be hashed and **cost** is the *cost parameter* that determines the computational cost to calculate the hash. Specifying a high cost makes it computationally intractable to use the hash to determine the original password, which is an important security precaution in a production environment, but in tests we want the **digest** method to be as fast as possible. The secure password source code has a line for this as well:

```
cost = ActiveModel::SecurePassword.min_cost ? BCrypt::Engine::MIN_COST :
                                               BCrypt::Engine.cost
```

This rather obscure code, which you don't need to understand in detail, arranges for precisely the behavior we want: It uses the minimum cost parameter in tests and a normal (high) cost parameter in production. (We'll learn more about the strange **?-:** notation in Section 9.2.)

There are several places we could put the resulting **digest** method, but we'll have an opportunity in Section 9.1.1 to reuse **digest** in the User model. This suggests placing the method in **user.rb**. Because we won't necessarily have access to a user object when calculating the digest (as will be the case in the fixtures file), we'll attach the **digest** method to the User class itself, which (as we saw briefly in Section 4.4.1) makes it a *class method*. The result appears in Listing 8.25.

Listing 8.25: Adding a digest method for use in fixtures.
app/models/user.rb

```ruby
class User < ApplicationRecord
  before_save { self.email = email.downcase }
  validates :name,  presence: true, length: { maximum: 50 }
  VALID_EMAIL_REGEX = /\A[\w+\-.]+@[a-z\d\-.]+\.[a-z]+\z/i
  validates :email, presence: true, length: { maximum: 255 },
                    format: { with: VALID_EMAIL_REGEX },
                    uniqueness: true
  has_secure_password
  validates :password, presence: true, length: { minimum: 6 }
```

```
  # Returns the hash digest of the given string.
  def User.digest(string)
    cost = ActiveModel::SecurePassword.min_cost ? BCrypt::Engine::MIN_COST :
                                                   BCrypt::Engine.cost
    BCrypt::Password.create(string, cost: cost)
  end
end
```

With the **digest** method from Listing 8.25, we are now ready to create a user fixture for a valid user, as shown in Listing 8.26.[17]

Listing 8.26: A fixture for testing user login.

test/fixtures/users.yml

```
michael:
  name: Michael Example
  email: michael@example.com
  password_digest: <%= User.digest('password') %>
```

Note that fixtures support embedded Ruby, which allows us to use

```
<%= User.digest('password') %>
```

to create the valid password digest for the test user.

Although we've defined the **password_digest** attribute required by **has_secure_password**, sometimes it's convenient to refer to the plain (virtual) password as well. Unfortunately, this is impossible to arrange with fixtures, and adding a **password** attribute to Listing 8.26 causes Rails to complain that there is no such column in the database (which is true). We'll make do by adopting the convention that all fixture users have the same password (**'password'**).

Having created a fixture with a valid user, we can retrieve it inside a test as follows:

```
user = users(:michael)
```

---

17. Indentation in fixture files must take the form of spaces, not tabs, so take care when copying code like that shown in Listing 8.26.

Here **users** corresponds to the fixture filename **users.yml**, while the symbol
:michael references user with the key shown in Listing 8.26.

Armed with our fixture user as above, we can now write a test for the layout links
by converting the sequence enumerated at the beginning of this section into code, as
shown in Listing 8.27.

Listing 8.27: A test for a user logging in with valid information. GREEN
`test/integration/users_login_test.rb`

```ruby
require 'test_helper'

class UsersLoginTest < ActionDispatch::IntegrationTest

  def setup
    @user = users(:michael)
  end

  test "login with valid information" do
    get login_path
    post login_path, params: { session: { email:    @user.email,
                                           password: 'password' } }
    assert_redirected_to @user
    follow_redirect!
    assert_template 'users/show'
    assert_select "a[href=?]", login_path, count: 0
    assert_select "a[href=?]", logout_path
    assert_select "a[href=?]", user_path(@user)
  end
end
```

Here we've used

```ruby
assert_redirected_to @user
```

to check the right redirect target and

```ruby
follow_redirect!
```

to actually visit the target page. Listing 8.27 also confirms that the login link disappears
by verifying that there are *zero* login path links on the page:

```ruby
assert_select "a[href=?]", login_path, count: 0
```

By including the extra **count: 0** option, we tell **assert_select** that we expect zero links matching the given pattern. (Compare this to **count: 2** in Listing 5.32, which checks for exactly two matching links.)

Because the application code was already working, this test should be GREEN:

Listing 8.28: GREEN

```
$ rails test test/integration/users_login_test.rb
```

Exercises

Solutions to the exercises are available to all Rails Tutorial purchasers at https://www.railstutorial.org/aw-solutions.

To see other people's answers and to record your own, subscribe to the Rails Tutorial course or to the Learn Enough All Access Bundle.

1. Confirm by commenting out everything after **if user** in line 8 of Listing 8.15 that the tests still pass even if we don't authenticate the user by email and password, as shown in Listing 8.29. This is because Listing 8.9 doesn't test the case of a correct user email but incorrect password. Fix this serious omission in our test suite by adding a valid email to the Users login test (Listing 8.30). Verify that the tests are RED, then remove the line 8 comment to get back to GREEN. (Because it's so important, we'll add this test to the main code in Section 8.3.)

2. Use the "safe navigation" operator **&.** to simplify the boolean test in line 8 of Listing 8.15, as shown in line 8 of Listing 8.31.[18] This Ruby feature allows us to condense the common pattern of **obj &&** obj.method into **obj&.method**. Confirm that the tests in Listing 8.30 still pass after the change.

Listing 8.29: Commenting out the authentication code, but tests still GREEN.
app/controllers/sessions_controller.rb

```
class SessionsController < ApplicationController

  def new
  end
```

---

18. Thanks to reader Aviv Levinsky for suggesting this addition.

```
  def create
    user = User.find_by(email: params[:session][:email].downcase)
    if user # && user.authenticate(params[:session][:password])
      log_in user
      redirect_to user
    else
      flash.now[:danger] = 'Invalid email/password combination'
      render 'new'
    end
  end

  def destroy
  end
end
```

Listing 8.30: Testing the case of valid user email, invalid password.
`test/integration/users_login_test.rb`

```
require 'test_helper'

class UsersLoginTest < ActionDispatch::IntegrationTest

  def setup
    @user = users(:michael)
  end
  test "login with valid email/invalid password" do
    get login_path
    assert_template 'sessions/new'
    post login_path, params: { session: { email:    FILL_IN,
                                           password: "invalid" } }
    assert_template 'sessions/new'
    assert_not flash.empty?
    get root_path
    assert flash.empty?
  end
  .
  .
  .
end
```

Listing 8.31: Using the "safe navigation" operator **&.** to simplify the login code.
`app/controllers/sessions_controller.rb`

```ruby
class SessionsController < ApplicationController

  def new
  end

  def create
    user = User.find_by(email: params[:session][:email].downcase)
    if user&.authenticate(params[:session][:password])
      log_in user
      redirect_to user
    else
      flash.now[:danger] = 'Invalid email/password combination'
      render 'new'
    end
  end

  def destroy
    log_out
    redirect_to root_url
  end
end
```

8.2.5 Login Upon Signup

Although our authentication system is now working, newly registered users might be confused, as they are not logged in by default. Because it would be strange to force users to log in immediately after signing up, we'll log in new users automatically as part of the signup process. To arrange this behavior, all we need to do is add a call to **log_in** in the Users controller **create** action, as shown in Listing 8.32.[19]

Listing 8.32: Logging in the user upon signup.
`app/controllers/users_controller.rb`

```ruby
class UsersController < ApplicationController

  def show
```

---

19. As with the Sessions controller, the **log_in** method is available in the Users controller because of the module inclusion in Listing 8.13.

```
    @user = User.find(params[:id])
  end

  def new
    @user = User.new
  end

  def create
    @user = User.new(user_params)
    if @user.save
      log_in @user
      flash[:success] = "Welcome to the Sample App!"
      redirect_to @user
    else
      render 'new'
    end
  end

  private

    def user_params
      params.require(:user).permit(:name, :email, :password,
                                   :password_confirmation)
    end
end
```

To test the behavior from Listing 8.32, we can add a line to the test from Listing 7.31 to check that the user is logged in. It's helpful in this context to define
an **is_logged_in?** helper method to parallel the **logged_in?** helper defined in
Listing 8.18, which returns **true** if there's a user id in the (test) session and false
otherwise (Listing 8.33). (Because helper methods aren't available in tests, we can't
use the **current_user** as in Listing 8.18, but the **session** method is available, so we
use that instead.) Here we use **is_logged_in?** instead of **logged_in?** so that the test
helper and Sessions helper methods have different names, which prevents them from
being mistaken for each other.[20] (In this case we could actually just include the Sessions helper and use **logged_in?** directly, but this technique would fail in Chapter 9

---

20. For example, I once had a test suite that was GREEN even after I accidentally deleted the main **log_in**
method in the Sessions helper. The reason is that the tests were happily using a test helper with the same
name, thereby passing even though the application was completely broken. As with **is_logged_in?**, we'll
avoid this issue by defining the test helper **log_in_as** in Listing 9.24.

due to details of how cookies are handled in tests, so instead we define a test-specific method that will work in all cases.)

Listing 8.33: A boolean method for checking login status inside tests.
`test/test_helper.rb`

```ruby
ENV['RAILS_ENV'] ||= 'test'
.
.
.
class ActiveSupport::TestCase
  fixtures :all

  # Returns true if a test user is logged in.
  def is_logged_in?
    !session[:user_id].nil?
  end
end
```

With the code in Listing 8.33, we can assert that the user is logged in after signup using the line shown in Listing 8.34.

Listing 8.34: A test of login after signup. GREEN
`test/integration/users_signup_test.rb`

```ruby
require 'test_helper'

class UsersSignupTest < ActionDispatch::IntegrationTest
  .
  .
  .
  test "valid signup information" do
    get signup_path
    assert_difference 'User.count', 1 do
      post users_path, params: { user: { name:  "Example User",
                                         email: "user@example.com",
                                         password:              "password",
                                         password_confirmation: "password" } }
    end
    follow_redirect!
    assert_template 'users/show'
    assert is_logged_in?
  end
end
```

At this point, the test suite should still be GREEN:

Listing 8.35: GREEN

```
$ rails test
```

Exercises

Solutions to the exercises are available to all Rails Tutorial purchasers at https://www.railstutorial.org/aw-solutions.

To see other people's answers and to record your own, subscribe to the Rails Tutorial course or to the Learn Enough All Access Bundle.

1. Is the test suite RED or GREEN if you comment out the **log_in** line in Listing 8.32?

2. By using your text editor's ability to comment out code, toggle back and forth between commenting out code in Listing 8.32 and confirm that the test suite toggles between RED and GREEN. (You will need to save the file between toggles.)

8.3 Logging Out

As discussed in Section 8.1, our authentication model is to keep users logged in until they log out explicitly. In this section, we'll add this necessary logout capability. Because the "Log out" link has already been defined (Listing 8.19), all we need is to write a valid controller action to destroy user sessions.

So far, the Sessions controller actions have followed the RESTful convention of using **new** for a login page and **create** to complete the login. We'll continue this theme by using a **destroy** action to delete sessions, in other words, to log out. Unlike with the login functionality, which we use in both Listing 8.15 and Listing 8.32, we'll be logging out only in one place, so we'll put the relevant code directly in the **destroy** action. As we'll see in Section 9.3, this design (with a little refactoring) will also make the authentication machinery easier to test.

Logging out involves undoing the effects of the **log_in** method from Listing 8.14, which involves deleting the user id from the session.[21] To do this, we use the **delete** method as follows:

```
session.delete(:user_id)
```

We'll also set the current user to **nil**, although in the present case this won't matter because of an immediate redirect to the root URL.[22] As with **log_in** and associated methods, we'll put the resulting **log_out** method in the Sessions helper module, as shown in Listing 8.36.

Listing 8.36: The **log_out** method.
app/helpers/sessions_helper.rb

```
module SessionsHelper

  # Logs in the given user.
  def log_in(user)
    session[:user_id] = user.id
  end
  .
  .
  .
  # Logs out the current user.
  def log_out
    session.delete(:user_id)
    @current_user = nil
  end
end
```

We can put the **log_out** method to use in the Sessions controller's **destroy** action, as shown in Listing 8.37.

---

21. Some browsers offer a "remember where I left off" feature, which restores the session automatically, so be sure to disable any such feature before trying to log out.

22. Setting **@current_user** to **nil** would matter only if **@current_user** were created before the **destroy** action (which it isn't) *and* if we didn't issue an immediate redirect (which we do). This is an unlikely combination of events, and with the application as presently constructed it isn't necessary, but because it's security-related I include it for completeness.

Listing 8.37: Destroying a session (user logout).
`app/controllers/sessions_controller.rb`

```ruby
class SessionsController < ApplicationController

  def new
  end

  def create
    user = User.find_by(email: params[:session][:email].downcase)
    if user && user.authenticate(params[:session][:password])
      log_in user
      redirect_to user
    else
      flash.now[:danger] = 'Invalid email/password combination'
      render 'new'
    end
  end

  def destroy
    log_out
    redirect_to root_url
  end
end
```

To test the logout machinery, we can add some steps to the user login test from Listing 8.27. After logging in, we use **delete** to issue a DELETE request to the logout path (Table 8.1) and verify that the user is logged out and redirected to the root URL. We also check that the login link reappears and that the logout and profile links disappear. The new steps appear in Listing 8.38.

Listing 8.38: A test for user logout (and an improved test for invalid login). GREEN
`test/integration/users_login_test.rb`

```ruby
require 'test_helper'

class UsersLoginTest < ActionDispatch::IntegrationTest

  def setup
    @user = users(:michael)
  end

  test "login with valid email/invalid password" do
```

```
    get login_path
    assert_template 'sessions/new'
    post login_path, params: { session: { email:    @user.email,
                                           password: "invalid" } }
    assert_not is_logged_in?
    assert_template 'sessions/new'
    assert_not flash.empty?
    get root_path
    assert flash.empty?
  end

  test "login with valid information followed by logout" do
    get login_path
    post login_path, params: { session: { email:    @user.email,
                                           password: 'password' } }
    assert is_logged_in?
    assert_redirected_to @user
    follow_redirect!
    assert_template 'users/show'
    assert_select "a[href=?]", login_path, count: 0
    assert_select "a[href=?]", logout_path
    assert_select "a[href=?]", user_path(@user)
    delete logout_path
    assert_not is_logged_in?
    assert_redirected_to root_url
    follow_redirect!
    assert_select "a[href=?]", login_path
    assert_select "a[href=?]", logout_path,        count: 0
    assert_select "a[href=?]", user_path(@user), count: 0
  end
end
```

(Now that we have **is_logged_in?** available in tests, we've also thrown in a bonus **assert is_logged_in?** immediately after posting valid information to the sessions path. We've also added a similar assertion and the solution to the exercise from Section 8.2.4 by adding the results of Listing 8.30.)

With the session **destroy** action thus defined and tested, the initial signup/-login/logout triumvirate is complete, and the test suite should be GREEN:

Listing 8.39: GREEN

```
$ rails test
```

Exercises

Solutions to the exercises are available to all Rails Tutorial purchasers at https://www.railstutorial.org/aw-solutions.

To see other people's answers and to record your own, subscribe to the Rails Tutorial course or to the Learn Enough All Access Bundle.

1. Confirm in a browser that the "Log out" link causes the correct changes in the site layout. What is the correspondence between these changes and the final three steps in Listing 8.38?

2. By checking the site cookies, confirm that the session is correctly removed after logging out.

8.4 Conclusion

With the material in this chapter, our sample application has a fully functional login and authentication system. In the next chapter, we'll take our app to the next level by adding the ability to remember users for longer than a single browser session.

Before moving on, merge your changes back into the master branch:

```
$ rails test
$ git add -A
$ git commit -m "Implement basic login"
$ git checkout master
$ git merge basic-login
```

Then push up to the remote repository:

```
$ rails test
$ git push
```

Finally, deploy to Heroku as usual:

```
$ git push heroku
```

8.4.1 What We Learned in this Chapter

- Rails can maintain state from one page to the next using temporary cookies via the **session** method.

- The login form is designed to create a new session to log a user in.

- The **flash.now** method is used for flash messages on rendered pages.

- Test-driven development is useful when debugging by reproducing the bug in a test.

- Using the **session** method, we can securely place a user id on the browser to create a temporary session.

- We can change features such as links on the layouts based on login status.

- Integration tests can verify correct routes, database updates, and proper changes to the layout.

CHAPTER 9
Advanced Login

The basic login system developed in Chapter 8 is fully functional, but most modern websites include the ability to "remember" users when they visit the site again even if they've closed their browsers in the interim. In this chapter, we use *permanent cookies* to implement this behavior. We'll start by automatically remembering users when they log in (Section 9.1), a common model used by sites such as Bitbucket and GitHub. We'll then add the ability to *optionally* remember users using a "remember me" checkbox, a model used by sites such as Twitter and Facebook.

Because the Chapter 8 login system is complete by itself, the core of the sample application will work fine without it, and if desired you can skip right to Chapter 10 (and from there to Chapter 13). On the other hand, learning how to implement the "remember me" feature is both highly instructive by itself and lays an essential foundation for account activation (Chapter 11) and password reset (Chapter 12). Moreover, the result is an outstanding example of computer magic: You've seen a billion of these "remember me" login forms on the Web, and now's your chance to learn how to make one.

9.1 Remember Me

In this section, we'll add the ability to remember our users' login state even after they close and reopen their browsers. This "remember me" behavior will happen automatically, and users will automatically stay logged in until they explicitly log out. As we'll see, the resulting machinery will make it easy to add an optional "remember me" checkbox as well (Section 9.2).

As usual, I suggest switching to a topic branch before proceeding:

```
$ git checkout -b advanced-login
```

9.1.1 Remember Token and Digest

In Section 8.2, we used the Rails **session** method to store the user's id, but this information disappears when the user closes the browser. In this section, we'll take the first step toward persistent sessions by generating a *remember token* appropriate for creating permanent cookies using the **cookies** method, together with a secure *remember digest* for authenticating those tokens.

As noted in Section 8.2.1, information stored using **session** is automatically secure, but this is not the case with information stored using **cookies**. In particular, persistent cookies are vulnerable to session hijacking, in which an attacker uses a stolen remember token to log in as a particular user. There are four main ways to steal cookies: (1) using a packet sniffer to detect cookies being passed over insecure networks,[1] (2) compromising a database containing remember tokens, (3) using cross-site scripting (XSS), and (4) gaining physical access to a machine with a logged-in user.

We prevented the first problem in Section 7.5 by using Secure Sockets Layer (SSL) site-wide, which protects network data from packet sniffers. We'll prevent the second problem by storing a hash digest of the remember tokens instead of the token itself, in much the same way that we stored password digests instead of raw passwords in Section 6.3.[2] Rails automatically prevents the third problem by escaping any content inserted into view templates. Finally, although there's no iron-clad way to stop attackers who have physical access to a logged-in computer, we'll minimize the fourth problem by changing tokens every time a user logs out and by taking care to *cryptographically sign* any potentially sensitive information we place on the browser.

With these design and security considerations in mind, our plan for creating persistent sessions appears as follows:

---

1. Session hijacking was widely publicized by the Firesheep application, which showed that remember tokens at many high-profile sites were visible from devices connected to public Wi-Fi networks.

2. Rails 5 introduced a **has_secure_token** method that automatically generates random tokens, but it stores the *unhashed* values in the database, and hence is unsuitable for our present purposes.

1. Create a random string of digits for use as a remember token.

2. Place the token in the browser cookies with an expiration date far in the future.

3. Save the hash digest of the token to the database.

4. Place an encrypted version of the user's id in the browser cookies.

5. When presented with a cookie containing a persistent user id, find the user in the database using the given id, and verify that the remember token cookie matches the associated hash digest from the database.

Note how similar the final step is to logging a user in, where we retrieve the user by email address and then verify (using the **authenticate** method) that the submitted password matches the password digest (Listing 8.7). As a result, our implementation will parallel aspects of **has_secure_password**.

We'll start by adding the required **remember_digest** attribute to the User model, as shown in Figure 9.1. To add the data model from Figure 9.1 to our application, we'll generate a migration:

```
$ rails generate migration add_remember_digest_to_users remember_digest:string
```

(Compare this to the password digest migration in Section 6.3.1.) As in previous migrations, we've used a migration name that ends in **_to_users** to tell Rails that

users	
`id`	integer
`name`	string
`email`	string
`created_at`	datetime
`updated_at`	datetime
`password_digest`	string
`remember_digest`	string

Figure 9.1: The User model with an added **remember_digest** attribute.

the migration is designed to alter the **users** table in the database. Because we also included the attribute (**remember_digest**) and type (**string**), Rails generates a default migration for us, as shown in Listing 9.1.

Listing 9.1: The generated migration for the remember digest.
db/migrate/[timestamp]_add_remember_digest_to_users.rb

```
class AddRememberDigestToUsers < ActiveRecord::Migration[6.0]
  def change
    add_column :users, :remember_digest, :string
  end
end
```

Because we don't expect to retrieve users by remember digest, there's no need to put an index on the **remember_digest** column, and we can use the default migration:

```
$ rails db:migrate
```

Now we have to decide what to use as a remember token. There are many mostly equivalent possibilities—essentially, any long random string will do. The **urlsafe_base64** method from the **SecureRandom** module in the Ruby standard library fits the bill:[3] It returns a random string of length 22 composed of the characters A–Z, a–z, 0–9, "-", and "_" (for a total of 64 possibilities, thus "base64"). A typical base64 string appears as follows:

```
$ rails console
>> SecureRandom.urlsafe_base64
=> "brl_446-8bqHv87AQzUj_Q"
```

Just as it's perfectly fine if two users have the same password,[4] there's no need for remember tokens to be unique—but it's more secure if they are.[5] In the case of our base64 string, each of the 22 characters has 64 possibilities, so the probability of two

---

3. This choice is based on the RailsCast on remember me.

4. In any case, with bcrypt's salted hashes there's no way for us to tell if two users' passwords match.

5. With unique remember tokens, an attacker always needs *both* the user id and the remember token cookies to hijack the session.

remember tokens colliding is a negligibly small $1/64^{22} = 2^{-132} \approx 10^{-40}$.[6] As a bonus, by using base64 strings specifically designed to be safe in URLs (as indicated by the name **urlsafe_base64**), we'll be able to use the same token generator to make account activation and password reset links in Chapter 12.

Remembering users involves creating a remember token and saving the digest of the token to the database. We've already defined a **digest** method for use in the test fixtures (Listing 8.25), and we can use the results of the preceding discussion to create a **new_token** method to create a new token. As with **digest**, the new token method doesn't need a user object, so we'll make it a class method.[7] The result is the User model shown in Listing 9.2.

Listing 9.2: Adding a method for generating tokens.
app/models/user.rb

```ruby
class User < ApplicationRecord
  before_save { self.email = email.downcase }
  validates :name,  presence: true, length: { maximum: 50 }
  VALID_EMAIL_REGEX = /\A[\w+\-.]+@[a-z\d\-.]+\.[a-z]+\z/i
  validates :email, presence: true, length: { maximum: 255 },
                    format: { with: VALID_EMAIL_REGEX },
                    uniqueness: true
  has_secure_password
  validates :password, presence: true, length: { minimum: 6 }

  # Returns the hash digest of the given string.
  def User.digest(string)
    cost = ActiveModel::SecurePassword.min_cost ? BCrypt::Engine::MIN_COST :
                                                  BCrypt::Engine.cost
    BCrypt::Password.create(string, cost: cost)
  end

  # Returns a random token.
  def User.new_token
    SecureRandom.urlsafe_base64
  end
end
```

---

6. This hasn't stopped some developers from adding a check to verify that no collision has occurred, but such efforts result from failing to grasp just how small 10^{-40} is. For example, if we generated a billion tokens a second for the entire age of the universe (4.4×10^7 s), the expected number of collisions would still be on the order of 2×10^{-23}, which is zero in any operational sense of the word.

7. As a general rule, if a method doesn't need an instance of an object, it should be a class method. Indeed, this decision will prove to be wise in Section 11.2.

Our plan for the implementation is to make a **user.remember** method that associates a remember token with the user and saves the corresponding remember digest to the database. Because of the migration in Listing 9.1, the User model already has a **remember_digest** attribute, but it doesn't yet have a **remember_token** attribute. We need a way to make a token available via **user.remember_token** (for storage in the cookies) *without* storing it in the database. We solved a similar issue with secure passwords in Section 6.3, which paired a virtual **password** attribute with a secure **password_digest** attribute in the database. In that case, the virtual **password** attribute was created automatically by **has_secure_password**, but we'll have to write the code for a **remember_token** ourselves. The way to do this is to use **attr_accessor** to create an accessible attribute, as we saw in Section 4.4.5:

```
class User < ApplicationRecord
  attr_accessor :remember_token
  .
  .
  .
  def remember
    self.remember_token = ...
    update_attribute(:remember_digest, ...)
  end
end
```

Note the form of the assignment in the first line of the **remember** method. Because of the way Ruby handles assignments inside objects, without **self** the assignment would create a *local* variable called **remember_token**, which isn't what we want. Using **self** ensures that assignment sets the user's **remember_token** attribute. (Now you know why the **before_save** callback from Listing 6.32 uses **self.email** instead of just **email**.) Meanwhile, the second line of **remember** uses the **update_attribute** method to update the remember digest. (As noted in Section 6.1.5, this method bypasses the validations, which is necessary in this case because we don't have access to the user's password or confirmation.)

With these considerations in mind, we can create a valid token and associated digest by first making a new remember token using **User.new_token**, and then updating the remember digest with the result of applying **User.digest**. This procedure gives the **remember** method shown in Listing 9.3.

Listing 9.3: Adding a **remember** method to the User model. GREEN
`app/models/user.rb`

```ruby
class User < ApplicationRecord
  attr_accessor :remember_token
  before_save { self.email = email.downcase }
  validates :name,  presence: true, length: { maximum: 50 }
  VALID_EMAIL_REGEX = /\A[\w+\-.]+@[a-z\d\-.]+\.[a-z]+\z/i
  validates :email, presence: true, length: { maximum: 255 },
                    format: { with: VALID_EMAIL_REGEX },
                    uniqueness: true
  has_secure_password
  validates :password, presence: true, length: { minimum: 6 }

  # Returns the hash digest of the given string.
  def User.digest(string)
    cost = ActiveModel::SecurePassword.min_cost ? BCrypt::Engine::MIN_COST :
                                                  BCrypt::Engine.cost
    BCrypt::Password.create(string, cost: cost)
  end

  # Returns a random token.
  def User.new_token
    SecureRandom.urlsafe_base64
  end

  # Remembers a user in the database for use in persistent sessions.
  def remember
    self.remember_token = User.new_token
    update_attribute(:remember_digest, User.digest(remember_token))
  end
end
```

Exercises

Solutions to the exercises are available to all Rails Tutorial purchasers at https://www.railstutorial.org/aw-solutions.

To see other people's answers and to record your own, subscribe to the Rails Tutorial course or to the Learn Enough All Access Bundle.

1. In the console, assign **User** to the first user in the database, and verify by calling it directly that the **remember** method works. How do **remember_token** and **remember_digest** compare?

2. In Listing 9.3, we defined the new token and digest class methods by explicitly prefixing them with **User**. This works fine and, because they are actually

called using **User.new_token** and **User.digest**, it is probably the clearest way to define them. But there are two perhaps more idiomatically correct ways to define class methods, one slightly confusing and one extremely confusing. By running the test suite, verify that the implementations in Listing 9.4 (slightly confusing) and Listing 9.5 (extremely confusing) are correct. (Note that, in the context of Listing 9.4 and Listing 9.5, **self** is the **User** class, whereas the other uses of **self** in the User model refer to a user object *instance*. This is part of what makes them confusing.)

Listing 9.4: Defining the new token and digest methods using **self**. GREEN
`app/models/user.rb`

```
class User < ApplicationRecord
  .
  .
  .
  # Returns the hash digest of the given string.
  def self.digest(string)
    cost = ActiveModel::SecurePassword.min_cost ? BCrypt::Engine::MIN_COST :
                                                  BCrypt::Engine.cost
    BCrypt::Password.create(string, cost: cost)
  end

  # Returns a random token.
  def self.new_token
    SecureRandom.urlsafe_base64
  end
  .
  .
  .
end
```

Listing 9.5: Defining the new token and digest methods using **class << self**. GREEN
`app/models/user.rb`

```
class User < ApplicationRecord
  .
  .
  .
  class << self
    # Returns the hash digest of the given string.
    def digest(string)
```

```
    cost = ActiveModel::SecurePassword.min_cost ? BCrypt::Engine::MIN_COST :
                                                   BCrypt::Engine.cost
    BCrypt::Password.create(string, cost: cost)
  end

  # Returns a random token.
  def new_token
    SecureRandom.urlsafe_base64
  end
end
```
.
.
.

9.1.2   Login with Remembering

Having created a working **user.remember** method, we can now create a persistent
session by storing a user's (encrypted) id and remember token as permanent cookies
on the browser. We do this with the **cookies** method, which (as with **session**) we
can treat as a hash. A cookie consists of two pieces of information, a **value** and an
optional **expires** date. For example, we could make a persistent session by creating
a cookie with a value equal to the remember token that expires 20 years from now:

```
cookies[:remember_token] = { value:   remember_token,
                             expires: 20.years.from_now.utc }
```

(This uses one of the convenient Rails time helpers, as discussed in Box 9.1.) This
pattern of setting a cookie that expires 20 years in the future is so common that Rails
has a special **permanent** method to implement it, so that we can simply write

```
cookies.permanent[:remember_token] = remember_token
```

This causes Rails to set the expiration to **20.years.from_now** automatically.

Box 9.1:   Cookies Expire **20.years.from_now**

You may recall from Section 4.4.2 that Ruby lets you add methods to *any* class,
even built-in ones. In that section, we added a palindrome? method to the

String class (and discovered as a result that "deified" is a palindrome), and we also saw how Rails adds a blank? method to class Object (so that "".blank?, " ".blank?, and nil.blank? are all true). The cookies.permanent method, which creates "permanent" cookies with an expiration 20.years.from_now, provides yet another example of this practice through one of Rails' *time helpers*, which are methods added to Fixnum (the base class for integers):

```
$ rails console
>> 1.year.from_now
=> Wed, 21 Jun 2017 19:36:29 UTC +00:00
>> 10.weeks.ago
=> Tue, 12 Apr 2016 19:36:44 UTC +00:00
```

Rails adds other helpers, too:

```
>> 1.kilobyte
=> 1024
>> 5.megabytes
=> 5242880
```

These are useful for upload validations, making it easy to restrict, say, image uploads to 5.megabytes.

Although this flexibility should be used with caution, adding methods to built-in classes enables extraordinarily natural extensions to plain Ruby. Indeed, much of the elegance of Rails ultimately derives from the malleability of the underlying Ruby language.

To store the user's id in the cookies, we could follow the pattern used with the **session** method (Listing 8.14) using something like

```
cookies[:user_id] = user.id
```

Because it places the id as plain text, this method exposes the form of the application's cookies and makes it easier for an attacker to compromise user accounts. To avoid this problem, we'll use an *encrypted* cookie, which securely encrypts the cookie before placing it on the browser:

```
cookies.encrypted[:user_id] = user.id
```

Because we want the user id to be paired with the permanent remember token, we should make it permanent as well, which we can do by chaining the **encrypted** and **permanent** methods:

```
cookies.permanent.encrypted[:user_id] = user.id
```

After the cookies are set, on subsequent page views we can retrieve the user with code like

```
User.find_by(id: cookies.encrypted[:user_id])
```

where **cookies.encrypted[:user_id]** automatically decrypts the user id cookie. We can then use bcrypt to verify that **cookies[:remember_token]** matches the **remember_digest** generated in Listing 9.3. (In case you're wondering why we don't just use the encrypted user id, without the remember token, this would allow an attacker with possession of the encrypted id to log in as the user in perpetuity. In the present design, an attacker with both cookies can log in as the user only until the user logs out.)

The final piece of the puzzle is to verify that a given remember token matches the user's remember digest. In this context there are a couple of equivalent ways to use bcrypt to verify a match. If you look at the secure password source code, you'll find a comparison like this:[8]

```
BCrypt::Password.new(password_digest) == unencrypted_password
```

In our case, the analogous code would look like this:

```
BCrypt::Password.new(remember_digest) == remember_token
```

If you think about it, this code is really strange: It appears to be comparing a bcrypt password digest directly with a token, which would imply *decrypting* the digest in order to compare it using **==**. But the whole point of using bcrypt is for hashing to be irreversible, so this can't be right. Indeed, digging into the source code of the bcrypt

---

8. As noted in Section 6.3.1, "unencrypted password" is a misnomer, as the secure password is *hashed*, not encrypted.

gem verifies that the comparison operator **==** is being *redefined*, and under the hood the preceding comparison is equivalent to the following:

```
BCrypt::Password.new(remember_digest).is_password?(remember_token)
```

Instead of **==**, this uses the boolean method **is_password?** to perform the comparison. Because its meaning is a little clearer, we'll prefer this second comparison form in the application code.

This discussion suggests that we should put the digest–token comparison into an **authenticated?** method in the User model, which plays a role similar to that of the **authenticate** method provided by **has_secure_password** for authenticating a user (Listing 8.15). The implementation appears in Listing 9.6. (Although the **authenticated?** method in Listing 9.6 is tied specifically to the remember digest, it will turn out to be useful in other contexts as well, and we'll generalize it in Chapter 11.)

Listing 9.6: Adding an **authenticated?** method to the User model.
app/models/user.rb

```ruby
class User < ApplicationRecord
  attr_accessor :remember_token
  before_save { self.email = email.downcase }
  validates :name,  presence: true, length: { maximum: 50 }
  VALID_EMAIL_REGEX = /\A[\w+\-.]+@[a-z\d\-.]+\.[a-z]+\z/i
  validates :email, presence: true, length: { maximum: 255 },
                    format: { with: VALID_EMAIL_REGEX },
                    uniqueness: true
  has_secure_password
  validates :password, presence: true, length: { minimum: 6 }

  # Returns the hash digest of the given string.
  def User.digest(string)
    cost = ActiveModel::SecurePassword.min_cost ? BCrypt::Engine::MIN_COST :
                                                  BCrypt::Engine.cost
    BCrypt::Password.create(string, cost: cost)
  end

  # Returns a random token.
  def User.new_token
    SecureRandom.urlsafe_base64
  end
```

```
# Remembers a user in the database for use in persistent sessions.
def remember
  self.remember_token = User.new_token
  update_attribute(:remember_digest, User.digest(remember_token))
end

# Returns true if the given token matches the digest.
def authenticated?(remember_token)
  BCrypt::Password.new(remember_digest).is_password?(remember_token)
end
end
```

Note that the **remember_token** argument in the **authenticated?** method defined in Listing 9.6 is not the same as the accessor that we defined in Listing 9.3 using **attr_accessor :remember_token**; instead, it is a variable local to the method. (Because the argument refers to the remember token, it is not uncommon to use a method argument that has the same name.) Also note the use of the **remember_digest** attribute, which is the same as **self.remember_digest** and, like **name** and **email** in Chapter 6, is created automatically by Active Record based on the name of the corresponding database column (Listing 9.1).

We're now in a position to remember a logged-in user, which we'll do by adding a **remember** helper to go along with **log_in**, as shown in Listing 9.7.

Listing 9.7: Logging in and remembering a user. RED

app/controllers/sessions_controller.rb

```
class SessionsController < ApplicationController

  def new
  end

  def create
    user = User.find_by(email: params[:session][:email].downcase)
    if user && user.authenticate(params[:session][:password])
      log_in user
      remember user
      redirect_to user
    else
      flash.now[:danger] = 'Invalid email/password combination'
      render 'new'
    end
  end
```

```
    def destroy
      log_out
      redirect_to root_url
    end
end
```

As with **log_in**, Listing 9.7 defers the real work to the Sessions helper, where we define a **remember** method that calls **user.remember**, thereby generating a remember token and saving its digest to the database. It then uses **cookies** to create permanent cookies for the user id and remember token as described above. The result appears in Listing 9.8.

Listing 9.8: Remembering the user. GREEN
app/helpers/sessions_helper.rb

```
module SessionsHelper

  # Logs in the given user.
  def log_in(user)
    session[:user_id] = user.id
  end

  # Remembers a user in a persistent session.
  def remember(user)
    user.remember
    cookies.permanent.encrypted[:user_id] = user.id
    cookies.permanent[:remember_token] = user.remember_token
  end

  # Returns the current logged-in user (if any).
  def current_user
    if session[:user_id]
      @current_user ||= User.find_by(id: session[:user_id])
    end
  end

  # Returns true if the user is logged in, false otherwise.
  def logged_in?
    !current_user.nil?
  end

  # Logs out the current user.
  def log_out
```

```
    session.delete(:user_id)
    @current_user = nil
  end
end
```

With the code in Listing 9.8, a user logging in will be remembered in the sense that their browser will get a valid remember token, but it doesn't do us any good just yet because the **current_user** method defined in Listing 8.16 knows only about the temporary session:

```
@current_user ||= User.find_by(id: session[:user_id])
```

In the case of persistent sessions, we want to retrieve the user from the temporary session if **session[:user_id]** exists, but otherwise we should look for **cookies[:user_id]** to retrieve (and log in) the user corresponding to the persistent session. We can accomplish this as follows:

```
if session[:user_id]
  @current_user ||= User.find_by(id: session[:user_id])
elsif cookies.encrypted[:user_id]
  user = User.find_by(id: cookies.encrypted[:user_id])
  if user && user.authenticated?(cookies[:remember_token])
    log_in user
    @current_user = user
  end
end
```

(This follows the same **user && user.authenticated** pattern we saw in Listing 8.7.) This code will work, but note the repeated use of both **session** and **cookies**. We can eliminate this duplication as follows:

```
if (user_id = session[:user_id])
  @current_user ||= User.find_by(id: user_id)
elsif (user_id = cookies.encrypted[:user_id])
  user = User.find_by(id: user_id)
  if user && user.authenticated?(cookies[:remember_token])
    log_in user
    @current_user = user
  end
end
```

This uses the common but potentially confusing construction

```
if (user_id = session[:user_id])
```

Despite appearances, this is *not* a comparison (which would use double-equals **==**) but rather an *assignment*. If you were to read it in words, you wouldn't say, "If user id equals session of user id…," but rather something like "If session of user id exists (while setting user id to session of user id)…."[9]

Defining the **current_user** helper as just discussed leads to the implementation shown in Listing 9.9.

Listing 9.9: Updating **current_user** for persistent sessions. RED
app/helpers/sessions_helper.rb

```ruby
module SessionsHelper

  # Logs in the given user.
  def log_in(user)
    session[:user_id] = user.id
  end

  # Remembers a user in a persistent session.
  def remember(user)
    user.remember
    cookies.permanent.encrypted[:user_id] = user.id
    cookies.permanent[:remember_token] = user.remember_token
  end

  # Returns the user corresponding to the remember token cookie.
  def current_user
    if (user_id = session[:user_id])
      @current_user ||= User.find_by(id: user_id)
    elsif (user_id = cookies.encrypted[:user_id])
      user = User.find_by(id: user_id)
      if user && user.authenticated?(cookies[:remember_token])
        log_in user
        @current_user = user
      end
    end
  end
```

---

9. I generally use the convention of putting such assignments in parentheses, which is a visual reminder that it's not a comparison.

```
  # Returns true if the user is logged in, false otherwise.
  def logged_in?
    !current_user.nil?
  end

  # Logs out the current user.
  def log_out
    session.delete(:user_id)
    @current_user = nil
  end
end
```

With the code as in Listing 9.9, newly logged in users are correctly remembered, as you can verify by logging in, closing the browser, and checking that you're still logged in when you restart the sample application and revisit the sample application.[10] If you want, you can even inspect the browser cookies to see the result directly (Figure 9.2).[11]

There's only one problem with our application as it stands: Short of clearing their browser cookies (or waiting 20 years), there's no way for users to log out. This is exactly the sort of thing our test suite should catch, and indeed the tests should currently be RED:

---

10. Alert reader Jack Fahnestock has noted an edge case that isn't covered by the current design:

1. Log in with "remember me" checked in browser A (saving hashed remember token A to **remember_digest**).

2. Log in with "remember me" checked in browser B (saving hashed **remember_token** B to **remember_digest**, overwriting remember token A saved in browser A).

3. Close browser A (now relying on permanent cookies for login—second conditional in **current_user** method).

4. Reopen browser A (**logged_in?** returns false, even though permanent cookies are on the browser).

Although this is arguably a more secure design than remembering the user in multiple places, it violates the expectation that users can be permanently remembered on more than one browser. The solution, which is substantially more complicated than the present design, is to factor the remember digest into a separate table, where each row has a user id and a digest. Checking for the current user would then look through the table for a digest corresponding to a particular remember token. Furthermore, the **forget** in Listing 9.11 method would delete only the row corresponding to the digest of the current browser. For security purposes, logging out would remove all digests for that user.

11. Google "<your browser name> inspect cookies" to learn how to inspect the cookies on your system.

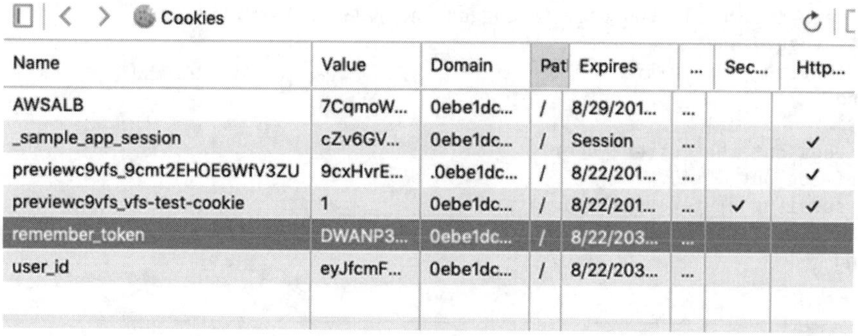

Name		Value	Domain	Pat	Expires	...	Sec...	Http...
AWSALB		7CqmoW...	0ebe1dc...	/	8/29/201...	...		
_sample_app_session		cZv6GV...	0ebe1dc...	/	Session	...		✓
previewc9vfs_9cmt2EHOE6WfV3ZU		9cxHvrE...	.0ebe1dc...	/	8/22/201...	...		✓
previewc9vfs_vfs-test-cookie		1	0ebe1dc...	/	8/22/201...	...	✓	✓
remember_token		DWANP3...	0ebe1dc...	/	8/22/203...	...		
user_id		eyJfcmF...	0ebe1dc...	/	8/22/203...	...		

Figure 9.2: The remember token cookie in the local browser.

Listing 9.10: RED

```
$ rails test
```

Exercises

Solutions to the exercises are available to all Rails Tutorial purchasers at https://www.railstutorial.org/aw-solutions.

To see other people's answers and to record your own, subscribe to the Rails Tutorial course or to the Learn Enough All Access Bundle.

1. By finding the cookie in your local browser, verify that a remember token and encrypted user id are present after logging in.

2. At the console, verify directly that the **authenticated?** method defined in Listing 9.6 works correctly.

9.1.3 Forgetting Users

To allow users to log out, we'll define methods to forget users in analogy with the methods to remember them. The resulting **user.forget** method just undoes **user.remember** by updating the remember digest with **nil**, as shown in Listing 9.11.

Listing 9.11: Adding a **forget** method to the User model. RED
app/models/user.rb

```ruby
class User < ApplicationRecord
  attr_accessor :remember_token
  before_save { self.email = email.downcase }
  validates :name,  presence: true, length: { maximum: 50 }
  VALID_EMAIL_REGEX = /\A[\w+\-.]+@[a-z\d\-.]+\.[a-z]+\z/i
  validates :email, presence: true, length: { maximum: 255 },
                    format: { with: VALID_EMAIL_REGEX },
                    uniqueness: true
  has_secure_password
  validates :password, presence: true, length: { minimum: 6 }

  # Returns the hash digest of the given string.
  def User.digest(string)
    cost = ActiveModel::SecurePassword.min_cost ? BCrypt::Engine::MIN_COST :
                                                  BCrypt::Engine.cost
    BCrypt::Password.create(string, cost: cost)
  end

  # Returns a random token.
  def User.new_token
    SecureRandom.urlsafe_base64
  end

  # Remembers a user in the database for use in persistent sessions.
  def remember
    self.remember_token = User.new_token
    update_attribute(:remember_digest, User.digest(remember_token))
  end

  # Returns true if the given token matches the digest.
  def authenticated?(remember_token)
    BCrypt::Password.new(remember_digest).is_password?(remember_token)
  end

  # Forgets a user.
  def forget
    update_attribute(:remember_digest, nil)
  end
end
```

With the code in Listing 9.11, we're now ready to forget a permanent session by
adding a **forget** helper and calling it from the **log_out** helper (Listing 9.12). As seen

in Listing 9.12, the **forget** helper calls **user.forget** and then deletes the **user_id** and **remember_token** cookies.

Listing 9.12: Logging out from a persistent session. GREEN
app/helpers/sessions_helper.rb

```
module SessionsHelper

  # Logs in the given user.
  def log_in(user)
    session[:user_id] = user.id
  end
  .
  .
  .
  # Forgets a persistent session.
  def forget(user)
    user.forget
    cookies.delete(:user_id)
    cookies.delete(:remember_token)
  end

  # Logs out the current user.
  def log_out
    forget(current_user)
    session.delete(:user_id)
    @current_user = nil
  end
end
```

At this point, the tests suite should be GREEN:

Listing 9.13: GREEN

```
$ rails test
```

Exercise

Solutions to the exercises are available to all Rails Tutorial purchasers at https://www.railstutorial.org/aw-solutions.

To see other people's answers and to record your own, subscribe to the Rails Tutorial course or to the Learn Enough All Access Bundle.

1. After logging out, verify that the corresponding cookies have been removed from your browser.

9.1.4 Two Subtle Bugs

There are two closely related subtleties left to address. The first subtlety is that, even though the "Log out" link appears only when logged-in, a user could potentially have multiple browser windows open to the site. If the user logged out in one window, thereby setting **current_user** to **nil**, clicking the "Log out" link in a second window would result in an error because of **forget(current_user)** in the **log_out** method (Listing 9.12).[12] We can avoid this by logging out only if the user is logged in.

The second subtlety is that a user could be logged in (and remembered) in multiple browsers, such as Chrome and Firefox, which causes a problem if the user logs out in the first browser but not the second, and then closes and re-opens the second one.[13] For example, suppose that the user logs out in Firefox, thereby setting the remember digest to **nil** (via **user.forget** in Listing 9.11). The application will still work in Firefox; because the **log_out** method in Listing 9.12 deletes the user's id, both highlighted conditionals are **false**:

```ruby
# Returns the user corresponding to the remember token cookie.
def current_user
  if (user_id = session[:user_id])
    @current_user ||= User.find_by(id: user_id)
  elsif (user_id = cookies.encrypted[:user_id])
    user = User.find_by(id: user_id)
    if user && user.authenticated?(cookies[:remember_token])
      log_in user
      @current_user = user
    end
  end
end
```

As a result, evaluation falls off the end of the **current_user** method, thereby returning **nil** as required.

---

12. Thanks to reader Paulo Célio Júnior for pointing this out.

13. Thanks to reader Niels de Ron for pointing this out.

In contrast, if we close Chrome, we set **session[:user_id]** to **nil** (because all **session** variables expire automatically on browser close), but the **user_id** *cookie* will still be present. This means that the corresponding user will still be pulled out of the database when Chrome is relaunched:

```
# Returns the user corresponding to the remember token cookie.
def current_user
  if (user_id = session[:user_id])
    @current_user ||= User.find_by(id: user_id)
  elsif (user_id = cookies.encrypted[:user_id])
    user = User.find_by(id: user_id)
    if user && user.authenticated?(cookies[:remember_token])
      log_in user
      @current_user = user
    end
  end
end
```

Consequently, the inner **if** conditional will be evaluated:

```
user && user.authenticated?(cookies[:remember_token])
```

In particular, because **user** isn't **nil**, the *second* expression will be evaluated, which raises an error. This is because the user's remember digest was deleted as part of logging out (Listing 9.11) in Firefox. So when we access the application in Chrome, we end up calling

```
BCrypt::Password.new(remember_digest).is_password?(remember_token)
```

with a **nil** remember digest, thereby raising an exception inside the bcrypt library. To fix this, we want **authenticated?** to return **false** instead.

These are exactly the sorts of subtleties that benefit from test-driven development, so we'll write tests to catch the two errors before correcting them. We first get the integration test from Listing 8.38 to RED, as shown in Listing 9.14.

Listing 9.14: A test for logging out in a second window. RED
test/integration/users_login_test.rb

```
require 'test_helper'

class UsersLoginTest < ActionDispatch::IntegrationTest
```

```
  .
  .
  .
test "login with valid information followed by logout" do
  get login_path
  post login_path, params: { session: { email:    @user.email,
                                         password: 'password' } }
  assert is_logged_in?
  assert_redirected_to @user
  follow_redirect!
  assert_template 'users/show'
  assert_select "a[href=?]", login_path, count: 0
  assert_select "a[href=?]", logout_path
  assert_select "a[href=?]", user_path(@user)
  delete logout_path
  assert_not is_logged_in?
  assert_redirected_to root_url
  # Simulate a user clicking logout in a second window.
  delete logout_path
  follow_redirect!
  assert_select "a[href=?]", login_path
  assert_select "a[href=?]", logout_path,      count: 0
  assert_select "a[href=?]", user_path(@user), count: 0
  end
end
```

The second call to **delete logout_path** in Listing 9.14 should raise an error due to the missing **current_user**, leading to a RED test suite:

Listing 9.15: RED

```
$ rails test
```

The application code simply involves calling **log_out** only if **logged_in?** is true, as shown in Listing 9.16.

Listing 9.16: Only logging out if logged in. GREEN
app/controllers/sessions_controller.rb

```
class SessionsController < ApplicationController
  .
  .
  .
  def destroy
```

```
    log_out if logged_in?
    redirect_to root_url
  end
end
```

The second case, involving a scenario with two different browsers, is harder to simulate with an integration test, but it's easy to check in the User model test directly. All we need is to start with a user that has no remember digest (which is true for the **@user** variable defined in the **setup** method) and then call **authenticated?**, as shown in Listing 9.17. (Note that we've left the remember token blank; it doesn't matter what its value is, because the error occurs before it ever gets used.)

Listing 9.17: A test of **authenticated?** with a nonexistent digest. RED
test/models/user_test.rb

```
require 'test_helper'

class UserTest < ActiveSupport::TestCase

  def setup
    @user = User.new(name: "Example User", email: "user@example.com",
                     password: "foobar", password_confirmation: "foobar")
  end
  .
  .
  .
  test "authenticated? should return false for a user with nil digest" do
    assert_not @user.authenticated?('')
  end
end
```

Because **BCrypt::Password.new(nil)** raises an error, the test suite should now be RED:

Listing 9.18: RED

```
$ rails test
```

To fix the error and get to GREEN, all we need to do is return **false** if the remember digest is **nil**, as shown in Listing 9.19.

Listing 9.19: Updating **authenticated?** to handle a nonexistent digest. GREEN
app/models/user.rb

```ruby
class User < ApplicationRecord
  .
  .
  .
  # Returns true if the given token matches the digest.
  def authenticated?(remember_token)
    return false if remember_digest.nil?
    BCrypt::Password.new(remember_digest).is_password?(remember_token)
  end

  # Forgets a user.
  def forget
    update_attribute(:remember_digest, nil)
  end
end
```

This uses the **return** keyword to return immediately if the remember digest is **nil**, which is a common way to emphasize that the rest of the method gets ignored in that case. The equivalent code

```ruby
if remember_digest.nil?
  false
else
  BCrypt::Password.new(remember_digest).is_password?(remember_token)
end
```

would also work fine, but I prefer the explicitness of the version in Listing 9.19 (which also happens to be slightly shorter).

With the code in Listing 9.19, our full test suite should be GREEN, and both subtleties should now be addressed:

Listing 9.20: GREEN

```
$ rails test
```

Exercises

Solutions to the exercises are available to all Rails Tutorial purchasers at https://www.railstutorial.org/aw-solutions.

To see other people's answers and to record your own, subscribe to the Rails Tutorial course or to the Learn Enough All Access Bundle.

1. Comment out the fix in Listing 9.16 and then verify that the first subtle bug is present by opening two logged-in tabs, logging out in one, and then clicking "Log out" link in the other.

2. Comment out the fix in Listing 9.19 and verify that the second subtle bug is present by logging out in one browser and closing and opening the second browser.

3. Uncomment the fixes and confirm that the test suite goes from RED to GREEN.

9.2 "Remember Me" Checkbox

With the code in Section 9.1.3, our application has a complete, professional-grade authentication system. As a final step, we'll see how to make staying logged in optional using a "remember me" checkbox. A mockup of the login form with such a checkbox appears in Figure 9.3.

To write the implementation, we start by adding a checkbox to the login form from Listing 8.4. As with labels, text fields, password fields, and submit buttons, checkboxes can be created with a Rails helper method. In order to get the styling right, though, we have to *nest* the checkbox inside the label, as follows:

```erb
<%= f.label :remember_me, class: "checkbox inline" do %>
  <%= f.check_box :remember_me %>
  <span>Remember me on this computer</span>
<% end %>
```

Putting this into the login form gives the code shown in Listing 9.21.

Listing 9.21: Adding a "remember me" checkbox to the login form.
app/views/sessions/new.html.erb

```erb
<% provide(:title, "Log in") %>
<h1>Log in</h1>

<div class="row">
```

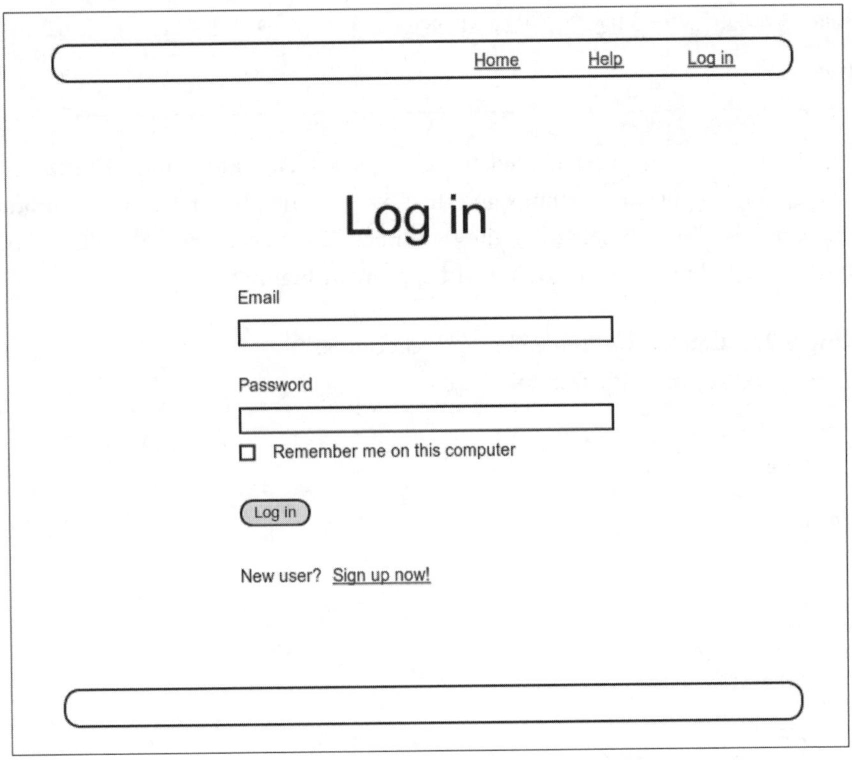

Figure 9.3: A mockup of a "remember me" checkbox.

```
<div class="col-md-6 col-md-offset-3">
  <%= form_with(url: login_path, scope: :session, local: true) do |f| %>

    <%= f.label :email %>
    <%= f.email_field :email, class: 'form-control' %>

    <%= f.label :password %>
    <%= f.password_field :password, class: 'form-control' %>

    <%= f.label :remember_me, class: "checkbox inline" do %>
      <%= f.check_box :remember_me %>
      <span>Remember me on this computer</span>
    <% end %>

    <%= f.submit "Log in", class: "btn btn-primary" %>
  <% end %>
```

```
    <p>New user? <%= link_to "Sign up now!", signup_path %></p>
  </div>
</div>
```

In Listing 9.21, we've included the CSS classes **checkbox** and **inline**, which Bootstrap uses to put the checkbox and the text ("Remember me on this computer") in the same line. To complete the styling, we need just a few more CSS rules, as shown in Listing 9.22. The resulting login form appears in Figure 9.4.

Listing 9.22: CSS for the "remember me" checkbox.
app/assets/stylesheets/custom.scss

```
.
.
.
/* forms */
.
.
.
.checkbox {
  margin-top: -10px;
  margin-bottom: 10px;
  span {
    margin-left: 20px;
    font-weight: normal;
  }
}

#session_remember_me {
  width: auto;
  margin-left: 0;
}
```

Having edited the login form, we're now ready to remember users if they check the checkbox and forget them otherwise. Incredibly, because of all our work in the previous sections, the implementation can be reduced to one line. We start by noting that the **params** hash for submitted login forms now includes a value based on the checkbox (as you can verify by submitting the form in Listing 9.21 with invalid information and inspecting the values in the debug section of the page). In particular, the value of

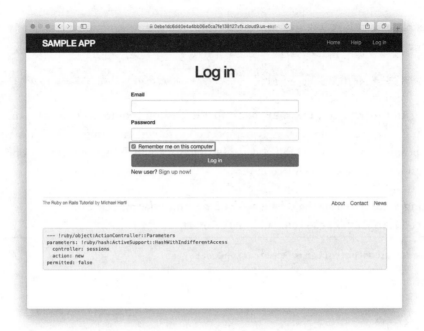

Figure 9.4: The login form with an added "remember me" checkbox.

```
params[:session][:remember_me]
```

is `'1'` if the box is checked and `'0'` if it isn't.

By testing the relevant value of the **params** hash, we can now remember or forget the user based on the value of the submission:[14]

```
if params[:session][:remember_me] == '1'
  remember(user)
else
  forget(user)
end
```

---

14. This means unchecking the box will log out the user on all browsers on all computers. The alternative design of remembering user login sessions on each browser independently is potentially more convenient for users, but less secure as well as more complicated to implement. Ambitious readers are invited to try their hand at implementing it.

As explained in Box 9.2, this sort of **if-then** branching structure can be converted to one line using the *ternary operator* as follows:[15]

```
params[:session][:remember_me] == '1' ? remember(user) : forget(user)
```

Using this to replace **remember user** in the Sessions controller's **create** method (Listing 9.7) leads to the amazingly compact code shown in Listing 9.23. (Now you're in a position to understand the code in Listing 8.25, which uses the ternary operator to define the bcrypt **cost** variable.)

Listing 9.23: Handling the submission of the "remember me" checkbox.
app/controllers/sessions_controller.rb

```ruby
class SessionsController < ApplicationController

  def new
  end

  def create
    user = User.find_by(email: params[:session][:email].downcase)
    if user && user.authenticate(params[:session][:password])
      log_in user
      params[:session][:remember_me] == '1' ? remember(user) : forget(user)
      redirect_to user
    else
      flash.now[:danger] = 'Invalid email/password combination'
      render 'new'
    end
  end

  def destroy
    log_out if logged_in?
    redirect_to root_url
  end
end
```

With the implementation in Listing 9.23, our login system is complete, as you can verify by checking or unchecking the box in your browser.

---

15. Earlier we wrote **remember user** without parentheses, but when used with the ternary operator, omitting them results in a syntax error.

Box 9.2: 10 Types of People

There's an old joke that there are 10 kinds of people in the world: those who understand binary and those who don't (10, of course, being 2 in binary). In this spirit, we can say that there are 10 kinds of people in the world: those who like the ternary operator, those who don't, and those who don't yet know about it. (If you happen to be in the third category, soon you won't be any longer.)

When you do a lot of programming, you quickly learn that one of the most common bits of control flow goes something like this:

```
if boolean?
  do_one_thing
else
  do_something_else
end
```

Ruby, like many other languages (including C/C++, Perl, PHP, and Java), allows you to replace this with a much more compact expression using the *ternary operator* (so called because it consists of three parts):

```
boolean? ? do_one_thing : do_something_else
```

You can also use the ternary operator to replace assignment, so that

```
if boolean?
  var = foo
else
  var = bar
end
```

becomes

```
var = boolean? ? foo : bar
```

Finally, it's often convenient to use the ternary operator in a function's return value:

```
def foo
  do_stuff
  boolean? ? "bar" : "baz"
end
```

Since Ruby implicitly returns the value of the last expression in a function, here the foo method returns "bar" or "baz" depending on whether boolean? is true or false.

Exercises

Solutions to the exercises are available to all Rails Tutorial purchasers at https://www.railstutorial.org/aw-solutions.

To see other people's answers and to record your own, subscribe to the Rails Tutorial course or to the Learn Enough All Access Bundle.

1. By inspecting your browser's cookies directly, verify that the "remember me" checkbox is having its intended effect.

2. At the console, invent examples showing both possible behaviors of the ternary operator (Box 9.2).

9.3 Remember Tests

Although our "remember me" functionality is now working, it's important to write some tests to verify its behavior. One reason is to catch implementation errors, as discussed in a moment. Even more important, though, is that the core user persistence code is completely untested at present. Fixing these issues will require some trickery, but the result will be a far more powerful test suite.

9.3.1 Testing the "Remember Me" Checkbox

When I originally implemented the checkbox handling in Listing 9.23, instead of the correct

```
params[:session][:remember_me] == '1' ? remember(user) : forget(user)
```

I actually used

```
params[:session][:remember_me] ? remember(user) : forget(user)
```

In this context, **params[:session][:remember_me]** is either **'0'** or **'1'**, both of which are **true** in a boolean context, so the resulting expression is *always true*, and the application acts as if the checkbox is always checked. This is exactly the kind of error a test should catch.

Because remembering users requires that they be logged in, our first step is to define a helper to log users in inside tests. In Listing 8.27, we logged a user in using the **post** method and a valid **session** hash, but it's cumbersome to do this every time. To avoid needless repetition, we'll write a helper method called **log_in_as** to log in for us.

Our method for logging a user in depends on the type of test. Inside controller tests, we can manipulate the **session** method directly, assigning **user.id** to the **:user_id** key (as first seen in Listing 8.14):

```
def log_in_as(user)
  session[:user_id] = user.id
end
```

We call the method **log_in_as** to avoid any confusion with the application code's **log_in** method as defined in Listing 8.14. Its location is in the **ActiveSupport::-TestCase** class inside the **test_helper** file, the same location as the **is_logged_in?** helper from Listing 8.33:

```
class ActiveSupport::TestCase
  fixtures :all

  # Returns true if a test user is logged in.
  def is_logged_in?
    !session[:user_id].nil?
  end

  # Log in as a particular user.
  def log_in_as(user)
    session[:user_id] = user.id
  end
end
```

We won't actually need this version of the method in this chapter, but we'll put it to use in Chapter 10.

Inside integration tests, we can't manipulate **session** directly, but we can **post** to the sessions path as in Listing 8.27, which leads to the **log_in_as** method shown here:

```
class ActionDispatch::IntegrationTest

  # Log in as a particular user.
  def log_in_as(user, password: 'password', remember_me: '1')
    post login_path, params: { session: { email: user.email,
```

```
                                       password: password,
                                       remember_me: remember_me } }
    end
end
```

Because it's located inside the **ActionDispatch::IntegrationTest** class, this version of **log_in_as** will be called inside integration tests. We use the same method name in both cases because it lets us do things like use code from a controller test in an integration without making any changes to the login method.

Putting these two methods together yields the parallel **log_in_as** helpers shown in Listing 9.24.

Listing 9.24: Adding a **log_in_as** helper.
test/test_helper.rb

```
ENV['RAILS_ENV'] ||= 'test'
.
.
.
class ActiveSupport::TestCase
  fixtures :all

  # Returns true if a test user is logged in.
  def is_logged_in?
    !session[:user_id].nil?
  end

  # Log in as a particular user.
  def log_in_as(user)
    session[:user_id] = user.id
  end
end

class ActionDispatch::IntegrationTest

  # Log in as a particular user.
  def log_in_as(user, password: 'password', remember_me: '1')
    post login_path, params: { session: { email: user.email,
                                           password: password,
                                           remember_me: remember_me } }
  end
end
```

Note that, for maximum flexibility, the second **log_in_as** method in Listing 9.24 accepts keyword arguments (as in Listing 7.13), with default values for the password and for the "remember me" checkbox set to **'password'** and **'1'**, respectively.

To verify the behavior of the "remember me" checkbox, we'll write two tests, one each for submitting user information with and without the checkbox checked. This is easy using the login helper defined in Listing 9.24, with the two cases appearing as

```
log_in_as(@user, remember_me: '1')
```

and

```
log_in_as(@user, remember_me: '0')
```

(Because **'1'** is the default value of **remember_me**, we could omit the corresponding option in the first case here, but I've included it to make the parallel structure more apparent.)

After logging in, we can check if the user has been remembered by looking for the **remember_token** key in the **cookies**. Ideally, we would check that the cookie's value is equal to the user's remember token, but as currently designed there's no way for the test to get access to it: The **user** variable in the controller has a remember token attribute, but (because **remember_token** is virtual) the **@user** variable in the test doesn't. Fixing this minor blemish is left as an exercise (Section 9.3.1), but for now we can just test to see whether the relevant cookie is **nil**. The results appear in Listing 9.25. (Recall from Listing 8.27 that **users(:michael)** references the fixture user from Listing 8.26.)

Listing 9.25: A test of the "remember me" checkbox. GREEN
test/integration/users_login_test.rb

```
require 'test_helper'

class UsersLoginTest < ActionDispatch::IntegrationTest

  def setup
    @user = users(:michael)
  end
  .
  .
  .
  test "login with remembering" do
```

```
    log_in_as(@user, remember_me: '1')
    assert_not_nil cookies['remember_token']
  end

  test "login without remembering" do
    # Log in to set the cookie.
    log_in_as(@user, remember_me: '1')
    # Log in again and verify that the cookie is deleted.
    log_in_as(@user, remember_me: '0')
    assert_nil cookies['remember_token']
  end
end
```

Assuming you didn't make the same implementation mistake I did, the tests should be GREEN:

Listing 9.26: GREEN

```
$ rails test
```

Exercise

Solutions to the exercises are available to all Rails Tutorial purchasers at https://www.railstutorial.org/aw-solutions.

To see other people's answers and to record your own, subscribe to the Rails Tutorial course or to the Learn Enough All Access Bundle.

1. As mentioned in this section, the application currently doesn't have any way to access the virtual **remember_token** attribute in the integration test in Listing 9.25. It is possible, though, using a special test method called **assigns**. Inside a test, you can access *instance* variables defined in the controller by using **assigns** with the corresponding symbol. For example, if the **create** action defines an **@user** variable, we can access it in the test using **assigns(:user)**. Right now, the Sessions controller **create** action defines a normal (non-instance) variable called **user**, but if we change it to an instance variable we can test that **cookies** correctly contains the user's remember token. By filling in the missing elements in Listing 9.27 and Listing 9.28 (indicated with question marks **?** and **FILL_IN**), complete this improved test of the "remember me" checkbox.

Listing 9.27: A template for using an instance variable in the **create** action.
app/controllers/sessions_controller.rb

```
class SessionsController < ApplicationController

  def new
  end

  def create
    ?user = User.find_by(email: params[:session][:email].downcase)
    if ?user && ?user.authenticate(params[:session][:password])
      log_in ?user
      params[:session][:remember_me] == '1' ? remember(?user) : forget(?user)
      redirect_to ?user
    else
      flash.now[:danger] = 'Invalid email/password combination'
      render 'new'
    end
  end

  def destroy
    log_out if logged_in?
    redirect_to root_url
  end
end
```

Listing 9.28: A template for an improved "remember me" test. GREEN
test/integration/users_login_test.rb

```
require 'test_helper'

class UsersLoginTest < ActionDispatch::IntegrationTest

  def setup
    @user = users(:michael)
  end
  .
  .
  .
  test "login with remembering" do
    log_in_as(@user, remember_me: '1')
    assert_equal FILL_IN, assigns(:user).FILL_IN
  end

  test "login without remembering" do
    # Log in to set the cookie.
    log_in_as(@user, remember_me: '1')
```

```
    # Log in again and verify that the cookie is deleted.
    log_in_as(@user, remember_me: '0')
    assert_empty cookies[:remember_token]
  end
  .
  .
  .
end
```

9.3.2 Testing the Remember Branch

In Section 9.1.2, we verified by hand that the persistent session implemented in the preceding sections is working, but in fact the relevant branch in the **current_user** method is currently completely untested. My favorite way to handle this kind of situation is to raise an exception in the suspected untested block of code: If the code isn't covered, the tests will still pass; if it is covered, the resulting error will identify the relevant test. The result in the present case appears in Listing 9.29.

Listing 9.29: Raising an exception in an untested branch. GREEN
`app/helpers/sessions_helper.rb`

```
module SessionsHelper
  .
  .
  .
  # Returns the user corresponding to the remember token cookie.
  def current_user
    if (user_id = session[:user_id])
      @current_user ||= User.find_by(id: user_id)
    elsif (user_id = cookies.encrypted[:user_id])
      raise        # The tests still pass, so this branch is currently untested.
      user = User.find_by(id: user_id)
      if user && user.authenticated?(cookies[:remember_token])
        log_in user
        @current_user = user
      end
    end
  end
  .
  .
  .
end
```

At this point, the tests are GREEN:

Listing 9.30: GREEN

```
$ rails test
```

This is a problem, of course, because the code in Listing 9.29 is broken. Moreover, persistent sessions are cumbersome to check by hand, so if we ever want to refactor the **current_user** method (as we will in Chapter 11) it's important to test it.

Because both versions of the **log_in_as** helper method defined in Listing 9.24 automatically set **session[:user_id]** (either explicitly or by posting to the login path), testing the "remember" branch of the **current_user** method is difficult in an integration test. Luckily, we can bypass this restriction by testing the **current_user** method directly in a Sessions helper test, whose file we have to create:

```
$ touch test/helpers/sessions_helper_test.rb
```

The test sequence is simple:

1. Define a **user** variable using the fixtures.
2. Call the **remember** method to remember the given user.
3. Verify that **current_user** is equal to the given user.

Because the **remember** method doesn't set **session[:user_id]**, this procedure will test the desired "remember" branch. The result appears in Listing 9.31.

Listing 9.31: A test for persistent sessions. RED
test/helpers/sessions_helper_test.rb

```
require 'test_helper'

class SessionsHelperTest < ActionView::TestCase

  def setup
    @user = users(:michael)
    remember(@user)
  end
```

```
test "current_user returns right user when session is nil" do
  assert_equal @user, current_user
  assert is_logged_in?
end

test "current_user returns nil when remember digest is wrong" do
  @user.update_attribute(:remember_digest, User.digest(User.new_token))
  assert_nil current_user
end
end
```

Note that we've added a second test, which checks that the current user is **nil** if the user's remember digest doesn't correspond correctly to the remember token, thereby testing the **authenticated?** expression in the nested **if** statement:

```
if user && user.authenticated?(cookies[:remember_token])
```

Incidentally, in Listing 9.31 we could write

```
assert_equal current_user, @user
```

instead, and it would work just the same. As mentioned briefly in Section 5.3.4, though, the conventional order for the arguments to **assert_equal** is *expected*, *actual*:

```
assert_equal <expected>, <actual>
```

which in the case of Listing 9.31 gives

```
assert_equal @user, current_user
```

With the code as in Listing 9.31, the test is RED as required:

Listing 9.32: RED

```
$ rails test test/helpers/sessions_helper_test.rb
```

We can get the tests in Listing 9.31 to pass by removing the **raise** and restoring the original **current_user** method, as shown in Listing 9.33.

Listing 9.33: Removing the raised exception. GREEN

`app/helpers/sessions_helper.rb`

```ruby
module SessionsHelper
  .
  .
  .
  # Returns the user corresponding to the remember token cookie.
  def current_user
    if (user_id = session[:user_id])
      @current_user ||= User.find_by(id: user_id)
    elsif (user_id = cookies.encrypted[:user_id])
      user = User.find_by(id: user_id)
      if user && user.authenticated?(cookies[:remember_token])
        log_in user
        @current_user = user
      end
    end
  end
  .
  .
  .
end
```

At this point, the test suite should be GREEN:

Listing 9.34: GREEN

```
$ rails test
```

Now that the "remember" branch of **current_user** is tested, we can be confident of catching regressions without having to check by hand.

Exercise

Solutions to the exercises are available to all Rails Tutorial purchasers at https://www.railstutorial.org/aw-solutions.

To see other people's answers and to record your own, subscribe to the Rails Tutorial course or to the Learn Enough All Access Bundle.

1. Verify by removing the **authenticated?** expression in Listing 9.33 that the second test in Listing 9.31 fails, thereby confirming that it tests the right thing.

9.4 Conclusion

We've covered a lot of ground in the last three chapters, transforming our promising but unformed application into a site capable of the full suite of signup and login behaviors. All that is needed to complete the authentication functionality is to restrict access to pages based on login status and user identity. We'll accomplish this task en route to giving users the ability to edit their information, which is the main goal of Chapter 10.

Before moving on, merge your changes back into the master branch:

```
$ rails test
$ git add -A
$ git commit -m "Implement advanced login"
$ git checkout master
$ git merge advanced-login
$ git push
```

Before deploying to Heroku, it's worth noting that the application will briefly be in an invalid state after pushing but before the migration is finished. On a production site with significant traffic, it's a good idea to turn on *maintenance mode* before making the changes:

```
$ heroku maintenance:on
$ git push heroku
$ heroku run rails db:migrate
$ heroku maintenance:off
```

This arranges to show a standard error page during the deployment and migration (Figure 9.5). (We won't bother with this step again, but it's good to see it at least once.) For more information, see the Heroku documentation on error pages.

9.4.1 What We Learned in this Chapter

- Rails can maintain state from one page to the next using persistent cookies via the **cookies** method.

- We associate to each user a remember token and a corresponding remember digest for use in persistent sessions.

Figure 9.5: The production app in maintenance mode.

- Using the **cookies** method, we create a persistent session by placing a permanent remember token cookie on the browser.
- Login status is determined by the presence of a current user based on the temporary session's user id or the permanent session's unique remember token.
- The application signs users out by deleting the session's user id and removing the permanent cookie from the browser.
- The ternary operator is a compact way to write simple if-then statements.

CHAPTER 10

Updating, Showing, and Deleting Users

In this chapter, we complete the REST actions for the Users resource (Table 7.1) by adding **edit**, **update**, **index**, and **destroy** actions. We'll start by giving users the ability to update their profiles, which will also provide a natural opportunity to enforce an authorization model (made possible by the authentication code in Chapter 8). Then we'll make a listing of all users (also requiring authentication), which will motivate the introduction of sample data and pagination. Finally, we'll add the ability to destroy users, wiping them clear from the database. Since we can't allow just any user to have such dangerous powers, we'll take care to create a privileged class of administrative users authorized to delete other users.

10.1 Updating Users

The pattern for editing user information closely parallels that for creating new users (Chapter 7). Instead of a **new** action rendering a view for new users, we have an **edit** action rendering a view to edit users; instead of **create** responding to a POST request, we have an **update** action responding to a PATCH request (Box 3.2). The biggest difference is that, while anyone can sign up, only the current user should be able to update their information. The authentication machinery from Chapter 8 will allow us to use a *before filter* to ensure that this is the case.

To get started, let's start work on an **updating-users** topic branch:

```
$ git checkout -b updating-users
```

10.1.1 Edit Form

We start with the edit form, whose mockup appears in Figure 10.1.[1] To turn the
mockup in Figure 10.1 into a working page, we need to fill in both the Users controller
edit action and the user edit view. We start with the **edit** action, which requires
pulling the relevant user out of the database. Note from Table 7.1 that the proper
URL for a user's edit page is /users/1/edit (assuming the user's id is 1). Recall that

Figure 10.1: A mockup of the user edit page.

1. Image retrieved from https://www.flickr.com/photos/sashawolff/4598355045/ on 2014-08-25. Copyright © 2010 by Sasha Wolff and used unaltered under the terms of the Creative Commons Attribution 2.0 Generic license.

the id of the user is available in the **params[:id]** variable, which means that we can find the user with the code in Listing 10.1.

Listing 10.1: The user **edit** action.
app/controllers/users_controller.rb

```ruby
class UsersController < ApplicationController

  def show
    @user = User.find(params[:id])
  end

  def new
    @user = User.new
  end

  def create
    @user = User.new(user_params)
    if @user.save
      log_in @user
      flash[:success] = "Welcome to the Sample App!"
      redirect_to @user
    else
      render 'new'
    end
  end

  def edit
    @user = User.find(params[:id])
  end

  private

    def user_params
      params.require(:user).permit(:name, :email, :password,
                                   :password_confirmation)
    end
end
```

The corresponding user edit view (which you will have to create by hand) is shown in Listing 10.2. Note how closely it resembles the new user view from Listing 7.15; the large overlap suggests factoring the repeated code into a partial, which is left as an exercise (Section 10.1.1).

Listing 10.2: The user edit view.
app/views/users/edit.html.erb

```erb
<% provide(:title, "Edit user") %>
<h1>Update your profile</h1>

<div class="row">
  <div class="col-md-6 col-md-offset-3">
    <%= form_with(model: @user, local: true) do |f| %>
      <%= render 'shared/error_messages' %>

      <%= f.label :name %>
      <%= f.text_field :name, class: 'form-control' %>

      <%= f.label :email %>
      <%= f.email_field :email, class: 'form-control' %>

      <%= f.label :password %>
      <%= f.password_field :password, class: 'form-control' %>

      <%= f.label :password_confirmation, "Confirmation" %>
      <%= f.password_field :password_confirmation, class: 'form-control' %>

      <%= f.submit "Save changes", class: "btn btn-primary" %>
    <% end %>

    <div class="gravatar_edit">
      <%= gravatar_for @user %>
      <a href="https://gravatar.com/emails" target="_blank">change</a>
    </div>
  </div>
</div>
```

Here we have reused the shared **error_messages** partial introduced in Section 7.3.3. By the way, the use of **target="_blank"** in the Gravatar link is a neat trick to get the browser to open the page in a new window or tab, which is sometimes convenient behavior when linking to third-party sites. (There's a minor security issue associated with **target="_blank"**; dealing with this detail is left as an exercise (Section 10.1.1).)

With the **@user** instance variable from Listing 10.1, the edit page should render properly, as shown in Figure 10.2. The "Name" and "Email" fields in Figure 10.2 also show how Rails automatically prefills the Name and Email fields using the attributes of the existing **@user** variable.

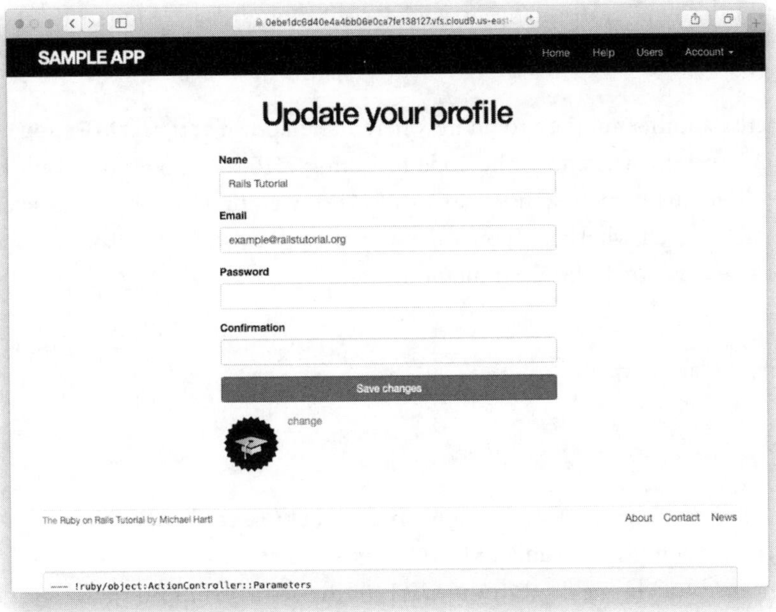

Figure 10.2: The initial user edit page with pre-filled name and email.

Looking at the HTML source for Figure 10.2, we see a form tag as expected, as in Listing 10.3 (slight details may differ).

Listing 10.3: HTML for the edit form defined in Listing 10.2 and shown in Figure 10.2.

```
<form accept-charset="UTF-8" action="/users/1" class="edit_user"
    id="edit_user_1" method="post">
  <input name="_method" type="hidden" value="patch" />
  .
  .
  .
</form>
```

Note here the hidden input field:

```
<input name="_method" type="hidden" value="patch" />
```

Since web browsers can't natively send PATCH requests (as required by the REST conventions from Table 7.1), Rails fakes it with a POST request and a hidden **input** field.[2]

There's another subtlety to address here: The code **form_with(@user)** in Listing 10.2 is *exactly* the same as the code in Listing 7.15—so how does Rails know to use a POST request for new users and a PATCH for editing users? The answer is that it is possible to tell whether a user is new or already exists in the database via Active Record's **new_record?** boolean method:

```
$ rails console
>> User.new.new_record?
=> true
>> User.first.new_record?
=> false
```

When constructing a form using **form_with(@user)**, Rails uses POST if **@user.new_record?** is **true** and PATCH if it is **false**.

As a final touch, we'll fill in the URL of the settings link in the site navigation. This is easy using the named route **edit_user_path** from Table 7.1, together with the handy **current_user** helper method defined in Listing 9.9:

```
<%= link_to "Settings", edit_user_path(current_user) %>
```

The full application code appears in Listing 10.4.

Listing 10.4: Adding a URL to the "Settings" link in the site layout.
app/views/layouts/_header.html.erb

```
<header class="navbar navbar-fixed-top navbar-inverse">
  <div class="container">
    <%= link_to "sample app", root_path, id: "logo" %>
    <nav>
      <ul class="nav navbar-nav navbar-right">
        <li><%= link_to "Home", root_path %></li>
        <li><%= link_to "Help", help_path %></li>
        <% if logged_in? %>
          <li><%= link_to "Users", '#' %></li>
          <li class="dropdown">
```

---

2. Don't worry about how this works; the details are of interest to developers of the Rails framework itself, and by design are not important for Rails application developers.

```
      <a href="#" class="dropdown-toggle" data-toggle="dropdown">
        Account <b class="caret"></b>
      </a>
      <ul class="dropdown-menu">
        <li><%= link_to "Profile", current_user %></li>
        <li><%= link_to "Settings", edit_user_path(current_user) %></li>
        <li class="divider"></li>
        <li>
          <%= link_to "Log out", logout_path, method: :delete %>
        </li>
      </ul>
    </li>
  <% else %>
    <li><%= link_to "Log in", login_path %></li>
  <% end %>
    </ul>
  </nav>
 </div>
</header>
```

Exercises

Solutions to the exercises are available to all Rails Tutorial purchasers at https://www.railstutorial.org/aw-solutions.

To see other people's answers and to record your own, subscribe to the Rails Tutorial course or to the Learn Enough All Access Bundle.

1. As noted earlier, there's a minor security issue associated with using **target="_blank"** to open URLs—namely, the target site gains control of the "**window** object" associated with the HTML document. As a result, the target site could potentially introduce malicious content, such as a phishing page. This is extremely unlikely to happen when linking to a reputable site like Gravatar, but it turns out that we can eliminate the risk entirely by setting the **rel** attribute ("relationship") to **"noopener"** in the origin link. Add this attribute to the Gravatar edit link in Listing 10.2.

2. Remove the duplicated form code by refactoring the **new.html.erb** and **edit.html.erb** views to use the partial in Listing 10.5, as shown in Listing 10.6 and Listing 10.7. Note the use of the **provide** method, which we used in Section 3.4.3 to eliminate duplication in the layout.[3]

---

3. Thanks to Jose Carlos Montero Gómez for a suggestion that further reduced duplication in the **new** and **edit** partials.

Listing 10.5: A partial for the **new** and **edit** form.
app/views/users/_form.html.erb

```erb
<%= form_with(model: @user, local: true) do |f| %>
  <%= render 'shared/error_messages', object: @user %>

  <%= f.label :name %>
  <%= f.text_field :name, class: 'form-control' %>

  <%= f.label :email %>
  <%= f.email_field :email, class: 'form-control' %>

  <%= f.label :password %>
  <%= f.password_field :password, class: 'form-control' %>

  <%= f.label :password_confirmation %>
  <%= f.password_field :password_confirmation, class: 'form-control' %>

  <%= f.submit yield(:button_text), class: "btn btn-primary" %>
<% end %>
```

Listing 10.6: The signup view with partial.
app/views/users/new.html.erb

```erb
<% provide(:title, 'Sign up') %>
<% provide(:button_text, 'Create my account') %>
<h1>Sign up</h1>
<div class="row">
  <div class="col-md-6 col-md-offset-3">
    <%= render 'form' %>
  </div>
</div>
```

Listing 10.7: The edit view with partial.
app/views/users/edit.html.erb

```erb
<% provide(:title, 'Edit user') %>
<% provide(:button_text, 'Save changes') %>
<h1>Update your profile</h1>
<div class="row">
  <div class="col-md-6 col-md-offset-3">
```

```
<%= render 'form' %>
  <div class="gravatar_edit">
    <%= gravatar_for @user %>
    <a href="https://gravatar.com/emails" target="_blank">Change</a>
  </div>
  </div>
</div>
```

10.1.2 Unsuccessful Edits

In this section we'll handle unsuccessful edits, following ideas similar to what we applied to unsuccessful signups (Section 7.3). We start by creating an **update** action, which uses **update** (Section 6.1.5) to update the user based on the submitted **params** hash, as shown in Listing 10.8. With invalid information, the update attempt returns **false**, so the **else** branch renders the edit page. We've seen this pattern before: The structure closely parallels the first version of the **create** action (Listing 7.18).

Listing 10.8: The initial user **update** action.
app/controllers/users_controller.rb

```
class UsersController < ApplicationController

  def show
    @user = User.find(params[:id])
  end

  def new
    @user = User.new
  end

  def create
    @user = User.new(user_params)
    if @user.save
      log_in @user
      flash[:success] = "Welcome to the Sample App!"
      redirect_to @user
    else
      render 'new'
    end
  end

  def edit
```

```
    @user = User.find(params[:id])
  end

  def update
    @user = User.find(params[:id])
    if @user.update(user_params)
      # Handle a successful update.
    else
      render 'edit'
    end
  end

  private

    def user_params
      params.require(:user).permit(:name, :email, :password,
                                   :password_confirmation)
    end
end
```

Note the use of **user_params** in the call to **update**, which uses strong parameters to prevent mass assignment vulnerability (as described in Section 7.3.2).

Because of the existing User model validations and the error-messages partial in Listing 10.2, submission of invalid information results in helpful error messages (Figure 10.3).

Exercise

Solutions to the exercises are available to all Rails Tutorial purchasers at https://www.railstutorial.org/aw-solutions.

To see other people's answers and to record your own, subscribe to the Rails Tutorial course or to the Learn Enough All Access Bundle.

1. Confirm by submitting various invalid combinations of username, email, and password that the edit form won't accept invalid submissions.

10.1.3 Testing Unsuccessful Edits

We left Section 10.1.2 with a working edit form. Following the testing guidelines from Box 3.3, we'll now write an integration test to catch any regressions. Our first step is to generate an integration test as usual:

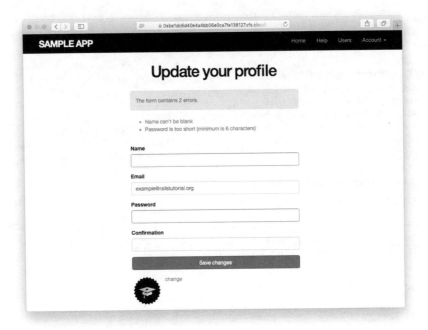

Figure 10.3: Error messages from submitting the update form.

```
$ rails generate integration_test users_edit
    invoke   test_unit
    create     test/integration/users_edit_test.rb
```

Then we'll write a simple test of an unsuccessful edit, as shown in Listing 10.9. The test in Listing 10.9 checks for the correct behavior by verifying that the edit template is rendered after getting the edit page and re-rendered upon submission of invalid information. Note the use of the **patch** method to issue a PATCH request, which follows the same pattern as **get**, **post**, and **delete**.

Listing 10.9: A test for an unsuccessful edit. GREEN
test/integration/users_edit_test.rb

```
require 'test_helper'

class UsersEditTest < ActionDispatch::IntegrationTest
```

```
  def setup
    @user = users(:michael)
  end

  test "unsuccessful edit" do
    get edit_user_path(@user)
    assert_template 'users/edit'
    patch user_path(@user), params: { user: { name:  "",
                                              email: "foo@invalid",
                                              password:              "foo",
                                              password_confirmation: "bar" } }

    assert_template 'users/edit'
  end
end
```

At this point, the test suite should still be GREEN:

Listing 10.10: GREEN

```
$ rails test
```

Exercise

Solutions to the exercises are available to all Rails Tutorial purchasers at https://www.railstutorial.org/aw-solutions.

To see other people's answers and to record your own, subscribe to the Rails Tutorial course or to the Learn Enough All Access Bundle.

1. Add a line in Listing 10.9 to test for the correct *number* of error messages. *Hint*: Use an **assert_select** (Table 5.2) that tests for a **div** with class **alert** containing the text "The form contains 4 errors."

10.1.4 Successful Edits (with TDD)

Now it's time to get the edit form to work. Editing the profile images is already functional since we've outsourced image upload to the Gravatar website: We can edit a Gravatar by clicking on the "change" link in Figure 10.2, which opens the Gravatar site in a new tab (due to **target="_blank"** in Listing 10.2), as shown in Figure 10.4. Let's get the rest of the user edit functionality working as well.

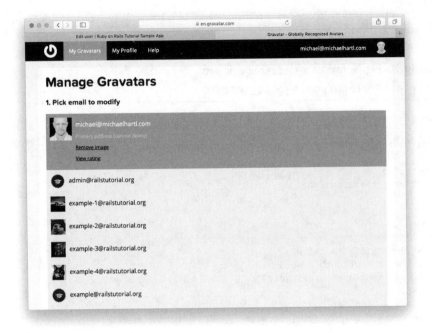

Figure 10.4: The Gravatar image-editing interface.

As you become more comfortable with testing, you might find that it's useful to write integration tests before you write the application code, instead of after. Such tests are sometimes known as *acceptance tests*, since they determine when a particular feature should be accepted as complete. To see how this works, we'll complete the user edit feature using test-driven development.

We'll test for the correct behavior of updating users by writing a test similar to the one shown in Listing 10.9, except this time we'll submit valid information. Then we'll check for a non-empty flash message and a successful redirect to the profile page, while also verifying that the user's information correctly changed in the database. The result appears in Listing 10.11. Note that the password and confirmation in Listing 10.11 are blank, which is convenient for users who don't want to update their passwords every time they update their names or email addresses. Note also the use of **@user.reload** (first seen in Section 6.1.5) to reload the user's values from the database and confirm that they were successfully updated. (This is the kind of detail you could easily forget

initially, which is why acceptance testing—and TDD generally—require a certain level
of experience to be effective.)

Listing 10.11: A test of a successful edit. RED
`test/integration/users_edit_test.rb`

```ruby
require 'test_helper'

class UsersEditTest < ActionDispatch::IntegrationTest

  def setup
    @user = users(:michael)
  end
  .
  .
  .
  test "successful edit" do
    get edit_user_path(@user)
    assert_template 'users/edit'
    name  = "Foo Bar"
    email = "foo@bar.com"
    patch user_path(@user), params: { user: { name:  name,
                                               email: email,
                                               password:              "",
                                               password_confirmation: "" } }
    assert_not flash.empty?
    assert_redirected_to @user
    @user.reload
    assert_equal name,  @user.name
    assert_equal email, @user.email
  end
end
```

The **update** action needed to get the tests in Listing 10.11 to pass is similar to the
final form of the **create** action (Listing 8.32), as seen in Listing 10.12.

Listing 10.12: The user **update** action. RED
`app/controllers/users_controller.rb`

```ruby
class UsersController < ApplicationController
  .
  .
  .
  def update
```

```
    @user = User.find(params[:id])
    if @user.update(user_params)
      flash[:success] = "Profile updated"
      redirect_to @user
    else
      render 'edit'
    end
  end
  .
  .
  .
end
```

As indicated in the Listing 10.12 caption, the test suite is still RED because the password length validation (Listing 6.43) fails due to the empty password and confirmation in Listing 10.11. To get the tests to GREEN, we need to make an exception to the password validation if the password is empty. We can do this by passing the **allow_nil: true** option to **validates**, as seen in Listing 10.13.

Listing 10.13: Allowing empty passwords on update. GREEN

app/models/user.rb

```
class User < ApplicationRecord
  attr_accessor :remember_token
  before_save { self.email = email.downcase }
  validates :name, presence: true, length: { maximum: 50 }
  VALID_EMAIL_REGEX = /\A[\w+\-.]+@[a-z\d\-.]+\.[a-z]+\z/i
  validates :email, presence: true, length: { maximum: 255 },
                    format: { with: VALID_EMAIL_REGEX },
                    uniqueness: true
  has_secure_password
  validates :password, presence: true, length: { minimum: 6 }, allow_nil: true
  .
  .
  .
end
```

In case you're worried that Listing 10.13 might allow new users to sign up with empty passwords, recall from Section 6.3.3 that **has_secure_password** includes a separate presence validation that specifically catches **nil** passwords. (Because **nil** passwords now bypass the main presence validation but are still caught by

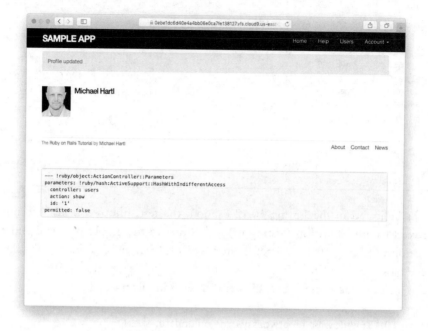

Figure 10.5: The result of a successful edit.

has_secure_password, this also fixes the duplicate error message mentioned in Section 7.3.3.)

With the code in this section, the user edit page should be working (Figure 10.5). You can double-check this by rerunning the test suite, which should now be GREEN:

Listing 10.14: GREEN

```
$ rails test
```

Exercises

Solutions to the exercises are available to all Rails Tutorial purchasers at https://www.railstutorial.org/aw-solutions.

To see other people's answers and to record your own, subscribe to the Rails Tutorial course or to the Learn Enough All Access Bundle.

1. Double-check that you can now make edits by making a few changes on the development version of the application.

2. What happens when you change the email address to one without an associated Gravatar?

10.2 Authorization

In the context of web applications, *authentication* allows us to identify users of our site, while *authorization* lets us control what they can do. One nice effect of building the authentication machinery in Chapter 8 is that we are now in a position to implement authorization as well.

Although the edit and update actions from Section 10.1 are functionally complete, they suffer from a ridiculous security flaw: They allow anyone (even non-logged-in users) to access either action and update the information for any user. In this section, we'll implement a security model that requires users to be logged in and prevents them from updating any information other than their own.

In Section 10.2.1, we'll handle the case of non-logged-in users who try to access a protected page to which they might normally have access. Because this could easily happen in the normal course of using the application, such users will be forwarded to the login page with a helpful message, as mocked up in Figure 10.6. In contrast, users who try to access a page for which they would never be authorized (such as a logged-in user trying to access a different user's edit page) will be redirected to the root URL (Section 10.2.2).

10.2.1 Requiring Logged-in Users

To implement the forwarding behavior shown in Figure 10.6, we'll use a *before filter* in the Users controller. Before filters use the **before_action** command to arrange for a particular method to be called before the given actions.[4] To require users to be logged in, we define a **logged_in_user** method and invoke it using **before_action :logged_in_user**, as shown in Listing 10.15.

---

4. The command for before filters used to be called **before_filter**, but the Rails core team decided to rename it to emphasize that the filter takes place before particular controller actions.

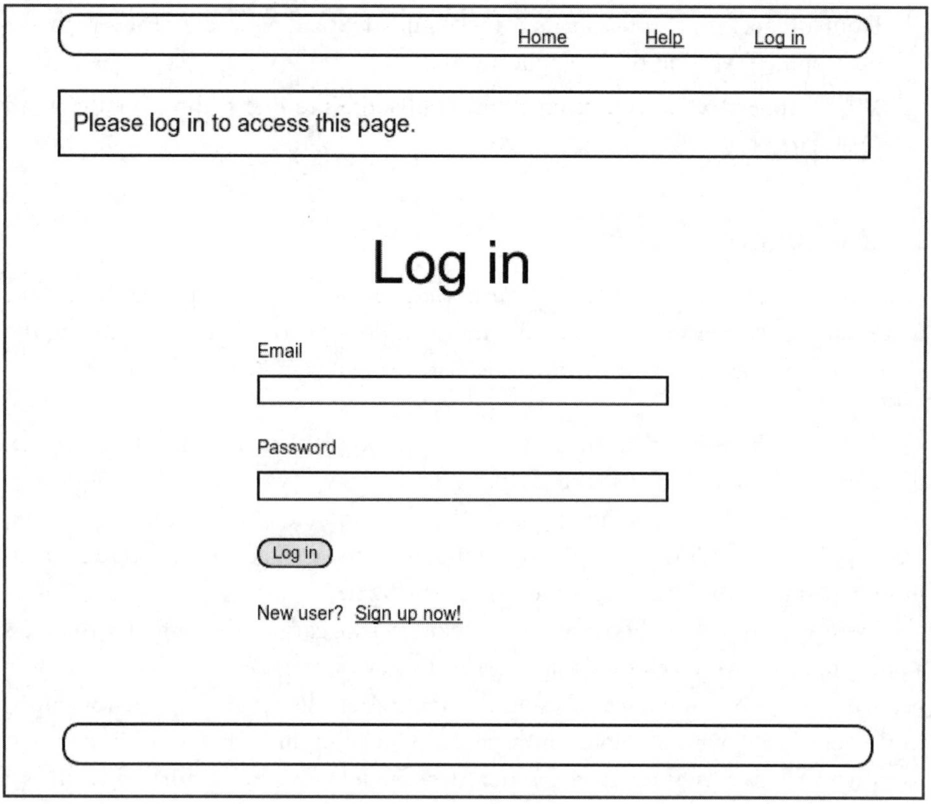

Figure 10.6: A mockup of the result of visiting a protected page.

Listing 10.15: Adding a **logged_in_user** before filter. RED
app/controllers/users_controller.rb

```ruby
class UsersController < ApplicationController
  before_action :logged_in_user, only: [:edit, :update]
  .
  .
  .
  private

    def user_params
      params.require(:user).permit(:name, :email, :password,
                                   :password_confirmation)
    end
```

```
# Before filters

# Confirms a logged-in user.
def logged_in_user
  unless logged_in?
    flash[:danger] = "Please log in."
    redirect_to login_url
  end
end
end
```

By default, before filters apply to *every* action in a controller, so here we restrict the filter to act only on the `:edit` and `:update` actions by passing the appropriate `only:` options hash.

We can see the result of the before filter in Listing 10.15 by logging out and attempting to access the user edit page /users/1/edit, as seen in Figure 10.7.

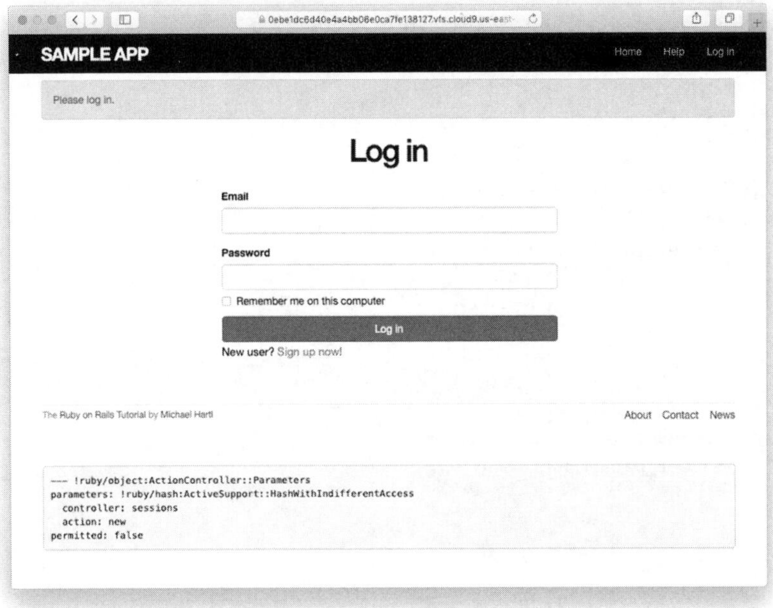

Figure 10.7: The login form after trying to access a protected page.

As indicated in the caption of Listing 10.15, our test suite is currently RED:

Listing 10.16: RED

```
$ rails test
```

The reason is that the edit and update actions now require a logged-in user, but no user is logged in inside the corresponding tests.

We'll fix our test suite by logging the user in before hitting the edit or update actions. This is easy using the **log_in_as** helper developed in Section 9.3 (Listing 9.24), as shown in Listing 10.17.

Listing 10.17: Logging in a test user. GREEN
test/integration/users_edit_test.rb

```
require 'test_helper'

class UsersEditTest < ActionDispatch::IntegrationTest

  def setup
    @user = users(:michael)
  end

  test "unsuccessful edit" do
    log_in_as(@user)
    get edit_user_path(@user)
    .
    .
    .
  end

  test "successful edit" do
    log_in_as(@user)
    get edit_user_path(@user)
    .
    .
    .
  end
end
```

(We could eliminate some duplication by putting the test login in the **setup** method of Listing 10.17, but in Section 10.2.3 we'll change one of the tests to visit the edit page *before* logging in, which isn't possible if the login step happens during the test setup.)

At this point, our test suite should be GREEN:

Listing 10.18: GREEN

```
$ rails test
```

Even though our test suite is now passing, we're not finished with the before filter, because the suite is still GREEN even if we remove our security model, as you can verify by commenting it out (Listing 10.19). This is a Bad Thing—of all the regressions we'd like our test suite to catch, a massive security hole is probably 1, so the code in Listing 10.19 should definitely be RED. Let's write tests to arrange that.

Listing 10.19: Commenting out the before filter to test our security model. GREEN
`app/controllers/users_controller.rb`

```
class UsersController < ApplicationController
  # before_action :logged_in_user, only: [:edit, :update]
  .
  .
  .
end
```

Because the before filter operates on a per-action basis, we'll put the corresponding tests in the Users controller test. The plan is to hit the **edit** and **update** actions with the right kinds of requests and verify that the flash is set and that the user is redirected to the login path. From Table 7.1, we see that the proper requests are GET and PATCH, respectively, which means using the **get** and **patch** methods inside the tests. The results (which include adding a **setup** method to define an **@user** variable) appear in Listing 10.20.

Listing 10.20: Testing that **edit** and **update** are protected. RED
`test/controllers/users_controller_test.rb`

```
require 'test_helper'

class UsersControllerTest < ActionDispatch::IntegrationTest
```

```
  def setup
    @user = users(:michael)
  end
  .
  .
  .

  test "should redirect edit when not logged in" do
    get edit_user_path(@user)
    assert_not flash.empty?
    assert_redirected_to login_url
  end

  test "should redirect update when not logged in" do
    patch user_path(@user), params: { user: { name: @user.name,
                                              email: @user.email } }
    assert_not flash.empty?
    assert_redirected_to login_url
  end
end
```

Note that the second test shown in Listing 10.20 involves using the **patch** method to send a PATCH request to **user_path(@user)**. According to Table 7.1, such a request gets routed to the **update** action in the Users controller, as required.

The test suite should now be RED, as required. To get it to GREEN, just uncomment the before filter (Listing 10.21).

Listing 10.21: Uncommenting the before filter. GREEN
`app/controllers/users_controller.rb`

```
class UsersController < ApplicationController
  before_action :logged_in_user, only: [:edit, :update]
  .
  .
  .
end
```

With that, our test suite should be GREEN:

Listing 10.22: GREEN

```
$ rails test
```

Any accidental exposure of the edit methods to unauthorized users will now be caught immediately by our test suite.

Exercise

Solutions to the exercises are available to all Rails Tutorial purchasers at https://www.railstutorial.org/aw-solutions.

To see other people's answers and to record your own, subscribe to the Rails Tutorial course or to the Learn Enough All Access Bundle.

1. By default before filters apply to every action in a controller, which in our cases is an error (requiring, for example, that users log in to hit the signup page, which is absurd). By commenting out the **only:** hash in Listing 10.15, confirm that the test suite catches this error.

10.2.2 Requiring the Right User

Of course, requiring users to log in isn't quite enough; users should be allowed to edit only their *own* information. As we saw in Section 10.2.1, it's easy to have a test suite that misses an essential security flaw, so we'll proceed using test-driven development to ensure our code implements the security model correctly. To do this, we'll add tests to the Users controller test to complement the ones shown in Listing 10.20.

To make sure users can't edit other users' information, we need to be able to log in as a second user. This means adding a second user to our users fixture file, as shown in Listing 10.23.

Listing 10.23: Adding a second user to the fixture file.
`test/fixtures/users.yml`

```
michael:
  name: Michael Example
  email: michael@example.com
  password_digest: <%= User.digest('password') %>

archer:
  name: Sterling Archer
  email: duchess@example.gov
  password_digest: <%= User.digest('password') %>
```

By using the **log_in_as** method defined in Listing 9.24, we can test the **edit** and **update** actions as shown in Listing 10.24. Note that we expect to redirect users to the root path instead of the login path because a user trying to edit a different user would already be logged in.

Listing 10.24: Tests for trying to edit as the wrong user. RED
test/controllers/users_controller_test.rb

```ruby
require 'test_helper'

class UsersControllerTest < ActionDispatch::IntegrationTest

  def setup
    @user       = users(:michael)
    @other_user = users(:archer)
  end
  .
  .
  .
  test "should redirect edit when logged in as wrong user" do
    log_in_as(@other_user)
    get edit_user_path(@user)
    assert flash.empty?
    assert_redirected_to root_url
  end

  test "should redirect update when logged in as wrong user" do
    log_in_as(@other_user)
    patch user_path(@user), params: { user: { name: @user.name,
                                              email: @user.email } }
    assert flash.empty?
    assert_redirected_to root_url
  end
end
```

To redirect users trying to edit another user's profile, we'll add a second method called **correct_user**, together with a before filter to call it (Listing 10.25). Note that the **correct_user** before filter defines the **@user** variable, so Listing 10.25 also shows that we can eliminate the **@user** assignments in the **edit** and **update** actions.

Listing 10.25: A before filter to protect the edit/update pages. GREEN
app/controllers/users_controller.rb

```ruby
class UsersController < ApplicationController
  before_action :logged_in_user, only: [:edit, :update]
  before_action :correct_user,   only: [:edit, :update]
  .
  .
  .
  def edit
  end

  def update
    if @user.update(user_params)
      flash[:success] = "Profile updated"
      redirect_to @user
    else
      render 'edit'
    end
  end
  .
  .
  .
  private

    def user_params
      params.require(:user).permit(:name, :email, :password,
                                   :password_confirmation)
    end

    # Before filters

    # Confirms a logged-in user.
    def logged_in_user
      unless logged_in?
        flash[:danger] = "Please log in."
        redirect_to login_url
      end
    end

    # Confirms the correct user.
    def correct_user
      @user = User.find(params[:id])
      redirect_to(root_url) unless @user == current_user
    end
end
```

At this point, our test suite should be GREEN:

Listing 10.26: GREEN

```
$ rails test
```

As a final refactoring, we'll adopt a common convention and define a **current_user?** boolean method for use in the **correct_user** before filter. We'll use this method to replace code like

```
unless @user == current_user
```

with the more expressive

```
unless current_user?(@user)
```

The result appears in Listing 10.27. Note that by writing **user && user == current_user**, we also catch the edge case where **user** is **nil**.[5]

Listing 10.27: The **current_user?** method.
app/helpers/sessions_helper.rb

```
module SessionsHelper

  # Logs in the given user.
  def log_in(user)
    session[:user_id] = user.id
  end

  # Remembers a user in a persistent session.
  def remember(user)
    user.remember
    cookies.permanent.encrypted[:user_id] = user.id
    cookies.permanent[:remember_token] = user.remember_token
  end

  # Returns the user corresponding to the remember token cookie.
```

---

5. Thanks to reader Andrew Moor for pointing this out. Andrew also noted that we can use the safe navigation operator introduced in Section 8.2.4 to write this as **user&. == current_user**.

```ruby
  def current_user
    if (user_id = session[:user_id])
      @current_user ||= User.find_by(id: user_id)
    elsif (user_id = cookies.encrypted[:user_id])
      user = User.find_by(id: user_id)
      if user && user.authenticated?(cookies[:remember_token])
        log_in user
        @current_user = user
      end
    end
  end

  # Returns true if the given user is the current user.
  def current_user?(user)
    user && user == current_user
  end
  .
  .
  .
end
```

Replacing the direct comparison with the boolean method yields the code shown in
Listing 10.28.

Listing 10.28: The final **correct_user** before filter. GREEN
app/controllers/users_controller.rb

```ruby
class UsersController < ApplicationController
  before_action :logged_in_user, only: [:edit, :update]
  before_action :correct_user,   only: [:edit, :update]
  .
  .
  .
  def edit
  end

  def update
    if @user.update(user_params)
      flash[:success] = "Profile updated"
      redirect_to @user
    else
      render 'edit'
    end
  end
```

.
.
.

```
  private

    def user_params
      params.require(:user).permit(:name, :email, :password,
                                   :password_confirmation)
    end

    # Before filters

    # Confirms a logged-in user.
    def logged_in_user
      unless logged_in?
        flash[:danger] = "Please log in."
        redirect_to login_url
      end
    end

    # Confirms the correct user.
    def correct_user
      @user = User.find(params[:id])
      redirect_to(root_url) unless current_user?(@user)
    end
end
```

Exercises

Solutions to the exercises are available to all Rails Tutorial purchasers at https://www.railstutorial.org/aw-solutions.

To see other people's answers and to record your own, subscribe to the Rails Tutorial course or to the Learn Enough All Access Bundle.

1. Why is it important to protect both the **edit** and **update** actions?

2. Which action could you more easily test in a browser?

10.2.3 Friendly Forwarding

Our site authorization is complete as written, but it has one minor blemish: When users try to access a protected page, they are redirected to their profile pages regardless of where they were trying to go. In other words, if a non-logged-in user tries to visit the edit page, after logging in the user will be redirected to /users/1 instead of /users/1/edit. It would be much friendlier to redirect users to their intended destination instead.

The application code will turn out to be relatively complicated, but we can write a ridiculously simple test for friendly forwarding just by reversing the order of logging in and visiting the edit page in Listing 10.17. As seen in Listing 10.29, the resulting test tries to visit the edit page, then logs in, and then checks that the user is redirected to the *edit* page instead of the default profile page. (Listing 10.29 also removes the test for rendering the edit template since that's no longer the expected behavior.)

Listing 10.29: A test for friendly forwarding. RED
test/integration/users_edit_test.rb

```
require 'test_helper'

class UsersEditTest < ActionDispatch::IntegrationTest

  def setup
    @user = users(:michael)
  end
  .
  .
  .
  test "successful edit with friendly forwarding" do
    get edit_user_path(@user)
    log_in_as(@user)
    assert_redirected_to edit_user_path(@user)
    name  = "Foo Bar"
    email = "foo@bar.com"
    patch user_path(@user), params: { user: { name:  name,
                                              email: email,
                                              password:             "",
                                              password_confirmation: "" } }
    assert_not flash.empty?
    assert_redirected_to @user
    @user.reload
    assert_equal name,  @user.name
    assert_equal email, @user.email
  end
end
```

Now that we have a failing test, we're ready to implement friendly forwarding.[6] To forward users to their intended destination, we need to store the location of

---

6. The code in this section is adapted from the Clearance gem (github.com/thoughtbot/clearance) by thoughtbot (thoughtbot.com).

the requested page somewhere, and then redirect to that location instead of to the default. We accomplish this with a pair of methods, **store_location** and **redirect_back_or**, both defined in the Sessions helper (Listing 10.30).

Listing 10.30: Code to implement friendly forwarding. RED
app/helpers/sessions_helper.rb

```
module SessionsHelper
  .
  .
  .
  # Redirects to stored location (or to the default).
  def redirect_back_or(default)
    redirect_to(session[:forwarding_url] || default)
    session.delete(:forwarding_url)
  end

  # Stores the URL trying to be accessed.
  def store_location
    session[:forwarding_url] = request.original_url if request.get?
  end
end
```

Here the storage mechanism for the forwarding URL is the same **session** facility we used in Section 8.2.1 to log the user in. Listing 10.30 also uses the **request** object (via **request.original_url**) to get the URL of the requested page.

The **store_location** method in Listing 10.30 puts the requested URL in the **session** variable under the key **:forwarding_url**, but only for a **GET** request. This prevents storing the forwarding URL if a user, say, submits a form when not logged in (which is an edge case but could happen if, for example, a user deleted the session cookies by hand before submitting the form). In such a case, the resulting redirect would issue a **GET** request to a URL expecting **POST**, **PATCH**, or **DELETE**, thereby causing an error. Including **if request.get?** prevents this from happening.[7]

To make use of **store_location**, we need to add it to the **logged_in_user** before filter, as shown in Listing 10.31.

---

7. Thanks to reader Yoel Adler for pointing out this subtle issue, and for discovering the solution.

Listing 10.31: Adding **store_location** to the logged-in user before filter. RED
app/controllers/users_controller.rb

```ruby
class UsersController < ApplicationController
  before_action :logged_in_user, only: [:edit, :update]
  before_action :correct_user,   only: [:edit, :update]
  .
  .
  .
  def edit
  end
  .
  .
  .
  private

    def user_params
      params.require(:user).permit(:name, :email, :password,
                                   :password_confirmation)
    end

    # Before filters

    # Confirms a logged-in user.
    def logged_in_user
      unless logged_in?
        store_location
        flash[:danger] = "Please log in."
        redirect_to login_url
      end
    end

    # Confirms the correct user.
    def correct_user
      @user = User.find(params[:id])
      redirect_to(root_url) unless current_user?(@user)
    end
end
```

To implement the forwarding itself, we use the **redirect_back_or** method to
redirect to the requested URL if it exists, or to some default URL otherwise. We add
to this default URL the Sessions controller **create** action to redirect after success-
ful login (Listing 10.32). The **redirect_back_or** method uses the or operator ||
through

```
session[:forwarding_url] || default
```

This evaluates to **session[:forwarding_url]** unless it's **nil**, in which case it evaluates to the given default URL. Note that Listing 10.30 is careful to remove the forwarding URL (via **session.delete(:forwarding_url)**); otherwise, subsequent login attempts would forward the user to the protected page until the user closed the browser. (Testing for this case is left as an exercise (Section 10.2.3).) Also note that the session deletion occurs even though the line with the redirect appears first; redirects don't happen until an explicit **return** or the end of the method, so any code appearing after the redirect is still executed.

Listing 10.32: The Sessions **create** action with friendly forwarding. GREEN
`app/controllers/sessions_controller.rb`

```ruby
class SessionsController < ApplicationController
  .
  .
  .
  def create
    user = User.find_by(email: params[:session][:email].downcase)
    if user && user.authenticate(params[:session][:password])
      log_in user
      params[:session][:remember_me] == '1' ? remember(user) : forget(user)
      redirect_back_or user
    else
      flash.now[:danger] = 'Invalid email/password combination'
      render 'new'
    end
  end
  .
  .
  .
end
```

With that, the friendly forwarding integration test in Listing 10.29 should pass, and the basic user authentication and page protection implementation is complete. As usual, it's a good idea to verify that the test suite is GREEN before proceeding:

Listing 10.33: GREEN

```
$ rails test
```

Exercises

Solutions to the exercises are available to all Rails Tutorial purchasers at https://
www.railstutorial.org/aw-solutions.

To see other people's answers and to record your own, subscribe to the Rails
Tutorial course or to the Learn Enough All Access Bundle.

1. Write a test to confirm that friendly forwarding forwards to the given URL only
   the first time. On subsequent login attempts, the forwarding URL should revert
   to the default (i.e., the profile page). *Hint*: Add to the test in Listing 10.29 by
   checking for the right value of `session[:forwarding_url]`.

2. Put a **debugger** (Section 7.1.3) in the Sessions controller's **new** action, then log
   out and try to visit /users/1/edit. Confirm in the debugger that the value of
   `session[:forwarding_url]` is correct. What is the value of **request.get?** for
   the **new** action? (Sometimes the terminal can freeze up or act strangely when
   you're using the debugger; use your technical sophistication (Box 1.2) to resolve
   any issues.)

10.3 Showing All Users

In this section, we'll add the penultimate user action, the **index** action, which is
designed to display *all* the users instead of just one. Along the way, we'll learn how
to seed the database with sample users and how to *paginate* the user output so that the
index page can scale up to display a potentially large number of users. A mockup
of the result—users, pagination links, and a "Users" navigation link—appears in
Figure 10.8.[8] In Section 10.4, we'll add an administrative interface to the users index
so that users can also be destroyed.

10.3.1 Users Index

To get started with the users index, we'll first implement a security model. Although
we'll keep individual user **show** pages visible to all site visitors, the user **index** will be
restricted to logged-in users so that there's a limit to how much unregistered users can
see by default.[9]

---

8. Image retrieved from https://www.flickr.com/photos/glasgows/338937124/ on 2014-08-25. Copyright
© 2008 by M&R Glasgow and used unaltered under the terms of the Creative Commons Attribution 2.0
Generic license.

9. This is the same authorization model used by Twitter.

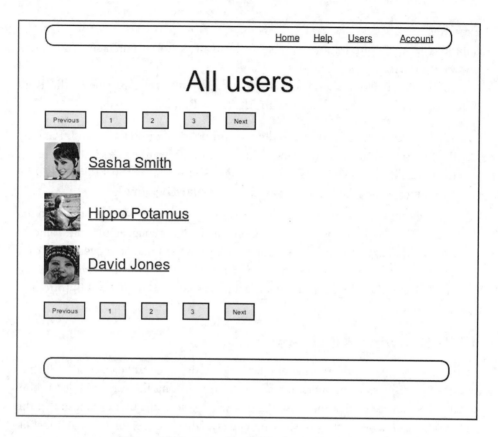

Figure 10.8: A mockup of the users index page.

To protect the **index** page from unauthorized access, we'll first add a short test to verify that the **index** action is redirected properly (Listing 10.34).

Listing 10.34: Testing the **index** action redirect. RED
test/controllers/users_controller_test.rb

```
require 'test_helper'

class UsersControllerTest < ActionDispatch::IntegrationTest

  def setup
    @user       = users(:michael)
    @other_user = users(:archer)
```

```
    end

    test "should get new" do
      get signup_path
      assert_response :success
    end

    test "should redirect index when not logged in" do
      get users_path
      assert_redirected_to login_url
    end
    .
    .
    .
end
```

Then we just need to add an **index** action and include it in the list of actions protected by the **logged_in_user** before filter (Listing 10.35).

Listing 10.35: Requiring a logged-in user for the **index** action. GREEN
app/controllers/users_controller.rb

```
class UsersController < ApplicationController
  before_action :logged_in_user, only: [:index, :edit, :update]
  before_action :correct_user,   only: [:edit, :update]

  def index
  end

  def show
    @user = User.find(params[:id])
  end
  .
  .
  .
end
```

To display the users themselves, we need to make a variable containing all the site's users and then render each one by iterating through them in the index view. As you may recall from the corresponding action in the toy app (Listing 2.9), we can use **User.all** to pull all the users out of the database, assigning them to an **@users** instance variable for use in the view, as seen in Listing 10.36. (If displaying all the users at once seems like a bad idea, you're right—we'll remove this blemish in Section 10.3.3.)

Listing 10.36: The user **index** action.
`app/controllers/users_controller.rb`

```ruby
class UsersController < ApplicationController
  before_action :logged_in_user, only: [:index, :edit, :update]
    .
    .
    .
  def index
    @users = User.all
  end
    .
    .
    .
end
```

To make the actual index page, we'll make a view (which you'll have to create) that iterates through the users and wraps each one in an **li** tag. We do this with the **each** method, displaying each user's Gravatar and name, while wrapping the whole thing in a **ul** tag (Listing 10.37).

Listing 10.37: The users index view.
`app/views/users/index.html.erb`

```erb
<% provide(:title, 'All users') %>
<h1>All users</h1>

<ul class="users">
  <% @users.each do |user| %>
    <li>
      <%= gravatar_for user, size: 50 %>
      <%= link_to user.name, user %>
    </li>
  <% end %>
</ul>
```

The code in Listing 10.37 uses the result from Section 7.1.4, which allows us to pass an option to the Gravatar helper specifying a size other than the default. If you didn't do that exercise, update your Users helper file with the contents of Listing 10.38 before proceeding. (You are also welcome to use the Ruby 2.0–style version from Listing 7.13 instead.)

Listing 10.38: Adding an options hash in the **gravatar_for** helper.
app/helpers/users_helper.rb

```
module UsersHelper

  # Returns the Gravatar for the given user.
  def gravatar_for(user, options = { size: 80 })
    size         = options[:size]
    gravatar_id  = Digest::MD5::hexdigest(user.email.downcase)
    gravatar_url = "https://secure.gravatar.com/avatar/#{gravatar_id}?s=#{size}"
    image_tag(gravatar_url, alt: user.name, class: "gravatar")
  end
end
```

Let's also add a little CSS (or, rather, SCSS) for style (Listing 10.39).

Listing 10.39: CSS for the users index.
app/assets/stylesheets/custom.scss

```
.
.
.
/* Users index */

.users {
  list-style: none;
  margin: 0;
  li {
    overflow: auto;
    padding: 10px 0;
    border-bottom: 1px solid $gray-lighter;
  }
}
```

Finally, we'll add the URL to the users link in the site's navigation header using **users_path**, thereby using the last of the unused named routes in Table 7.1. The result appears in Listing 10.40.

Listing 10.40: Adding the URL to the users link.

`app/views/layouts/_header.html.erb`

```erb
<header class="navbar navbar-fixed-top navbar-inverse">
  <div class="container">
    <%= link_to "sample app", root_path, id: "logo" %>
    <nav>
      <ul class="nav navbar-nav navbar-right">
        <li><%= link_to "Home", root_path %></li>
        <li><%= link_to "Help", help_path %></li>
        <% if logged_in? %>
          <li><%= link_to "Users", users_path %></li>
          <li class="dropdown">
            <a href="#" class="dropdown-toggle" data-toggle="dropdown">
              Account <b class="caret"></b>
            </a>
            <ul class="dropdown-menu">
              <li><%= link_to "Profile", current_user %></li>
              <li><%= link_to "Settings", edit_user_path(current_user) %></li>
              <li class="divider"></li>
              <li>
                <%= link_to "Log out", logout_path, method: :delete %>
              </li>
            </ul>
          </li>
        <% else %>
          <li><%= link_to "Log in", login_path %></li>
        <% end %>
      </ul>
    </nav>
  </div>
</header>
```

With that, the users index is fully functional, with all tests GREEN:

Listing 10.41: GREEN

```
$ rails test
```

On the other hand, as seen in Figure 10.9, it is a bit ... lonely. We'll remedy this sad situation in the next edition.

Figure 10.9: The users index page with only one user.

Exercise

Solutions to the exercises are available to all Rails Tutorial purchasers at https://www.railstutorial.org/aw-solutions.

To see other people's answers and to record your own, subscribe to the Rails Tutorial course or to the Learn Enough All Access Bundle.

1. We've now filled in all the links in the site layout. Write an integration test for all the layout links, including the proper behavior for logged-in and non-logged-in users. *Hint*: Use the `log_in_as` helper and add to the steps shown in Listing 5.32.

10.3.2 Sample Users

In this section, we'll give our lonely sample user some company. Of course, to create enough users to make a decent users index, we *could* use our web browser to visit the signup page and make the new users one by one, but a far better solution is to use Ruby to make the users for us.

First, we'll add the `Faker` gem to the **Gemfile**, which will allow us to make sample users with semi-realistic names and email addresses (Listing 10.42).[10] (Ordinarily, you'd probably want to restrict the `faker` gem to a development environment, but in the case of the sample app we'll be using it on our production site as well (Section 10.5).)

Listing 10.42: Adding the Faker gem to the **Gemfile**.

```
source 'https://rubygems.org'

gem 'rails',          '6.0.2.1'
gem 'bcrypt',         '3.1.13'
gem 'faker',          '2.1.2'
gem 'bootstrap-sass', '3.4.1'
  .
  .
  .
```

Then install as usual:

```
$ bundle install
```

Next, we'll add a Ruby program to seed the database with sample users, for which Rails uses the standard file **db/seeds.rb**. The result appears in Listing 10.43. (The code in Listing 10.43 is a bit advanced, so don't worry too much about the details.)

Listing 10.43: A program for seeding the database with sample users.
db/seeds.rb

```
# Create a main sample user.
User.create!(name:  "Example User",
             email: "example@railstutorial.org",
             password:              "foobar",
             password_confirmation: "foobar")

# Generate a bunch of additional users.
99.times do |n|
  name  = Faker::Name.name
  email = "example-#{n+1}@railstutorial.org"
```

---

10. As always, you should use the version numbers listed at gemfiles-6th-ed.railstutorial.org instead of the ones listed here.

```
    password = "password"
    User.create!(name:  name,
                 email: email,
                 password:                 password,
                 password_confirmation: password)
end
```

The code in Listing 10.43 creates an example user with a name and an email address replicating the information for our previous user, and then makes 99 more. The **create!** method is just like the **create** method, except it raises an exception (Section 6.1.4) for an invalid user rather than returning **false**. This behavior makes debugging easier by avoiding silent errors.

With the code as in Listing 10.43, we can reset the database and then invoke the Rake task using **db:seed**:[11]

```
$ rails db:migrate:reset
$ rails db:seed
```

Seeding the database can be slow, and on some systems could take a few minutes. Also, some readers have reported that they are unable to run the reset command if the Rails server is running, so you may have to stop the server first before proceeding (Box 1.2).

After running the **db:seed** Rake task, our application should have 100 sample users. As seen in Figure 10.10, I've taken the liberty of associating the first few sample addresses with Gravatars so that they're not all the default Gravatar image.

Exercise

Solutions to the exercises are available to all Rails Tutorial purchasers at https:// www.railstutorial.org/aw-solutions.

To see other people's answers and to record your own, subscribe to the Rails Tutorial course or to the Learn Enough All Access Bundle.

1. Verify that trying to visit the edit page of another user results in a redirect as required by Section 10.2.2.

---

11. In principle, these two tasks can be combined in **rails db:reset**, but as of this writing this command doesn't work with the latest version of Rails.

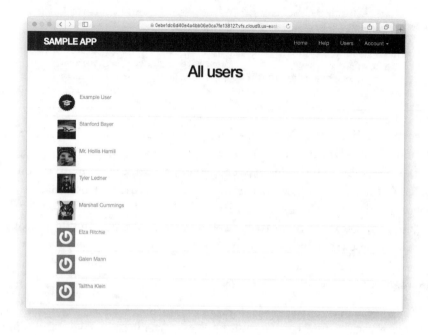

Figure 10.10: The users index page with 100 sample users.

10.3.3 Pagination

Our original user doesn't suffer from loneliness any more, but now we have the opposite problem: Our user has *too many* companions, and they all appear on the same page.
Right now there are a hundred users, which is already a reasonably large number, and
on a real site there could be thousands. The solution is to *paginate* the users, so that
(for example) only 30 show up on a page at any one time.

Several pagination methods are available in Rails; we'll use one of the simplest and most robust, called will_paginate. To use it, we need to include
both the `will_paginate` gem and `bootstrap-will_paginate`, which configures
`will_paginate` to use Bootstrap's pagination styles. The updated **Gemfile** appears
in Listing 10.44.[12]

---

12. As always, you should use the version numbers listed at gemfiles-6th-ed.railstutorial.org instead of the
ones listed here.

Listing 10.44: Including `will_paginate` in the **Gemfile**.

```
source 'https://rubygems.org'

gem 'rails',                      '6.0.2.1'
gem 'bcrypt',                     '3.1.13'
gem 'faker',                      '2.1.2'
gem 'will_paginate',              '3.1.8'
gem 'bootstrap-will_paginate', '1.0.0'
.
.
.
```

Then run **bundle install**:

```
$ bundle install
```

You should also restart the webserver to ensure that the new gems are loaded properly.

To get pagination working, we need to add some code to the index view telling Rails to paginate the users, and we need to replace **User.all** in the **index** action with an object that knows about pagination. We'll start by adding the special **will_paginate** method in the view (Listing 10.45); we'll see in a moment why the code appears both above and below the user list.

Listing 10.45: The users index with pagination.
`app/views/users/index.html.erb`

```erb
<% provide(:title, 'All users') %>
<h1>All users</h1>

<%= will_paginate %>

<ul class="users">
  <% @users.each do |user| %>
    <li>
      <%= gravatar_for user, size: 50 %>
      <%= link_to user.name, user %>
    </li>
  <% end %>
</ul>

<%= will_paginate %>
```

The **will_paginate** method is a little magical: Inside a **users** view, it automatically looks for an **@users** object, and then displays pagination links to access other pages. The view in Listing 10.45 doesn't work yet, though, because currently **@users** contains the results of **User.all** (Listing 10.36), whereas **will_paginate** requires that we paginate the results explicitly using the **paginate** method:

```
$ rails console
>> User.paginate(page: 1)
  User Load (1.5ms)  SELECT "users".* FROM "users" LIMIT 11 OFFSET 0
   (1.7ms)  SELECT COUNT(*) FROM "users"
=> #<ActiveRecord::Relation [#<User id: 1,...
>> User.paginate(page: 1).length
  User Load (3.0ms)  SELECT "users".* FROM "users" LIMIT ? OFFSET ?
   [["LIMIT", 30], ["OFFSET", 0]]
=> 30
```

Note that **paginate** takes a hash argument with key **:page** and value equal to the page requested. **User.paginate** pulls the users out of the database one chunk at a time (30 by default), based on the **:page** parameter. So, for example, page 1 is users 1–30, page 2 is users 31–60, and so forth. If **page** is **nil**, **paginate** simply returns the first page. (The console result just shown presents 11 results rather than 30 due to a console limit in Active Record itself, but calling the **length** method bypasses this restriction.)

Using the **paginate** method, we can paginate the users in the sample application by using **paginate** in place of **all** in the **index** action (Listing 10.46). Here the **page** parameter comes from **params[:page]**, which is generated automatically by **will_paginate**.

Listing 10.46: Paginating the users in the **index** action.
app/controllers/users_controller.rb

```
class UsersController < ApplicationController
  before_action :logged_in_user, only: [:index, :edit, :update]
  .
  .
  .
  def index
    @users = User.paginate(page: params[:page])
```

```
  end
  .
  .
  .
end
```

The users index page should now be working, appearing as in Figure 10.11. (On some systems, you may have to restart the Rails server at this point.) Because we included **will_paginate** both above and below the user list, the pagination links appear in both places.

If you now click on either the 2 link or Next link, you'll get the second page of results, as shown in Figure 10.12.

Exercises

Solutions to the exercises are available to all Rails Tutorial purchasers at https:// www.railstutorial.org/aw-solutions.

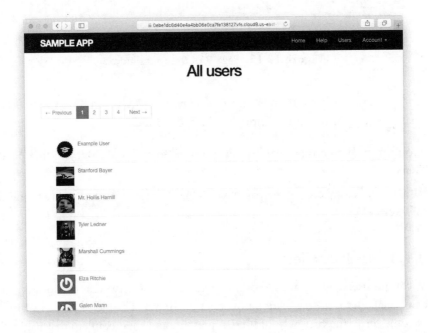

Figure 10.11: The users index page with pagination.

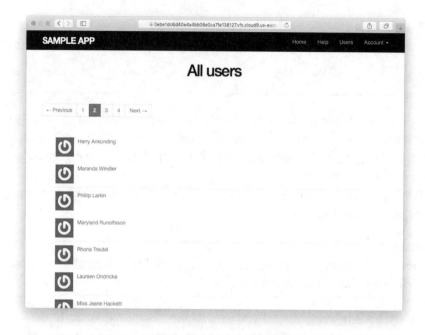

Figure 10.12: Page 2 of the users index.

To see other people's answers and to record your own, subscribe to the Rails Tutorial course or to the Learn Enough All Access Bundle.

1. Confirm at the console that setting the page to **nil** pulls out the first page of users.

2. What is the Ruby class of the pagination object? How does it compare to the class of **User.all**?

10.3.4 Users Index Test

Now that our users index page is working, we'll write a lightweight test for it, including a minimal test for the pagination from Section 10.3.3. The idea is to log in, visit the index path, verify the first page of users is present, and then confirm that pagination is present on the page. For these last two steps to work, we need to have enough users in the test database to invoke pagination, that is, more than 30.

We created a second user in the fixtures in Listing 10.23, but 30 or so more users is a lot to create by hand. Luckily, as we've seen with the user fixture's **password_digest** attribute, fixture files support embedded Ruby. Thus, we can create 30 additional users as shown in Listing 10.47. (Listing 10.47 also creates a couple of other named users for future reference.)

Listing 10.47: Adding 30 extra users to the fixture.
`test/fixtures/users.yml`

```
michael:
  name: Michael Example
  email: michael@example.com
  password_digest: <%= User.digest('password') %>

archer:
  name: Sterling Archer
  email: duchess@example.gov
  password_digest: <%= User.digest('password') %>

lana:
  name: Lana Kane
  email: hands@example.gov
  password_digest: <%= User.digest('password') %>

malory:
  name: Malory Archer
  email: boss@example.gov
  password_digest: <%= User.digest('password') %>

<% 30.times do |n| %>
user_<%= n %>:
  name:  <%= "User #{n}" %>
  email: <%= "user-#{n}@example.com" %>
  password_digest: <%= User.digest('password') %>
<% end %>
```

With the fixtures defined in Listing 10.47, we're ready to write a test of the users index. First we generate the relevant test:

```
$ rails generate integration_test users_index
    invoke  test_unit
    create    test/integration/users_index_test.rb
```

The test itself involves checking for a **div** with the required **pagination** class and verifying that the first page of users is present. The result appears in Listing 10.48.

Listing 10.48: A test of the users index, including pagination. GREEN
`test/integration/users_index_test.rb`

```
require 'test_helper'

class UsersIndexTest < ActionDispatch::IntegrationTest

  def setup
    @user = users(:michael)
  end

  test "index including pagination" do
    log_in_as(@user)
    get users_path
    assert_template 'users/index'
    assert_select 'div.pagination'
    User.paginate(page: 1).each do |user|
      assert_select 'a[href=?]', user_path(user), text: user.name
    end
  end
end
```

The result should be a GREEN test suite:

Listing 10.49: GREEN

```
$ rails test
```

Exercises

Solutions to the exercises are available to all Rails Tutorial purchasers at https://www.railstutorial.org/aw-solutions.

To see other people's answers and to record your own, subscribe to the Rails Tutorial course or to the Learn Enough All Access Bundle.

1. By commenting out the pagination links in Listing 10.45, confirm that the test in Listing 10.48 goes RED.

2. Confirm that commenting out only *one* of the calls to `will_paginate` leaves the tests GREEN. How would you test for the presence of both sets of `will_paginate` links? *Hint*: Use a count from Table 5.2.

10.3.5 Partial Refactoring

The paginated users index is now complete, but there's one improvement I can't resist including: Rails has some incredibly slick tools for making compact views, and in this section we'll refactor the index page to use them. Because our code is well tested, we can refactor with confidence, assured that we are unlikely to break our site's functionality.

The first step in our refactoring is to replace the user **li** from Listing 10.45 with a **render** call (Listing 10.50).

Listing 10.50: The first refactoring attempt in the index view. RED
`app/views/users/index.html.erb`

```erb
<% provide(:title, 'All users') %>
<h1>All users</h1>

<%= will_paginate %>

<ul class="users">
  <% @users.each do |user| %>
    <%= render user %>
  <% end %>
</ul>

<%= will_paginate %>
```

Here we call **render** not on a string with the name of a partial, but rather on a **user** variable of class **User**.[13] In this context, Rails automatically looks for a partial called **_user.html.erb**, which we must create (Listing 10.51).

---

13. The name **user** is immaterial—we could have written **@users.each do |foobar|** and then used **render foobar**. The key is the *class* of the object—in this case, **User**.

Listing 10.51: A partial to render a single user. GREEN
`app/views/users/_user.html.erb`

```
<li>
  <%= gravatar_for user, size: 50 %>
  <%= link_to user.name, user %>
</li>
```

This is a definite improvement, but we can do even better: We can call **render** *directly* on the **@users** variable (Listing 10.52).

Listing 10.52: The fully refactored users index. GREEN
`app/views/users/index.html.erb`

```
<% provide(:title, 'All users') %>
<h1>All users</h1>

<%= will_paginate %>

<ul class="users">
  <%= render @users %>
</ul>

<%= will_paginate %>
```

Here Rails infers that **@users** is a list of **User** objects; moreover, when called with a collection of users, Rails automatically iterates through them and renders each one with the **_user.html.erb** partial (inferring the name of the partial from the name of the class). The result is the impressively compact code in Listing 10.52.

As with any refactoring, you should verify that the test suite is still GREEN after changing the application code:

Listing 10.53: GREEN

```
$ rails test
```

Exercise

Solutions to the exercises are available to all Rails Tutorial purchasers at https://www.railstutorial.org/aw-solutions.

To see other people's answers and to record your own, subscribe to the Rails Tutorial course or to the Learn Enough All Access Bundle.

1. Comment out the **render** line in Listing 10.52 and confirm that the resulting tests are RED.

10.4 Deleting Users

Now that the users index is complete, there's only one canonical REST action left: **destroy**. In this section, we'll add links to delete users, as mocked up in Figure 10.13,

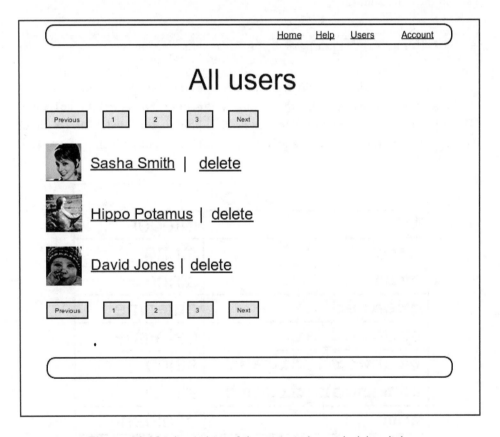

Figure 10.13: A mockup of the users index with delete links.

and define the **destroy** action necessary to accomplish the deletion. But first, we'll create the class of administrative users, or *admins*, authorized to do so. In the context of authorization, such a set of special privileges is known as a *role*.

10.4.1 Administrative Users

We will identify privileged administrative users with a boolean **admin** attribute in the User model, which will lead automatically to an **admin?** boolean method to test for admin status. The resulting data model appears in Figure 10.14.

As usual, we add the **admin** attribute with a migration, indicating the **boolean** type on the command line:

```
$ rails generate migration add_admin_to_users admin:boolean
```

The migration adds the **admin** column to the **users** table, as shown in Listing 10.54. Note that we've added the argument **default: false** to **add_column** in Listing 10.54, which means that users will *not* be administrators by default. (Without the **default: false** argument, **admin** will be **nil** by default, which is still **false**,

users	
`id`	integer
`name`	string
`email`	string
`created_at`	datetime
`updated_at`	datetime
`password_digest`	string
`remember_digest`	string
`admin`	boolean

Figure 10.14: The User model with an added **admin** boolean attribute.

so this step is not strictly necessary. It is more explicit, though, and communicates our intentions more clearly both to Rails and to readers of our code.)

Listing 10.54: The migration to add a boolean **admin** attribute to users.
`db/migrate/[timestamp]_add_admin_to_users.rb`

```
class AddAdminToUsers < ActiveRecord::Migration[6.0]
  def change
    add_column :users, :admin, :boolean, default: false
  end
end
```

Next, we migrate as usual:

```
$ rails db:migrate
```

As expected, Rails figures out the boolean nature of the **admin** attribute and automatically adds the question-mark method **admin?**:

```
$ rails console --sandbox
>> user = User.first
>> user.admin?
=> false
>> user.toggle!(:admin)
=> true
>> user.admin?
=> true
```

Here we've used the **toggle!** method to flip the **admin** attribute from **false** to **true**.

As a final step, let's update our seed data to make the first user an admin by default (Listing 10.55).

Listing 10.55: The seed data code with an admin user.
`db/seeds.rb`

```
# Create a main sample user.
User.create!(name:  "Example User",
             email: "example@railstutorial.org",
             password:              "foobar",
             password_confirmation: "foobar",
             admin: true)
```

```
# Generate a bunch of additional users.
99.times do |n|
  name  = Faker::Name.name
  email = "example-#{n+1}@railstutorial.org"
  password = "password"
  User.create!(name:  name,
               email: email,
               password:                password,
               password_confirmation: password)
end
```

Then reset and reseed the database:

```
$ rails db:migrate:reset
$ rails db:seed
```

Revisiting Strong Parameters

You might have noticed that Listing 10.55 makes the user an admin by including **admin: true** in the initialization hash. This underscores the danger of exposing our objects to the wild web—if we simply passed an initialization hash in from an arbitrary web request, a malicious user could send a PATCH request as follows:[14]

```
patch /users/17?admin=1
```

This request would make user 17 an admin, which would be a potentially serious security breach.

Because of this danger, it is essential that we update only attributes that are safe to edit through the web. As noted in Section 7.3.2, this is accomplished using *strong parameters* by calling **require** and **permit** on the **params** hash:

```
def user_params
  params.require(:user).permit(:name, :email, :password,
                               :password_confirmation)
end
```

---

14. Command-line tools such as curl can issue PATCH requests of this form.

Note that **admin** is *not* in the list of permitted attributes. This prevents arbitrary users from granting themselves administrative access to our application. Because of its importance, it's a good idea to write a test for any attribute that isn't editable, and writing such a test for the **admin** attribute is left as an exercise (Section 10.4.1).

Exercise

Solutions to the exercises are available to all Rails Tutorial purchasers at https://www.railstutorial.org/aw-solutions.

To see other people's answers and to record your own, subscribe to the Rails Tutorial course or to the Learn Enough All Access Bundle.

1. By issuing a PATCH request directly to the user path as shown in Listing 10.56, verify that the **admin** attribute isn't editable through the web. To be sure your test is covering the right thing, your first step should be to *add* **admin** to the list of permitted parameters in **user_params** so that the initial test is RED. For the final line, make sure to load the updated user information from the database (Section 6.1.5).

Listing 10.56: Testing that the **admin** attribute is forbidden.
`test/controllers/users_controller_test.rb`

```
require 'test_helper'

class UsersControllerTest < ActionDispatch::IntegrationTest

  def setup
    @user       = users(:michael)
    @other_user = users(:archer)
  end
  .
  .
  .
  test "should redirect update when not logged in" do
    patch user_path(@user), params: { user: { name: @user.name,
                                              email: @user.email } }
    assert_not flash.empty?
    assert_redirected_to login_url
  end

  test "should not allow the admin attribute to be edited via the web" do
    log_in_as(@other_user)
    assert_not @other_user.admin?
```

```
      patch user_path(@other_user), params: {
                                  user: { password:              "password",
                                          password_confirmation: "password",
                                          admin: FILL_IN } }
    assert_not @other_user.FILL_IN.admin?
  end
  .
  .
  .
end
```

10.4.2 The destroy Action

The final step needed to complete the Users resource is to add delete links and a **destroy** action. We'll start by adding a delete link for each user on the users index page, restricting access to administrative users. The resulting **"delete"** links will be displayed only if the current user is an admin (Listing 10.57).

Listing 10.57: User delete links (viewable only by admins).
app/views/users/_user.html.erb

```erb
<li>
  <%= gravatar_for user, size: 50 %>
  <%= link_to user.name, user %>
  <% if current_user.admin? && !current_user?(user) %>
    | <%= link_to "delete", user, method: :delete,
                            data: { confirm: "You sure?" } %>
  <% end %>
</li>
```

Note the **method: :delete** argument, which arranges for the link to issue the necessary DELETE request. We've also wrapped each link inside an **if** statement so that only admins can see them. The result for our admin user appears in Figure 10.15.

Web browsers can't send DELETE requests natively, so Rails fakes them with JavaScript. As a consequence, the delete links won't work if the user has JavaScript disabled. If you must support non-JavaScript-enabled browsers, you can fake a DELETE request using a form and a POST request, which works even without JavaScript.[15]

---

15. See the RailsCast on "Destroy Without JavaScript" (railscasts.com/episodes/77-destroy-without-javascript) for details.

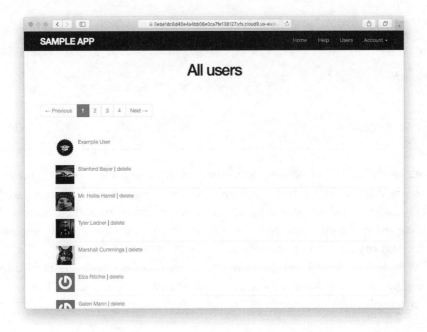

Figure 10.15: The users index with delete links.

To get the delete links to work, we need to add a **destroy** action (Table 7.1), which finds the corresponding user and destroys it with the Active Record **destroy** method, then redirects to the users index, as seen in Listing 10.58. Because users have to be logged in to delete users, Listing 10.58 also adds **:destroy** to the **logged_in_user** before filter.

Listing 10.58: Adding a working **destroy** action.
app/controllers/users_controller.rb

```ruby
class UsersController < ApplicationController
  before_action :logged_in_user, only: [:index, :edit, :update, :destroy]
  before_action :correct_user,   only: [:edit, :update]
  .
  .
  .
  def destroy
    User.find(params[:id]).destroy
```

```
    flash[:success] = "User deleted"
    redirect_to users_url
  end

  private
    .
    .
    .
end
```

As constructed, only admins can destroy users through the web since only they can see the delete links, but there's still a terrible security hole: Any sufficiently sophisticated attacker could simply issue a DELETE request directly from the command line to delete any user on the site. To secure the site properly, we also need access control on the **destroy** action, so that *only* admins can delete users.

As in Section 10.2.1 and Section 10.2.2, we'll enforce access control using a before filter, this time to restrict access to the **destroy** action to admins. The resulting **admin_user** before filter appears in Listing 10.59.

Listing 10.59: A before filter restricting the **destroy** action to admins.
`app/controllers/users_controller.rb`

```
class UsersController < ApplicationController
  before_action :logged_in_user, only: [:index, :edit, :update, :destroy]
  before_action :correct_user,    only: [:edit, :update]
  before_action :admin_user,      only: :destroy
    .
    .
    .
  private
    .
    .
    .
  # Confirms an admin user.
  def admin_user
    redirect_to(root_url) unless current_user.admin?
  end
end
```

Exercise

Solutions to the exercises are available to all Rails Tutorial purchasers at https://www.railstutorial.org/aw-solutions.

To see other people's answers and to record your own, subscribe to the Rails Tutorial course or to the Learn Enough All Access Bundle.

1. As the admin user, destroy a few sample users through the web interface. What are the corresponding entries in the server log?

10.4.3 User Destroy Tests

With something as dangerous as destroying users, it's important to have good tests for the expected behavior. We start by arranging for one of our fixture users to be an admin, as shown in Listing 10.60.

Listing 10.60: Making one of the fixture users an admin.
`test/fixtures/users.yml`

```
michael:
  name: Michael Example
  email: michael@example.com
  password_digest: <%= User.digest('password') %>
  admin: true

archer:
  name: Sterling Archer
  email: duchess@example.gov
  password_digest: <%= User.digest('password') %>

lana:
  name: Lana Kane
  email: hands@example.gov
  password_digest: <%= User.digest('password') %>

malory:
  name: Malory Archer
  email: boss@example.gov
  password_digest: <%= User.digest('password') %>

<% 30.times do |n| %>
user_<%= n %>:
  name:  <%= "User #{n}" %>
  email: <%= "user-#{n}@example.com" %>
  password_digest: <%= User.digest('password') %>
<% end %>
```

Following the practice from Section 10.2.1, we'll put action-level tests of access control in the Users controller test file. As with the logout test in Listing 8.38, we'll use **delete** to issue a DELETE request directly to the **destroy** action. We need to check two cases: (1) users who aren't logged in should be redirected to the login page and (2) users who are logged in but who aren't admins should be redirected to the Home page. The result appears in Listing 10.61.

Listing 10.61: Action-level tests for admin access control. GREEN
`test/controllers/users_controller_test.rb`

```ruby
require 'test_helper'

class UsersControllerTest < ActionDispatch::IntegrationTest

  def setup
    @user       = users(:michael)
    @other_user = users(:archer)
  end
  .
  .
  .
  test "should redirect destroy when not logged in" do
    assert_no_difference 'User.count' do
      delete user_path(@user)
    end
    assert_redirected_to login_url
  end

  test "should redirect destroy when logged in as a non-admin" do
    log_in_as(@other_user)
    assert_no_difference 'User.count' do
      delete user_path(@user)
    end
    assert_redirected_to root_url
  end
end
```

Note that Listing 10.61 also makes sure that the user count doesn't change using the **assert_no_difference** method (seen earlier in Listing 7.23).

The tests in Listing 10.61 verify the behavior in the case of an unauthorized (non-admin) user, but we also want to check that an admin can use a delete link to successfully destroy a user. Since the delete links appear on the users index, we'll add

these tests to the users index test from Listing 10.48. The only really tricky part is
verifying that a user gets deleted when an admin clicks on a delete link, which we'll
accomplish as follows:

```
assert_difference 'User.count', -1 do
  delete user_path(@other_user)
end
```

This uses the **assert_difference** method first seen in Listing 7.31 when creating a
user, this time verifying that a user is *destroyed* by checking that **User.count** changes
by −1 when issuing a **delete** request to the corresponding user path.

Putting everything together gives the pagination and delete test in Listing 10.62,
which includes tests for both admins and non-admins.

Listing 10.62: An integration test for delete links and destroying users. GREEN
test/integration/users_index_test.rb

```
require 'test_helper'

class UsersIndexTest < ActionDispatch::IntegrationTest

  def setup
    @admin     = users(:michael)
    @non_admin = users(:archer)
  end

  test "index as admin including pagination and delete links" do
    log_in_as(@admin)
    get users_path
    assert_template 'users/index'
    assert_select 'div.pagination'
    first_page_of_users = User.paginate(page: 1)
    first_page_of_users.each do |user|
      assert_select 'a[href=?]', user_path(user), text: user.name
      unless user == @admin
        assert_select 'a[href=?]', user_path(user), text: 'delete'
      end
    end
    assert_difference 'User.count', -1 do
      delete user_path(@non_admin)
    end
  end
```

```
   test "index as non-admin" do
     log_in_as(@non_admin)
     get users_path
     assert_select 'a', text: 'delete', count: 0
   end
end
```

Note that Listing 10.62 checks for the right delete links, including skipping the test if the user happens to be the admin (which lacks a delete link due to Listing 10.57).

At this point, our deletion code is well tested, and the test suite should be GREEN:

Listing 10.63: GREEN

```
$ rails test
```

Exercise

Solutions to the exercises are available to all Rails Tutorial purchasers at https://www.railstutorial.org/aw-solutions.

To see other people's answers and to record your own, subscribe to the Rails Tutorial course or to the Learn Enough All Access Bundle.

1. By commenting out the admin user before filter in Listing 10.59, confirm that the tests go RED.

10.5 Conclusion

We've come a long way since we introduced the Users controller way back in Section 5.4. Those users couldn't even sign up; now users can sign up, log in, log out, view their profiles, edit their settings, and see an index of all users—and some can even destroy other users.

As it presently stands, the sample application forms a solid foundation for any website requiring users with authentication and authorization. In Chapter 11 and Chapter 12, we'll add two additional refinements: an account activation link for newly registered users (verifying a valid email address in the process) and password resets to help users who forget their passwords.

Before moving on, be sure to merge all the changes into the master branch:

```
$ git add -A
$ git commit -m "Finish user edit, update, index, and destroy actions"
$ git checkout master
$ git merge updating-users
$ git push
```

You can also deploy the application and even populate the production database with sample users (using the **pg:reset** task to reset the production database):

```
$ rails test
$ git push heroku
$ heroku pg:reset DATABASE
$ heroku run rails db:migrate
$ heroku run rails db:seed
```

Of course, you probably wouldn't want to seed a real site with sample data, but I include this step here for purposes of illustration (Figure 10.16). Incidentally, the order of the sample users in Figure 10.16 may vary, and on my system it doesn't match the local version from Figure 10.11; because we haven't specified a default ordering for users when retrieved from the database, the current order is database-dependent. This doesn't matter much for users, but it will for microposts, and we'll address this issue further in Section 13.1.4.

10.5.1 What We Learned in this Chapter

- Users can be updated using an edit form, which sends a PATCH request to the **update** action.

- Safe updating through the web is enforced using strong parameters.

- Before filters give a standard way to run methods before particular controller actions.

- We implement an authorization using before filters.

- Authorization tests use both low-level commands to submit particular HTTP requests directly to controller actions and high-level integration tests.

- Friendly forwarding redirects users where they wanted to go after logging in.

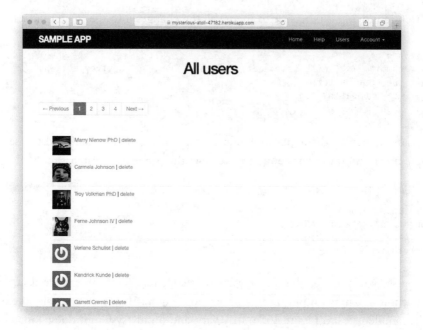

Figure 10.16: The sample users in production.

- The users index page shows all users, one page at a time.

- Rails uses the standard file **db/seeds.rb** to seed the database with sample data using **rails db:seed**.

- Running **render @users** automatically calls the **_user.html.erb** partial on each user in the collection.

- A boolean attribute called **admin** on the User model automatically creates an **admin?** boolean method on user objects.

- Admins can delete users through the web by clicking on delete links that issue DELETE requests to the Users controller **destroy** action.

- We can create a large number of test users by using embedded Ruby inside fixtures.

CHAPTER 11

Account Activation

At present, newly registered users immediately have full access to their accounts (Chapter 7); in this chapter, we'll implement an account activation step to verify that the user controls the email address they used to sign up.[1] This will involve associating an activation token and digest with a user, sending the user an email with a link including the token, and activating the user upon clicking the link. In Chapter 12, we'll apply similar ideas to allow users to reset their passwords if they forget them. Each of these two features will involve creating a new resource, thereby giving us a chance to see further examples of controllers, routing, and database migrations. In the process, we'll also have a chance to learn how to send email in Rails, both in development and in production.

Our strategy for handling account activation parallels user login (Section 8.2) and especially remembering users (Section 9.1). The basic sequence appears as follows:[2]

1. Start users in an "unactivated" state.

2. When a user signs up, generate an activation token and corresponding activation digest.

---

1. This chapter is independent of the others, apart from the mailer generation in Listing 11.6, which is used in Chapter 12. Readers can skip to Chapter 12 or to Chapter 13 with minimal discontinuity, although the former will be substantially more challenging due to substantial overlap with this chapter.

2. In addition to this basic sequence, another nice feature to have is the ability to resend account activation emails in case the initial confirmation gets lost, marked as spam, and so forth. Adding such a feature should be within your capabilities by the time you finish this tutorial. You might also consider using a solution such as Devise, already includes the ability to resend confirmation emails.

3. Save the activation digest to the database, and then send an email to the user with a link containing the activation token and user's email address.[3]

4. When the user clicks the link, find the user by email address, and then authenticate the token by comparing with the activation digest.

5. If the user is authenticated, change the status from "unactivated" to "activated."

Because of the similarity with passwords and remember tokens, we will be able to reuse many of the same ideas for account activation (as well as password reset), including the **User.digest** and **User.new_token** methods and a modified version of the **user.authenticated?** method. Table 11.1 illustrates the analogy (including the password reset from Chapter 12).

In Section 11.1, we'll make a resource and data model for account activations and in Section 11.2 we'll add a *mailer* for sending account activation emails. We'll implement the actual account activation, including a generalized version of the **authenticated?** method from Table 11.1, in Section 11.3.

Table 11.1: The analogy between login, remembering, account activation, and password reset.

find by	string	digest	authentication
email	password	password_digest	authenticate (password)
id	remember_token	remember_digest	authenticated? (:remember, token)
email	activation_token	activation_digest	authenticated? (:activation, token)
email	reset_token	reset_digest	authenticated? (:reset, token)

---

3. We could use the user's id instead, since it's already exposed in the URLs of our application, but using email addresses is more future-proof in case we want to obfuscate user ids for any reason (e.g., to prevent competitors from knowing how many users our application has).

11.1 Account Activations Resource

As with sessions (Section 8.1), we'll model account activations as a resource even though they won't be associated with an Active Record model. Instead, we'll include the relevant data (including the activation token and activation status) in the User model itself.

Because we'll be treating account activations as a resource, we'll interact with them via a standard REST URL. The activation link will be modifying the user's activation status, and for such modifications the standard REST practice is to issue a PATCH request to the **update** action (Table 7.1). The activation link needs to be sent in an email, though, and hence will involve a regular browser click, which issues a GET request instead of PATCH. This design constraint means that we can't use the **update** action, but we'll do the next-best thing and use the **edit** action instead, which does respond to GET requests.

As usual, we'll make a topic branch for the new feature:

```
$ git checkout -b account-activation
```

11.1.1 Account Activations Controller

As with Users and Sessions, the actions (or, in this case, the sole action) for the Account Activations resource will live inside an Account Activations controller, which we can generate as follows:[4]

```
$ rails generate controller AccountActivations
```

As we'll see in Section 11.2.1, the activation email will involve a URL of the form

```
edit_account_activation_url(activation_token, ...)
```

which means we'll need a named route for the **edit** action. We can arrange for this with the **resources** line shown in Listing 11.1, which gives the RESTful route shown in Table 11.2.

---

4. Because we'll be using an **edit** action, we could include **edit** on the command line, but this would also generate both an edit view and a test, neither of which we'll actually need.

Table 11.2: RESTful route provided by the Account Activations resource in Listing 11.1.

HTTP request	URL	Action	Named route
GET	/account_activation/ <token>/edit	**edit**	**edit_account_activation_url(token)**

Listing 11.1: Adding a route for the Account Activations **edit** action.
`config/routes.rb`

```
Rails.application.routes.draw do
  root   'static_pages#home'
  get    '/help',    to: 'static_pages#help'
  get    '/about',   to: 'static_pages#about'
  get    '/contact', to: 'static_pages#contact'
  get    '/signup',  to: 'users#new'
  get    '/login',   to: 'sessions#new'
  post   '/login',   to: 'sessions#create'
  delete '/logout',  to: 'sessions#destroy'
  resources :users
  resources :account_activations, only: [:edit]
end
```

We'll define the **edit** action itself in Section 11.3.2, after we've finished the Account Activations data model and mailers.

Exercises

Solutions to the exercises are available to all Rails Tutorial purchasers at https://www.railstutorial.org/aw-solutions.

To see other people's answers and to record your own, subscribe to the Rails Tutorial course or to the Learn Enough All Access Bundle.

1. Verify that the test suite is still GREEN.

2. Why does Table 11.2 list the **_url** form of the named route instead of the **_path** form? *Hint*: We're going to use it in an email.

11.1.2 Account Activation Data Model

As discussed in the introduction, we need a unique activation token for use in the activation email. One possibility would be to use a string that's both stored in the database and included in the activation URL, but this raises security concerns if our database is compromised. For example, an attacker with access to the database could immediately activate newly created accounts (thereby logging in as the user), and could then change the password to gain control.[5]

To prevent such scenarios, we'll follow the example of passwords (Chapter 6) and remember tokens (Chapter 9) by pairing a publicly exposed virtual attribute with a secure hash digest saved to the database. This way we can access the activation token using

```
user.activation_token
```

and authenticate the user with code like

```
user.authenticated?(:activation, token)
```

(This will require a modification of the **authenticated?** method defined in Listing 9.6.)

We'll also add a boolean attribute called **activated** to the User model, which will allow us to test if a user is activated using the same kind of auto-generated boolean method we saw in Section 10.4.1:

```
if user.activated? ...
```

Finally, although we won't use it in this tutorial, we'll record the time and date of the activation in case we want it for future reference. The full data model appears in Figure 11.1.

The migration to add the data model from Figure 11.1 adds all three attributes at the command line:

```
$ rails generate migration add_activation_to_users \
> activation_digest:string activated:boolean activated_at:datetime
```

(Here the **>** on the second line is a "line continuation" character inserted automatically by the shell; it should not be typed literally.) As with the **admin** attribute (Listing 10.54), we'll add a default boolean value of **false** to the **activated** attribute, as shown in Listing 11.2.

---

5. It's mainly for this reason that we won't be using the (perhaps slightly misnamed) **has_secure_token** facility added in Rails 5, which stores the corresponding token in the database as unhashed cleartext.

users	
id	integer
name	string
email	string
created_at	datetime
updated_at	datetime
password_digest	string
remember_digest	string
admin	boolean
activation_digest	string
activated	boolean
activated_at	datetime

Figure 11.1: The User model with added account activation attributes.

Listing 11.2: A migration for account activation (with added index).
`db/migrate/[timestamp]_add_activation_to_users.rb`

```ruby
class AddActivationToUsers < ActiveRecord::Migration[6.0]
  def change
    add_column :users, :activation_digest, :string
    add_column :users, :activated, :boolean, default: false
    add_column :users, :activated_at, :datetime
  end
end
```

We then apply the migration as usual:

```
$ rails db:migrate
```

Activation Token Callback

Because every newly signed-up user will require activation, we should assign an activation token and digest to each user object before it's created. We saw a similar idea in Section 6.2.5, where we needed to convert an email address to lowercase before saving a user to the database. In that case, we used a **before_save** callback combined with the **downcase** method (Listing 6.32). A **before_save** callback is automatically called before the object is saved, which includes both object creation and updates. In the case of the activation digest, though, we want the callback to fire only when the user is created. This requires a **before_create** callback, which we'll define as follows:

```
before_create :create_activation_digest
```

This code, called a *method reference*, arranges for Rails to look for a method called **create_activation_digest** and run it before creating the user. (In Listing 6.32, we passed **before_save** an explicit block, but the method reference technique is generally preferred.) Because the **create_activation_digest** method itself is only used internally by the User model, there's no need to expose it to outside users; as we saw in Section 7.3.2, the Ruby way to accomplish this is to use the **private** keyword:

```
private

  def create_activation_digest
    # Create the token and digest.
  end
```

All methods defined in a class after **private** are automatically hidden, as seen in this console session:

```
$ rails console
>> User.first.create_activation_digest
NoMethodError: private method `create_activation_digest' called for #<User>
```

The purpose of the **before_create** callback is to assign the token and corresponding digest, which we can accomplish as follows:

```
self.activation_token  = User.new_token
self.activation_digest = User.digest(activation_token)
```

This code simply reuses the token and digest methods used for the remember token, as we can see by comparing it with the **remember** method from Listing 9.3:

```
# Remembers a user in the database for use in persistent sessions.
def remember
  self.remember_token = User.new_token
  update_attribute(:remember_digest, User.digest(remember_token))
end
```

The main difference is the use of **update_attribute** in the latter case. The reason for the difference is that remember tokens and digests are created for users that already exist in the database, whereas the **before_create** callback happens *before* the user has been created, so there's not yet any attribute to update. As a result of the callback, when a new user is defined with **User.new** (as in user signup, Listing 7.19), it will automatically get both **activation_token** and **activation_digest** attributes; because the latter is associated with a column in the database (Figure 11.1), it will be written to the database automatically when the user is saved.

Putting all this information together yields the User model shown in Listing 11.3. As required by the virtual nature of the activation token, we've added a second **attr_accessor** to our model. Note that we've taken the opportunity to replace the email downcasing callback from Listing 6.32 with a method reference.

Listing 11.3: Adding account activation code to the User model. GREEN
app/models/user.rb

```
class User < ApplicationRecord
  attr_accessor :remember_token, :activation_token
  before_save    :downcase_email
  before_create :create_activation_digest
  validates :name,  presence: true, length: { maximum: 50 }
  .
  .
  .
  private

    # Converts email to all lower-case.
    def downcase_email
```

```
      self.email = email.downcase
  end

  # Creates and assigns the activation token and digest.
  def create_activation_digest
    self.activation_token  = User.new_token
    self.activation_digest = User.digest(activation_token)
  end
end
```

Seed and Fixture Users

Before moving on, we should also update our seed data and fixtures so that our sample and test users are initially activated, as shown in Listing 11.4 and Listing 11.5. (The **Time.zone.now** method is a built-in Rails helper that returns the current timestamp, taking into account the time zone on the server.)

Listing 11.4: Activating seed users by default.
db/seeds.rb

```
# Create a main sample user.
User.create!(name:  "Example User",
             email: "example@railstutorial.org",
             password:                "foobar",
             password_confirmation: "foobar",
             admin:    true,
             activated: true,
             activated_at: Time.zone.now)


# Generate a bunch of additional users.
99.times do |n|
  name  = Faker::Name.name
  email = "example-#{n+1}@railstutorial.org"
  password = "password"
  User.create!(name:  name,
               email: email,
               password:                password,
               password_confirmation: password,
               activated: true,
               activated_at: Time.zone.now)
end
```

Listing 11.5: Activating fixture users.
`test/fixtures/users.yml`

```
michael:
  name: Michael Example
  email: michael@example.com
  password_digest: <%= User.digest('password') %>
  admin: true
  activated: true
  activated_at: <%= Time.zone.now %>

archer:
  name: Sterling Archer
  email: duchess@example.gov
  password_digest: <%= User.digest('password') %>
  activated: true
  activated_at: <%= Time.zone.now %>

lana:
  name: Lana Kane
  email: hands@example.gov
  password_digest: <%= User.digest('password') %>
  activated: true
  activated_at: <%= Time.zone.now %>

malory:
  name: Malory Archer
  email: boss@example.gov
  password_digest: <%= User.digest('password') %>
  activated: true
  activated_at: <%= Time.zone.now %>

<% 30.times do |n| %>
user_<%= n %>:
  name:  <%= "User #{n}" %>
  email: <%= "user-#{n}@example.com" %>
  password_digest: <%= User.digest('password') %>
  activated: true
  activated_at: <%= Time.zone.now %>
<% end %>
```

To apply the changes in Listing 11.4, reset the database to reseed the data as usual:

```
$ rails db:migrate:reset
$ rails db:seed
```

Exercises

Solutions to the exercises are available to all Rails Tutorial purchasers at https://www.railstutorial.org/aw-solutions.

To see other people's answers and to record your own, subscribe to the Rails Tutorial course or to the Learn Enough All Access Bundle.

1. Verify that the test suite is still GREEN after the changes made in this section.

2. By instantiating a User object in the console, confirm that calling the **create_activation_digest** method raises a **NoMethodError** due to its being a private method. What is the value of the user's activation digest?

3. In Listing 6.35, we saw that email downcasing can be written more simply as **email.downcase!** (without any assignment). Make this change to the **downcase_email** method in Listing 11.3 and verify by running the test suite that it works.

11.2 Account Activation Emails

With the data modeling complete, we're now ready to add the code needed to send an account activation email. The method is to add a User *mailer* using the Action Mailer library, which we'll use in the Users controller **create** action to send an email with an activation link. Mailers are structured much like controller actions, with email templates defined as views. These templates will include links with the activation token and email address associated with the account to be activated.

11.2.1 Mailer Templates

As with models and controllers, we can generate a mailer using **rails generate**, as shown in Listing 11.6.

Listing 11.6: Generating the User mailer.

```
$ rails generate mailer UserMailer account_activation password_reset
```

In addition to the necessary **account_activation** method, Listing 11.6 generates the **password_reset** method we'll need in Chapter 12.

The command in Listing 11.6 also generates two view templates for each mailer, one for plain-text email and one for HTML email. For the account activation mailer method, they appear as in Listing 11.7 and Listing 11.8. (We'll take care of the corresponding password reset templates in Chapter 12.)

Listing 11.7: The generated account activation text view.
`app/views/user_mailer/account_activation.text.erb`

```
UserMailer#account_activation

<%= @greeting %>, find me in app/views/user_mailer/account_activation.text.erb
```

Listing 11.8: The generated account activation HTML view.
`app/views/user_mailer/account_activation.html.erb`

```
<h1>UserMailer#account_activation</h1>

<p>
  <%= @greeting %>, find me in app/views/user_mailer/account_activation.html.erb
</p>
```

Let's take a look at the generated mailers to get a sense of how they work (Listing 11.9 and Listing 11.10). We see in Listing 11.9 that there is a default **from** address common to all mailers in the application, and each method in Listing 11.10 has a recipient's address as well. (Listing 11.9 uses a mailer layout corresponding to the email format; although it won't ever matter in this tutorial, the resulting HTML and plain-text mailer layouts can be found in **app/views/layouts**.) The generated code also includes an instance variable (**@greeting**), which is available in the mailer views in much the same way that instance variables in controllers are available in ordinary views.

Listing 11.9: The generated application mailer.
`app/mailers/application_mailer.rb`

```
class ApplicationMailer < ActionMailer::Base
  default from: "from@example.com"
  layout 'mailer'
end
```

Listing 11.10: The generated User mailer.
app/mailers/user_mailer.rb

```ruby
class UserMailer < ApplicationMailer

  # Subject can be set in your I18n file at config/locales/en.yml
  # with the following lookup:
  #
  #   en.user_mailer.account_activation.subject
  #
  def account_activation
    @greeting = "Hi"

    mail to: "to@example.org"
  end

  # Subject can be set in your I18n file at config/locales/en.yml
  # with the following lookup:
  #
  #   en.user_mailer.password_reset.subject
  #
  def password_reset
    @greeting = "Hi"

    mail to: "to@example.org"
  end
end
```

To make a working activation email, we'll first customize the generated template as shown in Listing 11.11. Next, we'll create an instance variable containing the user (for use in the view), and then mail the result to **user.email** (Listing 11.12). As seen in Listing 11.12, the **mail** method also takes a **subject** key, whose value is used as the email's subject line.

Listing 11.11: The application mailer with a new default **from** address.
app/mailers/application_mailer.rb

```ruby
class ApplicationMailer < ActionMailer::Base
  default from: "noreply@example.com"
  layout 'mailer'
end
```

Listing 11.12: Mailing the account activation link. RED
`app/mailers/user_mailer.rb`

```ruby
class UserMailer < ApplicationMailer

  def account_activation(user)
    @user = user
    mail to: user.email, subject: "Account activation"
  end

  def password_reset
    @greeting = "Hi"

    mail to: "to@example.org"
  end
end
```

As indicated in the Listing 11.12 caption, the tests are currently RED (due to our changing **account_activation** to take an argument); we'll get them to GREEN in Section 11.2.3.

As with ordinary views, we can use embedded Ruby to customize the template views, in this case greeting the user by name and including a link to a custom activation link. Our plan is to find the user by email address and then authenticate the activation token, so the link needs to include both the email and the token. Because we're modeling activations using an Account Activations resource, the token itself can appear as the argument of the named route defined in Listing 11.1:

```ruby
edit_account_activation_url(@user.activation_token, ...)
```

Recalling that

```ruby
edit_user_url(user)
```

produces a URL of the form

```
http://www.example.com/users/1/edit
```

the corresponding account activation link's base URL will look like this:

```
http://www.example.com/account_activations/q5lt38hQDc_959PVoo6b7A/edit
```

Here **q5lt38hQDc_959PVoo6b7A** is a URL-safe base64 string generated by the **new_token** method (Listing 9.2). It plays the same role as the user id in /users/1/edit. In particular, in the Activations controller **edit** action, the token will be available in the **params** hash as **params[:id]**.

To include the email as well, we need to use a *query parameter*, which in a URL appears as a key-value pair following a question mark:[6]

```
account_activations/q5lt38hQDc_959PVoo6b7A/edit?email=foo%40example.com
```

Notice that the "@" in the email address appears as **%40**, that is, it's "escaped out" to guarantee a valid URL. The way to set a query parameter in Rails is to include a hash in the named route:

```
edit_account_activation_url(@user.activation_token, email: @user.email)
```

When using named routes in this way to define query parameters, Rails automatically escapes out any special characters. The resulting email address will also be unescaped automatically in the controller, and will be available via **params[:email]**.

With the **@user** instance variable as defined in Listing 11.12, we can create the necessary links using the named edit route and embedded Ruby, as shown in Listing 11.13 and Listing 11.14. Note that the HTML template in Listing 11.14 uses the **link_to** method to construct a valid link.

Listing 11.13: The account activation text view.
app/views/user_mailer/account_activation.text.erb

```
Hi <%= @user.name %>,

Welcome to the Sample App! Click on the link below to activate your account:

<%= edit_account_activation_url(@user.activation_token, email: @user.email) %>
```

---

6. URLs can contain multiple query parameters, consisting of multiple key-value pairs separated by the ampersand character **&**, as in **/edit?name=Foo%20Bar&email=foo%40example.com**.

Listing 11.14: The account activation HTML view.
`app/views/user_mailer/account_activation.html.erb`

```erb
<h1>Sample App</h1>

<p>Hi <%= @user.name %>,</p>

<p>
Welcome to the Sample App! Click on the link below to activate your account:
</p>

<%= link_to "Activate", edit_account_activation_url(@user.activation_token,
                                          email: @user.email) %>
```

Exercise

Solutions to the exercises are available to all Rails Tutorial purchasers at https://www.railstutorial.org/aw-solutions.

To see other people's answers and to record your own, subscribe to the Rails Tutorial course or to the Learn Enough All Access Bundle.

1. At the console, verify that the **escape** method in the **CGI** module escapes out the email address as shown in Listing 11.15. What is the escaped value of the string **"Don't panic!"**?

Listing 11.15: Escaping an email with `CGI.escape`.

```
>> CGI.escape('foo@example.com')
=> "foo%40example.com"
```

11.2.2 Email Previews

To see the results of the templates defined in Listing 11.13 and Listing 11.14, we can use *email previews*, which are special URLs exposed by Rails to let us see what our email messages look like. First, we need to add some configuration to our application's development environment, as shown in Listing 11.16.

Listing 11.16: Email settings in development.
`config/environments/development.rb`

```ruby
Rails.application.configure do
  .
  .
  .
  config.action_mailer.raise_delivery_errors = false

  host = 'example.com' # Don't use this literally; use your local dev host instead
  # Use this on the cloud IDE.
  config.action_mailer.default_url_options = { host: host, protocol: 'https' }
  # Use this if developing on localhost.
  # config.action_mailer.default_url_options = { host: host, protocol: 'http' }
  .
  .
  .
end
```

Listing 11.16 uses a host name of **'example.com'**, but as indicated in the comment you should use the actual host of your development environment. For example, on the cloud IDE you should use

```
host = '<hex string>.vfs.cloud9.us-east-2.amazonaws.com'    # Cloud IDE
config.action_mailer.default_url_options = { host: host, protocol: 'https' }
```

where the exact URL is based on what you see in your browser (Figure 11.2).

On a local system, you should use this instead:

```
host = 'localhost:3000'                      # Local server
config.action_mailer.default_url_options = { host: host, protocol: 'http' }
```

Note especially in this second example that **https** has changed to plain **http**.

After restarting the development server to activate the configuration in Listing 11.16, we next need to update the User mailer *preview file*. It was automatically generated in Section 11.2, as shown in Listing 11.17.

Figure 11.2: The host URL for the cloud IDE.

Listing 11.17: The generated User mailer previews.
`test/mailers/previews/user_mailer_preview.rb`

```ruby
# Preview all emails at http://localhost:3000/rails/mailers/user_mailer
class UserMailerPreview < ActionMailer::Preview

  # Preview this email at
  # http://localhost:3000/rails/mailers/user_mailer/account_activation
  def account_activation
    UserMailer.account_activation
  end

  # Preview this email at
  # http://localhost:3000/rails/mailers/user_mailer/password_reset
  def password_reset
    UserMailer.password_reset
  end

end
```

Because the **account_activation** method defined in Listing 11.12 requires a
valid user object as an argument, the code in Listing 11.17 won't work as written. To
fix it, we define a **user** variable equal to the first user in the development database, and
then pass it as an argument to **UserMailer.account_activation** (Listing 11.18).
Note that Listing 11.18 also assigns a value to **user.activation_token**, which is
necessary because the account activation templates in Listing 11.13 and Listing 11.14
need an account activation token. (Because **activation_token** is a virtual attribute
(Section 11.1), the user from the database doesn't have one.)

Listing 11.18: A working preview method for account activation.
`test/mailers/previews/user_mailer_preview.rb`

```ruby
# Preview all emails at http://localhost:3000/rails/mailers/user_mailer
class UserMailerPreview < ActionMailer::Preview

  # Preview this email at
  # http://localhost:3000/rails/mailers/user_mailer/account_activation
  def account_activation
    user = User.first
    user.activation_token = User.new_token
    UserMailer.account_activation(user)
```

```
  end

  # Preview this email at
  # http://localhost:3000/rails/mailers/user_mailer/password_reset
  def password_reset
    UserMailer.password_reset
  end
end
```

With the preview code as in Listing 11.18, we can visit the suggested URLs to preview the account activation emails. (If you are using the cloud IDE, you should replace **localhost:3000** with the corresponding base URL.) The resulting HTML and text emails appear as in Figure 11.3 and Figure 11.4.

Figure 11.3: A preview of the HTML version of the account activation email.

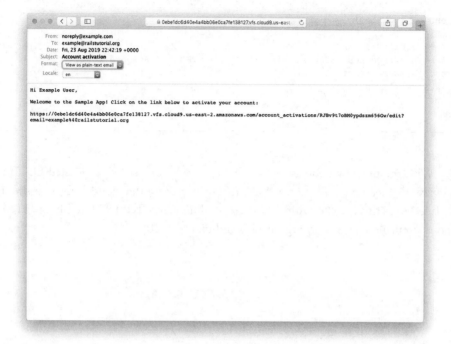

Figure 11.4: A preview of the text version of the account activation email.

Exercise

Solutions to the exercises are available to all Rails Tutorial purchasers at https://www.railstutorial.org/aw-solutions.

To see other people's answers and to record your own, subscribe to the Rails Tutorial course or to the Learn Enough All Access Bundle.

1. Preview the email templates in your browser. What do the Date fields read for your previews?

11.2.3 Email Tests

As a final step, we'll write a couple of tests to double-check the results shown in the email previews. This isn't as hard as it sounds, because Rails has generated useful example tests for us (Listing 11.19).

Listing 11.19: The User mailer test generated by Rails. RED
`test/mailers/user_mailer_test.rb`

```ruby
require 'test_helper'

class UserMailerTest < ActionMailer::TestCase

  test "account_activation" do
    mail = UserMailer.account_activation
    assert_equal "Account activation", mail.subject
    assert_equal ["to@example.org"], mail.to
    assert_equal ["from@example.com"], mail.from
    assert_match "Hi", mail.body.encoded
  end

  test "password_reset" do
    mail = UserMailer.password_reset
    assert_equal "Password reset", mail.subject
    assert_equal ["to@example.org"], mail.to
    assert_equal ["from@example.com"], mail.from
    assert_match "Hi", mail.body.encoded
  end
end
```

As mentioned in Section 11.2.1, the tests in Listing 11.19 are currently RED.

The tests in Listing 11.19 use the powerful **assert_match** method, which can be used with either a string or a regular expression:

```ruby
assert_match 'foo', 'foobar'    # true
assert_match 'baz', 'foobar'    # false
assert_match /\w+/, 'foobar'    # true
assert_match /\w+/, '$#!*+@'    # false
```

The test in Listing 11.20 uses **assert_match** to check that the name, activation token, and escaped email appear in the email's body. For the last of these, note the use of

```ruby
CGI.escape(user.email)
```

to escape the test user's email, which we encountered briefly in Section 11.2.1.[7]

---

7. When I originally wrote this chapter, I couldn't recall offhand how to escape URLs in Rails, and figuring it out was pure technical sophistication (Box 1.2). What I did was Google "ruby rails escape url," which led

Listing 11.20: A test of the current email implementation. RED
`test/mailers/user_mailer_test.rb`

```ruby
require 'test_helper'

class UserMailerTest < ActionMailer::TestCase

  test "account_activation" do
    user = users(:michael)
    user.activation_token = User.new_token
    mail = UserMailer.account_activation(user)
    assert_equal "Account activation", mail.subject
    assert_equal [user.email], mail.to
    assert_equal ["noreply@example.com"], mail.from
    assert_match user.name,                mail.body.encoded
    assert_match user.activation_token,    mail.body.encoded
    assert_match CGI.escape(user.email),   mail.body.encoded
  end
end
```

Note that Listing 11.20 takes care to add an activation token to the fixture user, which would otherwise be blank. (Listing 11.20 also removes the generated password reset test, which we'll add back—in modified form—in Section 12.2.2.)

To get the test in Listing 11.20 to pass, we have to configure our test file with the proper domain host, as shown in Listing 11.21.

Listing 11.21: Setting the test domain host. GREEN
`config/environments/test.rb`

```ruby
Rails.application.configure do
  .
  .
  .
  config.action_mailer.delivery_method = :test
```

---

me to find two main possibilities, **URI.encode(str)** and **CGI.escape(str)**. Trying them both revealed that the latter works. (It turns out there's a third possibility. The **ERB::Util** library supplies a url_encode method that has the same effect.)

```
config.action_mailer.default_url_options = { host: 'example.com' }
  .
  .
  .
end
```

With this code, the mailer test should be GREEN:

Listing 11.22: GREEN

```
$ rails test:mailers
```

Exercises

Solutions to the exercises are available to all Rails Tutorial purchasers at https://www.railstutorial.org/aw-solutions.

To see other people's answers and to record your own, subscribe to the Rails Tutorial course or to the Learn Enough All Access Bundle.

1. Verify that the full test suite is still GREEN.

2. Confirm that the test goes RED if you remove the call to **CGI.escape** in Listing 11.20.

11.2.4 Updating the Users `create` Action

To use the mailer in our application, we just need to add a couple of lines to the **create** action that signs users up, as shown in Listing 11.23. Note that Listing 11.23 has changed the redirect behavior upon signing up. Before, we redirected to the user's profile page (Section 7.4), but that doesn't make sense now that we're requiring account activation. Instead, we now redirect to the root URL.

Listing 11.23: Adding account activation to user signup. RED
app/controllers/users_controller.rb

```
class UsersController < ApplicationController
  .
  .
  .
  def create
```

```
    @user = User.new(user_params)
    if @user.save
      UserMailer.account_activation(@user).deliver_now
      flash[:info] = "Please check your email to activate your account."
      redirect_to root_url
    else
      render 'new'
    end
  end
    .
    .
    .
end
```

Because Listing 11.23 redirects to the root URL instead of to the profile page and doesn't log the user in as before, the test suite is currently RED, even though the application is working as designed. We'll fix this by temporarily commenting out the failing lines, as shown in Listing 11.24. We'll uncomment these lines and write passing tests for account activation in Section 11.3.3.

Listing 11.24: Temporarily commenting out failing tests. GREEN
`test/integration/users_signup_test.rb`

```
require 'test_helper'

class UsersSignupTest < ActionDispatch::IntegrationTest

  test "invalid signup information" do
    get signup_path
    assert_no_difference 'User.count' do
      post users_path, params: { user: { name:  "",
                                         email: "user@invalid",
                                         password:               "foo",
                                         password_confirmation: "bar" } }
    end
    assert_template 'users/new'
    assert_select 'div#error_explanation'
    assert_select 'div.field_with_errors'
  end

  test "valid signup information" do
    get signup_path
    assert_difference 'User.count', 1 do
      post users_path, params: { user: { name:  "Example User",
```

```
                                            email: "user@example.com",
                                            password:                "password",
                                            password_confirmation: "password" } }
     end
     follow_redirect!
     # assert_template 'users/show'
     # assert is_logged_in?
   end
end
```

If you now try signing up as a new user, you should be redirected as shown in Figure 11.5, and an email like the one shown in Listing 11.25 should be generated. Note that you will *not* receive an actual email in a development environment, but it will show up in your server logs. (You may have to scroll up a bit to see it.) Section 11.4 discusses how to send email for real in a production environment.

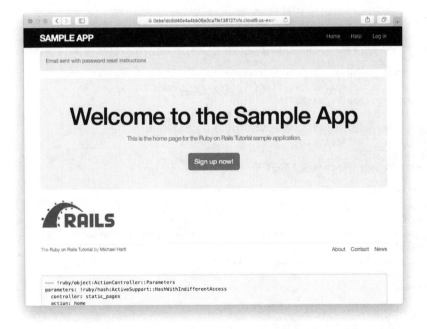

Figure 11.5: The Home page with an activation message after signup.

Listing 11.25: A sample account activation email from the server log.

```
UserMailer#account_activation: processed outbound mail in 5.1ms
Delivered mail 5d606e97b7a44_28872b106582df988776a@ip-172-31-25-202.mail (3.2ms)
Date: Fri, 23 Aug 2019 22:54:15 +0000
From: noreply@example.com
To: michael@michaelhartl.com
Message-ID: <5d606e97b7a44_28872b106582df988776a@ip-172-31-25-202.mail>
Subject: Account activation
Mime-Version: 1.0
Content-Type: multipart/alternative;
 boundary="--==_mimepart_5d606e97b6f16_28872b106582df98876dd";
 charset=UTF-8
Content-Transfer-Encoding: 7bit


----==_mimepart_5d606e97b6f16_28872b106582df98876dd
Content-Type: text/plain;
 charset=UTF-8
Content-Transfer-Encoding: 7bit

Hi Michael Hartl,

Welcome to the Sample App! Click on the link below to activate your account:

https://0ebe1dc6d40e4a4bb06e0ca7fe138127.vfs.cloud9.us-east-2.
amazonaws.com/account_activations/zdqs6sF7BMiDfXBaC7-6vA/
edit?email=michael%40michaelhartl.com

----==_mimepart_5d606e97b6f16_28872b106582df98876dd
Content-Type: text/html;
 charset=UTF-8
Content-Transfer-Encoding: 7bit

<!DOCTYPE html>
<html>
  <head>
    <meta http-equiv="Content-Type" content="text/html; charset=utf-8" />
    <style>
      /* Email styles need to be inline */
    </style>
  </head>

  <body>
    <h1>Sample App</h1>

<p>Hi Michael Hartl,</p>
```

```
<p>
Welcome to the Sample App! Click on the link below to activate your account:
</p>

<a href="https://0ebe1dc6d40e4a4bb06e0ca7fe138127.vfs.cloud9.us-east-2.
amazonaws.com/account_activations/zdqs6sF7BMiDfXBaC7-6vA/
edit?email=michael%40michaelhartl.com">Activate</a>
  </body>
</html>

------==_mimepart_5d606e97b6f16_28872b106582df98876dd--
```

Exercises

Solutions to the exercises are available to all Rails Tutorial purchasers at https://
www.railstutorial.org/aw-solutions.

To see other people's answers and to record your own, subscribe to the Rails
Tutorial course or to the Learn Enough All Access Bundle.

1. Sign up as a new user and verify that you're properly redirected. What is the
   content of the generated email in the server log? What is the value of the activation
   token?

2. Verify at the console that the new user has been created but is not yet activated.

11.3 Activating the Account

Now that we have a correctly generated email as in Listing 11.25, we need to write
the **edit** action in the Account Activations controller that actually activates the user.
As usual, we'll write a test for this action, and once the code is tested we'll refactor
it to move some functionality out of the Account Activations controller and into the
User model.

11.3.1 Generalizing the authenticated? Method

Recall from the discussion in Section 11.2.1 that the activation token and email are
available as **params[:id]** and **params[:email]**, respectively. Following the model
of passwords (Listing 8.7) and remember tokens (Listing 9.9), we plan to find and
authenticate the user with code something like this:

```
user = User.find_by(email: params[:email])
if user && user.authenticated?(:activation, params[:id])
```

(As we'll see in a moment, there will be one extra boolean in this expression. See if you can guess what it will be.)

The preceding code uses the **authenticated?** method to test if the account activation digest matches the given token. At present this won't work because that method is specialized to the remember token (Listing 9.6):

```
# Returns true if the given token matches the digest.
def authenticated?(remember_token)
  return false if remember_digest.nil?
  BCrypt::Password.new(remember_digest).is_password?(remember_token)
end
```

Here **remember_digest** is an attribute on the User model, and inside the model we can rewrite it as follows:

```
self.remember_digest
```

Somehow, we want to be able to make this *variable*, so we can call

```
self.activation_digest
```

instead by passing in the appropriate parameter to the **authenticated?** method.

The solution involves our first example of *metaprogramming*, which is essentially a program that writes a program. (Metaprogramming is one of Ruby's strongest suits, and many of the "magic" features of Rails are due to its use of Ruby metaprogramming.) The key in this case is the powerful **send** method, which lets us call a method with a name of our choice by "sending a message" to a given object. For example, in this console session we use **send** on a native Ruby object to find the length of an array:

```
$ rails console
>> a = [1, 2, 3]
>> a.length
=> 3
>> a.send(:length)
=> 3
>> a.send("length")
=> 3
```

Here we see that passing the symbol **:length** or the string **"length"** to **send** is equivalent to calling the **length** method on the given object. As a second example, we'll access the **activation_digest** attribute of the first user in the database:

```
>> user = User.first
>> user.activation_digest
=> "$2a$10$4e6TFzEJAVNyjLv8Q5u22ensMt28qEkx0roaZvtRcp6UZKRM6N9Ae"
>> user.send(:activation_digest)
=> "$2a$10$4e6TFzEJAVNyjLv8Q5u22ensMt28qEkx0roaZvtRcp6UZKRM6N9Ae"
>> user.send("activation_digest")
=> "$2a$10$4e6TFzEJAVNyjLv8Q5u22ensMt28qEkx0roaZvtRcp6UZKRM6N9Ae"
>> attribute = :activation
>> user.send("#{attribute}_digest")
=> "$2a$10$4e6TFzEJAVNyjLv8Q5u22ensMt28qEkx0roaZvtRcp6UZKRM6N9Ae"
```

Note that we've defined an **attribute** variable equal to the symbol **:activation** and used string interpolation to build up the proper argument to **send**. This also would work with the string **'activation'**, but using a symbol is more conventional. In either case,

```
"#{attribute}_digest"
```

becomes

```
"activation_digest"
```

once the string is interpolated. (We saw how symbols are interpolated as strings in Section 7.4.2.)

Based on this discussion of **send**, we can rewrite the current **authenticated?** method as follows:

```
def authenticated?(remember_token)
  digest = self.send("remember_digest")
  return false if digest.nil?
  BCrypt::Password.new(digest).is_password?(remember_token)
end
```

With this template in place, we can generalize the method by adding a function argument with the name of the digest, and then use string interpolation as we did earlier:

```
def authenticated?(attribute, token)
  digest = self.send("#{attribute}_digest")
  return false if digest.nil?
  BCrypt::Password.new(digest).is_password?(token)
end
```

(Here we have renamed the second argument **token** to emphasize that it's now generic.) Because we're inside the user model, we can also omit **self**, yielding the most idiomatically correct version:

```
def authenticated?(attribute, token)
  digest  = send("#{attribute}_digest")
  return false if digest.nil?
  BCrypt::Password.new(digest).is_password?(token)
end
```

We can now reproduce the previous behavior of **authenticated?** by invoking it like this:

```
user.authenticated?(:remember, remember_token)
```

Applying this discussion to the User model yields the generalized **authenticated?** method shown in Listing 11.26.

Listing 11.26: A generalized **authenticated?** method. RED
`app/models/user.rb`

```
class User < ApplicationRecord
  .
  .
  .
  # Returns true if the given token matches the digest.
  def authenticated?(attribute, token)
    digest = send("#{attribute}_digest")
    return false if digest.nil?
    BCrypt::Password.new(digest).is_password?(token)
  end
```

.

.

.

end

The Listing 11.26 caption indicates a RED test suite:

Listing 11.27: RED

```
$ rails test
```

The reason for the failure is that the **current_user** method (Listing 9.9) and the test for **nil** digests (Listing 9.17) both use the old version of **authenticated?**, which expects one argument instead of two. Note that this is exactly the kind of error a test suite is supposed to catch.

To fix the issue, we simply update the two cases to use the generalized method, as shown in Listing 11.28 and Listing 11.29.

Listing 11.28: Using the generalized **authenticated?** method in **current_user**. RED
app/helpers/sessions_helper.rb

```
module SessionsHelper
  .
  .
  .
  # Returns the current logged-in user (if any).
  def current_user
    if (user_id = session[:user_id])
      @current_user ||= User.find_by(id: user_id)
    elsif (user_id = cookies.encrypted[:user_id])
      user = User.find_by(id: user_id)
      if user && user.authenticated?(:remember, cookies[:remember_token])
        log_in user
        @current_user = user
      end
    end
  end
  .
  .
  .
end
```

Listing 11.29: Using the generalized **authenticated?** method in the User test. GREEN
test/models/user_test.rb

```
require 'test_helper'

class UserTest < ActiveSupport::TestCase

  def setup
    @user = User.new(name: "Example User", email: "user@example.com",
                     password: "foobar", password_confirmation: "foobar")
  end
  .
  .
  .
  test "authenticated? should return false for a user with nil digest" do
    assert_not @user.authenticated?(:remember, '')
  end
end
```

At this point, the tests should be GREEN:

Listing 11.30: GREEN

```
$ rails test
```

Refactoring the code shown here is incredibly more error-prone without a solid test suite, which is why we went to such trouble to write good tests in Section 9.1.2 and Section 9.3.

Exercises

Solutions to the exercises are available to all Rails Tutorial purchasers at https://www.railstutorial.org/aw-solutions.

To see other people's answers and to record your own, subscribe to the Rails Tutorial course or to the Learn Enough All Access Bundle.

1. Create and remember a new user at the console. What are the user's remember and activation tokens? What are the corresponding digests?

2. Using the generalized **authenticated?** method from Listing 11.26, verify that the user is authenticated according to both the remember token and the activation token.

11.3.2 Activation `edit` Action

With the **authenticated?** method as in Listing 11.26, we're now ready to write an **edit** action that authenticates the user corresponding to the email address in the **params** hash. Our test for validity will look like this:

```
if user && !user.activated? && user.authenticated?(:activation, params[:id])
```

Note the presence of **!user.activated?**, which is the extra boolean alluded to earlier in this section. It prevents our code from activating users who have already been activated, which is important because we'll be logging in users upon confirmation, and we don't want to allow attackers who manage to obtain the activation link to log in as the user.

If the user is authenticated according to our booleans, we need to activate the user and update the **activated_at** timestamp:[8]

```
user.update_attribute(:activated,    true)
user.update_attribute(:activated_at, Time.zone.now)
```

This leads to the **edit** action shown in Listing 11.31. Note also that Listing 11.31 handles the case of an invalid activation token; this should rarely happen, but it's easy enough to redirect in this case to the root URL.

Listing 11.31: An **edit** action to activate accounts.
`app/controllers/account_activations_controller.rb`

```ruby
class AccountActivationsController < ApplicationController

  def edit
    user = User.find_by(email: params[:email])
    if user && !user.activated? && user.authenticated?(:activation, params[:id])
      user.update_attribute(:activated,    true)
      user.update_attribute(:activated_at, Time.zone.now)
      log_in user
      flash[:success] = "Account activated!"
      redirect_to user
```

---

8. Here we use two calls to **update_attribute** rather than a single call to **update_attributes** because (per Section 6.1.5) the latter would run the validations. When missing the user password, as in this case, these validations would fail.

```
    else
      flash[:danger] = "Invalid activation link"
      redirect_to root_url
    end
  end
end
```

With the code in Listing 11.31, you should now be able to paste in the URL from Listing 11.25 to activate the relevant user. For example, on my system I visited the URL

```
https://0ebe1dc6d40e4a4bb06e0ca7fe138127.vfs.cloud9.us-east-2.
amazonaws.com/account_activations/zdqs6sF7BMiDfXBaC7-6vA/
edit?email=michael%40michaelhartl.com
```

and got the result shown in Figure 11.6.

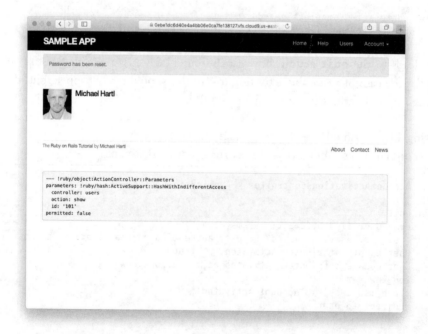

Figure 11.6: The profile page after a successful activation.

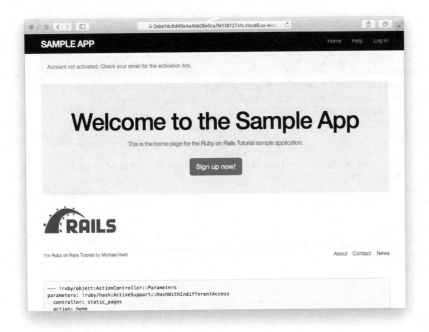

Figure 11.7: The warning message for a not-yet-activated user.

Of course, currently user activation doesn't actually *do* anything, because we haven't changed how users log in. To have account activation mean something, we need to allow users to log in only if they are activated. As shown in Listing 11.32, the way to do this is to log the user in as usual if **user.activated?** is true; otherwise, we redirect to the root URL with a **warning** message (Figure 11.7).

Listing 11.32: Preventing unactivated users from logging in.
`app/controllers/sessions_controller.rb`

```ruby
class SessionsController < ApplicationController

  def new
  end

  def create
    user = User.find_by(email: params[:session][:email].downcase)
    if user && user.authenticate(params[:session][:password])
```

```
      if user.activated?
        log_in user
        params[:session][:remember_me] == '1' ? remember(user) : forget(user)
        redirect_back_or user
      else
        message  = "Account not activated. "
        message += "Check your email for the activation link."
        flash[:warning] = message
        redirect_to root_url
      end
    else
      flash.now[:danger] = 'Invalid email/password combination'
      render 'new'
    end
  end

  def destroy
    log_out if logged_in?
    redirect_to root_url
  end
end
```

With that, apart from one refinement, we've finished the basic functionality of user activation. (That refinement is preventing unactivated users from being displayed, which is left as an exercise (Section 11.3.3).) In Section 11.3.3, we'll complete the process by adding some tests and then doing a little refactoring.

Exercises

Solutions to the exercises are available to all Rails Tutorial purchasers at https://www.railstutorial.org/aw-solutions.

To see other people's answers and to record your own, subscribe to the Rails Tutorial course or to the Learn Enough All Access Bundle.

1. Paste in the URL from the email generated in Section 11.2.4. What is the activation token?

2. Verify at the console that the user is authenticated according to the activation token in the URL from the previous exercise. Is the user now activated?

11.3.3 Activation Test and Refactoring

In this section, we'll add an integration test for account activation. Because we already have a test for signing up with valid information, we'll add the steps to the test developed in Section 7.4.4 (Listing 7.31). There are quite a few steps, but they are mostly straightforward; see if you can follow along in Listing 11.33. (The highlights in Listing 11.33 indicate lines that are especially important or easy to miss, but there are other new lines as well, so take care to add them all.)

Listing 11.33: Adding account activation to the user signup test. GREEN
`test/integration/users_signup_test.rb`

```ruby
require 'test_helper'

class UsersSignupTest < ActionDispatch::IntegrationTest

  def setup
    ActionMailer::Base.deliveries.clear
  end

  test "invalid signup information" do
    get signup_path
    assert_no_difference 'User.count' do
      post users_path, params: { user: { name:  "",
                                         email: "user@invalid",
                                         password:              "foo",
                                         password_confirmation: "bar" } }
    end
    assert_template 'users/new'
    assert_select 'div#error_explanation'
    assert_select 'div.field_with_errors'
  end

  test "valid signup information with account activation" do
    get signup_path
    assert_difference 'User.count', 1 do
      post users_path, params: { user: { name:  "Example User",
                                         email: "user@example.com",
                                         password:              "password",
                                         password_confirmation: "password" } }
    end
    assert_equal 1, ActionMailer::Base.deliveries.size
    user = assigns(:user)
    assert_not user.activated?
    # Try to log in before activation.
    log_in_as(user)
    assert_not is_logged_in?
    # Invalid activation token
    get edit_account_activation_path("invalid token", email: user.email)
    assert_not is_logged_in?
```

```
      # Valid token, wrong email
      get edit_account_activation_path(user.activation_token, email: 'wrong')
      assert_not is_logged_in?
      # Valid activation token
      get edit_account_activation_path(user.activation_token, email: user.email)
      assert user.reload.activated?
      follow_redirect!
      assert_template 'users/show'
      assert is_logged_in?
    end
end
```

There's a lot of code in Listing 11.33, but the only completely novel code is in the line

```
assert_equal 1, ActionMailer::Base.deliveries.size
```

This code verifies that exactly one message was delivered. Because the **deliveries** array is global, we have to reset it in the **setup** method to prevent our code from breaking if any other tests deliver email (as will be the case in Chapter 12).

Listing 11.33 also uses the **assigns** method for the first time in the main tutorial. As explained in a Chapter 9 exercise (Section 9.3.1), **assigns** lets us access instance variables in the corresponding action. For example, the Users controller's **create** action defines an **@user** variable (Listing 11.23), so we can access it in the test using **assigns(:user)**. The **assigns** method is deprecated in default Rails tests as of Rails 5, but I still find it useful in many contexts, and it's available via the `rails-controller-testing` gem we included in Listing 3.2.

Finally, note that Listing 11.33 restores the lines we commented out in Listing 11.24.

At this point, the test suite should be GREEN:

Listing 11.34: GREEN

```
$ rails test
```

With the test in Listing 11.33, we're ready to refactor a little by moving some of the user manipulation out of the controller and into the model. In particular, we'll make an **activate** method to update the user's activation attributes and a

send_activation_email to send the activation email. The extra methods appear in Listing 11.35, and the refactored application code appears in Listing 11.36 and Listing 11.37.

Listing 11.35: Adding user activation methods to the User model.
app/models/user.rb

```ruby
class User < ApplicationRecord
  .
  .
  .
  # Activates an account.
  def activate
    update_attribute(:activated,    true)
    update_attribute(:activated_at, Time.zone.now)
  end

  # Sends activation email.
  def send_activation_email
    UserMailer.account_activation(self).deliver_now
  end

  private
    .
    .
    .
end
```

Listing 11.36: Sending email via the user model object.
app/controllers/users_controller.rb

```ruby
class UsersController < ApplicationController
  .
  .
  .
  def create
    @user = User.new(user_params)
    if @user.save
      @user.send_activation_email
      flash[:info] = "Please check your email to activate your account."
      redirect_to root_url
    else
      render 'new'
```

```
      end
    end
      .
      .
      .

end
```

Listing 11.37: Account activation via the user model object.
`app/controllers/account_activations_controller.rb`

```ruby
class AccountActivationsController < ApplicationController

  def edit
    user = User.find_by(email: params[:email])
    if user && !user.activated? && user.authenticated?(:activation, params[:id])
      user.activate
      log_in user
      flash[:success] = "Account activated!"
      redirect_to user
    else
      flash[:danger] = "Invalid activation link"
      redirect_to root_url
    end
  end
end
```

Note that Listing 11.35 eliminates the use of **user.**, which would break inside the User model because there is no such variable:

```
-user.update_attribute(:activated,    true)
-user.update_attribute(:activated_at, Time.zone.now)
+update_attribute(:activated,    true)
+update_attribute(:activated_at, Time.zone.now)
```

(We could have switched from **user** to **self**, but recall from Section 6.2.5 that **self** is optional inside the model.) It also changes **@user** to **self** in the call to the User mailer:

```
-UserMailer.account_activation(@user).deliver_now
+UserMailer.account_activation(self).deliver_now
```

These are *exactly* the kinds of details that are easy to miss during even a simple refactoring but will be caught by a good test suite. Speaking of which, the test suite should still be GREEN:

Listing 11.38: GREEN

```
$ rails test
```

Exercises

Solutions to the exercises are available to all Rails Tutorial purchasers at https://www.railstutorial.org/aw-solutions.

To see other people's answers and to record your own, subscribe to the Rails Tutorial course or to the Learn Enough All Access Bundle.

1. In Listing 11.35, the **activate** method makes two calls to the **update_attribute**, each of which requires a separate database transaction. By filling in the template shown in Listing 11.39, replace the two **update_attribute** calls with a single call to **update_columns**, which hits the database only once. (Note that, like **update_attribute**, **update_columns** doesn't run the model callbacks or validations.) After making the changes, verify that the test suite is still GREEN.

2. Right now *all* users are displayed on the user index page at /users and are visible via the URL /users/:id, but it makes sense to show users only if they are activated. Arrange for this behavior by filling in the template shown in Listing 11.40.[9] (This template uses the Active Record **where** method, which we'll learn more about in Section 13.3.3.)

3. To test the code in the previous exercise, write integration tests for both /users and /users/:id.

---

9. Note that Listing 11.40 uses **and** in place of **&&**. The two are nearly identical, but the latter operator has a higher *precedence*, which binds too tightly to **root_url** in this case. We could fix the problem by putting **root_url** in parentheses, but the idiomatically correct way to do it is to use **and** instead.

Listing 11.39: A template for using **update_columns**.
app/models/user.rb

```ruby
class User < ApplicationRecord
  attr_accessor :remember_token, :activation_token
  before_save   :downcase_email
  before_create :create_activation_digest
  .
  .
  .
  # Activates an account.
  def activate
    update_columns(activated: FILL_IN, activated_at: FILL_IN)
  end

  # Sends activation email.
  def send_activation_email
    UserMailer.account_activation(self).deliver_now
  end

  private

    # Converts email to all lowercase.
    def downcase_email
      self.email = email.downcase
    end

    # Creates and assigns the activation token and digest.
    def create_activation_digest
      self.activation_token  = User.new_token
      self.activation_digest = User.digest(activation_token)
    end
end
```

Listing 11.40: A template for code to show only active users.
app/controllers/users_controller.rb

```ruby
class UsersController < ApplicationController
  .
  .
  .
  def index
    @users = User.where(activated: FILL_IN).paginate(page: params[:page])
```

```
  end

  def show
    @user = User.find(params[:id])
    redirect_to root_url and return unless FILL_IN
  end
  .
  .
  .
end
```

11.4 Email in Production

Now that we've got account activations working in development, in this section we'll configure our application so that it can actually send email in production. We'll first get set up with a free service to send email, and then configure and deploy our application.

To send email in production, we'll use SendGrid, which is available as an add-on at Heroku for verified accounts. (Using SendGrid requires adding credit card information to your Heroku account, but there is no charge when verifying an account.) For our purposes, the "starter" tier (which as of this writing is limited to 400 emails a day but costs nothing) is the best fit. We can add it to our app as follows:

```
$ heroku addons:create sendgrid:starter
```

(This might fail on systems with an older version of Heroku's command-line interface. In this case, either upgrade to the latest Heroku toolbelt or try the older syntax **heroku addons:add sendgrid:starter**.)

To configure our application to use SendGrid, we need to fill out the SMTP settings for our production environment. As shown in Listing 11.41, you will also have to define a **host** variable with the address of your production website.

Listing 11.41: Configuring Rails to use SendGrid in production.
config/environments/production.rb

```
Rails.application.configure do
  .
  .
  .
```

```
config.action_mailer.raise_delivery_errors = true
config.action_mailer.delivery_method = :smtp
host = '<your heroku app>.herokuapp.com'
config.action_mailer.default_url_options = { host: host }
ActionMailer::Base.smtp_settings = {
  :address            => 'smtp.sendgrid.net',
  :port               => '587',
  :authentication     => :plain,
  :user_name          => ENV['SENDGRID_USERNAME'],
  :password           => ENV['SENDGRID_PASSWORD'],
  :domain             => 'heroku.com',
  :enable_starttls_auto => true
}
  .
  .
  .
end
```

The email configuration in Listing 11.41 includes the **user_name** and **password** of the SendGrid account, but note that they are accessed via the **ENV** environment variable instead of being hard-coded. This is a best practice for production applications, which for security reasons should never expose sensitive information such as raw passwords in source code. In the present case, these variables are configured automatically via the SendGrid add-on, but we'll see an example in Section 13.4.4 where we'll have to define them ourselves. In case you're curious, you can view the environment variables used in Listing 11.41 as follows:

```
$ heroku config:get SENDGRID_USERNAME
$ heroku config:get SENDGRID_PASSWORD
```

At this point, you should merge the topic branch into master:

```
$ rails test
$ git add -A
$ git commit -m "Add account activation"
$ git checkout master
$ git merge account-activation
```

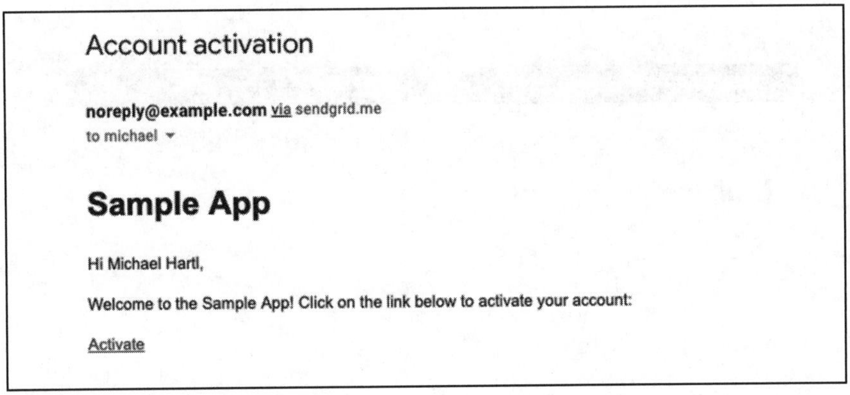

Figure 11.8: An account activation email sent in production.

Then push up to the remote repository and deploy to Heroku:

```
$ rails test
$ git push && git push heroku
$ heroku run rails db:migrate
```

Once the Heroku deploy has finished, try signing up for the sample application in production using an email address you control. You should get an activation email as implemented in Section 11.2, as shown in Figure 11.8. Clicking on the link should activate the account as promised, as shown in Figure 11.9.

Exercises

Solutions to the exercises are available to all Rails Tutorial purchasers at https://www.railstutorial.org/aw-solutions.

To see other people's answers and to record your own, subscribe to the Rails Tutorial course or to the Learn Enough All Access Bundle.

1. Sign up for a new account in production. Did you get the email?
2. Click on the link in the activation email to confirm that it works. What is the corresponding entry in the server log? *Hint*: Run **heroku logs** at the command line.

Figure 11.9: Successful account activation in production.

11.5 Conclusion

With the added account activation, our sample application's signup, login, and logout machinery is nearly complete. The only significant feature left is allowing users to reset their passwords if they forget them. As we'll see in Chapter 12, password reset shares many features with account activation, which means that we'll be able to put the knowledge we've gained in this chapter to good use.

11.5.1 What We Learned in this Chapter

- Like sessions, account activations can be modeled as a resource despite not being Active Record objects.

- Rails can generate Action Mailer actions and views to send email.

- Action Mailer supports both plain-text and HTML mail.

- As with ordinary actions and views, instance variables defined in mailer actions are available in mailer views.

- Account activations use a generated token to create a unique URL for activating users.

- Account activations use a hashed activation digest to securely identify valid activation requests.

- Both mailer tests and integration tests are useful for verifying the behavior of the User mailer.

- We can send email in production using SendGrid.

CHAPTER 12

Password Reset

Having completed account activation (and thereby verified the user's email address) in Chapter 11, we're now in a good position to implement *password reset*, which enables us to handle the common case of users forgetting their passwords.[1] As we'll see, many of the steps are similar to those for account activation, and we will have several opportunities to apply the lessons learned in Chapter 11. The beginning is different, though: Unlike account activation, implementing password resets requires both a change to one of our views and two new forms (to handle email and new password submission).

Before writing any code, let's mock up the expected sequence for resetting passwords. We'll start by adding a "forgot password" link to the sample application's login form (Figure 12.1). The "forgot password" link will go to a page with a form that takes an email address as input and sends an email containing a password reset link (Figure 12.2). The reset link will go to a form for resetting the user's password (with confirmation), as shown in Figure 12.3.

If you worked through Chapter 11, you already have a mailer for password resets, which was generated in Section 11.2 (Listing 11.6). In this section, we'll complete the necessary preliminaries by adding a resource and data model for password resets (Section 12.1) to go along with the mailer. We'll implement the actual password reset in Section 12.3.

---

1. This chapter is independent of the others apart from using the mailer generation in Listing 11.6, but it closely parallels Chapter 11, so it's much easier if you've completed that chapter first.

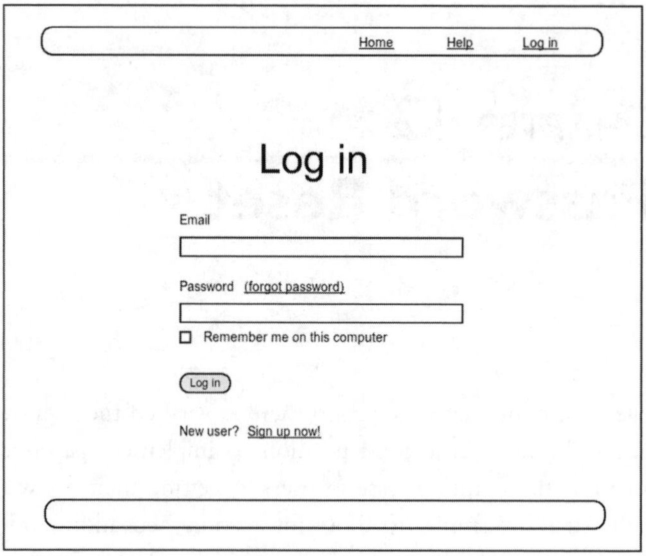

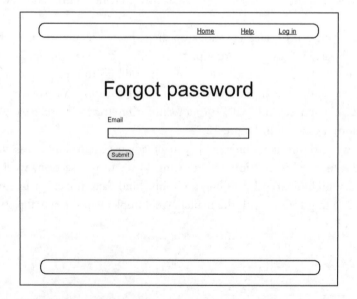

Figure 12.1: A mockup of a "forgot password" link.

Figure 12.2: A mockup of the "forgot password" form.

Figure 12.3: A mockup of the reset password form.

In analogy with account activations, our general plan is to make a Password Resets resource, with each password reset consisting of a reset token and corresponding reset digest. The primary sequence goes like this:

1. When a user requests a password reset, find the user by the submitted email address.

2. If the email address exists in the database, generate a reset token and corresponding reset digest.

3. Save the reset digest to the database, and then send an email to the user with a link containing the reset token and user's email address.

4. When the user clicks the link, find the user by email address, and then authenticate the token by comparing it to the reset digest.

5. If authenticated, present the user with the form for changing the password.

12.1   Password Resets Resource

As with sessions (Section 8.1) and account activations (Chapter 11), we'll model password resets as a resource even though they won't be associated with an Active Record model. Instead, we'll include the relevant data (including the reset token) in the User model itself.

Because we'll be treating password resets as a resource, we'll interact with them via the standard REST URLs. Unlike the activation link, which required only an **edit** action, in this case we'll be rendering both **new** and **edit** forms for manipulating password resets, as well as creating and updating them, so we'll end up using four RESTful routes in total.

As usual, we'll make a topic branch for the new feature:

```
$ git checkout -b password-reset
```

12.1.1 Password Resets Controller

Our first step is to generate a controller for the Password Resets resource, in this case making both **new** and **edit** actions per our earlier discussion:

```
$ rails generate controller PasswordResets new edit --no-test-framework
```

Note that we've included a flag to skip generating tests. This is because we don't need the controller tests, preferring instead to build on the integration test from Section 11.3.3.

Because we'll need forms both for creating new password resets (Figure 12.2) and for updating them by changing the password in the User model (Figure 12.3), we need routes for **new**, **create**, **edit**, and **update**. We can arrange this with the **resources** line shown in Listing 12.1.

Listing 12.1: Adding a resource for password resets.
config/routes.rb

```
Rails.application.routes.draw do
  root    'static_pages#home'
  get     '/help',    to: 'static_pages#help'
  get     '/about',   to: 'static_pages#about'
```

```
get    '/contact', to: 'static_pages#contact'
get    '/signup', to: 'users#new'
get    '/login',  to: 'sessions#new'
post   '/login',  to: 'sessions#create'
delete '/logout', to: 'sessions#destroy'
resources :users
resources :account_activations, only: [:edit]
resources :password_resets,       only: [:new, :create, :edit, :update]
end
```

The code in Listing 12.1 arranges for the RESTful routes shown in Table 12.1. In particular, the first route in Table 12.1 gives a link to the "forgot password" form via

```
new_password_reset_path
```

as seen in Listing 12.2 and Figure 12.4.

Listing 12.2: Adding a link to password resets.

app/views/sessions/new.html.erb

```erb
<% provide(:title, "Log in") %>
<h1>Log in</h1>

<div class="row">
  <div class="col-md-6 col-md-offset-3">
    <%= form_with(url: login_path, scope: :session, local: true) do |f| %>

      <%= f.label :email %>
      <%= f.email_field :email, class: 'form-control' %>

      <%= f.label :password %>
      <%= link_to "(forgot password)", new_password_reset_path %>
      <%= f.password_field :password, class: 'form-control' %>

      <%= f.label :remember_me, class: "checkbox inline" do %>
        <%= f.check_box :remember_me %>
        <span>Remember me on this computer</span>
      <% end %>

      <%= f.submit "Log in", class: "btn btn-primary" %>
    <% end %>

    <p>New user? <%= link_to "Sign up now!", signup_path %></p>
  </div>
</div>
```

Table 12.1: RESTful routes provided by the Password Resets resource in Listing 12.1.

HTTP request	URL	Action	Named route
GET	/password_resets/new	**new**	**new_password_reset_path**
POST	/password_resets	**create**	**password_resets_path**
GET	/password_resets/<token>/edit	**edit**	**edit_password_reset_url (token)**
PATCH	/password_resets/<token>	**update**	**password_reset_path (token)**

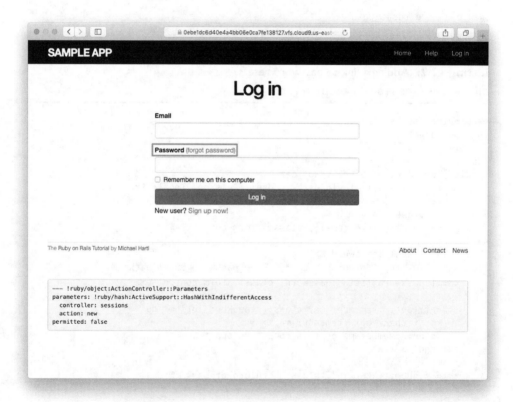

Figure 12.4: The login page with a "forgot password" link.

Exercises

Solutions to the exercises are available to all Rails Tutorial purchasers at https://www.railstutorial.org/aw-solutions.

To see other people's answers and to record your own, subscribe to the Rails Tutorial course or to the Learn Enough All Access Bundle.

1. Verify that the test suite is still GREEN.

2. Why does Table 12.1 list the **_url** form of the **edit** named route instead of the **_path** form? *Hint*: The answer is the same as for the similar account activations exercise (Section 11.1.1).

12.1.2 New Password Resets

To create new password resets, we first need to define the data model, which is similar to the one used for account activation (Figure 11.1). Following the pattern set by remember tokens (Chapter 9) and account activation tokens (Chapter 11), password resets will pair a virtual reset token for use in the reset email with a corresponding reset digest for retrieving the user. If we instead stored an unhashed token, an attacker with access to the database could send a reset request to the user's email address and then use the token and email to visit the corresponding password reset link, thereby gaining control of the account. Using a digest for password resets is thus essential. As an additional security precaution, we'll plan to *expire* the reset link after a couple of hours, which requires recording the time when the reset gets sent. The resulting **reset_digest** and **reset_sent_at** attributes appear in Figure 12.5.

The migration to add the attributes from Figure 12.5 appears as follows:

```
$ rails generate migration add_reset_to_users reset_digest:string \
> reset_sent_at:datetime
```

(As in Section 11.1.2, the **>** on the second line is a "line continuation" character inserted automatically by the shell, and should not be typed literally.) We then migrate as usual:

```
$ rails db:migrate
```

To make the view for new password resets, we'll work in analogy with the previous form for making a new non–Active Record resource—namely, the login

users	
`id`	integer
`name`	string
`email`	string
`created_at`	datetime
`updated_at`	datetime
`password_digest`	string
`remember_digest`	string
`admin`	boolean
`activation_digest`	string
`activated`	boolean
`activated_at`	datetime
`reset_digest`	string
`reset_sent_at`	datetime

Figure 12.5: The User model with added password reset attributes.

form (Listing 8.4) for creating a new session, shown again in Listing 12.3 for reference.

Listing 12.3: Reviewing the code for the login form.
`app/views/sessions/new.html.erb`

```erb
<% provide(:title, "Log in") %>
<h1>Log in</h1>

<div class="row">
  <div class="col-md-6 col-md-offset-3">
    <%= form_with(url: login_path, scope: :session, local: true) do |f| %>
```

```
    <%= f.label :email %>
    <%= f.email_field :email, class: 'form-control' %>

    <%= f.label :password %>
    <%= link_to "(forgot password)", new_password_reset_path %>
    <%= f.password_field :password, class: 'form-control' %>

    <%= f.label :remember_me, class: "checkbox inline" do %>
      <%= f.check_box :remember_me %>
      <span>Remember me on this computer</span>
    <% end %>

    <%= f.submit "Log in", class: "btn btn-primary" %>
  <% end %>

  <p>New user? <%= link_to "Sign up now!", signup_path %></p>
  </div>
</div>
```

The new password resets form has a lot in common with Listing 12.3; the most important differences are the use of a different resource and URL in the call to **form_with** and the omission of the password attribute. The result appears in Listing 12.4 and Figure 12.6.

Listing 12.4: A new password reset view.
app/views/password_resets/new.html.erb

```
<% provide(:title, "Forgot password") %>
<h1>Forgot password</h1>

<div class="row">
  <div class="col-md-6 col-md-offset-3">
    <%= form_with(url: password_resets_path, scope: :password_reset,
                  local: true) do |f| %>
      <%= f.label :email %>
      <%= f.email_field :email, class: 'form-control' %>

      <%= f.submit "Submit", class: "btn btn-primary" %>
    <% end %>
  </div>
</div>
```

Exercise

Solutions to the exercises are available to all Rails Tutorial purchasers at https://www.railstutorial.org/aw-solutions.

To see other people's answers and to record your own, subscribe to the Rails Tutorial course or to the Learn Enough All Access Bundle.

1. Why does the **form_with** in Listing 12.4 use **:password_reset** instead of **@password_reset**?

12.1.3 Password Reset `create` Action

Upon submitting the form in Figure 12.6, we need to find the user by email address and update its attributes with the password reset token and sent-at time-stamp. We then redirect to the root URL with an informative flash message. As with login (Listing 8.11), in the case of an invalid submission we re-render the **new** page with a **flash.now** message.[2] The results appear in Listing 12.5.

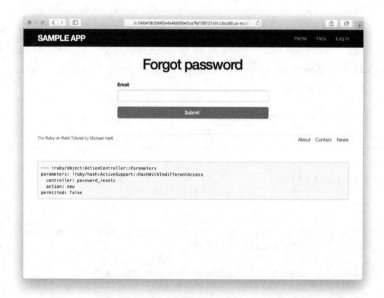

Figure 12.6: The "forgot password" form.

2. Security concerns about revealing the absence of the given email address are commonly misplaced. In fact, this property is already present in every website that won't let you sign up with an email address that's already in use, which is practically all of them. Thus, indicating that a given email address isn't available for password resets gives potential attackers no additional information.

Listing 12.5: A **create** action for password resets.
app/controllers/password_resets_controller.rb

```ruby
class PasswordResetsController < ApplicationController

  def new
  end

  def create
    @user = User.find_by(email: params[:password_reset][:email].downcase)
    if @user
      @user.create_reset_digest
      @user.send_password_reset_email
      flash[:info] = "Email sent with password reset instructions"
      redirect_to root_url
    else
      flash.now[:danger] = "Email address not found"
      render 'new'
    end
  end

  def edit
  end
end
```

The code in the User model parallels the **create_activation_digest** method used in the **before_create** callback (Listing 11.3), as seen in Listing 12.6.

Listing 12.6: Adding password reset methods to the User model.
app/models/user.rb

```ruby
class User < ApplicationRecord
  attr_accessor : remember_token, :activation_token, :reset_token
  before_save    :downcase_email
  before_create  :create_activation_digest
  .
  .
  .
  # Activates an account.
  def activate
    update_attribute(:activated,    true)
    update_attribute(:activated_at, Time.zone.now)
  end

  # Sends activation email.
```

```ruby
  def send_activation_email
    UserMailer.account_activation(self).deliver_now
  end

  # Sets the password reset attributes.
  def create_reset_digest
    self.reset_token =  User.new_token
    update_attribute(:reset_digest, User.digest(reset_token))
    update_attribute(:reset_sent_at, Time.zone.now)
  end

  # Sends password reset email.
  def send_password_reset_email
    UserMailer.password_reset(self).deliver_now
  end

  private

    # Converts email to all lowercase.
    def downcase_email
      self.email = email.downcase
    end

    # Creates and assigns the activation token and digest.
    def create_activation_digest
      self.activation_token  = User.new_token
      self.activation_digest = User.digest(activation_token)
    end
end
```

As shown in Figure 12.7, at this point the application's behavior for invalid email addresses is already working. To get the application working upon submission of a valid email address as well, we need to define a password reset mailer method.

Exercises

Solutions to the exercises are available to all Rails Tutorial purchasers at https://www.railstutorial.org/aw-solutions.

To see other people's answers and to record your own, subscribe to the Rails Tutorial course or to the Learn Enough All Access Bundle.

1. Submit a valid email address to the form shown in Figure 12.6. What error message do you get?

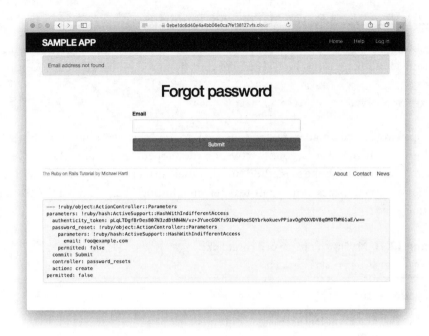

Figure 12.7: The "forgot password" form for an invalid email address.

2. Confirm at the console that the user in the previous exercise has valid
   reset_digest and **reset_sent_at** attributes, despite the error. What are the
   attribute values?

12.2 Password Reset Emails

We left Section 12.1 with a nearly working **create** action in the Password Resets
controller. The only thing missing is the method to deliver valid password reset
emails.

If you worked through Section 11.1, you already have a default **password_reset**
method in **app/mailers/user_mailer.rb** as a result of the User mailer generation
in Listing 11.6. If you skipped Chapter 11, you can just copy the code provided in
this section (omitting the **account_activation** and related methods) and create the
missing files as necessary.

12.2.1 Password Reset Mailer and Templates

In Listing 12.6, we applied the design pattern implemented as a refactoring in Section 11.3.3 by putting the User mailer directly in the model (Listing 12.6):

```
UserMailer.password_reset(self).deliver_now
```

The password reset mailer method needed to get this working is nearly identical to the mailer for account activation developed in Section 11.2. We first create a **password_reset** method in the user mailer (Listing 12.7), and then define view templates for plain-text email (Listing 12.8) and HTML email (Listing 12.9).

Listing 12.7: Mailing the password reset link.
app/mailers/user_mailer.rb

```ruby
class UserMailer < ApplicationMailer

  def account_activation(user)
    @user = user
    mail to: user.email, subject: "Account activation"
  end

  def password_reset(user)
    @user = user
    mail to: user.email, subject: "Password reset"
  end
end
```

Listing 12.8: The password reset plain-text email template.
app/views/user_mailer/password_reset.text.erb

```erb
To reset your password click the link below:

<%= edit_password_reset_url(@user.reset_token, email: @user.email) %>

This link will expire in two hours.

If you did not request your password to be reset, please ignore this email and
your password will stay as it is.
```

Listing 12.9: The password reset HTML email template.
app/views/user_mailer/password_reset.html.erb

```
<h1>Password reset</h1>

<p>To reset your password click the link below:</p>

<%= link_to "Reset password", edit_password_reset_url(@user.reset_token,
                                                email: @user.email) %>

<p>This link will expire in two hours.</p>

<p>
If you did not request your password to be reset, please ignore this email and
your password will stay as it is.
</p>
```

As with account activation emails (Section 11.2), we can preview password reset emails using the Rails email previewer. The code is exactly analogous to Listing 11.18, as shown in Listing 12.10.

Listing 12.10: A working preview method for password reset.
test/mailers/previews/user_mailer_preview.rb

```
# Preview all emails at http://localhost:3000/rails/mailers/user_mailer
class UserMailerPreview < ActionMailer::Preview

  # Preview this email at
  # http://localhost:3000/rails/mailers/user_mailer/account_activation
  def account_activation
    user = User.first
    user.activation_token = User.new_token
    UserMailer.account_activation(user)
  end

  # Preview this email at
  # http://localhost:3000/rails/mailers/user_mailer/password_reset
  def password_reset
    user = User.first
    user.reset_token = User.new_token
    UserMailer.password_reset(user)
  end
end
```

Figure 12.8: A preview of the HTML version of the password reset email.

With the code in Listing 12.10, the HTML and text email previews appear as in Figure 12.8 and Figure 12.9.

With the code in Listing 12.7, Listing 12.8, and Listing 12.9, submission of a valid email address appears as shown in Figure 12.10. The corresponding email appears in the server log and should look something like Listing 12.11.

Listing 12.11: A sample password reset email from the server log.

```
UserMailer#password_reset: processed outbound mail in 6.0ms
Delivered mail 5d609328d5d29_28872b106582ddf4886d8@ip-172-31-25-202.mail (2.8ms)
Date: Sat, 24 Aug 2019 01:30:16 +0000
From: noreply@example.com
To: michael@michaelhartl.com
Message-ID: <5d609328d5d29_28872b106582ddf4886d8@ip-172-31-25-202.mail>
Subject: Password reset
Mime-Version: 1.0
Content-Type: multipart/alternative;
```

```
 boundary="--==_mimepart_5d609328d5404_28872b106582ddf488531";
 charset=UTF-8
Content-Transfer-Encoding: 7bit


----==_mimepart_5d609328d5404_28872b106582ddf488531
Content-Type: text/plain;
 charset=UTF-8
Content-Transfer-Encoding: 7bit

To reset your password click the link below:

https://0ebe1dc6d40e4a4bb06e0ca7fe138127.vfs.cloud9.us-east-2.
amazonaws.com/password_resets/cT3mB4pwu7o-hrg6qEDfKg/
edit?email=michael%40michaelhartl.com

This link will expire in two hours.

If you did not request your password to be reset, please ignore this email and
your password will stay as it is.

----==_mimepart_5d609328d5404_28872b106582ddf488531
Content-Type: text/html;
 charset=UTF-8
Content-Transfer-Encoding: 7bit

<!DOCTYPE html>
<html>
  <head>
    <meta http-equiv="Content-Type" content="text/html; charset=utf-8" />
    <style>
      /* Email styles need to be inline */
    </style>
  </head>

  <body>
    <h1>Password reset</h1>

<p>To reset your password click the link below:</p>

<a href="https://0ebe1dc6d40e4a4bb06e0ca7fe138127.vfs.cloud9.us-east-2.
amazonaws.com/password_resets/cT3mB4pwu7o-hrg6qEDfKg/
edit?email=michael%40michaelhartl.com">Reset password</a>

<p>This link will expire in two hours.</p>

<p>
If you did not request your password to be reset, please ignore this email and
your password will stay as it is.
```

```
</p>
  </body>
</html>

-----==_mimepart_5d609328d5404_28872b106582ddf488531--
```

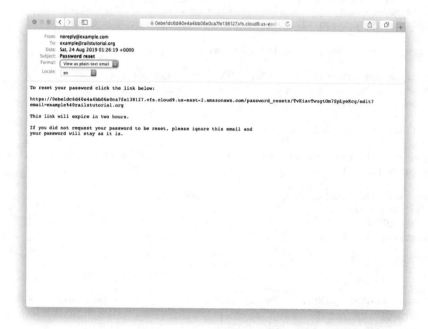

Figure 12.9: A preview of the text version of the password reset email.

Exercises

Solutions to the exercises are available to all Rails Tutorial purchasers at https://www.railstutorial.org/aw-solutions.

To see other people's answers and to record your own, subscribe to the Rails Tutorial course or to the Learn Enough All Access Bundle.

1. Preview the email templates in your browser. What do the Date fields read for your previews?

2. Submit a valid email address to the new password reset form. What is the content of the generated email in the server log?

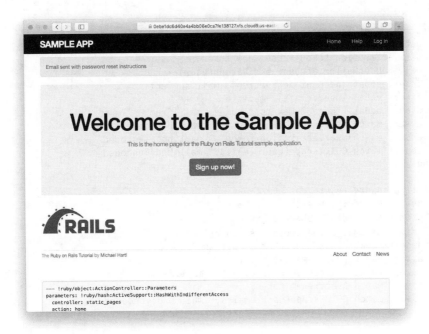

Figure 12.10: The result of submitting a valid email address.

3. At the console, find the user object corresponding to the email address from the previous exercise and verify that it has valid **reset_digest** and **reset_sent_at** attributes.

12.2.2 Email Tests

In analogy with the account activation mailer method test (Listing 11.20), we'll write a test of the password reset mailer method, as shown in Listing 12.12.

Listing 12.12: Adding a test of the password reset mailer method. GREEN
`test/mailers/user_mailer_test.rb`

```
require 'test_helper'

class UserMailerTest < ActionMailer::TestCase
```

```
  test "account_activation" do
    user = users(:michael)
    user.activation_token = User.new_token
    mail = UserMailer.account_activation(user)
    assert_equal "Account activation", mail.subject
    assert_equal [user.email], mail.to
    assert_equal ["noreply@example.com"], mail.from
    assert_match user.name,                mail.body.encoded
    assert_match user.activation_token,    mail.body.encoded
    assert_match CGI.escape(user.email),   mail.body.encoded
  end

  test "password_reset" do
    user = users(:michael)
    user.reset_token = User.new_token
    mail = UserMailer.password_reset(user)
    assert_equal "Password reset", mail.subject
    assert_equal [user.email], mail.to
    assert_equal ["noreply@example.com"], mail.from
    assert_match user.reset_token,         mail.body.encoded
    assert_match CGI.escape(user.email),   mail.body.encoded
  end
end
```

At this point, the test suite should be GREEN:

Listing 12.13: GREEN

```
$ rails test
```

Exercises

Solutions to the exercises are available to all Rails Tutorial purchasers at https://www.railstutorial.org/aw-solutions.

To see other people's answers and to record your own, subscribe to the Rails Tutorial course or to the Learn Enough All Access Bundle.

1. Run just the mailer tests. Are they GREEN?

2. Confirm that the test goes RED if you remove the second call to **CGI.escape** in Listing 12.12.

12.3 Resetting the Password

Now that we have a correctly generated email as in Listing 12.11, we need to write the **edit** action in the Password Resets controller that actually resets the user's password. As in Section 11.3.3, we'll write a thorough integration test as well.

12.3.1 Reset edit Action

Password reset emails such as that shown in Listing 12.11 contain links of the following form:

```
https://example.com/password_resets/3BdBrXeQZSWqFIDRN8cxHA/edit?email=fu%40bar.com
```

To get these links to work, we need a form for resetting passwords. This task is similar to updating users via the user edit view (Listing 10.2) but involves only password and confirmation fields.

There's an additional complication, though: We expect to find the user by email address, which means we need its value in both the **edit** and **update** actions. The email will automatically be available in the **edit** action because of its presence in the link just given, but after we submit the form its value will be lost. The solution is to use a *hidden field* to place (but not display) the email on the page, and then submit it along with the rest of the form's information. The result appears in Listing 12.14.

Listing 12.14: The form to reset a password.
app/views/password_resets/edit.html.erb

```erb
<% provide(:title, 'Reset password') %>
<h1>Reset password</h1>

<div class="row">
  <div class="col-md-6 col-md-offset-3">
    <%= form_with(model: @user, url: password_reset_path(params[:id]),
                  local: true) do |f| %>
      <%= render 'shared/error_messages' %>

      <%= hidden_field_tag :email, @user.email %>

      <%= f.label :password %>
      <%= f.password_field :password, class: 'form-control' %>
```

```
        <%= f.label :password_confirmation, "Confirmation" %>
        <%= f.password_field :password_confirmation, class: 'form-control' %>

        <%= f.submit "Update password", class: "btn btn-primary" %>
      <% end %>
    </div>
  </div>
```

Note that Listing 12.14 uses the form tag helper

```
hidden_field_tag :email, @user.email
```

instead of

```
f.hidden_field :email, @user.email
```

because the reset link puts the email in **params[:email]**, whereas the latter would put it in **params[:user][:email]**.

To get the form to render, we need to define an **@user** variable in the Password Resets controller's **edit** action. As with account activation (Listing 11.31), this involves finding the user corresponding to the email address in **params[:email]**. We then need to verify that the user is valid—that is, that it exists, is activated, and is authenticated according to the reset token from **params[:id]** (using the generalized **authenticated?** method defined in Listing 11.26). Because confirmation of the existence of a valid **@user** is needed in both the **edit** and **update** actions, we'll put the code to find and validate it in a couple of before filters, as shown in Listing 12.15.

Listing 12.15: The **edit** action for password reset.
app/controllers/password_resets_controller.rb

```
class PasswordResetsController < ApplicationController
  before_action :get_user,    only: [:edit, :update]
  before_action :valid_user,  only: [:edit, :update]
  .
  .
  .
  def edit
  end

  private
```

```
def get_user
  @user = User.find_by(email: params[:email])
end

# Confirms a valid user.
def valid_user
  unless ( @user && @user.activated? &&
           @user.authenticated?( :reset, params[:id]))
    redirect_to root_url
  end
end
end
```

In Listing 12.15, compare the use of

```
authenticated?(:reset, params[:id])
```

to

```
authenticated?(:remember, cookies[:remember_token])
```

in Listing 11.28 and to

```
authenticated?(:activation, params[:id])
```

in Listing 11.31. Together, these three uses complete the authentication methods shown in Table 11.1.

With this code, following the link from Listing 12.11 should render a password reset form. The result of pasting the link from the log (Listing 12.11) appears in Figure 12.11.

Exercises

Solutions to the exercises are available to all Rails Tutorial purchasers at https://www.railstutorial.org/aw-solutions.

To see other people's answers and to record your own, subscribe to the Rails Tutorial course or to the Learn Enough All Access Bundle.

1. Follow the link in the email from the server log in Section 12.2.1. Does it properly render the form as shown in Figure 12.11?

2. What happens if you submit the form from the previous exercise?

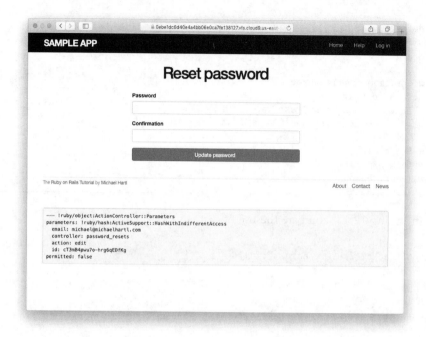

Figure 12.11: The password reset form.

12.3.2 Updating the Reset

Unlike the Account Activations **edit** method, which simply toggles the user from "inactive" to "active," the **edit** method for Password Resets is a form, which must therefore submit to a corresponding **update** action. To define this **update** action, we need to consider four cases:

1. An expired password reset
2. A failed update due to an invalid password
3. A failed update (which initially looks "successful") due to an empty password and confirmation
4. A successful update

Cases (1), (2), and (4) are fairly straightforward, but Case (3) is non-obvious and is explained in more detail below.

Case (1) applies to both the **edit** and **update** actions, and so logically belongs in a before filter:

```
before_action :check_expiration, only: [:edit, :update]     # Case (1)
```

This requires defining a private **check_expiration** method:

```
# Checks expiration of reset token.
def check_expiration
  if @user.password_reset_expired?
    flash[:danger] = "Password reset has expired."
    redirect_to new_password_reset_url
  end
end
```

In the **check_expiration** method, we've deferred the expiration check to the instance method **password_reset_expired?**, which is a little tricky and will be defined in a moment.

Listing 12.16 shows the implementation of these filters, together with the **update** action that implements Cases (2)–(4). Case (2) gets handled by a failed update, with the error messages from the shared partial in Listing 12.14 being displayed automatically when the **edit** form is re-rendered. Case (4) corresponds to a successful change, and the result is similar to a successful login (Listing 8.32).

The only failure case not handled by Case (2) is when the password is empty, which is currently allowed by our User model (Listing 10.13); thus, this error needs to be caught and handled explicitly.[3] This is Case (3). Our method in this case is to add an error directly to the **@user** object's error messages using **errors.add**:

```
@user.errors.add(:password, :blank)
```

This arranges to use the default message for blank content when the password is empty.[4]

---

3. We need handle only the case where the password is empty because if the confirmation is empty, the confirmation validation (which is skipped if the password is empty) will catch the problem and supply a relevant error message.

4. Alert reader Khaled Teilab has noted that one advantage of using **errors.add(:password, :blank)** is that the resulting message is automatically rendered in the correct language when using the `rails-i18n` gem.

The result of putting Cases (1)–(4) together is the **update** action shown in Listing 12.16.

Listing 12.16: The **update** action for password reset.
`app/controllers/password_resets_controller.rb`

```ruby
class PasswordResetsController < ApplicationController
  before_action :get_user,         only: [:edit, :update]
  before_action :valid_user,       only: [:edit, :update]
  before_action :check_expiration, only: [:edit, :update]    # Case (1)

  def new
  end

  def create
    @user = User.find_by(email: params[:password_reset][:email].downcase)
    if @user
      @user.create_reset_digest
      @user.send_password_reset_email
      flash[:info] = "Email sent with password reset instructions"
      redirect_to root_url
    else
      flash.now[:danger] = "Email address not found"
      render 'new'
    end
  end

  def edit
  end

  def update
    if params[ :user][ :password].empty?                      # Case (3)
      @user.errors.add(:password, "can't be empty")
      render 'edit'
    elsif @user.update(user_params)                          # Case (4)
      log_in @user
      flash[:success] = "Password has been reset."
      redirect_to @user
    else
      render 'edit'                                          # Case (2)
    end
  end

  private

    def user_params
```

```
      params.require( :user).permit( :password,   :password_confirmation)
    end

    # Before filters

    def get_user
      @user = User.find_by(email: params[:email])
    end

    # Confirms a valid user.
    def valid_user
      unless (@user && @user.activated? &&
              @user.authenticated?(:reset, params[:id]))
        redirect_to root_url
      end
    end

    # Checks expiration of reset token.
    def check_expiration
      if @user.password_reset_expired?
        flash[:danger] = "Password reset has expired."
        redirect_to new_password_reset_url
      end
    end
  end
end
```

Note that we've added a **user_params** method permitting both the password and password confirmation attributes (Section 7.3.2).

As noted earlier, the implementation in Listing 12.16 delegates the boolean test for password reset expiration to the User model via the code

```
@user.password_reset_expired?
```

To get this to work, we need to define the **password_reset_expired?** method. As indicated in the email templates from Section 12.2.1, we'll consider a password reset to be expired if it was sent more than two hours ago. We can express this condition in Ruby as follows:

```
reset_sent_at < 2.hours.ago
```

This can be confusing if you read **<** as "less than," because then it sounds like "Password reset sent less than two hours ago," which is the opposite of what we want. In this context, it's better to read **<** as "earlier than," which gives something like "Password reset sent earlier than two hours ago." That *is* what we want, and it leads to the **password_reset_expired?** method in Listing 12.17. (For a formal demonstration that the comparison is correct, see the proof in Section 12.6.)

Listing 12.17: Adding password reset methods to the User model.
`app/models/user.rb`

```ruby
class User < ApplicationRecord
  .
  .
  .
  # Returns true if a password reset has expired.
  def password_reset_expired?
    reset_sent_at < 2.hours.ago
  end

  private
  .
  .
  .
end
```

With the code in Listing 12.17, the **update** action in Listing 12.16 should be working. The results for invalid and valid submissions are shown in Figure 12.12 and Figure 12.13, respectively. (Lacking the patience to wait two hours, we'll cover the third branch in a test, which is left as an exercise (Section 12.3.3).)

Exercises

Solutions to the exercises are available to all Rails Tutorial purchasers at https://www.railstutorial.org/aw-solutions.

To see other people's answers and to record your own, subscribe to the Rails Tutorial course or to the Learn Enough All Access Bundle.

1. Follow the email link from Section 12.2.1 again and submit mismatched passwords to the form. What is the error message?

2. In the console, find the user belonging to the email link, and retrieve the value of the **password_digest** attribute. Now submit valid matching passwords to the form shown in Figure 12.12. Did the submission appear to work? How did it affect the value of **password_digest**? *Hint*: Use **user.reload** to retrieve the new value.

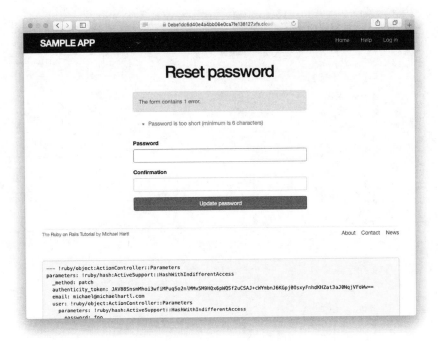

Figure 12.12: A failed password reset.

12.3.3 Password Reset Test

In this section, we'll write an integration test covering two of the three branches in Listing 12.16, invalid and valid submission. (As noted earlier, testing the third branch is left as an exercise (Section 12.3.3).) We'll get started by generating a test file for password resets:

```
$ rails generate integration_test password_resets
      invoke  test_unit
      create    test/integration/password_resets_test.rb
```

The steps to test password resets broadly parallel the test for account activation from Listing 11.33, though there is a difference at the outset: We first visit the "forgot password" form and submit invalid and then valid email addresses, the latter of which creates a password reset token and sends the reset email. We then visit the link from the

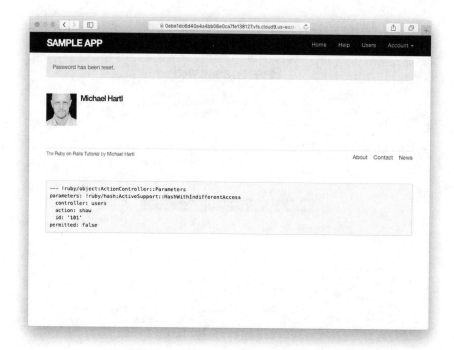

Figure 12.13: A successful password reset.

email and again submit invalid and valid information, verifying the correct behavior in each case. The resulting test, shown in Listing 12.18, is an excellent exercise in reading code.

Listing 12.18: An integration test for password resets.
`test/integration/password_resets_test.rb`

```ruby
require 'test_helper'

class PasswordResetsTest < ActionDispatch::IntegrationTest

  def setup
    ActionMailer::Base.deliveries.clear
    @user = users(:michael)
  end
```

```ruby
test "password resets" do
  get new_password_reset_path
  assert_template 'password_resets/new'
  assert_select 'input[name=?]', 'password_reset[email]'
  # Invalid email
  post password_resets_path, params: { password_reset: { email: "" } }
  assert_not flash.empty?
  assert_template 'password_resets/new'
  # Valid email
  post password_resets_path,
      params: { password_reset: { email: @user.email } }
  assert_not_equal @user.reset_digest, @user.reload.reset_digest
  assert_equal 1, ActionMailer::Base.deliveries.size
  assert_not flash.empty?
  assert_redirected_to root_url
  # Password reset form
  user = assigns(:user)
  # Wrong email
  get edit_password_reset_path(user.reset_token, email: "")
  assert_redirected_to root_url
  # Inactive user
  user.toggle!(:activated)
  get edit_password_reset_path(user.reset_token, email: user.email)
  assert_redirected_to root_url
  user.toggle!(:activated)
  # Right email, wrong token
  get edit_password_reset_path('wrong token', email: user.email)
  assert_redirected_to root_url
  # Right email, right token
  get edit_password_reset_path(user.reset_token, email: user.email)
  assert_template 'password_resets/edit'
  assert_select "input[name=email][type=hidden][value=?]", user.email
  # Invalid password & confirmation
  patch password_reset_path(user.reset_token),
        params: { email: user.email,
                  user: { password:              "foobaz",
                          password_confirmation: "barquux" } }
  assert_select 'div#error_explanation'
  # Empty password
  patch password_reset_path(user.reset_token),
        params: { email: user.email,
                  user: { password:              "",
                          password_confirmation: "" } }
  assert_select 'div#error_explanation'
  # Valid password & confirmation
  patch password_reset_path(user.reset_token),
        params: { email: user.email,
                  user: { password:              "foobaz",
```

```
                              password_confirmation: "foobaz" } }
    assert is_logged_in?
    assert_not flash.empty?
    assert_redirected_to user
  end
end
```

Most of the ideas in Listing 12.18 have appeared previously in this tutorial; the only really novel element is the test of the **input** tag:

```
assert_select "input[name=email][type=hidden][value=?]", user.email
```

This makes sure that there is an **input** tag with the right name, (hidden) type, and email address:

```
<input id="email" name="email" type="hidden" value="michael@example.com" />
```

With the code as in Listing 12.18, our test suite should be GREEN:

Listing 12.19: GREEN

```
$ rails test
```

Exercises

Solutions to the exercises are available to all Rails Tutorial purchasers at https://www.railstutorial.org/aw-solutions.

To see other people's answers and to record your own, subscribe to the Rails Tutorial course or to the Learn Enough All Access Bundle.

1. In Listing 12.6, the **create_reset_digest** method makes two calls to **update_attribute**, each of which requires a separate database operation. By filling in the template shown in Listing 12.20, replace the two **update_attribute** calls with a single call to **update_columns**, which hits the database only once. After making the changes, verify that the test suite is still GREEN. (For convenience, Listing 12.20 includes the results of solving the exercise in Listing 11.39.)

2. Write an integration test for the expired password reset branch in Listing 12.16 by filling in the template shown in Listing 12.21. (This code introduces **response.body**, which returns the full HTML body of the page.) There are

many ways to test for the result of an expiration, but the method suggested by Listing 12.21 is to (case-insensitively) check that the response body includes the word "expired."

3. Expiring password resets after a couple of hours is a nice security precaution, but an even more secure solution is available for cases where a public computer is used. The reason is that the password reset link remains active for two hours and can be used even if logged out. If a user reset their password from a public machine, anyone could press the back button and change the password (and get logged in to the site). To fix this, add the code shown in Listing 12.22 to clear the reset digest on successful password update.[5]

4. Add a line to Listing 12.18 to test for the clearing of the reset digest in the previous exercise. *Hint*: Combine **assert_nil** (first seen in Listing 9.25) with **user.reload** (Listing 11.33) to test the **reset_digest** attribute directly.

Listing 12.20: A template for using **update_columns**.
app/models/user.rb

```
class User < ApplicationRecord
  attr_accessor :remember_token, :activation_token, :reset_token
  before_save    :downcase_email
  before_create  :create_activation_digest
  .
  .
  .
  # Activates an account.
  def activate
    update_columns(activated: true, activated_at: Time.zone.now)
  end

  # Sends activation email.
  def send_activation_email
    UserMailer.account_activation(self).deliver_now
  end

  # Sets the password reset attributes.
  def create_reset_digest
    self.reset_token = User.new_token
```

---

5. Thanks to reader Tristan Ludowyk for suggesting this feature and for providing both a detailed description and a suggested implementation.

```
    update_columns( reset_digest:  FILL_IN,  reset_sent_at: FILL_IN)
  end

  # Sends password reset email.
  def send_password_reset_email
    UserMailer.password_reset(self).deliver_now
  end

  private

    # Converts email to all lowercase.
    def downcase_email
      self.email = email.downcase
    end

    # Creates and assigns the activation token and digest.
    def create_activation_digest
      self.activation_token  = User.new_token
      self.activation_digest = User.digest(activation_token)
    end
end
```

Listing 12.21: A test for an expired password reset. GREEN
test/integration/password_resets_test.rb

```
require 'test_helper'

class PasswordResetsTest < ActionDispatch::IntegrationTest

  def setup
    ActionMailer::Base.deliveries.clear
    @user = users(:michael)
  end
  .
  .
  .
  test "expired token" do
    get new_password_reset_path
    post password_resets_path,
        params: { password_reset: { email: @user.email } }

    @user = assigns(:user)
    @user.update_attribute(:reset_sent_at, 3.hours.ago)
    patch password_reset_path(@user.reset_token),
        params: { email: @user.email,
                  user: { password:              "foobar",
```

```
                                 password_confirmation: "foobar" } }
    assert_response :redirect
    follow_redirect!
    assert_match /FILL_IN/i, response.body
  end
end
```

Listing 12.22: Clearing the reset digest on successful password reset.
app/controllers/password_resets_controller.rb

```
class PasswordResetsController < ApplicationController
  .
  .
  .
  def update
    if params[:user][:password].empty?
      @user.errors.add(:password, "can't be empty")
      render 'edit'
    elsif @user.update(user_params)
      log_in @user
      @user.update_attribute(:reset_digest, nil)
      flash[:success] = "Password has been reset."
      redirect_to @user
    else
      render 'edit'
    end
  end
  .
  .
  .
end
```

12.4 Email in Production (Take Two)

Now that we've got password resets working in development, in this section we'll get them working in production as well. The steps are exactly the same as for account activations, so if you already worked through Section 11.4 you can skip right to Listing 12.24.

To send email in production, we'll use SendGrid, which is available as an add-on at Heroku for verified accounts. (Using SendGrid requires adding credit card information to your Heroku account, but there is no charge when verifying an account.) For our purposes, the "starter" tier (which as of this writing is limited to 400 emails a day but costs nothing) is the best fit. We can add it to our app as follows:

```
$ heroku addons:create sendgrid:starter
```

(This might fail on systems with older version of Heroku's command-line interface. In this case, either upgrade to the latest Heroku toolbelt or try the older syntax **heroku addons:add sendgrid:starter**.)

To configure our application to use SendGrid, we need to fill out the SMTP settings for our production environment. As shown in Listing 12.23, you will also have to define a **host** variable with the address of your production website.

Listing 12.23: Configuring Rails to use SendGrid in production.
config/environments/production.rb

```
Rails.application.configure do
  .
  .
  .
  config.action_mailer.raise_delivery_errors = true
  config.action_mailer.delivery_method = :smtp
  host = '<your heroku app>.herokuapp.com'
  config.action_mailer.default_url_options = { host: host }
  ActionMailer::Base.smtp_settings = {
    :address        => 'smtp.sendgrid.net',
    :port           => '587',
    :authentication => :plain,
    :user_name      => ENV['SENDGRID_USERNAME'],
    :password       => ENV['SENDGRID_PASSWORD'],
    :domain         => 'heroku.com',
    :enable_starttls_auto => true
  }
  .
  .
  .
end
```

The email configuration in Listing 11.41 includes the **user_name** and **password** of the SendGrid account, but note that they are accessed via the **ENV** environment variable instead of being hard-coded. This is a best practice for production applications, which for security reasons should never expose sensitive information such as raw passwords in source code. In the present case, these variables are configured automatically via the SendGrid add-on, but we'll see an example in Section 13.4.4 where we'll have to define them ourselves.

At this point, you should merge the topic branch into **master** (Listing 12.24).

Listing 12.24: Merging the **password-reset** branch into **master**.

```
$ rails test
$ git add -A
$ git commit -m "Add password reset"
$ git checkout master
$ git merge password-reset
```

Then push up to the remote repository and deploy to Heroku:

```
$ rails test
$ git push && git push heroku
$ heroku run rails db:migrate
```

Once the Heroku deploy has finished, you can reset your password by clicking the "(forgot password)" link (Figure 12.4). The result should be a reset email, as shown in Figure 12.14. Following the link and making invalid or valid submissions should work as it did in development (Figure 12.12 and Figure 12.13). Likewise, upon successfully changing the password, the user should be redirected to the profile page (Figure 12.15).

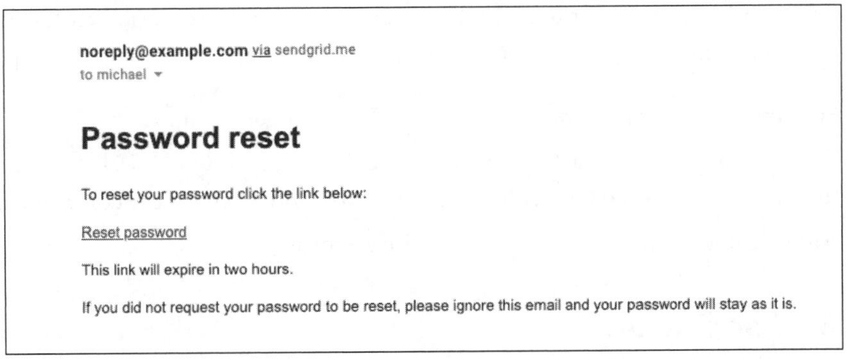

Figure 12.14: A password reset email sent in production.

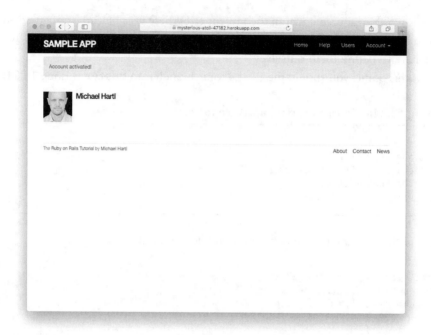

Figure 12.15: The result of a successful password reset in production.

Exercises

Solutions to the exercises are available to all Rails Tutorial purchasers at https:// www.railstutorial.org/aw-solutions.

To see other people's answers and to record your own, subscribe to the Rails Tutorial course or to the Learn Enough All Access Bundle.

1. Sign up for a new account in production. Did you get the email?
2. Click on the link in the activation email to confirm that it works. What is the corresponding entry in the server log? *Hint*: Run **heroku logs** at the command line.
3. Are you able to successfully update your password?

12.5 Conclusion

With the added password resets, our sample application's signup, login, and logout machinery is complete and professional-grade. The rest of the *Ruby on Rails Tutorial* builds on this foundation to make a site with Twitter-like microposts (Chapter 13) and a status feed of posts from followed users (Chapter 14). In the process, we'll learn about some of the most powerful features of Rails, including image upload, custom database queries, and advanced data modeling with **has_many** and **has_many :through**.

12.5.1   What We Learned in this Chapter

- Like sessions and account activations, password resets can be modeled as a resource despite not being Active Record objects.

- Rails can generate Action Mailer actions and views to send email.

- Action Mailer supports both plain-text and HTML mail.

- As with ordinary actions and views, instance variables defined in mailer actions are available in mailer views.

- Password resets use a generated token to create a unique URL for resetting passwords.

- Password resets use a hashed reset digest to securely identify valid reset requests.

- Both mailer tests and integration tests are useful for verifying the behavior of the User mailer.

- We can send email in production using SendGrid.

12.6   Proof of Expiration Comparison

We saw in Section 12.3 that the comparison test for determining when a password reset has expired is

```
reset_sent_at < 2.hours.ago
```

as seen in Listing 12.17. This looks likes it might be read as "reset sent less than two hours ago," which is the opposite of what we want. In this section, we'll prove that the above comparison is correct.[6]

---

6. This proof is the price you pay for reading a web development tutorial written by a Ph.D. physicist. Just be grateful I couldn't find a way to work $\left(-\frac{\hbar^2}{2m} \nabla^2 + V \right) \psi = E\psi$ or $G^{\mu\nu} = 8\pi T^{\mu\nu} (= 4\tau T^{\mu\nu})$ into the exposition.

We start by defining two time intervals. Let Δt_r be the time interval since sending the password reset and let Δt_e be the expiration time limit (e.g., two hours). A password reset has expired if the time interval since the reset was sent is greater than the expiration limit:

$$\Delta t_r > \Delta t_e \tag{12.1}$$

If we write the time now as t_N, the password reset sending time as t_r, and the expiration time as t_e (e.g., two hours ago), then we have

$$\Delta t_r = t_N - t_r \tag{12.2}$$

and

$$\Delta t_e = t_N - t_e \tag{12.3}$$

Plugging Eq. (12.2) and Eq. (12.3) into Eq. (12.1) then gives

$$\begin{aligned} \Delta t_r &> \Delta t_e \\ t_N - t_r &> t_N - t_e \\ -t_r &> -t_e \end{aligned}$$

Multiplying through by -1 then yields

$$t_r < t_e \tag{12.4}$$

Converting Eq. (12.4) to code with the value $t_e = 2$ hours ago gives the **password_reset_expired?** method shown in Listing 12.17:

```
def password_reset_expired?
  reset_sent_at < 2.hours.ago
end
```

As noted in Section 12.3, if we read **<** as "earlier than" instead of "less than," this code makes sense as the English sentence "The password reset was sent earlier than two hours ago."

CHAPTER 13
User Microposts

In the course of developing the core sample application, we've now encountered four resources—users, sessions, account activations, and password resets—but only the first of these is backed by an Active Record model with a table in the database. The time has finally come to add a second such resource: user *microposts*, which are short messages associated with a particular user.[1] We first saw microposts in larval form in Chapter 2. In this chapter we will make a full-strength version of the sketch from Section 2.3 by constructing the Micropost data model, associating it with the User model using the **has_many** and **belongs_to** methods, and then making the forms and partials needed to manipulate and display the results (including, in Section 13.4, uploaded images). In Chapter 14, we'll complete our tiny Twitter clone by adding the notion of *following* users to receive a *feed* of their microposts.

13.1 A Micropost Model

We begin the Microposts resource by creating a Micropost model, which captures the essential characteristics of microposts. What follows builds on the work from Section 2.3; as with the model in that section, our new Micropost model will include data validations and an association with the User model. Unlike that model, the present Micropost model will be fully tested, and will also have a default *ordering* and automatic *destruction* if its parent user is destroyed.

---

1. The name is motivated by the common description of Twitter as a *microblog*; since blogs have posts, microblogs should have *microposts*, which can be thought of as the generic equivalent of "tweets."

If you're using Git for version control, I suggest making a topic branch at this time:

```
$ git checkout -b user-microposts
```

13.1.1 The Basic Model

The Micropost model needs only two attributes: a **content** attribute to hold the micropost's content and a **user_id** to associate a micropost with a particular user. The result is a Micropost model with the structure shown in Figure 13.1.

It's worth noting that the model in Figure 13.1 uses the **text** data type for micropost content (instead of **string**), which is capable of storing an arbitrary amount of text. Even though the content will be restricted to fewer than 140 characters (Section 13.1.2) and hence would fit inside the 255-character **string** type, using **text** better expresses the nature of microposts, which are more naturally thought of as blocks of text. Indeed, in Section 13.3.2 we'll use a text *area* instead of a text field for submitting microposts. In addition, using **text** gives us greater flexibility should we wish to increase the length limit at a future date (as part of internationalization, for example). Finally, using the **text** type results in no performance difference in production,[2] so it costs us nothing to use it here.

microposts	
id	integer
content	text
user_id	integer
created_at	datetime
updated_at	datetime

Figure 13.1: The Micropost data model.

---

2. www.postgresql.org/docs/9.1/static/datatype-character.html

As with the case of the User model (Listing 6.1), we generate the Micropost model using **generate model** (Listing 13.1).

Listing 13.1: Generating the Micropost model.

```
$ rails generate model Micropost content:text user:references
```

This migration leads to the creation of the Micropost model shown in Listing 13.2. In addition to inheriting from **ApplicationRecord** as usual (Section 6.1.2), the generated model includes a line indicating that a micropost **belongs_to** a user, which is included as a result of the **user:references** argument in Listing 13.1. We'll explore the implications of this line in Section 13.1.3.

Listing 13.2: The generated Micropost model.
app/models/micropost.rb

```
class Micropost < ApplicationRecord
  belongs_to :user
end
```

The **generate** command in Listing 13.1 also produces a migration to create a **microposts** table in the database (Listing 13.3); compare it to the analogous migration for the **users** table from Listing 6.2. The biggest difference is the use of **references**, which automatically adds a **user_id** column (along with an index and a foreign key reference)[3] for use in the user/micropost association. As with the User model, the Micropost model migration automatically includes the **t.timestamps** line, which (as mentioned in Section 6.1.1) adds the magic **created_at** and **updated_at** columns shown in Figure 13.1. (We'll put the **created_at** column to work starting in Section 13.1.4.)

---

3. The foreign key reference is a database-level constraint indicating that the user id in the microposts table refers to the id column in the users table. This detail will never be important in this tutorial, and the foreign key constraint isn't even supported by all databases. (It's supported by PostgreSQL, which we use in production, but not by the development SQLite database adapter.) We'll learn more about foreign keys in Section 14.1.2.

Listing 13.3: The Micropost migration with added index.
db/migrate/[timestamp]_create_microposts.rb

```ruby
class CreateMicroposts < ActiveRecord::Migration[6.0]
  def change
    create_table :microposts do |t|
      t.text :content
      t.references :user, null: false, foreign_key: true

      t.timestamps
    end
    add_index :microposts, [:user_id, :created_at]
  end
end
```

Because we expect to retrieve all the microposts associated with a given user id in reverse order of creation, Listing 13.3 adds an index (Box 6.2) on the **user_id** and **created_at** columns:

```ruby
add_index :microposts, [:user_id, :created_at]
```

By including both the **user_id** and **created_at** columns as an array, we arrange for Rails to create a *multiple key index*, which means that Active Record uses *both* keys at the same time.

With the migration in Listing 13.3, we can update the database as usual:

```
$ rails db:migrate
```

Exercises

Solutions to the exercises are available to all Rails Tutorial purchasers at https://www.railstutorial.org/aw-solutions.

To see other people's answers and to record your own, subscribe to the Rails Tutorial course or to the Learn Enough All Access Bundle.

1. Using **Micropost.new** in the console, instantiate a new Micropost object called **micropost** with content "Lorem ipsum" and user id equal to the id of the first user in the database. What are the values of the magic columns **created_at** and **updated_at**?

2. What is **micropost.user** for the micropost in the previous exercise? What about **micropost.user.name**?

3. Save the micropost to the database. What are the values of the magic columns now?

13.1.2 Micropost Validations

Now that we've created the basic model, we'll add some validations to enforce the desired design constraints. One of the necessary aspects of the Micropost model is the presence of a user id to indicate which user made the micropost. The idiomatically correct way to do this is to use Active Record *associations*, which we'll implement in Section 13.1.3. For now, though, we'll work with the **Micropost** model directly.

The initial micropost tests parallel those for the User model (Listing 6.7). In the **setup** step, we create a new micropost while associating it with a valid user from the fixtures, and then check that the result is valid. Because every micropost should have a user id, we'll add a test for a **user_id** presence validation. Putting these elements together yields the test in Listing 13.4.

Listing 13.4: Tests for the validity of a new micropost. GREEN
test/models/micropost_test.rb

```
require 'test_helper'

class MicropostTest < ActiveSupport::TestCase

  def setup
    @user = users(:michael)
    # This code is not idiomatically correct.
    @micropost = Micropost.new(content: "Lorem ipsum", user_id: @user.id)
  end

  test "should be valid" do
    assert @micropost.valid?
  end

  test "user id should be present" do
    @micropost.user_id = nil
    assert_not @micropost.valid?
  end
end
```

As indicated by the comment in the **setup** method, the code to create the micropost is not idiomatically correct. We'll fix this problem in Section 13.1.3.

As with the original User model test (Listing 6.5), the first test in Listing 13.4 is just a reality check, but the second is a test of the presence of the user id, for which we'll add the presence validation shown in Listing 13.5.

Listing 13.5: A validation for the micropost's **user_id**. GREEN
`app/models/micropost.rb`

```
class Micropost < ApplicationRecord
  belongs_to :user
  validates :user_id, presence: true
end
```

By the way, as of Rails 5 the tests in Listing 13.4 actually pass without the valida-tion in Listing 13.5, but only when using the idiomatically incorrect line highlighted in Listing 13.4. The user id presence validation is necessary after switching to the idiomatically correct code in Listing 13.12, so we include it here for convenience.

With the code in Listing 13.5 the tests should (still) be GREEN:

Listing 13.6: GREEN

```
$ rails test:models
```

Next, we'll add validations for the micropost's **content** attribute (following the example from Section 2.3.2). As with the **user_id**, the **content** attribute must be present, and it is further constrained to be no longer than 140 characters (which is what puts the *micro* in micropost).

As with the User model validations (Section 6.2), we'll add the micropost content validations using test-driven development. The resulting tests generally follow the examples from the User model validation tests, as shown in Listing 13.7.

Listing 13.7: Tests for the Micropost model validations. RED
`test/models/micropost_test.rb`

```
require 'test_helper'

class MicropostTest < ActiveSupport::TestCase

  def setup
    @user = users(:michael)
```

```
    @micropost = Micropost.new(content: "Lorem ipsum", user_id: @user.id)
  end

  test "should be valid" do
    assert @micropost.valid?
  end

  test "user id should be present" do
    @micropost.user_id = nil
    assert_not @micropost.valid?
  end

  test "content should be present" do
    @micropost.content = "   "
    assert_not @micropost.valid?
  end

  test "content should be at most 140 characters" do
    @micropost.content = "a" * 141
    assert_not @micropost.valid?
  end
end
```

As in Section 6.2, the code in Listing 13.7 uses string multiplication to test the micropost length validation:

```
$ rails console
>> "a" * 10
=> "aaaaaaaaaa"
>> "a" * 141
=> "aaaaaaaaaaaaaaaaaaaaaaaaaaaaaaaaaaaaaaaaaaaaaaaaaaaaaaaaaaaaaaaaaaaaaaaaaaaa
aaaaaaaaaaaaaaaaaaaaaaaaaaaaaaaaaaaaaaaaaaaaaaaaaaaaaaaaaaaaaaaaaaaaaaaa"
```

The corresponding application code is virtually identical to the **name** validation for users (Listing 6.16), as shown in Listing 13.8.

Listing 13.8: The Micropost model validations. GREEN
app/models/micropost.rb

```
class Micropost < ApplicationRecord
  belongs_to :user
  validates :user_id, presence: true
  validates :content, presence: true, length: { maximum: 140 }
end
```

At this point, the full test suite should be GREEN:

Listing 13.9: GREEN

```
$ rails test
```

Exercises

Solutions to the exercises are available to all Rails Tutorial purchasers at https://www.railstutorial.org/aw-solutions.

To see other people's answers and to record your own, subscribe to the Rails Tutorial course or to the Learn Enough All Access Bundle.

1. At the console, instantiate a micropost with no user id and blank content. Is it valid? What are the full error messages?

2. At the console, instantiate a second micropost with no user id and content that's too long. Is it valid? What are the full error messages?

13.1.3 User/Micropost Associations

When constructing data models for web applications, it is essential to be able to make *associations* between individual models. In the present case, each micropost is associated with one user, and each user is associated with (potentially) many microposts—a relationship seen briefly in Section 2.3.3 and shown schematically in Figure 13.2 and Figure 13.3. As part of implementing these associations, we'll write tests for the Micropost model and add a couple of tests to the User model.

Using the **belongs_to/has_many** association defined in this section, Rails constructs the methods shown in Table 13.1. Note from Table 13.1 that instead of

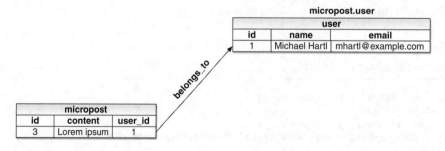

Figure 13.2: The **belongs_to** relationship between a micropost and its associated user.

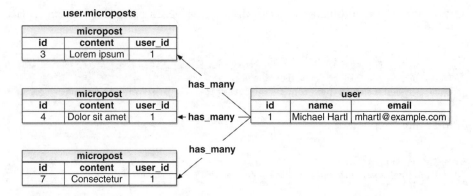

Figure 13.3: The **has_many** relationship between a user and its microposts.

Table 13.1: A summary of user/micropost association methods.

Method	Purpose
micropost.user	Returns the User object associated with the micropost
user.microposts	Returns a collection of the user's microposts
user.microposts.create(arg)	Creates a micropost associated with **user**
user.microposts.create!(arg)	Creates a micropost associated with **user** (exception on failure)
user.microposts.build(arg)	Returns a new Micropost object associated with **user**
user.microposts.find_by(id: 1)	Finds the micropost with id **1** and **user_id** equal to **user.id**

```
Micropost.create
Micropost.create!
Micropost.new
```

we have

```
user.microposts.create
user.microposts.create!
user.microposts.build
```

These latter methods constitute the idiomatically correct way to make a micropost—namely, *through* its association with a user. When a new micropost is made in this

way, its **user_id** is automatically set to the right value. In particular, we can replace
the code

```
@user = users(:michael)
# This code is not idiomatically correct.
@micropost = Micropost.new(content: "Lorem ipsum", user_id: @user.id)
```

from Listing 13.4 with this:

```
@user = users(:michael)
@micropost = @user.microposts.build(content: "Lorem ipsum")
```

(As with **new**, **build** returns an object in memory but doesn't modify the database.)[4]
Once we define the proper associations, the resulting **@micropost** variable will
automatically have a **user_id** attribute equal to its associated user's id.

To get code like **@user.microposts.build** to work, we need to update the User
and Micropost models with code to associate them. The first part of this code was
included automatically by the migration in Listing 13.3 via **belongs_to :user**, as
shown in Listing 13.10. The second half of the association, **has_many :microposts**,
needs to be added by hand, as shown in Listing 13.11.

Listing 13.10: A micropost **belongs_to** a user. GREEN
app/models/micropost.rb

```
class Micropost < ApplicationRecord
  belongs_to :user
  validates :user_id, presence: true
  validates :content, presence: true, length: { maximum: 140 }
end
```

Listing 13.11: A user **has_many** microposts. GREEN
app/models/user.rb

```
class User < ApplicationRecord
  has_many :microposts
```

---

4. In fact, if you look at the source, you'll see that **build** is actually just an alias for **new**. Thanks to reader
Abdullah Budri for pointing this out.

.
.
.
end

___

With the association thus made, we can update the **setup** method in Listing 13.4 with the idiomatically correct way to build a new micropost, as shown in Listing 13.12.

Listing 13.12: Using idiomatically correct code to build a micropost. GREEN
`test/models/micropost_test.rb`

___

```ruby
require 'test_helper'

class MicropostTest < ActiveSupport::TestCase

  def setup
    @user = users(:michael)
    @micropost = @user.microposts.build(content: "Lorem ipsum")
  end

  test "should be valid" do
    assert @micropost.valid?
  end

  test "user id should be present" do
    @micropost.user_id = nil
    assert_not @micropost.valid?
  end
  .
  .
  .
end
```

___

Of course, after this minor refactoring the test suite should still be GREEN:

Listing 13.13: GREEN

___

```
$ rails test
```

___

Exercises
Solutions to the exercises are available to all Rails Tutorial purchasers at https://www.railstutorial.org/aw-solutions.

To see other people's answers and to record your own, subscribe to the Rails Tutorial course or to the Learn Enough All Access Bundle.

1. Set **user** to the first user in the database. What happens when you execute the command **micropost = user.microposts.create(content: "Lorem ipsum")**?

2. The previous exercise should have created a micropost in the database. Confirm this by running **user.microposts.find(micropost.id)**. What if you write **micropost** instead of **micropost.id**?

3. What is the value of **user == micropost.user**? How about **user.microposts.first == micropost**?

13.1.4 Micropost Refinements

In this section, we'll add a couple of refinements to the user/micropost association. In particular, we'll arrange for a user's microposts to be retrieved in a specific *order*, and we'll make microposts *dependent* on users so that they will be automatically destroyed if their associated user is destroyed.

Default Scope

By default, the **user.microposts** method makes no guarantees about the order of the posts, but (following the convention of blogs and Twitter) we want the microposts to come out in reverse order of when they were created so that the most recent post appears first.[5] We'll arrange for this to happen using a *default scope*.

This is exactly the sort of feature that could easily lead to a spurious passing test (i.e., a test that would pass even if the application code were wrong), so we'll proceed using test-driven development to be sure we're testing the right thing. In particular, let's write a test to verify that the first micropost in the database is the same as a fixture micropost we'll call **most_recent**, as shown in Listing 13.14.

Listing 13.14: Testing the micropost order. RED
test/models/micropost_test.rb

```
require 'test_helper'

class MicropostTest < ActiveSupport::TestCase
```

---

5. We briefly encountered a similar issue in Section 10.5 in the context of the users index.

```
                .
                .
                .
  test "order should be most recent first" do
    assert_equal microposts(:most_recent), Micropost.first
  end
end
```

Listing 13.14 relies on having some micropost fixtures, which we can define in analogy with the user fixtures, last seen in Listing 11.5. In addition to the **content** attribute defined in Section 13.1.1, we need to define the associated **user**. Conveniently, Rails includes a way to build associations in fixtures, like this:

```
orange:
  content: "I just ate an orange!"
  created_at: <%= 10.minutes.ago %>
  user: michael
```

By identifying the **user** as **michael**, we tell Rails to associate this micropost with the corresponding user in the users fixture:

```
michael:
  name: Michael Example
  email: michael@example.com
    .
    .
    .
```

The full micropost fixtures appear in Listing 13.15.

Listing 13.15: Micropost fixtures.
```
test/fixtures/microposts.yml
```

```
orange:
  content: "I just ate an orange!"
  created_at: <%= 10.minutes.ago %>
  user: michael

tau_manifesto:
  content: "Check out the @tauday site by @mhartl: https://tauday.com"
  created_at: <%= 3.years.ago %>
  user: michael
```

```
cat_video:
  content: "Sad cats are sad: https://youtu.be/PKffm2uI4dk"
  created_at: <%= 2.hours.ago %>
  user: michael

most_recent:
  content: "Writing a short test"
  created_at: <%= Time.zone.now %>
  user: michael
```

Note that Listing 13.15 explicitly sets the **created_at** column using embedded Ruby. Because it's a "magic" column automatically updated by Rails, setting **created_at** by hand isn't ordinarily possible, but it is possible in fixtures.[6]

With the code in Listing 13.14 and Listing 13.15, the test suite should be RED:

Listing 13.16: RED

```
$ rails test test/models/micropost_test.rb
```

We'll get the test to pass using a Rails method called **default_scope**, which among other things can be used to set the default order in which elements are retrieved from the database. To enforce a particular order, we'll include the **order** argument in **default_scope**, which lets us order by the **created_at** column:

```
order(:created_at)
```

Unfortunately, this orders the results in *ascending* order from smallest to biggest, which means that the oldest microposts come out first. To pull them out in reverse order, we can push down one level deeper and include a string with some raw SQL:

```
order('created_at DESC')
```

Here **DESC** is SQL for "descending"—that is, in descending order from newest to oldest.[7] In older versions of Rails, using this raw SQL used to be the only option to

---

6. In practice this might not be necessary, and in fact on many systems the fixtures are created in the order in which they appear in the file. In this case, the final fixture in the file is created last (and hence is most recent), but it would be foolish to rely on this behavior, which is brittle and probably system-dependent.

7. SQL is case-insensitive, but the convention is to write SQL keywords (such as **DESC**) in all-caps.

get the desired behavior, but as of Rails 4.0 we can use a more natural pure-Ruby syntax as well:

```
order(created_at: :desc)
```

Adding this in a default scope for the Micropost model gives Listing 13.17.

Listing 13.17: Ordering the microposts with **default_scope**. GREEN
app/models/micropost.rb

```
class Micropost < ApplicationRecord
  belongs_to :user
  default_scope -> { order(created_at: :desc) }
  validates :user_id, presence: true
  validates :content, presence: true, length: { maximum: 140 }
end
```

Listing 13.17 introduces the "stabby lambda" syntax for an object called a *Proc* (procedure) or *lambda*, which is an *anonymous function* (a function created without a name). The stabby lambda **->** takes in a block (Section 4.3.2) and returns a Proc, which can then be evaluated with the **call** method. We can see how it works at the console:

```
>> -> { puts "foo" }
=> #<Proc:0x007fab938d0108@(irb):1 (lambda)>
>> -> { puts "foo" }.call
foo
=> nil
```

(This is a somewhat advanced Ruby topic, so don't worry if it doesn't make sense right away.)

With the code in Listing 13.17, the tests should be GREEN:

Listing 13.18: GREEN

```
$ rails test
```

Dependent: Destroy

Apart from proper ordering, there is a second refinement we'd like to add to microposts. Recall from Section 10.4 that site administrators have the power to *destroy* users.

It stands to reason that, if a user is destroyed, the user's microposts should be destroyed as well.

We can arrange for this behavior by passing an option to the **has_many** association method, as shown in Listing 13.19.

Listing 13.19: Ensuring that a user's microposts are destroyed along with the user. app/models/user.rb

```
class User < ApplicationRecord
  has_many :microposts, dependent: :destroy
  .
  .
  .
end
```

Here the option **dependent: :destroy** arranges for the dependent microposts to be destroyed when the user itself is destroyed. This prevents userless microposts from being stranded in the database when admins choose to remove users from the system.

We can verify that Listing 13.19 is working with a test for the User model. All we need to do is save the user (so it gets an id) and create an associated micropost. Then we check that destroying the user reduces the micropost count by 1. The result appears in Listing 13.20. (Compare this code to the integration test for "delete" links in Listing 10.62.)

Listing 13.20: A test of **dependent: :destroy**. GREEN
test/models/user_test.rb

```
require 'test_helper'

class UserTest < ActiveSupport::TestCase

  def setup
    @user = User.new(name: "Example User", email: "user@example.com",
                     password: "foobar", password_confirmation: "foobar")
  end
  .
  .
  .
  test "associated microposts should be destroyed" do
    @user.save
    @user.microposts.create!(content: "Lorem ipsum")
    assert_difference 'Micropost.count', -1 do
```

```
      @user.destroy
    end
  end
end
```

If the code in Listing 13.19 is working correctly, the test suite should still be GREEN:

Listing 13.21: GREEN

```
$ rails test
```

Exercises

Solutions to the exercises are available to all Rails Tutorial purchasers at https://www.railstutorial.org/aw-solutions.

To see other people's answers and to record your own, subscribe to the Rails Tutorial course or to the Learn Enough All Access Bundle.

1. How does the value of `Micropost.first.created_at` compare to `Micropost.last.created_at`?

2. What are the SQL queries for `Micropost.first` and `Micropost.last`? *Hint*: They are printed out by the console.

3. Let **user** be the first user in the database. What is the id of its first micropost? Destroy the first user in the database using the **destroy** method, then confirm using `Micropost.find` that the user's first micropost was also destroyed.

13.2 Showing Microposts

Although we don't yet have a way to create microposts through the web—that comes in Section 13.3.2—this won't stop us from displaying them (and testing that display). Following Twitter's lead, we'll plan to display a user's microposts not on a separate microposts **index** page but rather directly on the user **show** page itself, as mocked up in Figure 13.4.[8] We'll start with fairly simple ERb templates for adding a micropost display to the user profile, and then we'll add microposts to the seed data from Section 10.3.2 so that we have something to display.

---

8. This and other figures in this chapter: Baby photo was retrieved from https://www.flickr.com/photos/glasgows/338937124/ on 2014-08-25. Copyright © 2008 by M&R Glasgow and used unaltered under the terms of the CC BY license.

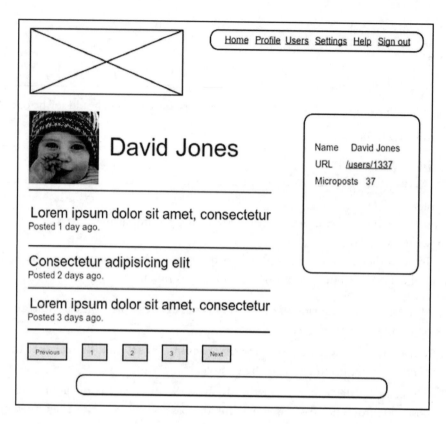

Figure 13.4: A mockup of a profile page with microposts.

13.2.1 Rendering Microposts

Our plan is to display the microposts for each user on the user's profile page (**show. html.erb**), together with a running count of how many microposts they've made. As we'll see, many of the ideas are similar to our work in Section 10.3 on showing all users.

In case you've added some microposts in the exercises, it's a good idea to reset and reseed the database at this time:

```
$ rails db:migrate:reset
$ rails db:seed
```

Although we won't need the Microposts controller until Section 13.3, we will need the views directory in just a moment, so let's generate the controller now:

```
$ rails generate controller Microposts
```

Our primary purpose in this section is to render all the microposts for each user. We saw in Section 10.3.5 that the code

```
<ul class="users">
  <%= render @users %>
</ul>
```

automatically renders each of the users in the **@users** variable using the **_user. html.erb** partial. We'll define an analogous **_micropost.html.erb** partial so that we can use the same technique on a collection of microposts as follows:

```
<ol class="microposts">
  <%= render @microposts %>
</ol>
```

Note that we've used the *ordered list* tag **ol** (as opposed to an unordered list **ul**) because microposts are listed in a particular order (reverse-chronological). The corresponding partial appears in Listing 13.22.

Listing 13.22: A partial for showing a single micropost.
`app/views/microposts/_micropost.html.erb`

```
<li id="micropost-<%= micropost.id %>">
  <%= link_to gravatar_for(micropost.user, size: 50), micropost.user %>
  <span class="user"><%= link_to micropost.user.name, micropost.user %></span>
  <span class="content"><%= micropost.content %></span>
  <span class="timestamp">
    Posted <%= time_ago_in_words(micropost.created_at) %> ago.
  </span>
</li>
```

This uses the awesome **time_ago_in_words** helper method, whose meaning is probably clear and whose effect we will see in Section 13.2.2. Listing 13.22 also adds a CSS id for each micropost using

```
<li id="micropost-<%= micropost.id %>">
```

This is a generally good practice, as it opens up the possibility of manipulating individual microposts at a future date (using JavaScript, for example).

The next step is to address the difficulty of displaying a potentially large number of microposts. We'll solve this problem the same way we solved it for users in Section 10.3.3—namely, using pagination. As before, we'll use the **will_paginate** method:

```
<%= will_paginate @microposts %>
```

If you compare this with the analogous line on the user index page, Listing 10.45, you'll see that before we had just

```
<%= will_paginate %>
```

This worked because, in the context of the Users controller, **will_paginate** *assumes* the existence of an instance variable called **@users** (which, as we saw in Section 10.3.3, should be of class **ActiveRecord::Relation**). In the present case, since we are still in the Users controller but want to paginate *microposts* instead, we'll pass an explicit **@microposts** variable to **will_paginate**. Of course, this means that we will have to define such a variable in the user **show** action (Listing 13.23).

Listing 13.23: Adding an **@microposts** instance variable to the user **show** action.
`app/controllers/users_controller.rb`

```
class UsersController < ApplicationController
  .
  .
  .
  def show
    @user = User.find(params[:id])
    @microposts = @user.microposts.paginate(page: params[:page])
  end
  .
  .
  .
end
```

Notice here how clever **paginate** is: It even works *through* the microposts association, reaching into the microposts table and pulling out the desired page of microposts.

Our final task is to display the number of microposts for each user, which we can do with the **count** method:

```
user.microposts.count
```

As with **paginate**, we can use the **count** method through the association. In particular, **count** does *not* pull all the microposts out of the database and then call **length** on the resulting array, as this would become inefficient as the number of microposts grew. Instead, it performs the calculation directly in the database, asking the database to count the microposts with the given **user_id** (an operation for which all databases are highly optimized). (In the unlikely event that finding the count is still a bottleneck in your application, you can make it even faster using a *counter cache*.)

Putting all the elements together, we are now in a position to add microposts to the profile page, as shown in Listing 13.24. Note the use of **if @user.microposts.any?** (a construction we saw in Listing 7.21), which makes sure that an empty list won't be displayed when the user has no microposts.

Listing 13.24: Adding microposts to the user **show** page.
app/views/users/show.html.erb

```erb
<% provide(:title, @user.name) %>
<div class="row">
  <aside class="col-md-4">
    <section class="user_info">
      <h1>
        <%= gravatar_for @user %>
        <%= @user.name %>
      </h1>
    </section>
  </aside>
  <div class="col-md-8">
    <% if @user.microposts.any? %>
      <h3>Microposts (<%= @user.microposts.count %>)</h3>
      <ol class="microposts">
        <%= render @microposts %>
      </ol>
      <%= will_paginate @microposts %>
    <% end %>
  </div>
</div>
```

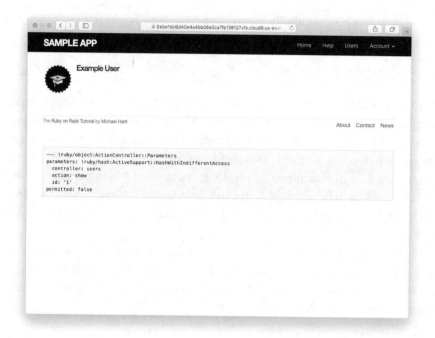

Figure 13.5: The user profile page with code for microposts—but no microposts.

At this point, we can get a look at our updated user profile page in Figure 13.5. It's rather … disappointing. Of course, we do not currently have any microposts. It's time to change that.

Exercises

Solutions to the exercises are available to all Rails Tutorial purchasers at https://www.railstutorial.org/aw-solutions.

To see other people's answers and to record your own, subscribe to the Rails Tutorial course or to the Learn Enough All Access Bundle.

1. As mentioned briefly in Section 7.3.3, helper methods like `time_ago_in_words` are available in the Rails console via the `helper` object. Using `helper`, apply `time_ago_in_words` to `3.weeks.ago` and `6.months.ago`.

2. What is the result of `helper.time_ago_in_words(1.year.ago)`?

3. What is the Ruby class for a page of microposts? *Hint*: Use the code in Listing 13.23 as your model, and call the **class** method on **paginate** with the argument **page: nil**.

13.2.2 Sample Microposts

With all the work making templates for user microposts in Section 13.2.1, the ending was rather anticlimactic. We can rectify this sad situation by adding microposts to the seed data from Section 10.3.2.

Adding sample microposts for *all* the users actually takes a rather long time, so for now we'll select just the first six users (i.e., the five users with custom Gravatars, and one with the default Gravatar) using the **take** method:

```
User.order(:created_at).take(6)
```

The call to **order** ensures that we find the first six users that were created.

For each of the selected users, we'll make 50 microposts (plenty to overflow the pagination limit of 30). To generate sample content for each micropost, we'll use the Faker gem's handy `Lorem.sentence` method.[9] The result is the new seed data method shown in Listing 13.25. (The reason for the order of the loops in Listing 13.25 is to intermix the microposts for use in the status feed (Section 14.3). Looping over the users first gives feeds with big runs of microposts from the same user, which is visually unappealing.)

Listing 13.25: Adding microposts to the sample data.
db/`seeds.rb`

```
  .
  .
  .
# Generate microposts for a subset of users.
users = User.order(:created_at).take(6)
50.times do
  content = Faker::Lorem.sentence(word_count: 5)
  users.each { |user| user.microposts.create!(content: content) }
end
```

9. **Faker::Lorem.sentence** returns *lorem ipsum* text; as noted in Chapter 6, *lorem ipsum* has a fascinating back story, see www.straightdope.com/columns/read/2290/what-does-the-filler-text-lorem-ipsum-mean.

At this point, we can reseed the development database as usual:

```
$ rails db:migrate:reset
$ rails db:seed
```

You should also quit and restart the Rails development server.

With that, we are in a position to enjoy the fruits of our Section 13.2.1 labors by displaying information for each micropost.[10] The preliminary results appear in Figure 13.6.

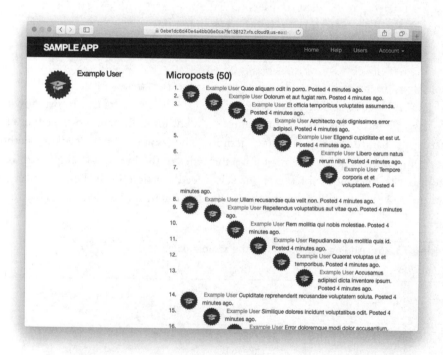

Figure 13.6: The user profile with unstyled microposts.

---

10. By design, the Faker gem's *lorem ipsum* text is randomized, so the contents of your sample microposts will differ.

The page shown in Figure 13.6 has no micropost-specific styling, so let's add some (Listing 13.26) and take a look at the resulting pages.[11]

Listing 13.26: The CSS for microposts (including all the CSS for this chapter).
`app/assets/stylesheets/custom.scss`

```scss
.
.
.
/* microposts */

.microposts {
  list-style: none;
  padding: 0;
  li {
    padding: 10px 0;
    border-top: 1px solid #e8e8e8;
  }
  .user {
    margin-top: 5em;
    padding-top: 0;
  }
  .content {
    display: block;
    margin-left: 60px;
    img {
      display: block;
      padding: 5px 0;
    }
  }
  .timestamp {
    color: $gray-light;
    display: block;
    margin-left: 60px;
  }
  .gravatar {
    float: left;
    margin-right: 10px;
    margin-top: 5px;
  }
}

aside {
  textarea {
```

---

11. For convenience, Listing 13.26 actually has *all* the CSS needed for this chapter.

```
    height: 100px;
    margin-bottom: 5px;
  }
}

span.image {
  margin-top: 10px;
  input {
    border: 0;
  }
}
```

Figure 13.7 shows the user profile page for the first user, while Figure 13.8 shows the profile for a second user. Finally, Figure 13.9 shows the *second* page of microposts for the first user, along with the pagination links at the bottom of the display. In all three cases, observe that each micropost display indicates the time since it was created

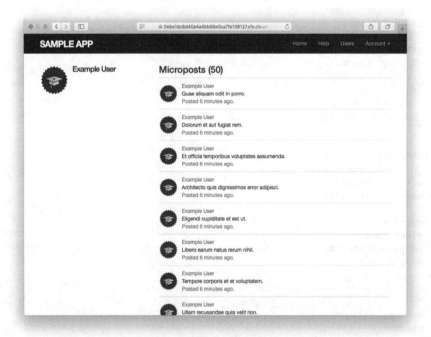

Figure 13.7: The user profile with microposts (/users/1).

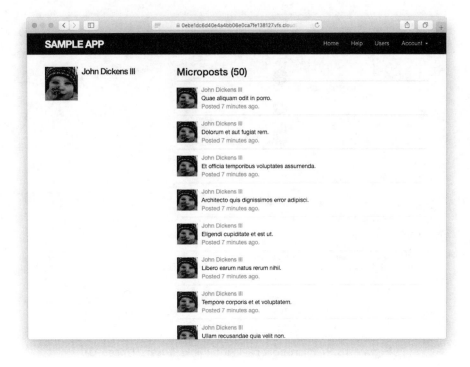

Figure 13.8: The profile of a different user, also with microposts (/users/5).

(e.g., "Posted 1 minute ago."); this is the work of the **time_ago_in_words** method from Listing 13.22. If you wait a couple of minutes and reload the pages, you'll see how the text gets automatically updated based on the new time.

Exercises

Solutions to the exercises are available to all Rails Tutorial purchasers at https://www.railstutorial.org/aw-solutions.

To see other people's answers and to record your own, subscribe to the Rails Tutorial course or to the Learn Enough All Access Bundle.

1. See if you can guess the result of running **(1..10).to_a.take(6)**. Check at the console to see if your guess is right.

2. Is the **to_a** method in the previous exercise necessary?

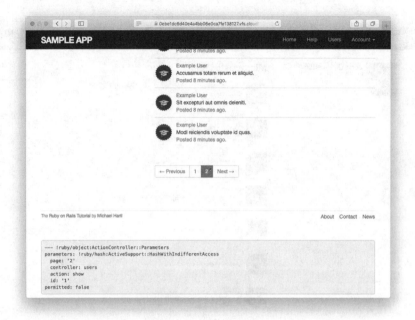

Figure 13.9: Micropost pagination links (/users/1?page=2).

3. Faker has a huge number of occasionally amusing applications. By consulting the Faker documentation (github.com/stympy/faker), learn how to print out a fake university name, a fake phone number, a fake Hipster Ipsum sentence, and a fake Chuck Norris fact.

13.2.3 Profile Micropost Tests

Because newly activated users get redirected to their profile pages, we already have a test that the profile page renders correctly (Listing 11.33). In this section, we'll write a short integration test for some of the other elements on the profile page, including the work from this section. We'll start by generating an integration test for the profiles of our site's users:

```
$ rails generate integration_test users_profile
      invoke  test_unit
      create    test/integration/users_profile_test.rb
```

To test micropost pagination, we'll also generate some additional micropost fixtures using the same embedded Ruby technique we used to make additional users in Listing 10.47:

```
<% 30.times do |n| %>
micropost_<%= n %>:
  content: <%= Faker::Lorem.sentence(5) %>
  created_at: <%= 42.days.ago %>
  user: michael
<% end %>
```

Adding this to the code from Listing 13.15 gives the updated micropost fixtures in Listing 13.27.

Listing 13.27: Micropost fixtures with generated microposts.
`test/fixtures/microposts.yml`

```
orange:
  content: "I just ate an orange!"
  created_at: <%= 10.minutes.ago %>
  user: michael

tau_manifesto:
  content: "Check out the @tauday site by @mhartl: https://tauday.com"
  created_at: <%= 3.years.ago %>
  user: michael

cat_video:
  content: "Sad cats are sad: https://youtu.be/PKffm2uI4dk"
  created_at: <%= 2.hours.ago %>
  user: michael

most_recent:
  content: "Writing a short test"
  created_at: <%= Time.zone.now %>
  user: michael

<% 30.times do |n| %>
micropost_<%= n %>:
  content: <%= Faker::Lorem.sentence(word_count: 5) %>
  created_at: <%= 42.days.ago %>
  user: michael
<% end %>
```

With the test data thus prepared, the test itself is fairly straightforward: We visit the user profile page and check for the page title and the user's name, Gravatar, micropost count, and paginated microposts. The result appears in Listing 13.28. Note the use of the **full_title** helper from Listing 4.2 to test the page's title, which we gain access to by including the Application Helper module into the test.[12]

Listing 13.28: A test for the user profile. GREEN
`test/integration/users_profile_test.rb`

```ruby
require 'test_helper'

class UsersProfileTest < ActionDispatch::IntegrationTest
  include ApplicationHelper

  def setup
    @user = users(:michael)
  end

  test "profile display" do
    get user_path(@user)
    assert_template 'users/show'
    assert_select 'title', full_title(@user.name)
    assert_select 'h1', text: @user.name
    assert_select 'h1>img.gravatar'
    assert_match @user.microposts.count.to_s, response.body
    assert_select 'div.pagination'
    @user.microposts.paginate(page: 1).each do |micropost|
      assert_match micropost.content, response.body
    end
  end
end
```

The micropost count assertion in Listing 13.28 uses **response.body**, which we saw briefly in the Chapter 12 exercises (Section 12.3.3). Despite its name, **response.body** contains the full HTML source of the page—and not just the page's body. So, if all we care about is that the number of microposts appears *somewhere* on the page, we can look for a match as follows:

---

12. If you'd like to refactor other tests to use **full_title** (such as those in Listing 3.32), you should include the Application Helper in **test_helper.rb** instead.

```
assert_match @user.microposts.count.to_s, response.body
```

This is a much less specific assertion than **assert_select**; in particular, unlike **assert_select**, using **assert_match** in this context doesn't require us to indicate which HTML tag we're looking for.

Listing 13.28 also introduces the nesting syntax for **assert_select**:

```
assert_select 'h1>img.gravatar'
```

This checks for an **img** tag with class **gravatar** *inside* a top-level heading tag (**h1**).

Because the application code was working, the test suite should be GREEN:

Listing 13.29: GREEN

```
$ rails test
```

Exercises

Solutions to the exercises are available to all Rails Tutorial purchasers at https://www.railstutorial.org/aw-solutions.

To see other people's answers and to record your own, subscribe to the Rails Tutorial course or to the Learn Enough All Access Bundle.

1. Comment out the application code needed to change the two **'h1'** lines in Listing 13.28 from GREEN to RED.

2. Update Listing 13.28 to test that **will_paginate** appears only *once*. *Hint*: Refer to Table 5.2.

13.3 Manipulating Microposts

Having finished both the data modeling and display templates for microposts, we now turn our attention to the interface for creating them through the web. In this section, we'll also see the first hint of a *status feed*—a notion brought to full fruition in Chapter 14. Finally, as with users, we'll make it possible to destroy microposts through the web.

There is one break with past convention worth noting: The interface to the Microposts resource will run principally through the Profile and Home pages, so we

Table 13.2: RESTful routes provided by the Microposts resource in Listing 13.30.

HTTP request	URL	Action	Named route
POST	/microposts	**create**	`microposts_path`
DELETE	/microposts/1	**destroy**	`micropost_path(micropost)`

won't need actions like **new** or **edit** in the Microposts controller; we'll need only **create** and **destroy**. This leads to the routes for the Microposts resource shown in Listing 13.30. The code in Listing 13.30 leads in turn to the RESTful routes shown in Table 13.2, which is a small subset of the full set of routes seen in Table 2.3. Of course, this simplicity is a sign of being *more* advanced, not less: We've come a long way since our reliance on scaffolding in Chapter 2, and we no longer need most of its complexity.

Listing 13.30: Routes for the Microposts resource.
`config/routes.rb`

```ruby
Rails.application.routes.draw do
  root   'static_pages#home'
  get    '/help',    to: 'static_pages#help'
  get    '/about',   to: 'static_pages#about'
  get    '/contact', to: 'static_pages#contact'
  get    '/signup',  to: 'users#new'
  get    '/login',   to: 'sessions#new'
  post   '/login',   to: 'sessions#create'
  delete '/logout',  to: 'sessions#destroy'
  resources :users
  resources :account_activations, only: [:edit]
  resources :password_resets,     only: [:new, :create, :edit, :update]
  resources :microposts,          only: [:create, :destroy]
end
```

13.3.1 Micropost Access Control

We begin our development of the Microposts resource with some access control in the Microposts controller. In particular, because we access microposts through their associated users, both the **create** and **destroy** actions must require users to be logged in.

Tests to enforce logged-in status mirror those for the Users controller (Listing 10.20 and Listing 10.61). We simply issue the correct request to each action and confirm that the micropost count is unchanged and the result is redirected to the login URL, as seen in Listing 13.31.

Listing 13.31: Authorization tests for the Microposts controller. RED
`test/controllers/microposts_controller_test.rb`

```ruby
require 'test_helper'

class MicropostsControllerTest < ActionDispatch::IntegrationTest

  def setup
    @micropost = microposts(:orange)
  end

  test "should redirect create when not logged in" do
    assert_no_difference 'Micropost.count' do
      post microposts_path, params: { micropost: { content: "Lorem ipsum" } }
    end
    assert_redirected_to login_url
  end

  test "should redirect destroy when not logged in" do
    assert_no_difference 'Micropost.count' do
      delete micropost_path(@micropost)
    end
    assert_redirected_to login_url
  end
end
```

Writing the application code needed to get the tests in Listing 13.31 to pass requires a little refactoring first. Recall from Section 10.2.1 that we enforced the login requirement using a before filter that called the **logged_in_user** method (Listing 10.15). At the time, we needed that method only in the Users controller, but now we find that we need it in the Microposts controller as well, so we'll move it into the Application controller, which is the base class of all controllers (Section 4.4.4).[13] The result appears in Listing 13.32.

---

13. Unlike the behavior in languages like Java or C++, private methods in Ruby can be called from derived classes. Thanks to reader Vishal Antony for bringing this difference to my attention.

Listing 13.32: Moving the **logged_in_user** method into the Application controller.
RED

app/controllers/application_controller.rb

```ruby
class ApplicationController < ActionController::Base
  include SessionsHelper

  private

    # Confirms a logged-in user.
    def logged_in_user
      unless logged_in?
        store_location
        flash[:danger] = "Please log in."
        redirect_to login_url
      end
    end
end
```

To avoid code repetition, you should also remove **logged_in_user** from the Users controller at this time (Listing 13.33).

Listing 13.33: The Users controller with the logged-in user filter removed. RED

app/controllers/users_controller.rb

```ruby
class UsersController < ApplicationController
  before_action :logged_in_user, only: [:index, :edit, :update, :destroy]
  .
  .
  .
  private

    def user_params
      params.require(:user).permit(:name, :email, :password,
                                   :password_confirmation)
    end

    # Before filters

    # Confirms the correct user.
    def correct_user
      @user = User.find(params[:id])
      redirect_to(root_url) unless current_user?(@user)
    end
```

```
  # Confirms an admin user.
  def admin_user
    redirect_to(root_url) unless current_user.admin?
  end
end
```

With the code in Listing 13.32, the **logged_in_user** method is now available in the Microposts controller, which means that we can add **create** and **destroy** actions and then restrict access to them using a before filter, as shown in Listing 13.34.

Listing 13.34: Adding authorization to the Microposts controller actions. GREEN
`app/controllers/microposts_controller.rb`

```
class MicropostsController < ApplicationController
  before_action :logged_in_user, only: [:create, :destroy]

  def create
  end

  def destroy
  end
end
```

At this point, the tests should pass:

Listing 13.35: GREEN

```
$ rails test
```

Exercise

Solutions to the exercises are available to all Rails Tutorial purchasers at https://www.railstutorial.org/aw-solutions.

To see other people's answers and to record your own, subscribe to the Rails Tutorial course or to the Learn Enough All Access Bundle.

1. Why is it a bad idea to leave a copy of **logged_in_user** in the Users controller?

13.3.2 Creating Microposts

In Chapter 7, we implemented user signup by making an HTML form that issued an HTTP POST request to the **create** action in the Users controller. The implementation of micropost creation is similar; the main difference is that, rather than using a separate page at /microposts/new, we will put the form on the Home page itself (i.e., the root path /), as mocked up in Figure 13.10.

When we last left the Home page, it appeared as in Figure 5.8—that is, it had a "Sign up now!" button in the middle. Since a micropost creation form makes sense only in the context of a particular logged-in user, one goal of this section will be to serve different versions of the Home page depending on a visitor's login status. We'll implement this in Listing 13.37 later in this section.

Figure 13.10: A mockup of the Home page with a form for creating microposts.

We'll start with the **create** action for microposts, which is similar to its user analogue (Listing 7.26); the principal difference lies in the use of the user/micropost association to **build** the new micropost, as seen in Listing 13.36. Note the use of strong parameters via **micropost_params**, which permits only the micropost's **content** attribute to be modified through the web.

Listing 13.36: The Microposts controller **create** action.
app/controllers/microposts_controller.rb

```
class MicropostsController < ApplicationController
  before_action :logged_in_user, only: [:create, :destroy]

  def create
    @micropost = current_user.microposts.build(micropost_params)
    if @micropost.save
      flash[:success] = "Micropost created!"
      redirect_to root_url
    else
      render 'static_pages/home'
    end
  end

  def destroy
  end

  private

    def micropost_params
      params.require(:micropost).permit(:content)
    end
end
```

To build a form for creating microposts, we use the code in Listing 13.37, which serves up different HTML based on whether the site visitor is logged in or not.

Listing 13.37: Adding microposts creation to the Home page (/).
app/views/static_pages/home.html.erb

```
<% if logged_in? %>
<div class="row">
  <aside class="col-md-4">
    <section class="user_info">
```

```erb
      <%= render 'shared/user_info' %>
    </section>
    <section class="micropost_form">
      <%= render 'shared/micropost_form' %>
    </section>
  </aside>
</div>
<% else %>
  <div class="center jumbotron">
    <h1>Welcome to the Sample App</h1>

    <h2>
      This is the home page for the
      <a href="https://www.railstutorial.org/">Ruby on Rails Tutorial</a>
      sample application.
    </h2>

    <%= link_to "Sign up now!", signup_path, class: "btn btn-lg btn-primary" %>
  </div>

  <%= link_to image_tag("rails.svg", alt: "Rails logo", width: "200"),
                        "https://rubyonrails.org/" %>
<% end %>
```

(Having so much code in each branch of the **if-else** conditional is a bit messy, and cleaning it up using partials is left as an exercise (Section 13.3.2).)

To get the page defined in Listing 13.37 working, we need to create and fill in a couple of partials. The first is the new Home page sidebar, as shown in Listing 13.38.

Listing 13.38: The partial for the user info sidebar.
app/views/shared/_user_info.html.erb

```erb
<%= link_to gravatar_for(current_user, size: 50), current_user %>
<h1><%= current_user.name %></h1>
<span><%= link_to "view my profile", current_user %></span>
<span><%= pluralize(current_user.microposts.count, "micropost") %></span>
```

Note that, as in the profile sidebar (Listing 13.24), the user info in Listing 13.38 displays the total number of microposts for the user. There's a slight difference in the display, though. In the profile sidebar, "Microposts" is a label, and showing "Microposts (1)" makes sense. In the present case, saying "1 microposts" is ungrammatical, so we arrange to display "1 micropost" and "2 microposts" using the **pluralize** method we saw in Section 7.3.3.

We next define the form for creating microposts (Listing 13.39), which is similar to the signup form in Listing 7.15.

Listing 13.39: The form partial for creating microposts.
`app/views/shared/_micropost_form.html.erb`

```erb
<%= form_with(model: @micropost, local: true) do |f| %>
  <%= render 'shared/error_messages', object: f.object %>
  <div class="field">
    <%= f.text_area :content, placeholder: "Compose new micropost..." %>
  </div>
  <%= f.submit "Post", class: "btn btn-primary" %>
<% end %>
```

We need to make two changes before the form in Listing 13.39 will work. First, we need to define **@micropost**, which (as before) we do through the association:

```ruby
@micropost = current_user.microposts.build
```

The result appears in Listing 13.40.

Listing 13.40: Adding a micropost instance variable to the **home** action.
`app/controllers/static_pages_controller.rb`

```ruby
class StaticPagesController < ApplicationController

  def home
    @micropost = current_user.microposts.build if logged_in?
  end

  def help
  end

  def about
  end

  def contact
  end
end
```

Of course, **current_user** exists only if the user is logged in, so the **@micropost** variable should be defined only in this case.

The second change needed to get Listing 13.39 to work is to redefine the error-messages partial so the following code from Listing 13.39 works:

```
<%= render 'shared/error_messages', object: f.object %>
```

You may recall from Listing 7.20 that the error-messages partial references the **@user** variable explicitly, but in the present case we have an **@micropost** variable instead. To unify these cases, we can pass the form variable **f** to the partial and access the associated object through **f.object**, so that in

```
form_with(model: @user, local: true) do |f|
```

f.object is **@user**; in

```
form_with(model: @micropost, local: true) do |f|
```

f.object is **@micropost**; and so on.

To pass the object to the partial, we use a hash with a value equal to the object and a key equal to the desired name of the variable in the partial, which is what the second line in Listing 13.39 accomplishes. In other words, **object: f.object** creates a variable called **object** in the **error_messages** partial, and we can use it to construct a customized error message, as shown in Listing 13.41.

Listing 13.41: Error messages that work with other objects. RED
app/views/shared/_error_messages.html.erb

```erb
<% if object.errors.any? %>
  <div id="error_explanation">
    <div class="alert alert-danger">
      The form contains <%= pluralize(object.errors.count, "error") %>.
    </div>
    <ul>
    <% object.errors.full_messages.each do |msg| %>
      <li><%= msg %></li>
    <% end %>
```

```
    </ul>
  </div>
<% end %>
```

At this point, you should verify that the test suite is RED:

Listing 13.42: RED

```
$ rails test
```

This is a hint that we need to update the other occurrences of the error-messages partial, which we used when signing up users (Listing 7.20), resetting passwords (Listing 12.14), and editing users (Listing 10.2). The updated versions are shown in Listing 13.43, Listing 13.45, and Listing 13.44.

Listing 13.43: Updating the rendering of user signup errors. RED
app/views/users/new.html.erb

```erb
<% provide(:title, 'Sign up') %>
<h1>Sign up</h1>

<div class="row">
  <div class="col-md-6 col-md-offset-3">
    <%= form_with(model: @user, local: true) do |f| %>
      <%= render 'shared/error_messages', object: f.object %>

      <%= f.label :name %>
      <%= f.text_field :name, class: 'form-control' %>

      <%= f.label :email %>
      <%= f.email_field :email, class: 'form-control' %>

      <%= f.label :password %>
      <%= f.password_field :password, class: 'form-control' %>

      <%= f.label :password_confirmation, "Confirmation" %>
      <%= f.password_field :password_confirmation, class: 'form-control' %>

      <%= f.submit "Create my account", class: "btn btn-primary" %>
    <% end %>
  </div>
</div>
```

Listing 13.44: Updating the errors for password resets. GREEN
`app/views/password_resets/edit.html.erb`

```erb
<% provide(:title, 'Reset password') %>
<h1>Reset password</h1>

<div class="row">
  <div class="col-md-6 col-md-offset-3">
    <%= form_with(model: @user, url: password_reset_path(params[:id]),
                  local: true) do |f| %>
      <%= render 'shared/error_messages', object: f.object %>

      <%= hidden_field_tag :email, @user.email %>

      <%= f.label :password %>
      <%= f.password_field :password, class: 'form-control' %>

      <%= f.label :password_confirmation, "Confirmation" %>
      <%= f.password_field :password_confirmation, class: 'form-control' %>

      <%= f.submit "Update password", class: "btn btn-primary" %>
    <% end %>
  </div>
</div>
```

Listing 13.45: Updating the errors for editing users. RED
`app/views/users/edit.html.erb`

```erb
<% provide(:title,. "Edit user") %>
<h1>Update your profile</h1>

<div class="row">
  <div class="col-md-6 col-md-offset-3">
    <%= form_with(model: @user, local: true) do |f| %>
      <%= render 'shared/error_messages', object: f.object %>

      <%= f.label :name %>
      <%= f.text_field :name, class: 'form-control' %>

      <%= f.label :email %>
      <%= f.email_field :email, class: 'form-control' %>

      <%= f.label :password %>
      <%= f.password_field :password, class: 'form-control' %>

      <%= f.label :password_confirmation, "Confirmation" %>
```

```
    <%= f.password_field :password_confirmation, class: 'form-control' %>

    <%= f.submit "Save changes", class: "btn btn-primary" %>
  <% end %>

  <div class="gravatar_edit">
    <%= gravatar_for @user %>
    <a href="https://gravatar.com/emails">change</a>
  </div>
 </div>
</div>
```

At this point, all the tests should be GREEN:

Listing 13.46: GREEN

```
$ rails test
```

Additionally, all the HTML in this section should render properly, showing the form as in Figure 13.11, and a form with a submission error as in Figure 13.12.

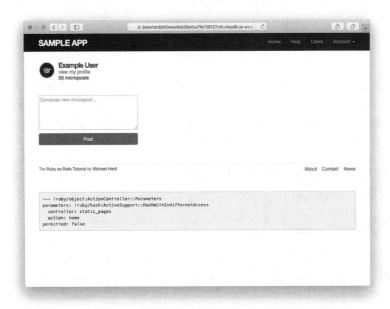

Figure 13.11: The Home page with a new micropost form.

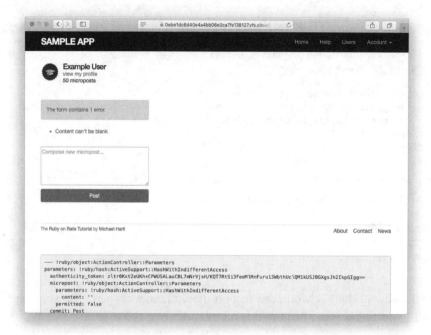

Figure 13.12: The Home page with a form error.

Exercise

Solutions to the exercises are available to all Rails Tutorial purchasers at https://www.railstutorial.org/aw-solutions.

To see other people's answers and to record your own, subscribe to the Rails Tutorial course or to the Learn Enough All Access Bundle.

1. Refactor the Home page to use separate partials for the two branches of the **if**-**else** statement.

13.3.3 A Proto-Feed

Although the micropost form is actually now working, users can't immediately see the results of a successful submission because the current Home page doesn't display any microposts. If you like, you can verify that the form shown in Figure 13.11 is working by submitting a valid entry and then navigating to the profile page to see the post, but that's rather cumbersome. It would be far better to have a *feed* of microposts that

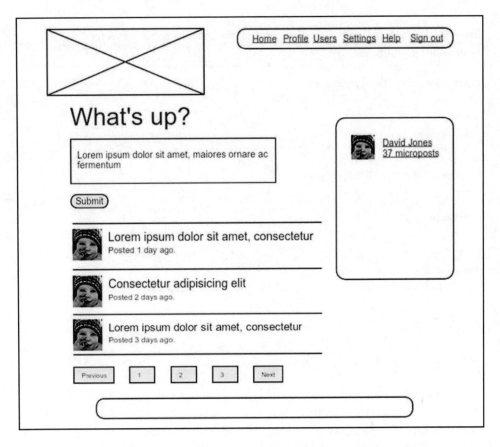

Figure 13.13: A mockup of the Home page with a proto-feed.

includes the user's own posts, as mocked up in Figure 13.13. (In Chapter 14, we'll generalize this feed to include the microposts of users being *followed* by the current user, à la Twitter.)

Since each user should have a feed, we are led naturally to a **feed** method in the User model, which will initially just select all the microposts belonging to the current user. We'll accomplish this using the **where** method on the **Micropost** model (seen briefly before in Section 11.3.3), as shown in Listing 13.47.[14]

---

14. See the Rails Guide on the Active Record Query Interface for more on **where** and related methods.

Listing 13.47: A preliminary implementation for the micropost status feed.
`app/models/user.rb`

```
class User < ApplicationRecord
  .
  .
  .
  # Defines a proto-feed.
  # See "Following users" for the full implementation.
  def feed
    Micropost.where("user_id = ?", id)
  end

  private
    .
    .
    .
end
```

The question mark in

```
Micropost.where("user_id = ?", id)
```

ensures that **id** is properly *escaped* before being included in the underlying SQL query, thereby avoiding a serious security hole called *SQL injection*. The **id** attribute here is just an integer (i.e., **self.id**, the unique id of the user), so there is no danger of SQL injection in this case. But this practice does no harm, and *always* escaping variables injected into SQL statements is a good habit to cultivate.

Alert readers might note at this point that the code in Listing 13.47 is essentially equivalent to writing

```
def feed
  microposts
end
```

We've used the code in Listing 13.47 instead because it generalizes much more naturally to the full status feed needed in Chapter 14.

To use the feed in the sample application, we add an **@feed_items** instance variable for the current user's (paginated) feed, as in Listing 13.48, and then add a status feed partial (Listing 13.49) to the Home page (Listing 13.50). Note that now two lines need to be run when the user is logged in, so Listing 13.48 changes

```
@micropost = current_user.microposts.build if logged_in?
```

from Listing 13.40 to

```
if logged_in?
  @micropost  = current_user.microposts.build
  @feed_items = current_user.feed.paginate(page: params[:page])
end
```

thereby moving the conditional from the end of the line to an if-end statement.

Listing 13.48: Adding a feed instance variable to the **home** action.
`app/controllers/static_pages_controller.rb`

```ruby
class StaticPagesController < ApplicationController

  def home
    if logged_in?
      @micropost  = current_user.microposts.build
      @feed_items = current_user.feed.paginate(page: params[:page])
    end
  end

  def help
  end

  def about
  end

  def contact
  end
end
```

Listing 13.49: The status feed partial.
`app/views/shared/_feed.html.erb`

```erb
<% if @feed_items.any? %>
  <ol class="microposts">
    <%= render @feed_items %>
```

```
    </ol>
    <%= will_paginate @feed_items %>
<% end %>
```

The status feed partial defers the rendering to the micropost partial defined in Listing 13.22:

```
<%= render @feed_items %>
```

Here Rails knows to call the micropost partial because each element of **@feed_items** has class **Micropost**. This causes Rails to look for a partial with the corresponding name in the views directory of the given resource:

```
app/views/microposts/_micropost.html.erb
```

We can add the feed to the Home page by rendering the feed partial as usual (Listing 13.50). The result is a display of the feed on the Home page, as required (Figure 13.14).

Listing 13.50: Adding a status feed to the Home page.
`app/views/static_pages/home.html.erb`

```erb
<% if logged_in? %>
  <div class="row">
    <aside class="col-md-4">
      <section class="user_info">
        <%= render 'shared/user_info' %>
      </section>
      <section class="micropost_form">
        <%= render 'shared/micropost_form' %>
      </section>
    </aside>
    <div class="col-md-8">
      <h3>Micropost Feed</h3>
      <%= render 'shared/feed' %>
    </div>
  </div>
<% else %>
  .
  .
  .
<% end %>
```

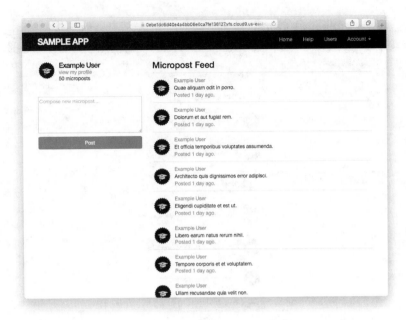

Figure 13.14: The Home page with a proto-feed.

At this point, creating a new micropost works as expected, as seen in Figure 13.15. There is one subtlety, though. On a *failed* micropost submission, the Home page expects an **@feed_items** instance variable, so failed submissions currently break. The solution is to create the necessary feed variable in the branch for failed submissions in the Microposts controller **create** action, as shown in Listing 13.51.

Listing 13.51: Adding an (empty) **@feed_items** instance variable to the **create** action.
`app/controllers/microposts_controller.rb`

```
class MicropostsController < ApplicationController
  before_action :logged_in_user, only: [:create, :destroy]

  def create
    @micropost = current_user.microposts.build(micropost_params)
    if @micropost.save
      flash[:success] = "Micropost created!"
      redirect_to root_url
    else
```

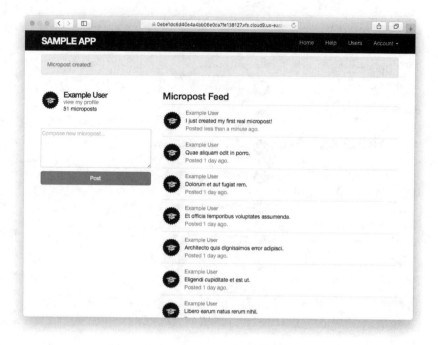

Figure 13.15: The Home page after creating a new micropost.

```
    @feed_items current_user.feed.paginate(page: params[:page])
    render 'static_pages/home'
  end
end

def destroy
end

private

  def micropost_params
    params.require(:micropost).permit(:content)
  end
end
```

Unfortunately, pagination still doesn't quite work. We can see why by submitting an invalid micropost—say, one whose length is too long (Figure 13.16).

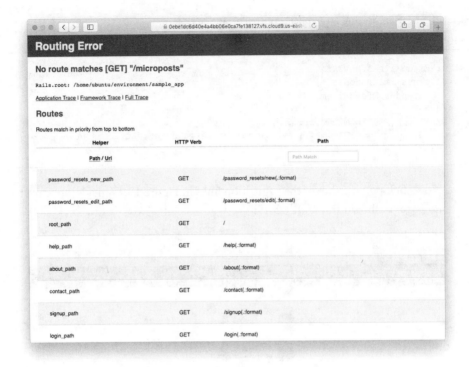

Figure 13.16: An invalid micropost on the Home page.

Scrolling down to the pagination links, we see links on both "2" and "Next" pointing to the next page (Figure 13.17). Because the **create** action is in the Microposts controller (Listing 13.51), the URL is /microposts?page=2, which tries to go to the nonexistent Microposts index action. As a result, clicking on either link gives a routing error (Figure 13.18).

We can solve this problem by giving **will_paginate** explicit **controller** and **action** parameters corresponding to the Home page—that is, the **static_pages** controller and the **home** action.[15] The result appears in Listing 13.52.

---

15. Thanks to reader Martin Francl for pointing out this solution.

Listing 13.52: Setting an explicit controller and action.
`app/views/shared/_feed.html.erb`

```erb
<% if @feed_items.any? %>
  <ol class="microposts">
    <%= render @feed_items %>
  </ol>
  <%= will_paginate @feed_items,
                    params: { controller: :static_pages, action: :home } %>
<% end %>
```

Now clicking on either of the pagination links in Figure 13.17 yields the expected second page, as shown in Figure 13.19.

Figure 13.17: The "Next" link on the Home page.

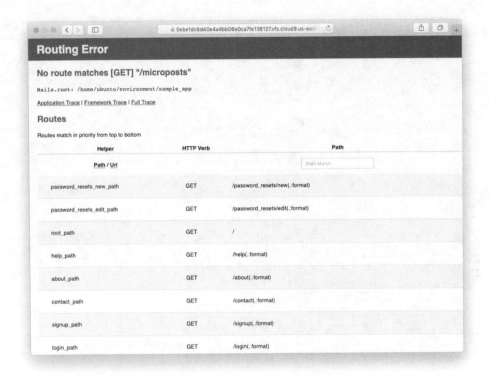

Figure 13.18: A routing error on page 2.

Exercises

Solutions to the exercises are available to all Rails Tutorial purchasers at https://www.railstutorial.org/aw-solutions.

To see other people's answers and to record your own, subscribe to the Rails Tutorial course or to the Learn Enough All Access Bundle.

1. Use the newly created micropost UI to create the first real micropost. What are the contents of the **INSERT** command in the server log?

2. In the console, set **user** to the first user in the database. Confirm that the values of **Micropost.where("user_id = ?", user.id)**, **user.microposts**, and **user.feed** are all the same. *Hint*: It's probably easiest to compare them directly using **==**.

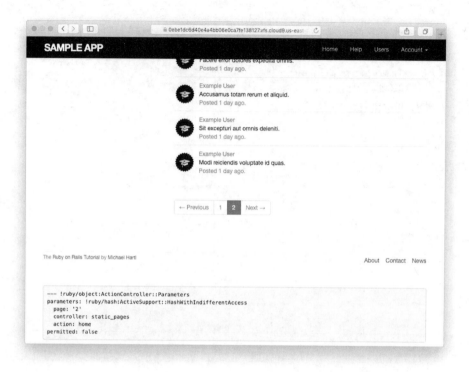

Figure 13.19: The result of a working pagination link to the second page.

13.3.4 Destroying Microposts

The last piece of functionality to add to the Microposts resource is the ability to destroy posts. As with user deletion (Section 10.4.2), we accomplish this with "delete" links, as mocked up in Figure 13.20. Unlike that case, which restricted user destruction to admin users, the delete links will work only for microposts created by the current user.

Our first step is to add a delete link to the micropost partial as in Listing 13.22. The result appears in Listing 13.53.

Listing 13.53: Adding a delete link to the micropost partial.
`app/views/microposts/_micropost.html.erb`

```
<li id="micropost-<%= micropost.id %>">
  <%= link_to gravatar_for(micropost.user, size: 50), micropost.user %>
```

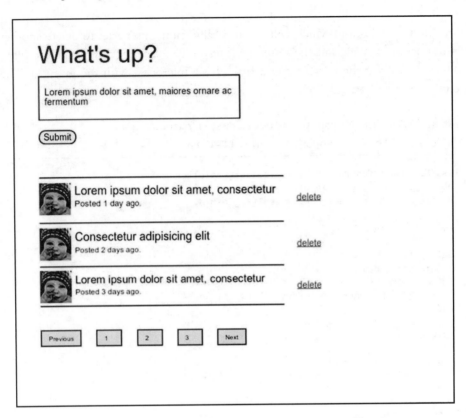

Figure 13.20: A mockup of the proto-feed with micropost delete links.

```
<span class="user"><%= link_to micropost.user.name, micropost.user %></span>
<span class="content"><%= micropost.content %></span>
<span class="timestamp">
  Posted <%= time_ago_in_words(micropost.created_at) %> ago.
  <% if current_user?(micropost.user) %>
    <%= link_to "delete", micropost, method: :delete,
                               data: { confirm: "You sure?" } %>
  <% end %>
</span>
</li>
```

The next step is to define a **destroy** action in the Microposts controller, which is analogous to the user case in Listing 10.59. The main difference is that, rather than using an **@user** variable with an **admin_user** before filter, we'll find the micropost through the association, which will automatically fail if a user tries to delete another user's micropost. We'll put the resulting **find** inside a **correct_user** before filter, which checks that the current user actually has a micropost with the given id. The result appears in Listing 13.54.

Listing 13.54: The Microposts controller **destroy** action.
app/controllers/microposts_controller.rb

```ruby
class MicropostsController < ApplicationController
  before_action :logged_in_user, only: [:create, :destroy]
  before_action :correct_user,   only: :destroy
  .
  .
  .
  def destroy
    @micropost.destroy
    flash[:success] = "Micropost deleted"
    redirect_to request.referrer || root_url
  end

  private

    def micropost_params
      params.require(:micropost).permit(:content)
    end

    def correct_user
      @micropost = current_user.microposts.find_by(id: params[:id])
      redirect_to root_url if @micropost.nil?
    end
end
```

Note that the **destroy** method in Listing 13.54 redirects to the URL

```
request.referrer || root_url
```

This uses the **request.referrer** method,[16] which is related to the **request.original_url** variable used in friendly forwarding (Section 10.2.3), and is just

---

16. This corresponds to HTTP_REFERER, as defined by the specification for HTTP. Note that "referer" is not a typo—the word is actually misspelled in the spec. Rails corrects this error by writing "referrer" instead.

the previous URL (in this case, the Home page).[17] This is convenient because microposts appear on both the Home page and the user's profile page, so by using **request.referrer** we arrange to redirect back to the page issuing the delete request in both cases. If the referring URL is **nil** (as is the case inside some tests), Listing 13.54 sets the **root_url** as the default using the **||** operator. (Compare this to the default options defined in Listing 9.24.)

With the code shown in this section, the Home page has working delete links (Figure 13.21), which you can verify by deleting, for example, the second post (Figure 13.22).

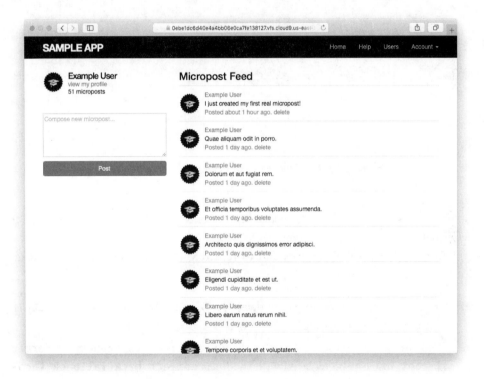

Figure 13.21: The Home page with delete links.

---

17. I didn't remember offhand how to get this URL inside a Rails application, so I Googled "rails request previous url" and found a Stack Overflow thread with the answer.

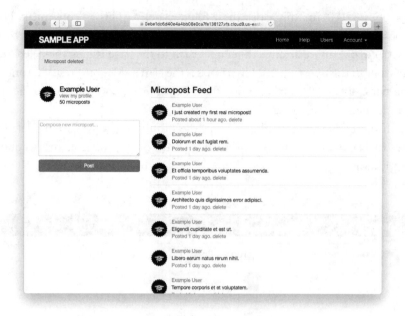

Figure 13.22: The result of deleting the second post.

Exercises

Solutions to the exercises are available to all Rails Tutorial purchasers at https://www.railstutorial.org/aw-solutions.

To see other people's answers and to record your own, subscribe to the Rails Tutorial course or to the Learn Enough All Access Bundle.

1. Create a new micropost and then delete it. What are the contents of the **DELETE** command in the server log?

2. Confirm directly in the browser that the line **redirect_to request.referrer || root_url** can be replaced with the line **redirect_back(fallback_location: root_url)**. (This method was added in Rails 5.)

13.3.5 Micropost Tests

With the code in Section 13.3.4, the Micropost model and interface are complete. All that's left is writing a short Microposts controller test to check authorization and a micropost integration test to tie it all together.

We'll start by adding a few microposts with different owners to the micropost
fixtures, as shown in Listing 13.55. (We'll be using only one for now, but we've put
in the others for future reference.)

Listing 13.55: Adding a micropost with a different owner.
`test/fixtures/microposts.yml`

```
.
.
.
ants:
  content: "Oh, is that what you want? Because that's how you get ants!"
  created_at: <%= 2.years.ago %>
  user: archer

zone:
  content: "Danger zone!"
  created_at: <%= 3.days.ago %>
  user: archer

tone:
  content: "I'm sorry. Your words made sense, but your sarcastic tone did not."
  created_at: <%= 10.minutes.ago %>
  user: lana

van:
  content: "Dude, this van's, like, rolling probable cause."
  created_at: <%= 4.hours.ago %>
  user: lana
```

We next write a short test to make sure one user can't delete the microposts of a
different user, and we also check for the proper redirect, as seen in Listing 13.56.

Listing 13.56: Testing micropost deletion with a user mismatch. GREEN
`test/controllers/microposts_controller_test.rb`

```
require 'test_helper'

class MicropostsControllerTest < ActionDispatch::IntegrationTest

  def setup
    @micropost = microposts(:orange)
  end
```

```ruby
  test "should redirect create when not logged in" do
    assert_no_difference 'Micropost.count' do
      post microposts_path, params: { micropost: { content: "Lorem ipsum" } }
    end
    assert_redirected_to login_url
  end

  test "should redirect destroy when not logged in" do
    assert_no_difference 'Micropost.count' do
      delete micropost_path(@micropost)
    end
    assert_redirected_to login_url
  end

  test "should redirect destroy for wrong micropost" do
    log_in_as(users(:michael))
    micropost = microposts(:ants)
    assert_no_difference 'Micropost.count' do
      delete micropost_path(micropost)
    end
    assert_redirected_to root_url
  end
end
```

Finally, we'll write an integration test to log in, check the micropost pagination, make an invalid submission, make a valid submission, delete a post, and then visit a second user's page to make sure there are no "delete" links. We start by generating a test as usual:

```
$ rails generate integration_test microposts_interface
      invoke  test_unit
      create    test/integration/microposts_interface_test.rb
```

The test appears in Listing 13.57. See if you can connect the lines in Listing 13.12 to the steps just mentioned.

Listing 13.57: An integration test for the micropost interface. GREEN
`test/integration/microposts_interface_test.rb`

```ruby
require 'test_helper'

class MicropostsInterfaceTest < ActionDispatch::IntegrationTest
```

```
  def setup
    @user = users(:michael)
  end

  test "micropost interface" do
    log_in_as(@user)
    get root_path
    assert_select 'div.pagination'
    # Invalid submission
    assert_no_difference 'Micropost.count' do
      post microposts_path, params: { micropost: { content: "" } }
    end
    assert_select 'div#error_explanation'
    assert_select 'a[href=?]', '/?page=2'  # Correct pagination link
    # Valid submission
    content = "This micropost really ties the room together"
    assert_difference 'Micropost.count', 1 do
      post microposts_path, params: { micropost: { content: content } }
    end
    assert_redirected_to root_url
    follow_redirect!
    assert_match content, response.body
    # Delete post
    assert_select 'a', text: 'delete'
    first_micropost = @user.microposts.paginate(page: 1).first
    assert_difference 'Micropost.count', -1 do
      delete micropost_path(first_micropost)
    end
    # Visit different user (no delete links)
    get user_path(users(:archer))
    assert_select 'a', text: 'delete', count: 0
  end
end
```

Because we wrote working application code first, the test suite should be GREEN:

Listing 13.58: GREEN

```
$ rails test
```

Exercises

Solutions to the exercises are available to all Rails Tutorial purchasers at https://www.railstutorial.org/aw-solutions.

To see other people's answers and to record your own, subscribe to the Rails Tutorial course or to the Learn Enough All Access Bundle.

1. For each of the four scenarios indicated by comments in Listing 13.57 (starting with "Invalid submission"), comment out application code to get the corresponding test to RED, then uncomment to get back to GREEN.

2. Add tests for the sidebar micropost count (including proper pluralization). Listing 13.59 will help get you started.

Listing 13.59: A template for the sidebar micropost count test.
`test/integration/microposts_interface_test.rb`

```
require 'test_helper'

class MicropostInterfaceTest < ActionDispatch::IntegrationTest

  def setup
    @user = users(:michael)
  end
  .
  .
  .
  test "micropost sidebar count" do
    log_in_as(@user)
    get root_path
    assert_match "#{FILL_IN} microposts", response.body
    # User with zero microposts
    other_user = users(:malory)
    log_in_as(other_user)
    get root_path
    assert_match "0 microposts", response.body
    other_user.microposts.create!(content: "A micropost")
    get root_path
    assert_match FILL_IN, response.body
  end
end
```

13.4 Micropost Images

Now that we've added support for all relevant micropost actions, in this section we'll make it possible for microposts to include images as well as text. We'll start with a basic version good enough for development use, and then add a series of enhancements to make image upload production-ready.

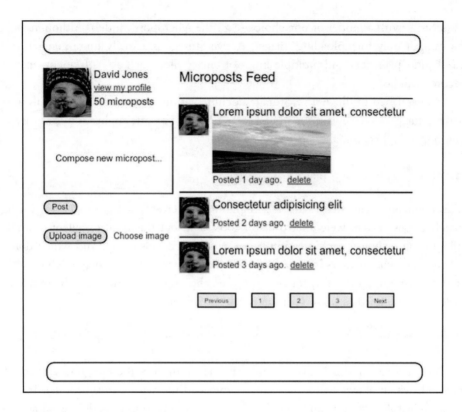

Figure 13.23: A mockup of micropost image upload (with an uploaded image).

Adding image upload involves two main visible elements: a form field for uploading an image and the micropost images themselves. A mockup of the resulting "Upload image" button and micropost photo appears in Figure 13.23.[18]

13.4.1   Basic Image Upload

The most convenient way to upload files in Rails is to use a built-in feature called Active Storage.[19] Active Storage makes it easy to handle an uploaded image and

---

18. Image retrieved from https://www.flickr.com/photos/grungepunk/14026922186 on 2014-09-19. Copyright © 2014 by Jussie D. Brito and used unaltered under the terms of the Creative Commons Attribution-ShareAlike 2.0 Generic license.

19. Active Storage was added in Rails 5.2.

associate it with a model of our choice (e.g., the Micropost model). Although we'll be using it only for uploading images, Active Storage is actually quite general, and can handle plain text and multiple kinds of binary files (such as PDF documents or recorded audio).

As described in the Active Storage documentation (edgeguides.rubyonrails.org/active_storage_overview.html), adding Active Storage to our application is as easy as running a single command:

```
$ rails active_storage:install
```

This command generates a database migration that creates a data model for storing attached files. You're welcome to take a look at it, but this is an excellent example of applying technical sophistication to know which details matter and which don't. In this case, what matters is the API for interacting with Active Storage, which we'll start covering in a moment; for our purposes, the implementation details are safe to ignore. All we need to do to set it up is run the migration:

```
$ rails db:migrate
```

The first part of the Active Storage API that we need is the **has_one_attached** method, which allows us to associate an uploaded file with a given model. In our case, we'll call it **image** and associate it with the Micropost model, as shown in Listing 13.60.

Listing 13.60: Adding an image to the Micropost model.
`app/models/micropost.rb`

```ruby
class Micropost < ApplicationRecord
  belongs_to        :user
  has_one_attached :image
  default_scope -> { order(created_at: :desc) }
  validates :user_id, presence: true
  validates :content, presence: true, length: { maximum: 140 }
end
```

We'll adopt a design of one image per micropost for our application, but Active Storage also offers a second option, **has_many_attached**, which enables multiple files to be attached to a single Active Record object.

To include image upload on the Home page as in Figure 13.23, we need to include a **file_field** tag in the micropost form, as shown in Listing 13.61 and Figure 13.24.

Listing 13.61: Adding image upload to the micropost create form.
`app/views/shared/_micropost_form.html.erb`

```erb
<%= form_with(model: @micropost, local: true) do |f| %>
  <%= render 'shared/error_messages', object: f.object %>
  <div class="field">
    <%= f.text_area :content, placeholder: "Compose new micropost..." %>
  </div>
  <%= f.submit "Post", class: "btn btn-primary" %>
  <span class="image">
    <%= f.file_field :image %>
  </span>
<% end %>
```

Finally, we need to update the Microposts controller to add the image to the newly created micropost object. We can do this using the **attach** method provided by the Active Storage API, which attaches the uploaded image to the **@micropost** object in the Microposts controller's **create** action. To allow the upload to go through, we also need to update the **micropost_params** method to add **:image** to the list of attributes permitted to be modified through the web. The result appears in Listing 13.62.

Listing 13.62: Adding **image** to the list of permitted attributes.
`app/controllers/microposts_controller.rb`

```ruby
class MicropostsController < ApplicationController
  before_action :logged_in_user, only: [:create, :destroy]
  before_action :correct_user,   only: :destroy

  def create
    @micropost = current_user.microposts.build(micropost_params)
    @micropost.image.attach(params[:micropost][:image])
    if @micropost.save
      flash[:success] = "Micropost created!"
      redirect_to root_url
    else
```

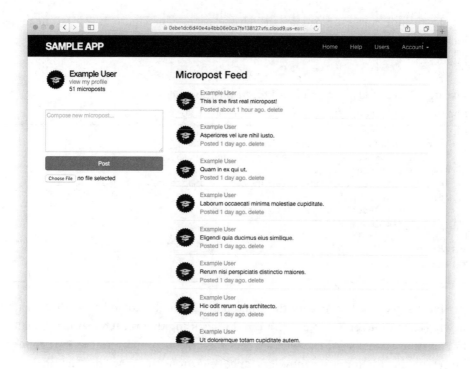

Figure 13.24: Adding an image upload field.

```ruby
    @feed_items = current_user.feed.paginate(page: params[:page])
    render 'static_pages/home'
  end
end

def destroy
  @micropost.destroy
  flash[:success] = "Micropost deleted"
  redirect_to request.referrer || root_url
end

private

  def micropost_params
    params.require(:micropost).permit(:content, :image)
  end
```

```ruby
    def correct_user
      @micropost = current_user.microposts.find_by(id: params[:id])
      redirect_to root_url if @micropost.nil?
    end
end
```

Once the image has been uploaded, we can render the associated **micro-post.image** using the **image_tag** helper in the micropost partial, as shown in Listing 13.63. Notice the use of the **attached?** boolean method to prevent the display of an image tag when there isn't an image.

Listing 13.63: Adding image display to microposts.
`app/views/microposts/_micropost.html.erb`

```erb
<li id="micropost-<%= micropost.id %>">
  <%= link_to gravatar_for(micropost.user, size: 50), micropost.user %>
  <span class="user"><%= link_to micropost.user.name, micropost.user %></span>
  <span class="content">
    <%= micropost.content %>
    <%= image_tag micropost.image if micropost.image.attached? %>
  </span>
  <span class="timestamp">
    Posted <%= time_ago_in_words(micropost.created_at) %> ago.
    <% if current_user?(micropost.user) %>
      <%= link_to "delete", micropost, method: :delete,
                                        data: { confirm: "You sure?" } %>
    <% end %>
  </span>
</li>
```

The result of making a micropost with an image appears in Figure 13.25. I'm always amazed when things like this actually work, but there's the proof! (It's also a good idea to write at least a basic automated test for image upload, which is left as an exercise (Section 13.4.1).)

Exercises

Solutions to the exercises are available to all Rails Tutorial purchasers at https:// www.railstutorial.org/aw-solutions.

To see other people's answers and to record your own, subscribe to the Rails Tutorial course or to the Learn Enough All Access Bundle.

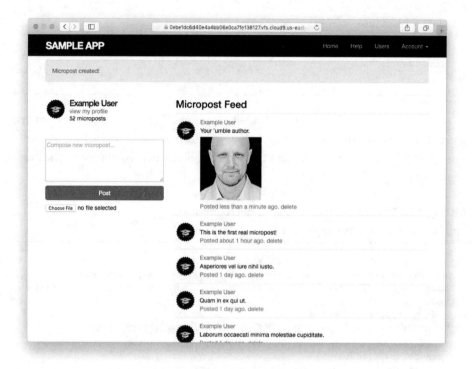

Figure 13.25: The result of submitting a micropost with an image.

1. Upload a micropost with attached image. Does the result look too big? (If so, don't worry; we'll fix it in Section 13.4.3.)

2. Write a test of the image uploader in Section 13.4. As preparation, you should add an image to the fixtures directory using Listing 13.64. The additional assertions in the template in Listing 13.65 check both for a file upload field on the Home page and for a valid image attribute on the micropost resulting from valid submission. Note the use of the special **fixture_file_upload** method for uploading files as fixtures inside tests.[20] *Hint*: To check for a valid **image** attribute, use the **assigns** method mentioned in Section 11.3.3 to access the micropost in the **create** action after valid submission.

---

20. Windows users should add a **:binary** parameter: **fixture_file_upload(file, type, :binary)**.

Listing 13.64: Downloading a fixture image for use in the tests.

```
$ curl -o test/fixtures/kitten.jpg -OL https://cdn.learnenough.com/kitten.jpg
```

Listing 13.65: A template for testing image upload.
test/integration/microposts_interface_test.rb

```ruby
require 'test_helper'

class MicropostInterfaceTest < ActionDispatch::IntegrationTest

  def setup
    @user = users(:michael)
  end

  test "micropost interface" do
    log_in_as(@user)
    get root_path
    assert_select 'div.pagination'
    assert_select 'input[type=FILL_IN]'
    # Invalid submission
    assert_no_difference 'Micropost.count' do
      post microposts_path, params: { micropost: { content: "" } }
    end
    assert_select 'div#error_explanation'
    assert_select 'a[href=?]', '/?page=2'  # Correct pagination link
    # Valid submission
    content = "This micropost really ties the room together"
    image = fixture_file_upload('test/fixtures/kitten.jpg', 'image/jpeg')
    assert_difference 'Micropost.count', 1 do
      post microposts_path, params:  { micropost:
                                        { content: content, image: image } }
    end
    assert FILL_IN.image.attached?
    follow_redirect!
    assert_match content, response.body
    # Delete a post.
    assert_select 'a', text: 'delete'
    first_micropost = @user.microposts.paginate(page: 1).first
    assert_difference 'Micropost.count', -1 do
      delete micropost_path(first_micropost)
    end
    # Visit a different user.
    get user_path(users(:archer))
```

```
    assert_select 'a', { text: 'delete', count: 0 }
  end
  .
  .
  .
end
```

13.4.2 Image Validation

The image upload code in Section 13.4.1 is a good start, but it has significant limitations. Among other things, it doesn't enforce any constraints on the uploaded file, which can cause problems if users try to upload large files or invalid file types. To remedy this defect, we'll add validations for the image size and format.

As of this writing, Active Storage (somewhat surprisingly) doesn't offer native support for things like format and size validations, but as is so often the case there is a gem that adds it for us (Listing 13.66).

Listing 13.66: Adding a gem for Active Storage validations.
`Gemfile`

```
source 'https://rubygems.org'
git_source(:github) { |repo| "https://github.com/#{repo}.git" }

gem 'rails',                    '6.0.2.1'
gem 'active_storage_validations', '0.8.2'
gem 'bcrypt',                    '3.1.13'
  .
  .
  .
```

Then **bundle install**:

```
$ bundle install
```

Following the gem documentation (github.com/igorkasyanchuk/active_storage_validations), we see that we can validate the image format by examining the **content_type** as follows:

```
content_type: { in: %w[image/jpeg image/gif image/png],
                message: "must be a valid image format" }
```

This checks that the MIME type of the image corresponds to a supported image format. (Recall the **%w[]** array-building syntax from Section 6.2.4.)

Similarly, we can validate the file size like this:

```
size: { less_than: 5.megabytes,
        message:   "should be less than 5MB" }
```

This sets a limit of 5 megabytes using a syntax we saw earlier in the context of time helpers (Box 9.1).

Adding these validations to the Micropost model gives the code in Listing 13.67.

Listing 13.67: Adding validations to images.
app/models/micropost.rb

```
class Micropost < ApplicationRecord
  belongs_to      :user
  has_one_attached :image
  default_scope -> { order(created_at: :desc) }
  validates :user_id, presence: true
  validates :content, presence: true, length: { maximum: 140 }
  validates :image,    content_type: { in: %w[image/jpeg image/gif image/png],
                                       message: "must be a valid image format" },
                       size:        { less_than: 5.megabytes,
                                      message:   "should be less than 5MB" }
end
```

The result of trying to upload a large, invalid image then appears as in Figure 13.26. (You may have to restart the Rails server first.)

To go along with the validations in Listing 13.67, we'll add client-side (in-browser) checks on the uploaded image size and format. We'll start by including a little Java-Script (or, more specifically, jQuery) to issue an alert if a user tries to upload an image that's too big (which prevents accidental time-consuming uploads and lightens the load on the server). The result appears in Listing 13.68.[21]

---

21. More advanced users of JavaScript would probably put the size check in its own function, but since this isn't a JavaScript tutorial the code in Listing 13.68 is fine for our purposes.

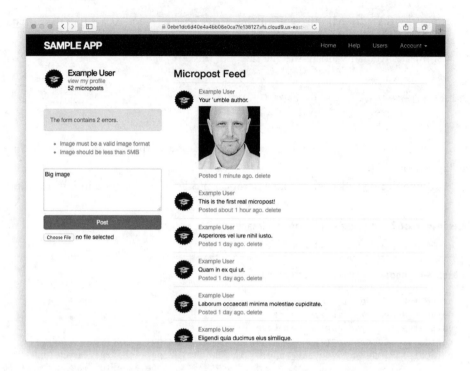

Figure 13.26: Trying to upload a large, invalid image.

Listing 13.68: Checking the file size with jQuery.

`app/views/shared/_micropost_form.html.erb`

```erb
<%= form_with(model: @micropost, local: true) do |f| %>
  <%= render 'shared/error_messages', object: f.object %>
  <div class="field">
    <%= f.text_area :content, placeholder: "Compose new micropost..." %>
  </div>
  <%= f.submit "Post", class: "btn btn-primary" %>
  <span class="image">
    <%= f.file_field :image %>
  </span>
<% end %>

<script type="text/javascript">
  $("#micropost_image").bind("change", function() {
    const size_in_megabytes = this.files[0].size/1024/1024;
```

```
    if (size_in_megabytes > 5) {
      alert("Maximum file size is 5MB. Please choose a smaller file.");
      $("#micropost_image").val("");
    }
  });
</script>
```

Although JavaScript isn't the focus of this book, you might be able to figure out that Listing 13.68 monitors the page element containing the CSS id **micropost_image** (as indicated by the hash mark **#**), which is the id of the micropost form in Listing 13.61. (The way to figure this out is to Ctrl-click and use your browser's web inspector.) When the element with that CSS id changes, the jQuery function fires and issues the **alert** method if the file is too big, as seen in Figure 13.27.[22]

Finally, by using the **accept** parameter in the **file_field** input tag, we can specify that only valid formats should be allowed (Listing 13.69).

Listing 13.69: Allowing only valid image formats.
app/views/shared/_micropost_form.html.erb

```
<%= form_with(model: @micropost, local: true) do |f| %>
  <%= render 'shared/error_messages', object: f.object %>
  <div class="field">
    <%= f.text_area :content, placeholder: "Compose new micropost..." %>
  </div>
  <%= f.submit "Post", class: "btn btn-primary" %>
  <span class="image">
    <%= f.file_field :image, accept: "image/jpeg,image/gif,image/png" %>
  </span>
<% end %>

<script type="text/javascript">
  $("#micropost_image").bind("change", function() {
    var size_in_megabytes = this.files[0].size/1024/1024;
    if (size_in_megabytes > 5) {
      alert("Maximum file size is 5MB. Please choose a smaller file.");
      $("#micropost_image").val("");
    }
  });
</script>
```

---

22. To learn how to do things like this, you can do what I did: Google for things like "javascript maximum file size" until you find something on Stack Overflow.

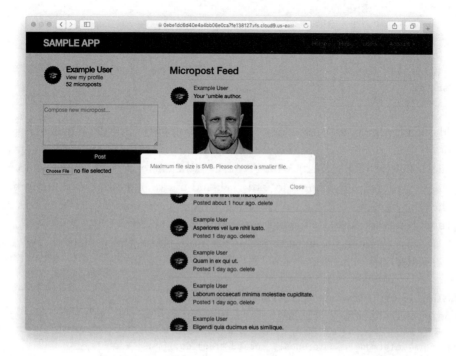

Figure 13.27: A JavaScript alert for a large file.

Listing 13.69 arranges to allow only valid image types to be selected in the first place, graying out any other file types (Figure 13.28).

Preventing invalid images from being uploaded in a browser is a nice touch, but it's important to understand that this sort of code can only make it *difficult* to upload an invalid format or large file; a user determined to upload an invalid file can always issue a direct POST request using, for example, **curl**. It is thus essential to include server-side validations of the type shown in Listing 13.67.

Exercises

Solutions to the exercises are available to all Rails Tutorial purchasers at https://www.railstutorial.org/aw-solutions.

To see other people's answers and to record your own, subscribe to the Rails Tutorial course or to the Learn Enough All Access Bundle.

Figure 13.28: Grayed-out invalid file types.

1. What happens if you try uploading an image bigger than 5 megabytes?
2. What happens if you try uploading a file with an invalid extension?

13.4.3 Image Resizing

The image size validations in Section 13.4.2 are a good start, but they still allow the uploading of images large enough to break our site's layout, sometimes with frightening results (Figure 13.29). Thus, while it's convenient to allow users to select fairly large images from their local disk, it's also a good idea to resize the images before displaying them.[23]

---

23. It's possible to constrain the *display* size with CSS, but this doesn't change the image size. In particular, large images would still take a while to load. (You've probably visited websites where "small" images seemingly take forever to load. This is why.)

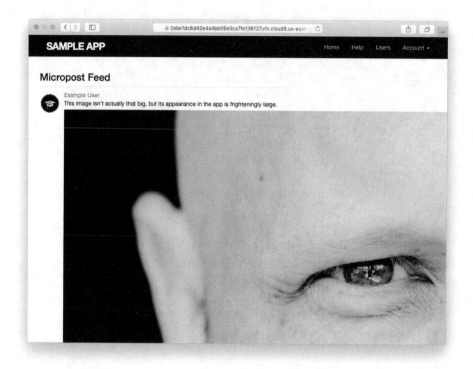

Figure 13.29: A frighteningly large uploaded image.

We'll be resizing images using the image manipulation program ImageMagick, which we need to install on the development environment. (As we'll see in Section 13.4.4, when we use Heroku for deployment, ImageMagick comes pre-installed in production.) On the cloud IDE, we can do this as follows:

```
$ sudo apt-get -y install imagemagick
```

(If you're not using the cloud IDE or an equivalent Linux system, do a Google search for "imagemagick <your platform>." On macOS, **brew install imagemagick** should work if you have Homebrew installed. Use your technical sophistication (Box 1.2) if you get stuck.)

Next, we need to add a couple of gems for image processing, including the aptly named `image_processing` gem and `mini_magick`, a Ruby processor for ImageMagick (Listing 13.70).

Listing 13.70: Adding gems for image processing.
`Gemfile`

```
source 'https://rubygems.org'
git_source(:github) { |repo| "https://github.com/#{repo}.git" }

gem 'rails',                    '6.0.2.1'
gem 'image_processing',         '1.9.3'
gem 'mini_magick',              '4.9.5'
gem 'active_storage_validations', '0.8.2'
  .
  .
  .
```

Then install as usual:

```
$ bundle install
```

You will probably need to restart the Rails server as well.

With the necessary software installed, we're now ready to use the **variant** method supplied by Active Storage for creating transformed images. In particular, we'll use the **resize_to_limit** option to ensure that neither the width nor the height of the image is greater than 500 pixels, as follows:

```
image.variant(resize_to_limit: [500, 500])
```

For convenience, we'll put this code in a separate **display_image** method, as shown in Listing 13.71.

Listing 13.71: Adding a resized display image.
`app/models/micropost.rb`

```
class Micropost < ApplicationRecord
  belongs_to        :user
  has_one_attached :image
  default_scope -> { order(created_at: :desc) }
  validates :user_id, presence: true
  validates :content, presence: true, length: { maximum: 140 }
  validates :image,   content_type: { in: %w[image/jpeg image/gif image/png],
                                       message: "must be a valid image format" },
                      size: { less_than: 5.megabytes,
                              message:    "should be less than 5MB" }
```

```
# Returns a resized image for display.
def display_image
    image.variant(resize_to_limit: [500, 500])
  end
end
```

Finally, we can use **display_image** in the micropost partial, as shown in Listing 13.72.

Listing 13.72: Using the resized **display_image**.
`app/views/microposts/_micropost.html.erb`

```erb
<li id="micropost-<%= micropost.id %>">
  <%= link_to gravatar_for(micropost.user, size: 50), micropost.user %>
  <span class="user"><%= link_to micropost.user.name, micropost.user %></span>
  <span class="content">
    <%= micropost.content %>
    <%= image_tag micropost.display_image if micropost.image.attached? %>
  </span>
  <span class="timestamp">
    Posted <%= time_ago_in_words(micropost.created_at) %> ago.
    <% if current_user?(micropost.user) %>
      <%= link_to "delete", micropost, method: :delete,
                                        data: { confirm: "You sure?" } %>
    <% end %>
  </span>
</li>
```

The **variant** resizing in Listing 13.71 will happen on demand when the method is first called in Listing 13.72, and will be cached for efficiency in subsequent uses.[24] The result is a properly resized display image, as seen in Figure 13.30.

Exercise

Solutions to the exercises are available to all Rails Tutorial purchasers at https:// www.railstutorial.org/aw-solutions.

---

24. For larger sites, it's probably better to defer such processing to a background process. This method is beyond the scope of this tutorial, but investigating Active Job will get you started if you need to go this route.

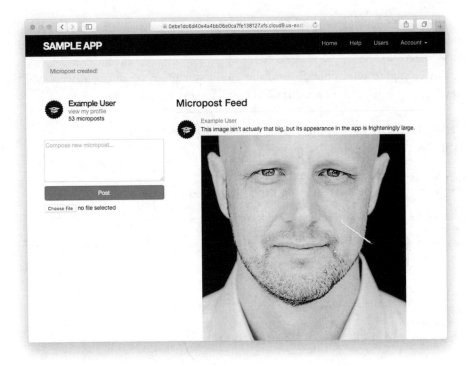

Figure 13.30: A nicely resized image.

To see other people's answers and to record your own, subscribe to the Rails Tutorial course or to the Learn Enough All Access Bundle.

1. Upload a large image and confirm directly that the resizing is working. Does the resizing work even if the image isn't square?

13.4.4 Image Upload in Production

The image uploading developed in Section 13.4.3 is good enough for development, but (as seen later in Listing 13.74) it uses the local disk for storing the images, which isn't a good practice in production. (Among other things, file storage on Heroku is temporary, so uploaded images will be deleted every time you deploy.) Instead, we'll use a cloud storage service to store images separately from our application.

There are many choices for cloud storage, but we'll use one of the most popular and well supported, Amazon.com's Simple Storage Service (S3), part of Amazon Web Services (AWS).[25]

To configure our application to use cloud storage in production, we'll add the `aws-sdk-s3` gem to the **:production** environment, as shown in Listing 13.73.

Listing 13.73: Adding a gem for Amazon Web Services (AWS).
`Gemfile`

```
source 'https://rubygems.org'
git_source(:github) { |repo| "https://github.com/#{repo}.git" }

gem 'rails',                      '6.0.2.1'
gem 'image_processing',           '1.9.3'
gem 'mini_magick',                '4.9.5'
gem 'active_storage_validations', '0.8.2'
 .
 .
 .
group :production do
  gem 'pg',           '1.1.4'
  gem 'aws-sdk-s3', '1.46.0', require: false
end
 .
 .
 .
```

Then **bundle** one more time:

```
$ bundle install
```

AWS Configuration

At this point, you'll need to configure your AWS system to use S3. Here are the basic steps:[26]

---

25. S3 is a paid service, but the storage needed to set up and test the Rails Tutorial sample application costs less than a cent per month.

26. The steps are current as of this writing, but services like AWS are constantly evolving, so the user interface may have changed in the interim. Use your technical sophistication to resolve any discrepancies.

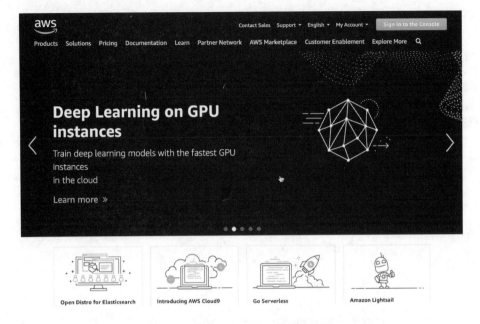

Figure 13.31: Signing up for AWS.

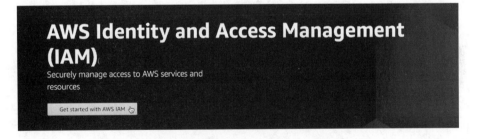

Figure 13.32: The AWS IAM interface.

1. Sign up for an Amazon Web Services account if you don't have one already (Figure 13.31). (If you signed up for the Cloud9 IDE in Section 1.1.1, you already have an AWS account and can skip this step.)

2. Create a user via AWS Identity and Access Management (IAM). This involves using the IAM users interface (Figure 13.32) to navigate to the "Add user" page (Figure 13.33), where you should create a user while enabling "programmatic

Identity and Access Management (IAM)

▼ **AWS Account (178692450841)**

Dashboard

Groups

Users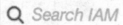

Roles

Policies

Identity providers

Account settings

Credential report

Q *Search IAM*

▼ **AWS Organizations**

Organization activity

Service control policies (SCPs)

Figure 13.33: Navigating to the "Add user" page.

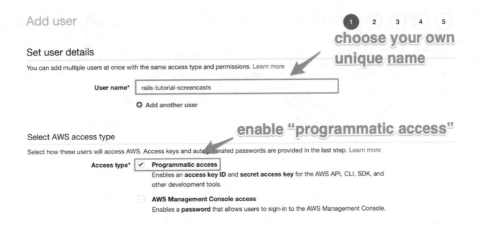

Figure 13.34: Creating a user with "programmatic access."

Figure 13.35: Granting the user administrator access.

access" (Figure 13.34), grant the user administrator access (Figure 13.35), and then skip the optional user tags (Figure 13.36).

3. After clicking "Create user," you should see the name of the user together with the access key ID and the secret access key (Figure 13.37). Copy these keys and store them someplace safe.

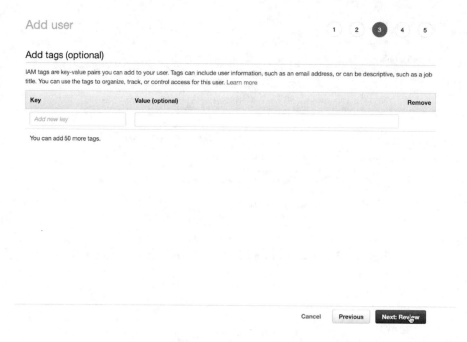

Figure 13.36: Skipping optional user tags.

Figure 13.37: Displaying the access key ID and the secret access key.

4. Create an S3 bucket using the AWS Console (Figure 13.38). S3 buckets exist in a global namespace, so the name has to be unique, but otherwise the default bucket settings should be fine.

You may find setting up S3 to be a challenging exercise in technical sophistication (Box 1.2). For further details on the steps presented here, consult the S3 documentation (aws.amazon.com/documentation/s3), the article "Setting up Rails 5 [or Higher] with Active Storage with Amazon S3" (medium.com/alturasoluciones/setting-up-rails-5-active-storage-with-amazon-s3-3d158cf021ff), and, if necessary, Google or Stack Overflow.

S3 buckets   ◻ Discover the console

| Q Search for buckets | All access types ⌄ |

+ Create bucket   Edit public access settings   Empty   Delete   **0** Buckets   **0** Regions   ⟳

You do not have any buckets. Here is how to get started with Amazon S3.

Figure 13.38: Creating an AWS bucket.

Figure 13.39: Getting the AWS region from the S3 console URL.

Production AWS

As with production email configuration (Listing 11.41), we'll be using Heroku **ENV**
variables to avoid hard-coding sensitive information like AWS keys. In Section 11.4
and Section 12.4, these variables were defined automatically via the SendGrid add-on,
but in this case we need to define them explicitly. Per the gem configuration documentation (github.com/aws/aws-sdk-ruby#configuration), these variables should be
named using the prefix **AWS**, which we can accomplish using **heroku config:set** as
follows:

```
$ heroku config:set AWS_ACCESS_KEY_ID=<access key>
$ heroku config:set AWS_SECRET_ACCESS_KEY=<secret key>
$ heroku config:set AWS_REGION=<region>
$ heroku config:set AWS_BUCKET=<bucket name>
```

You should paste in the values for your configuration in place of the placeholder
values shown here. To get the region, you can inspect the URL on the S3 console
page (Figure 13.39).

Once the Heroku variables are set, the next step is to use them in a special YAML
file for configuring storage options called **storage.yml**. We can create a storage
option for Amazon using the code in Listing 13.74.

Listing 13.74: Adding Amazon AWS as a storage option.
`config/storage.yml`

```
test:
  service: Disk
  root: <%= Rails.root.join("tmp/storage") %>

local:
  service: Disk
  root: <%= Rails.root.join("storage") %>

amazon:
  service: S3
  access_key_id:     <%= ENV['AWS_ACCESS_KEY_ID'] %>
  secret_access_key: <%= ENV['AWS_SECRET_ACCESS_KEY'] %>
  region:            <%= ENV['AWS_REGION'] %>
  bucket:            <%= ENV['AWS_BUCKET'] %>
```

Finally, we can put the option defined in Listing 13.74 to use in a production environment by adding the Active Storage service configuration parameter in **production.rb**. The result appears in Listing 13.75.

Listing 13.75: Configuring the production environment to use Amazon AWS (S3).
`config/environments/production.rb`

```
Rails.application.configure do
  .
  .
  .
  # Store uploaded files on Amazon AWS.
  config.active_storage.service = :amazon
  .
  .
  .
end
```

With this configuration, we are ready to commit our changes and deploy:

```
$ rails test
$ git add -A
$ git commit -m "Add user microposts"
```

Because so many things can go wrong with the configuration, we'll deploy the app directly from our current topic branch, making sure it's working before merging into

master. We can do this by including the branch name in the push to Heroku as follows:

```
$ git push heroku user-microposts:master
```

As usual, we then reset the database and reseed the sample data:

```
$ heroku pg:reset DATABASE
$ heroku run rails db:migrate
$ heroku run rails db:seed
```

Because Heroku comes with ImageMagick already installed, the result is successful image resizing and upload in production, as seen in Figure 13.40.

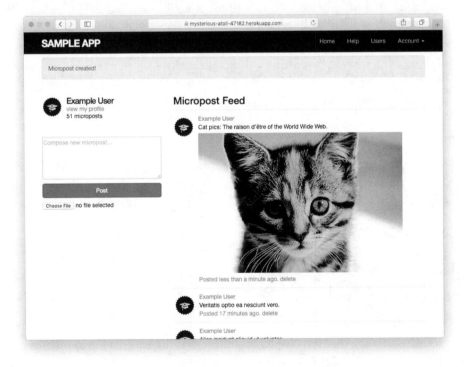

Figure 13.40: An uploaded image in production.

Exercise

Solutions to the exercises are available to all Rails Tutorial purchasers at https://www.railstutorial.org/aw-solutions.

To see other people's answers and to record your own, subscribe to the Rails Tutorial course or to the Learn Enough All Access Bundle.

1. Upload a large image and confirm directly that the resizing is working in production. Does the resizing work even if the image isn't square?

13.5 Conclusion

With the addition of the Microposts resource, we are nearly finished with our sample application. All that remains is to add a social layer by letting users follow each other. We'll learn how to model such user relationships, and see the implications for the microposts feed, in Chapter 14.

If you skipped Section 13.4.4, be sure to commit your changes:

```
$ rails test
$ git add -A
$ git commit -m "Add user microposts"
```

Then merge into **master**:

```
$ git checkout master
$ git merge user-microposts
$ git push
```

And finally deploy to production:

```
$ git push heroku
$ heroku pg:reset DATABASE
$ heroku run rails db:migrate
$ heroku run rails db:seed
```

It's worth noting that this chapter saw the last of the necessary gem installations. For reference, the final **Gemfile** is shown in Listing 13.76.[27]

---

27. As always, you should use the version numbers listed at gemfiles-6th-ed.railstutorial.org instead of the ones listed here.

Listing 13.76: The final **Gemfile** for the sample application.

```
source 'https://rubygems.org'
git_source(:github) { |repo| "https://github.com/#{repo}.git" }

gem 'rails',                        '6.0.2.1'
gem 'image_processing',             '1.9.3'
gem 'mini_magick',                  '4.9.5'
gem 'active_storage_validations',   '0.8.2'
gem 'bcrypt',                       '3.1.13'
gem 'faker',                        '2.1.2'
gem 'will_paginate',                '3.1.8'
gem 'bootstrap-will_paginate',      '1.0.0'
gem 'bootstrap-sass',               '3.4.1'
gem 'puma',                         '3.12.2'
gem 'sass-rails',                   '5.1.0'
gem 'webpacker',                    '4.0.7'
gem 'turbolinks',                   '5.2.0'
gem 'jbuilder',                     '2.9.1'
gem 'bootsnap',                     '1.4.5', require: false

group :development, :test do
  gem 'sqlite3', '1.4.1'
  gem 'byebug',  '11.0.1', platforms: [:mri, :mingw, :x64_mingw]
end

group :development do
  gem 'web-console',          '4.0.1'
  gem 'listen',               '3.1.5'
  gem 'spring',               '2.1.0'
  gem 'spring-watcher-listen', '2.0.1'
end

group :test do
  gem 'capybara',                 '3.28.0'
  gem 'selenium-webdriver',       '3.142.4'
  gem 'webdrivers',               '4.1.2'
  gem 'rails-controller-testing', '1.0.4'
  gem 'minitest',                 '5.11.3'
  gem 'minitest-reporters',       '1.3.8'
  gem 'guard',                    '2.15.0'
  gem 'guard-minitest',           '2.4.6'
end

group :production do
  gem 'pg',           '1.1.4'
```

```
  gem 'aws-sdk-s3', '1.46.0', require: false
end

# Windows does not include zoneinfo files, so bundle the tzinfo-data gem
gem 'tzinfo-data', platforms: [:mingw, :mswin, :x64_mingw, :jruby]
```

13.5.1 What We Learned in this Chapter

- Microposts, like Users, are modeled as a resource backed by an Active Record model.

- Rails supports multiple-key indices.

- We can model a user having many microposts using the **has_many** and **belongs_to** methods in the User and Micropost models, respectively.

- The **has_many**/**belongs_to** combination gives rise to methods that work through the association.

- The code **user.microposts.build(...)** returns a new Micropost object automatically associated with the given user.

- Rails supports default ordering via **default_scope**.

- Scopes take anonymous functions as arguments.

- The **dependent: :destroy** option causes objects to be destroyed at the same time as associated objects.

- Pagination and object counts can both be performed through associations, leading to automatically efficient code.

- Fixtures support the creation of associations.

- It is possible to pass variables to Rails partials.

- The **where** method can be used to perform Active Record selections.

- We can enforce secure operations by always creating and destroying dependent objects through their association.

- We can upload images using Active Storage.

CHAPTER 14
Following Users

In this chapter, we will complete the Rails Tutorial sample application by adding a social layer that allows users to follow (and unfollow) other users, resulting in each user's Home page displaying a status feed of the followed users' microposts. We'll start by learning how to model relationships between users in Section 14.1, and we'll build the corresponding web interface in Section 14.2 (including an introduction to Ajax). We'll end by developing a fully functional status feed in Section 14.3.

This final chapter contains some of the most challenging material in the tutorial, including some Ruby/SQL trickery to make the status feed. Through these examples, you will see how Rails can handle even rather intricate data models, which should serve you well as you go on to develop your own applications with their own specific requirements. To help with the transition from tutorial to independent development, Section 14.4 offers some pointers to more advanced resources.

Because the material in this chapter is particularly challenging, before writing any code we'll pause for a moment and take a tour of the interface. As in previous chapters, at this early stage we'll represent pages using mockups.[1] The full page flow runs as follows: A user (John Calvin) starts at his profile page (Figure 14.1) and navigates to the Users page (Figure 14.2) to select a user to follow. Calvin navigates to the profile of a second user, Thomas Hobbes (Figure 14.3), clicking on the "Follow" button to follow

---

[1]. Image of child retrieved from https://www.flickr.com/photos/john_lustig/2518452221/ on 2013-12-16. Copyright © 2008 by John Lustig and used unaltered under the terms of the Creative Commons Attribution 2.0 Generic license. Image of tiger retrieved from https://www.flickr.com/photos/renemensen/9187111340 on 2014-08-15. Copyright © 2013 by Rene Mesen and used unaltered under the terms of the Creative Commons Attribution 2.0 Generic license.

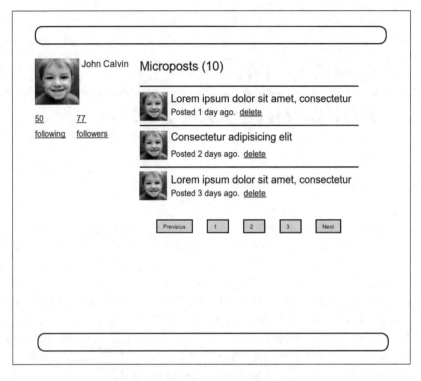

Figure 14.1: A current user's profile.

that user. This changes the "Follow" button to "Unfollow" and increments Hobbes's "followers" count by one (Figure 14.4). Navigating to his home page, Calvin now sees an incremented "following" count and finds Hobbes's microposts in his status feed (Figure 14.5). The rest of this chapter is dedicated to making this page flow actually work.

14.1 The Relationship Model

Our first step in implementing following users is to construct a data model, which is not as straightforward as it seems. Naïvely, it seems that a **has_many** relationship would do: A user **has_many** followed users and **has_many** followers. As we will see, there is a problem with this approach, and we'll learn how to fix it using **has_many :through**.

Figure 14.2: Finding a user to follow.

As usual, Git users should create a new topic branch:

```
$ git checkout -b following-users
```

14.1.1   A Problem with the Data Model (and a Solution)

As a first step toward constructing a data model for following users, let's examine a typical case. For instance, consider a user who follows a second user: We could say that, for example, Calvin is following Hobbes, and Hobbes is followed by Calvin, so that Calvin is the *follower* and Hobbes is *followed*. Using Rails' default pluralization convention, the set of all users following a given user is that user's *followers*, and **hobbes.followers** is an array of those users. Unfortunately, the reverse doesn't

Figure 14.3: The profile of a user to follow, with a Follow button.

work: By default, the set of all followed users would be called the *followeds*, which is ungrammatical and clumsy. We'll adopt Twitter's convention and call them *following* (as in "50 following, 75 followers"), with a corresponding **calvin.following** array.

This discussion suggests modeling the followed users as in Figure 14.6, with a **following** table and a **has_many** association. Since **user.following** should be a collection of users, each row of the **following** table would need to be a user, as identified by the **followed_id**, together with the **follower_id** to establish the association.[2] In addition, since each row is a user, we would need to include the user's other attributes, including the name, email, password, and so forth.

---

2. For simplicity, Figure 14.6 omits the **following** table's **id** column.

Figure 14.4: A profile with an Unfollow button and incremented followers count.

The problem with the data model in Figure 14.6 is that it is terribly redundant: Each row contains not only each followed user's id, but all their other information as well—all of which is *already* in the **users** table. Even worse, to model user *followers* we would need a separate, similarly redundant **followers** table. Finally, this data model is a maintainability nightmare: Each time a user changed (say) their name, we would need to update not just the user's record in the **users** table but also *every row containing that user* in both the **following** and **followers** tables.

The problem here is that we are missing an underlying abstraction. One way to find the proper model is to consider how we might implement the act of *following* in a web application. Recall from Section 7.1.2 that the REST architecture involves *resources* that are created and destroyed. This leads us to ask two questions: When a user follows another user, what is being created? When a user *un*follows another user,

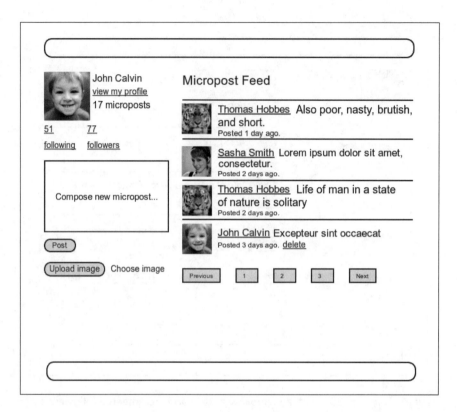

Figure 14.5: The Home page with status feed and incremented following count.

user		
id	**name**	**email**
1	Michael Hartl	mhartl@example.com

has_many

following			
follower_id	**followed_id**	**name**	**email**
1	2	...	...
1	7	...	...
1	10	...	...
1	8	...	...

Figure 14.6: A naïve implementation of user following.

what is being destroyed? Upon reflection, we see that in these cases the application should either create or destroy a *relationship* between two users. A user then has many relationships, and has many **following** (or **followers**) *through* these relationships.

There's an additional detail we need to address regarding our application's data model: Unlike symmetric Facebook-style friendships, which are always reciprocal (at least at the data-model level), Twitter-style following relationships are potentially *asymmetric*—Calvin can follow Hobbes without Hobbes following Calvin. To distinguish between these two cases, we'll adopt the terminology of *active* and *passive* relationships: If Calvin is following Hobbes but not vice versa, Calvin has an active relationship with Hobbes and Hobbes has a passive relationship with Calvin.[3]

We'll focus now on using active relationships to generate a list of followed users, and consider the passive case in Section 14.1.5. Figure 14.6 suggests how to implement it: Since each followed user is uniquely identified by **followed_id**, we could convert **following** to an **active_relationships** table, omit the user details, and use **followed_id** to retrieve the followed user from the **users** table. A diagram of the data model appears in Figure 14.7.

Because we'll end up using the same database table for both active and passive relationships, we'll use the generic term *relationship* for the table name, with a corresponding Relationship model. The result is the Relationship data model shown in

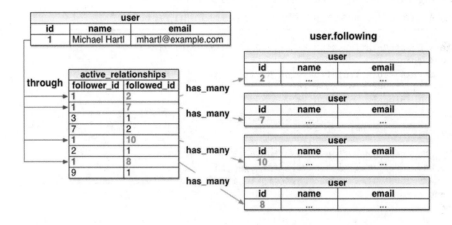

Figure 14.7: A model of followed users through active relationships.

---

3. Thanks to reader Paul Fioravanti for suggesting this terminology.

relationships	
id	integer
follower_id	integer
followed_id	integer
created_at	datetime
updated_at	datetime

Figure 14.8: The Relationship data model.

Figure 14.8. We'll see starting in Section 14.1.4 how to use the Relationship model to simulate both Active Relationship and Passive Relationship models.

To get started with the implementation, we first generate a migration corresponding to Figure 14.8:

```
$ rails generate model Relationship follower_id:integer followed_id:integer
```

Because we will be finding relationships by **follower_id** and by **followed_id**, we should add an index on each column for efficiency, as shown in Listing 14.1.

Listing 14.1: Adding indices for the **relationships** table.
db/migrate/[timestamp]_create_relationships.rb

```
class CreateRelationships < ActiveRecord::Migration[6.0]
  def change
    create_table :relationships do |t|
      t.integer :follower_id
      t.integer :followed_id

      t.timestamps
    end
    add_index :relationships, :follower_id
    add_index :relationships, :followed_id
    add_index :relationships, [:follower_id, :followed_id], unique: true
  end
end
```

Listing 14.1 also includes a multiple-key index that enforces uniqueness on (**follower_id**, **followed_id**) pairs, so that a user can't follow another user more than once. (Compare this to the email uniqueness index from Listing 6.29 and the multiple-key index in Listing 13.3.) As we'll see starting in Section 14.1.4, our user interface won't allow this to happen, but adding a unique index arranges to raise an error if a user tries to create duplicate relationships anyway (for example, by using a command-line tool such as **curl**).

To create the **relationships** table, we migrate the database as usual:

```
$ rails db:migrate
```

Exercises

Solutions to the exercises are available to all Rails Tutorial purchasers at https://www.railstutorial.org/aw-solutions.

To see other people's answers and to record your own, subscribe to the Rails Tutorial course or to the Learn Enough All Access Bundle.

1. For the user with id equal to **1** from Figure 14.7, what would the value of **user.following.map(&:id)** be? (Recall the **map(&:method_name)** pattern from Section 4.3.2; **user.following.map(&:id)** just returns the array of ids.)

2. By referring again to Figure 14.7, determine the ids of **user.following** for the user with id equal to **2**. What would the value of **user.following.map(&:id)** be for this user?

14.1.2 User/Relationship Associations

Before implementing user following and followers, we first need to establish the association between users and relationships. A user **has_many** relationships, and—since relationships involve *two* users—a relationship **belongs_to** both a follower and a followed user.

As with the microposts introduced in Section 13.1.3, we will create new relationships using the user association, with code such as

```
user.active_relationships.build(followed_id: ...)
```

At this point, you might expect application code as in Section 13.1.3. It's certainly similar, but there are two key differences.

First, in the case of the user/micropost association we could write

```
class User < ApplicationRecord
  has_many :microposts
  .
  .
  .
end
```

This works because by convention Rails looks for a Micropost model corresponding to the `:microposts` symbol.[4] In the present case, though, we want to write

```
has_many :active_relationships
```

even though the underlying model is called Relationship. We will thus have to tell Rails the model class name to look for.

Second, we wrote

```
class Micropost < ApplicationRecord
  belongs_to :user
  .
  .
  .
end
```

in the Micropost model. This works because the **microposts** table has a **user_id** attribute to identify the user (Section 13.1.1). An id used in this manner to connect two database tables is known as a *foreign key*. When the foreign key for a User model object is **user_id**, Rails infers the association automatically: By default, Rails expects a foreign key of the form **<class>_id**, where **<class>** is the lower-case version of the class name.[5] In the present case, although we are still dealing with users, the user following another user is now identified with the foreign key **follower_id**, so we have to tell that to Rails.

The result of this discussion is the user/relationship association shown in Listing 14.2 and Listing 14.3. As noted in the captions, the tests are currently RED (Why?);[6] we'll fix this issue in Section 14.1.3.

---

4. Technically, Rails converts the argument of **has_many** to a class name using the **classify** method, which converts **"foo_bars"** to **"FooBar"**.

5. Technically, Rails uses the **underscore** method to convert the class name to an id. For example, **"FooBar".underscore** is **"foo_bar"**, so the foreign key for a **FooBar** object would be **foo_bar_id**.

6. *Answer*: As in Listing 6.30, the generated fixtures don't satisfy the validations, which causes the tests to fail.

Listing 14.2: Implementing the active relationships **has_many** association. RED
app/models/user.rb

```
class User < ApplicationRecord
  has_many :microposts, dependent: :destroy
  has_many :active_relationships, class_name:  "Relationship",
                                  foreign_key: "follower_id",
                                  dependent:   :destroy
  .
  .
  .
end
```

(Since destroying a user should also destroy that user's relationships, we've added **dependent: :destroy** to the association.)

Listing 14.3: Adding the follower **belongs_to** association to the Relationship model.
RED
app/models/relationship.rb

```
class Relationship < ApplicationRecord
  belongs_to :follower, class_name: "User"
  belongs_to :followed, class_name: "User"
end
```

The **followed** association isn't actually needed until Section 14.1.4, but the parallel follower/followed structure is clearer if we implement them both at the same time.

The relationships in Listing 14.2 and Listing 14.3 give rise to methods analogous to the ones we saw in Table 13.1, as shown in Table 14.1.

Exercises

Solutions to the exercises are available to all Rails Tutorial purchasers at https://www.railstutorial.org/aw-solutions.

To see other people's answers and to record your own, subscribe to the Rails Tutorial course or to the Learn Enough All Access Bundle.

1. Using the **create** method from Table 14.1 in the console, create an active relationship for the first user in the database where the followed id is the second user.

Table 14.1: A summary of user/active relationship association methods.

Method	Purpose
`active_relationship.follower`	Returns the follower
`active_relationship.followed`	Returns the followed user
`user.active_relationships.create` `(followed_id: other_user.id)`	Creates an active relationship associated with **user**
`user.active_relationships.create!` `(followed_id: other_user.id)`	Creates an active relationship associated with **user** (exception on failure)
`user.active_relationships.build` `(followed_id: other_user.id)`	Returns a new Relationship object associated with **user**

2. Confirm that the values for **active_relationship.followed** and **active_re-lationship.follower** are correct.

14.1.3 Relationship Validations

Before moving on, we'll add a couple of Relationship model validations for completeness. The tests (Listing 14.4) and application code (Listing 14.5) are straightforward. As with the generated user fixture from Listing 6.30, the generated relationship fixture also violates the uniqueness constraint imposed by the corresponding migration (Listing 14.1). The solution—removing the fixture contents as in Listing 6.31—is also the same, as seen in Listing 14.6.

Listing 14.4: Testing the Relationship model validations. RED
test/models/relationship_test.rb

```
require 'test_helper'

class RelationshipTest < ActiveSupport::TestCase

  def setup
    @relationship = Relationship.new(follower_id: users(:michael).id,
                                     followed_id: users(:archer).id)
  end

  test "should be valid" do
    assert @relationship.valid?
  end
```

```
  test "should require a follower_id" do
    @relationship.follower_id = nil
    assert_not @relationship.valid?
  end

  test "should require a followed_id" do
    @relationship.followed_id = nil
    assert_not @relationship.valid?
  end
end
```

Listing 14.5: Adding the Relationship model validations. RED
app/models/relationship.rb

```
class Relationship < ApplicationRecord
  belongs_to :follower, class_name: "User"
  belongs_to :followed, class_name: "User"
  validates :follower_id, presence: true
  validates :followed_id, presence: true
end
```

Listing 14.6: Removing the contents of the relationship fixture. GREEN
test/fixtures/relationships.yml

```
# empty
```

At this point, the tests should be GREEN:

Listing 14.7: GREEN

```
$ rails test
```

Exercise

Solutions to the exercises are available to all Rails Tutorial purchasers at https://www.railstutorial.org/aw-solutions.

To see other people's answers and to record your own, subscribe to the Rails Tutorial course or to the Learn Enough All Access Bundle.

1. Verify by commenting out the validations in Listing 14.5 that the tests still pass. (This is a change as of Rails 5, and in previous versions of Rails the validations are required. We'll plan to leave them in for completeness, but it's worth bearing in mind that you may see these validations omitted in other people's code.)

14.1.4 Followed Users

We come now to the heart of the Relationship associations: **following** and **followers**. Here we will use **has_many :through** for the first time: A user has many following *through* relationships, as illustrated in Figure 14.7. By default, in a **has_many :through** association Rails looks for a foreign key corresponding to the singular version of the association. In other words, with code like

```
has_many :followeds, through: :active_relationships
```

Rails would see "followeds" and use the singular "followed," assembling a collection using the **followed_id** in the **relationships** table. But, as noted in Section 14.1.1, **user.followeds** is rather awkward, so we'll write **user.following** instead. Naturally, Rails allows us to override the default, in this case using the **source** parameter (as shown in Listing 14.8), which explicitly tells Rails that the source of the **following** array is the set of **followed** ids.

Listing 14.8: Adding the User model **following** association.
app/models/user.rb

```
class User < ApplicationRecord
  has_many :microposts, dependent: :destroy
  has_many :active_relationships, class_name:  "Relationship",
                                  foreign_key: "follower_id",
                                  dependent:   :destroy
  has_many :following, through: :active_relationships, source: :followed
  .
  .
  .
end
```

The association defined in Listing 14.8 leads to a powerful combination of Active Record and array-like behavior. For example, we can check if the followed users collection includes another user with the **include?** method (Section 4.3.1), and we can find objects through the association:

```
user.following.include?(other_user)
user.following.find(other_user)
```

We can also add and delete elements just as with arrays:

```
user.following << other_user
user.following.delete(other_user)
```

(Recall from Section 4.3.1 that the shovel operator **<<** appends an element to the end of an array.)

Although in many contexts we can effectively treat **following** as an array, Rails is smart about how it handles things under the hood. For example, code like

```
following.include?(other_user)
```

looks like it might have to pull all the followed users out of the database to apply the **include?** method, but in fact for efficiency Rails arranges for the comparison to happen directly in the database. (Compare this behavior to the code in Section 13.2.1, where we saw that

```
user.microposts.count
```

performs the count directly in the database.)

To manipulate following relationships, we'll introduce **follow** and **unfollow** utility methods so that we can write, for example, **user.follow(other_user)**. We'll also add an associated **following?** boolean method to test if one user is following another.[7]

This is exactly the kind of situation where I like to write some tests first. The reason is that we are quite far from writing a working web interface for following users,

---

7. Once you have a lot of experience modeling a particular domain, you can often guess such utility methods in advance, and even when you can't, you'll often find yourself writing them to make the tests cleaner. In this case, though, it's OK if you wouldn't have guessed them. Software development is usually an iterative process—you write code until it starts getting ugly, and then you refactor it—but for brevity the tutorial presentation is streamlined a bit.

but it's hard to proceed without some sort of *client* for the code we're developing. In this case, it's easy to write a short test for the User model, in which we use **following?** to make sure the user isn't following the other user, use **follow** to follow another user, use **following?** to verify that the operation succeeded, and finally **unfollow** and verify that it worked. The result appears in Listing 14.9.

Listing 14.9: Tests for some "following" utility methods. RED
`test/models/user_test.rb`

```
require 'test_helper'

class UserTest < ActiveSupport::TestCase
  .
  .
  .
  test "should follow and unfollow a user" do
    michael = users(:michael)
    archer  = users(:archer)
    assert_not michael.following?(archer)
    michael.follow(archer)
    assert michael.following?(archer)
    michael.unfollow(archer)
    assert_not michael.following?(archer)
  end
end
```

By treating the **following** association as an array, we can write the **follow**, **unfollow**, and **following?** methods as shown in Listing 14.10. (Note that we have omitted the user **self** variable whenever possible.)

Listing 14.10: Utility methods for following. GREEN
`app/models/user.rb`

```
class User < ApplicationRecord
  .
  .
  .
  def feed
    .
    .
    .
  end
```

```
# Follows a user.
def follow(other_user)
  following << other_user
end

# Unfollows a user.
def unfollow(other_user)
  following.delete(other_user)
end

# Returns true if the current user is following the other user.
def following?(other_user)
  following.include?(other_user)
end

private
  .
  .
  .
end
```

With the code in Listing 14.10, the tests should be GREEN:

Listing 14.11: GREEN

```
$ rails test
```

Exercises

Solutions to the exercises are available to all Rails Tutorial purchasers at https://www.railstutorial.org/aw-solutions.

To see other people's answers and to record your own, subscribe to the Rails Tutorial course or to the Learn Enough All Access Bundle.

1. At the console, replicate the steps shown in Listing 14.9.
2. What is the SQL for each of the commands in the previous exercise?

14.1.5 Followers

The final piece of the relationships puzzle is to add a **user.followers** method to go with **user.following**. You may have noticed from Figure 14.7 that all the information needed to extract an array of followers is already present in the

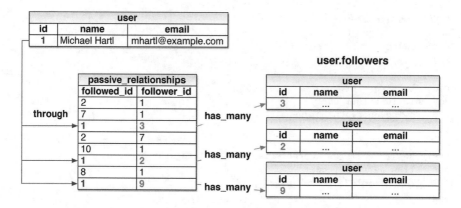

Figure 14.9: A model for user followers through passive relationships.

relationships table (which we are treating as the **active_relationships** table via the code in Listing 14.2). Indeed, the technique is exactly the same as that for followed users, with the roles of **follower_id** and **followed_id** reversed, and with **passive_relationships** in place of **active_relationships**. The data model then appears as in Figure 14.9.

The implementation of the data model in Figure 14.9 parallels Listing 14.8 exactly, as seen in Listing 14.12.

Listing 14.12: Implementing **user.followers** using passive relationships.
app/models/user.rb

```
class User < ApplicationRecord
  has_many :microposts, dependent: :destroy
  has_many :active_relationships,  class_name:  "Relationship",
                                   foreign_key: "follower_id",
                                   dependent:   :destroy
  has_many :passive_relationships, class_name:  "Relationship",
                                   foreign_key: "followed_id",
                                   dependent:   :destroy
  has_many :following, through: :active_relationships,  source: :followed
  has_many :followers, through: :passive_relationships, source: :follower
  .
  .
  .
end
```

It's worth noting that we could actually omit the **:source** key for **followers** in Listing 14.12, using simply

```
has_many :followers, through: :passive_relationships
```

This is because, in the case of a **:followers** attribute, Rails will singularize "followers" and automatically look for the foreign key **follower_id** in this case. Listing 14.12 keeps the **:source** key to emphasize the parallel structure with the **has_many :following** association.

We can conveniently test our data model using the **followers.include?** method, as shown in Listing 14.13. (Listing 14.13 might have used a **followed_by?** method to complement the **following?** method, but it turns out we won't need it in our application.)

Listing 14.13: A test for **followers**. GREEN
test/models/user_test.rb

```
require 'test_helper'

class UserTest < ActiveSupport::TestCase
  .
  .
  .
  test "should follow and unfollow a user" do
    michael = users(:michael)
    archer  = users(:archer)
    assert_not michael.following?(archer)
    michael.follow(archer)
    assert michael.following?(archer)
    assert archer.followers.include?(michael)
    michael.unfollow(archer)
    assert_not michael.following?(archer)
  end
end
```

Listing 14.13 adds only one line to the test from Listing 14.9, but so many things have to go right to get it to pass that it's a very sensitive test of the code in Listing 14.12.

At this point, the full test suite should be GREEN:

Listing 14.14: GREEN

```
$ rails test
```

Exercises

Solutions to the exercises are available to all Rails Tutorial purchasers at https://www.railstutorial.org/aw-solutions.

To see other people's answers and to record your own, subscribe to the Rails Tutorial course or to the Learn Enough All Access Bundle.

1. At the console, create several followers for the first user in the database (which you should call **user**). What is the value of **user.followers.map(&:id)**?

2. Confirm that **user.followers.count** matches the number of followers you created in the previous exercise.

3. What is the SQL used by **user.followers.count**? How is this different from **user.followers.to_a.count**? *Hint*: Suppose that the user had a million followers.

14.2 A Web Interface for Following Users

Section 14.1 placed some rather heavy demands on our data modeling skills, and it's fine if that information takes a while to soak in. In fact, one of the best ways to understand the associations is to use them in the web interface.

In the introduction to this chapter, we saw a preview of the page flow for user following. In this section, we will implement the basic interface and following/un-following functionality shown in those mockups. We will also make separate pages to show the user following and followers arrays. In Section 14.3, we'll complete our sample application by adding the user's status feed.

14.2.1 Sample Following Data

As in previous chapters, we will find it convenient to use **rails db:seed** to fill the database with sample relationships. This will allow us to design the look and feel of the web pages first, deferring the back-end functionality until later in this section.

Code to seed the following relationships appears in Listing 14.15. Here we somewhat arbitrarily arrange for the first user to follow users 3 through 51, and then have users 4 through 41 follow that user back. The resulting relationships will be sufficient for developing the application interface.

Listing 14.15: Adding following/follower relationships to the sample data.
db/seeds.rb

```
# Users
User.create!(name:  "Example User",
            email: "example@railstutorial.org",
            password:                "foobar",
            password_confirmation: "foobar",
            admin:     true,
            activated: true,
            activated_at: Time.zone.now)

99.times do |n|
  name  = Faker::Name.name
  email = "example-#{n+1}@railstutorial.org"
  password = "password"
  User.create!(name:  name,
              email: email,
              password:                password,
              password_confirmation: password,
              activated: true,
              activated_at: Time.zone.now)
end

# Microposts
users = User.order(:created_at).take(6)
50.times do
  content = Faker::Lorem.sentence(5)
  users.each { |user| user.microposts.create!(content: content) }
end

# Create following relationships.
users = User.all
user  = users.first
following = users[2..50]
followers = users[3..40]
following.each { |followed| user.follow(followed) }
followers.each { |follower| follower.follow(user) }
```

To execute the code in Listing 14.15, we reset and reseed the database as usual:

```
$ rails db:migrate:reset
$ rails db:seed
```

Exercises

Solutions to the exercises are available to all Rails Tutorial purchasers at https://www.railstutorial.org/aw-solutions.

To see other people's answers and to record your own, subscribe to the Rails Tutorial course or to the Learn Enough All Access Bundle.

1. Using the console, confirm that **User.first.followers.count** matches the value expected from Listing 14.15.

2. Confirm that **User.first.following.count** is correct as well.

14.2.2 Stats and a Follow Form

Now that our sample users have both followed users and followers, we need to update the profile page and Home page to reflect this. We'll start by making a partial to display the following and follower statistics on the profile and home pages. We'll next add a follow/unfollow form, and then make dedicated pages for showing "following" (followed users) and "followers".

As noted in Section 14.1.1, we'll adopt Twitter's convention of using "following" as a label for followed users, as in "50 following". This usage is reflected in the mockup sequence starting in Figure 14.1 and shown in close-up in Figure 14.10.

The stats in Figure 14.10 consist of the number of users the current user is following and the number of followers, each of which should be a link to its respective dedicated display page. In Chapter 5, we stubbed out such links with the dummy text '**#**', but that was before we had much experience with routes. This time, although we'll defer the creation of actual pages to Section 14.2.3, we'll make the routes now, as seen in Listing 14.16. This code uses the **:member** method inside a **resources** *block*, which we haven't seen before. Can you guess what it does?

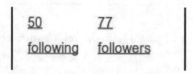

Figure 14.10: A mockup of the stats partial.

Listing 14.16: Adding `following` and `followers` actions to the Users controller.
`config/routes.rb`

```ruby
Rails.application.routes.draw do
  root    'static_pages#home'
  get     '/help',    to: 'static_pages#help'
  get     '/about',   to: 'static_pages#about'
  get     '/contact', to: 'static_pages#contact'
  get     '/signup',  to: 'users#new'
  get     '/login',   to: 'sessions#new'
  post    '/login',   to: 'sessions#create'
  delete  '/logout',  to: 'sessions#destroy'
  resources :users do
    member do
      get :following, :followers
    end
  end
  resources :account_activations, only: [:edit]
  resources :password_resets,     only: [:new, :create, :edit, :update]
  resources :microposts,          only: [:create, :destroy]
end
```

You might suspect that the URLs for following and followers will look like
/users/1/following and /users/1/followers, and that is exactly what the code in Listing 14.16 arranges. Since both pages will be *showing* data, the proper HTTP verb is a GET
request, so we use the **get** method to arrange for the URLs to respond appropriately.
Meanwhile, the **member** method arranges for the routes to respond to URLs containing
the user id. The other possibility, **collection**, works without the id, so that

```ruby
resources :users do
  collection do
    get :tigers
  end
end
```

would respond to the URL /users/tigers (presumably to display all the tigers in our
application).[8]

The routes generated by Listing 14.16 appear in Table 14.2. Note the named
routes for the followed user and followers pages, which we'll put to use shortly.

With the routes defined, we are now in a position to define the stats partial, which
involves a couple of links inside a div, as shown in Listing 14.17.

---

8. For more details on such routing options, see the Rails Guides article on "Rails Routing from the
Outside In" (guides.rubyonrails.org/routing.html).

Table 14.2: RESTful routes provided by the custom rules in the resource in Listing 14.16.

HTTP request	URL	Action	Named route
GET	/users/1/following	**following**	**following_user_path(1)**
GET	/users/1/followers	**followers**	**followers_user_path(1)**

Listing 14.17: A partial for displaying follower stats.
`app/views/shared/_stats.html.erb`

```erb
<% @user ||= current_user %>
<div class="stats">
  <a href="<%= following_user_path(@user) %>">
    <strong id="following" class="stat">
      <%= @user.following.count %>
    </strong>
    following
  </a>
  <a href="<%= followers_user_path(@user) %>">
    <strong id="followers" class="stat">
      <%= @user.followers.count %>
    </strong>
    followers
  </a>
</div>
```

Since we will be including the stats on both the user show pages and the Home page, the first line of Listing 14.17 picks the right one using

```erb
<% @user ||= current_user %>
```

As discussed in Box 8.1, this does nothing when **@user** is not **nil**, as on a profile page. When it is **nil**, though, as on the Home page, it sets **@user** to the current user. Note also that the following/follower counts are calculated through the associations using

```
@user.following.count
```

and

```
@user.followers.count
```

Compare these to the microposts count from Listing 13.24, where we wrote

```
@user.microposts.count
```

to count the microposts. As in that case, Rails calculates the count directly in the database for efficiency.

One final detail worth noting is the presence of CSS ids on some elements, as in

```
<strong id="following" class="stat">
...
</strong>
```

They are included for the benefit of the Ajax implementation in Section 14.2.5, which accesses elements on the page using their unique ids.

With the partial in hand, including the stats on the Home page is easy, as shown in Listing 14.18.

Listing 14.18: Adding follower stats to the Home page.
app/views/static_pages/home.html.erb

```erb
<% if logged_in? %>
  <div class="row">
    <aside class="col-md-4">
      <section class="user_info">
        <%= render 'shared/user_info' %>
      </section>
      <section class="stats">
        <%= render 'shared/stats' %>
      </section>
      <section class="micropost_form">
        <%= render 'shared/micropost_form' %>
      </section>
    </aside>
    <div class="col-md-8">
      <h3>Micropost Feed</h3>
      <%= render 'shared/feed' %>
    </div>
  </div>
<% else %>
  .
  .
  .
<% end %>
```

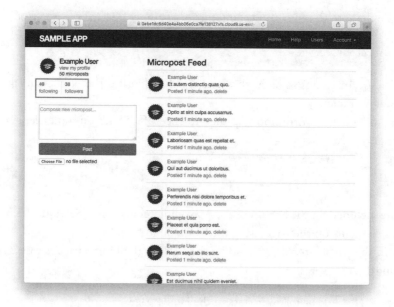

Figure 14.11: The Home page with follow stats.

To style the stats, we'll add some SCSS, as shown in Listing 14.19 (which contains all the stylesheet code needed in this chapter). The resulting Home page appears in Figure 14.11.

Listing 14.19: SCSS for the Home page sidebar.
`app/assets/stylesheets/custom.scss`

```
.
.
.
/* sidebar */
.
.
.
.gravatar {
  float: left;
  margin-right: 10px;
}

.gravatar_edit {
```

```scss
    margin-top: 15px;
}

.stats {
  overflow: auto;
  margin-top: 0;
  padding: 0;
  a {
    float: left;
    padding: 0 10px;
    border-left: 1px solid $gray-lighter;
    color: gray;
    &:first-child {
      padding-left: 0;
      border: 0;
    }
    &:hover {
      text-decoration: none;
      color: blue;
    }
  }
  strong {
    display: block;
  }
}

.user_avatars {
  overflow: auto;
  margin-top: 10px;
  .gravatar {
    margin: 1px 1px;
  }
  a {
    padding: 0;
  }
}

.users.follow {
  padding: 0;
}

/* forms */
    .
    .
    .
```

We'll render the stats partial on the profile page in a moment, but first let's make a partial for the follow/unfollow button, as shown in Listing 14.20.

Listing 14.20: A partial for a follow/unfollow form.
`app/views/users/_follow_form.html.erb`

```erb
<% unless current_user?(@user) %>
  <div id="follow_form">
  <% if current_user.following?(@user) %>
    <%= render 'unfollow' %>
  <% else %>
    <%= render 'follow' %>
  <% end %>
  </div>
<% end %>
```

This does nothing but defer the real work to the **follow** and **unfollow** partials. They need new routes for the Relationships resource, which follows the Microposts resource example (Listing 13.30), as seen in Listing 14.21.

Listing 14.21: Adding the routes for user relationships.
`config/routes.rb`

```ruby
Rails.application.routes.draw do
  root                    'static_pages#home'
  get    'help'     => 'static_pages#help'
  get    'about'    => 'static_pages#about'
  get    'contact'  => 'static_pages#contact'
  get    'signup'   => 'users#new'
  get    'login'    => 'sessions#new'
  post   'login'    => 'sessions#create'
  delete 'logout'   => 'sessions#destroy'
  resources :users do
    member do
      get :following, :followers
    end
  end
  resources :account_activations, only: [:edit]
  resources :password_resets,     only: [:new, :create, :edit, :update]
  resources :microposts,          only: [:create, :destroy]
  resources :relationships,       only: [:create, :destroy]
end
```

The follow and unfollow partials themselves are shown in Listing 14.22 and Listing 14.23, respectively.

Listing 14.22: A form for following a user.
app/views/users/_follow.html.erb

```
<%= form_with(model: current_user.active_relationships.build, local: true) do |f| %>
  <div><%= hidden_field_tag :followed_id, @user.id %></div>
  <%= f.submit "Follow", class: "btn btn-primary" %>
<% end %>
```

Listing 14.23: A form for unfollowing a user.
app/views/users/_unfollow.html.erb

```
<%= form_with(model: current_user.active_relationships.find_by(followed_id: @user.id),
           html: { method: :delete }, local: true) do |f| %>
  <%= f.submit "Unfollow", class: "btn" %>
<% end %>
```

Both of these forms use **form_with** to manipulate a Relationship model object; the main difference between the two is that Listing 14.22 builds a *new* relationship, whereas Listing 14.23 finds the existing relationship. Naturally, the former sends a POST request to the Relationships controller to **create** a relationship, while the latter sends a DELETE request to **destroy** a relationship. (We'll discuss these actions in more depty in Section 14.2.4.) Finally, note that the follow form doesn't have any content other than the button, but it still needs to send the **followed_id** to the controller. We accomplish this with the **hidden_field_tag** method in Listing 14.22, which produces HTML of the form

```
<input id="followed_id" name="followed_id" type="hidden" value="3" />
```

As we saw in Section 12.3 (Listing 12.14), the hidden **input** tag puts the relevant information on the page without displaying it in the browser.

We can now include the follow form and the following statistics on the user profile page simply by rendering the partials, as shown in Listing 14.24. Profiles with "Follow" and "Unfollow" buttons, respectively, appear in Figure 14.12 and Figure 14.13.

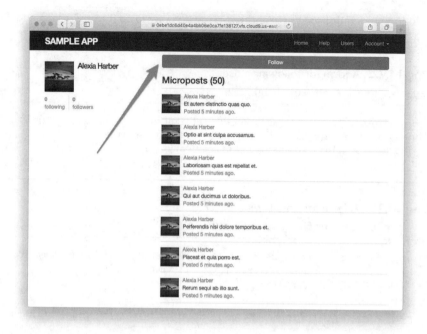

Figure 14.12: A user profile with a "Follow" button (/users/2).

Listing 14.24: Adding the follow form and follower stats to the user profile page.
`app/views/users/show.html.erb`

```
<% provide(:title, @user.name) %>
<div class="row">
  <aside class="col-md-4">
    <section>
      <h1>
        <%= gravatar_for @user %>
        <%= @user.name %>
      </h1>
    </section>
    <section class="stats">
      <%= render 'shared/stats' %>
    </section>
  </aside>
  <div class="col-md-8">
    <%= render 'follow_form' if logged_in? %>
```

```
<% if @user.microposts.any? %>
  <h3>Microposts (<%= @user.microposts.count %>)</h3>
  <ol class="microposts">
    <%= render @microposts %>
  </ol>
  <%= will_paginate @microposts %>
<% end %>
  </div>
</div>
```

We'll get these buttons working soon enough—in fact, we'll do it two ways, the standard way (Section 14.2.4) and using Ajax (Section 14.2.5). First, though, we'll finish the HTML interface by making the following and followers pages.

Exercises

Solutions to the exercises are available to all Rails Tutorial purchasers at https://www.railstutorial.org/aw-solutions.

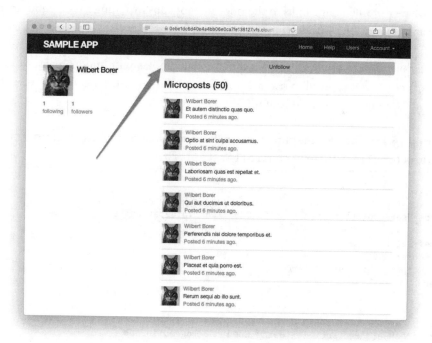

Figure 14.13: A user profile with an "Unfollow" button (/users/5).

To see other people's answers and to record your own, subscribe to the Rails Tutorial course or to the Learn Enough All Access Bundle.

1. Verify that /users/2 has a follow form and that /users/5 has an unfollow form. Is there a follow form on /users/1?

2. Confirm in the browser that the stats appear correctly on the Home page and on the profile page.

3. Write tests for the stats on the Home page. *Hint*: Add to the test in Listing 13.28. Why don't we also have to test the stats on the profile page?

14.2.3 Following and Followers Pages

Pages to display followed users and followers will resemble a hybrid of the user profile page and the user index page (Section 10.3.1), with a sidebar of user information (including the following stats) and a list of users. In addition, we'll include a raster of smaller user profile image links in the sidebar. Mockups matching these requirements appear in Figure 14.14 (following) and Figure 14.15 (followers).

Our first step is to get the following and followers links to work. We'll follow Twitter's lead and have both pages require user login. As with most previous examples of access control, we'll write the tests first, as shown in Listing 14.25. Note that Listing 14.25 uses the named routes from Table 14.2.

Listing 14.25: Tests for the authorization of the following and followers pages. RED
`test/controllers/users_controller_test.rb`

```
require 'test_helper'

class UsersControllerTest < ActionDispatch::IntegrationTest

  def setup
    @user = users(:michael)
    @other_user = users(:archer)
  end
  .
  .
  .
  test "should redirect following when not logged in" do
    get following_user_path(@user)
    assert_redirected_to login_url
```

```
  end

  test "should redirect followers when not logged in" do
    get followers_user_path(@user)
    assert_redirected_to login_url
  end
end
```

The only tricky part of the implementation is realizing that we need to add two new actions to the Users controller. Based on the routes defined in Listing 14.16, we need to call them **following** and **followers**. Each action needs to set a title, find the user, retrieve either **@user.following** or **@user.followers** (in paginated form), and then render the page. The result appears in Listing 14.26.

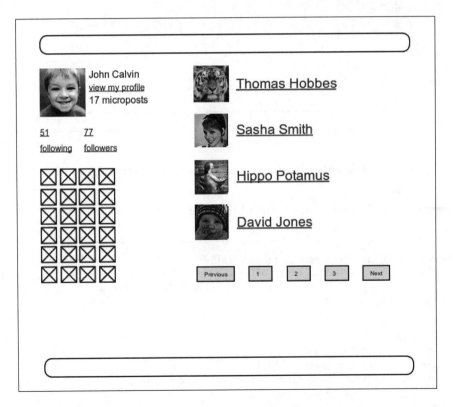

Figure 14.14: A mockup of the user following page.

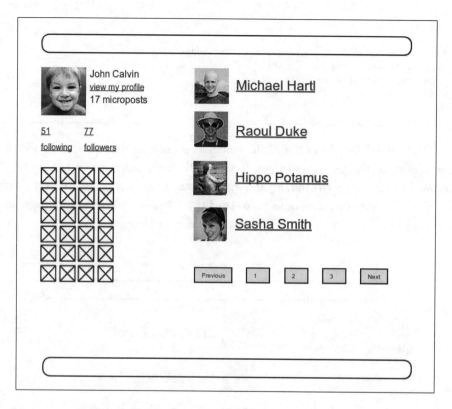

Figure 14.15: A mockup of the user followers page.

Listing 14.26: The **following** and **followers** actions. RED

`app/controllers/users_controller.rb`

```ruby
class UsersController < ApplicationController
  before_action :logged_in_user, only: [:index, :edit, :update, :destroy,
                                         :following, :followers]
  .
  .
  .
  def following
    @title = "Following"
    @user  = User.find(params[:id])
    @users = @user.following.paginate(page: params[:page])
    render 'show_follow'
  end
```

```
def followers
  @title = "Followers"
  @user  = User.find(params[:id])
  @users = @user.followers.paginate(page: params[:page])
  render 'show_follow'
end

private
  .
  .
  .
end
```

As we've seen throughout this tutorial, the usual Rails convention is to implicitly render the template corresponding to an action, such as rendering **show.html.erb** at the end of the **show** action. In contrast, both actions in Listing 14.26 make an *explicit* call to **render**, in this case rendering a view called **show_follow**, which we must create. The reason for the common view is that the ERb is nearly identical for the two cases, and Listing 14.27 covers them both.

Listing 14.27: The **show_follow** view used to render following and followers. GREEN
app/views/users/show_follow.html.erb

```
<% provide(:title, @title) %>
<div class="row">
  <aside class="col-md-4">
    <section class="user_info">
      <%= gravatar_for @user %>
      <h1><%= @user.name %></h1>
      <span><%= link_to "view my profile", @user %></span>
      <span><b>Microposts:</b> <%= @user.microposts.count %></span>
    </section>
    <section class="stats">
      <%= render 'shared/stats' %>
      <% if @users.any? %>
        <div class="user_avatars">
          <% @users.each do |user| %>
            <%= link_to gravatar_for(user, size: 30), user %>
          <% end %>
        </div>
      <% end %>
    </section>
  </aside>
  <div class="col-md-8">
```

```
<h3><%= @title %></h3>
<% if @users.any? %>
  <ul class="users follow">
    <%= render @users %>
  </ul>
  <%= will_paginate %>
<% end %>
</div>
</div>
```

The actions in Listing 14.26 render the view from Listing 14.27 in two contexts, "following" and "followers," with the results shown in Figure 14.16 and Figure 14.17, respectively Note that nothing in this code uses the current user, so the same links work for other users, as shown in Figure 14.18.

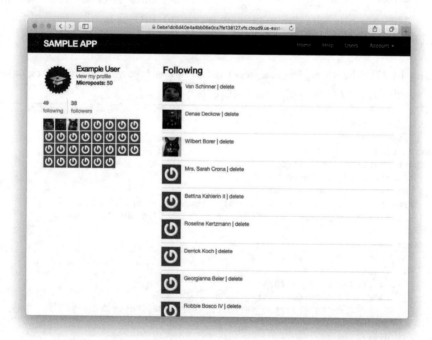

Figure 14.16: Showing the users the given user is following.

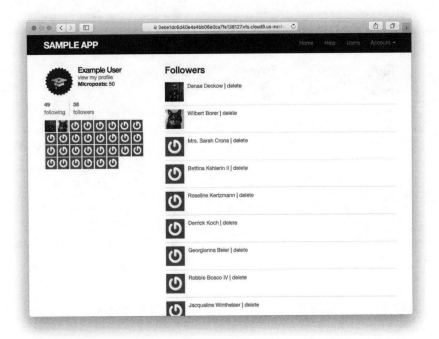

Figure 14.17: Showing the given user's followers.

At this point, the tests in Listing 14.25 should be GREEN due to the before filter in Listing 14.26:

Listing 14.28: GREEN

```
$ rails test
```

To test the **show_follow** rendering, we'll write a couple of short integration tests that verify the presence of working following and followers pages. They are designed to be a reality check, not to be comprehensive; indeed, as noted in Section 5.3.4, comprehensive tests of things like HTML structure are likely to be brittle and thus counter-productive. Our plan in the case of following/followers pages is to check that the number is correctly displayed and that links with the right URLs appear on the page.

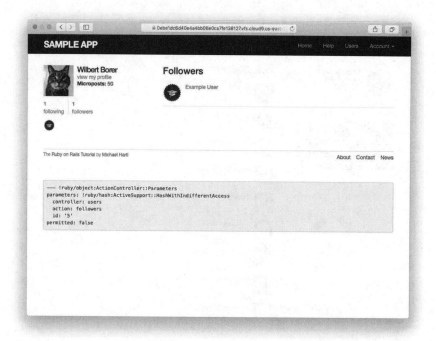

Figure 14.18: Showing a different user's followers.

To get started, we'll generate an integration test as usual:

```
$ rails generate integration_test following
      invoke  test_unit
      create    test/integration/following_test.rb
```

Next, we need to assemble some test data, which we can do by adding some relationships fixtures to create following/follower relationships. Recall from Section 13.2.3 that we can use code like

```
orange:
  content: "I just ate an orange!"
  created_at: <%= 10.minutes.ago %>
  user: michael
```

to associate a micropost with a given user. In particular, we can write

```
user: michael
```

instead of

```
user_id: 1
```

Applying this idea to the relationships fixtures gives the associations in Listing 14.29.

Listing 14.29: Relationships fixtures for use in following/follower tests.
`test/fixtures/relationships.yml`

```
one:
  follower: michael
  followed: lana

two:
  follower: michael
  followed: malory

three:
  follower: lana
  followed: michael

four:
  follower: archer
  followed: michael
```

The fixtures in Listing 14.29 first arrange for Michael to follow Lana and Malory, and then arrange for Michael to be followed by Lana and Archer. To test for the right count, we can use the same **assert_match** method we used in Listing 13.28 to test for the display of the number of microposts on the user profile page. Adding in assertions for the right links yields the tests shown in Listing 14.30.

Listing 14.30: Tests for following/follower pages. GREEN
`test/integration/following_test.rb`

```
require 'test_helper'

class FollowingTest < ActionDispatch::IntegrationTest

  def setup
    @user = users(:michael)
```

```
    log_in_as(@user)
  end

  test "following page" do
    get following_user_path(@user)
    assert_not @user.following.empty?
    assert_match @user.following.count.to_s, response.body
    @user.following.each do |user|
      assert_select "a[href=?]", user_path(user)
    end
  end

  test "followers page" do
    get followers_user_path(@user)
    assert_not @user.followers.empty?
    assert_match @user.followers.count.to_s, response.body
    @user.followers.each do |user|
      assert_select "a[href=?]", user_path(user)
    end
  end
end
```

In Listing 14.30, note that we include the assertion

```
assert_not @user.following.empty?
```

which is included to make sure that

```
@user.following.each do |user|
  assert_select "a[href=?]", user_path(user)
end
```

isn't vacuously true (and similarly for **followers**). In other words, if **@user. following.empty?** were true, not a single **assert_select** would execute in the loop, leading the tests to pass and thereby giving us a false sense of security.

The test suite should now be GREEN:

Listing 14.31: GREEN

```
$ rails test
```

Exercises

Solutions to the exercises are available to all Rails Tutorial purchasers at https://www.railstutorial.org/aw-solutions.

To see other people's answers and to record your own, subscribe to the Rails Tutorial course or to the Learn Enough All Access Bundle.

1. Verify in a browser that /users/1/followers and /users/1/following work. Do the image links in the sidebar work as well?

2. Comment out the application code needed to turn the **assert_select** tests in Listing 14.30 RED to confirm they're testing the right thing.

14.2.4   A Working Follow Button the Standard Way

Now that our views are in order, it's time to get the follow/unfollow buttons working. Because following and unfollowing involve creating and destroying relationships, we need a Relationships controller, which we generate as usual:

```
$ rails generate controller Relationships
```

As we'll see in Listing 14.33, enforcing access control on the Relationships controller actions won't much matter, but we'll still continue our previous practice of enforcing the security model as early as possible. In particular, we'll check that attempts to access actions in the Relationships controller require a logged-in user (and thus get redirected to the login page), while also not changing the Relationship count, as shown in Listing 14.32.

Listing 14.32: Basic access control tests for relationships. RED
`test/controllers/relationships_controller_test.rb`

```ruby
require 'test_helper'

class RelationshipsControllerTest < ActionDispatch::IntegrationTest

  test "create should require logged-in user" do
    assert_no_difference 'Relationship.count' do
      post relationships_path
    end
    assert_redirected_to login_url
  end
end
```

```ruby
    test "destroy should require logged-in user" do
      assert_no_difference 'Relationship.count' do
        delete relationship_path(relationships(:one))
      end
      assert_redirected_to login_url
    end
  end
```

We can get the tests in Listing 14.32 to pass by adding the **logged_in_user** before filter (Listing 14.33).

Listing 14.33: Access control for relationships. GREEN
app/controllers/relationships_controller.rb

```ruby
class RelationshipsController < ApplicationController
  before_action :logged_in_user

  def create
  end

  def destroy
  end
end
```

To get the "Follow" and "Unfollow" buttons to work, all we need to do is find the user associated with the **followed_id** in the corresponding form (i.e., Listing 14.22 or Listing 14.23), and then use the appropriate **follow** or **unfollow** method from Listing 14.10. The full implementation appears in Listing 14.34.

Listing 14.34: The Relationships controller. GREEN
app/controllers/relationships_controller.rb

```ruby
class RelationshipsController < ApplicationController
  before_action :logged_in_user

  def create
    user = User.find(params[:followed_id])
    current_user.follow(user)
    redirect_to user
```

```
  end

  def destroy
    user = Relationship.find(params[:id]).followed
    current_user.unfollow(user)
    redirect_to user
  end
end
```

We can see from Listing 14.34 why the security issue mentioned earlier is minor: If an unlogged-in user were to hit either action directly (e.g., using a command-line tool like **curl**), **current_user** would be **nil**, and in both cases the action's second line would raise an exception, resulting in an error but no harm to the application or its data. It's best not to rely on that behavior, though, so we've taken the extra step and added another layer of security.

With that, the core follow/unfollow functionality is complete, and any user can follow or unfollow any other user, as you can verify by clicking the corresponding buttons in your browser. (We'll write integration tests to verify this behavior in Section 14.2.6.) The result of following user #2 is shown in Figure 14.19 and Figure 14.20.

Exercises

Solutions to the exercises are available to all Rails Tutorial purchasers at https://www.railstutorial.org/aw-solutions.

To see other people's answers and to record your own, subscribe to the Rails Tutorial course or to the Learn Enough All Access Bundle.

1. Follow and unfollow /users/2 through the web. Did it work?

2. According to the server log, which templates are rendered in each case?

14.2.5 A Working Follow Button with Ajax

Although our user following implementation is complete as it stands, we have one bit of polish left to add before starting work on the status feed. You may have noticed in Section 14.2.4 that both the **create** and **destroy** actions in the Relationships controller simply redirect *back* to the original profile. In other words, a user starts on another user's profile page, follows the other user, and is immediately redirected back to the original page. It is reasonable to ask why the user needs to leave that page at all.

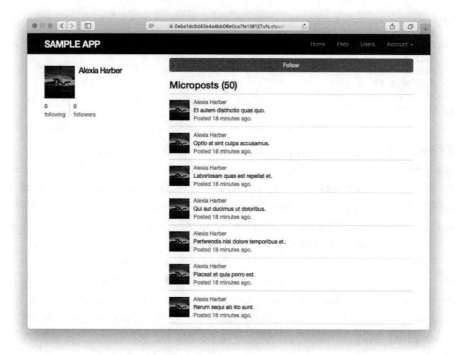

Figure 14.19: An unfollowed user.

This is exactly the problem solved by Ajax, which allows web pages to send requests asynchronously to the server without leaving the page.[9] Because adding Ajax to web forms is a common practice, Rails makes Ajax easy to implement. Indeed, updating the follow/unfollow form partials is trivial: Just change

```
form_with(model: ..., local: true)
```

to

```
form_with(model: ..., remote: true)
```

_____

9. Because it is nominally an acronym for *asynchronous JavaScript and XML*, Ajax is sometimes misspelled "AJAX," even though the original Ajax article spells it as "Ajax" throughout.

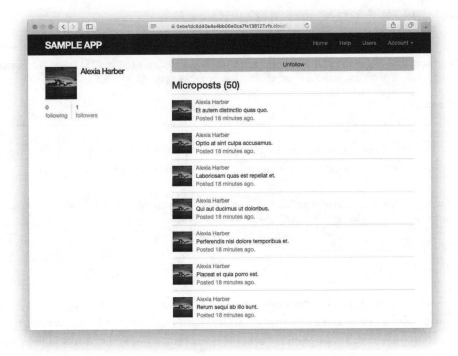

Figure 14.20: The result of following an unfollowed user.

and Rails automagically uses Ajax.[10] The updated partials appear in Listing 14.35 and Listing 14.36.

Listing 14.35: A form for following a user using Ajax.
`app/views/users/_follow.html.erb`

```erb
<%= form_for(model: current_user.active_relationships.build, remote: true) do |f| %>
  <div><%= hidden_field_tag :followed_id, @user.id %></div>
  <%= f.submit "Follow", class: "btn btn-primary" %>
<% end %>
```

---

10. In fact, the default behavior for **form_with** is to make remote submissions, but at least when starting out I prefer to be explicit.

Listing 14.36: A form for unfollowing a user using Ajax.
`app/views/users/_unfollow.html.erb`

```erb
<%= form_with(model: current_user.active_relationships.find_by(followed_id: @user.id),
              html: { method: :delete }, remote: true) do |f| %>
  <%= f.submit "Unfollow", class: "btn" %>
<% end %>
```

The actual HTML generated by this ERb isn't particularly relevant, but you might be curious, so here's a peek at a schematic view (details may differ):

```html
<form action="/relationships/117" class="edit_relationship" data-remote="true"
    id="edit_relationship_117" method="post">
  .
  .
  .
</form>
```

This sets the variable **data-remote="true"** inside the form tag, which tells Rails to allow the form to be handled by JavaScript. By using a simple HTML property instead of inserting the full JavaScript code (as in previous versions of Rails), Rails follows the philosophy of *unobtrusive JavaScript*.

Having updated the form, we now need to arrange for the Relationships controller to respond to Ajax requests. We can do this using the **respond_to** method, responding appropriately depending on the type of request. The general pattern looks like this:

```ruby
respond_to do |format|
  format.html { redirect_to user }
  format.js
end
```

This syntax is potentially confusing, and it's important to understand that only *one* of the lines gets executed. (In this sense, **respond_to** is more like an if-then-else statement than a series of sequential lines.) Adapting the Relationships controller to respond to Ajax involves adding **respond_to** as in the preceding code to the **create** and **destroy** actions from Listing 14.34. The result appears as in Listing 14.37. Note the change from the local variable **user** to the instance variable **@user**; in Listing 14.34

there was no need for an instance variable, but now such a variable is necessary in Listing 14.35 and Listing 14.36.

Listing 14.37: Responding to Ajax requests in the Relationships controller.
`app/controllers/relationships_controller.rb`

```ruby
class RelationshipsController < ApplicationController
  before_action :logged_in_user

  def create
    @user = User.find(params[:followed_id])
    current_user.follow(@user)
    respond_to do |format|
      format.html { redirect_to @user }
      format.js
    end
  end

  def destroy
    @user = Relationship.find(params[:id]).followed
    current_user.unfollow(@user)
    respond_to do |format|
      format.html { redirect_to @user }
      format.js
    end
  end
end
```

The actions in Listing 14.37 degrade gracefully, which means that they work fine in browsers that have JavaScript disabled (although a small amount of configuration is necessary, as shown in Listing 14.38).

Listing 14.38: Configuration needed for graceful degradation of form submission.
`config/application.rb`

```ruby
require_relative 'boot'
  .
  .
  .
module SampleApp
  class Application < Rails::Application
    .
```

```
      .
      .
    # Include the authenticity token in remote forms.
    config.action_view.embed_authenticity_token_in_remote_forms = true
  end
end
```

We have yet to respond properly when JavaScript is enabled, though. In the case of an Ajax request, Rails automatically calls a *JavaScript embedded Ruby* (**.js.erb**) file with the same name as the action—that is, **create.js.erb** or **destroy.js.erb**. As you might guess, such files allow us to mix JavaScript and embedded Ruby to perform actions on the current page. It is these files that we need to create and edit to update the user profile page upon being followed or unfollowed.

Inside a JS-ERb file, Rails automatically provides the jQuery JavaScript helpers needed to manipulate the page using the Document Object Model (DOM). The jQuery library (which we saw briefly in Section 13.4.2) provides a large number of methods for manipulating the DOM, but here we will need only two. First, we will need to know about the dollar-sign syntax to access a DOM element based on its unique CSS id. For example, to manipulate the **follow_form** element, we will use the syntax

```
$("#follow_form")
```

(Recall from Listing 14.20 that this is a **div** that wraps the form, not the form itself.) This syntax, inspired by CSS, uses the **#** symbol to indicate a CSS id. As you might guess, jQuery, like CSS, uses a dot **.** to manipulate CSS classes.

The second method we'll need is **html**, which updates the HTML inside the relevant element with the contents of its argument. For example, to replace the entire follow form with the string **"foobar"**, we would write

```
$("#follow_form").html("foobar")
```

Unlike plain JavaScript files, JS-ERb files also allow the use of embedded Ruby, which we apply in the **create.js.erb** file to update the follow form with the **unfollow** partial (which is what should be displayed after a successful following) and update the follower count. The result is shown in Listing 14.39. This uses the

escape_javascript method, which is needed to escape out the result when inserting HTML in a JavaScript file.

Listing 14.39: The JavaScript embedded Ruby to create a following relationship.
`app/views/relationships/create.js.erb`

```
$("#follow_form").html("<%= escape_javascript(render('users/unfollow')) %>");
$("#followers").html('<%= @user.followers.count %>');
```

Note the presence of line-ending semicolons, which are characteristic of languages with syntax descended from ALGOL.

The **destroy.js.erb** file is analogous (Listing 14.40).

Listing 14.40: The Ruby JavaScript (RJS) to destroy a following relationship.
`app/views/relationships/destroy.js.erb`

```
$("#follow_form").html("<%= escape_javascript(render('users/follow')) %>");
$("#followers").html('<%= @user.followers.count %>');
```

With that, you should navigate to a user profile page and verify that you can follow and unfollow without a page refresh.

Exercises

Solutions to the exercises are available to all Rails Tutorial purchasers at https://www.railstutorial.org/aw-solutions.

To see other people's answers and to record your own, subscribe to the Rails Tutorial course or to the Learn Enough All Access Bundle.

1. Unfollow and refollow /users/2 through the web. Did it work?
2. According to the server log, which templates are rendered in each case?

14.2.6 Following Tests

Now that the follow buttons are working, we'll write some simple tests to prevent regressions. To follow a user, we post to the relationships path and verify that the number of followed users increases by 1:

```
assert_difference '@user.following.count', 1 do
  post relationships_path, params: { followed_id: @other.id }
end
```

This tests the standard implementation, but testing the Ajax version is almost exactly the same; the only difference is the addition of the option **xhr: true**:

```
assert_difference '@user.following.count', 1 do
  post relationships_path, params: { followed_id: @other.id }, xhr: true
end
```

Here **xhr** stands for XmlHttpRequest; setting the **xhr** option to **true** issues an Ajax request in the test, which causes the **respond_to** block in Listing 14.37 to execute the proper JavaScript method.

A parallel structure applies to deleting users, with **delete** instead of **post**. Here we check that the followed user count goes down by 1 and include the relationship and followed user's id:

```
assert_difference '@user.following.count', -1 do
  delete relationship_path(relationship)
end
```

and

```
assert_difference '@user.following.count', -1 do
  delete relationship_path(relationship), xhr: true
end
```

Putting the two cases together gives the tests in Listing 14.41.

Listing 14.41: Tests for the follow/unfollow buttons. GREEN
test/integration/following_test.rb

```
require 'test_helper'

class FollowingTest < ActionDispatch::IntegrationTest

  def setup
    @user  = users(:michael)
    @other = users(:archer)
```

```
    log_in_as(@user)
  end
  .
  .
  .
  test "should follow a user the standard way" do
    assert_difference '@user.following.count', 1 do
      post relationships_path, params: { followed_id: @other.id }
    end
  end

  test "should follow a user with Ajax" do
    assert_difference '@user.following.count', 1 do
      post relationships_path, xhr: true, params: { followed_id: @other.id }
    end
  end

  test "should unfollow a user the standard way" do
    @user.follow(@other)
    relationship = @user.active_relationships.find_by(followed_id: @other.id)
    assert_difference '@user.following.count', -1 do
      delete relationship_path(relationship)
    end
  end

  test "should unfollow a user with Ajax" do
    @user.follow(@other)
    relationship = @user.active_relationships.find_by(followed_id: @other.id)
    assert_difference '@user.following.count', -1 do
      delete relationship_path(relationship), xhr: true
    end
  end
end
```

At this point, the tests should be GREEN:

Listing 14.42: GREEN

```
$ rails test
```

Exercises

Solutions to the exercises are available to all Rails Tutorial purchasers at https://www.railstutorial.org/aw-solutions.

To see other people's answers and to record your own, subscribe to the Rails Tutorial course or to the Learn Enough All Access Bundle.

1. By commenting and uncommenting each of the lines in the **respond_to** blocks (Listing 14.37), verify that the tests are testing the right things. Which test fails in each case?

2. What happens if you delete one of the occurrences of **xhr: true** in Listing 14.41? Explain why this is a problem, and why the procedure in the previous exercise would catch it.

14.3 The Status Feed

We come now to the pinnacle of our sample application: the status feed of microposts. Appropriately, this section contains some of the most advanced material in the entire tutorial. The full status feed builds on the proto-feed from Section 13.3.3 by assembling an array of the microposts from the users being followed by the current user, along with the current user's own microposts. Throughout this section, we'll proceed through a series of feed implementations of increasing sophistication. To accomplish this, we will need some fairly advanced Rails, Ruby, and even SQL programming techniques.

Because of the heavy lifting ahead, it's especially important to review where we're going. A recap of the final status feed, shown in Figure 14.5, appears again in Figure 14.21.

14.3.1 Motivation and Strategy

The basic idea behind the feed is simple. Figure 14.22 shows a sample **microposts** database table and the resulting feed. The purpose of a feed is to pull out the microposts whose user ids correspond to the users being followed by the current user (and the current user itself), as indicated by the arrows in the diagram.

Although we don't yet know how to implement the feed, the tests are relatively straightforward, so (following the guidelines in Box 3.3) we'll write them first. The key is to check all three requirements for the feed: Microposts for both followed users and the user itself should be included in the feed, but a post from an *unfollowed* user should not be included.

As we'll see in Listing 14.29, we'll be arranging for Michael to follow Lana but not Archer. Based on the fixtures in Listing 10.47 and Listing 13.55, this means that Michael should see Lana's posts and his own posts, but not Archer's posts. Converting

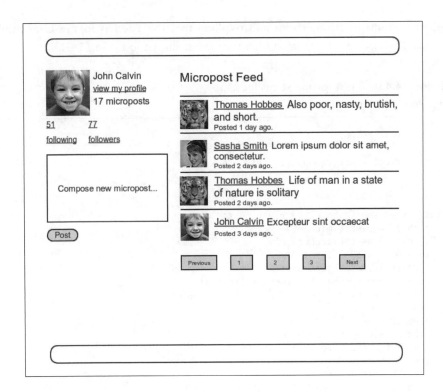

Figure 14.21: A mockup of a user's Home page with a status feed.

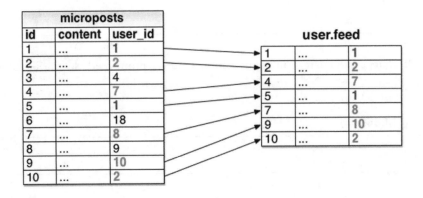

Figure 14.22: The feed for a user (id 1) following users with ids 2, 7, 8, and 10.

these requirements to assertions and recalling that the **feed** is in the User model
(Listing 13.47) gives the updated User model test shown in Listing 14.43.

Listing 14.43: A test for the status feed. RED
test/models/user_test.rb

```
require 'test_helper'

class UserTest < ActiveSupport::TestCase
  .
  .
  .
  test "feed should have the right posts" do
    michael = users(:michael)
    archer  = users(:archer)
    lana    = users(:lana)
    # Posts from followed user
    lana.microposts.each do |post_following|
      assert michael.feed.include?(post_following)
    end
    # Posts from self
    michael.microposts.each do |post_self|
      assert michael.feed.include?(post_self)
    end
    # Posts from unfollowed user
    archer.microposts.each do |post_unfollowed|
      assert_not michael.feed.include?(post_unfollowed)
    end
  end
end
```

Of course, the current implementation is just a proto-feed, so the new test is
initially RED:

Listing 14.44: RED

```
$ rails test
```

Exercise
Solutions to the exercises are available to all Rails Tutorial purchasers at https://
www.railstutorial.org/aw-solutions.

To see other people's answers and to record your own, subscribe to the Rails Tutorial course or to the Learn Enough All Access Bundle.

1. Assuming the micropost's ids are numbered sequentially, with larger numbers being more recent, what would **user.feed.map(&:id)** return for the feed shown in Figure 14.22? *Hint*: Recall the default scope from Section 13.1.4.

14.3.2 A First Feed Implementation

With the status feed design requirements captured in the test from Listing 14.43, we're ready to start writing the feed. Since the final feed implementation is rather intricate, we'll build up to it by introducing one piece at a time. The first step is to think of the kind of query we'll need. We need to select all the microposts from the **microposts** table with ids corresponding to the users being followed by a given user (or the user itself). We might write this schematically as follows:

```
SELECT * FROM microposts
WHERE user_id IN (<list of ids>) OR user_id = <user id>
```

In writing this code, we've guessed that SQL supports an **IN** keyword that allows us to test for set inclusion. (Happily, it does.)

Recall from the proto-feed in Section 13.3.3 that Active Record uses the **where** method to accomplish the kind of select shown here, as illustrated in Listing 13.47. In that listing, our select was very simple—we just picked out all the microposts with a user id corresponding to the current user:

```
Micropost.where("user_id = ?", id)
```

Here, we expect the select to be more complicated, something like this:

```
Micropost.where("user_id IN (?) OR user_id = ?", following_ids, id)
```

We see from these conditions that we'll need an array of ids corresponding to the users being followed. One way to do this is to use Ruby's **map** method, available on any "enumerable" object—that is, any object (such as an array or a hash) that consists of a collection of elements.[11] We saw an example of this method in Section 4.3.2; as another example, we'll use **map** to convert an array of integers to an array of strings:

```
$ rails console
>> [1, 2, 3, 4].map { |i| i.to_s }
=> ["1", "2", "3", "4"]
```

Situations like the one illustrated here, in which the same method gets called on each element in the collection, are common enough that there's a shorthand notation for it (seen briefly in Section 4.3.2). This uses an *ampersand* **&** and a symbol corresponding to the method:

```
>> [1, 2, 3, 4].map(&:to_s)
=> ["1", "2", "3", "4"]
```

Using the **join** method (Section 4.3.1), we can create a string composed of the ids by joining them on comma-space:

```
>> [1, 2, 3, 4].map(&:to_s).join(', ')
=> "1, 2, 3, 4"
```

We can use this method to construct the necessary array of followed user ids by calling **id** on each element in **user.following**. For example, for the first user in the database this array appears as follows:

```
>> User.first.following.map(&:id)
=> [3, 4, 5, 6, 7, 8, 9, 10, 11, 12, 13, 14, 15, 16, 17, 18, 19, 20, 21, 22,
23, 24, 25, 26, 27, 28, 29, 30, 31, 32, 33, 34, 35, 36, 37, 38, 39, 40, 41,
42, 43, 44, 45, 46, 47, 48, 49, 50, 51]
```

In fact, because this sort of construction is so useful, Active Record provides it by default:

```
>> User.first.following_ids
=> [3, 4, 5, 6, 7, 8, 9, 10, 11, 12, 13, 14, 15, 16, 17, 18, 19, 20, 21, 22,
```

---

11. The main requirement is that enumerable objects must implement an **each** method to iterate through the collection.

```
23, 24, 25, 26, 27, 28, 29, 30, 31, 32, 33, 34, 35, 36, 37, 38, 39, 40, 41,
42, 43, 44, 45, 46, 47, 48, 49, 50, 51]
```

Here the **following_ids** method is synthesized by Active Record based on the **has_many :following** association (Listing 14.8); the result is that we need to just append **_ids** to the association name to get the ids corresponding to the **user.following** collection. A string of followed user ids then appears as shown here:

```
>> User.first.following_ids.join(', ')
=> "3, 4, 5, 6, 7, 8, 9, 10, 11, 12, 13, 14, 15, 16, 17, 18, 19, 20, 21, 22,
23, 24, 25, 26, 27, 28, 29, 30, 31, 32, 33, 34, 35, 36, 37, 38, 39, 40, 41,
42, 43, 44, 45, 46, 47, 48, 49, 50, 51"
```

When inserting into an SQL string, though, you don't need to do this; the **?** interpolation takes care of it for you (and in fact eliminates some database-dependent incompatibilities). This means we can use **following_ids** by itself. As a result, the initial guess of

```
Micropost.where("user_id IN (?) OR user_id = ?", following_ids, id)
```

actually works! The result appears in Listing 14.45.

Listing 14.45: The initial working feed. GREEN
app/models/user.rb

```ruby
class User < ApplicationRecord
  .
  .
  .
  # Returns true if a password reset has expired.
  def password_reset_expired?
    reset_sent_at < 2.hours.ago
  end

  # Returns a user's status feed.
  def feed
    Micropost.where("user_id IN (?) OR user_id = ?", following_ids, id)
  end

  # Follows a user.
  def follow(other_user)
```

```
    following << other_user
  end
    .
    .
    .
end
```

The test suite should be GREEN:

Listing 14.46: GREEN

```
$ rails test
```

In some applications, this initial implementation might be good enough for most practical purposes, but Listing 14.45 isn't the final implementation. See if you can make a guess about why not before moving on to the next section. (*Hint*: What if a user is following 5,000 other users?)

Exercises

Solutions to the exercises are available to all Rails Tutorial purchasers at https://www.railstutorial.org/aw-solutions.

To see other people's answers and to record your own, subscribe to the Rails Tutorial course or to the Learn Enough All Access Bundle.

1. In Listing 14.45, remove the part of the query that finds the user's own posts. Which test in Listing 14.43 breaks?

2. In Listing 14.45, remove the part of the query that finds the followed users' posts. Which test in Listing 14.43 breaks?

3. How could you change the query in Listing 14.45 to have the feed erroneously return microposts of unfollowed users, thereby breaking the third test in Listing 14.43? *Hint*: Returning all the microposts would do the trick.

14.3.3 Subselects

As hinted at in the last section, the feed implementation in Section 14.3.2 doesn't scale well when the number of microposts in the feed is large, as would likely happen if a user were following, say, 5,000 other users. In this section, we'll reimplement the status feed in a way that scales better with the number of followed users.

The problem with the code in Section 14.3.2 is that **following_ids** pulls *all* the followed users' ids into memory, and creates an array the full length of the followed users array. Since the condition in Listing 14.45 actually just checks inclusion in a set, there must be a more efficient way to do this, and indeed SQL is optimized for just such set operations. The solution involves pushing the finding of followed user ids into the database using a *subselect*.

We'll start by refactoring the feed with the slightly modified code in Listing 14.47.

Listing 14.47: Using key-value pairs in the feed's **where** method. GREEN
app/models/user.rb

```
class User < ApplicationRecord
  .
  .
  .
  # Returns a user's status feed.
  def feed
    Micropost.where("user_id IN (:following_ids) OR user_id = :user_id",
                    following_ids: following_ids, user_id: id)
  end
  .
  .
  .
end
```

As preparation for the next step, we have replaced

```
Micropost.where("user_id IN (?) OR user_id = ?", following_ids, id)
```

with the equivalent

```
Micropost.where("user_id IN (:following_ids) OR user_id = :user_id",
                following_ids: following_ids, user_id: id)
```

The question-mark syntax is fine, but when we want the *same* variable inserted in more than one place, the second syntax is more convenient.

The preceding discussion implies that we will be adding a *second* occurrence of **user_id** in the SQL query. In particular, we can replace the Ruby code

```
following_ids
```

with the SQL snippet

```
following_ids = "SELECT followed_id FROM relationships
                 WHERE  follower_id = :user_id"
```

This code contains an SQL subselect, and internally the entire select for user 1 would look something like this:

```
SELECT * FROM microposts
WHERE user_id IN (SELECT followed_id FROM relationships
                  WHERE  follower_id = 1)
      OR user_id = 1
```

This subselect arranges for all the set logic to be pushed into the database, which is more efficient.

With this foundation, we are ready for a more efficient feed implementation, as seen in Listing 14.48. Note that, because it is now raw SQL, the **following_ids** string is *interpolated*, not escaped.

Listing 14.48: The final implementation of the feed. GREEN
app/models/user.rb

```
class User < ApplicationRecord
  .
  .
  .
  # Returns a user's status feed.
  def feed
    following_ids = "SELECT followed_id FROM relationships
                     WHERE  follower_id = :user_id"
    Micropost.where("user_id IN (#{following_ids})
                     OR user_id = :user_id", user_id: id)
  end
  .
  .
  .
end
```

This code contains a formidable combination of Rails, Ruby, and SQL, but it does the job, and does it well:

Listing 14.49: GREEN

```
$ rails test
```

Of course, even the subselect won't scale forever. For bigger sites, you would probably need to generate the feed asynchronously using a background job, but such scaling subtleties are beyond the scope of this tutorial.

With the code in Listing 14.48, our status feed is now complete. Recall from Section 13.3.3 that the Home page already includes the feed. In Chapter 13, the result was only a proto-feed (Figure 13.14), but with the implementation in Listing 14.48 as seen in Figure 14.23 the Home page now shows the full feed.

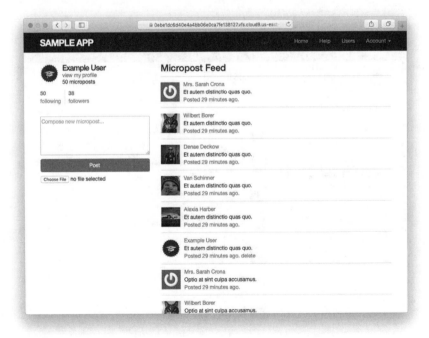

Figure 14.23: The Home page with a working status feed.

At this point, we're ready to merge our changes into the master branch:

```
$ rails test
$ git add -A
$ git commit -m "Add user following"
$ git checkout master
$ git merge following-users
```

We can then push the code to the remote repository and deploy the application to production:

```
$ git push
$ git push heroku
$ heroku pg:reset DATABASE
$ heroku run rails db:migrate
$ heroku run rails db:seed
```

The result is a working status feed on the live web (Figure 14.24).

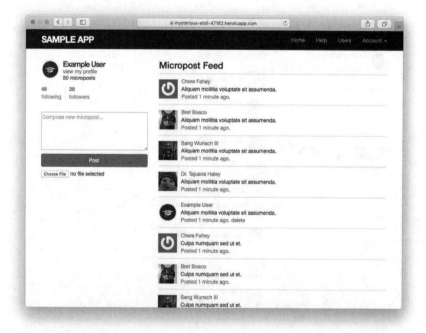

Figure 14.24: A working status feed on the live web.

Exercises

Solutions to the exercises are available to all Rails Tutorial purchasers at https://www.railstutorial.org/aw-solutions.

To see other people's answers and to record your own, subscribe to the Rails Tutorial course or to the Learn Enough All Access Bundle.

1. Write an integration test to verify that the first page of the feed appears on the Home page as required. A template appears in Listing 14.50.

2. Note that Listing 14.50 escapes the expected HTML using **CGI.escapeHTML** (which is closely related to the **CGI.escape** method we used in Section 11.2.3 to escape URLs). Why is escaping the HTML necessary in this case? *Hint*: Try removing the escaping and carefully inspect the page source for the micropost content that doesn't match. Using the search feature of your terminal shell (Cmd-F or Ctrl-F on most systems) to find the word "sorry" may prove particularly helpful.

3. The code in Listing 14.48 can be expressed directly in Rails using an *inner join* using the **join** method. By running the tests, show that the code in Listing 14.51 returns a valid feed.[12] What is the SQL query generated by this code? (*Hint*: Run **User.first.feed** in the console.)

Listing 14.50: Testing the feed HTML. GREEN
`test/integration/following_test.rb`

```
require 'test_helper'

class FollowingTest < ActionDispatch::IntegrationTest

  def setup
    @user = users(:michael)
    log_in_as(@user)
  end
  .
  .
  .
  test "feed on Home page" do
```

---

12. Thanks to reader Anna for suggesting this version.

```
    get root_path
    @user.feed.paginate(page: 1).each do |micropost|
      assert_match CGI.escapeHTML(FILL_IN), FILL_IN
    end
  end
end
```

Listing 14.51: Using a **join** to make the feed.
app/models/user.rb

```
class User < ApplicationRecord
  .
  .
  .
  # Returns a user's status feed.
  def feed
    part_of_feed = "relationships.follower_id = :id or microposts.user_id = :id"
    Micropost.joins(user: :followers).where(part_of_feed, { id: id })
  end
  .
  .
  .
end
```

14.4   Conclusion

With the addition of the status feed, we've finished the sample application for the *Ruby on Rails Tutorial*. This application includes examples of all the major features of Rails, including models, views, controllers, templates, partials, filters, validations, callbacks, **has_many**/**belongs_to** and **has_many :through** associations, security, testing, and deployment.

Despite this impressive list, there is still much to learn about web development. As a first step in this process, this section contains some suggestions for further learning.

14.4.1   Guide to Further Resources

A wealth of Rails resources are available in stores and on the web—indeed, the supply is so rich that it can be overwhelming. The good news is that, having gotten this far, you're ready for almost anything else out there. Here are some suggestions for further learning:

- Learn Enough All Access Bundle: Premium subscription service that includes a special enhanced version of the *Ruby on Rails Tutorial* book and 15-plus hours of streaming screencast lessons filled with the kind of tips, tricks, and live demos that you can't get from reading a book. Also includes text and videos for the other Learn Enough tutorials. Scholarship discounts are available.

- Launch School: Lots of in-person developer bootcamps have sprung up in recent years, and I recommend looking for one in your area, but Launch School is available online and so can be taken from anywhere. Launch School is an especially good choice if you want instructor feedback within the context of a structured curriculum.

- The Turing School of Software & Design: A full-time, 27-week Ruby/Rails/-JavaScript training program in Denver, Colorado. Most of its students start with limited programming experience but have the determination and drive needed to pick it up quickly. Turing guarantees its students will find a job after graduating or the school will refund the cost of tuition.

- Bloc: An online bootcamp with a structured curriculum, personalized mentorship, and a focus on learning through concrete projects. Use the coupon code BLOCLOVESHARTL to get $500 off the enrollment fee.

- Thinkful: An online class that pairs you with a professional engineer as you work through a project-based curriculum. Subjects include Ruby on Rails, front-end development, web design, and data science.

- Pragmatic Studio: Online Ruby and Rails courses from Mike and Nicole Clark.

- RailsApps: Instructive sample Rails apps.

- Lambda School: An innovative full-time online program that you pay for only if you land a high-paying job.

14.4.2 What We Learned in this Chapter

- Rails' `has_many :through` allows the modeling of complicated data relationships.

- The **has_many** method takes several optional arguments, including the object class name and the foreign key.

- Using **has_many** and **has_many :through** with properly chosen class names and foreign keys, we can model both active (following) and passive (being followed) relationships.

- Rails routing supports nested routes.

- The **where** method is a flexible and powerful way to create database queries.

- Rails supports issuing lower-level SQL queries if needed.

- By putting together everything we've learned in this book, we've successfully implemented user following with a status feed of microposts from followed users.

Index

Credits

Chapter 1, page 5: M&R Glasgow. Image retrieved from https://www.flickr.com/photos/glasgows/338937124/ on 2014-08-25. Copyright ©2008 by M&R Glasgow and used unaltered under the terms of the Creative Commons Attribution 2.0 Generic license.

Figure 1-1: Screenshot of The beginning hello app ©2020, Amazon Web Services, Inc.

Figure 1-2: Screenshot of An intermediate toy app ©2020, Amazon Web Services, Inc.

Figure 1-3: Screenshot of The final sample app ©2020, Amazon Web Services, Inc.

Figure 1-8: Screenshot of The final step before provisioning the IDE ©2020, Amazon Web Services, Inc.

Figure 1-9P Screenshot of The default cloud IDE ©2020, Amazon Web Services, Inc.

Figure 1-11: Screenshot of The directory structure for a newly created Rails app ©Ruby on Rails

Figure 1-12: Screenshot of The default Gemfile open in a text editor ©2020, Amazon Web Services, Inc.

Figure 1-18: Screenshot of The default Rails page served by rails server ©2020, Amazon Web Services, Inc.

Figure 1-19: FireFox logo ©1998–2020 by individual mozilla.org contributors

Figure 1-20: Screenshot of Viewing "hello, world!" in the browser ©2020, Amazon Web Services, Inc.

Figure 1-21: Screenshot of Changing the root route to return "¡Hola, mundo!" ©2020, Amazon Web Services, Inc.

Figure 1-22: Screenshot of Changing the root route to return "goodbye, world!" ©2020, Amazon Web Services, Inc.

Figure 1-23: Screenshot of Signing up for GitHub ©2020 GitHub, Inc.

Figure 1-27: Screenshot of A GitHub repository page ©2020 GitHub, Inc.

Figure 1-28: Screenshot of GitHub's rendering of the default Rails README ©2020 GitHub, Inc.

Figure 1-30: Screenshot of The improved README file at GitHub ©2020 GitHub, Inc.

Figure 1-31: Screenshot of The first Rails Tutorial application running on Heroku ©2020 Salesforce.com

Figure 2-4: Screenshot of The initial index page for the Users resource (/users) ©2020, Amazon Web Services, Inc.

Figure 2-5: Screenshot of The new user page (/users/new) ©2020, Amazon Web Services, Inc.

Figure 2-6: Screenshot of The page to show a user (/users/1) ©2020, Amazon Web Services, Inc.

Figure 2-7: Screenshot of The user edit page (/users/1/edit) ©2020, Amazon Web Services, Inc.

Figure 2-8: Screenshot of A user with updated information ©2020, Amazon Web Services, Inc.

Figure 2-9: Screenshot of The user index page (/users) with a second user ©2020, Amazon Web Services, Inc.

Figure 2-10: Screenshot of Destroying a user ©2020, Amazon Web Services, Inc.

Figure 2-11: Google logo ©2020 Google

Figure 2-12: Screenshot of The micropost index page (/microposts) ©2020, Amazon Web Services, Inc.

Figure 2-13: Screenshot of The new micropost page (/microposts/new) ©2020, Amazon Web Services, Inc.

Figure 2-14: Screenshot of The micropost index page with a couple of posts ©2020, Amazon Web Services, Inc.

Figure 2-15: Screenshot of Error messages for a failed micropost creation ©2020, Amazon Web Services, Inc.

Figure 2-17: Screenshot of The effect of a micropost presence validation ©2020, Amazon Web Services, Inc.

Figure 2-18: Screenshot of The effect of presence validations on the User model ©2020, Amazon Web Services, Inc.

Figure 2-21: Screenshot of An error page at Heroku ©2020 Salesforce.com

Figure 2-22: Screenshot of Running the toy app in production ©2020 Salesforce.com

Figure 3-2: Screenshot of The sample app README at GitHub ©2020 GitHub, Inc.

Figure 3-4: Screenshot of The raw home view (/static_pages/home) ©2020 Amazon Web Services, Inc.

Figure 3-5: Screenshot of A custom Home page ©2020 Amazon Web Services, Inc.

Figure 3-6: Screenshot of A custom Help page ©2020 Amazon Web Services, Inc.

Figure 3-7: Screenshot of The new About page (/static_pages/about) ©2020 Amazon Web Services, Inc.

Figure 3-9: Screenshot of The Home page at the root route ©2020 Amazon Web Services, Inc.

Chapter 5, page 214: Image retrieved from https://www.flickr.com/photos/deborah_s_perspective/14144861329 on 2016-01-09. Copyright ©2009 by Deborah and used unaltered under the terms of the Creative Commons Attribution 2.0 Generic license.

Figure 5-2: Screenshot of The Home page with no custom CSS ©2020, Amazon Web Services, Inc.

Figure 5-3: Image retrieved from https://www.flickr.com/photos/deborah_s_perspective/14144861329 on 2016-01-09. Copyright ©2009 by Deborah and used unaltered under the terms of the Creative Commons Attribution 2.0 Generic license.

Figure 5-4: Screenshot of The result of adding a kitten image to the Home page ©2020, Amazon Web Services, Inc.

Figure 5-5: Screenshot of The sample application with Bootstrap CSS ©2020, Amazon Web Services, Inc.

Figure 5-6: Screenshot of Adding some spacing and other universal styling ©2020, Amazon Web Services, Inc.

Figure 5-7: Screenshot of Adding some typographic styling ©2020, Amazon Web Services, Inc.

Figure 5-8: Screenshot of The sample app with nicely styled logo ©2020, Amazon Web Services, Inc.

Figure 5-9: Screenshot of The Home page with an added footer ©2020, Amazon Web Services, Inc.

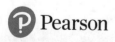

Photo by Marvent/Shutterstock

VIDEO TRAINING FOR THE **IT PROFESSIONAL**

LEARN QUICKLY
Learn a new technology in just hours. Video training can teach more in less time, and material is generally easier to absorb and remember.

WATCH AND LEARN
Instructors demonstrate concepts so you see technology in action.

TEST YOURSELF
Our Complete Video Courses offer self-assessment quizzes throughout.

CONVENIENT
Most videos are streaming with an option to download lessons for offline viewing.

Learn more, browse our store, and watch free, sample lessons at

informit.com/video

Save 50%* off the list price of video courses with discount code **VIDBOB**